AF479040

THE BIG BOOK OF LETTERHEADS

THE **BIG** BOOK OF

LETTERHEADS

Edited By

David E. Carter

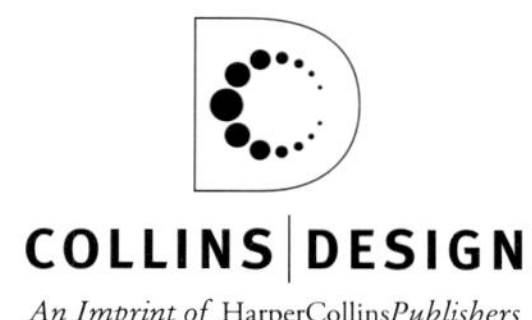

COLLINS | DESIGN

An Imprint of HarperCollins*Publishers*

THE BIG BOOK OF LETTERHEADS

First Edition

First published in 2007 by:
Collins Design
An Imprint of HarperCollins*Publishers*
10 East 53rd Street
New York, NY 10022
Tel: (212) 207-7000
Fax: (212) 207-7654
collinsdesign@harpercollins.com
www.harpercollins.com

Distributed throughout the world by:
HarperCollins*Publishers*
10 East 53rd Street
New York, NY 10022
Fax: (212) 207-7654

Produced by Crescent Hill Books, Louisville, KY

Book design by Designs on You!
Suzanna and Anthony Stephens

Library of Congress Control Number: 2006938762

ISBN-10: 0-06-125570-X
ISBN-13: 978-0-06-125570-0

Printed in China by Everbest Printing Company through Four Colour Imports, Louisville, Kentucky.

First Printing, 2007

"You've got mail"

Just a few short years ago, that phrase meant the postman had come and you had a bunch of stuff in envelopes and maybe a few catalogs. That was back in the *20TH CENTURY*, when business mail was printed on a letterhead, put into a business envelope, stamped, and sent through the post office. Then *ALONG CAME THE INTERNET* and business mail—and accompanying letterhead sets—became obsolete. **Right**?

Not so fast...although the importance of business mail has been reduced by the omnipresence of email communication, all email looks pretty much alike, so the letterhead just might be singing the song from *Spamalot*, "***I'm not dead yet***."

Letterheads haven't disappeared from the scene, but it's more important than ever for a letterhead design to *IMMEDIATELY CATCH THE READER'S ATTENTION*, making a positive impression. Because business letters are mailed less frequently, each one has the opportunity to have a **greater impact** on the reader than it would have in the pre-internet era.

So, the challenge for designers is to create a letterhead (or letterhead set) that will accomplish the following:

- *make a positive first impression for the business,*
- *be an appropriate design for the firm's personality and corporate culture,* and
- *leave a lasting impression in the mind of the recipient.*

Letterheads vs. Letterhead Sets

When I did a book on letterheads ten years ago, nearly every submission came with a letterhead, a business envelope, and a business card. (And those from Europe often came with a "with compliments" card included.)

This time, a number of submissions included *ONLY THE LETTERHEAD*. Why? The reasons are varied and complex, depending on the business. One good reason is that the firm who does business online has no personal contact with customers (therefore no business card), and no letters are sent out (therefore no business envelope.) The solo letterhead is included in the box with the merchandise. There are many other possible reasons why the letterhead now stands alone. We'll leave it up to you to conjecture about that issue.

Thanks to the many designers who sent work for this book

We present here a highly creative selection of letterheads and letterhead sets that make it almost fun to get a business letter. When I started this book, I wanted to include only examples that were truly **outstanding**, ones with a high level of **design quality**. Designs here were chosen from a large number of submissions, and each was selected for its ability to be **visually interesting** and make a positive statement about the business.

In *The Big Book of Letterheads* you will find nearly 400 pages of *EXCELLENT DESIGNS*, all selected for their unusual power to communicate.

As you use this book for what I call "solitary brainstorming," I hope you will find it a useful reference.

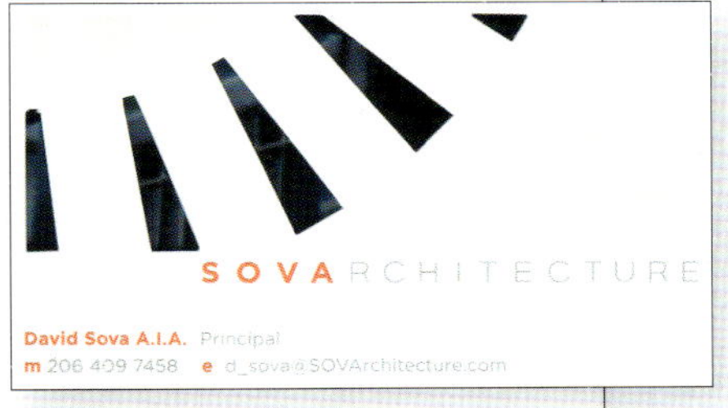

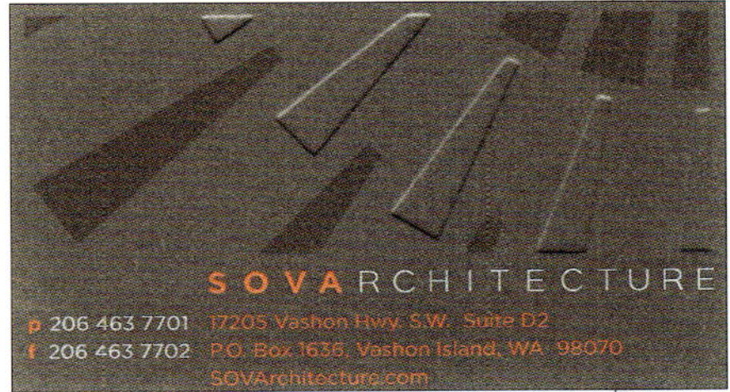

DESIGN FIRM
Hornall Anderson Design Works
Seattle, (WA) USA

PROJECT
SOVArchitecture

ART DIRECTORS
Jack Anderson,
Larry Anderson

DESIGNER
Henry Yiu

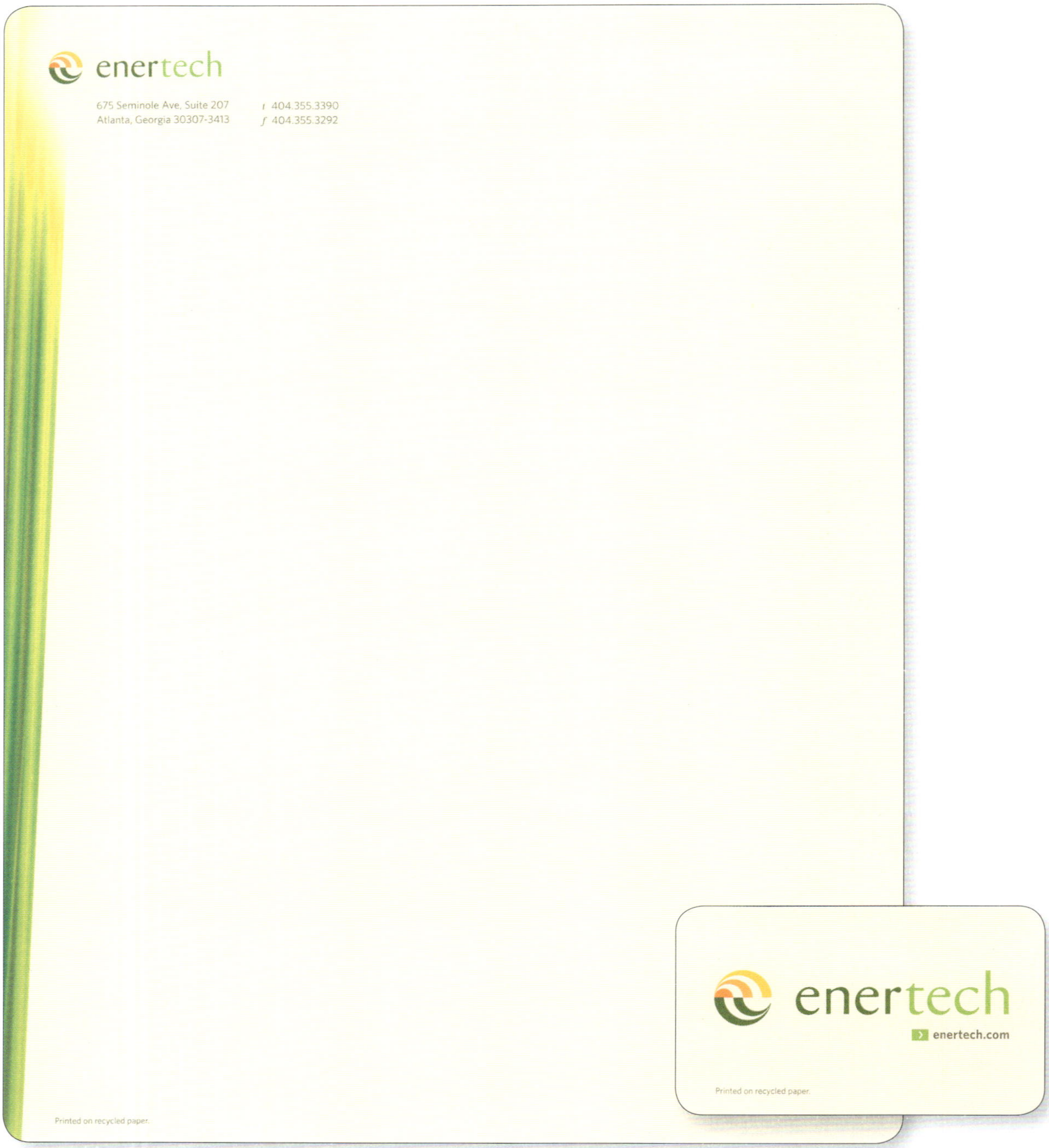

enertech

675 Seminole Ave, Suite 207
Atlanta, Georgia 30307-3413

t 404.355.3390
f 404.355.3292

Printed on recycled paper.

enertech

enertech.com

Printed on recycled paper.

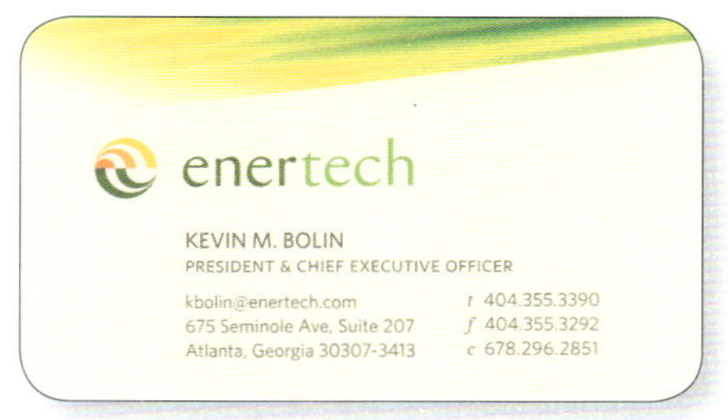

DESIGN FIRM
Hornall Anderson Design Works
Seattle, (WA) USA

PROJECT
Enertech

ART DIRECTORS
Jack Anderson,
James Tee

DESIGNERS
James Tee, Beth Grimm,
Elmer dela Cruz,
Sonja Max, Lauren DiRusso

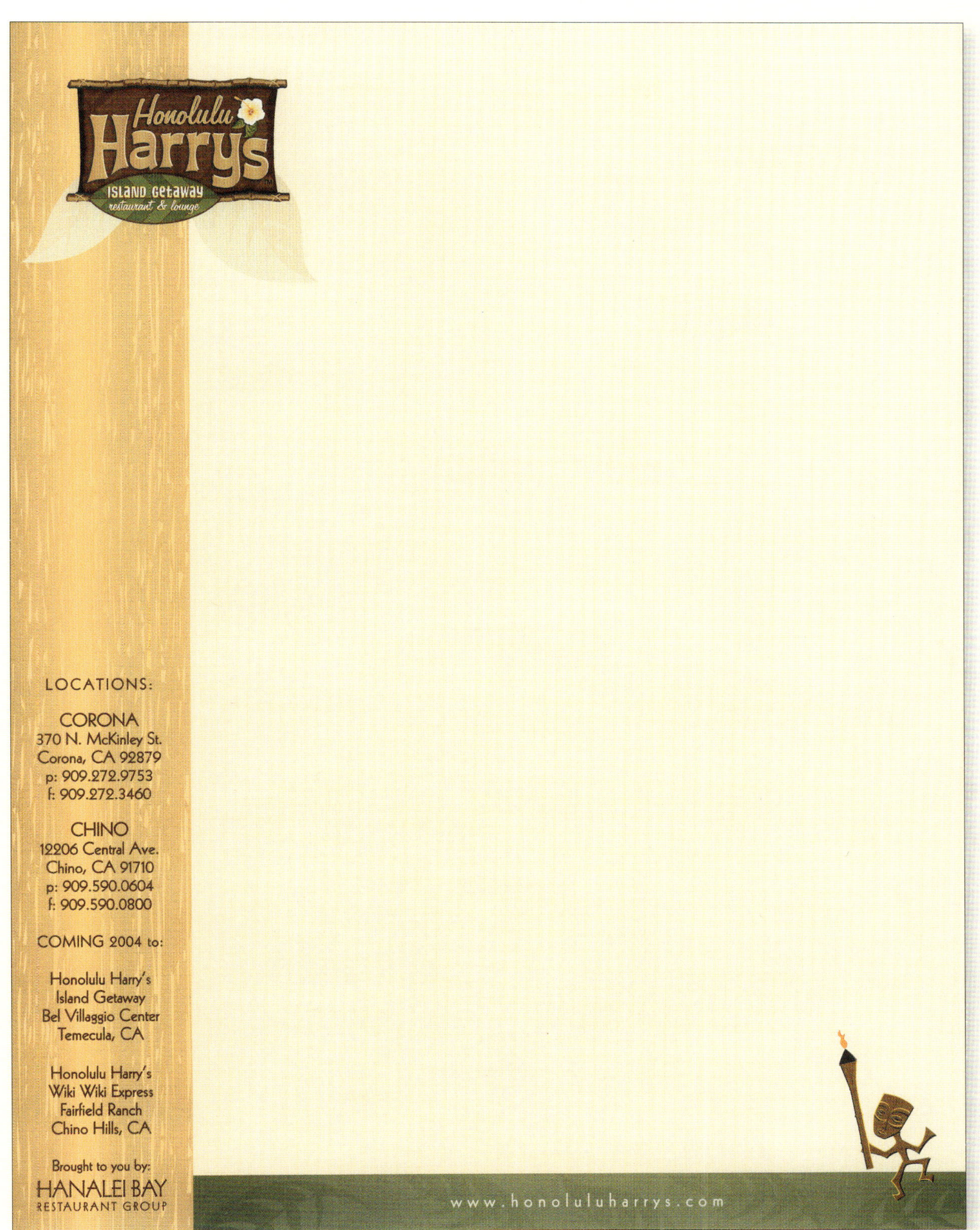

DESIGN FIRM
On The Edge Design
Newport Beach, (CA) USA
PROJECT
Honolulu Harry's
DESIGNER
Melanie Fujita

THE LODGE AT
Woodcliff

Resort & Conference Center

Woodcliff Drive Box 22850 Rochester, NY 14692
(716) 381-4000 Fax (716) 381-2673
e-Mail: welcome@woodclifflodge.com
Visit us at: www.woodclifflodge.com

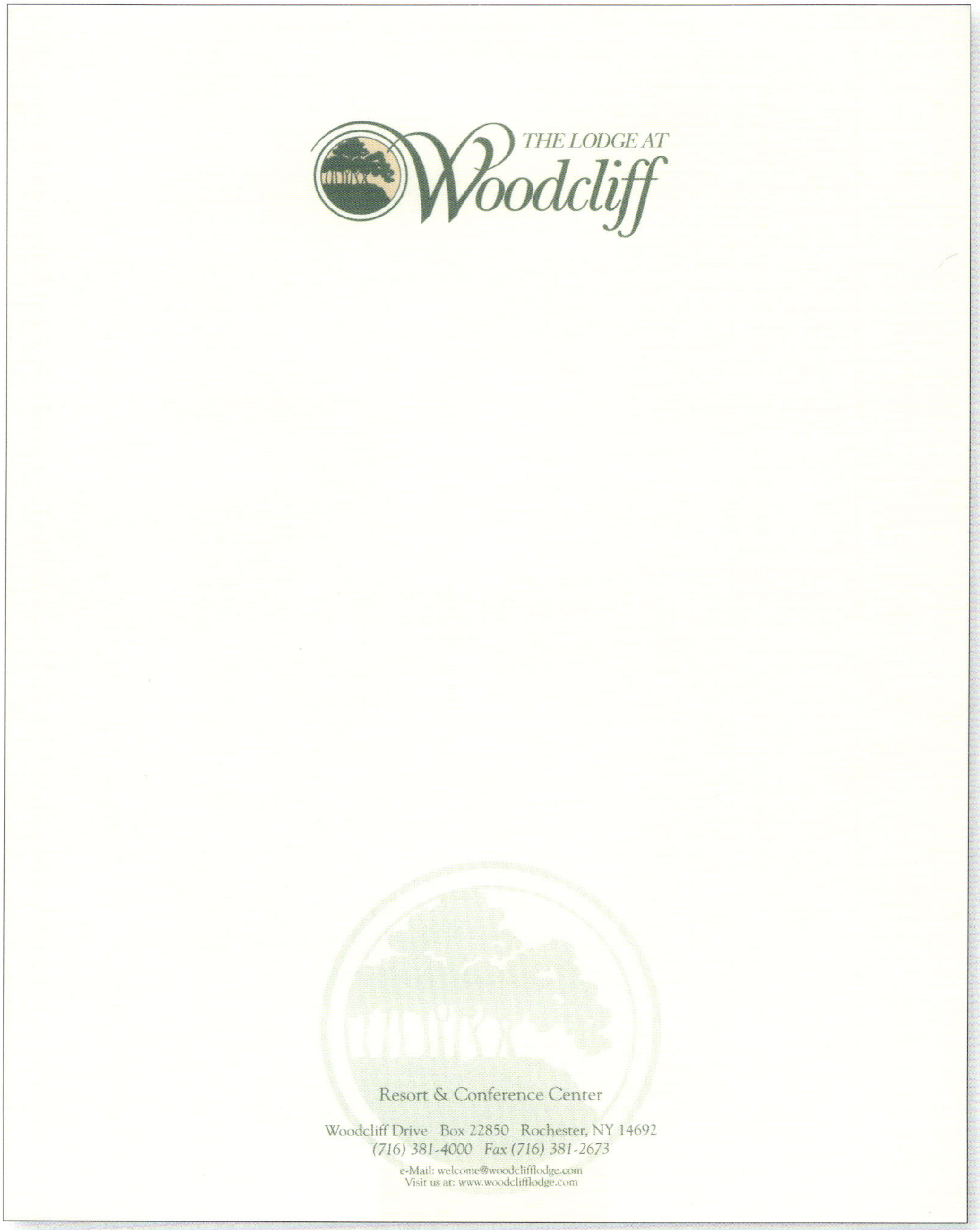

DESIGN FIRM
McElveney & Palozzi Design
Rochester, (NY) USA
PROJECT
The Lodge at Woodcliff
CREATIVE DIRECTOR
William McElveney
ART DIRECTOR
Ellen Johnson

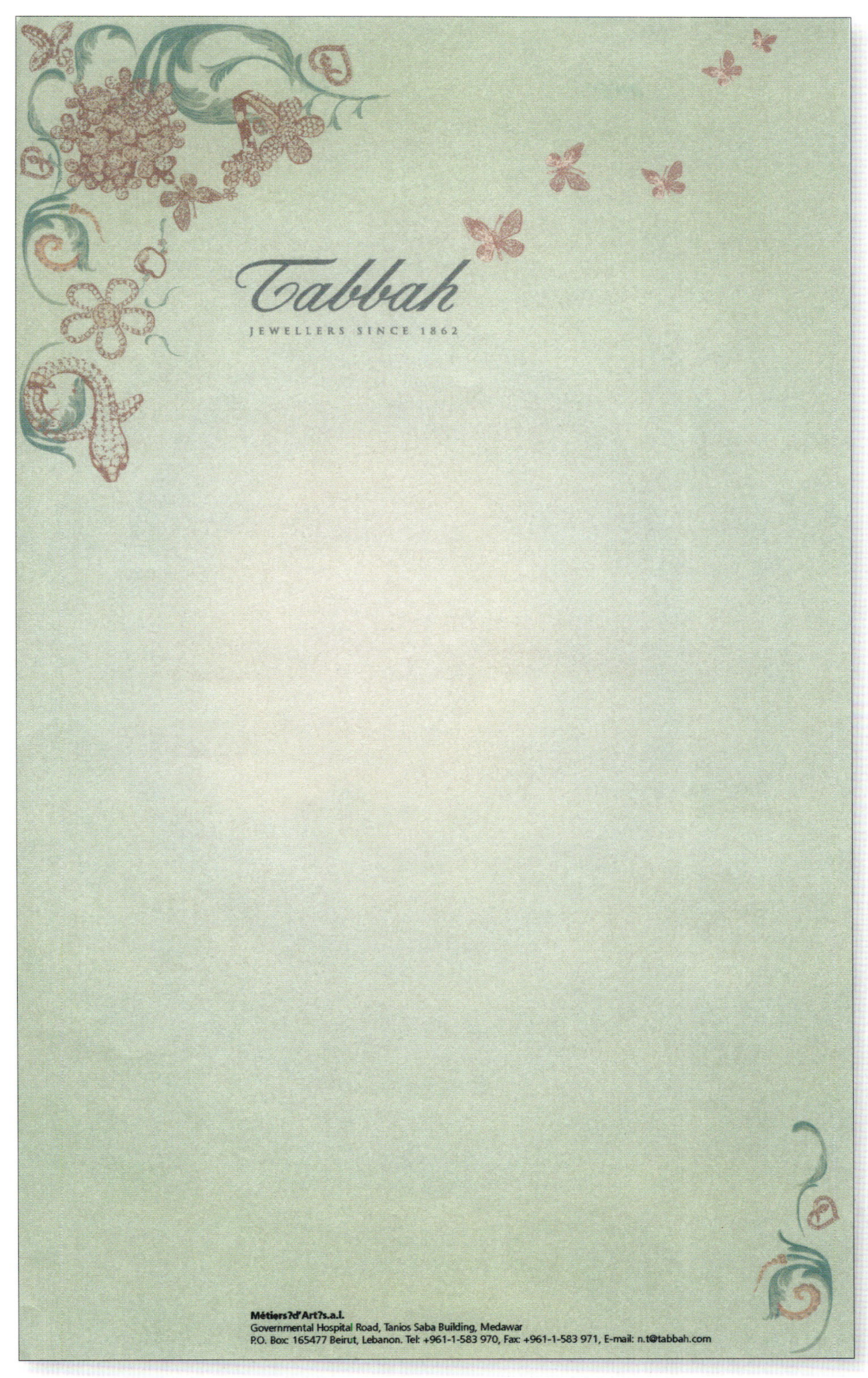

DESIGN FIRM
Go Graphic
Beirut, Lebanon
CLIENT
Métiers d'Art–Tabbah Jewellers
CREATIVE DIRECTOR
Maria Assi
DESIGNERS
Maria Assi
Rasha Jeaid

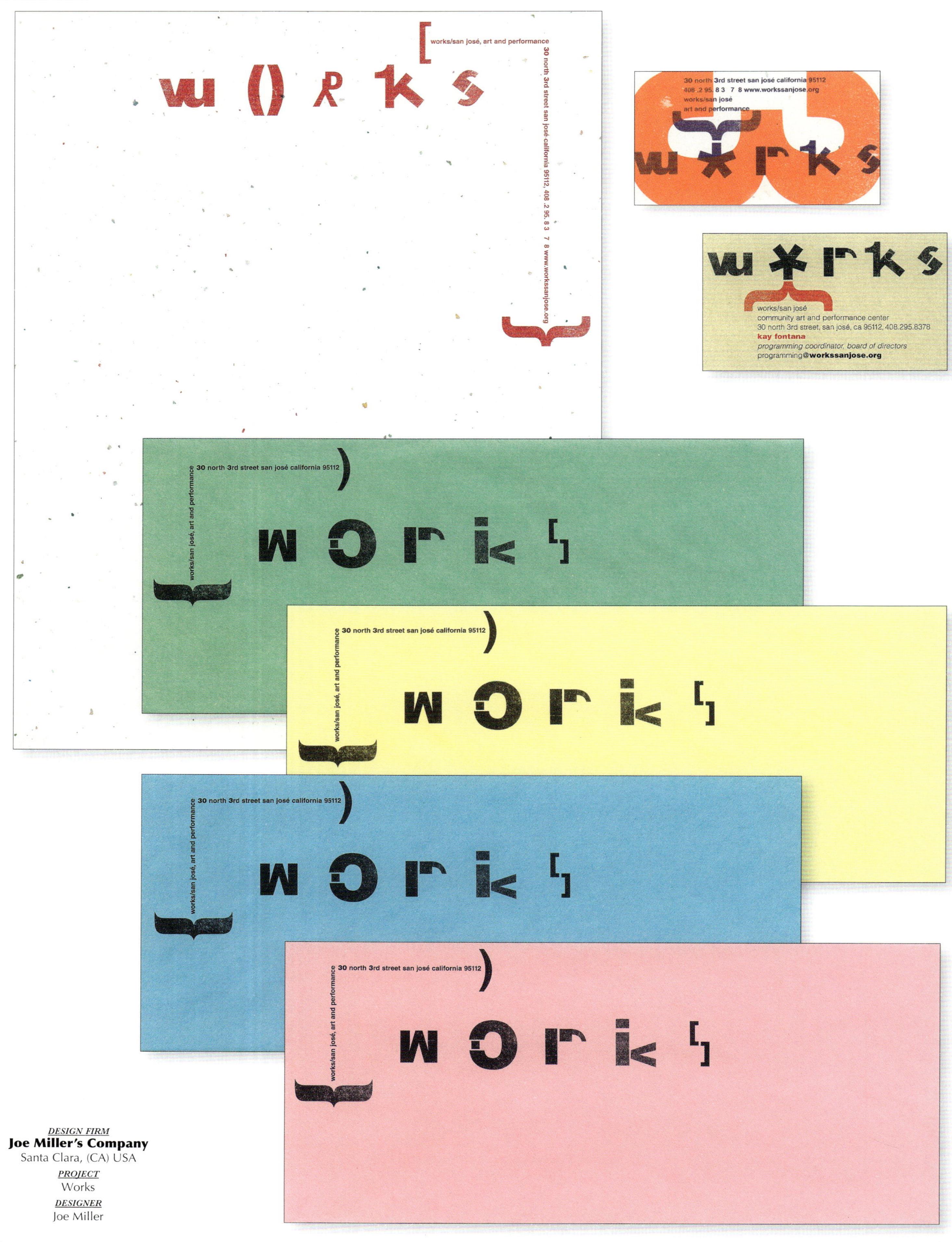

DESIGN FIRM
Joe Miller's Company
Santa Clara, (CA) USA

PROJECT
Works

DESIGNER
Joe Miller

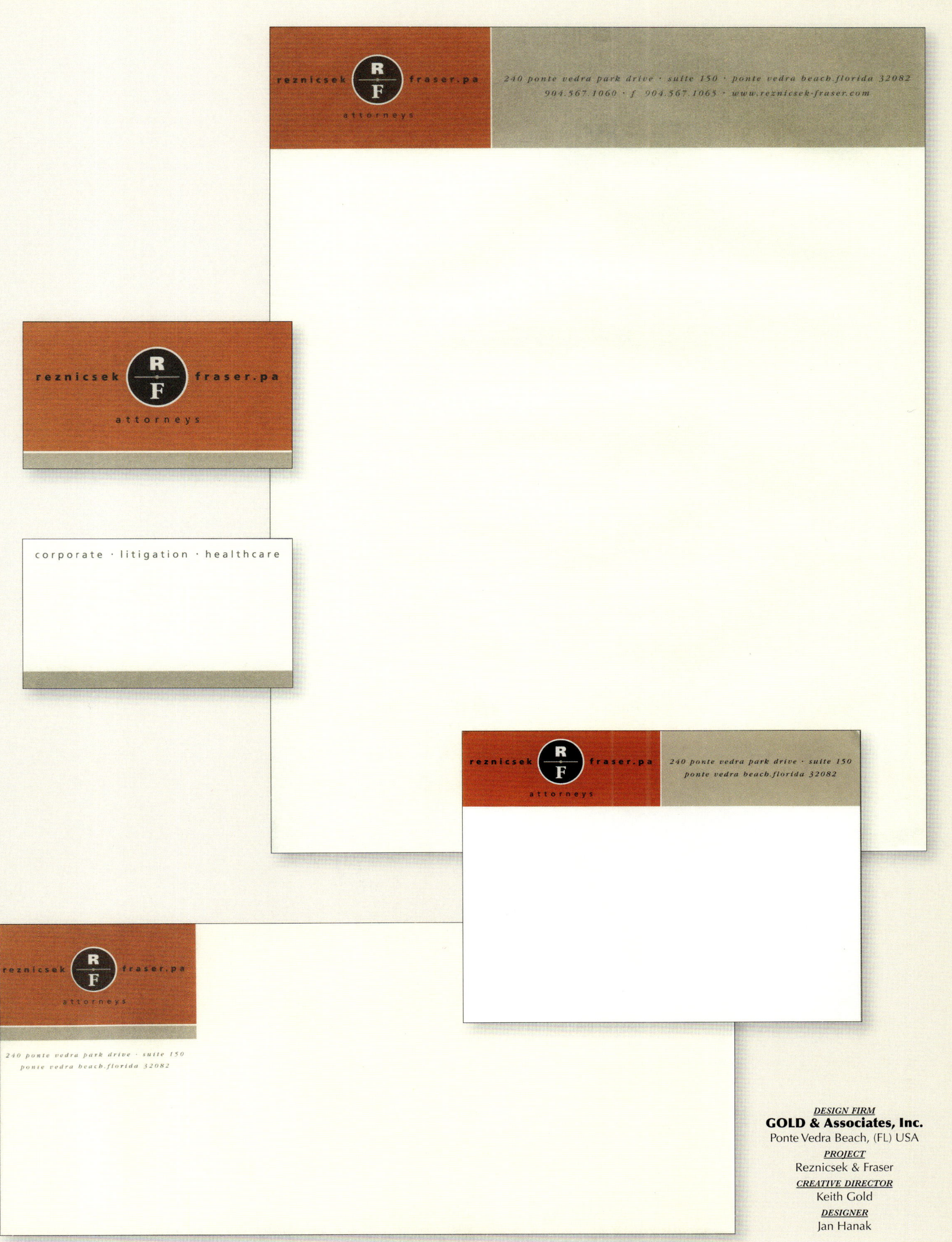

DESIGN FIRM
GOLD & Associates, Inc.
Ponte Vedra Beach, (FL) USA
PROJECT
Reznicsek & Fraser
CREATIVE DIRECTOR
Keith Gold
DESIGNER
Jan Hanak

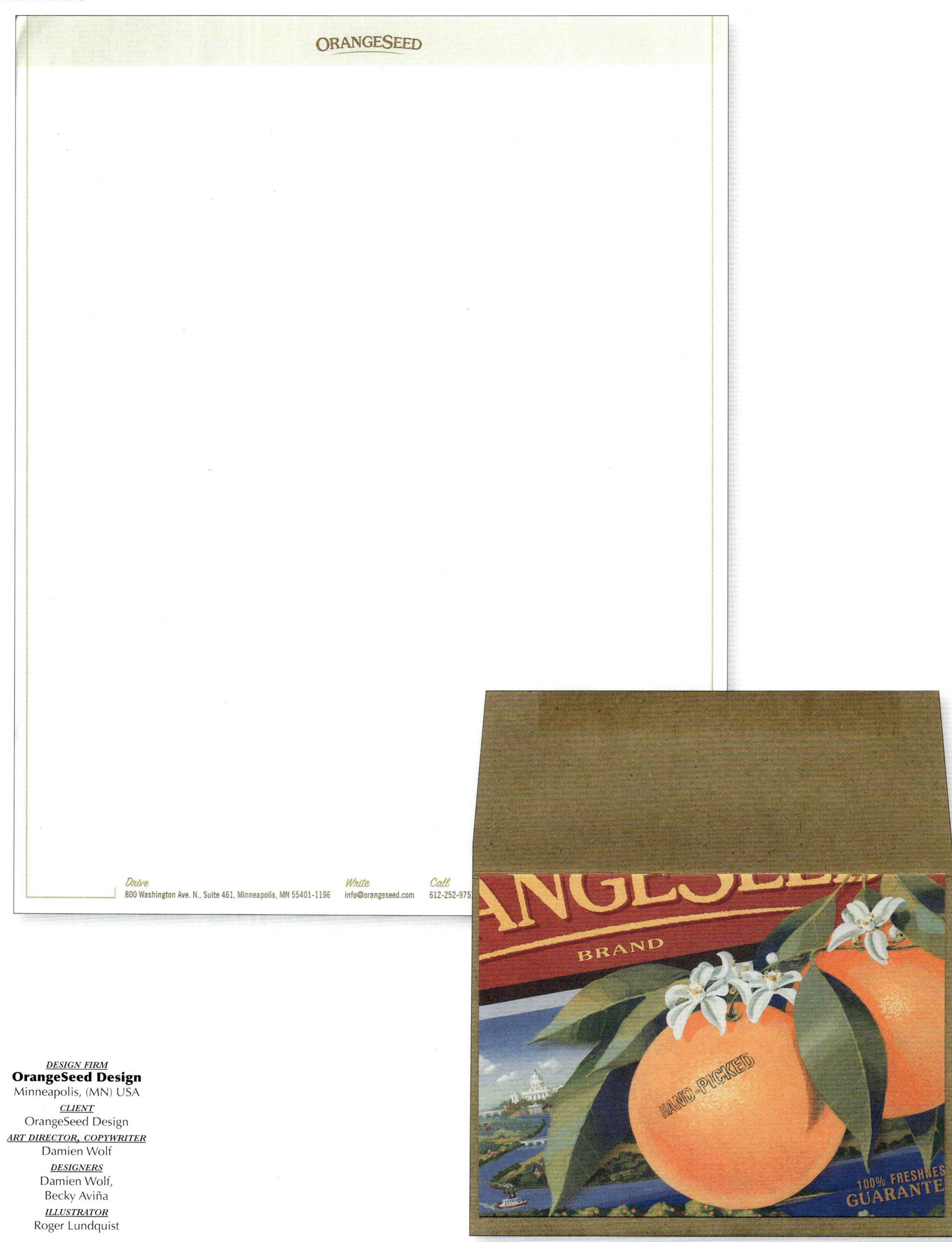

DESIGN FIRM
OrangeSeed Design
Minneapolis, (MN) USA
CLIENT
OrangeSeed Design
ART DIRECTOR, COPYWRITER
Damien Wolf
DESIGNERS
Damien Wolf,
Becky Aviña
ILLUSTRATOR
Roger Lundquist

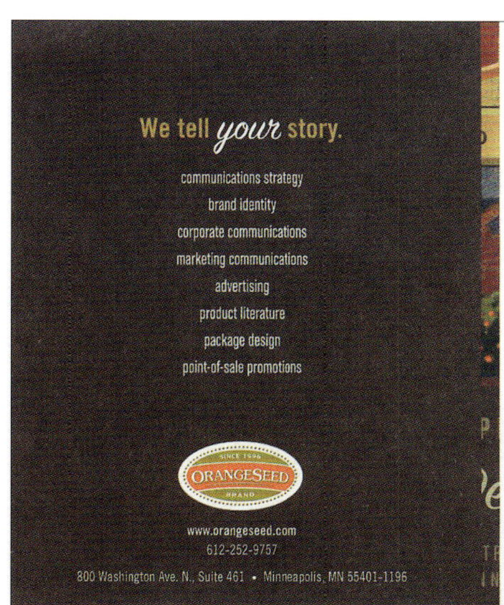
We tell your story.
communications strategy
brand identity
corporate communications
marketing communications
advertising
product literature
package design
point-of-sale promotions
ORANGESEED
www.orangeseed.com
612-252-9757
800 Washington Ave. N., Suite 461 • Minneapolis, MN 55401-1196

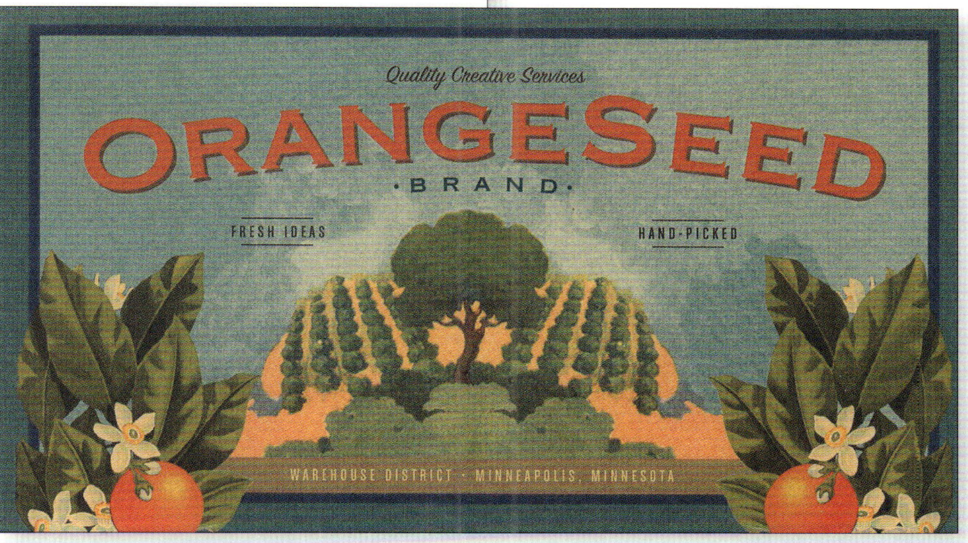
Quality Creative Services
ORANGESEED
BRAND
FRESH IDEAS
HAND-PICKED
WAREHOUSE DISTRICT · MINNEAPOLIS, MINNESOTA

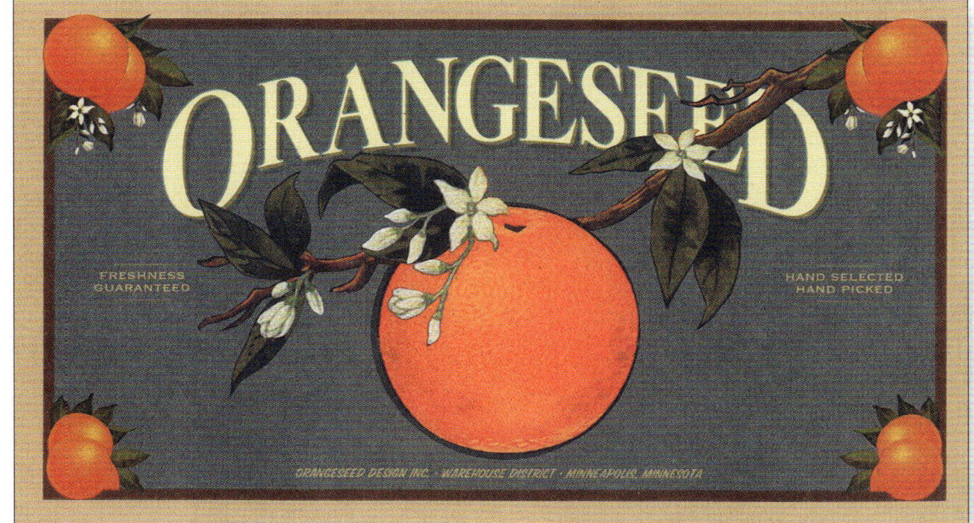
ORANGESEED
FRESHNESS GUARANTEED
HAND SELECTED HAND PICKED
ORANGESEED DESIGN INC. · WAREHOUSE DISTRICT · MINNEAPOLIS, MINNESOTA

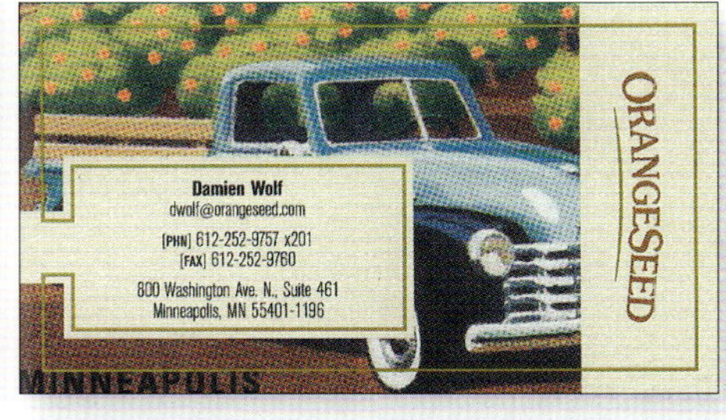
Damien Wolf
dwolf@orangeseed.com
[PHN] 612-252-9757 x201
[FAX] 612-252-9760
800 Washington Ave. N., Suite 461
Minneapolis, MN 55401-1196
ORANGESEED
MINNEAPOLIS

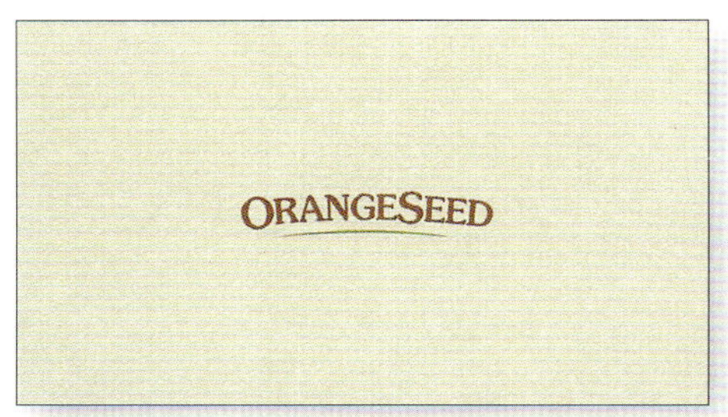
ORANGESEED

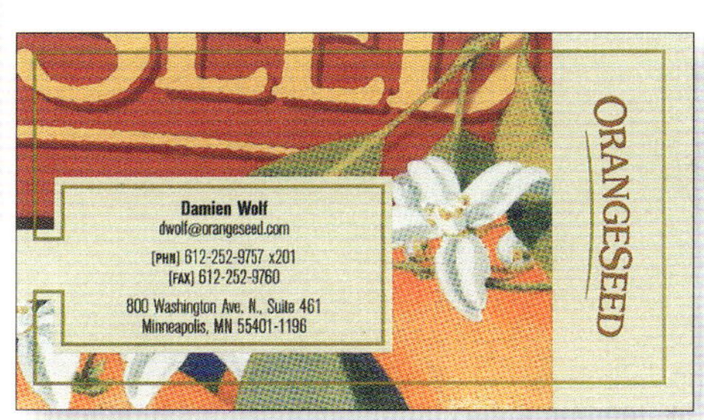
Damien Wolf
dwolf@orangeseed.com
[PHN] 612-252-9757 x201
[FAX] 612-252-9760
800 Washington Ave. N., Suite 461
Minneapolis, MN 55401-1196
ORANGESEED

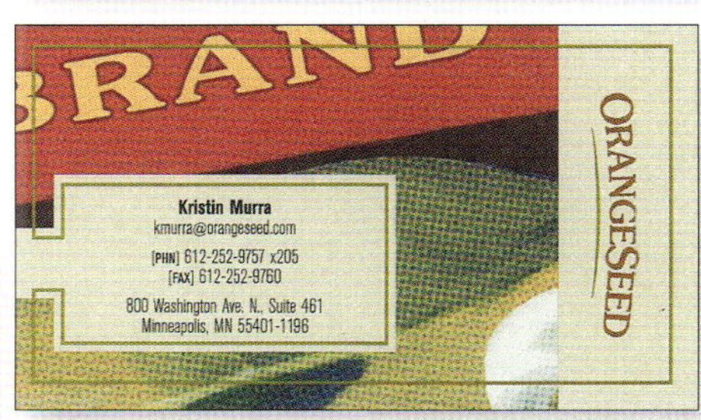
BRAND
Kristin Murra
kmurra@orangeseed.com
[PHN] 612-252-9757 x205
[FAX] 612-252-9760
800 Washington Ave. N., Suite 461
Minneapolis, MN 55401-1196
ORANGESEED

DESIGN FIRM
TrueFACES Creation Sdn. Bhd.
Selangor, Malaysia
DESIGNERS
TrueFACES Creative Team

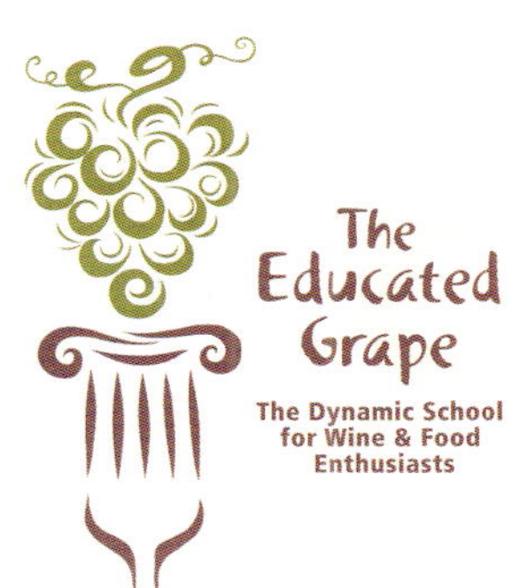

An Education Program from TopShelf
203 Main Street #259 Flemington, NJ 08822 t. 908.284.4930 f. 908.284.4931 TheEducatedGrape.com

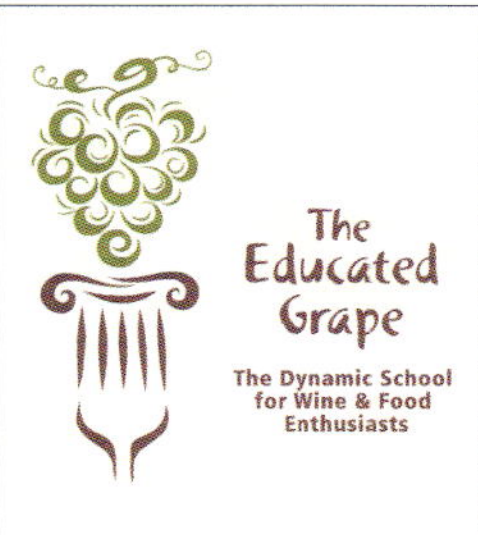

George Staikos
george@TheEducatedGrape.com

203 Main Street #259
Flemington, NJ 08822
t. 908.284.4930
f. 908.284.4931

TheEducatedGrape.com

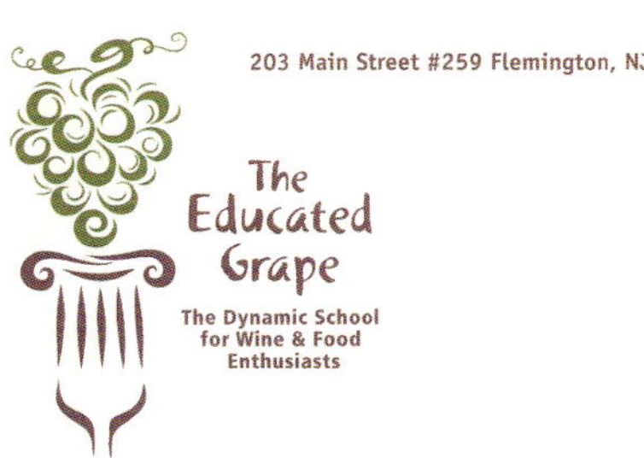

203 Main Street #259 Flemington, NJ 08822 TheEducatedGrape.com

DESIGN FIRM
PM Design
Berkeley Heights, (NJ) USA

PROJECT
The Educated Grape

ART DIRECTOR, DESIGNER
Phil Marzo

ILLUSTRATOR
Sandy Haight

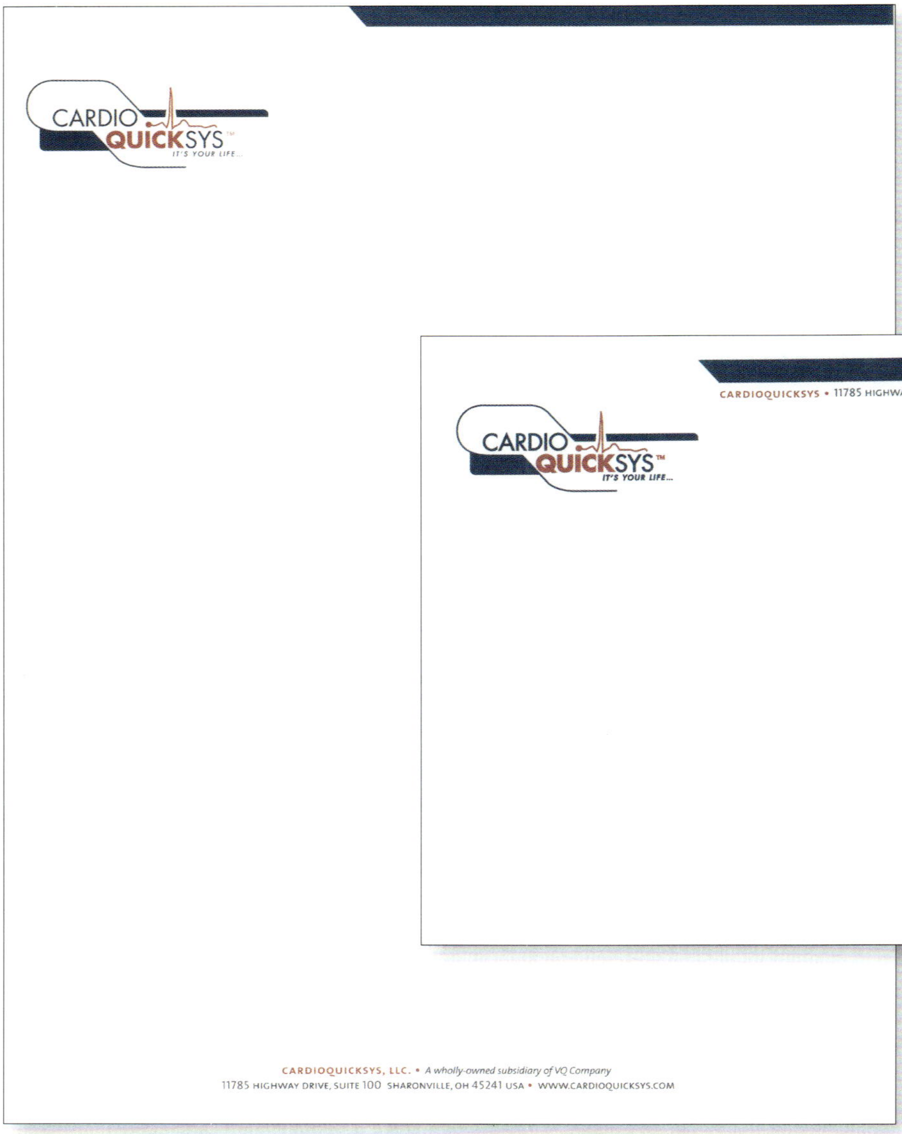

CARDIO QUICKSYS™
IT'S YOUR LIFE...

CARDIOQUICKSYS • 11785 HIGHWAY DRIVE, SUITE 100 SHARONVILLE, OH 45241 USA

CARDIOQUICKSYS, LLC. • *A wholly-owned subsidiary of VQ Company*
11785 HIGHWAY DRIVE, SUITE 100 SHARONVILLE, OH 45241 USA • WWW.CARDIOQUICKSYS.COM

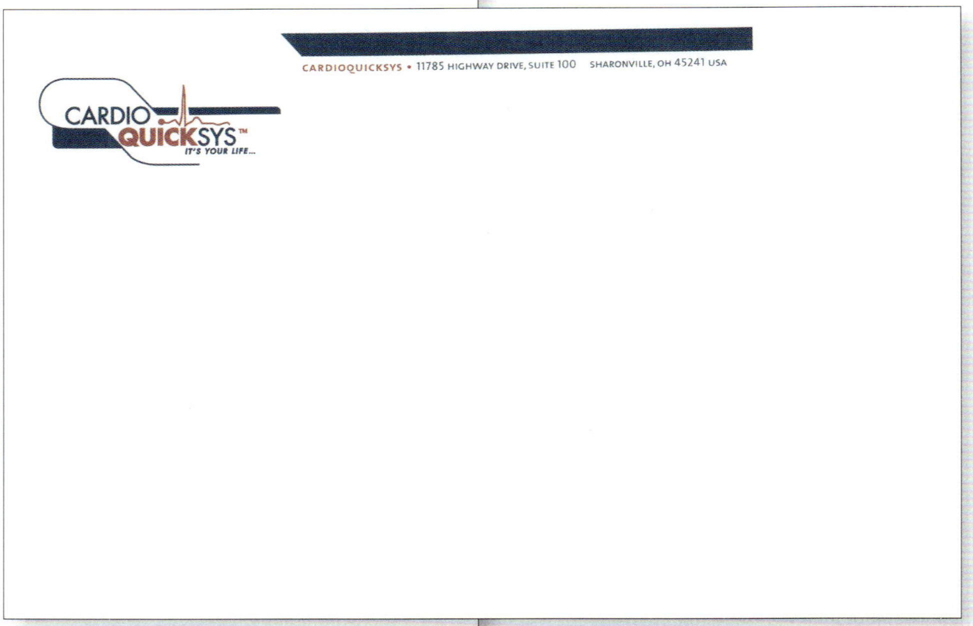

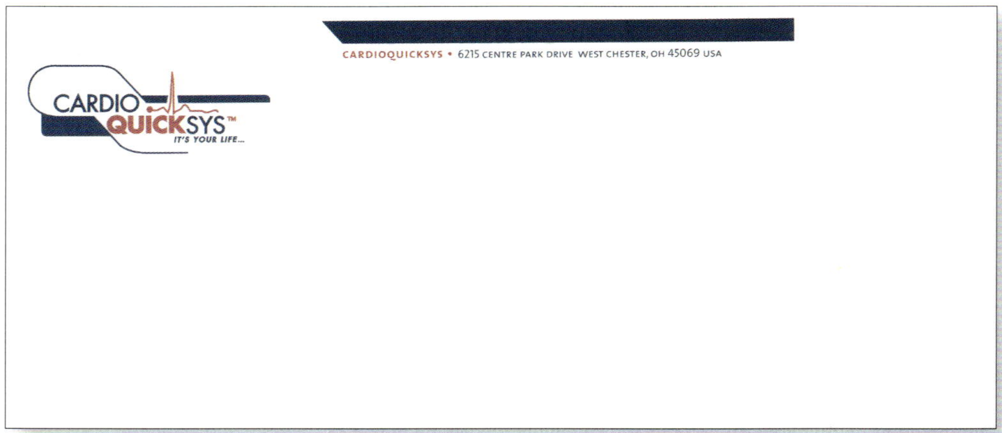

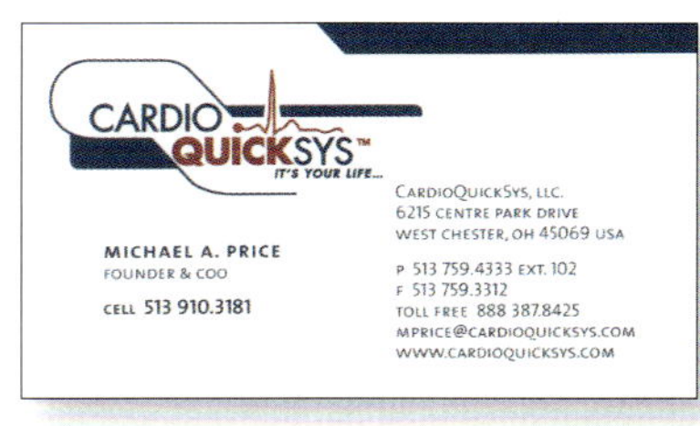

DESIGN FIRM
Five Visual Communication & Design
West Chester, (OH) USA

PROJECT
Cardio Quicksys

DESIGNERS
Rondi Tschopp,
Tonya Henry

DESIGN FIRM
On The Edge Design
Newport Beach, (CA) USA
PROJECT
Lazy Dog Cafe
DESIGNER
Melanie Fujita

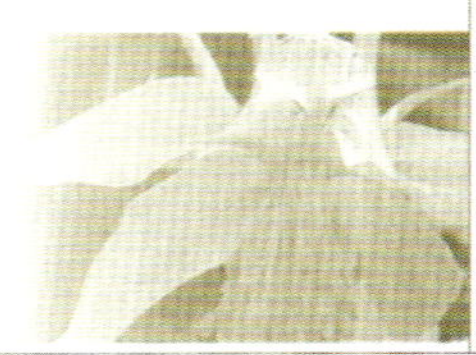

WhiteCounty

White County Industrial Foundation
P.O. Box 1031 · 110 North Main Street · Monticello, IN 47960

Pure Opportunity

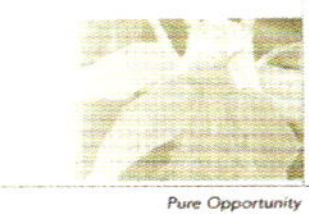

WhiteCounty

White County Industrial Foundation
P.O. Box 1031 · 110 North Main Street · Monticello, IN 47960

Pure Opportunity

Valerie A. Hunter
executive director

WhiteCounty

White County Industrial Foundation
P.O. Box 1031 · 110 North Main Street · Monticello, IN 47960

Pure Opportunity

574.583.6557 · fax / 574.583.6230 · cell / 219.613.0463
whiteco@monti.net · whitecountyin.org

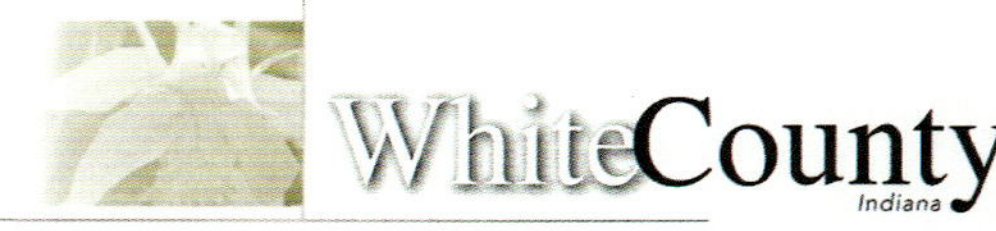

Pure Opportunity

DESIGN FIRM
Indiana Design Consortium, Inc.
Lafayette, (IN) USA

CLIENT
White County Industrial Foundation

DESIGNER
Kristy Blair

DESIGN FIRM
Studio Hill Design
Albuquerque (NM) USA
PROJECT
Healthcare Resource Providers
ART DIRECTOR
Sandy Hill
DESIGNERS
Sandy Hill,
Sean M. Chavez

s)g

scott group 3232 Kraft Avenue SE Grand Rapids, MI 49512 T 616.954.3200 F 616.954.9600 scottgroup.com

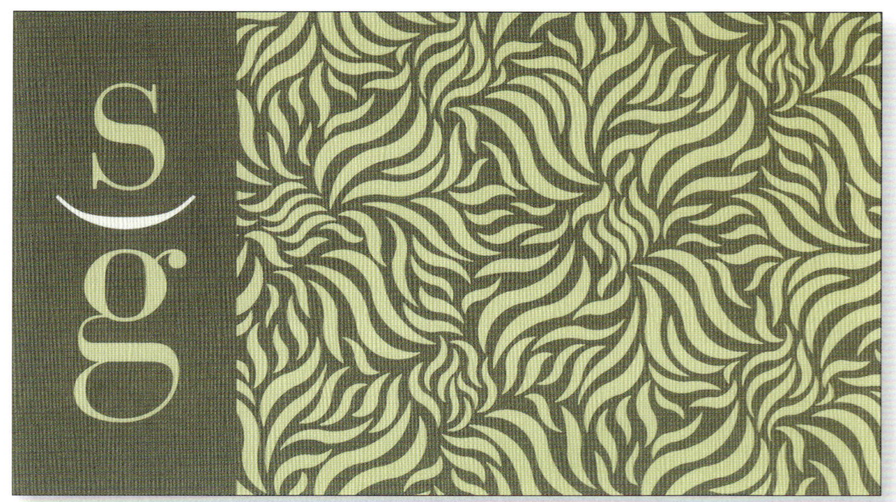

scott group

3232 Kraft Avenue SE Grand Rapids, MI 49512
T 616.954.3200 F 616.954.9600 scottgroup.com

Pattern Cirrus

scott group

Mike Sievers
Accounting Clerk

msievers@scottgroup.com
scottgroup.com

3232 Kraft Avenue SE
Grand Rapids, MI 49512
T 616.954.3200 x 222
F 616.954.9600

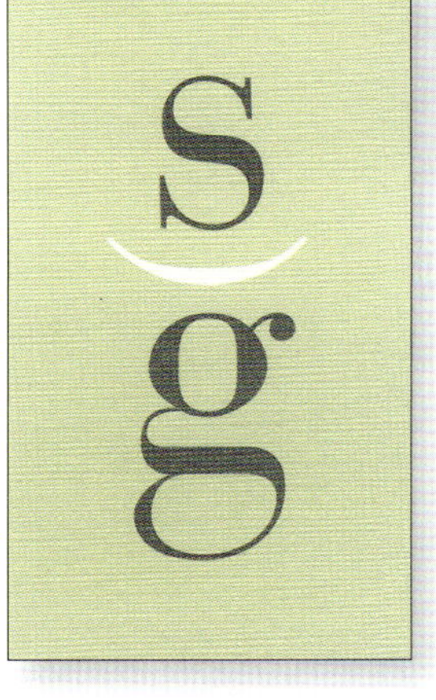

DESIGN FIRM
Square One Design
Grand Rapids, (MI) USA

PROJECT
Scott Group

ART DIRECTOR
Lin Ver Meulen

DESIGNER
Anna Huddleston

go
graphic s.a.r.l.

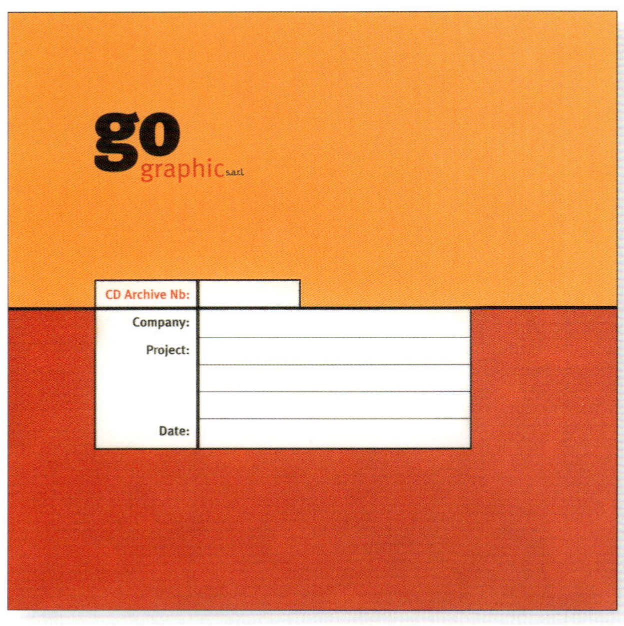
go
graphic s.a.r.l.
CD Archive Nb:
Company:
Project:
Date:

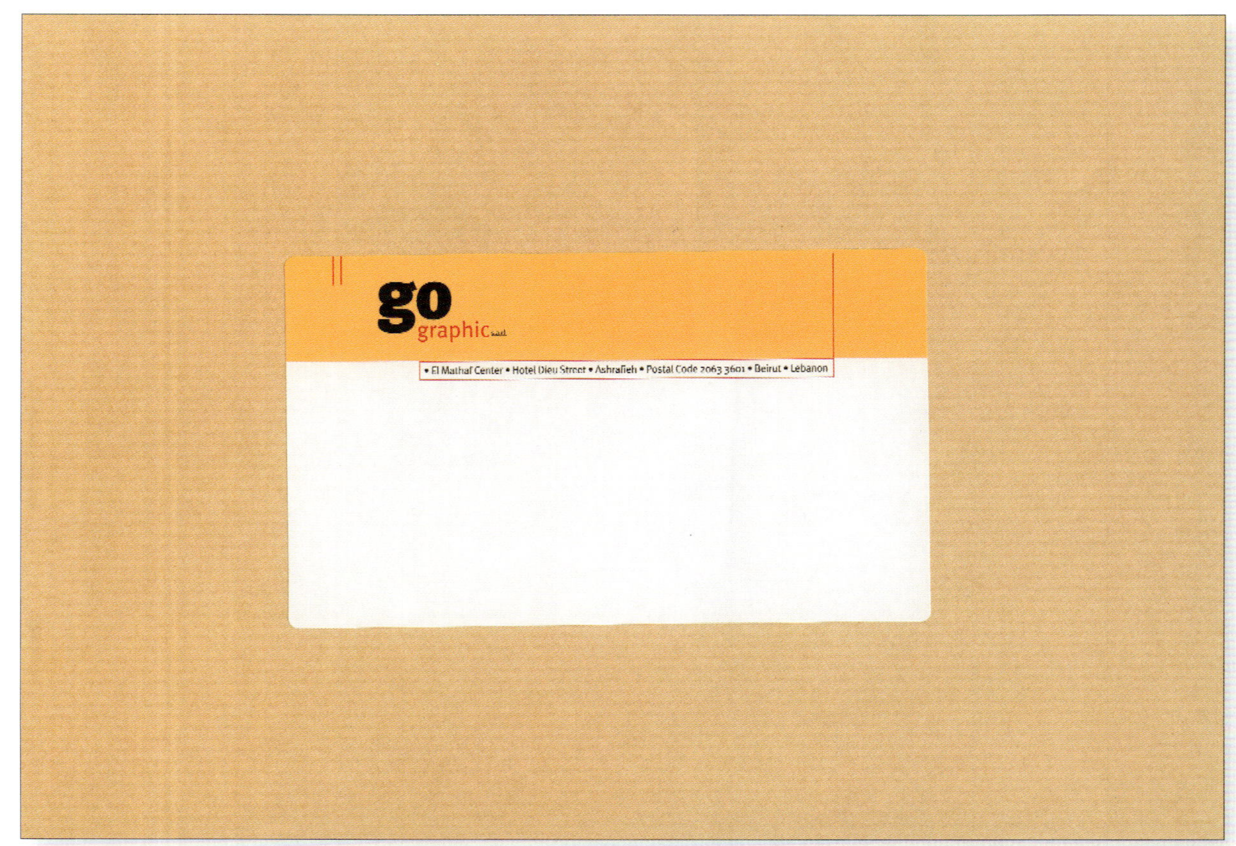
go
graphic s.a.r.l.
• El Mathaf Center • Hotel Dieu Street • Ashrafieh • Postal Code 2063 3601 • Beirut • Lebanon

DESIGN FIRM
Go Graphic
Beirut, Lebanon
CLIENT
Go Graphic
CREATIVE DIRECTOR, DESIGNER
Maria Assi

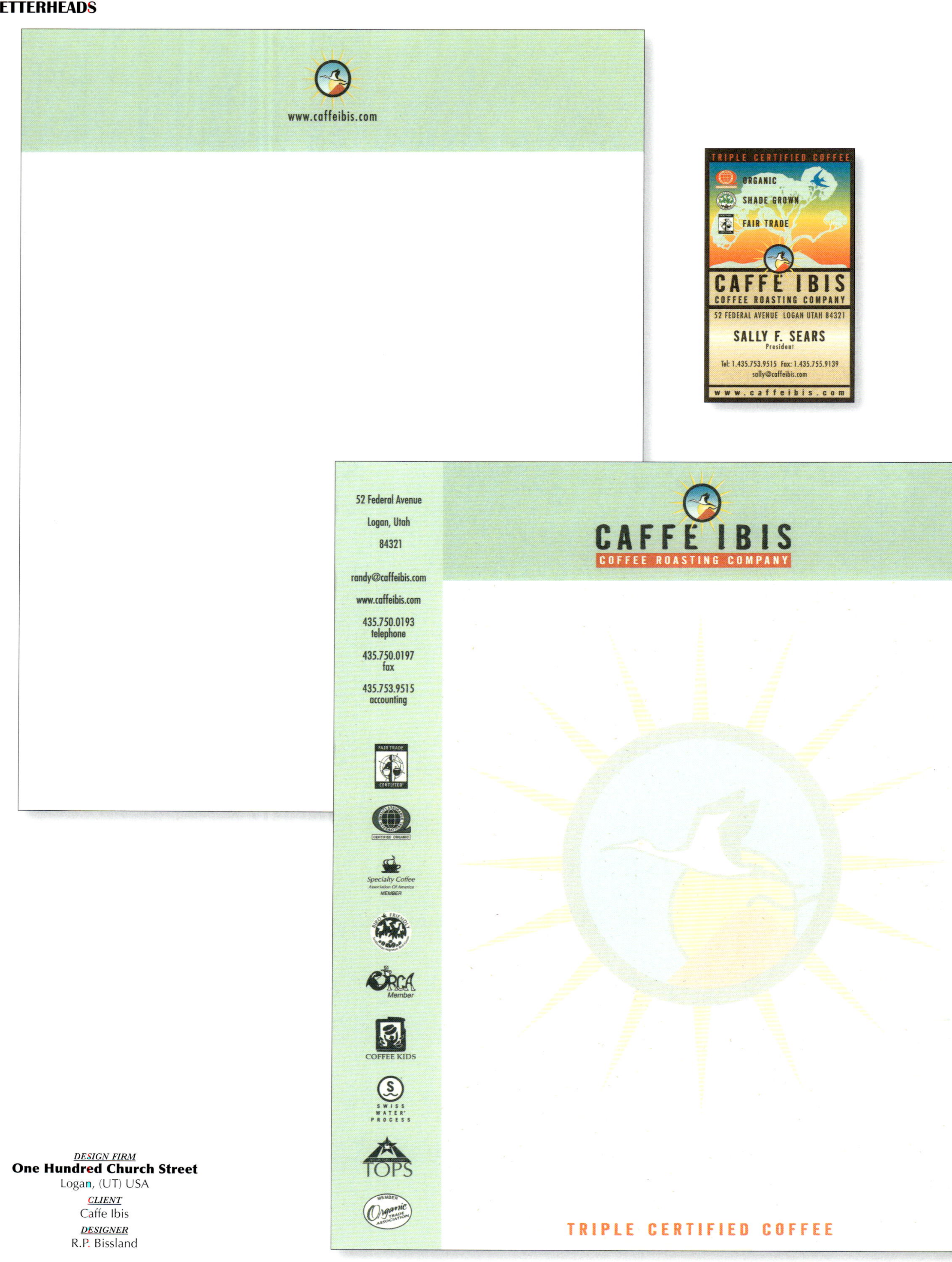

DESIGN FIRM
One Hundred Church Street
Logan, (UT) USA
CLIENT
Caffe Ibis
DESIGNER
R.P. Bissland

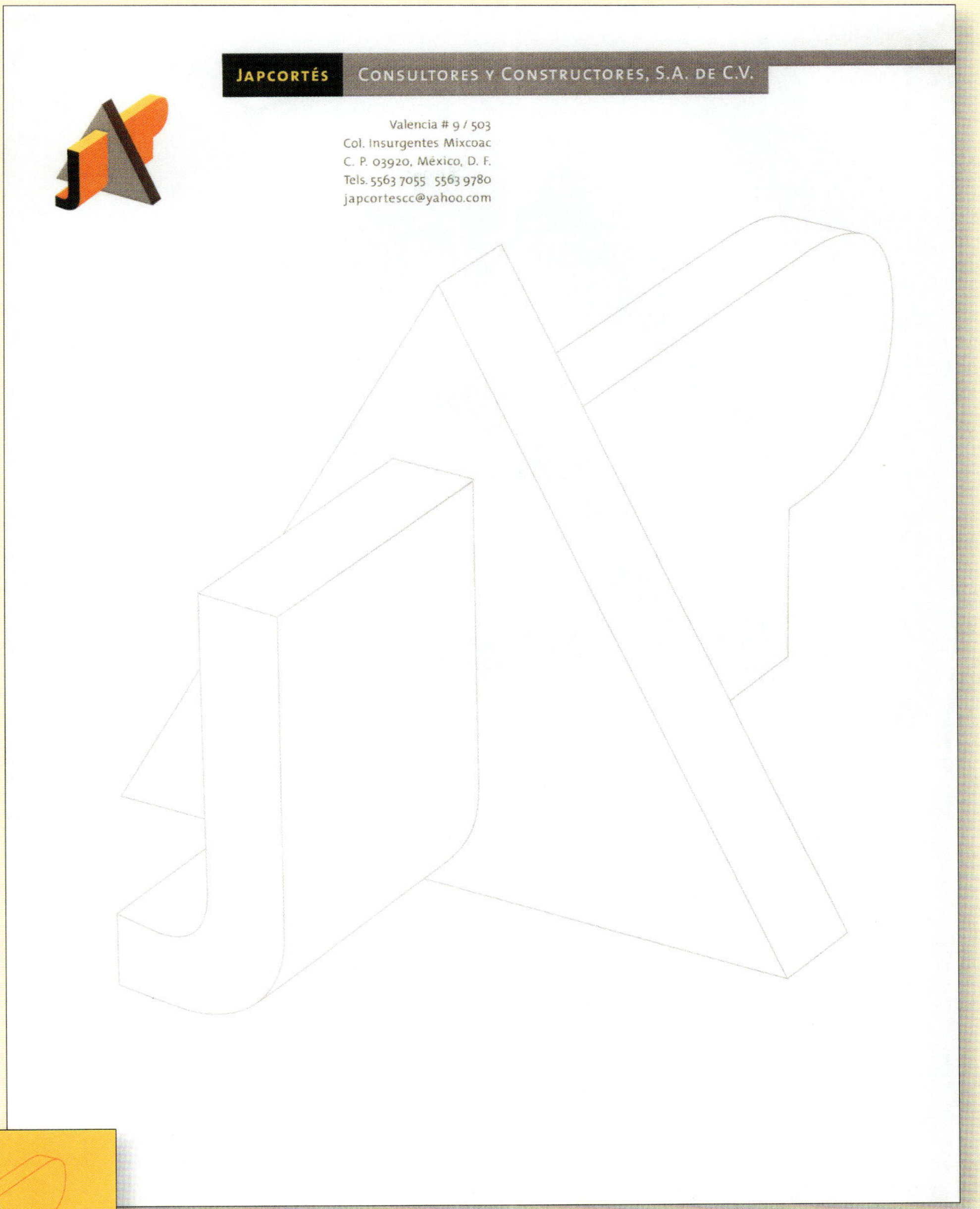

Japcortés Consultores y Constructores, S.A. de C.V.

Valencia # 9 / 503
Col. Insurgentes Mixcoac
C. P. 03920, México, D. F.
Tels. 5563 7055 5563 9780
japcortescc@yahoo.com

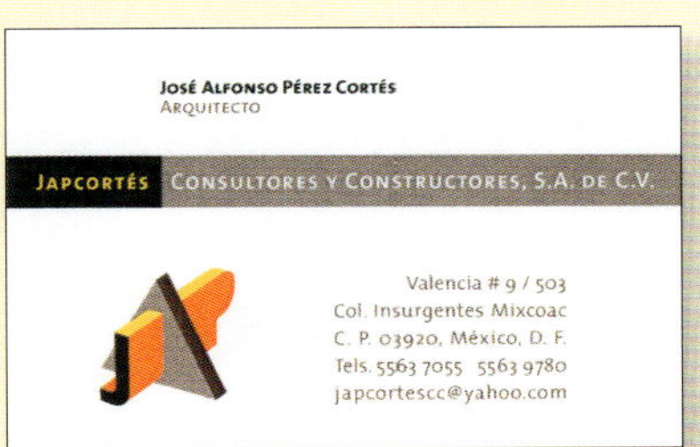

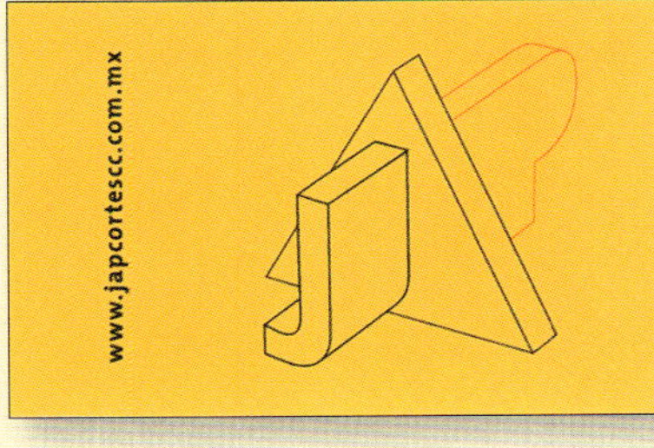

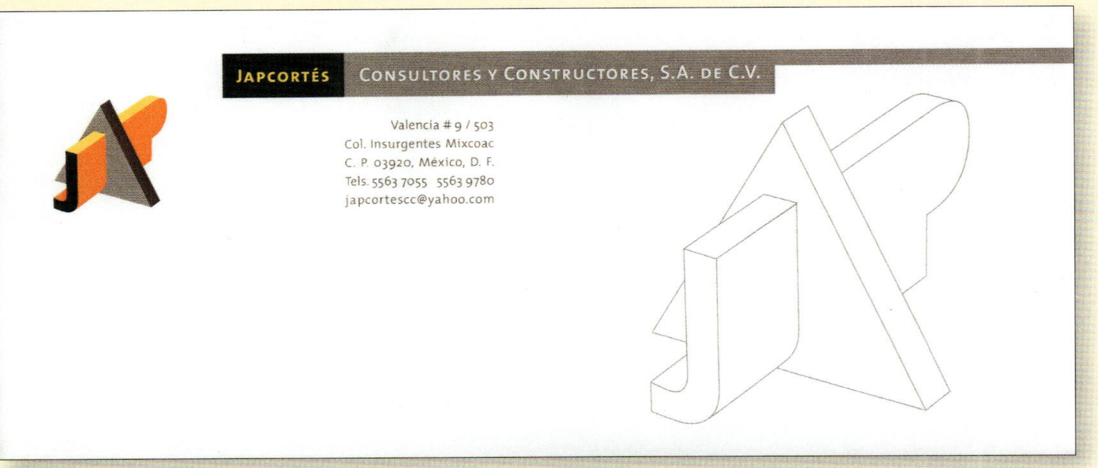

DESIGN FIRM
TD2
Mexico City, Mexico
CLIENT
Japcortes Architects
DESIGNER
Jose Luis Patiño

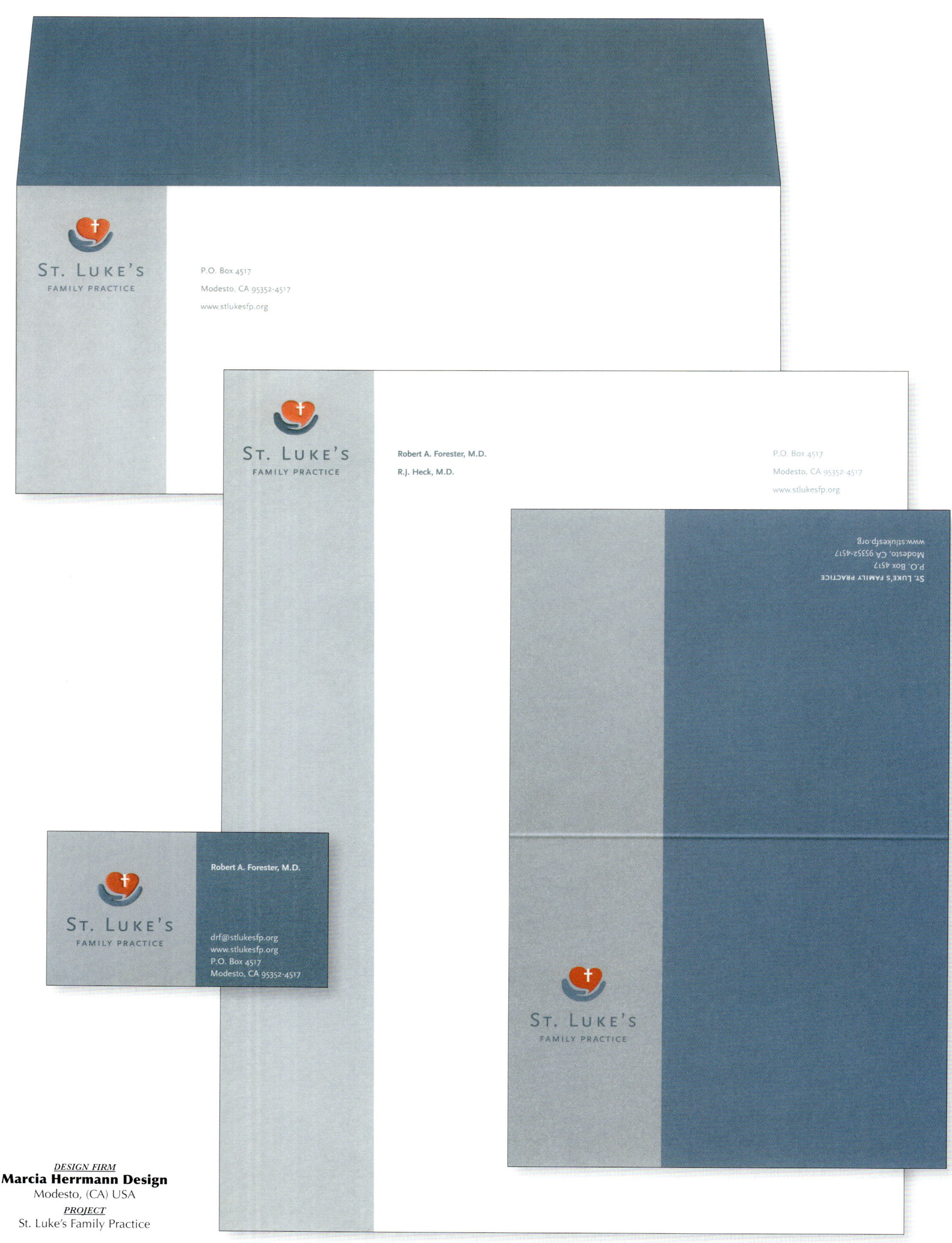

DESIGN FIRM
Marcia Herrmann Design
Modesto, (CA) USA
PROJECT
St. Luke's Family Practice

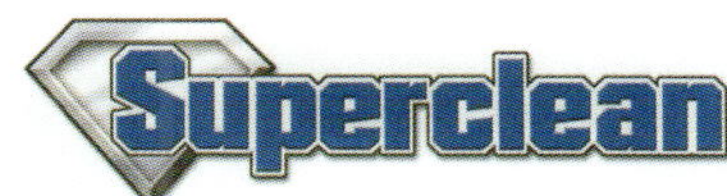

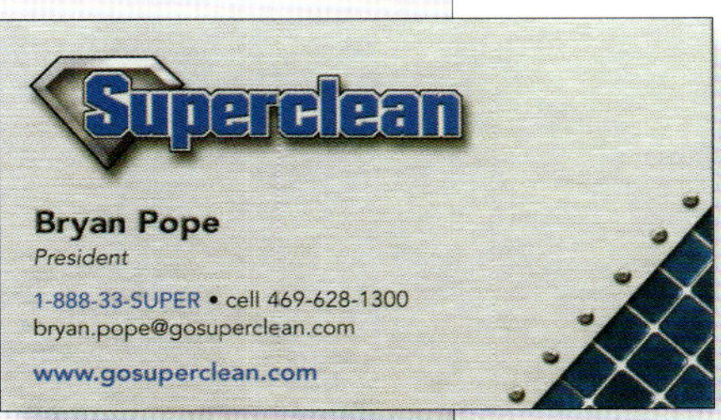

Superclean Service Company, Inc. • 2734 West Kingsley, Suite J2 • Garland, Texas 75041
1-888-33-SUPER • 972-926-1733 • Fax: 972-926-9733 • www.gosuperclean.com

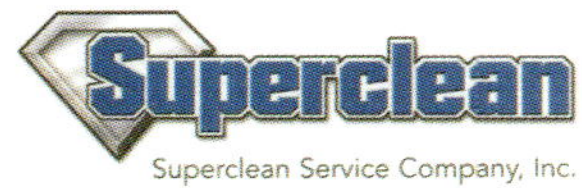

Superclean Service Company, Inc.
2734 West Kingsley, Suite J2
Garland, Texas 75041

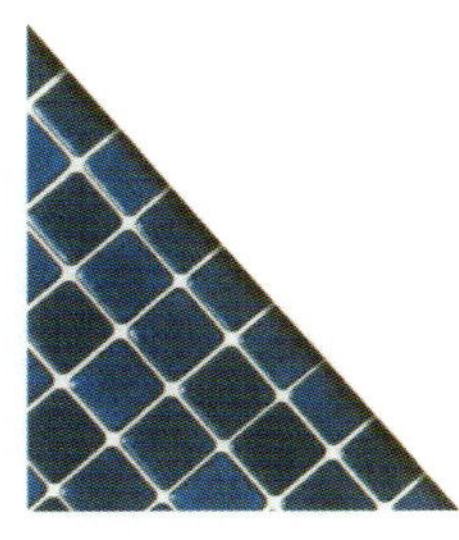

DESIGN FIRM
MDVC Creative
Dallas, (TX) USA
PROJECT
Superclean
CREATIVE DIRECTOR
Molly DeVoss

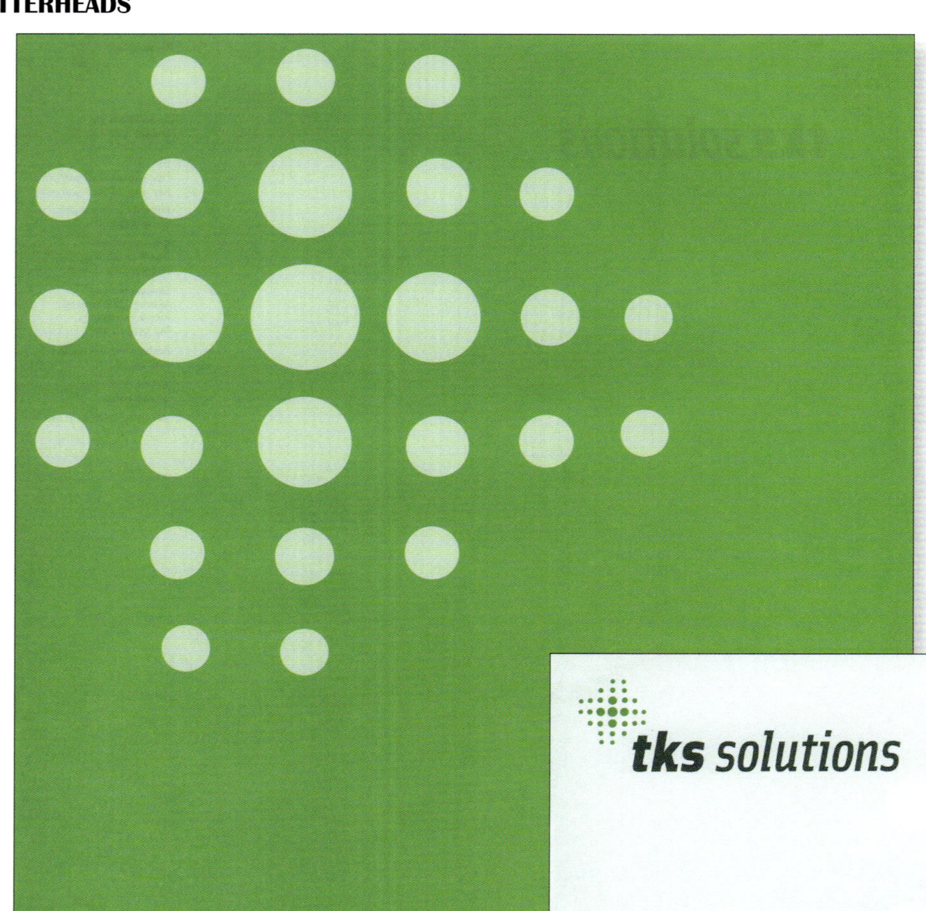

tks solutions

tks solutions gmbh
Ludwig-Beck-Ring 27
65239 Hochheim
Germany

Tel. +49 (0) 6146-906 961-2
Fax +49 (0) 6146-906 961-3

info@tks-solutions.com
www.tks-solutions.com

Geschäftsführer
Dipl.-Wirtsch.-Ing.
Thomas Katzenmeier

Bankverbindung
Mainzer Volksbank eG
Kto.Nr. 659 472 013
BLZ 551 900 00

Amtsgericht Wiesbaden
HRB 219 75

VAT-Nr. (Steuer-Nr.)
40 246 40072

VAT-ID-Nr. DE 81 44 71 610

DESIGN FIRM
Q
Wiesbaden, Germany
PROJECT
TKS Solutions
DESIGNERS
Marcel Kummerer,
Thilo von Debschitz

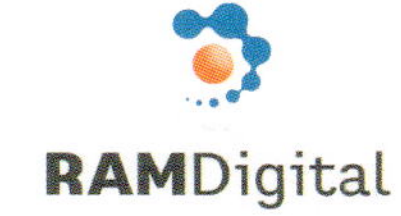

DESIGN FIRM
Octavo Designs
Frederick, (MD) USA

CLIENT
RAM Digital

ART DIRECTOR
Sue Hough

DESIGNERS
Sue Hough,
Mark Burrier

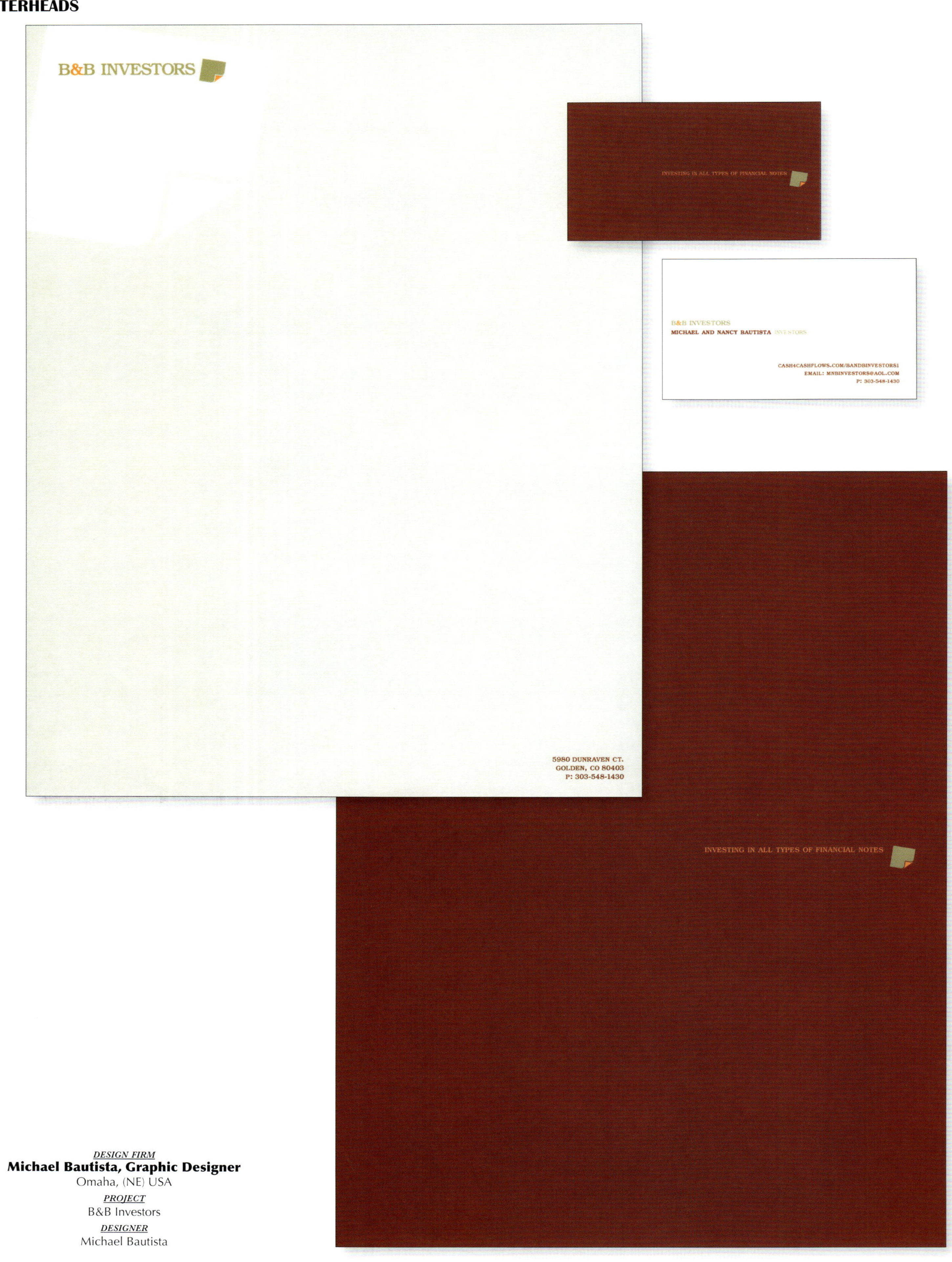

DESIGN FIRM
Michael Bautista, Graphic Designer
Omaha, (NE) USA
PROJECT
B&B Investors
DESIGNER
Michael Bautista

THIELEN DESIGNS
115 GOLD AVE. SUITE 209
*ALBUQUERQUE, NM
87104
SALE
·02¢
505 205 3157
WWW.THIELENDESIGNS.COM
49.95 USD
Tony Thielen
Tony@ThielenDesigns.com

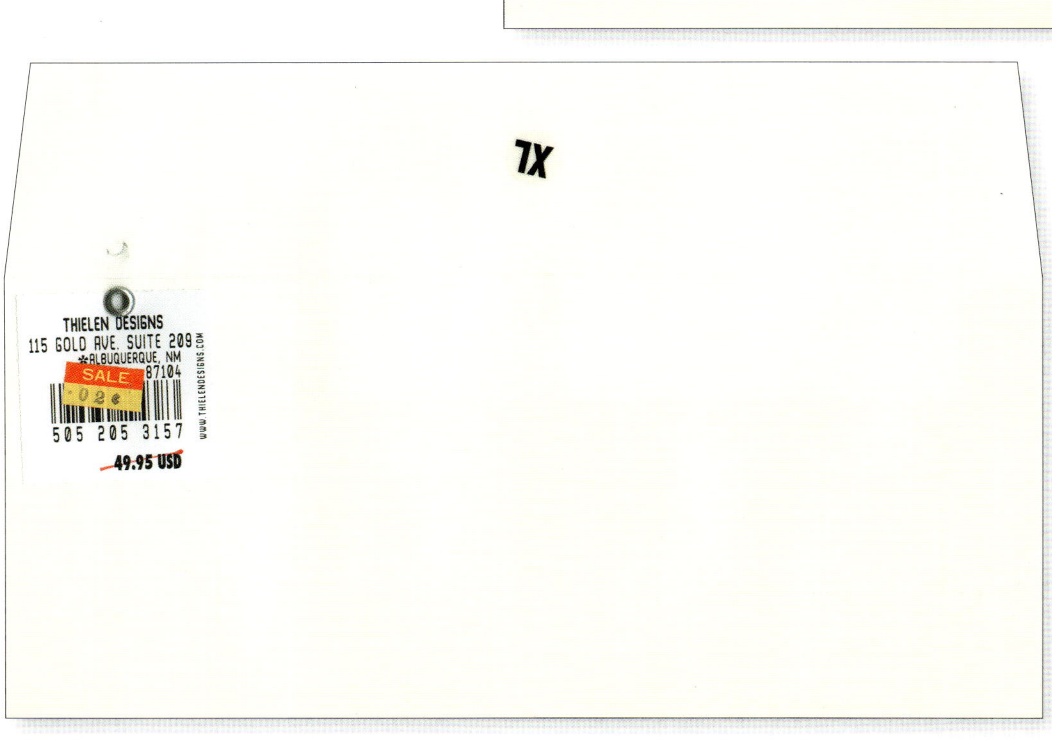

DESIGN FIRM
Thielen Designs
Albuquerque, (NM) USA
PROJECT
Thielen Designs Stationery
ART DIRECTOR, DESIGNER
Tony Thielen

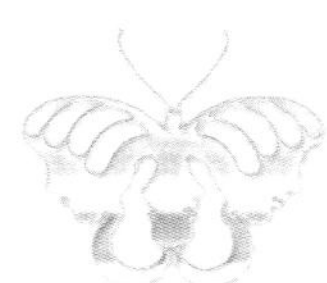

United States ✦ French Leave Resort ✦ 2121 Old Gatesburg Road ✦ State College ✦ Pennsylvania ✦ 16803

Bahamas ✦ French Leave Resort ✦ PO Box EL-80 ✦ Governor's Harbour ✦ Eleuthera ✦ Bahamas

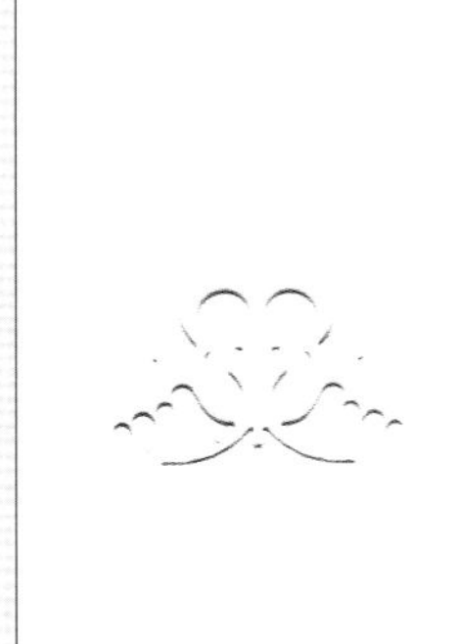

Eddie Lauth

485 Scenery Drive
State College, PA 16801
United States

814.234.2903
eddie@frenchleaveresort.com

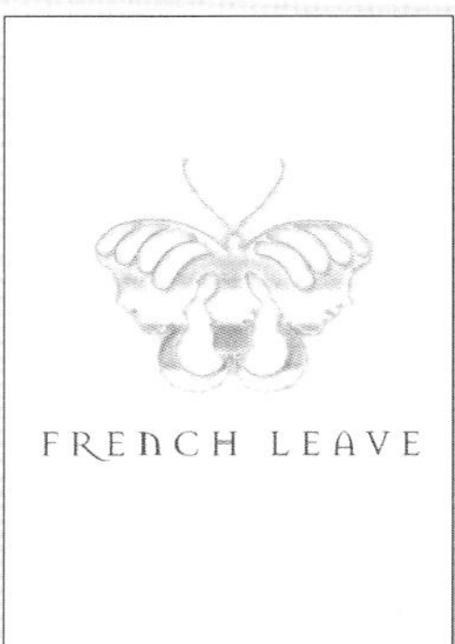

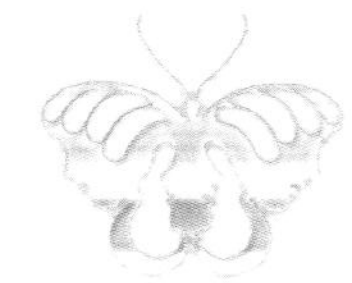

DESIGN FIRM
Sommese Design
Port Matilda, (PA) USA
PROJECT
French Leave
ART DIRECTORS
Kristen Sommese,
Lanny Sommese
DESIGNERS
Kristen Sommese,
Ryan Russell
ILLUSTRATOR
Lanny Sommese

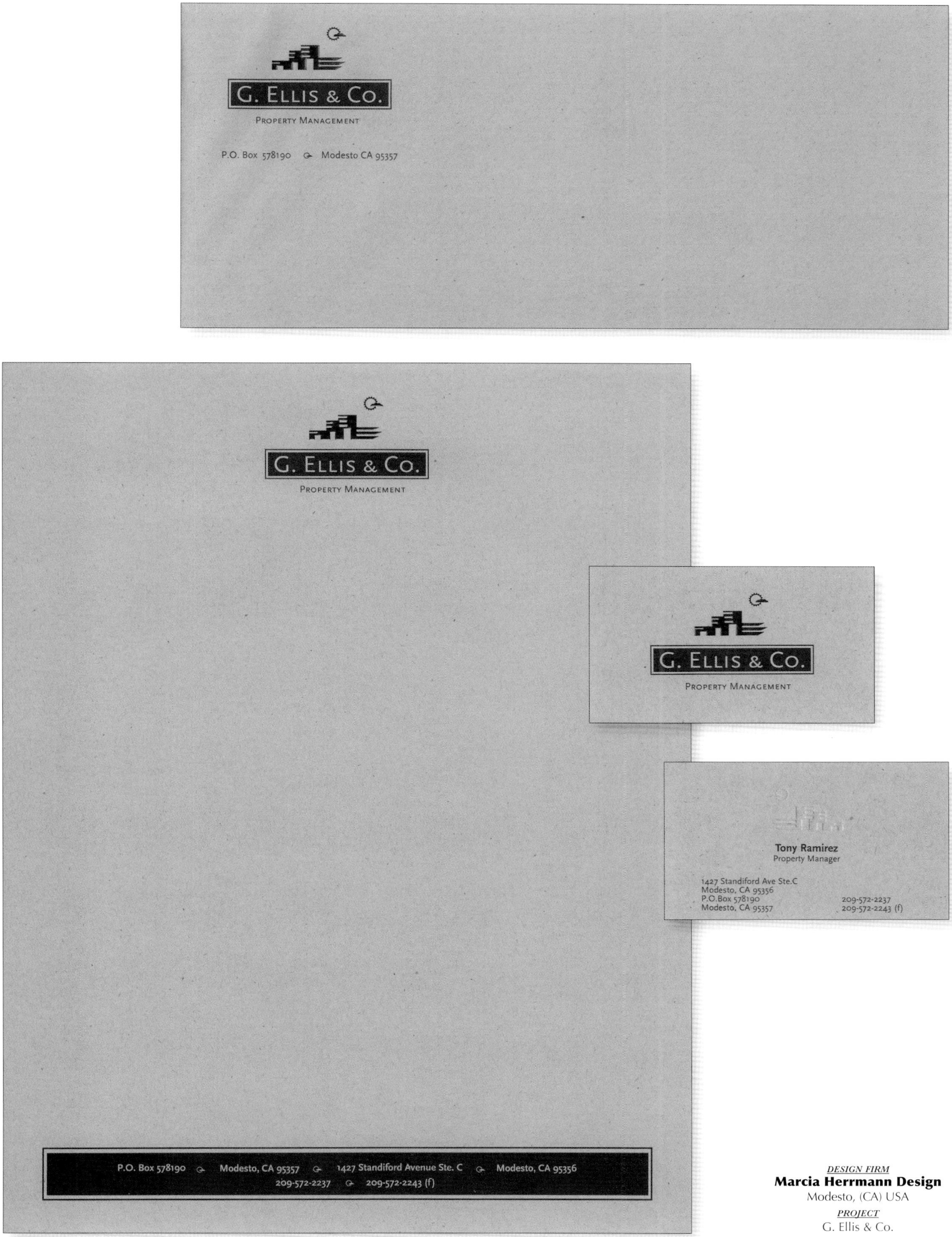

G. Ellis & Co.
Property Management

P.O. Box 578190 Modesto, CA 95357 1427 Standiford Avenue Ste. C Modesto, CA 95356
209-572-2237 209-572-2243 (f)

G. Ellis & Co.
Property Management

Tony Ramirez
Property Manager

1427 Standiford Ave Ste.C
Modesto, CA 95356
P.O.Box 578190
Modesto, CA 95357
209-572-2237
209-572-2243 (f)

DESIGN FIRM
Marcia Herrmann Design
Modesto, (CA) USA
PROJECT
G. Ellis & Co.

Saskia Ltd.
CULTURAL DOCUMENTATION

SASKIA LTD | Cultural Documentation

5 HORIZON LANE
FREEPORT, MAINE 04032

207.865-7080 voice
207.865-4336 facsimile

INFO@SASKIA.COM e-mail
www.saskia.com

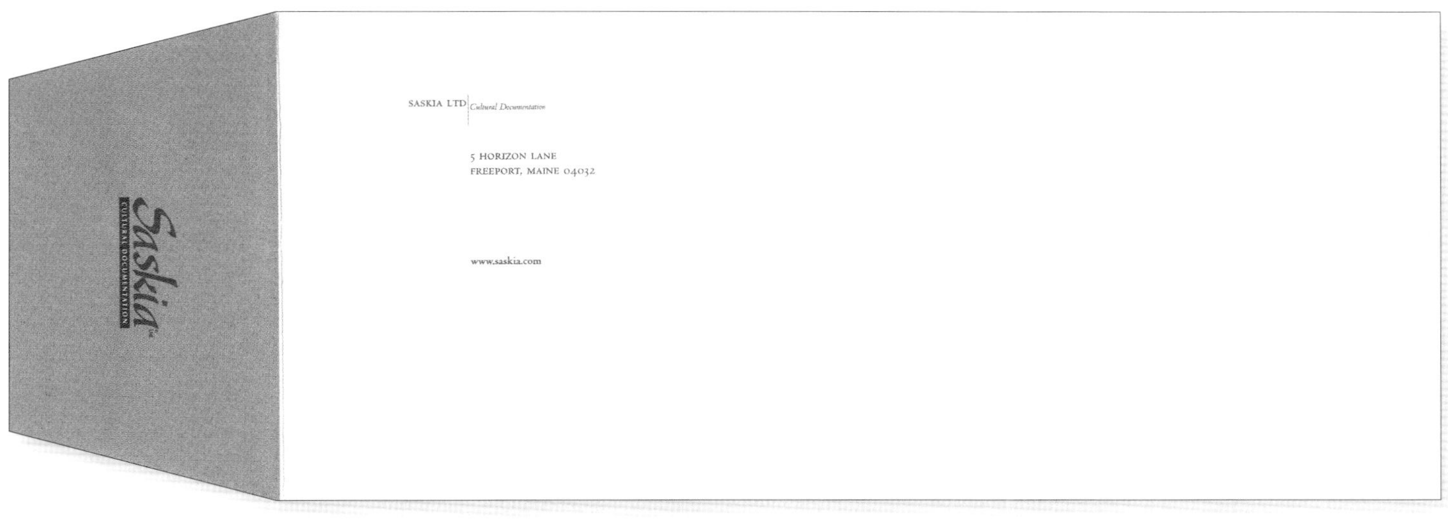

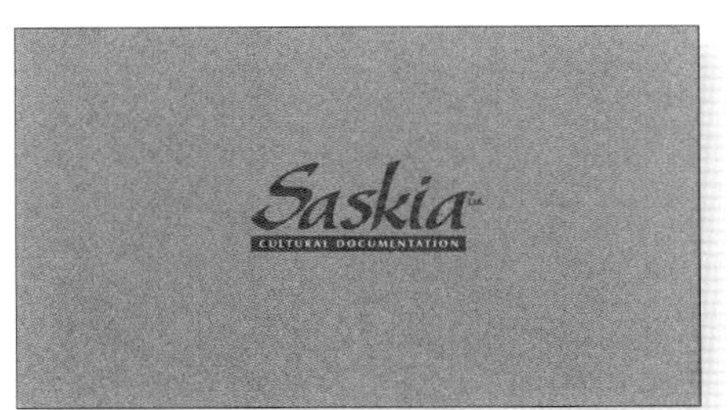

Maryann Ballotta
ACCOUNT MANAGER
SASKIA LTD Cultural Documentation
5 HORIZON LANE
FREEPORT, MAINE 04032
877.SASKIA-4 toll free
207.865-7080 voice
877.SASKIA-5 facsimile
MARYANN@SASKIA.COM e-mail
www.saskia.com

DESIGN FIRM
Gouthier Design: a brand collective
Fort Lauderdale, (FL) USA
CLIENT
Saskia, Ltd.
CREATIVE DIRECTOR
Jonathan Gouthier
DESIGNER
Kiley del Valle
PRINTER
Southeastern Printing

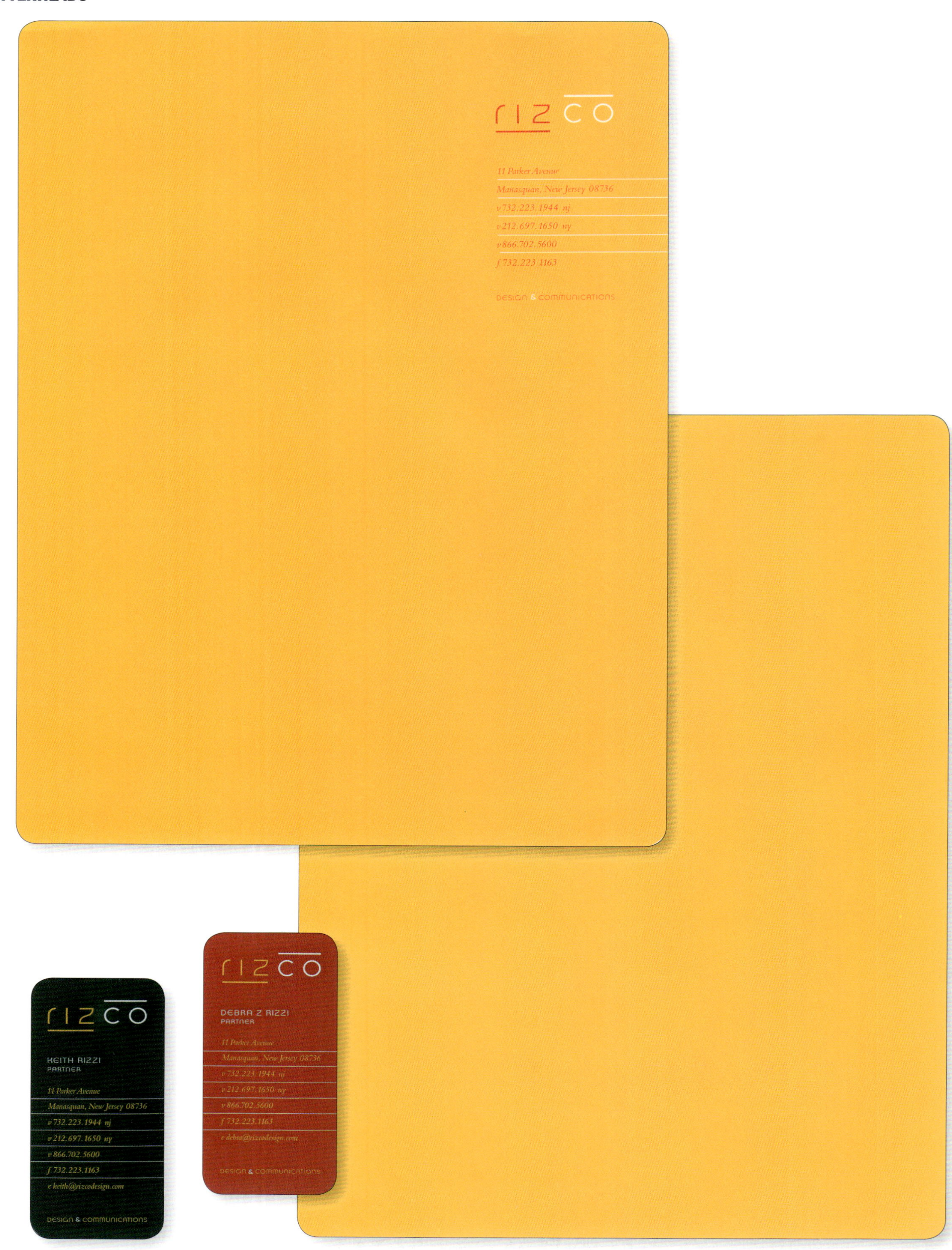
rizco
11 Parker Avenue
Manasquan, New Jersey 08736
v 732.223.1944 nj
v 212.697.1650 ny
v 866.702.5600
f 732.223.1163
DESIGN & COMMUNICATIONS
KEITH RIZZI
PARTNER
e keith@rizcodesign.com
DEBRA Z RIZZI
PARTNER
e debra@rizcodesign.com

rizco
11 Parker Avenue
Manasquan, New Jersey 08736
v732.223.1944 nj
v212.697.1650 ny
v866.702.5600
f732.223.1163
design & communications

content

rizco

DESIGN FIRM
Rizco Design & Communications
Manasquan, (NJ) USA
PROJECT
Rizco Design Identity Program
ART DIRECTOR, DESIGNER
Keith Rizzi

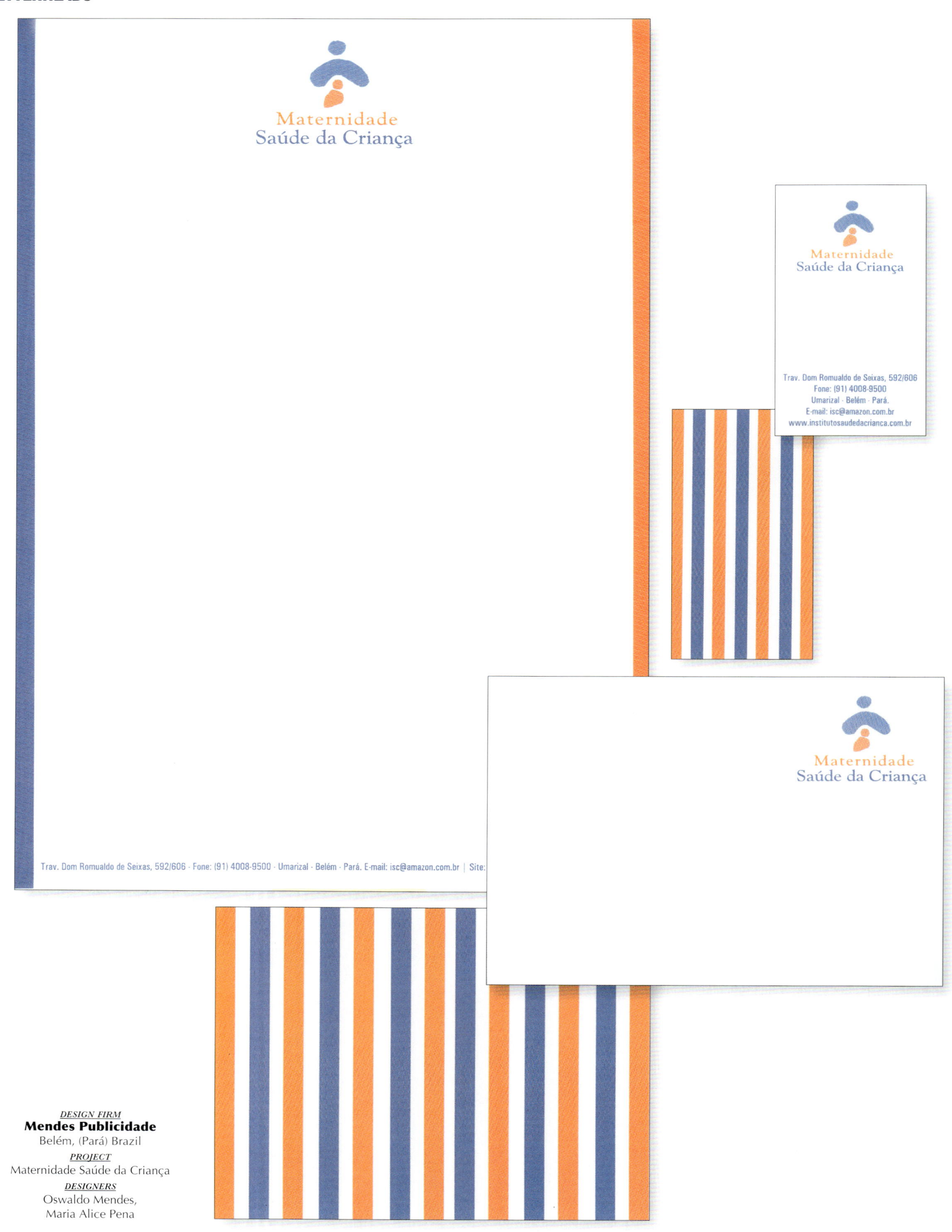

DESIGN FIRM
Mendes Publicidade
Belém, (Pará) Brazil
PROJECT
Maternidade Saúde da Criança
DESIGNERS
Oswaldo Mendes,
Maria Alice Pena

DESIGN FIRM
Octavo Designs
Frederick, (MD) USA
CLIENT
Healing Connections
ART DIRECTOR
Sue Hough
DESIGNERS
Sue Hough,
Mark Burrier

DESIGN FIRM
THiNK Ink & Design
Madison, (WI) USA
PROJECT
THiNK Ink & Design Stationery
DESIGNERS
THiNK Ink & Design Creative Team

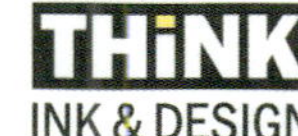
THiNK
INK & DESIGN
2819 Royal Avenue, Madison, WI 53713

2819 Royal Avenue, Madison, WI 53713 ■ 608.251.7300 ■ Fax 608.251.2141
thinkinkanddesign.com

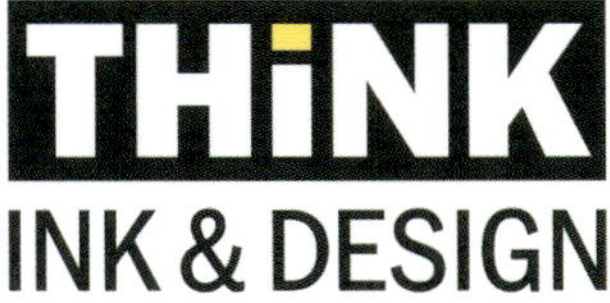
THiNK
INK & DESIGN

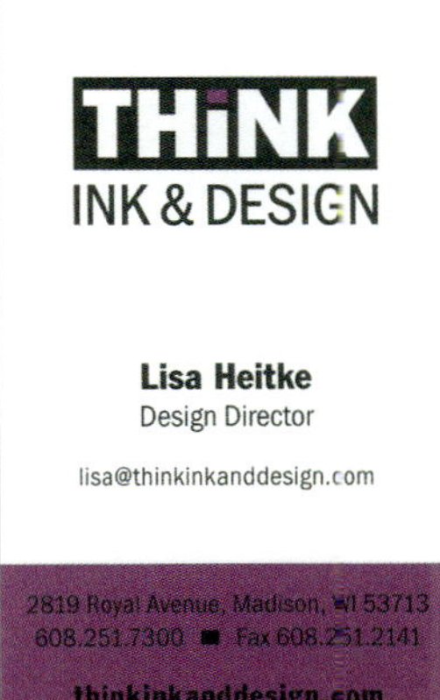
THiNK
INK & DESIGN
Lisa Heitke
Design Director
lisa@thinkinkanddesign.com
2819 Royal Avenue, Madison, WI 53713
608.251.7300 ■ Fax 608.251.2141
thinkinkanddesign.com

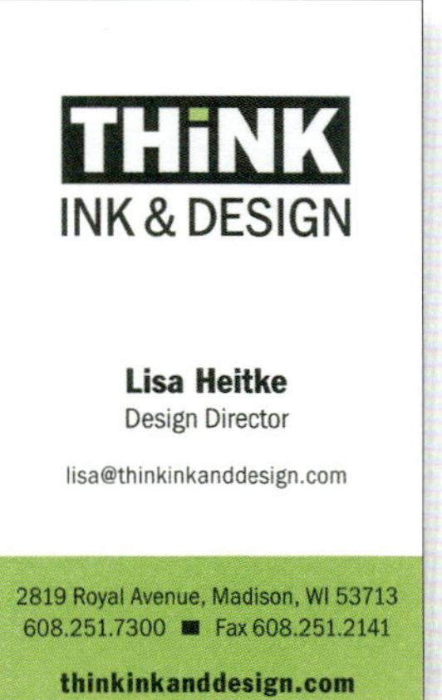
THiNK
INK & DESIGN
Lisa Heitke
Design Director
lisa@thinkinkanddesign.com
2819 Royal Avenue, Madison, WI 53713
608.251.7300 ■ Fax 608.251.2141
thinkinkanddesign.com

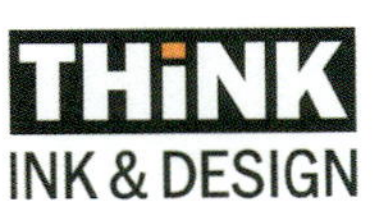
THiNK
INK & DESIGN
Lisa Heitke
Design Director
lisa@thinkinkanddesign.com
2819 Royal Avenue, Madison, WI 53713
608.251.7300 ■ Fax 608.251.2141
thinkinkanddesign.com

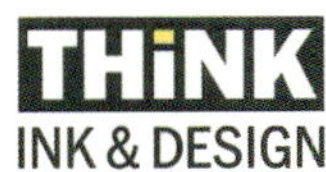
THiNK
INK & DESIGN
2819 Royal Avenue, Madison, WI 53713

DESIGN FIRM
At First Sight
Ormond, Australia
PROJECT
Madame Monarch
CREATIVE DIRECTOR
Olivia Brown
DESIGNER
Barry Selleck

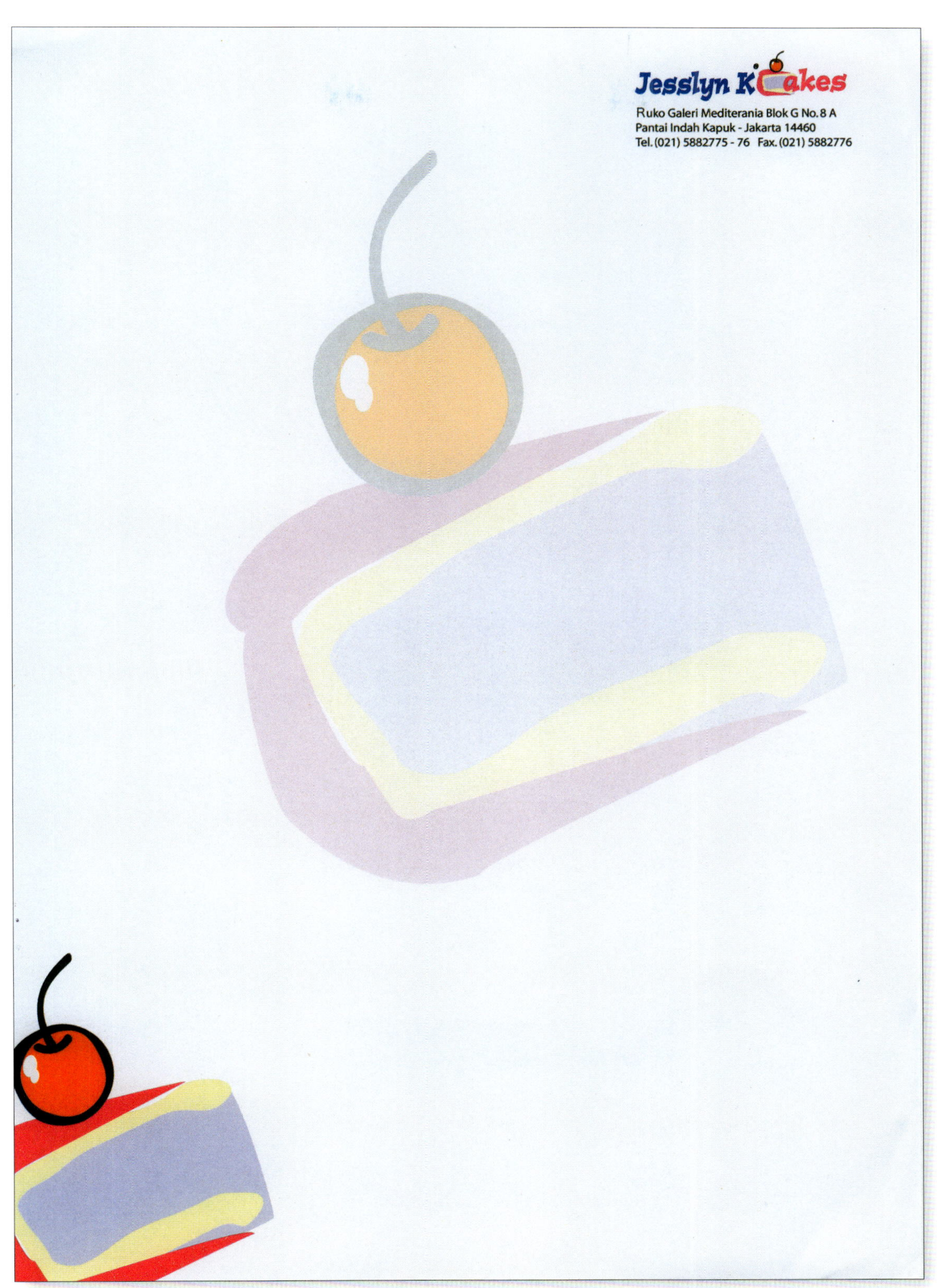

DESIGN FIRM
TrueFACES Creation Sdn. Bhd.
Selangor, Malaysia
PROJECT
Jesslyn K'akes
DESIGNERS
TrueFACES Creative Team

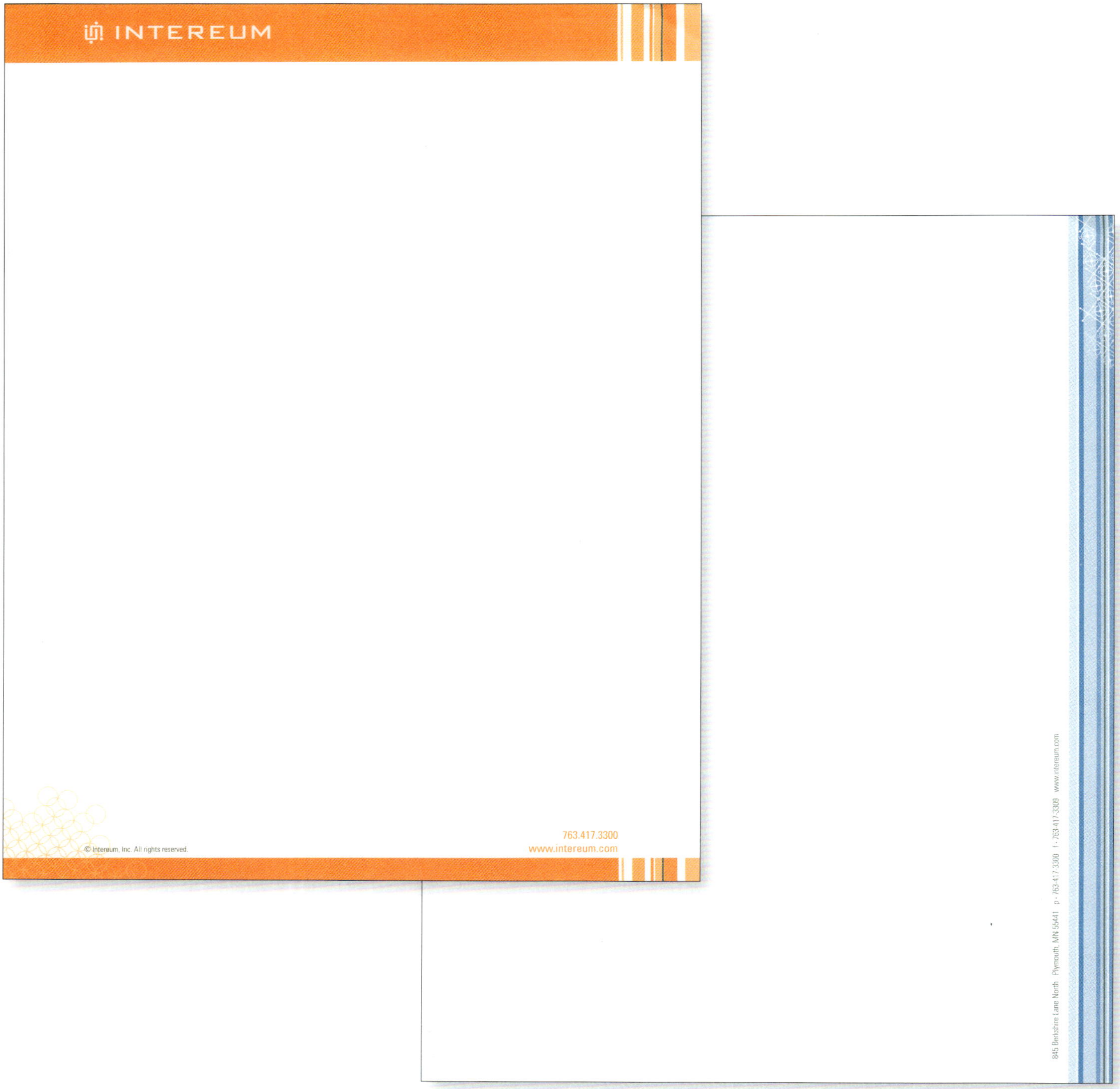

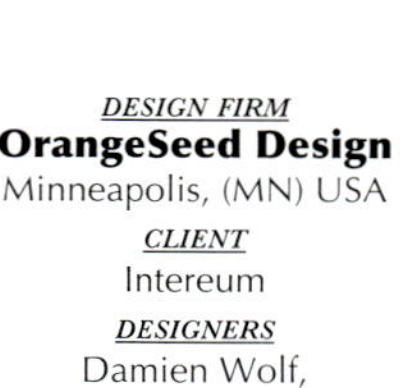

DESIGN FIRM
OrangeSeed Design
Minneapolis, (MN) USA
CLIENT
Intereum
DESIGNERS
Damien Wolf,
Phil Hoch

INTEREUM
845 Berkshire Lane North   Plymouth, MN 55441

INTEREUM
845 Berkshire Lane North   Plymouth, MN 55441

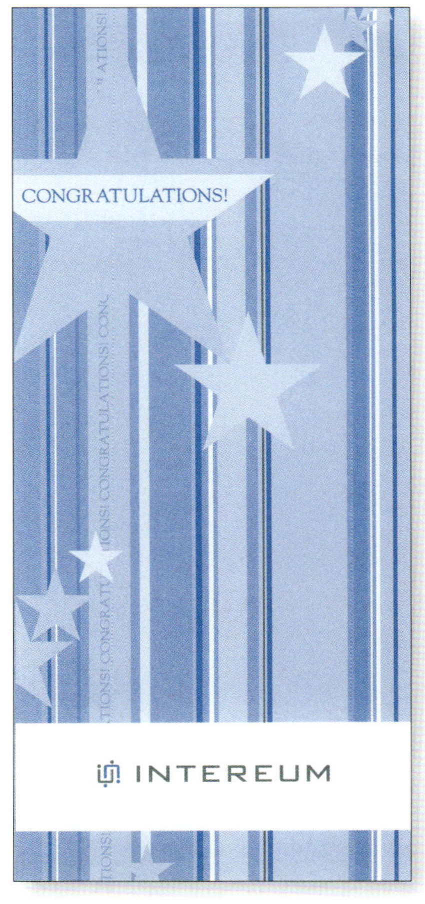
CONGRATULATIONS!
INTEREUM

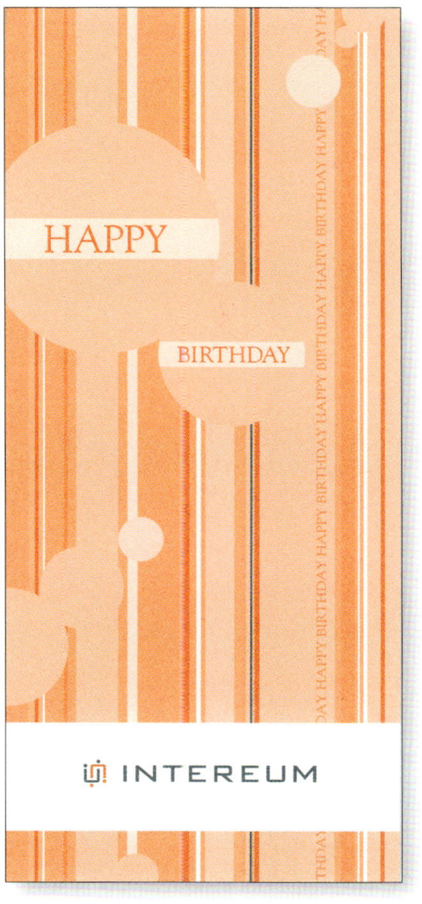
HAPPY
BIRTHDAY
INTEREUM

M

Mozambique
RESTAURANT • COASTAL LOUNGE
GREAT STEAKS ✦ GIANT PRAWNS ✦ CRISPED CHICKEN
T ✦ 949-715-7100 F ✦ 949-715-7101 1740 S. Coast Hwy Laguna Beach, CA 92651 www.MozambiqueOC.com

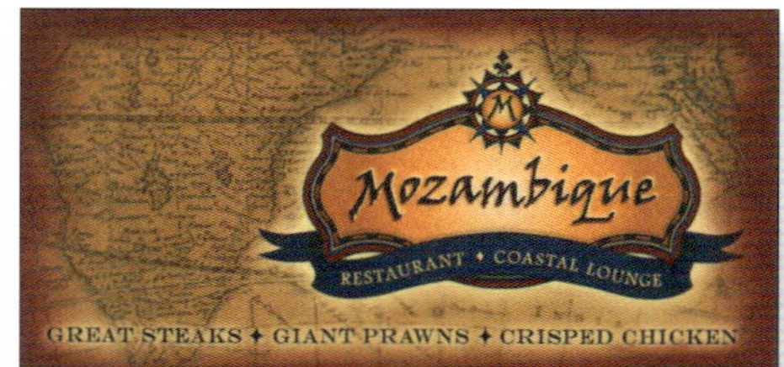

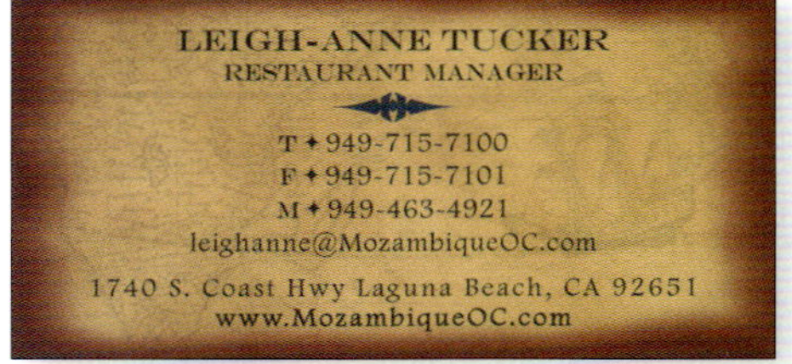

DESIGN FIRM
On The Edge Design
Newport Beach, (CA) USA
PROJECT
Mozambique Restaurant & Coastal Lounge
DESIGNER
Gina Mims

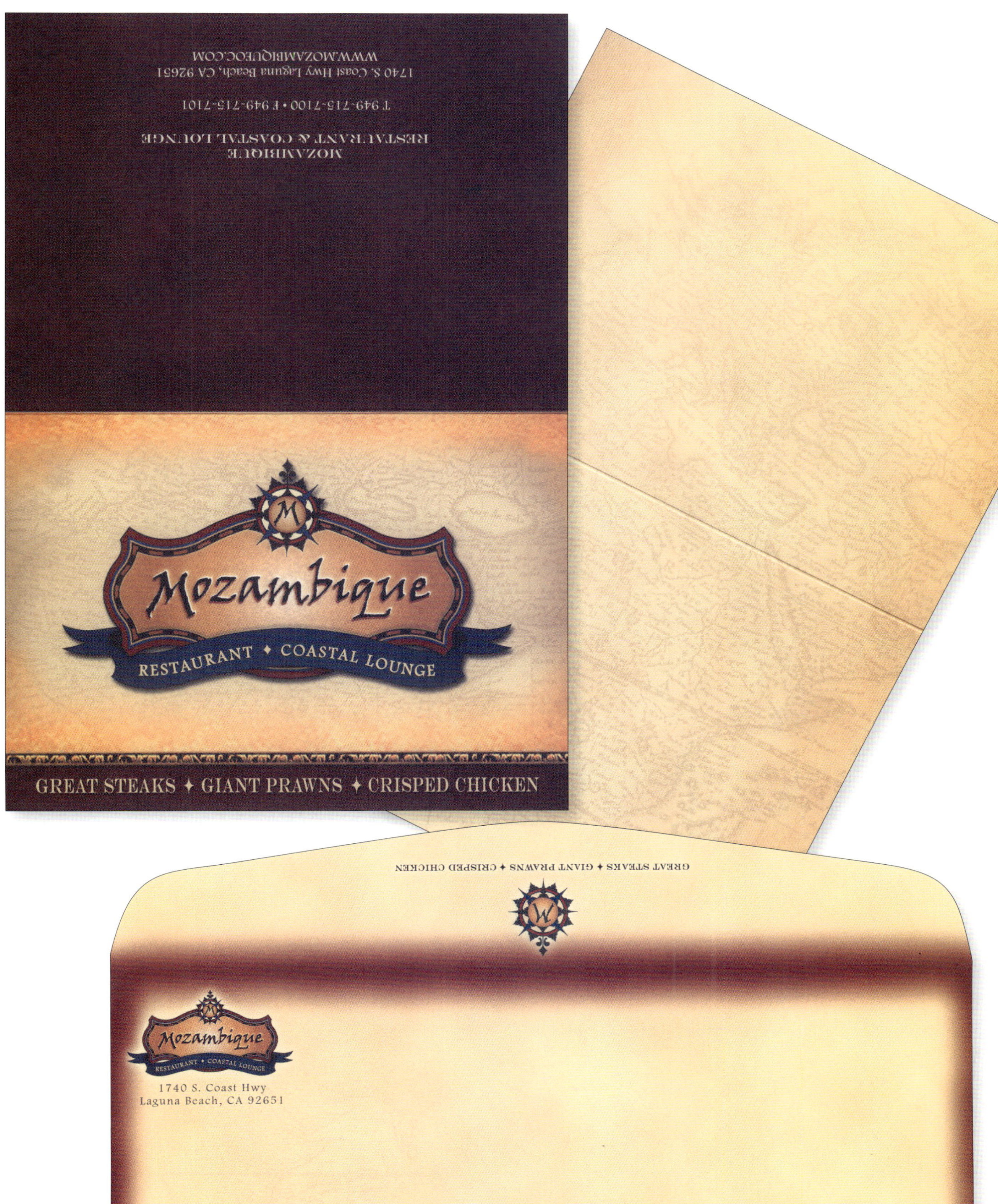
MOZAMBIQUE
RESTAURANT & COASTAL LOUNGE
T 949-715-7100 • F 949-715-7101
1740 S. Coast Hwy Laguna Beach, CA 92651
WWW.MOZAMBIQUEOC.COM
Mozambique
RESTAURANT ✦ COASTAL LOUNGE
GREAT STEAKS ✦ GIANT PRAWNS ✦ CRISPED CHICKEN
GREAT STEAKS ✦ GIANT PRAWNS ✦ CRISPED CHICKEN
Mozambique
RESTAURANT • COASTAL LOUNGE
1740 S. Coast Hwy
Laguna Beach, CA 92651

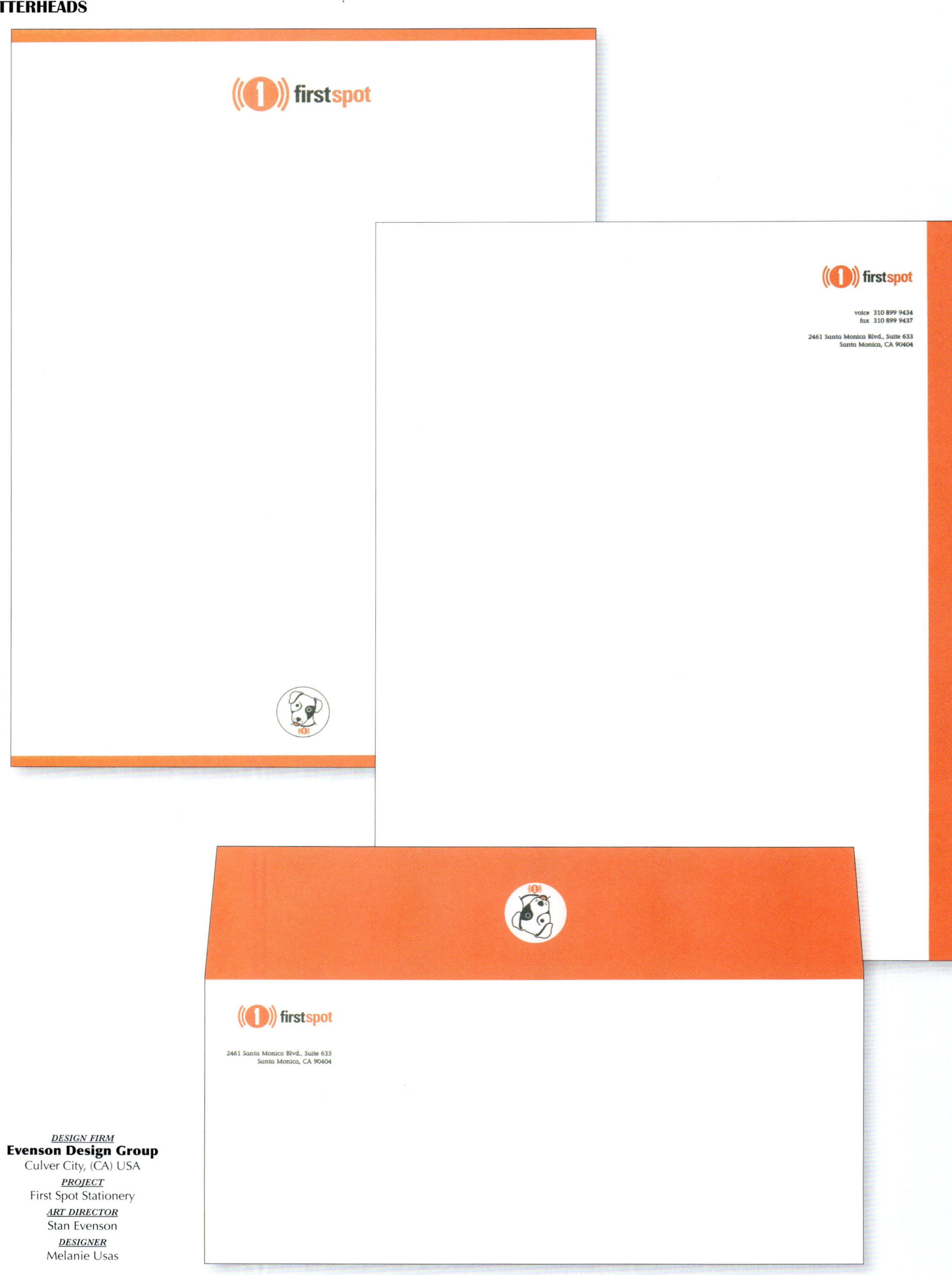

DESIGN FIRM
Evenson Design Group
Culver City, (CA) USA

PROJECT
First Spot Stationery

ART DIRECTOR
Stan Evenson

DESIGNER
Melanie Usas

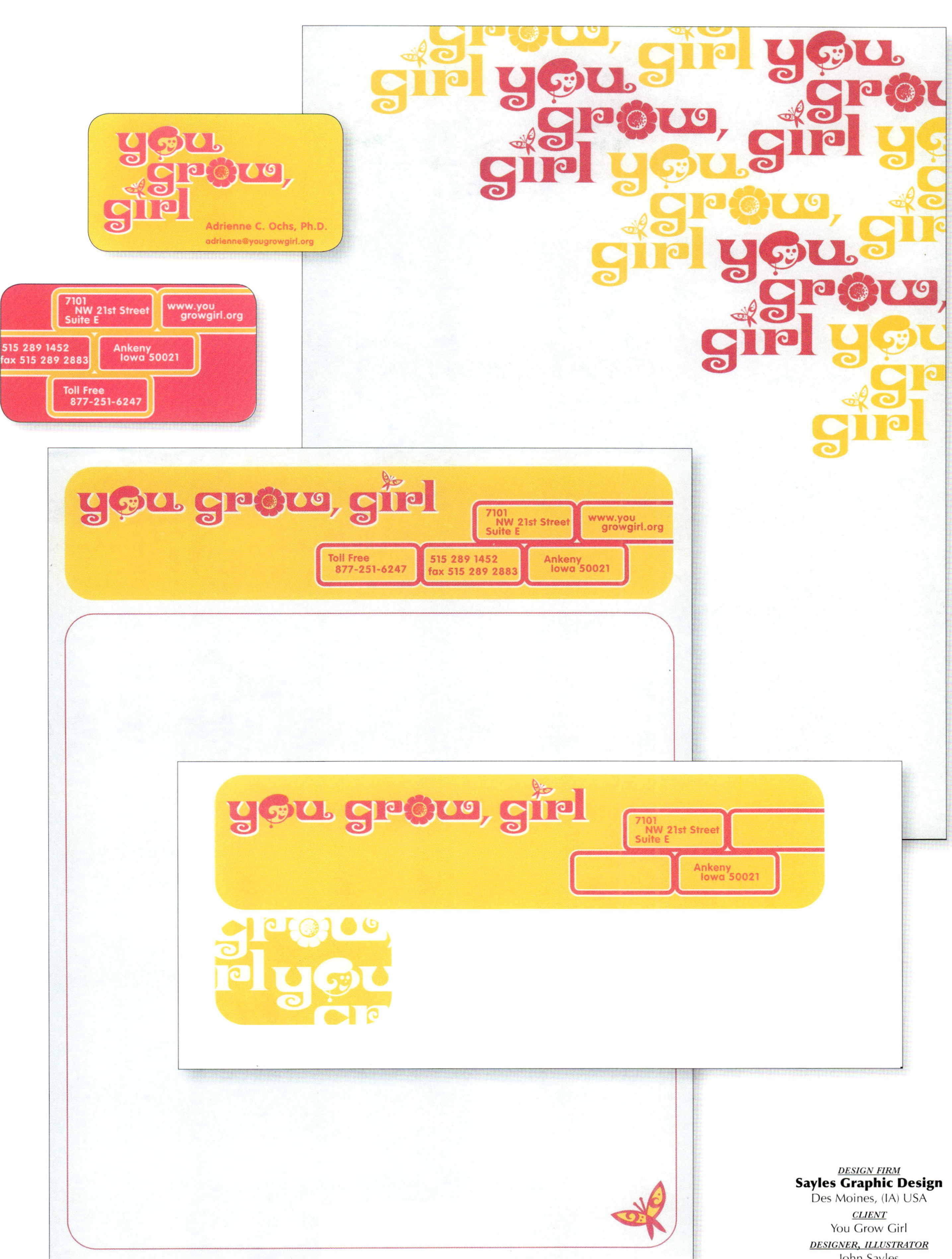

DESIGN FIRM
Sayles Graphic Design
Des Moines, (IA) USA
CLIENT
You Grow Girl
DESIGNER, ILLUSTRATOR
John Sayles

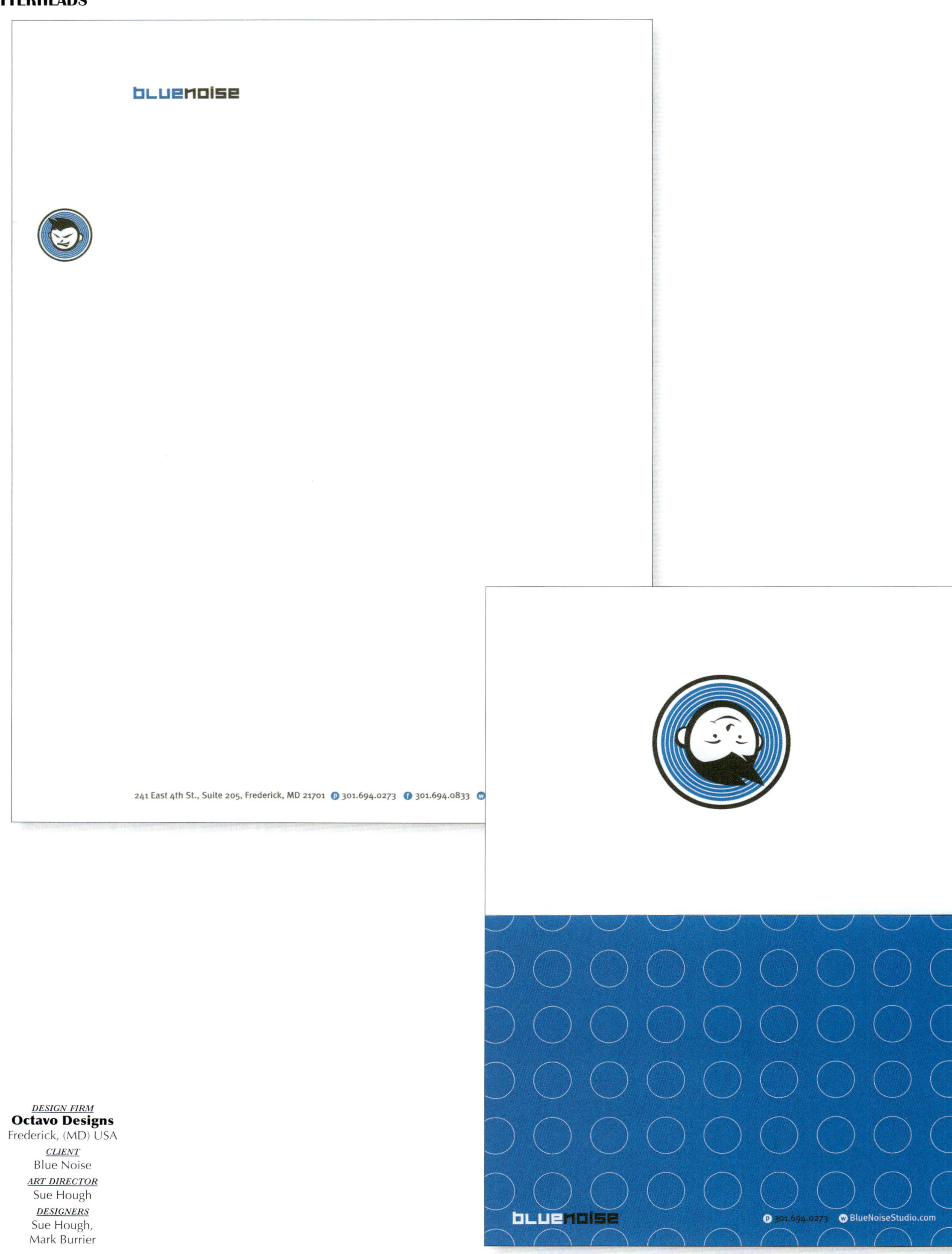

DESIGN FIRM
Octavo Designs
Frederick, (MD) USA
CLIENT
Blue Noise
ART DIRECTOR
Sue Hough
DESIGNERS
Sue Hough,
Mark Burrier

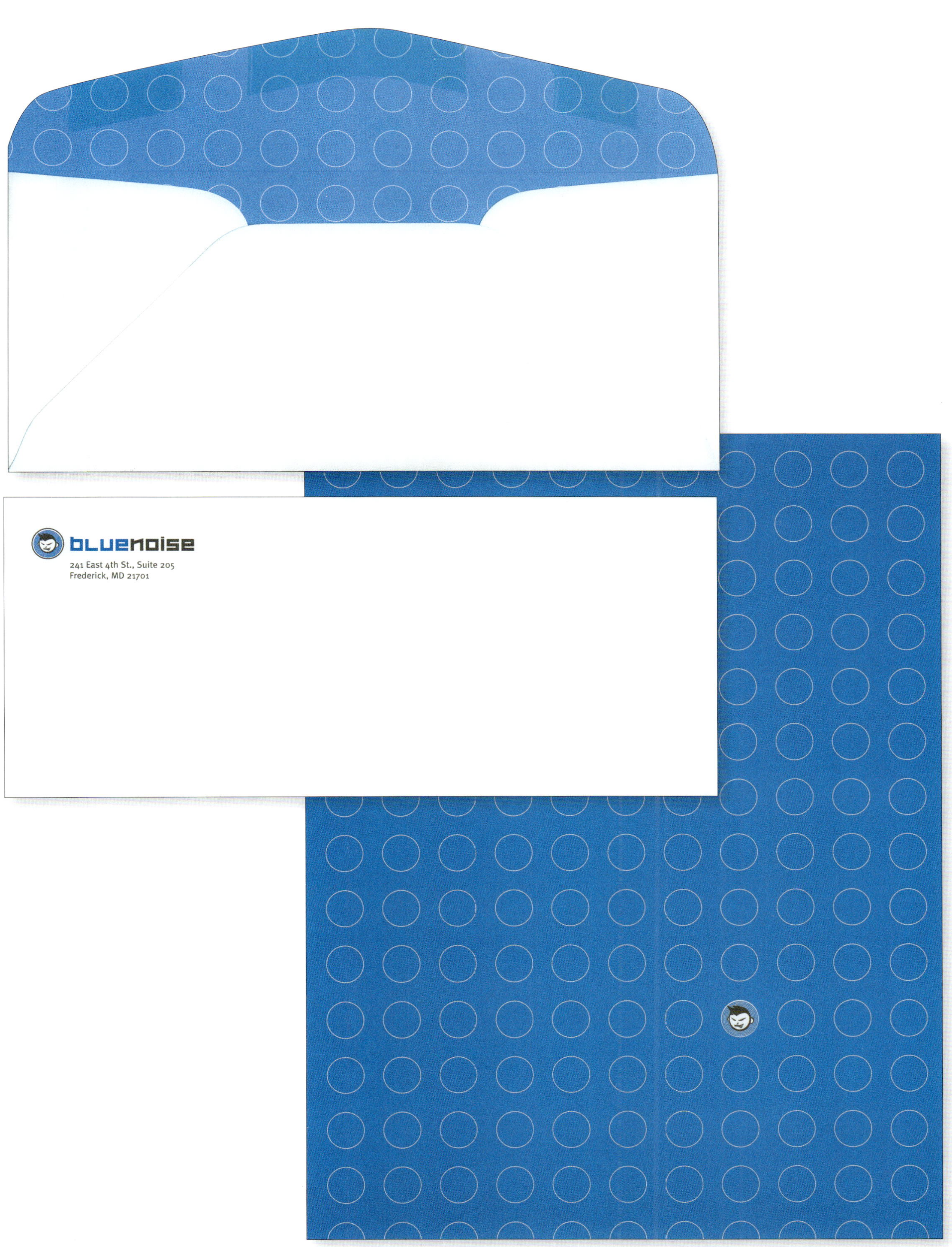
bluenoise
241 East 4th St., Suite 205
Frederick, MD 21701

159 South McClellan
Spokane, WA 99201

THINK

tel/509.624.4407
fax/509.624.4985

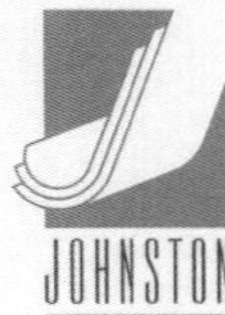

www.johnstonprinting.com

DESIGN FIRM
Klündt Hosmer
Spokane, (WA) USA
PROJECT
Johnston Printing Stationery
ART DIRECTOR
Darin Klündt
DESIGNER
Lorri Johnston

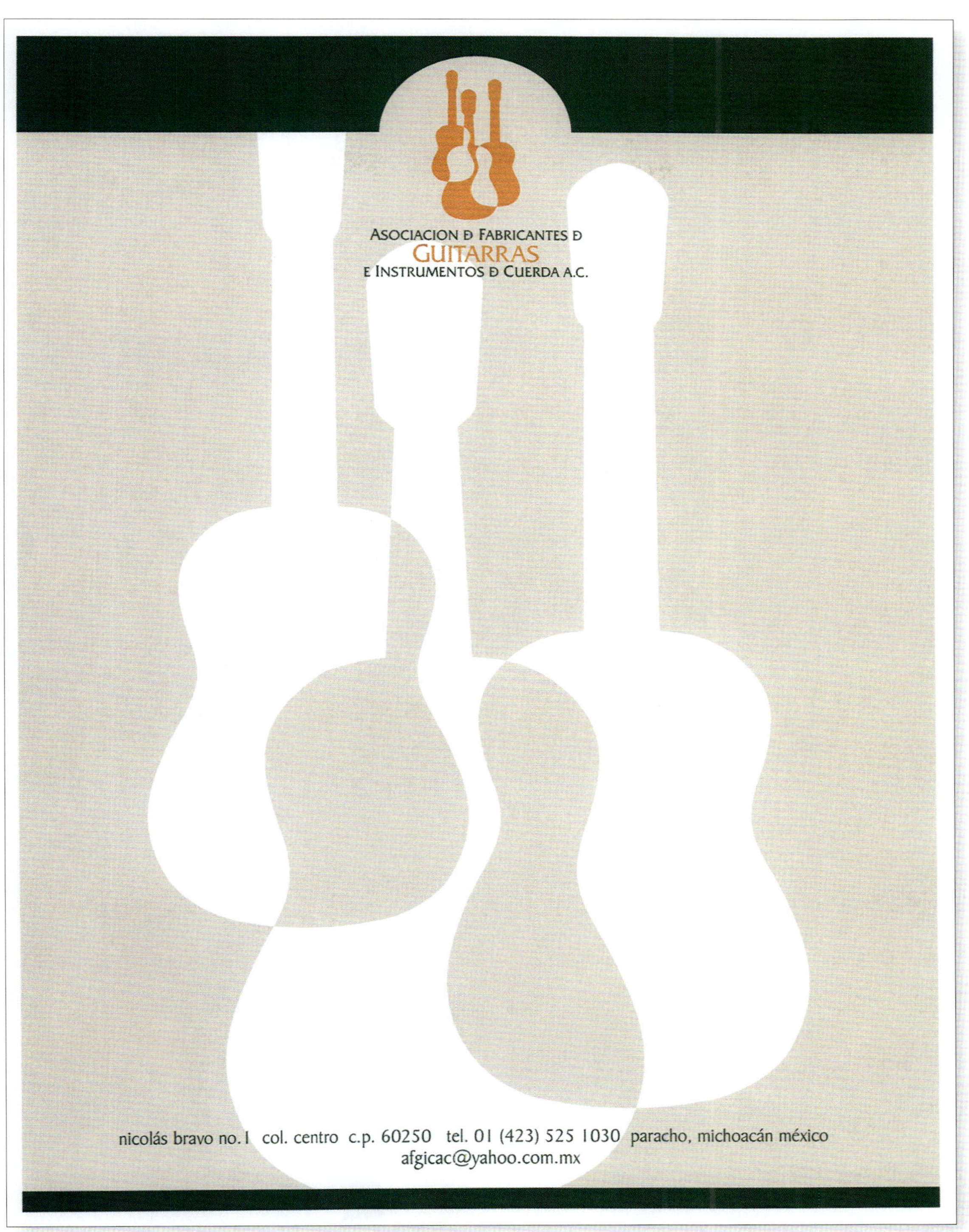

DESIGN FIRM
Kenneth Diseño
Uruapan (Michoacan), Mexico
PROJECT
Fabricantes De Guitarras De Paracho
DESIGNERS
Kenneth Treviño,
Minerva Galván

2100 Yakima Avenue
Tacoma, WA 98402
T 253 272 2505
F 253 272 2255

www.CITYSTEPSTACOMA.com

DESIGN FIRM
BCRA
Tacoma, (WA) USA
PROJECT
City Steps Stationery
DESIGNER
Danielle Larson

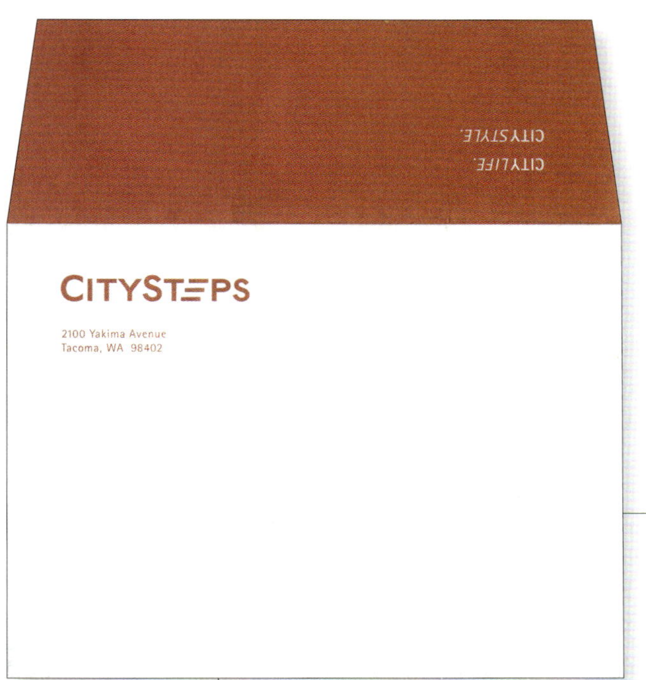

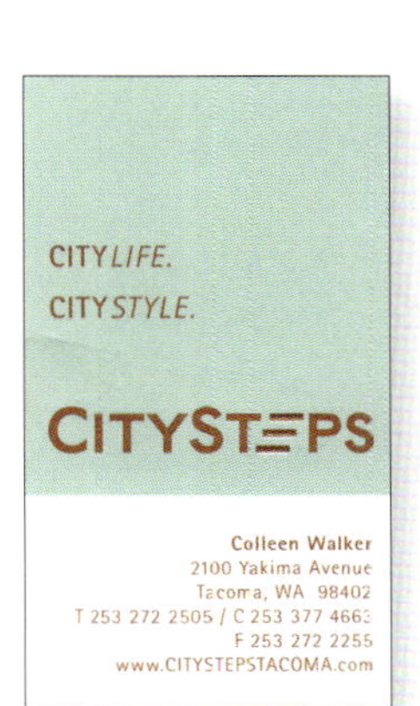

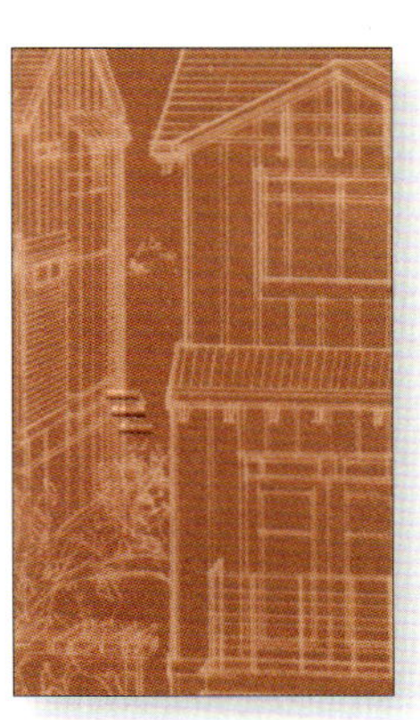

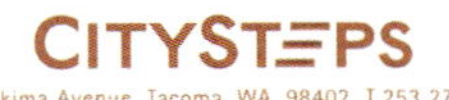

2100 Yakima Avenue Tacoma, WA 98402 T 253 272 2505

CITYLIFE.
CITYSTYLE.

CITYSTEPS

2100 Yakima Avenue
Tacoma, WA 98402

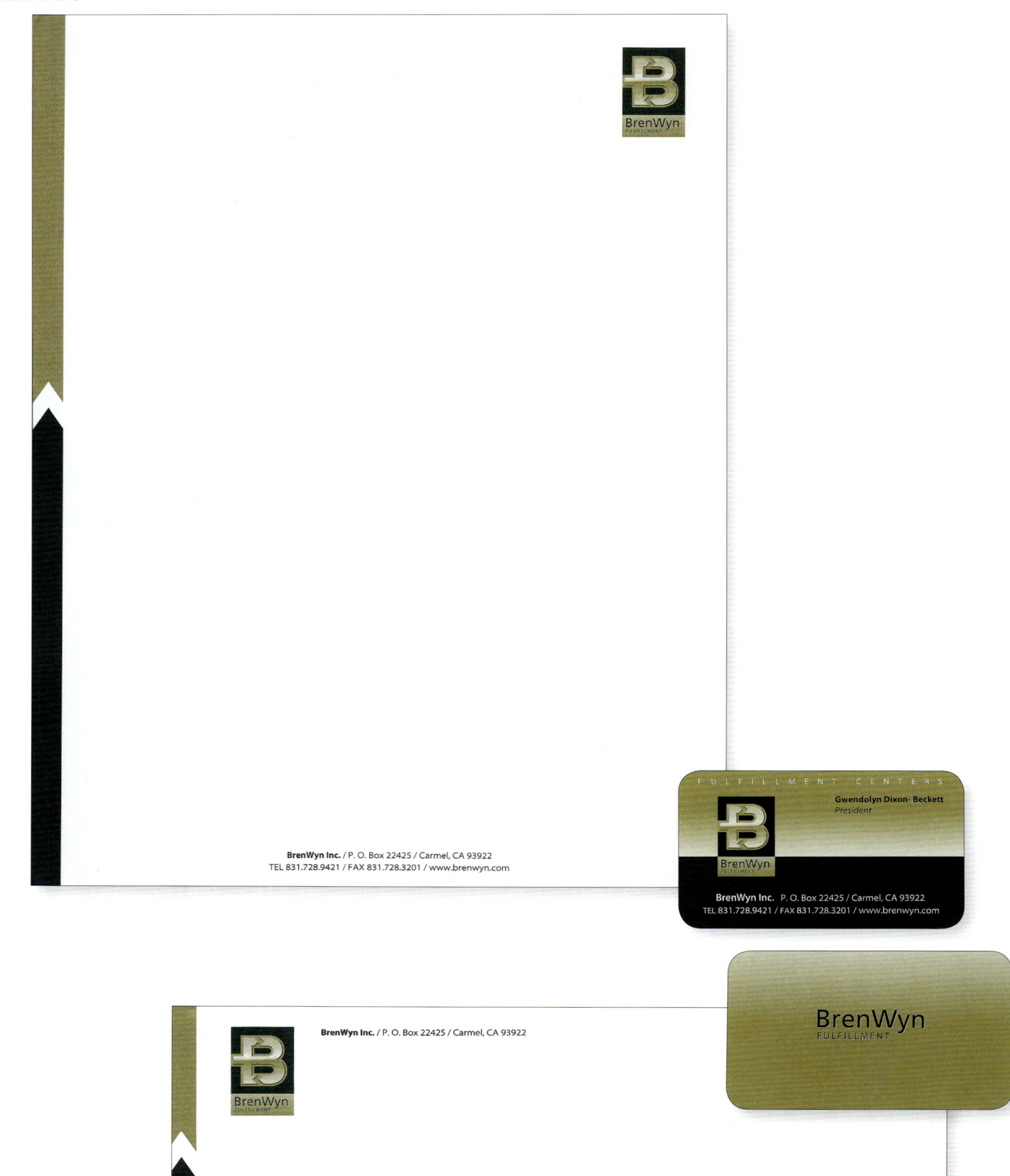

DESIGN FIRM
The Wecker Group
Monterey, (CA) USA
PROJECT
BrenWyn Inc.
DESIGNER
Robert Wecker

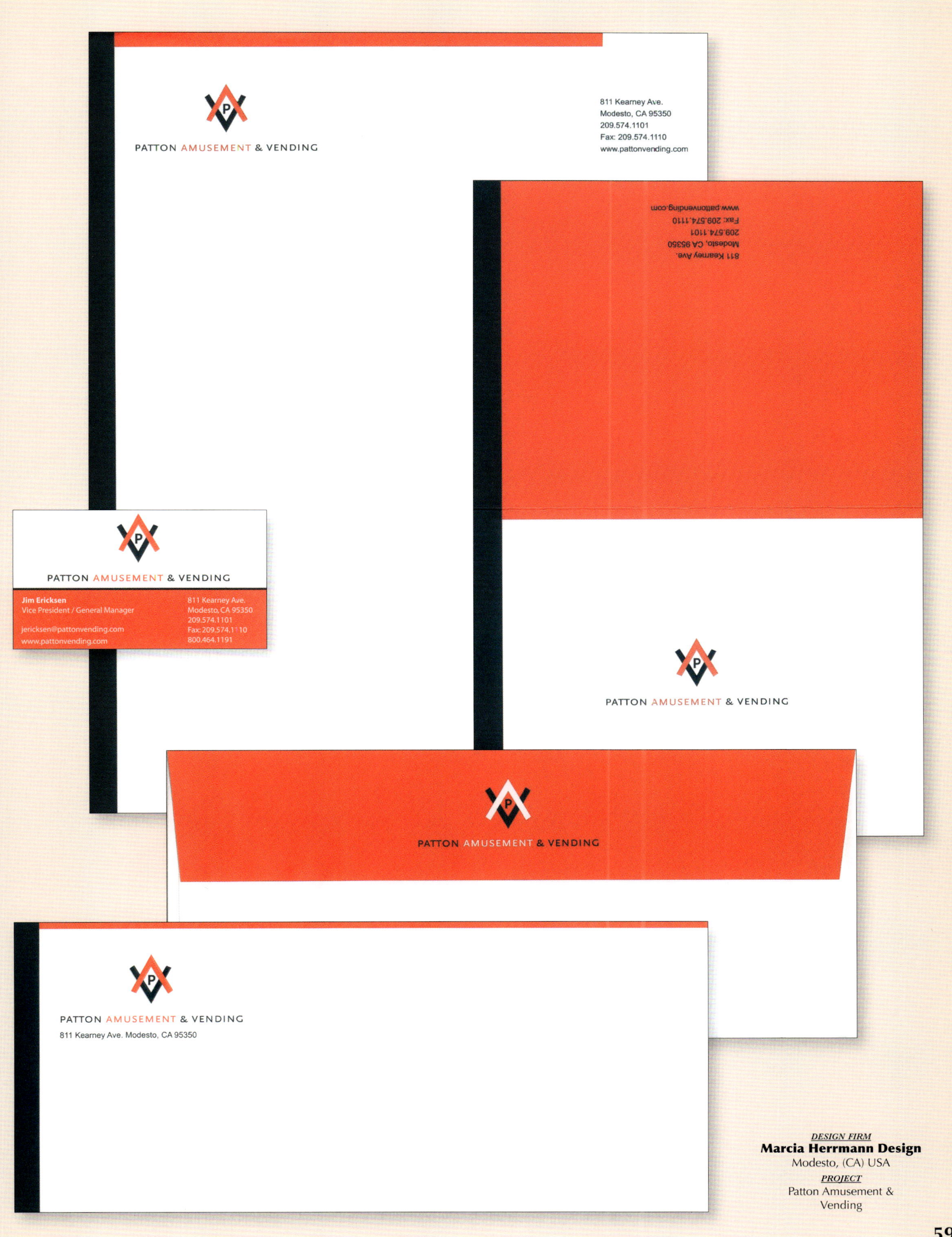

DESIGN FIRM
Marcia Herrmann Design
Modesto, (CA) USA
PROJECT
Patton Amusement & Vending

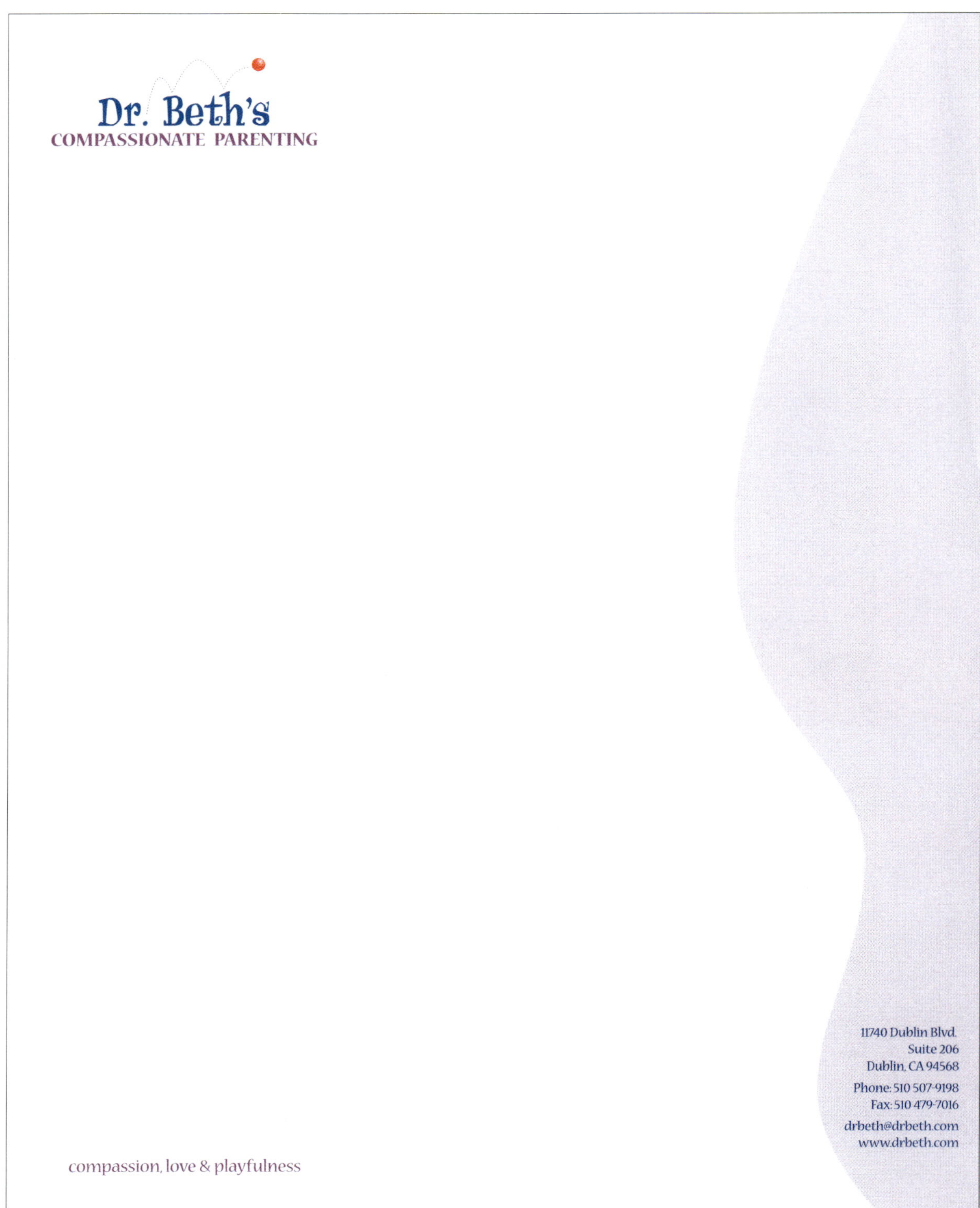

DESIGN FIRM
elf design
Belmont, (CA) USA
PROJECT
Dr. Beth's Compassionate Parenting
ART DIRECTOR, DESIGNER
Erin Ferree

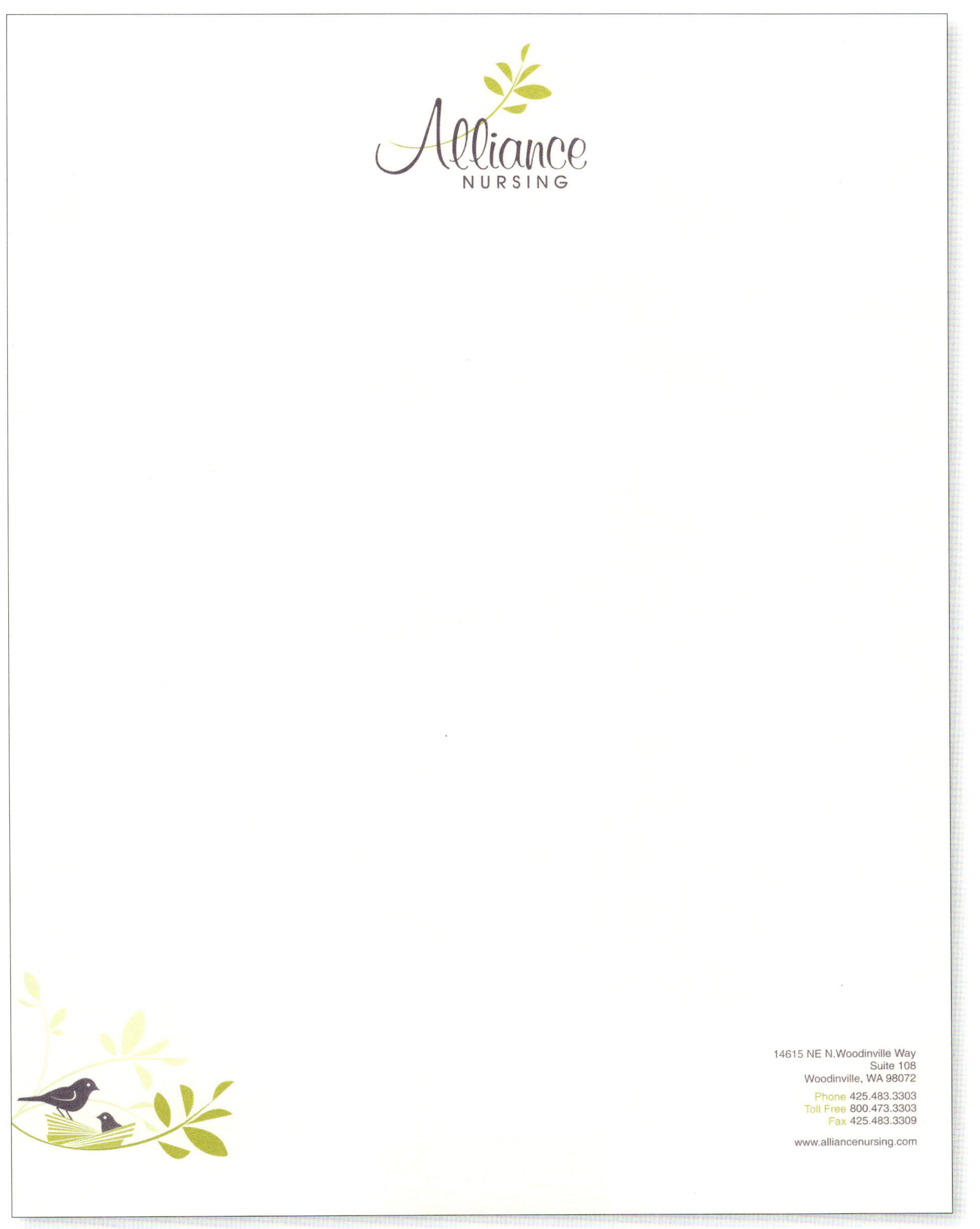

DESIGN FIRM
Eben Design
Seattle, (WA) USA
PROJECT
Alliance Nursing Stationery
ART DIRECTOR, DESIGNER, ILLUSTRATOR
Matthew Grimes

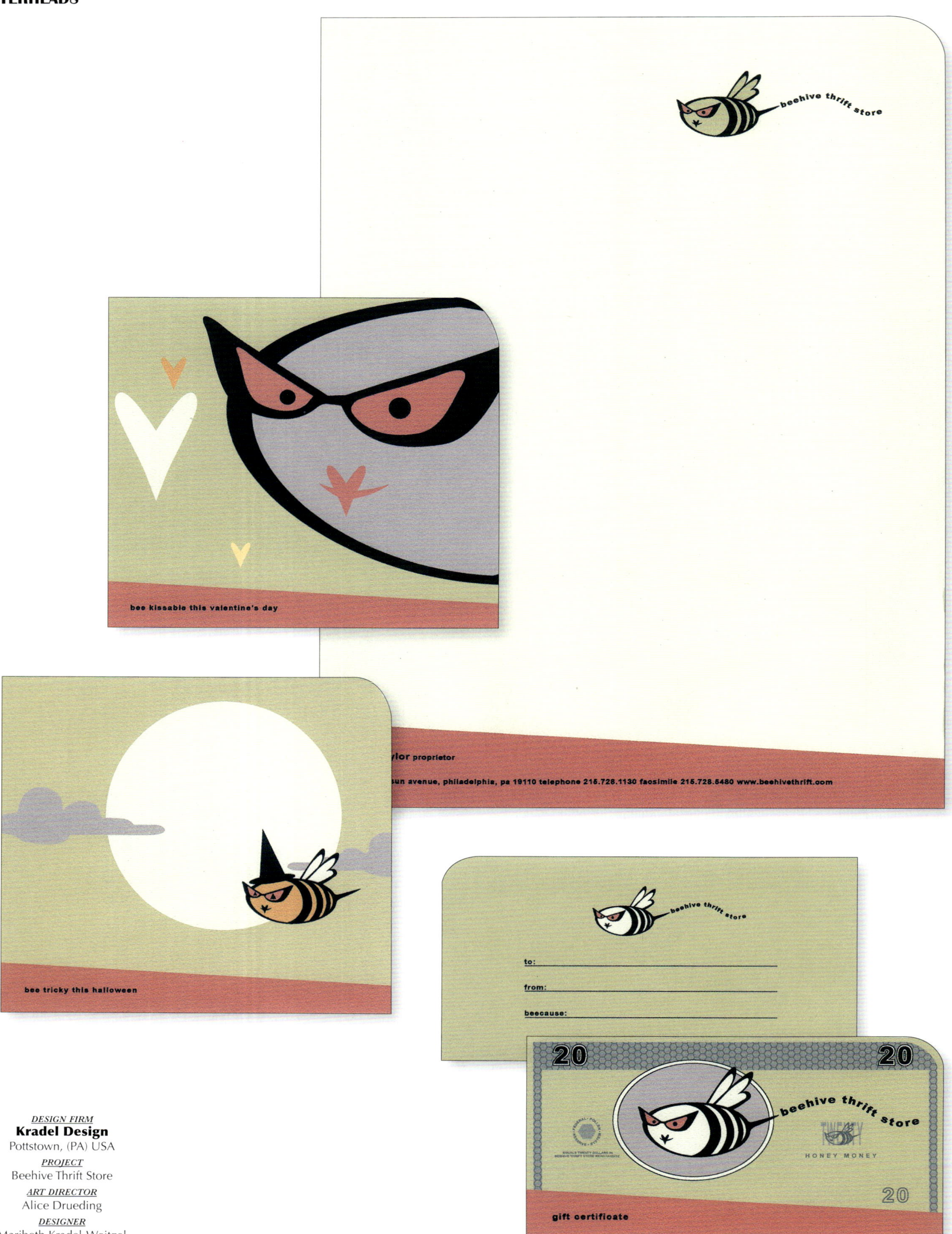

DESIGN FIRM
Kradel Design
Pottstown, (PA) USA
PROJECT
Beehive Thrift Store
ART DIRECTOR
Alice Drueding
DESIGNER
Maribeth Kradel-Weitzel

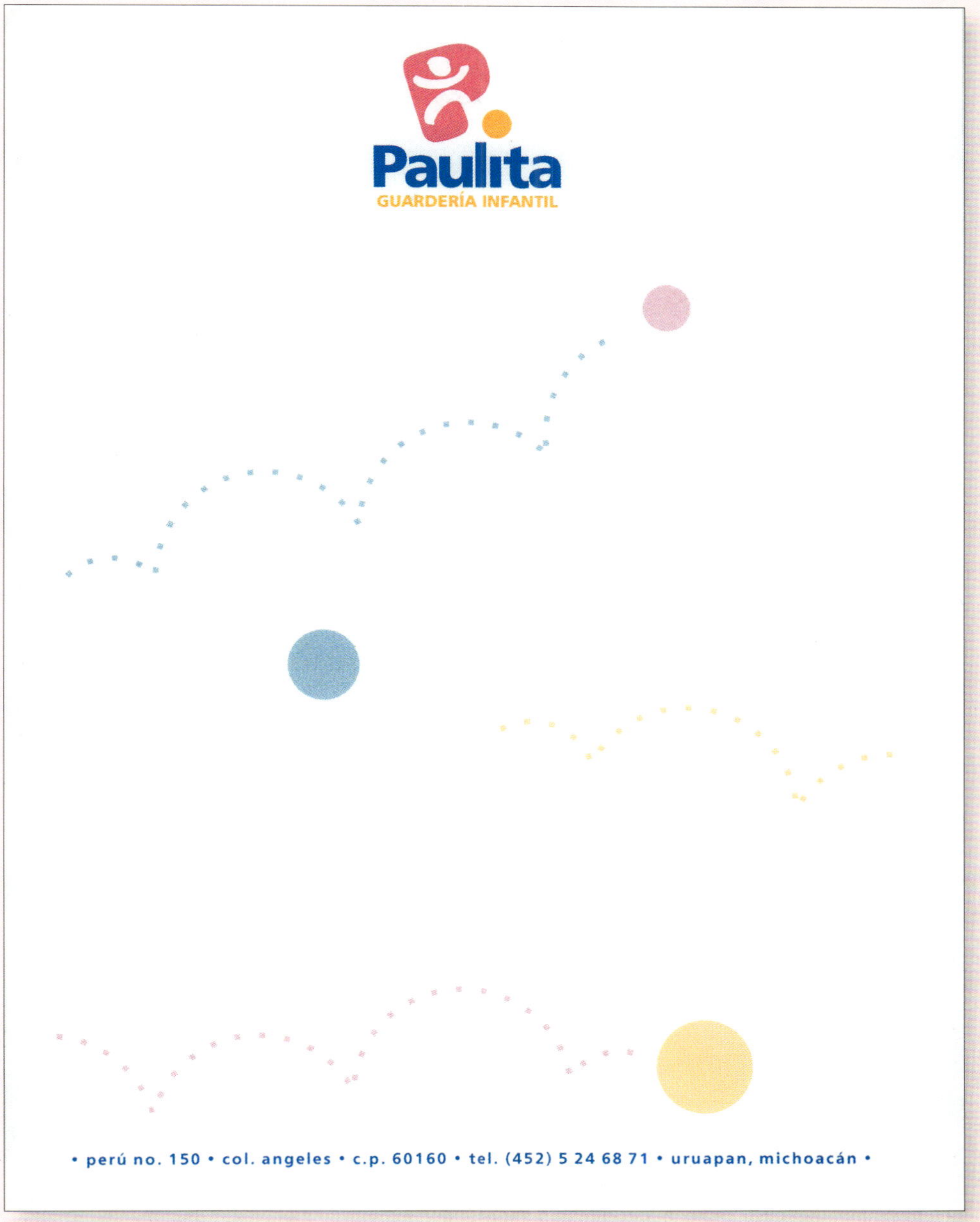

Paulita
GUARDERÍA INFANTIL

• perú no. 150 • col. angeles • c.p. 60160 • tel. (452) 5 24 68 71 • uruapan, michoacán •

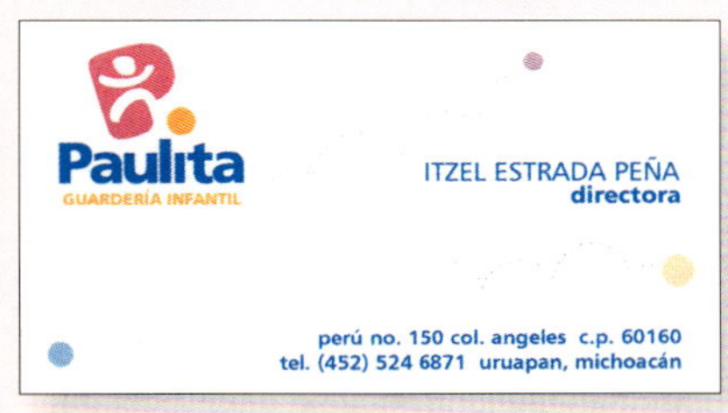

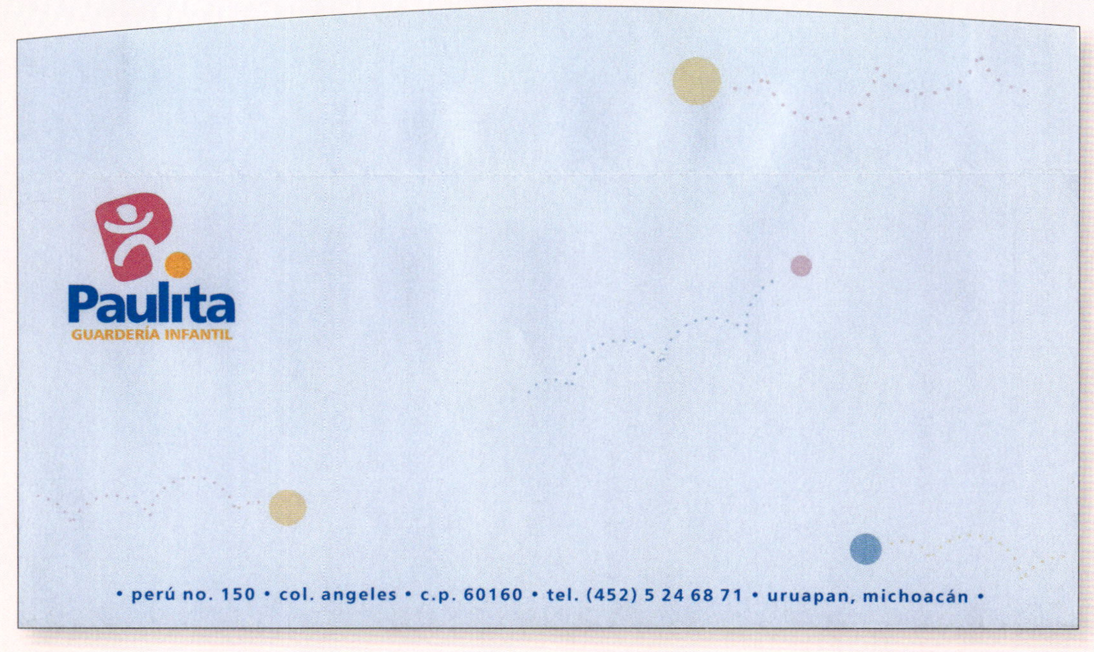

DESIGN FIRM
Kenneth Diseño
Uruapan (Michoacan), Mexico
PROJECT
Paulita
DESIGNERS
Kenneth Treviño,
Minerva Galván

DESIGN FIRM
Adventium Marketing & Design
New York, (NY) USA
PROJECT
Elevating
CREATIVE DIRECTOR, DESIGNER
Penny Chuang

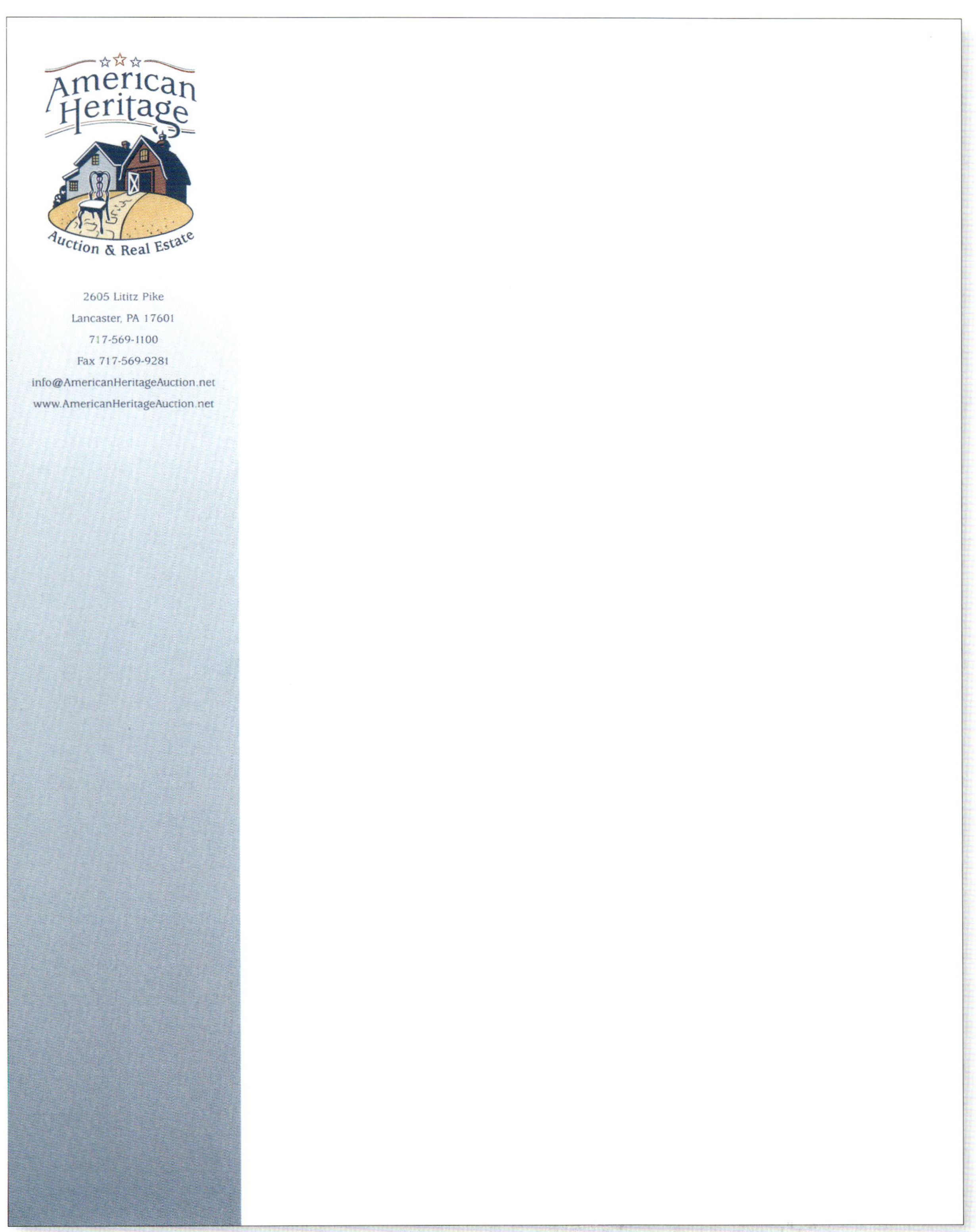

DESIGN FIRM
Dean Design/Marketing Group, Inc.
Lancaster, (PA) USA
PROJECT
Americam Heritage Auction
& Real Estate
SENIOR DESIGNER
Jeff Phillips

DESIGN FIRM
Indiana Design Consortium, Inc.
Lafayette, (IN) USA
CLIENT
Provision Living, LLC
DESIGNER
Debra Pohl Green

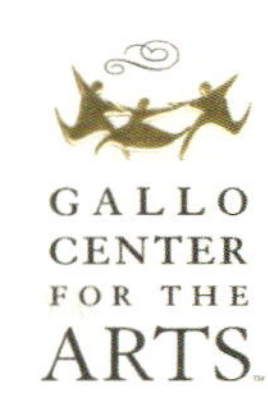

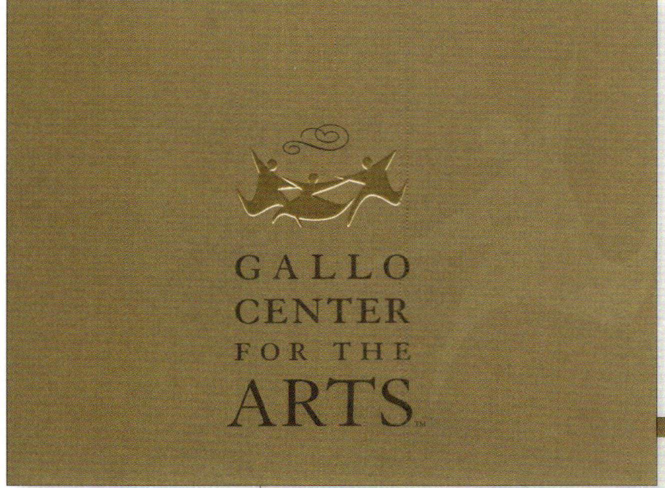

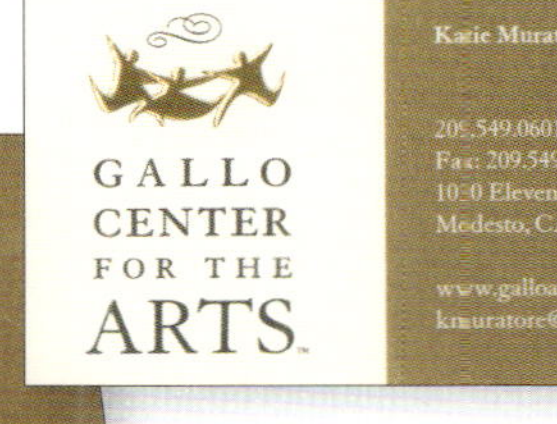

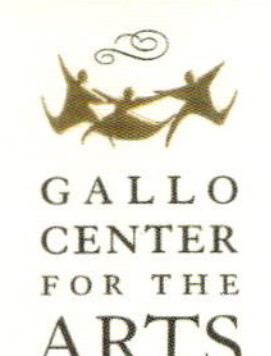

DESIGN FIRM
Marcia Herrmann Design
Modesto, (CA) USA
PROJECT
Gallo Center for the Arts

eliminating racism
empowering women ywca

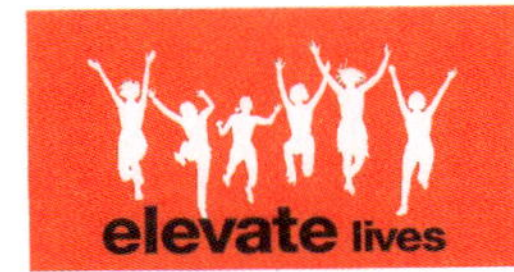

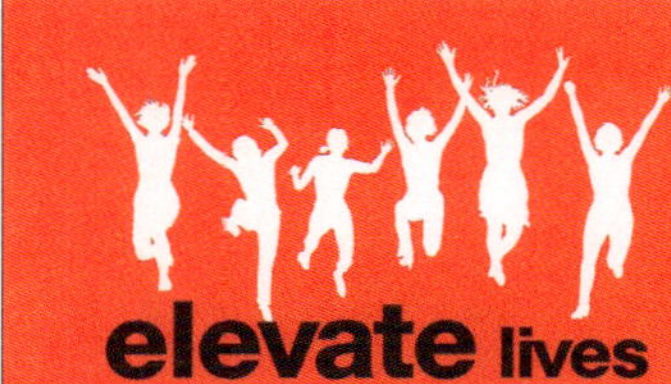

eliminating racism
empowering women
ywca

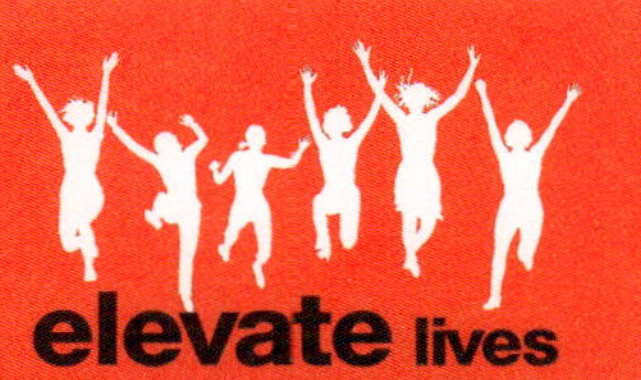

raise one roof
serve the needs of many

martella wilson-taylor
president / ceo

YWCA Boston
20 Park Plaza, Suite 1420
Boston, MA 02116
T: 617-585-5410
F: 617-585-5499
mwilson-taylor@ywcaboston.org
www.ywcaboston.org

eliminating racism
empowering women ywca

DESIGN FIRM
TSM Design
Springfield, (MA) USA
PROJECT
YWCA, Boston
Elevate Lives Campaign
DESIGNER
Noël Szado

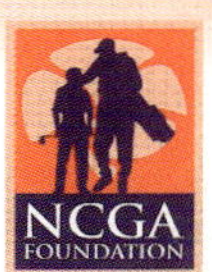

NCGA Foundation
P. O. Box 1157
Pebble Beach, CA 93953
Toll Free 877-624-2577
Fax 831-625-0150
www.ncgafoundation.org

"The NCGA Foundation is about kids and their futures."

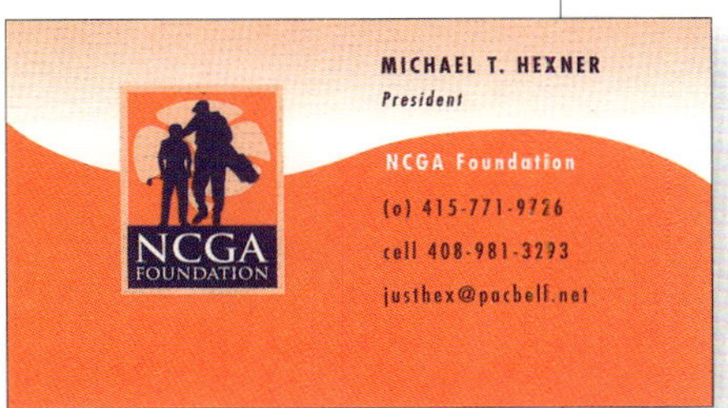

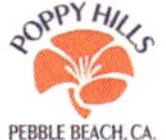

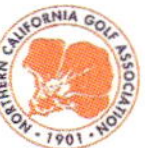

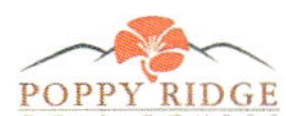

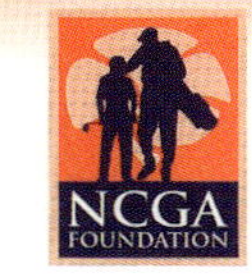

www.ncgafoundation.org

NCGA Foundation
P. O. Box 1157
Pebble Beach, CA 93953

DESIGN FIRM
The Wecker Group
Monterey, (CA) USA
PROJECT
NCGA Foundation
DESIGNERS
Robert Wecker,
Matt Guinbus

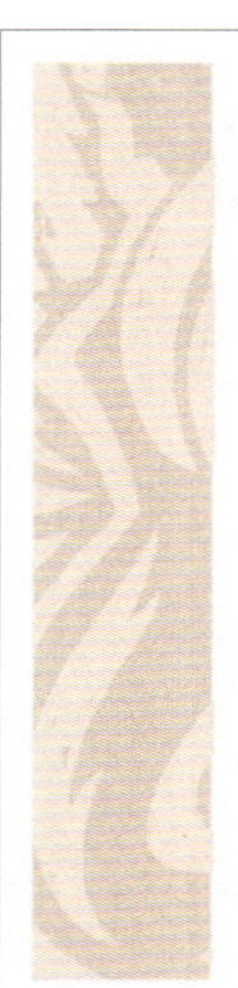

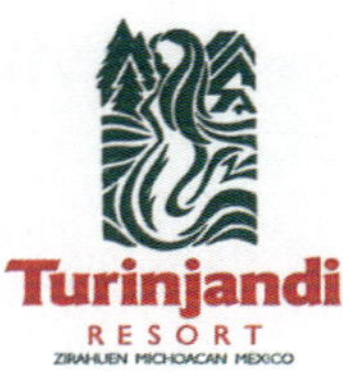

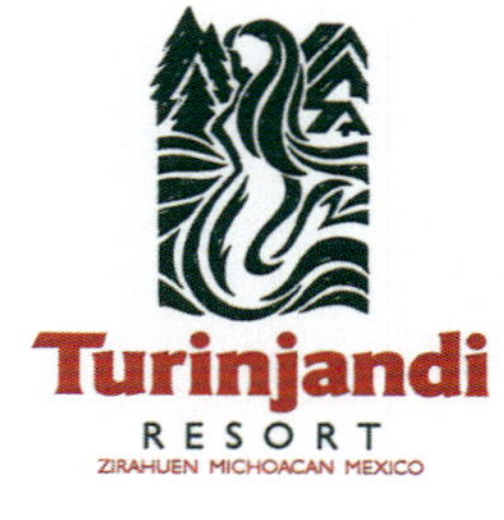

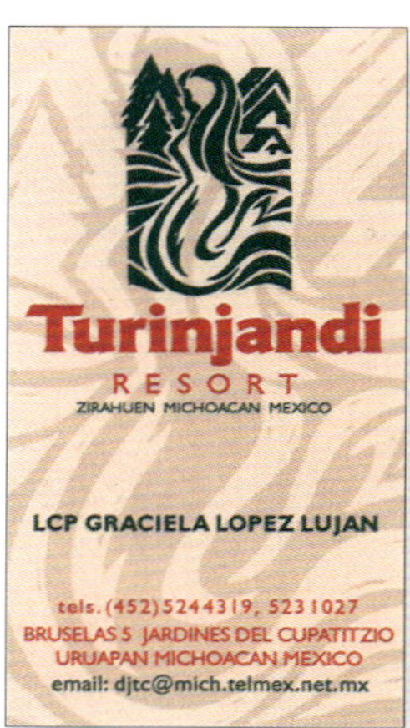

DESIGN FIRM
Kenneth Diseño
Uruapan, (Michoacan) Mexico
PROJECT
Turinjandi
DESIGNERS
Kenneth Treviño,
Minerva Galván

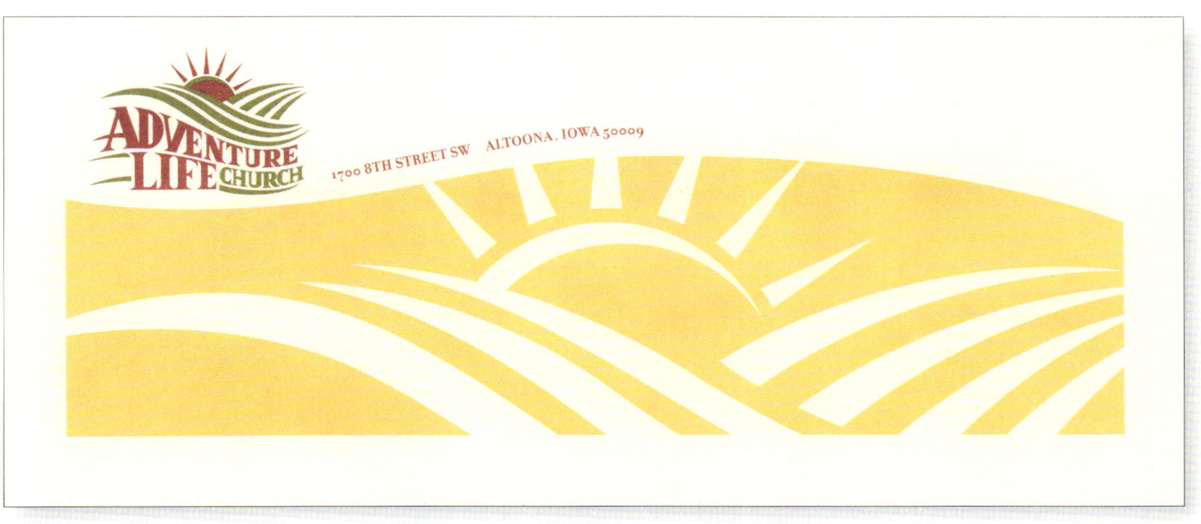

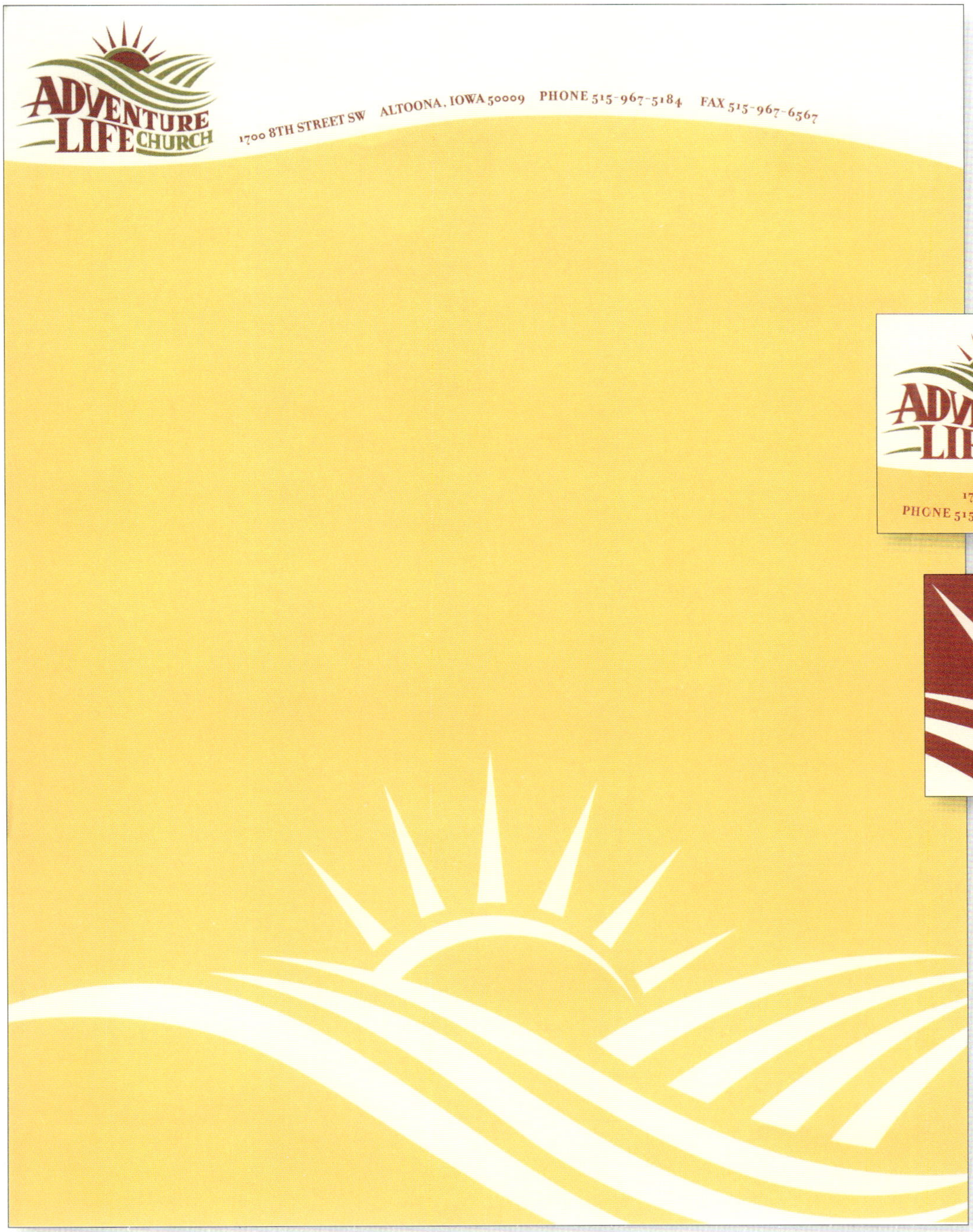

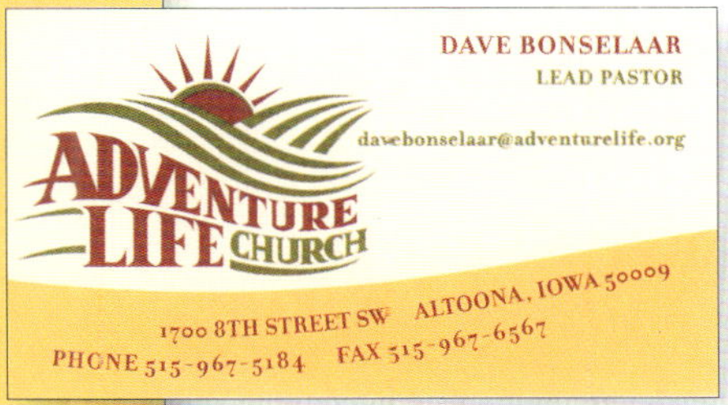

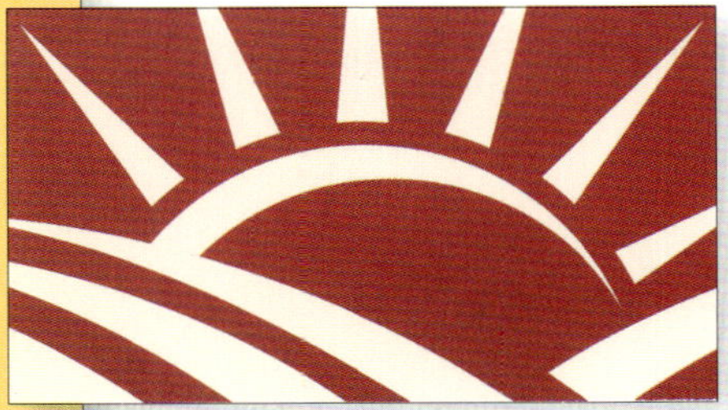

ADVENTURE
LIFE CHURCH
1700 8TH STREET SW ALTOONA, IOWA 50009 PHONE 515-967-5184 FAX 515-967-6567

DAVE BONSELAAR
LEAD PASTOR
davebonselaar@adventurelife.org
ADVENTURE
LIFE CHURCH
1700 8TH STREET SW ALTOONA, IOWA 50009
PHONE 515-967-5184 FAX 515-967-6567

DESIGN FIRM
Sayles Graphic Design
Des Moines (IA) USA
CLIENT
Adventure Life Reformed Church
DESIGNER, ILLUSTRATOR
John Sayles

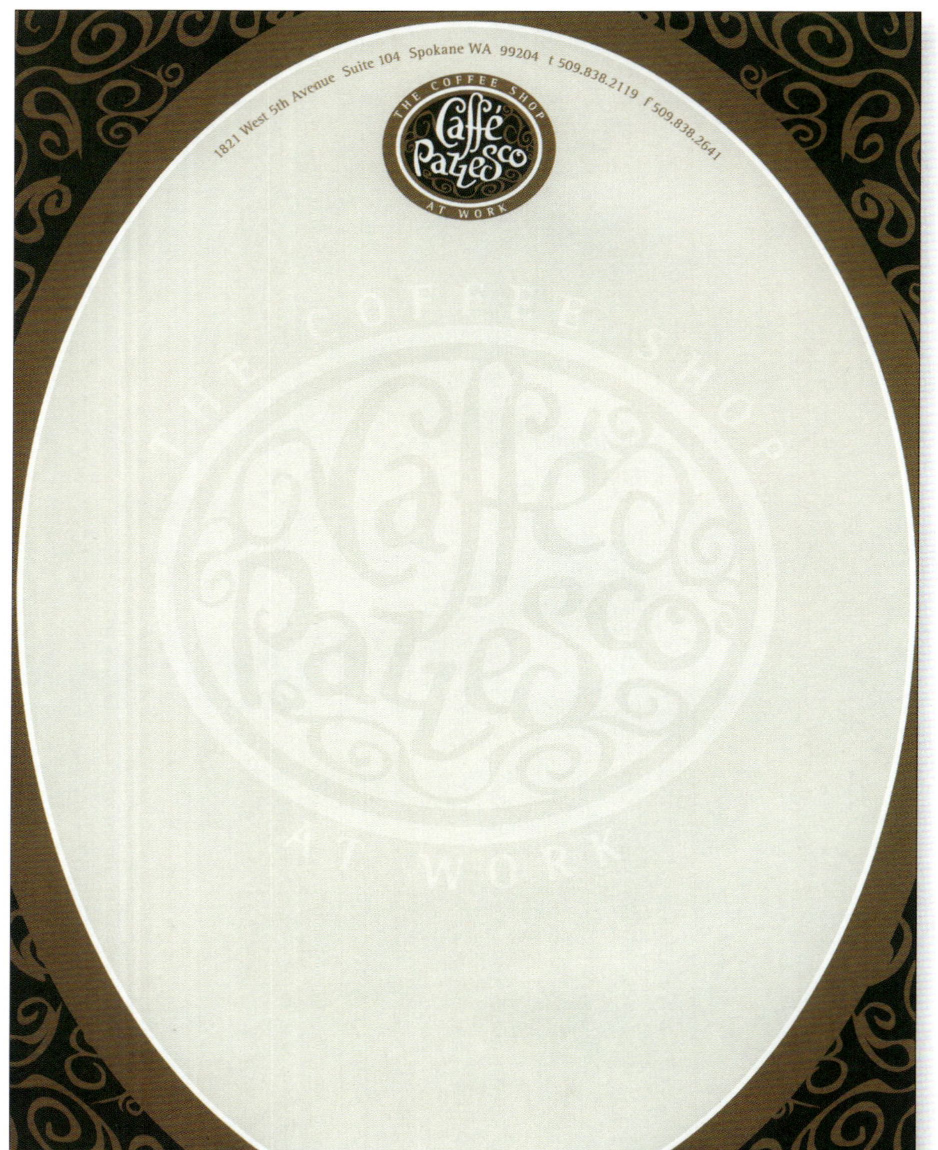

DESIGN FIRM
Kländt Hosmer
Spokane, (WA) USA
PROJECT
Caffe Pazzesco Stationery
ART DIRECTOR
Darin Kländt
DESIGNER
Diane Mahan

THE COFFEE SHOP
Caffé Pazzesco
AT WORK
1821 West 5th Avenue Suite 104 Spokane WA 99204
TRICIA PETRINOVICH
tpetrinovich@caffepazzesco.com
t 509.838.2119 f 509.838.2641

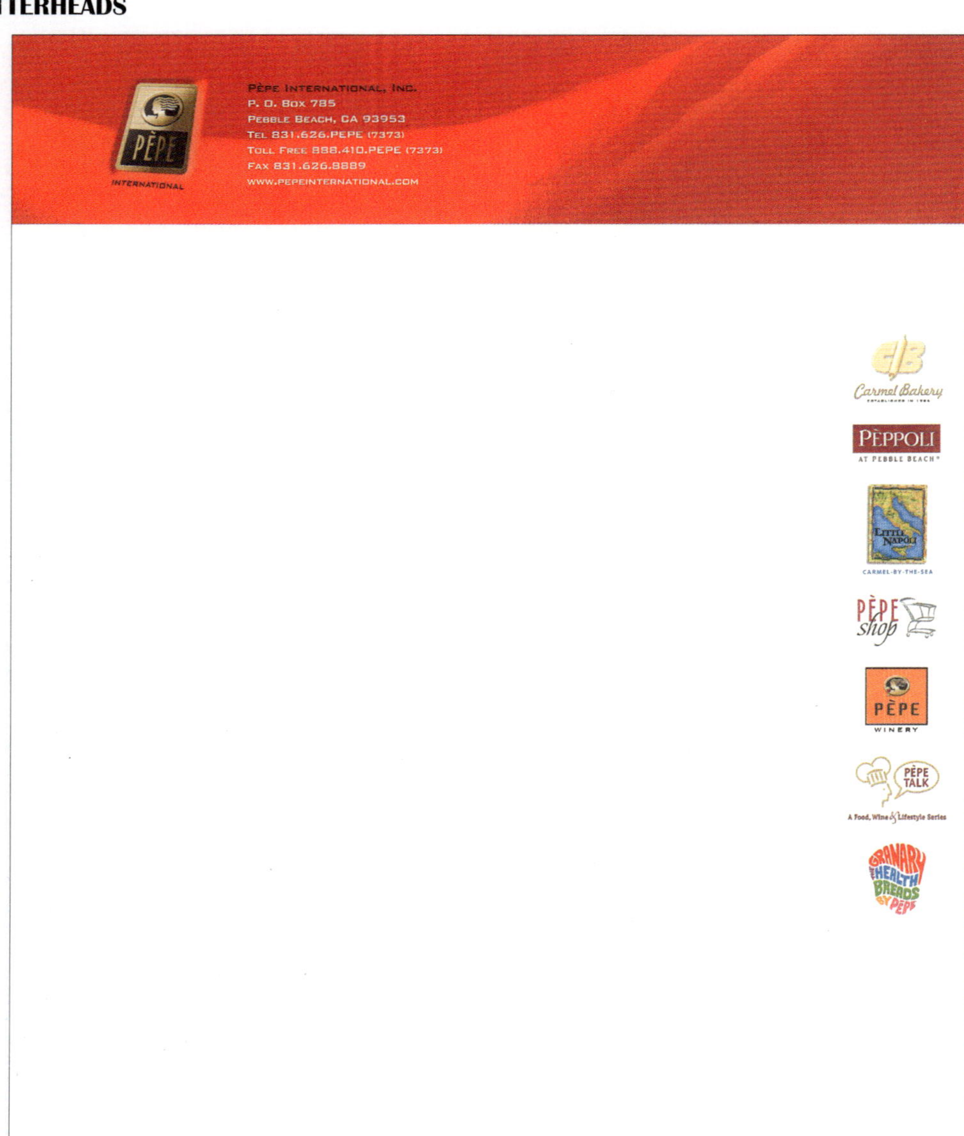

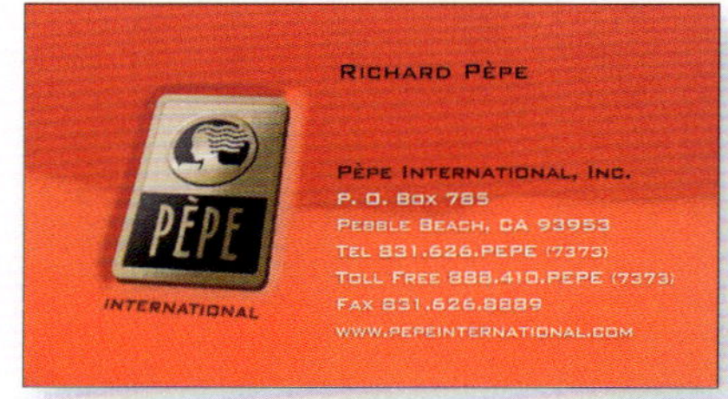

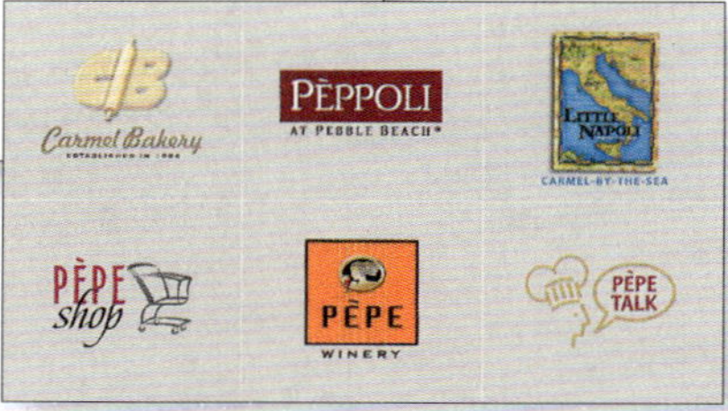

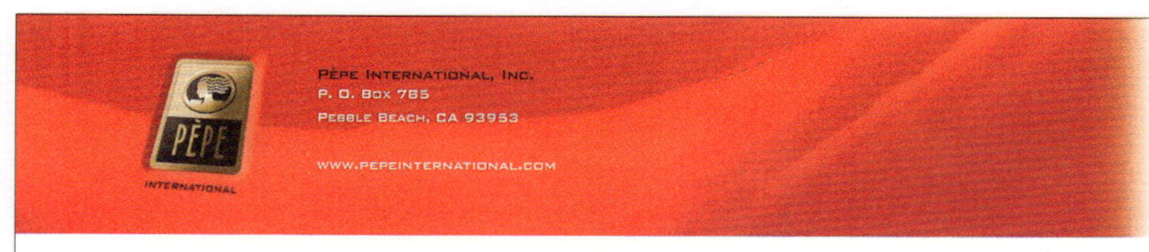

DESIGN FIRM
The Wecker Group
Monterey, (CA) USA
PROJECT
Pépe International, Inc.
DESIGNER
Robert Wecker

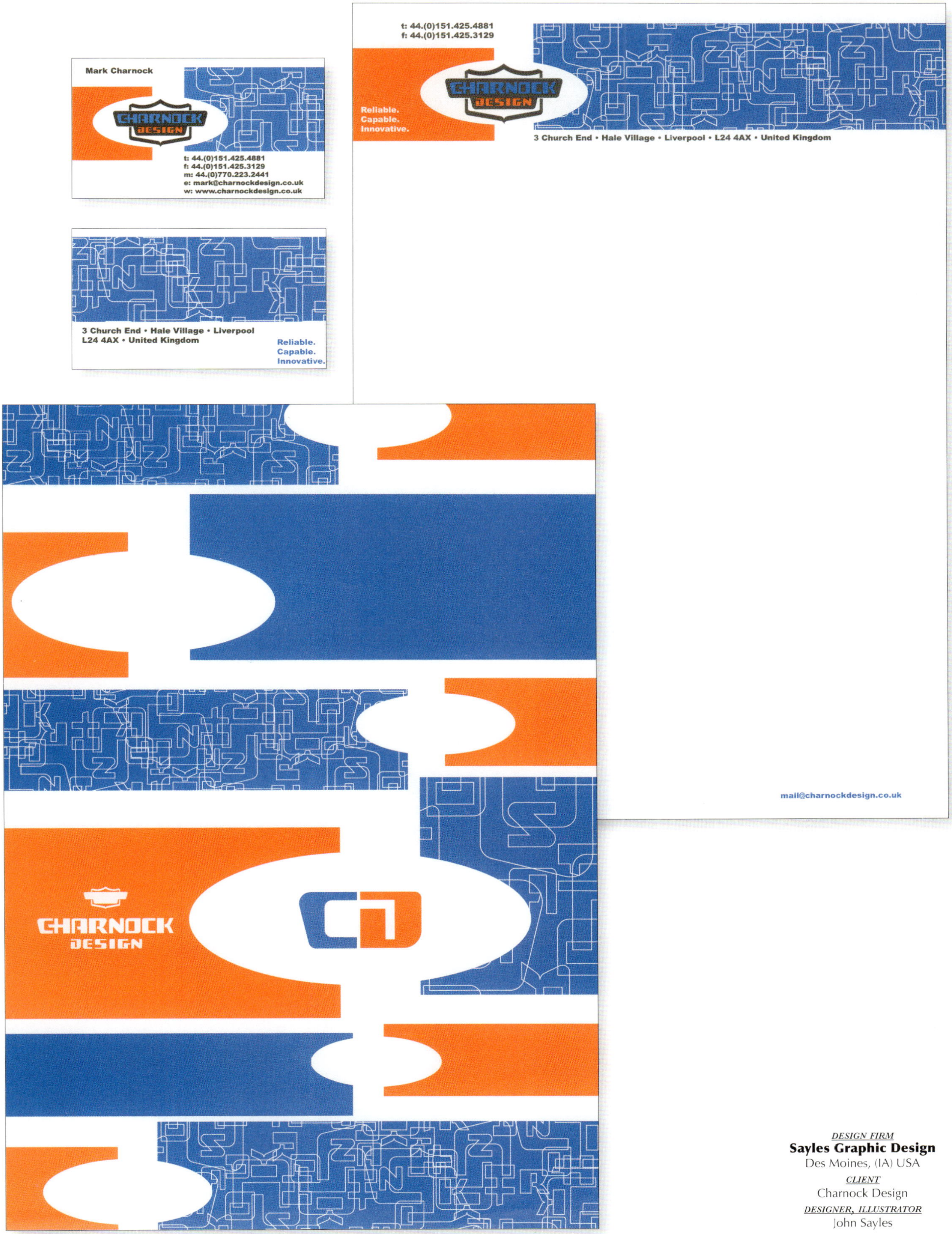

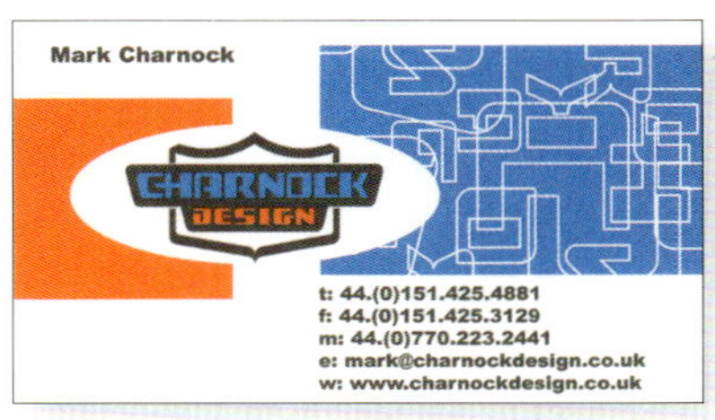

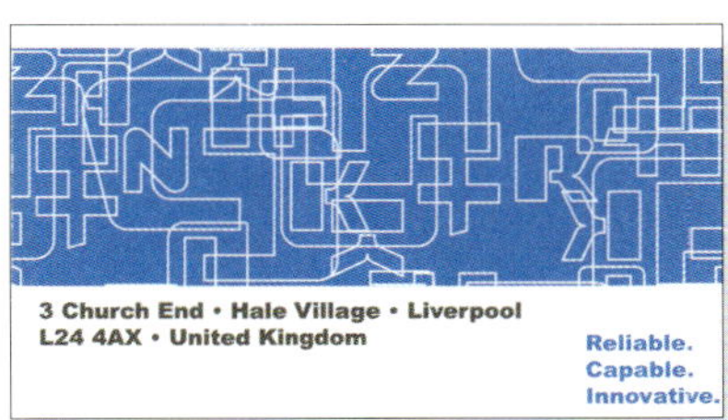

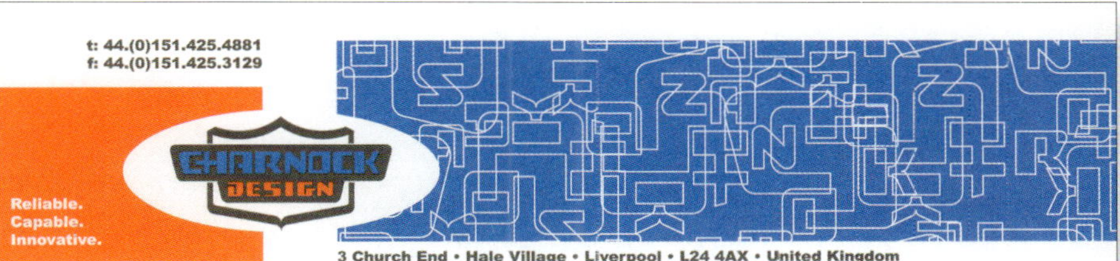

mail@charnockdesign.co.uk

CHARNOCK
DESIGN

DESIGN FIRM
Sayles Graphic Design
Des Moines, (IA) USA

CLIENT
Charnock Design

DESIGNER, ILLUSTRATOR
John Sayles

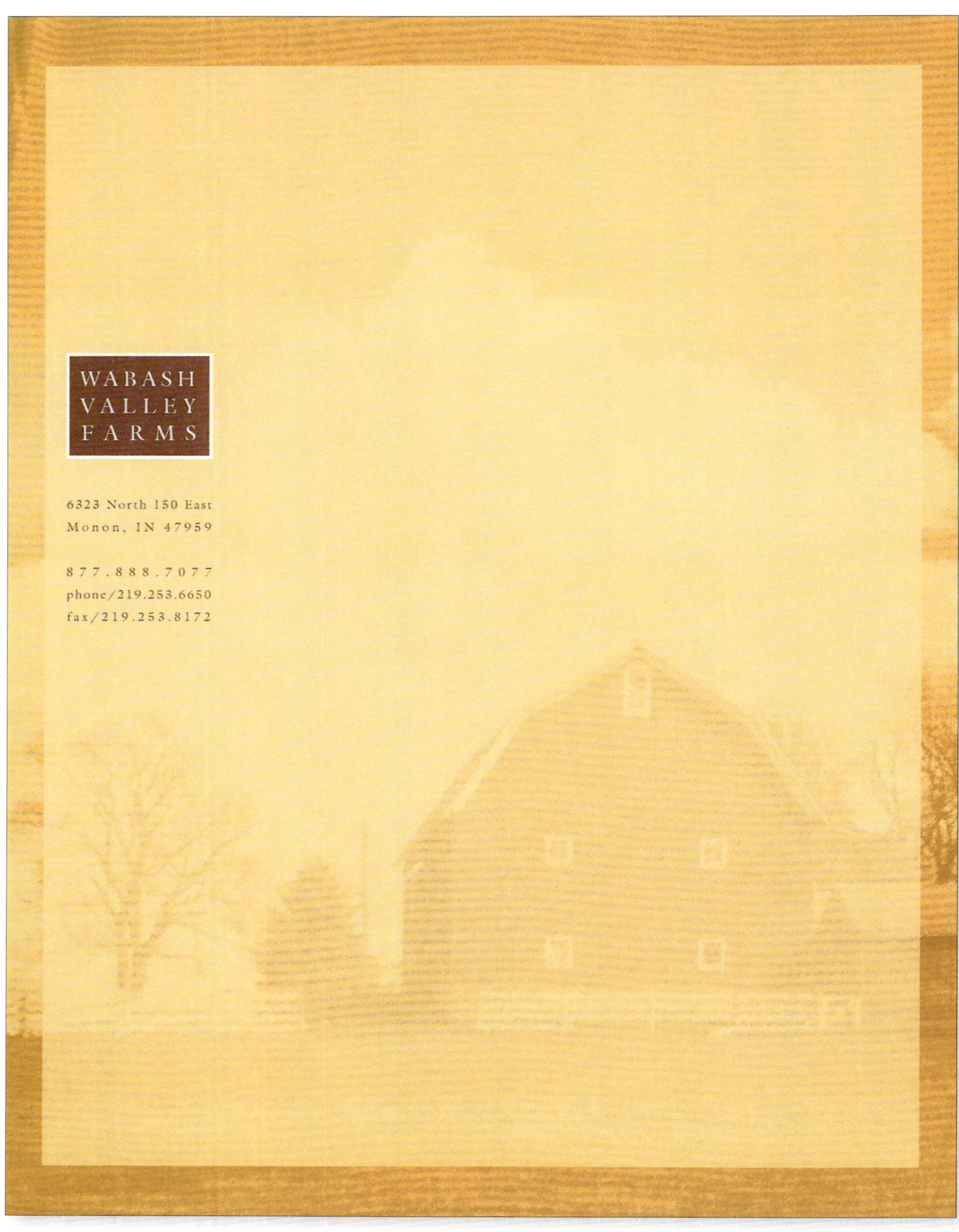

DESIGN FIRM
Indiana Design Consortium, Inc.
Lafayette, (IN) USA
CLIENT
Wabash Valley Farms
DESIGNER
Kristy Blair

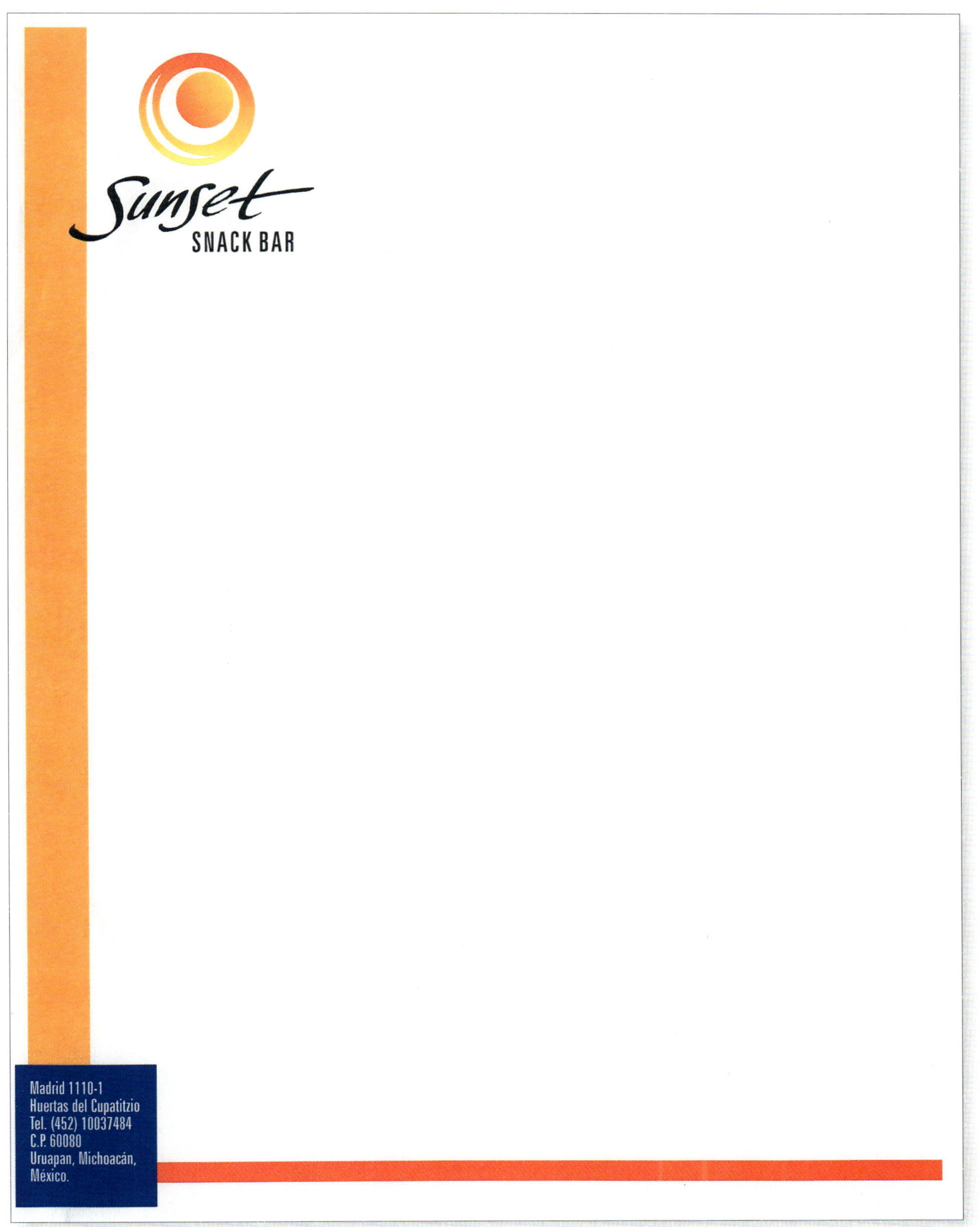

DESIGN FIRM
Kenneth Diseño
Uruapan, (Michoacan) Mexico
PROJECT
Sunset Snack Bar
DESIGNERS
Kenneth Treviño,
Minerva Galván

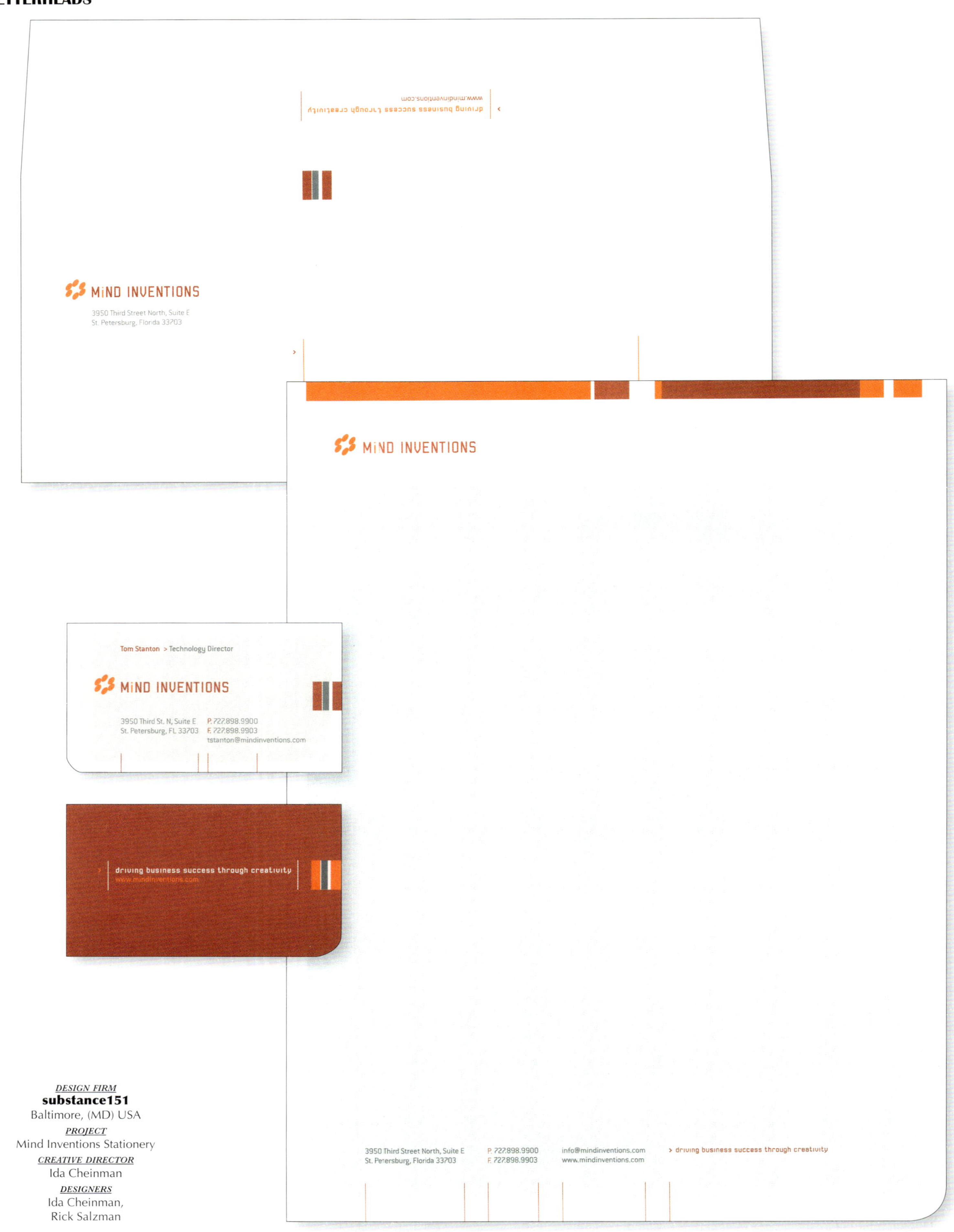

DESIGN FIRM
substance151
Baltimore, (MD) USA
PROJECT
Mind Inventions Stationery
CREATIVE DIRECTOR
Ida Cheinman
DESIGNERS
Ida Cheinman,
Rick Salzman

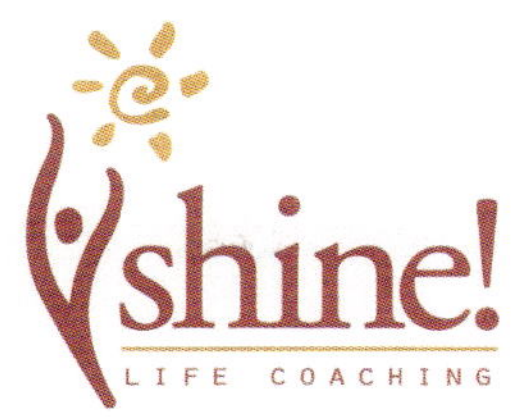

303.344.1181
www.ShineForResults.com
Anne@ShineForResults.com

Transforming stress – Increasing performance – Empowering lives!

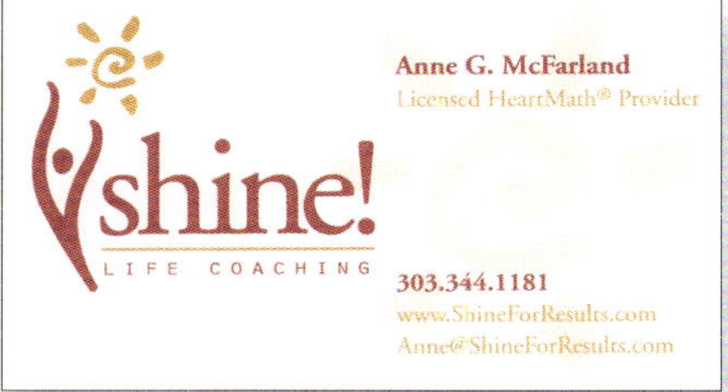

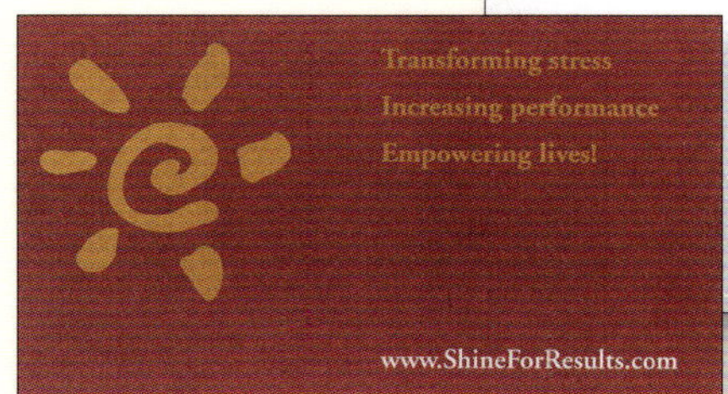

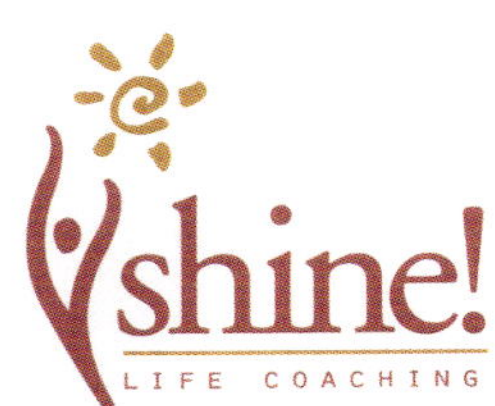

175 Rampart Way #902
Denver, Colorado 80230

DESIGN FIRM
CATALYST creative, inc.
Denver, (CO) USA
ART DIRECTOR, DESIGNER
Jeanna Pool

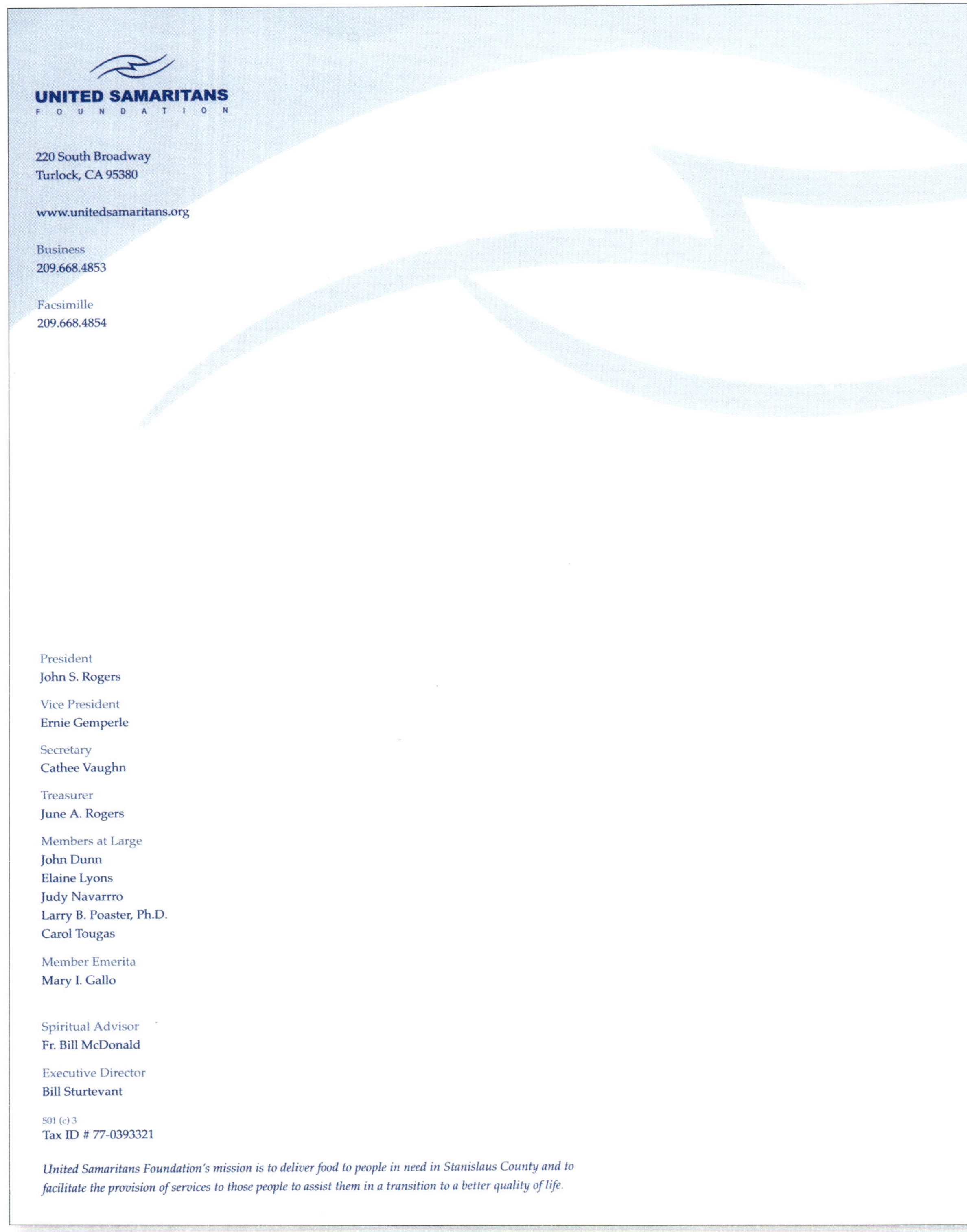
UNITED SAMARITANS
FOUNDATION

220 South Broadway
Turlock, CA 95380

www.unitedsamaritans.org

Business
209.668.4853

Facsimille
209.668.4854

President
John S. Rogers

Vice President
Ernie Gemperle

Secretary
Cathee Vaughn

Treasurer
June A. Rogers

Members at Large
John Dunn
Elaine Lyons
Judy Navarrro
Larry B. Poaster, Ph.D.
Carol Tougas

Member Emerita
Mary I. Gallo

Spiritual Advisor
Fr. Bill McDonald

Executive Director
Bill Sturtevant

501 (c) 3
Tax ID # 77-0393321

United Samaritans Foundation's mission is to deliver food to people in need in Stanislaus County and to facilitate the provision of services to those people to assist them in a transition to a better quality of life.

DESIGN FIRM
Never Boring Design Associates
Modesto, (CA) USA
PROJECT
United Samaritans
DESIGNER
Shawna Bayers

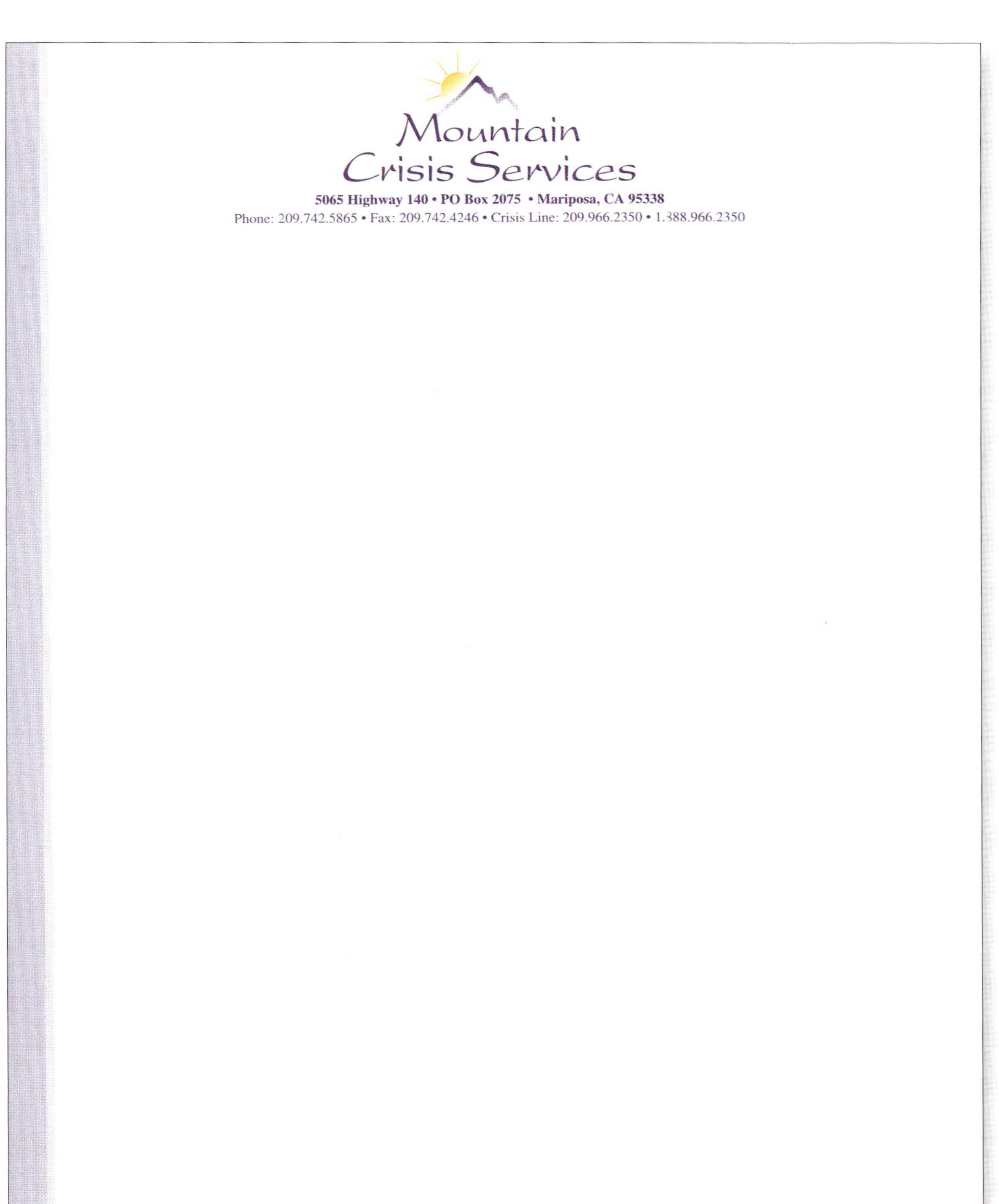

DESIGN FIRM
Ontarget Marketing
Merced, (CA) USA
CLIENT
Mountain Crisis Services
ART DIRECTOR
Jesse Bloodworth
DESIGNER
Dusty Dahlgren

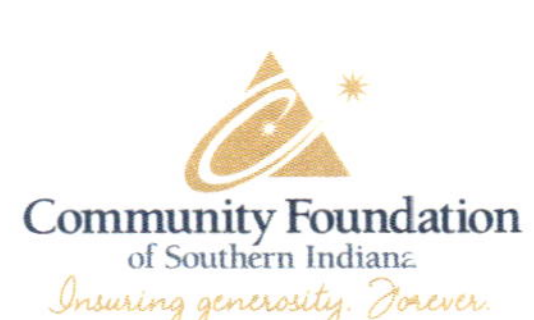

888.388.2374 • www.cfsouthernindiana.com

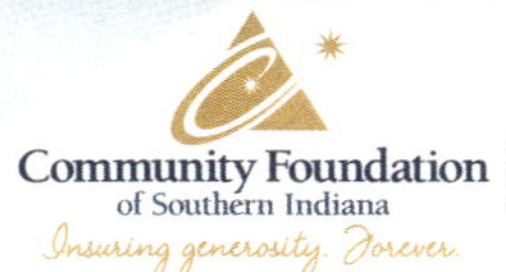

4104 Charlestown Road • New Albany, Indiana • 47150

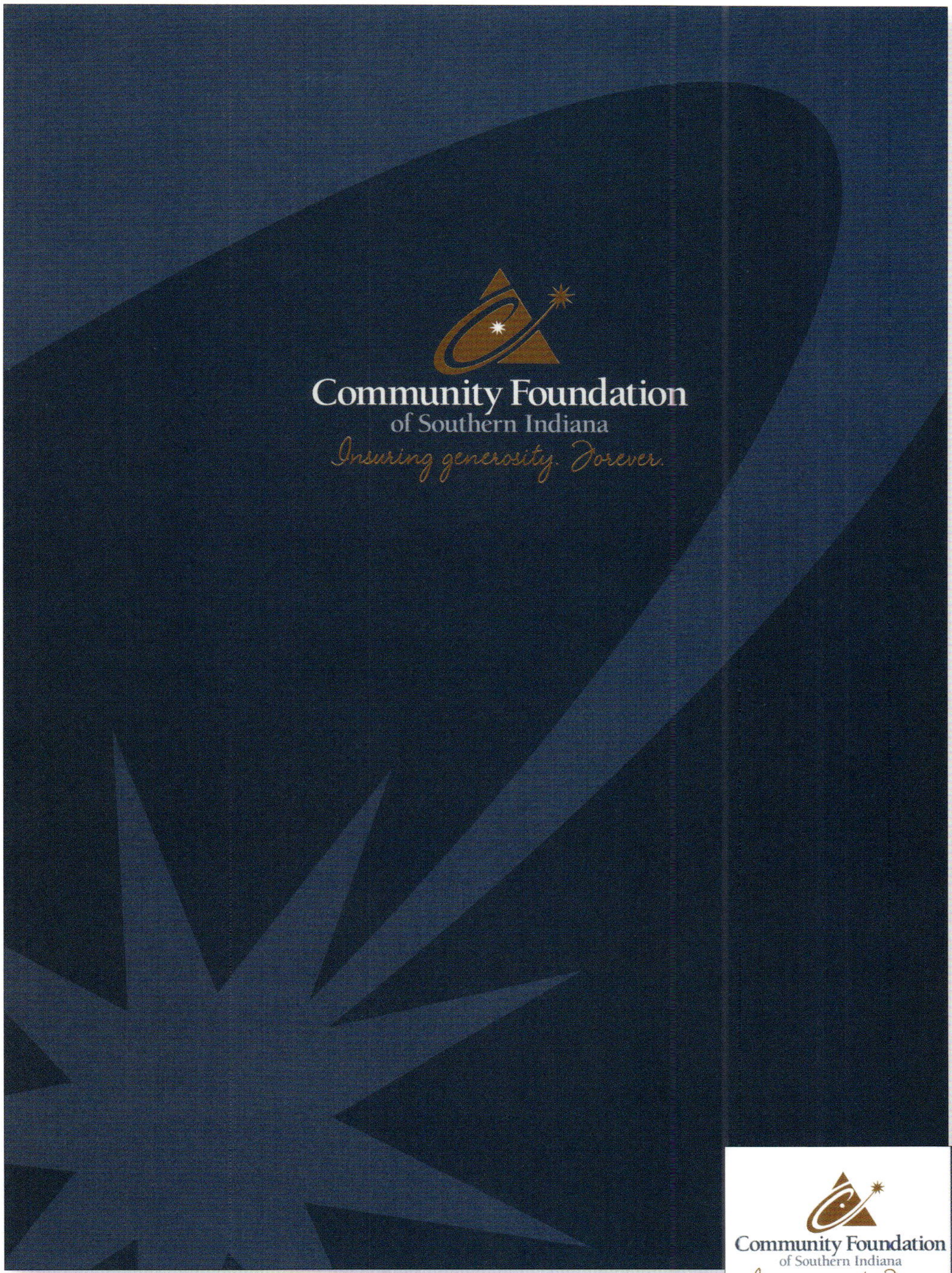

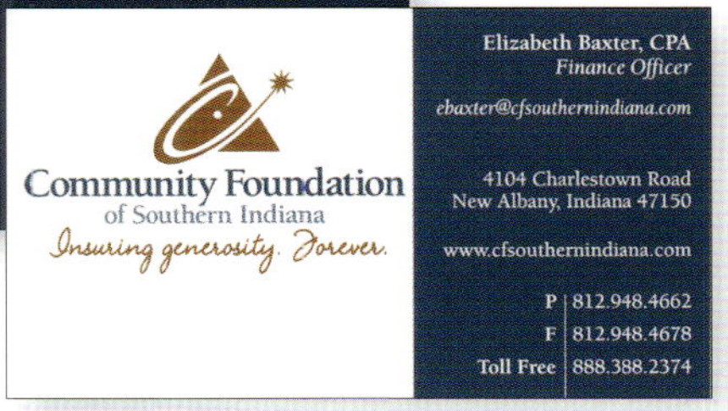

Community Foundation
of Southern Indiana
Insuring generosity. Forever.

Community Foundation
of Southern Indiana
Insuring generosity. Forever.

Elizabeth Baxter, CPA
Finance Officer
ebaxter@cfsouthernindiana.com
4104 Charlestown Road
New Albany, Indiana 47150
www.cfsouthernindiana.com
P 812.948.4662
F 812.948.4678
Toll Free 888.388.2374

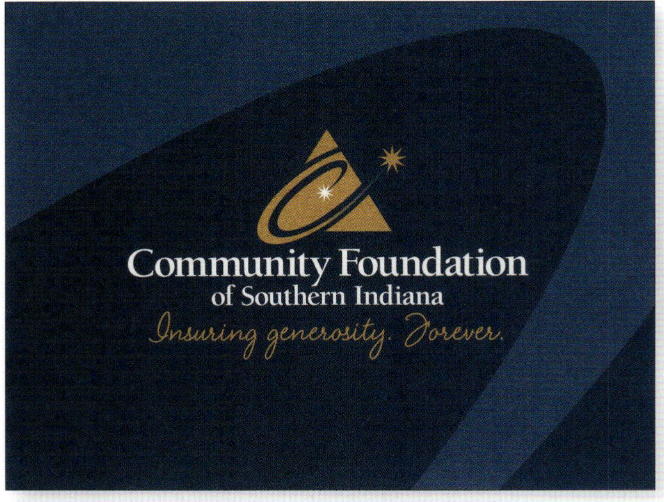

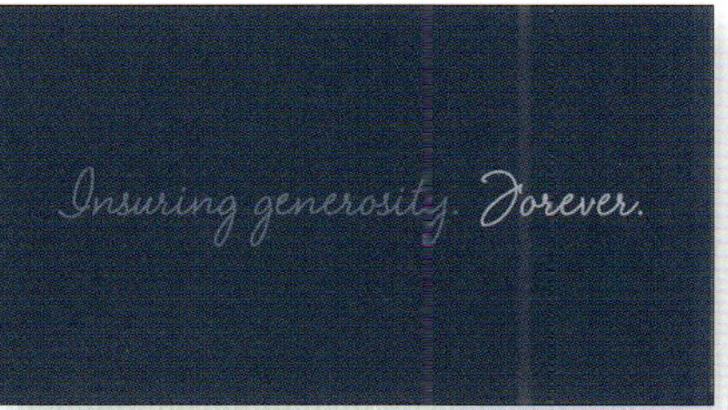

DESIGN FIRM
Mind's Eye Creative
New Albany, (IN) USA
CLIENT
Community Foundation of Southern Indiana
DESIGNERS
Stephen Brown, Doreen Dehart

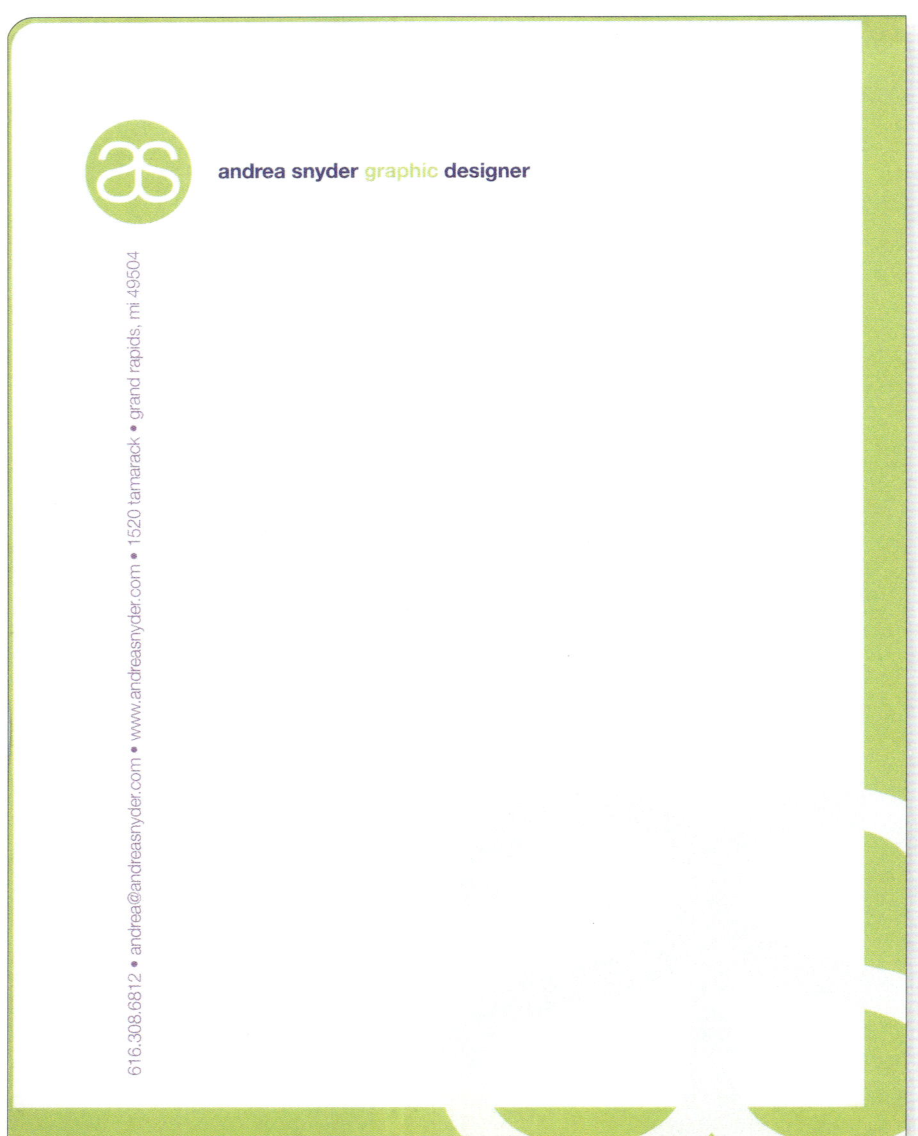

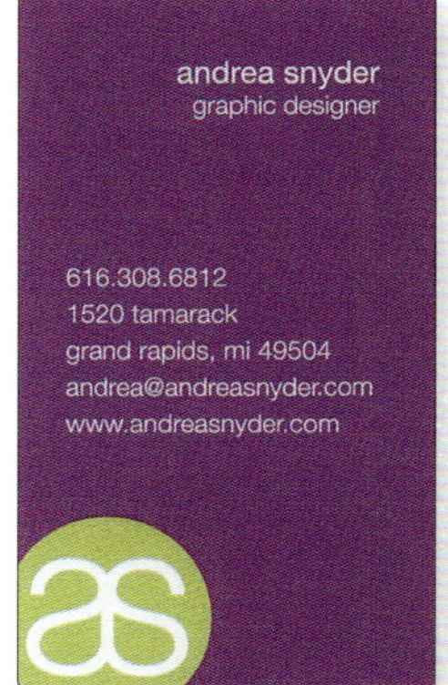

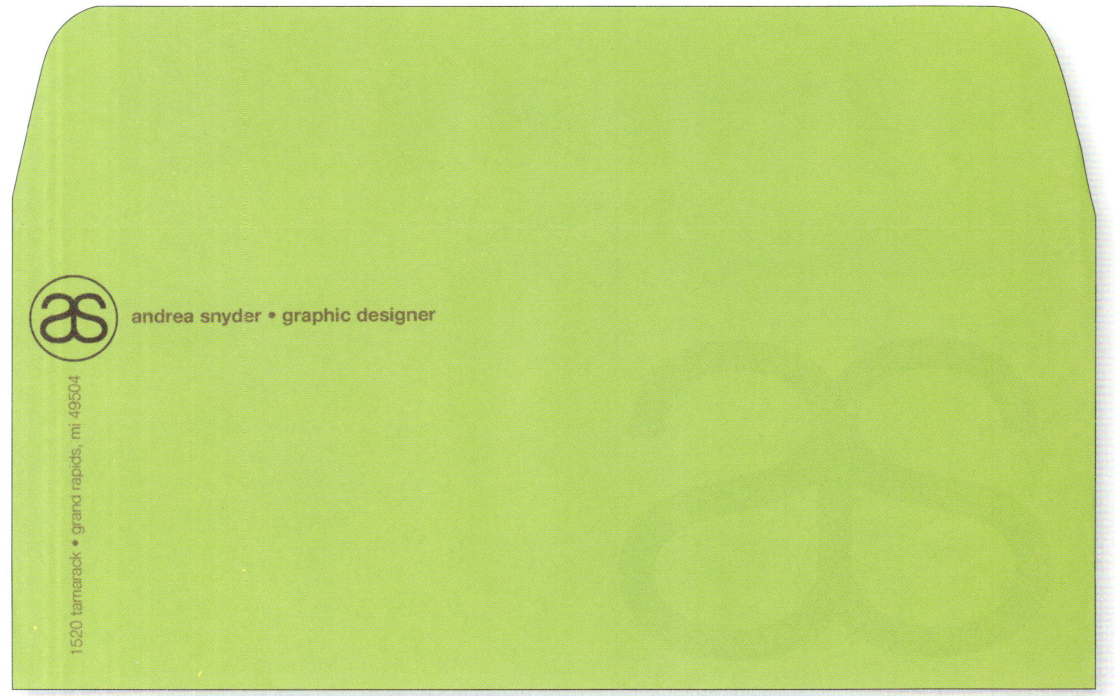

DESIGN FIRM
Andrea Snyder Design
Grand Rapids, (MI) USA
PROJECT
Andrea Snyder Graphic Design
CREATIVE DIRECTOR, DESIGNER
Andrea Snyder

DESIGN FIRM
McElveney & Palozzi Design
Rochester, (NY) USA
PROJECT
Atwater Foods
CREATIVE DIRECTOR
William McElveney
ART DIRECTOR
Lisa Gates

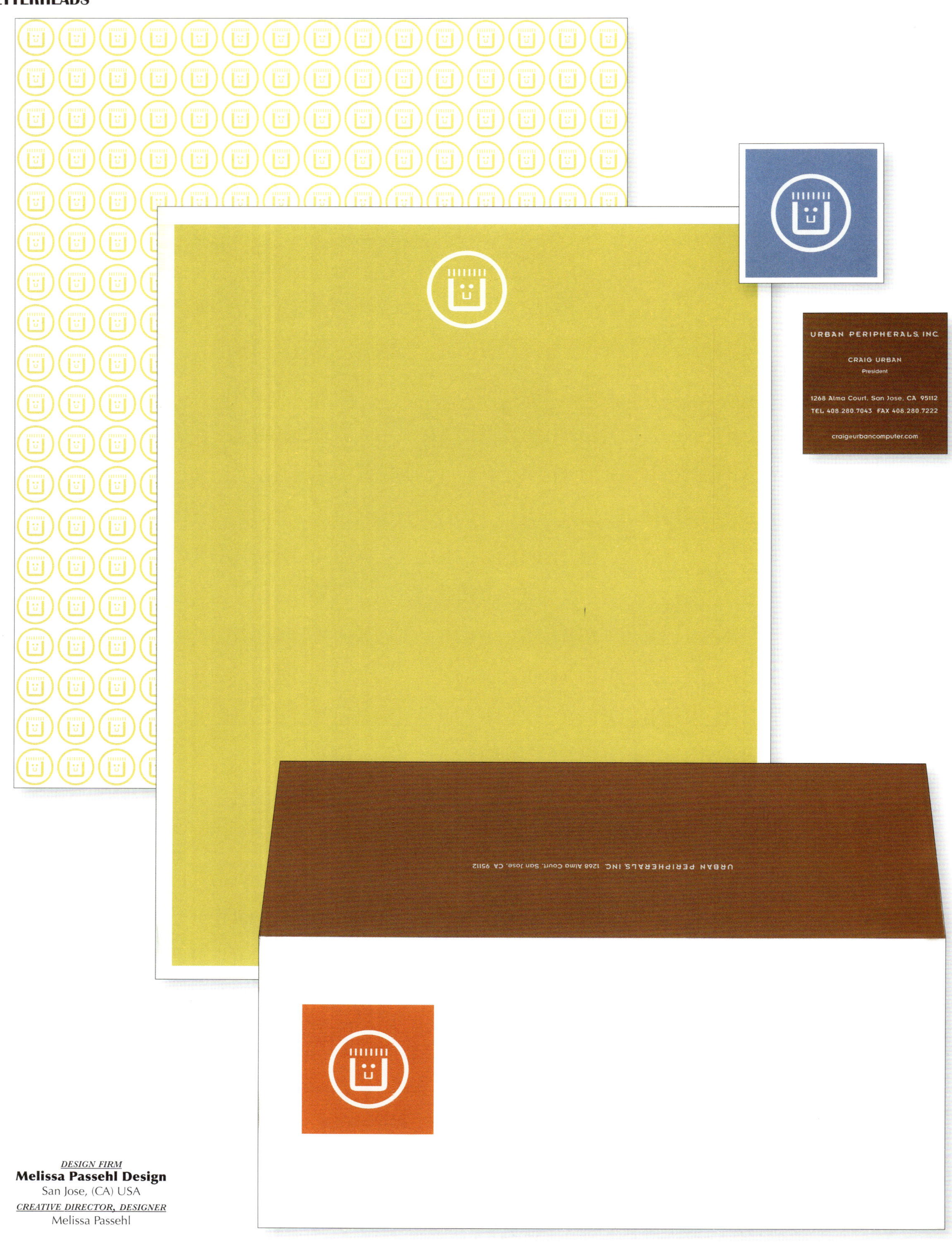

DESIGN FIRM
Melissa Passehl Design
San Jose, (CA) USA
CREATIVE DIRECTOR, DESIGNER
Melissa Passehl

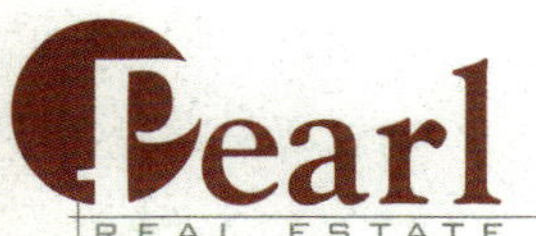

1001 NW 14th Avenue • Portland, Oregon 97209 • Phone: 503.223.2255 • Fax: 503.224.2255 • www.pearlrealestate.com

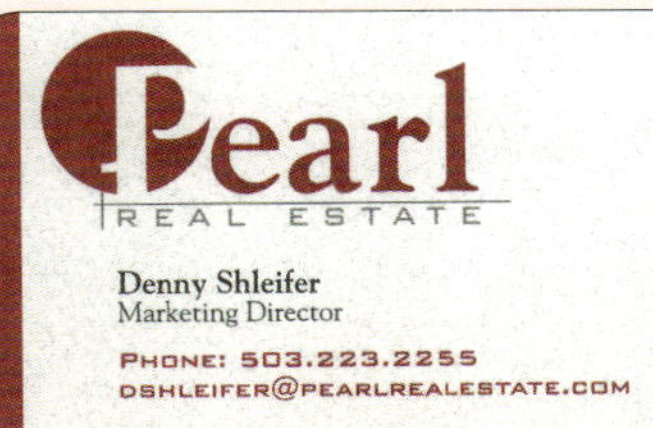

Denny Shleifer
Marketing Director

PHONE: 503.223.2255
DSHLEIFER@PEARLREALESTATE.COM

1001 NW 14th Avenue
Portland, Oregon 97209
Phone: 503.223.2255
Fax: 503.224.2255
www.pearlrealestate.com

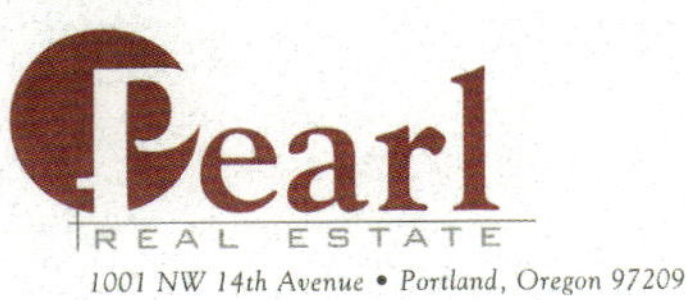

1001 NW 14th Avenue • Portland, Oregon 97209

DESIGN FIRM
Jeff Fisher LogoMotives
Portland, (OR) USA

CLIENT
Pearl Real Estate

ART DIRECTOR, DESIGNER
Jeff Fisher

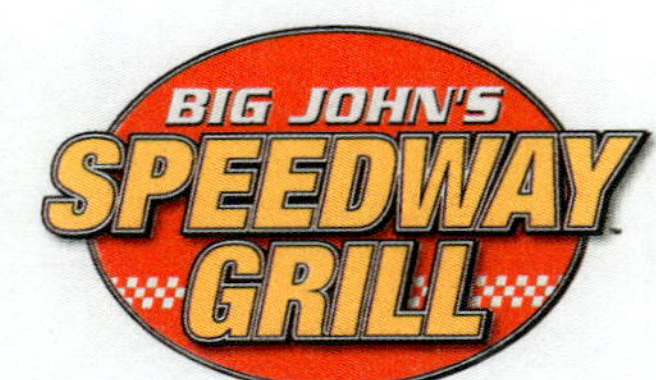

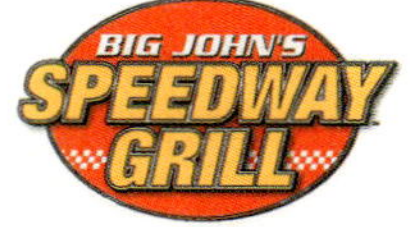

301 E. Alvarado Road
Phoenix, AZ 85004

301 E. Alvarado Road Phoenix, AZ 85004
ph 602-307-9207 **fx** 602-712-9561
www.speedwaygrill.com

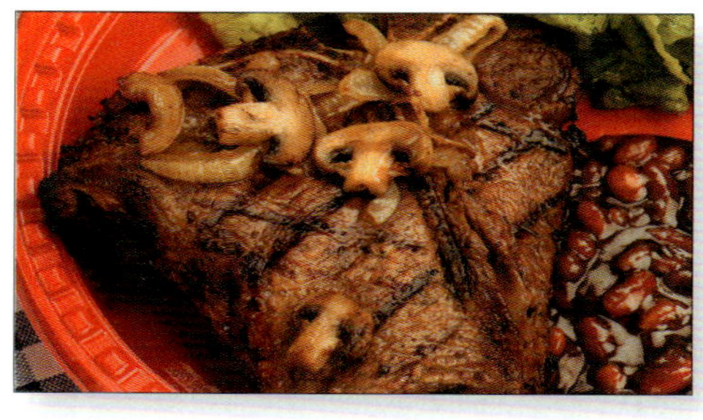

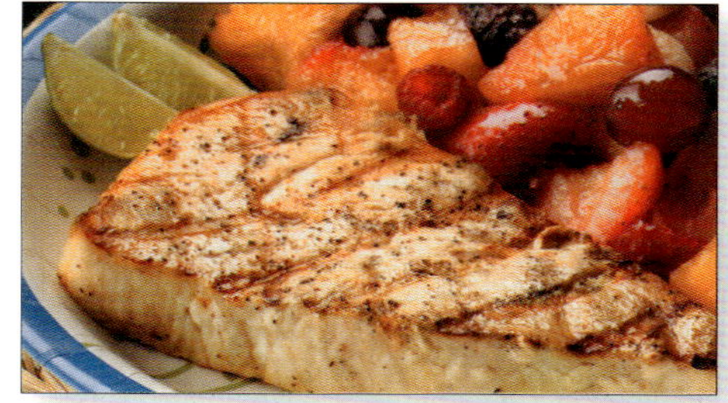

DESIGN FIRM
After Hours Creative
Phoenix, (AZ) USA
CLIENT
Big John's Speedway Grill
CREATIVE DIRECTOR
Russ Haan
DESIGNERS
Aaron Thompson,
Bradley Smith

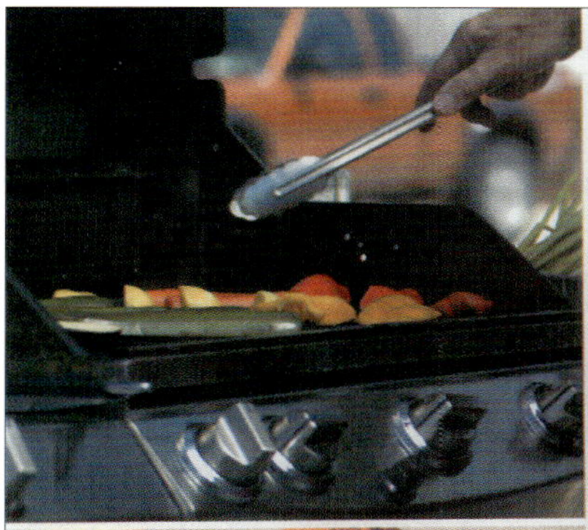

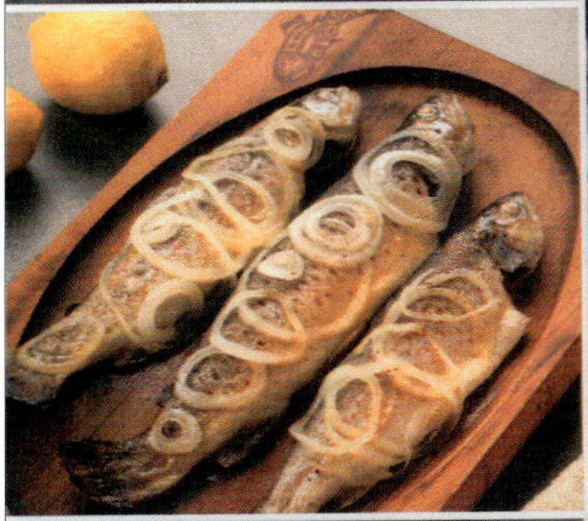

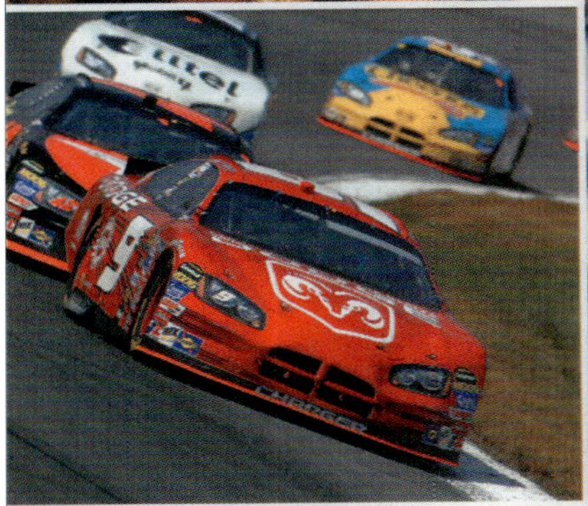

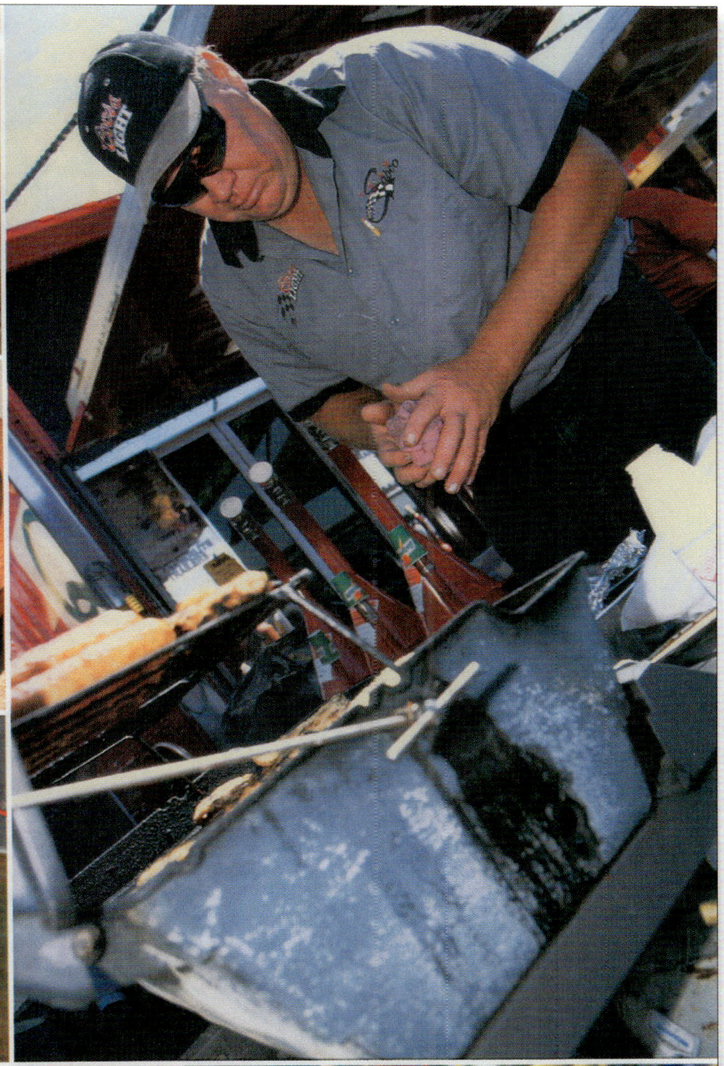

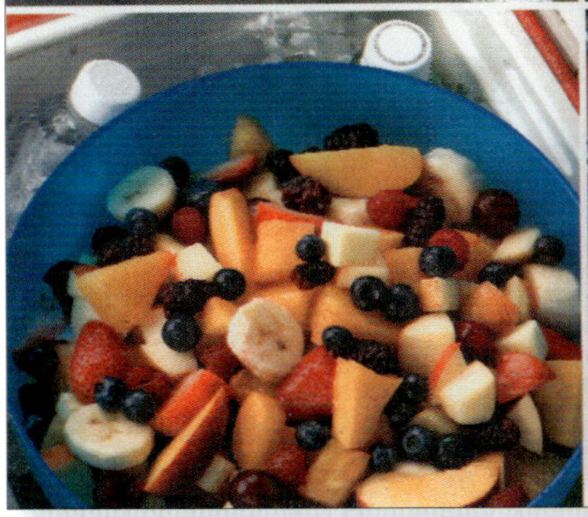

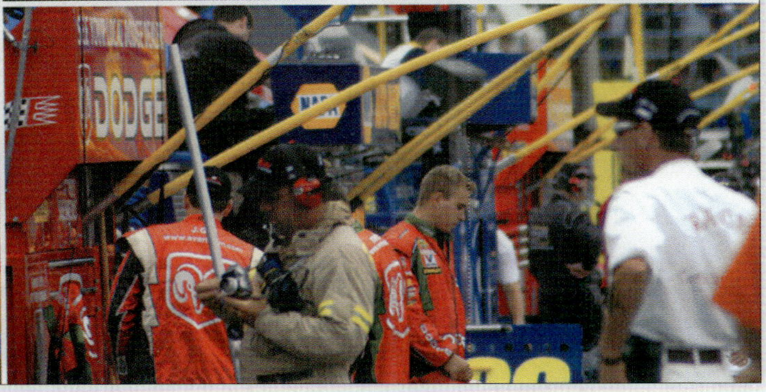

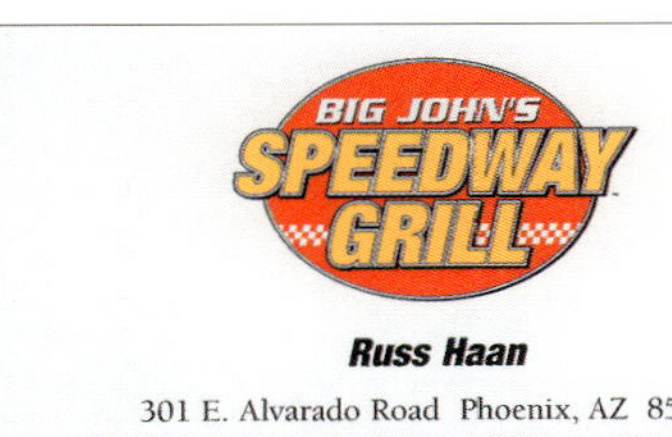
BIG JOHN'S
SPEEDWAY GRILL
Russ Haan
301 E. Alvarado Road Phoenix, AZ 85004
ph 602-307-9207 fx 602-712-9561 m 602-318-8958
www.speedwaygrill.com

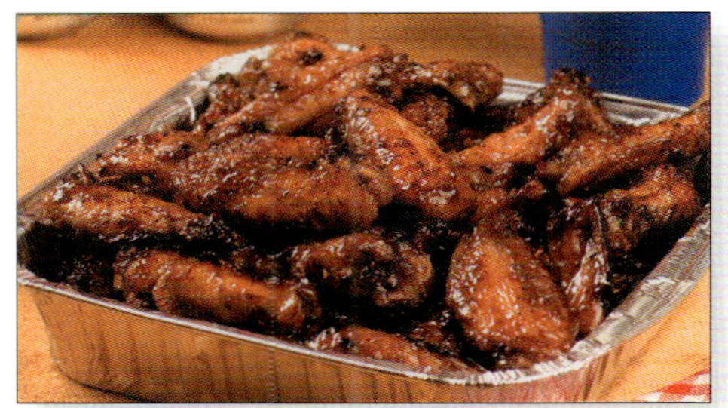

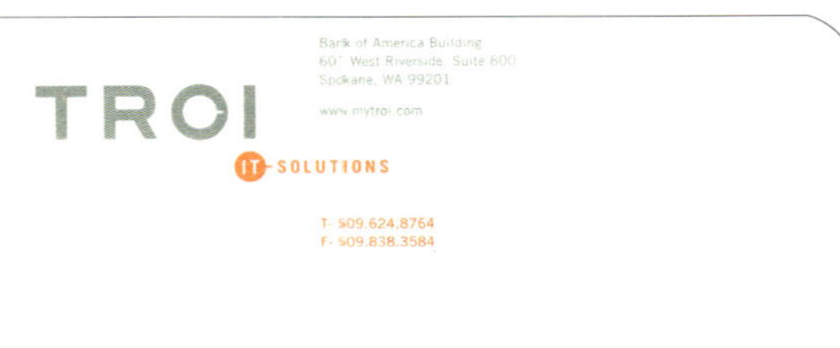

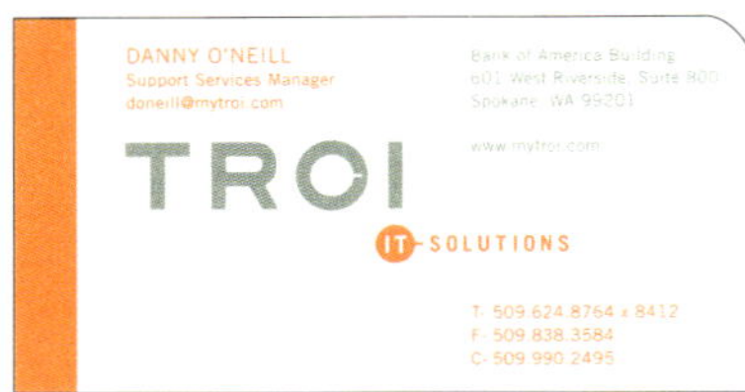

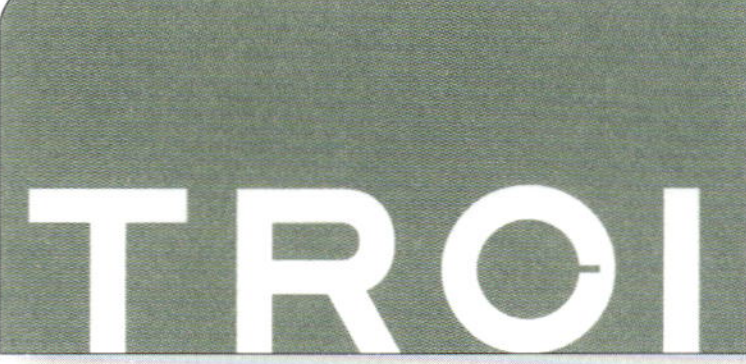

DESIGN FIRM
Klündt Hosmer
Spokane, (WA) USA

PROJECT
TROI IT SOLUTIONS

ART DIRECTOR
Darin Klündt

DESIGNER
Lorri Johnston

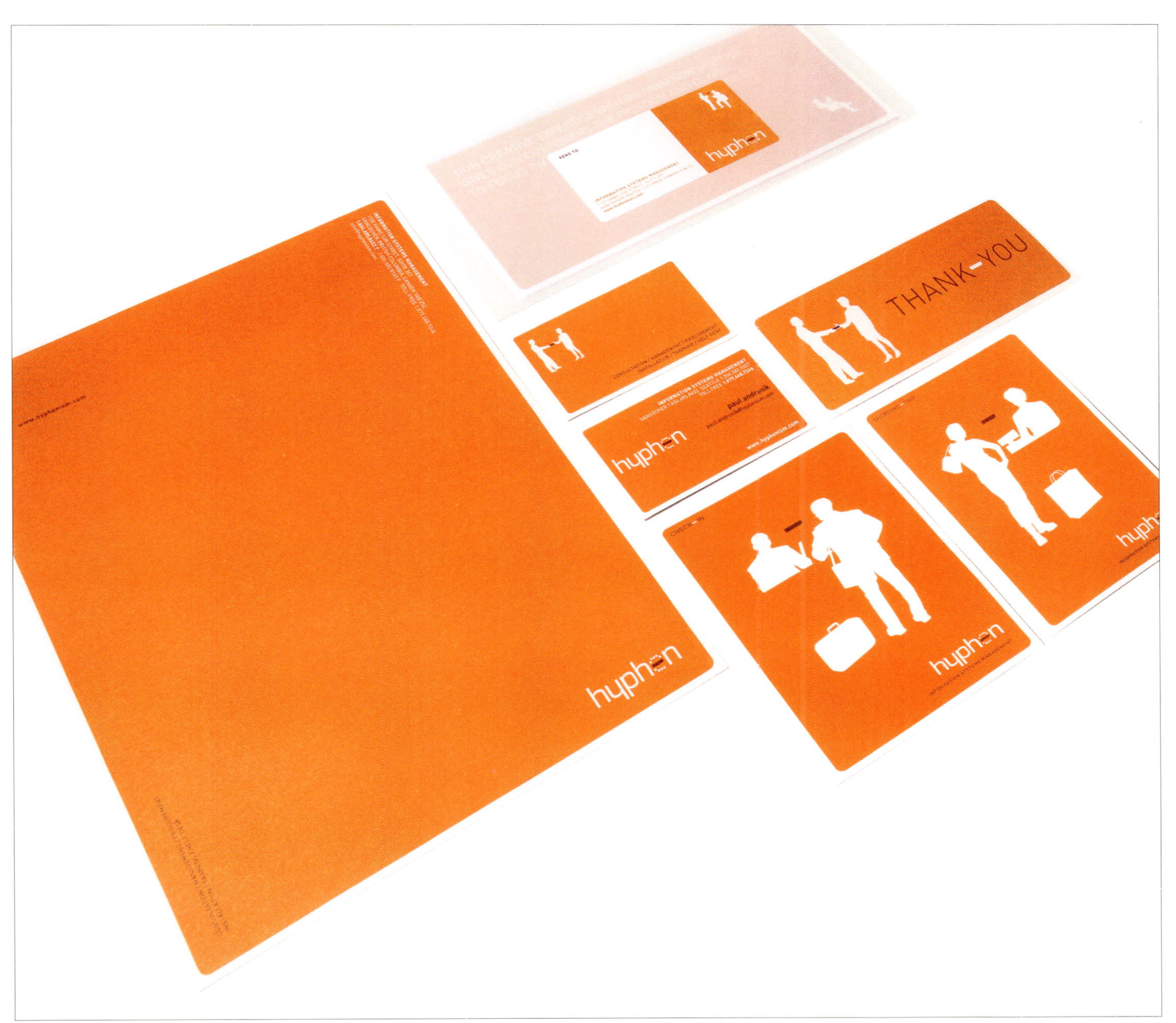

DESIGN FIRM
Subplot Design Inc.
Vancouver, (British Columbia) Canada
PROJECT
Hyphen Stationery
DESIGNER
Roy White

DESIGN FIRM
Market Street Marketing
Redding, (CA) USA
PROJECT
Market Street Marketing
DESIGNER
Kathleen Downs

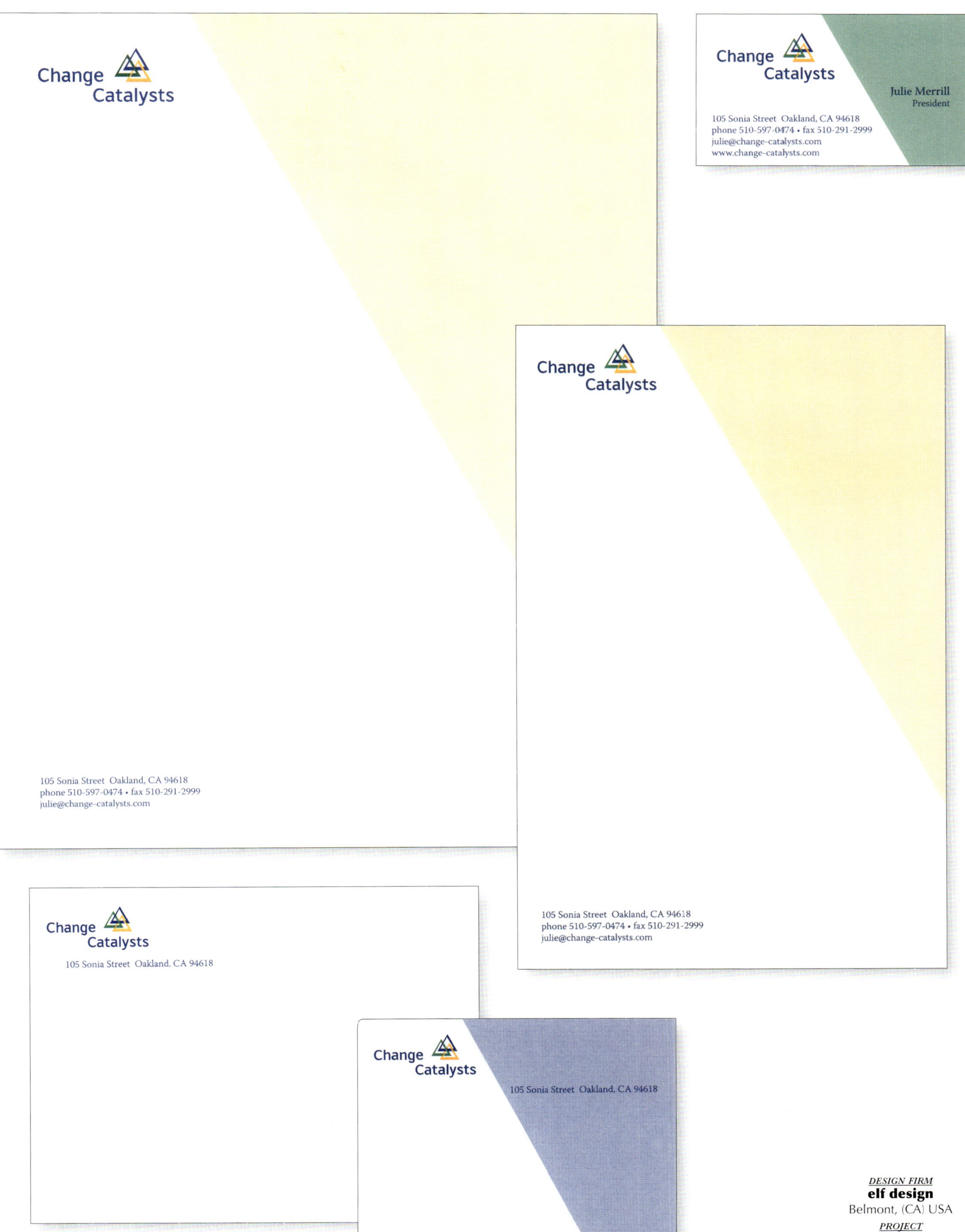

DESIGN FIRM
elf design
Belmont, (CA) USA
PROJECT
Change Catalysts
ART DIRECTOR, DESIGNER
Erin Ferree

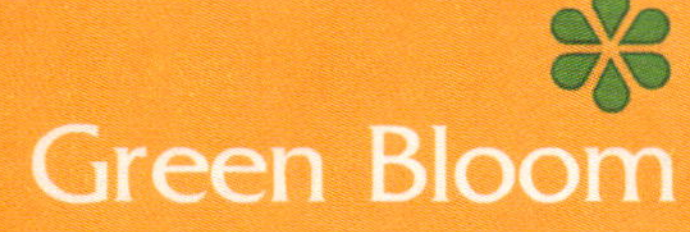

Tel. +971 4 2955800 fax. +971 4 2955811 email. greenbloom@alnaboodah.com P.O.Box 1200, Dubai, U.A.E

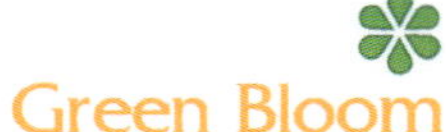

Mohammed Ahmed
Marketing Manager

P.O.Box 1200, Dubai, U.A.E
tel. +971 4 2955800 fax. +971 4 2955811
email. greenbloom@alnaboodah.com

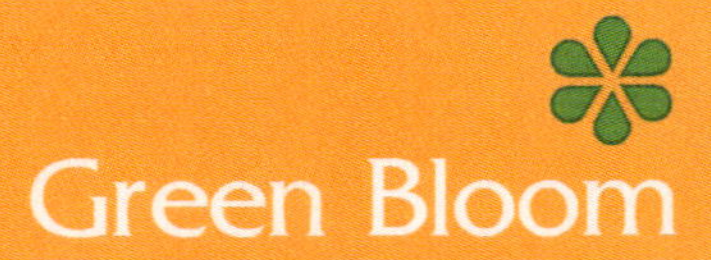

Tel. +971 4 2955800 fax. +971 4 2955811 email. greenbloom@alnaboodah.com P.O.Box 1200, Dubai, U.A.E

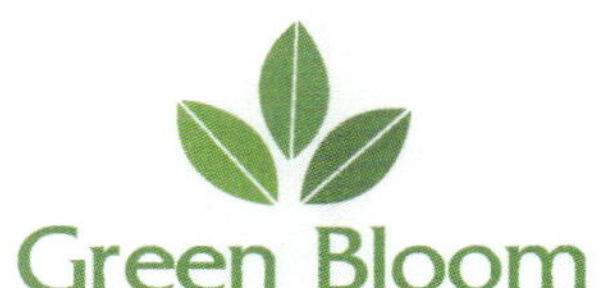

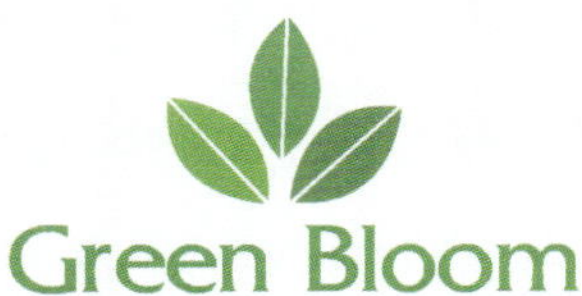

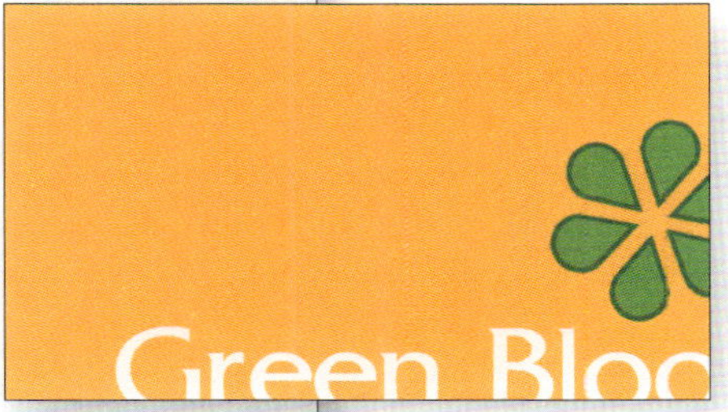

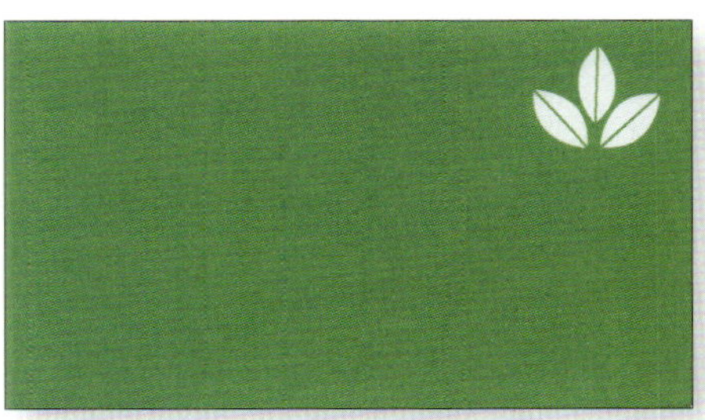

DESIGN FIRM
Riham M. AlGhussein
Abu Dhabi, UAE
PROJECT
Green Bloom
DESIGNER
Riham M. AlGhussein

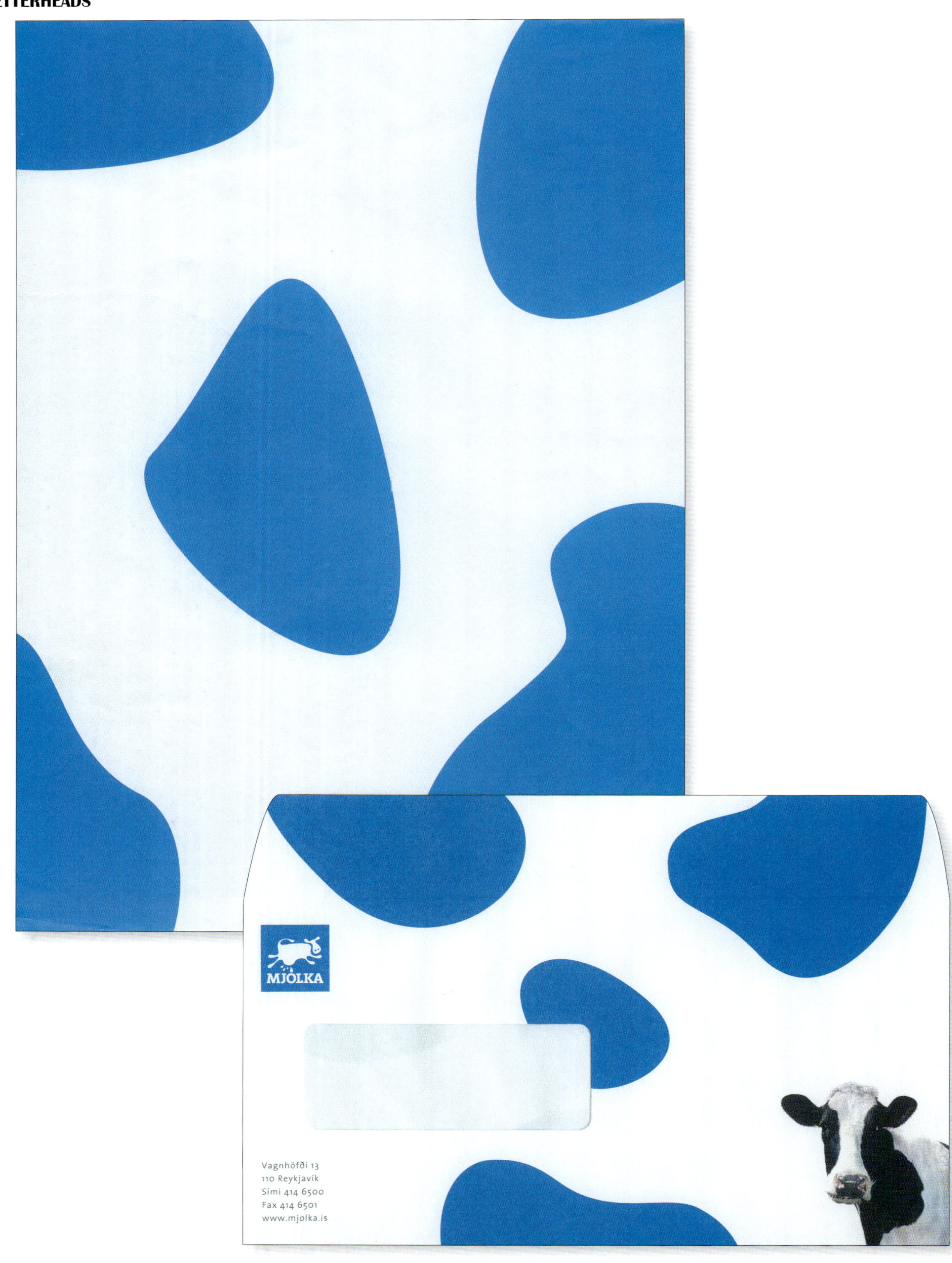
MJÖLKA
Vagnhöfði 13
110 Reykjavík
Sími 414 6500
Fax 414 6501
www.mjolka.is

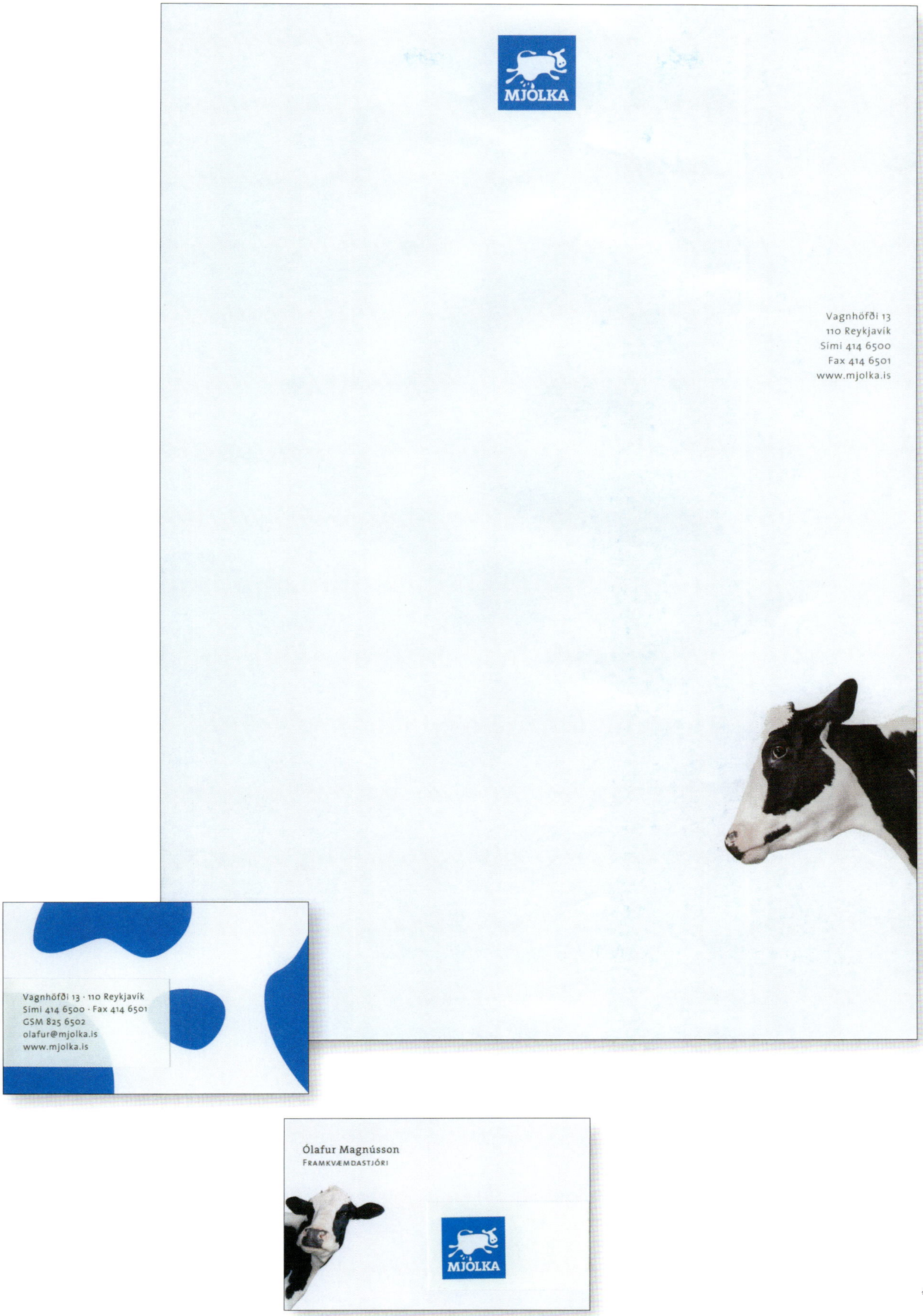

MJÓLKA

Vagnhöfði 13
110 Reykjavík
Sími 414 6500
Fax 414 6501
www.mjolka.is

Vagnhöfði 13 · 110 Reykjavík
Sími 414 6500 · Fax 414 6501
GSM 825 6502
olafur@mjolka.is
www.mjolka.is

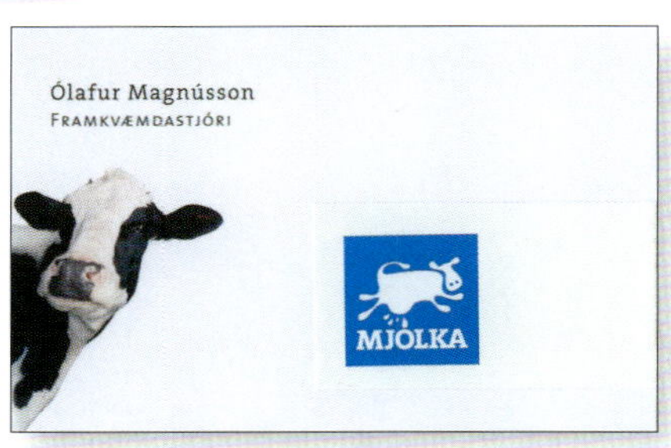

DESIGN FIRM
Ó!
Reykjavík, Iceland
CLIENT
Mjólka
ART DIRECTOR, DESIGNER
Einar Gylfason

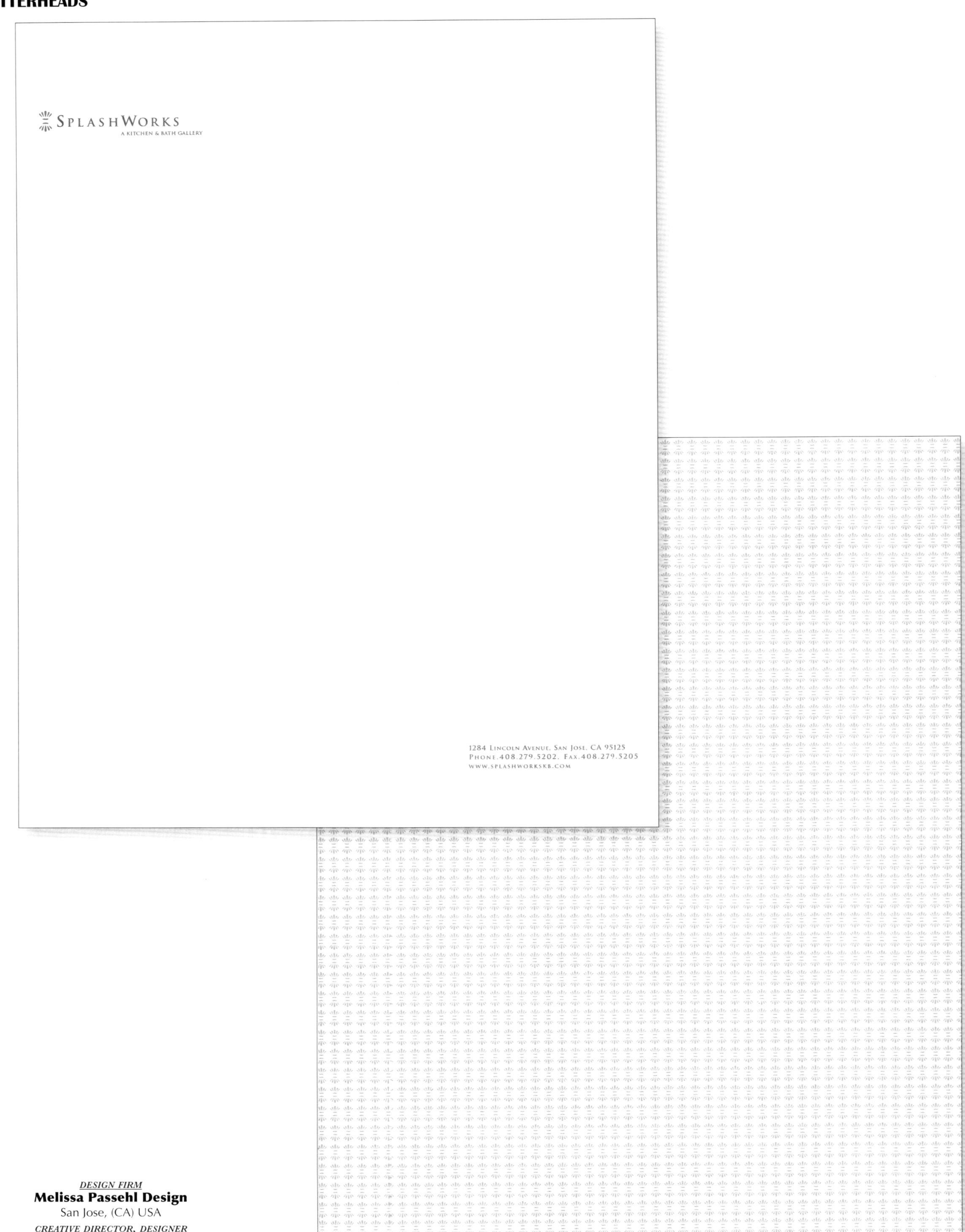

DESIGN FIRM
Melissa Passehl Design
San Jose, (CA) USA
CREATIVE DIRECTOR, DESIGNER
Melissa Passehl

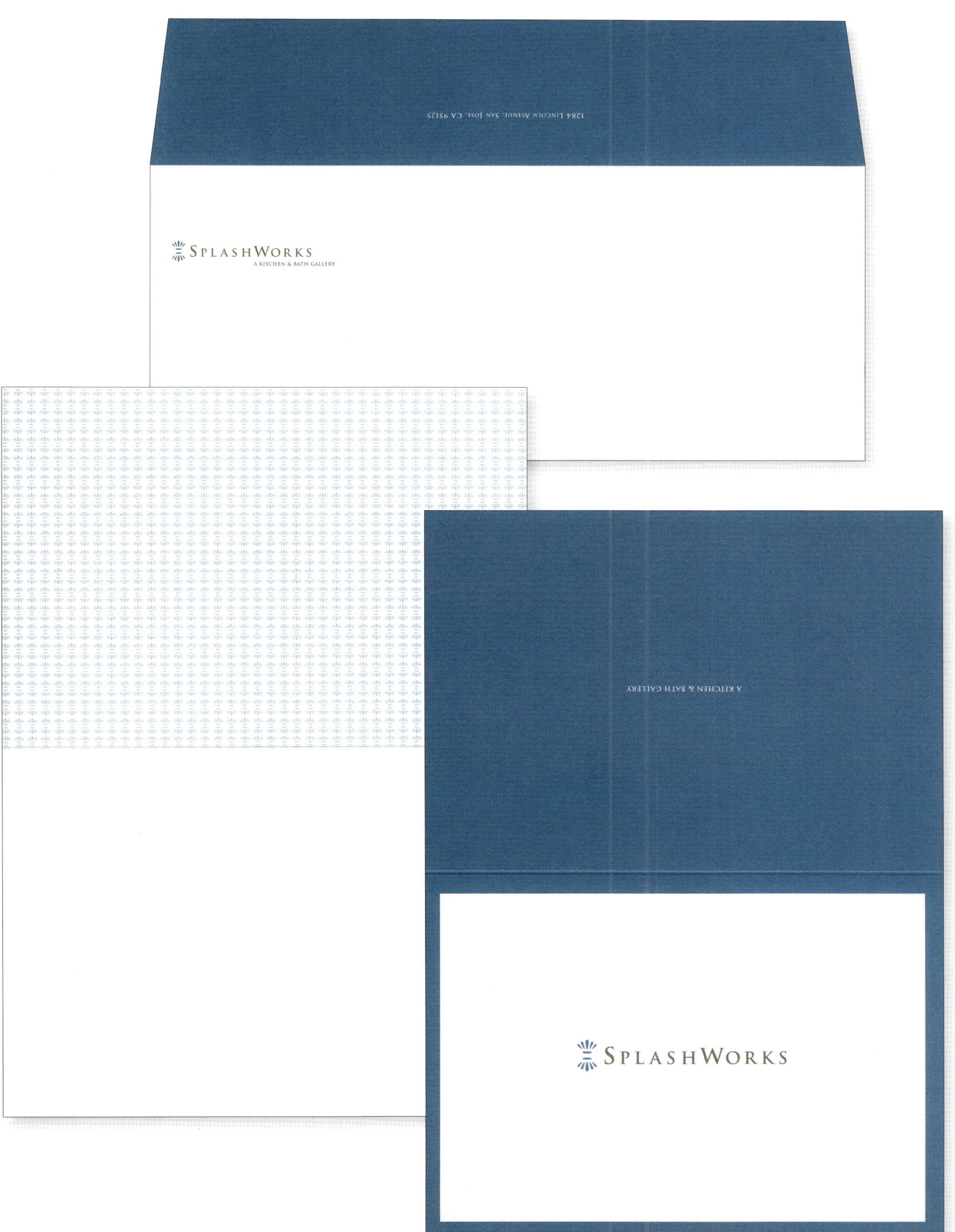
1284 Lincoln Avenue, San Jose, CA 95125
SplashWorks
A Kitchen & Bath Gallery
A Kitchen & Bath Gallery
SplashWorks

embellish
EMBELLISH
330 Frazier Avenue Suite C Chattanooga, TN 37405

embellish
EMBELLISH

Terri M. Holley
terri@embellishshoes.com
Tel 423 752 7463 Fax 423 752 8017
330 Frazier Avenue Suite C Chattanooga, TN 37405
www.embellishshoes.com

embellish
EMBELLISH

www.embellishshoes.com
Tel 423 752 7463 Fax 423 752 8017
330 Frazier Ave Suite C Chattanooga, TN 37405

DESIGN FIRM
Maycreate
Chattanooga, (TN) USA
PROJECT
Embellish
CREATIVE DIRECTOR, DESIGNER
Brian May
PRINTING
Creative Printing

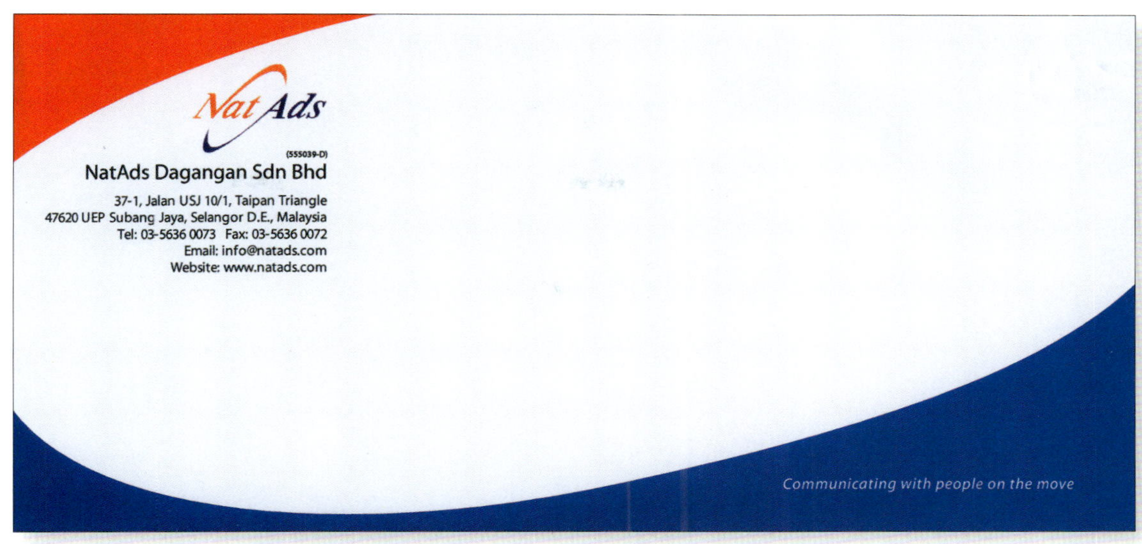

Nat Ads
(555039-D)
NatAds Dagangan Sdn Bhd
37-1, Jalan USJ 10/1, Taipan Triangle
47620 UEP Subang Jaya, Selangor D.E., Malaysia
Tel: 03-5636 0073 Fax: 03-5636 0072
Email: info@natads.com
Website: www.natads.com
Communicating with people on the move

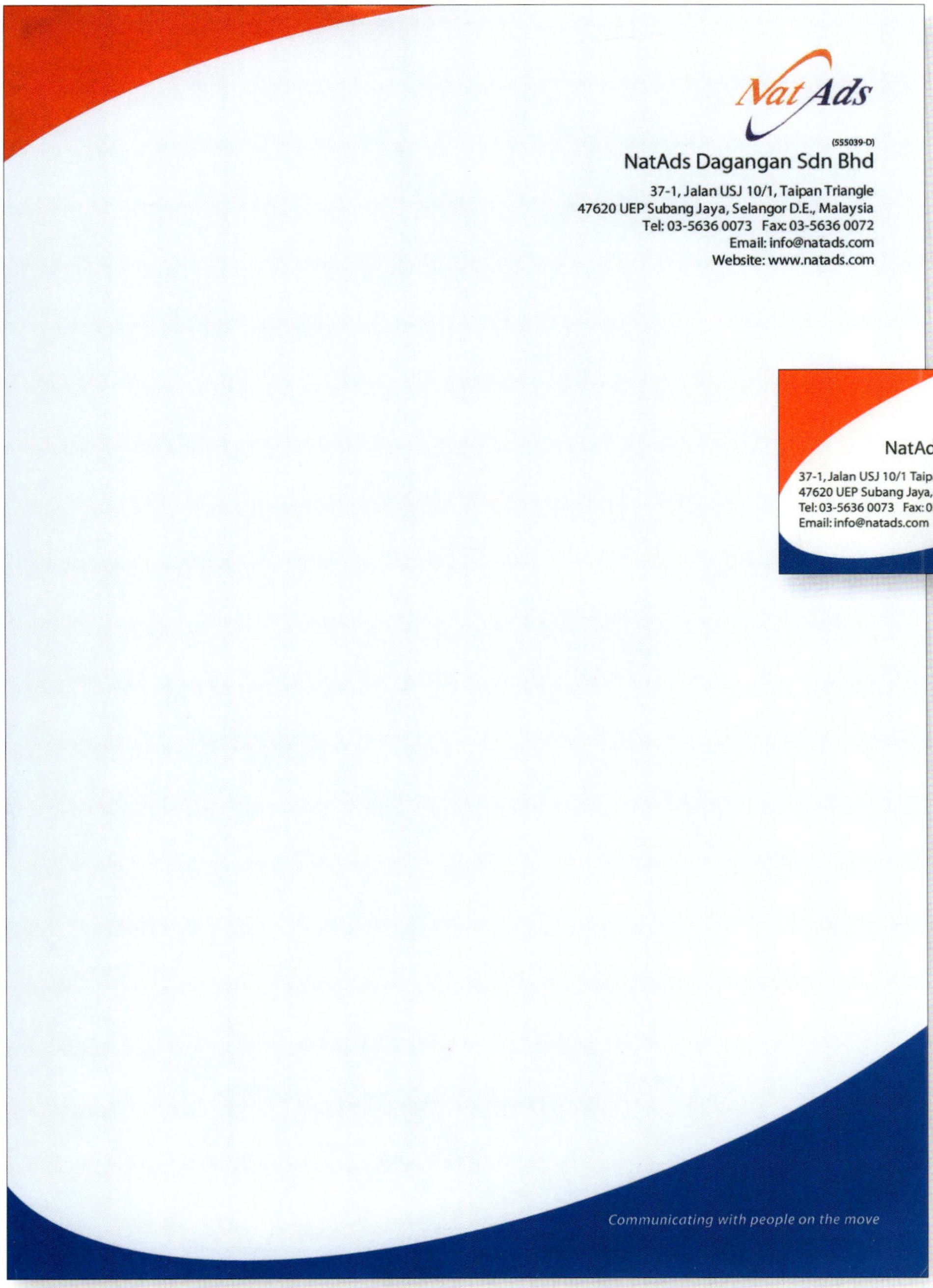

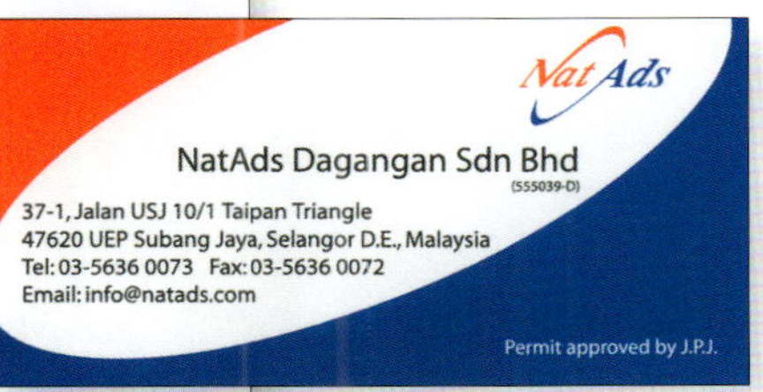

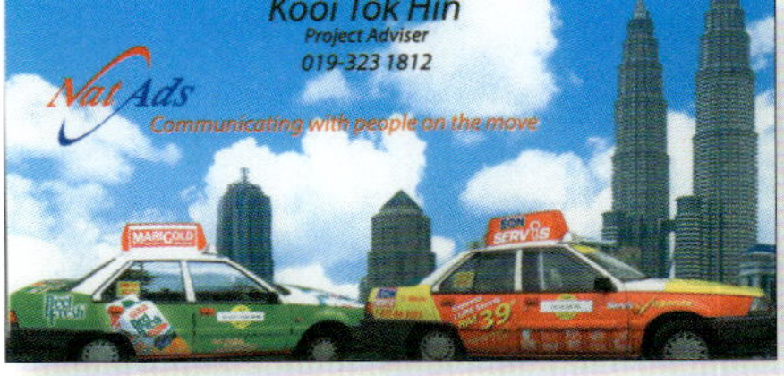

DESIGN FIRM
TrueFACES Creation Sdn. Bhd.
Subang Jaya, Malaysia
DESIGNERS
TrueFACES Creative Team

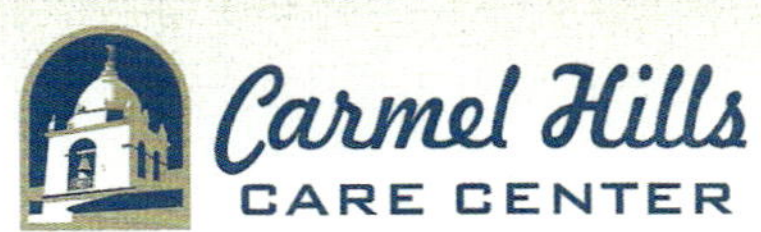

23795 W. R. Holman Highway / Monterey, CA 93940 / TEL 831-624-1875 / FAX 831-624-7138 / www.carmelhillscarecenter.com

DESIGN FIRM
The Wecker Group
Monterey, (CA) USA
PROJECT
Carmel Hills Care Center
DESIGNER
Robert Wecker

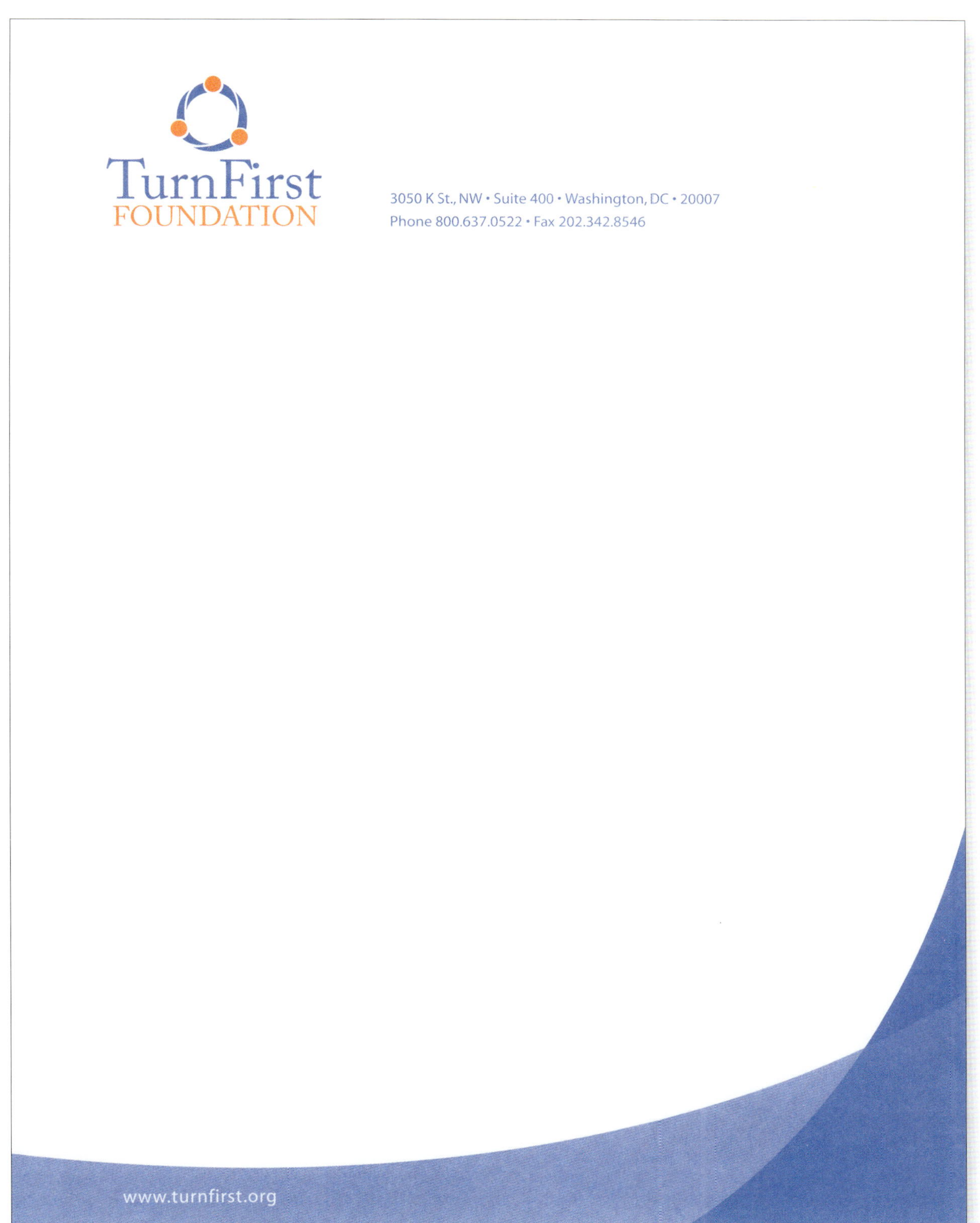

DESIGN FIRM
Sightline Marketing
Washington, (DC) USA
PROJECT
Turn First Foundation
DESIGNER
Anthony Begnoche

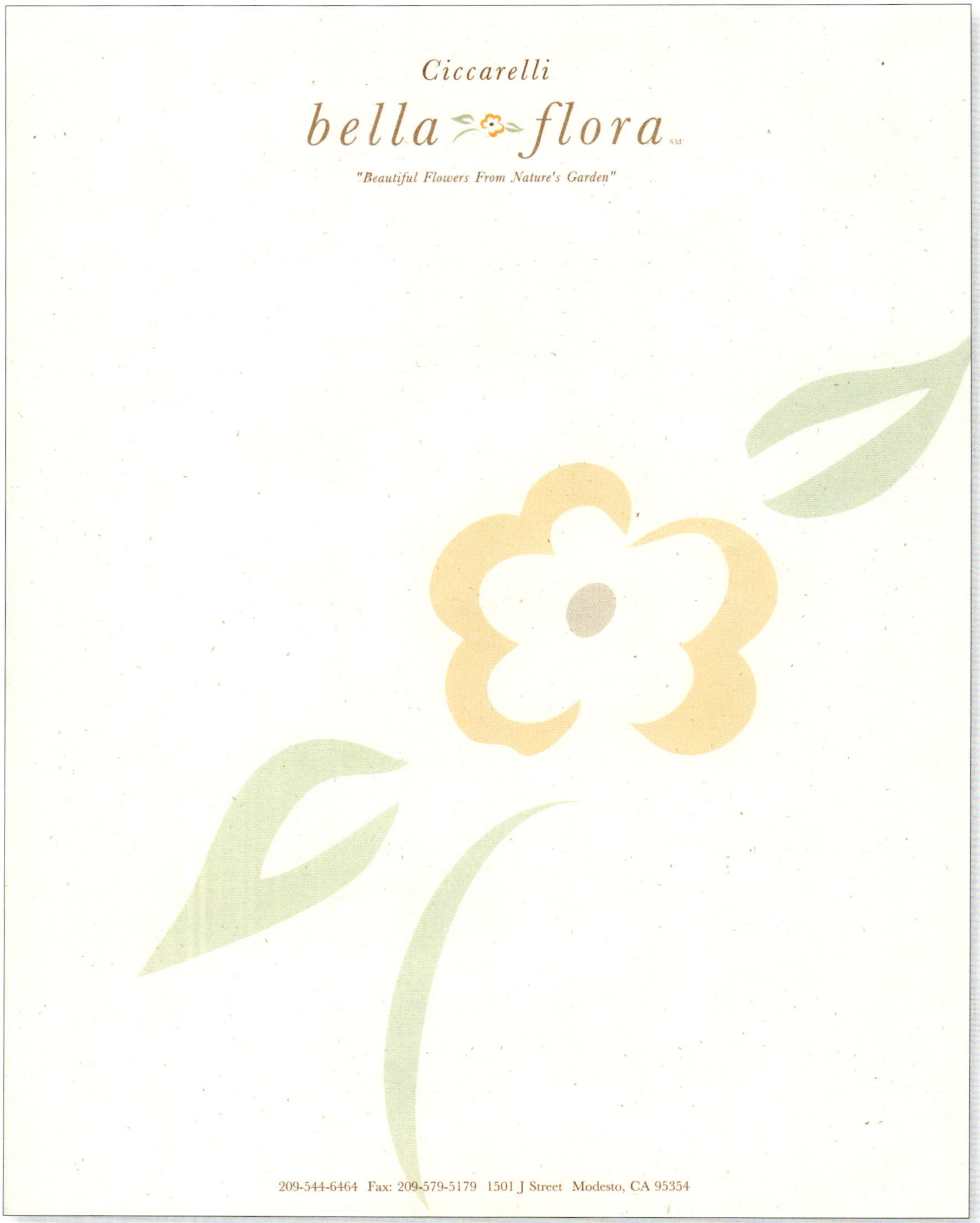

Ciccarelli
bella flora SM
"Beautiful Flowers From Nature's Garden"

209-544-6464 Fax: 209-579-5179 1501 J Street Modesto, CA 95354

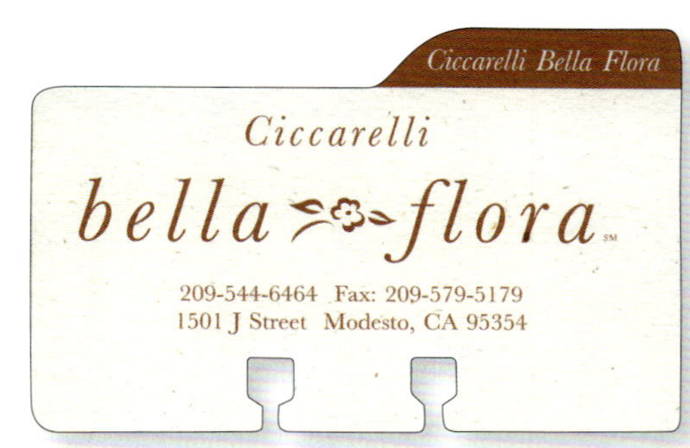

DESIGN FIRM
Marcia Herrmann Design
Modesto, (CA) USA
PROJECT
Ciccarelli

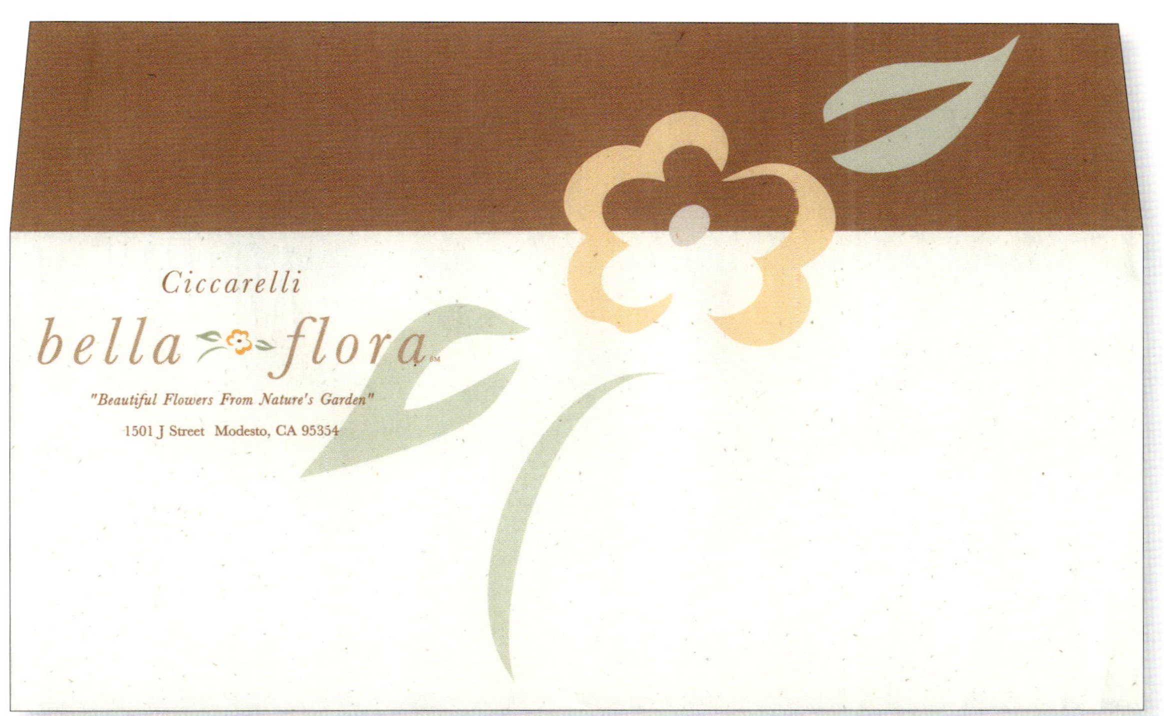
Ciccarelli
bella flora
"Beautiful Flowers From Nature's Garden"
1501 J Street Modesto, CA 95354

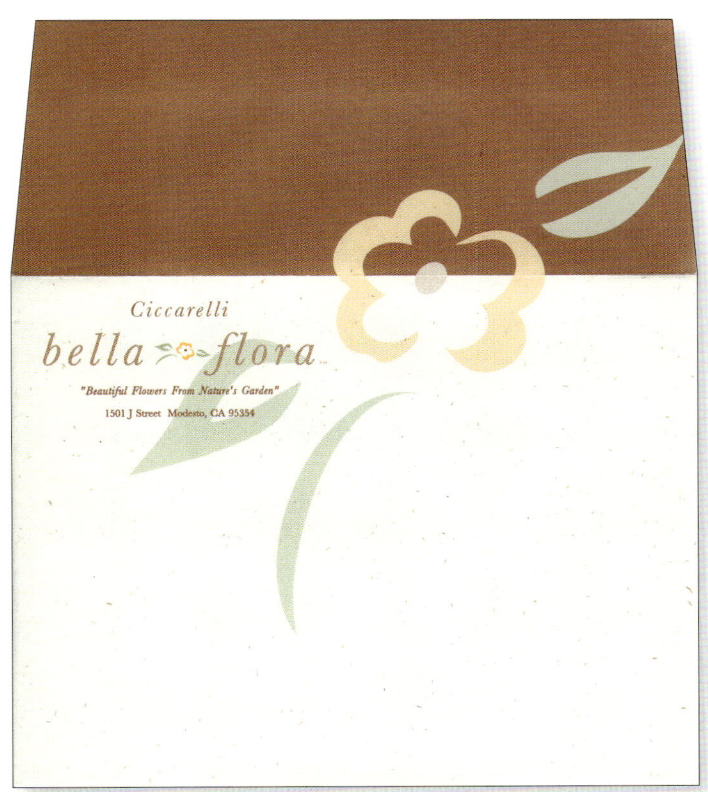
Ciccarelli
bella flora
"Beautiful Flowers From Nature's Garden"
1501 J Street Modesto, CA 95354

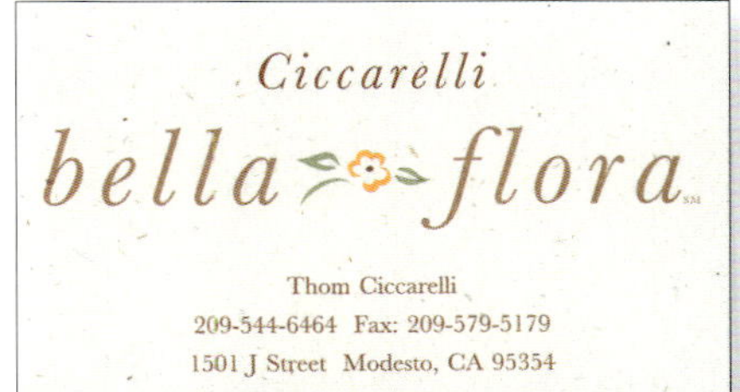
Ciccarelli
bella flora
Thom Ciccarelli
209-544-6464 Fax: 209-579-5179
1501 J Street Modesto, CA 95354

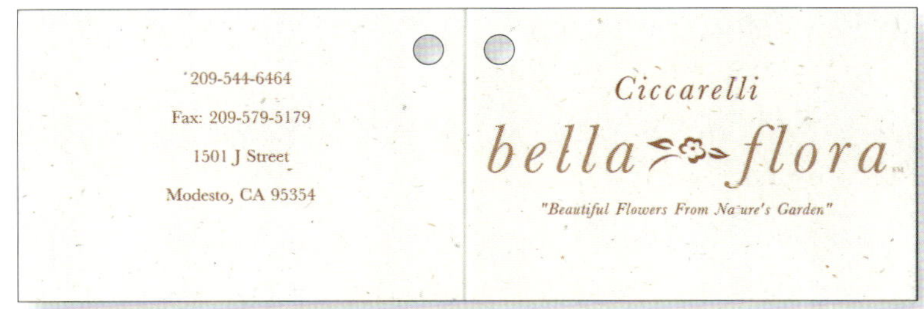
209-544-6464
Fax: 209-579-5179
1501 J Street
Modesto, CA 95354
Ciccarelli
bella flora
"Beautiful Flowers From Nature's Garden"

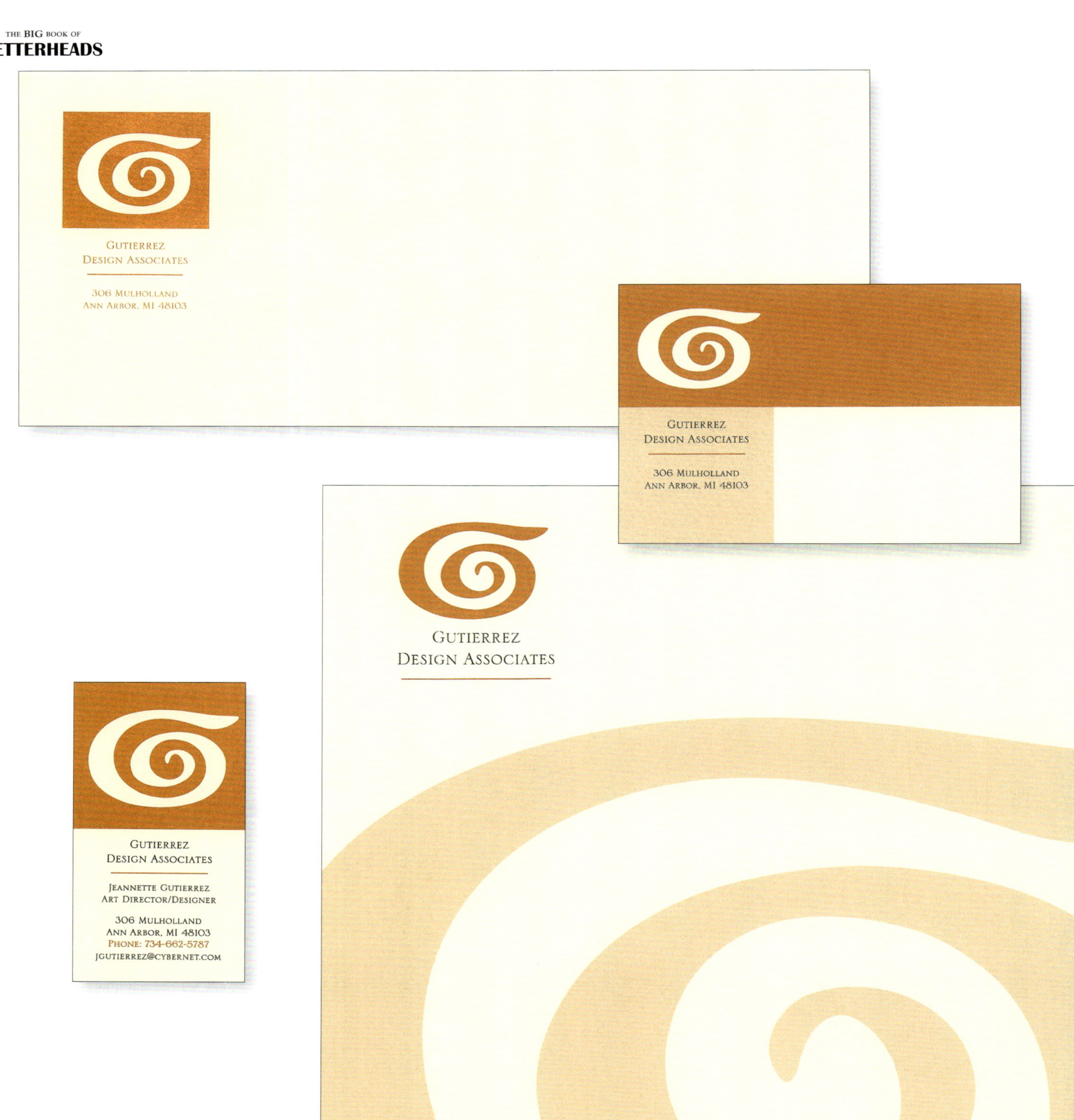

DESIGN FIRM
Gutierrez Design Associates
Ann Arbor, (MI) USA
CLIENT
Gutierrez Design Associates
DESIGNER
Jeannette Gutierrez

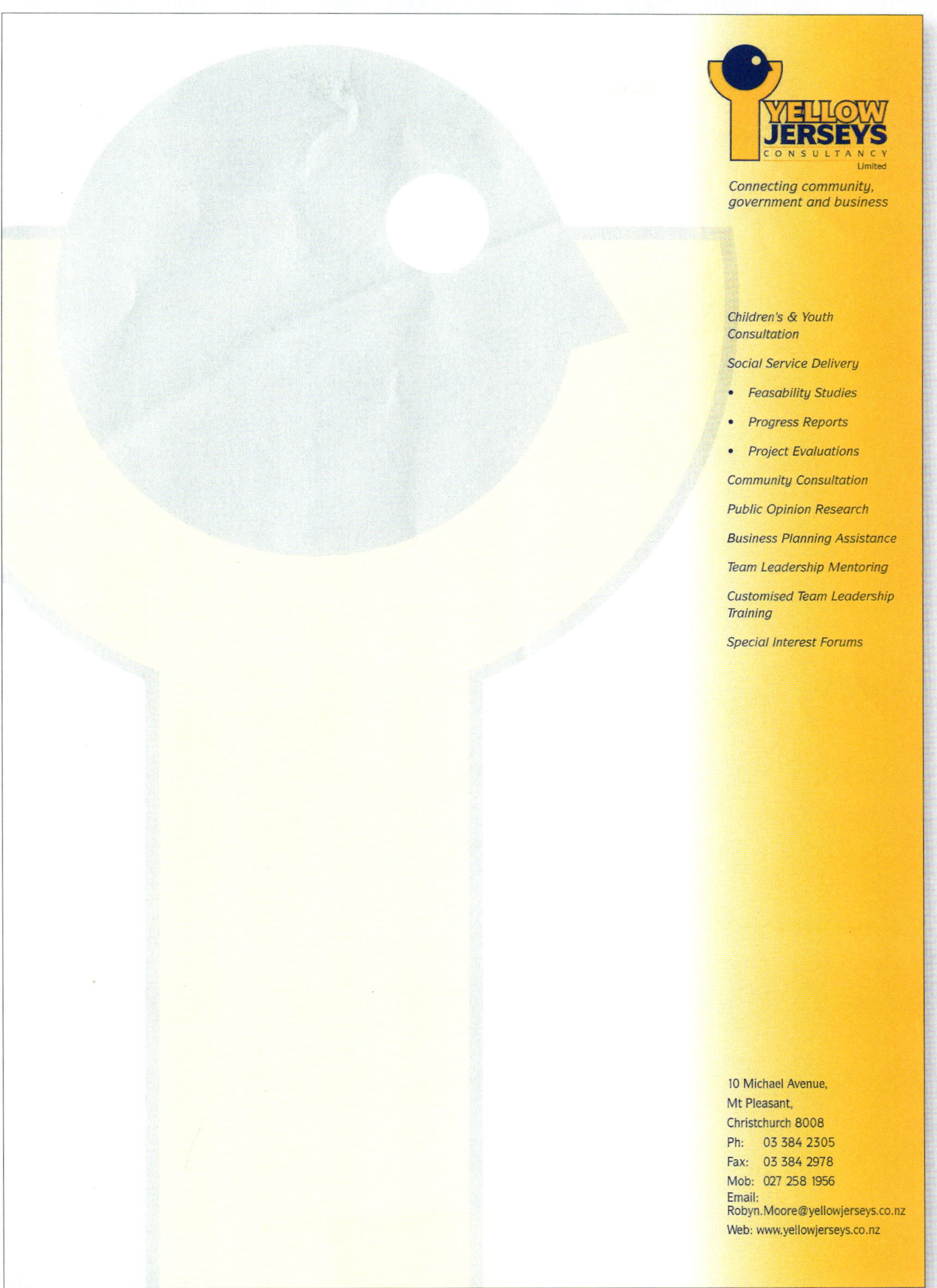

DESIGN FIRM
ArtnSoul Graphic Design
Christ Church, New Zealand
PROJECT
Yellow Jerseys
ART DIRECTOR, DESIGNER
Piers Le Sueur

Marine Repair Services
Container Maintenance
CORPORATION

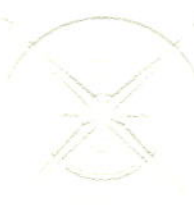

340 Commerce Dr.
Rincon, GA 31326
Tel: 912-966-1716
Fax: 912-826-4775
e-mail: jcooley@mrs-cmc.com

Joshua H. Cooley
Vice President

Container Maintenance Corporation, Wilmington, NC, Nashville, TN, Charleston, SC, Atlanta, GA, Savannah, GA, Jacksonville, FL, New Orleans, LA, Houston, TX, **Marine Repair Services, Inc.**, Staten Island, NY, Baltimore, MD, Norfolk, VA, **Marco Enterprises**, Staten Island, NY

DESIGN FIRM
Longwater & Company, Inc.
Savannah, (GA) USA
CLIENT
Marine Repair Services
Container Maintenance Corporation
CREATIVE DIRECTOR
Elaine Longwater
DESIGNER
Patrick Grone

LETTER

Adress Wurster Strasse 86 · 27580 Bremerhaven · Germany
Phone +49-471-80 60 792 · Facsimile +49-471-80 60 793
E-Mail fast.service@candy-station.com · www.candy-station.com

DON'T DO IT YOURSELF... LET OUR SKILLED MECHANICS FIX THE GROOVE FOR YOU!

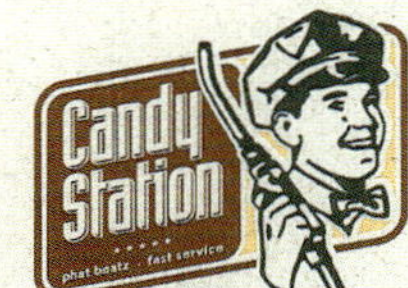

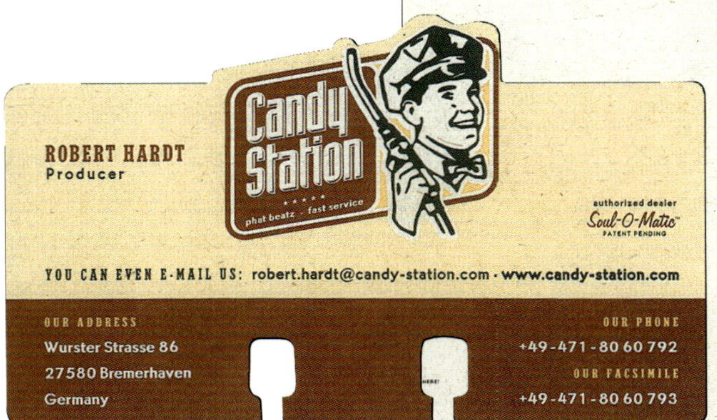

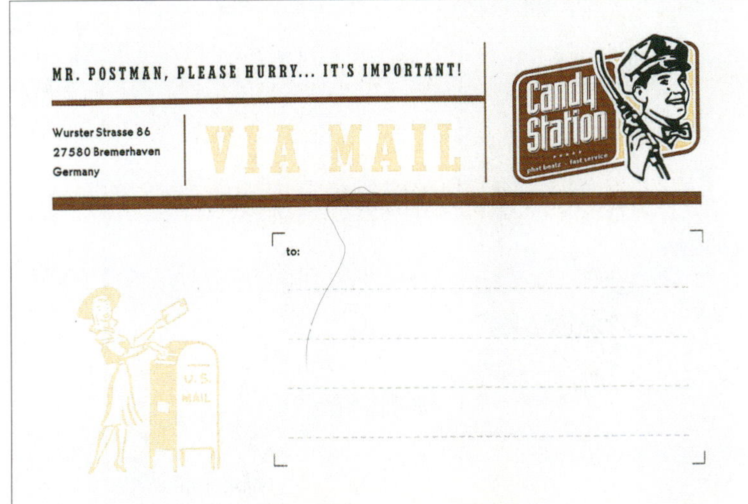

DESIGN FIRM
Braue: Branding & Corporate Design
Bremerhaven, Germany

CLIENT
Candy Station

CREATIVE DIRECTOR
Kai Braue

ART DIRECTOR
Marcel Robbers

DESIGNERS
Kai Braue,
Marcel Robbers

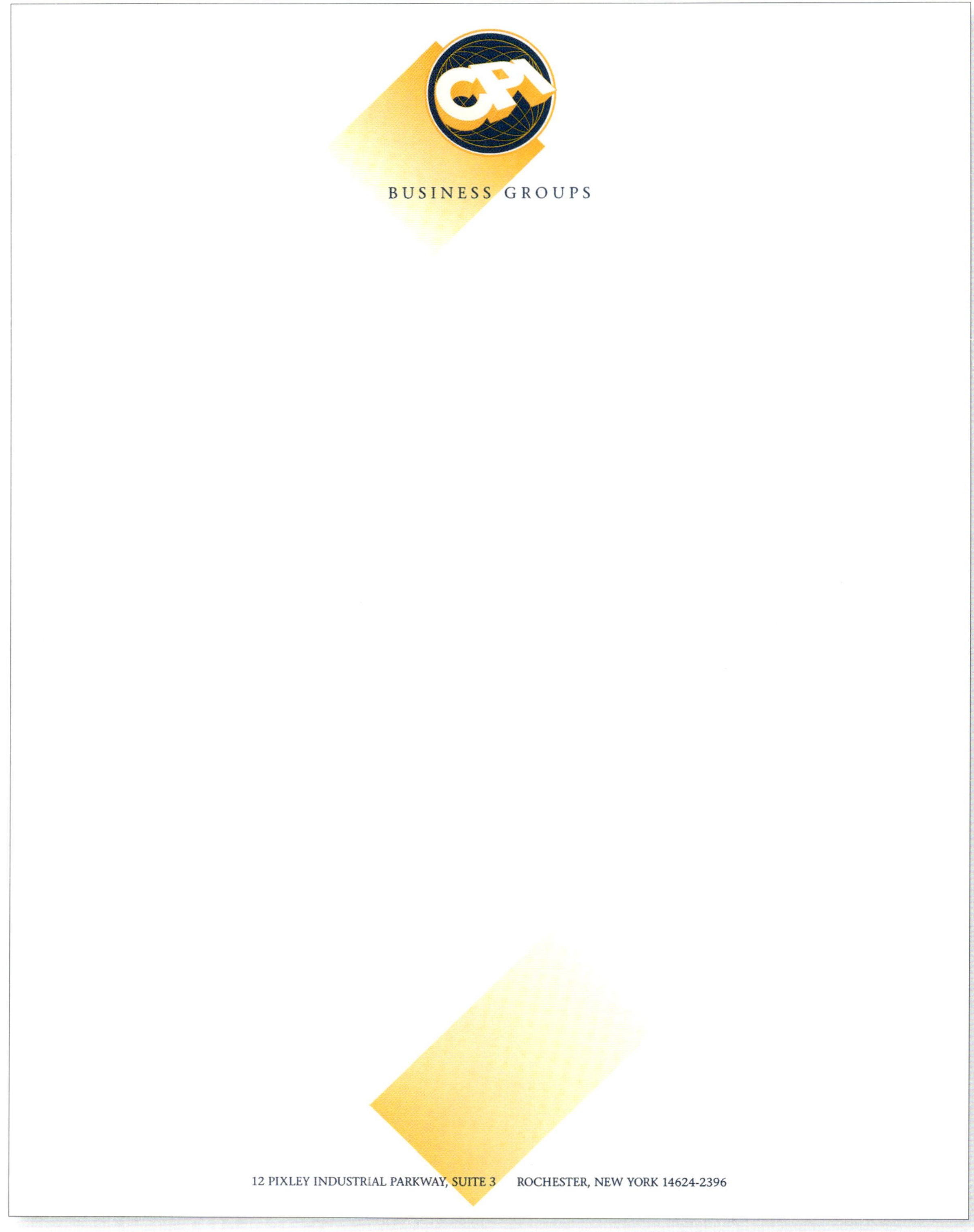

DESIGN FIRM
McElveney & Palozzi Design
Rochester, (NY) USA
PROJECT
CPI Business Groups
CREATIVE DIRECTOR
Steve Palozzi

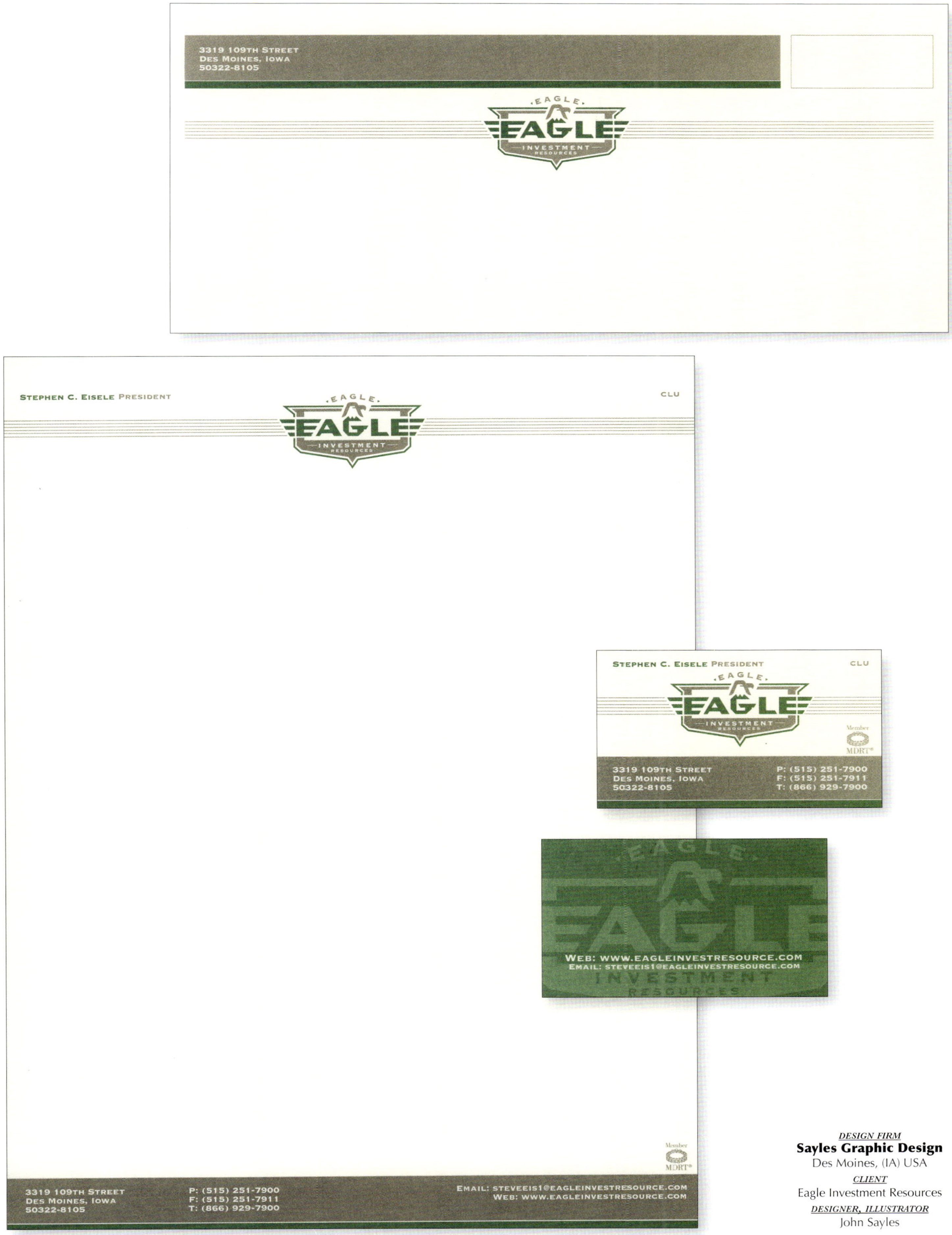

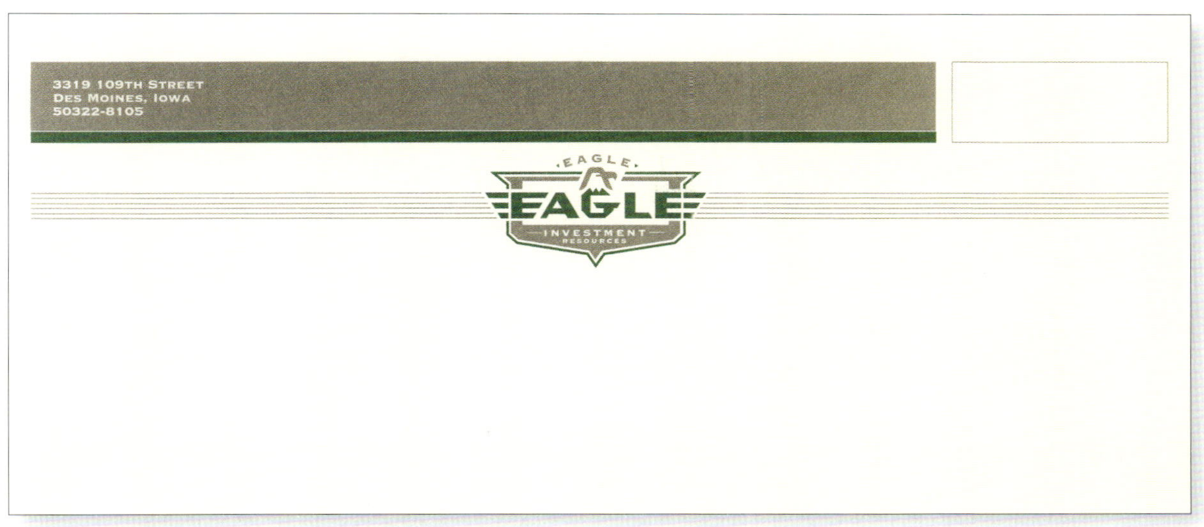

Stephen C. Eisele President
CLU
Eagle
Eagle
Investment
Resources
Member
MDRT®
3319 109th Street
Des Moines, Iowa
50322-8105
P: (515) 251-7900
F: (515) 251-7911
T: (866) 929-7900
Email: steveeis1@eagleinvestresource.com
Web: www.eagleinvestresource.com

Stephen C. Eisele President
CLU
Eagle
Eagle
Investment
Resources
Member
MDRT®
3319 109th Street
Des Moines, Iowa
50322-8105
P: (515) 251-7900
F: (515) 251-7911
T: (866) 929-7900

Web: www.eagleinvestresource.com
Email: steveeis1@eagleinvestresource.com

DESIGN FIRM
Sayles Graphic Design
Des Moines, (IA) USA
CLIENT
Eagle Investment Resources
DESIGNER, ILLUSTRATOR
John Sayles

Island
MARINE

SALES ▪ VALET STORAGE ▪ BROKERAGE ▪ BOAT BUTLER ▪ TRANSPORT ▪ DYNO SERVICE ▪ RACE RIGGING ▪ 24 HR SERVICE

AT YOUR SERVICE

26500 South Highway 125 ▪ Monkey Island, OK 74331 P 918-257-5300 F 918-257-4429 W islandmarine.biz

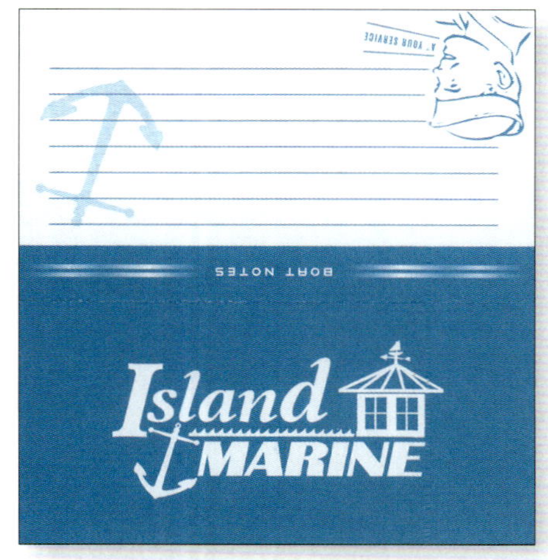

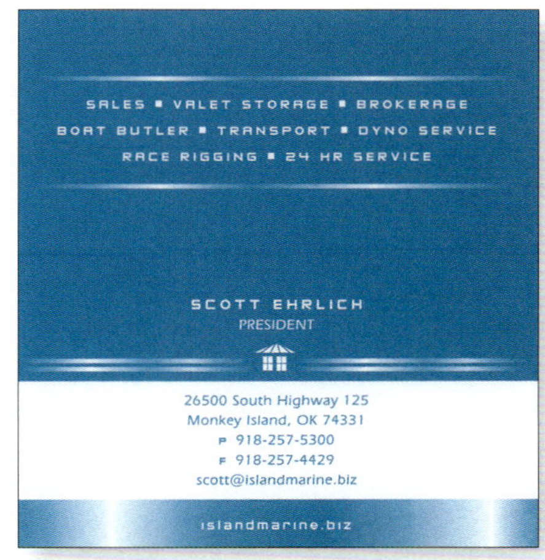

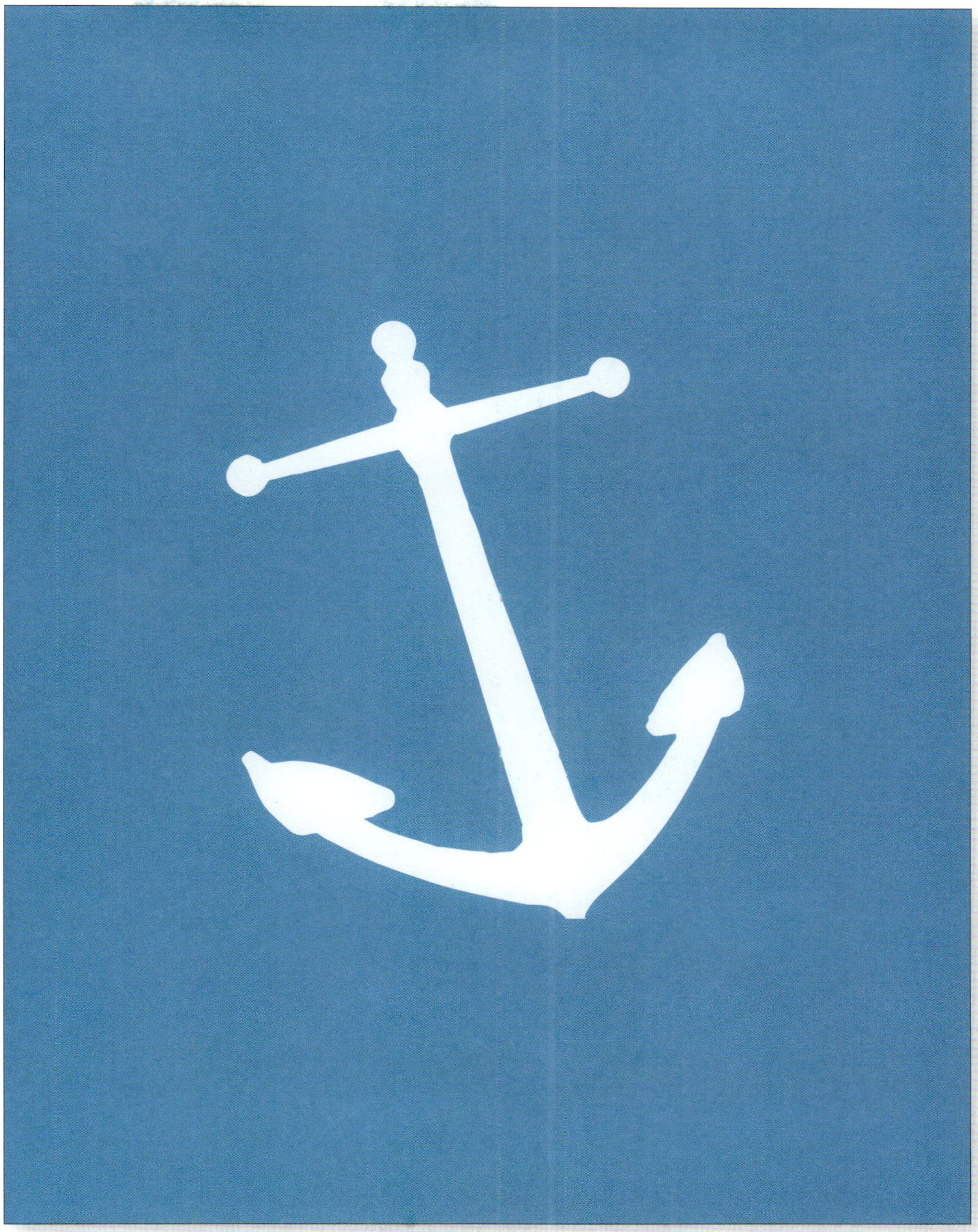

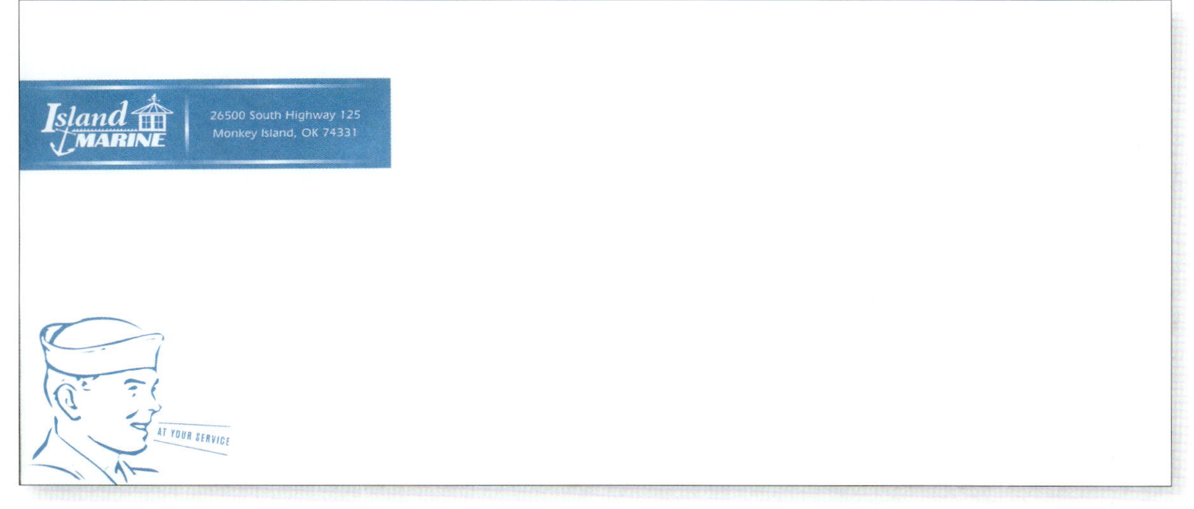

DESIGN FIRM
Entermotion Design Studio
Wichita, (KS) USA
PROJECT
Island Marine Stationery
DESIGNER
Lea Carmichael

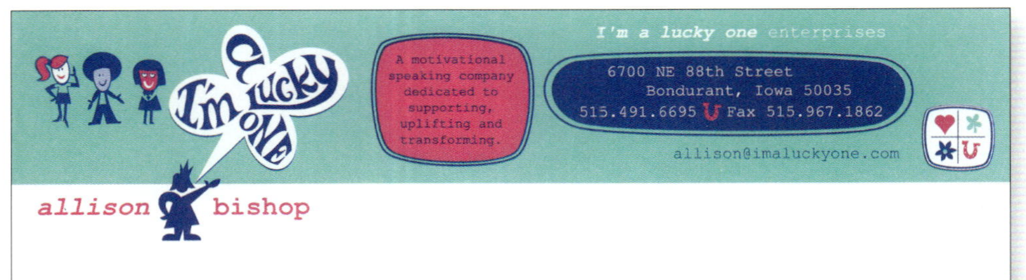

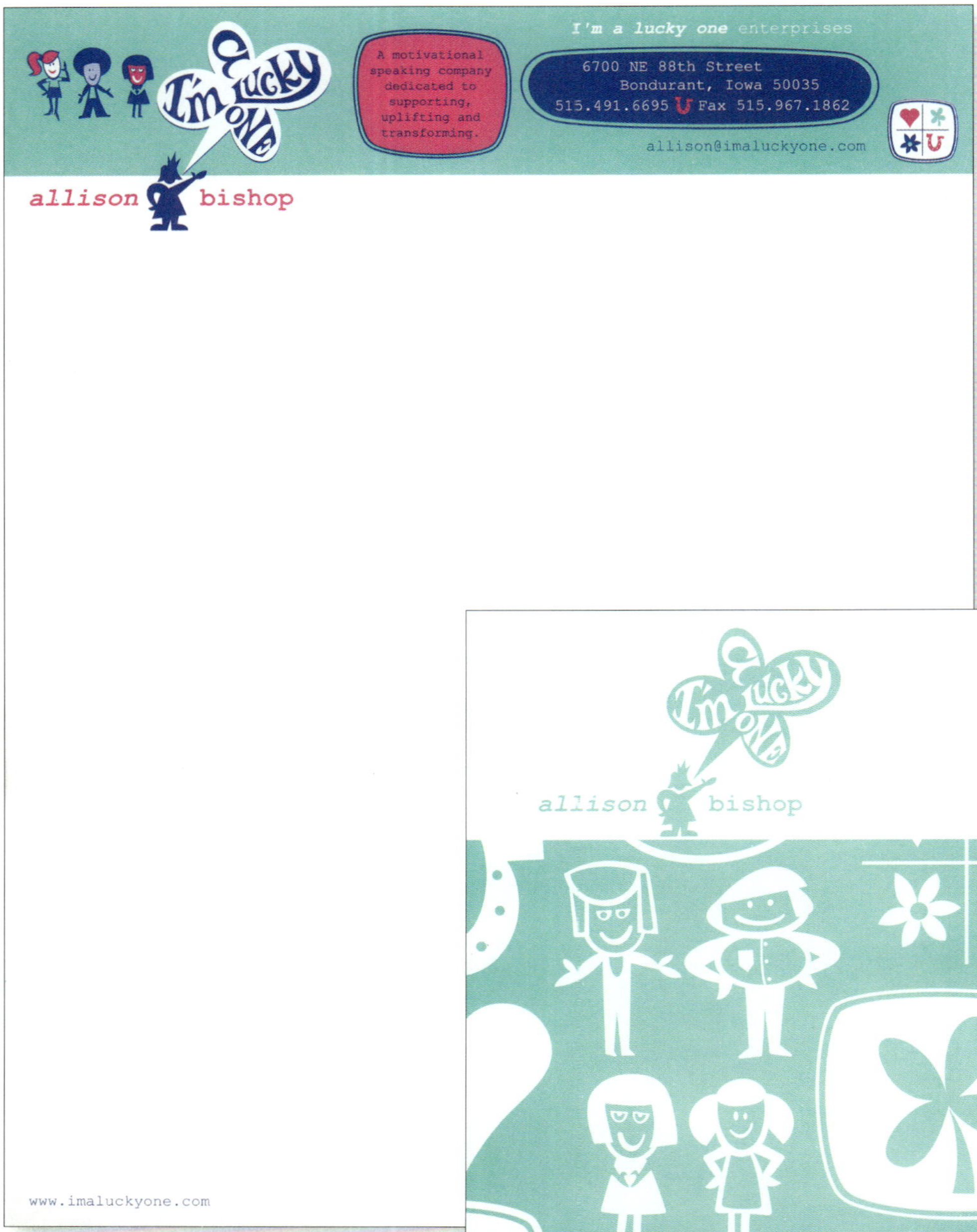

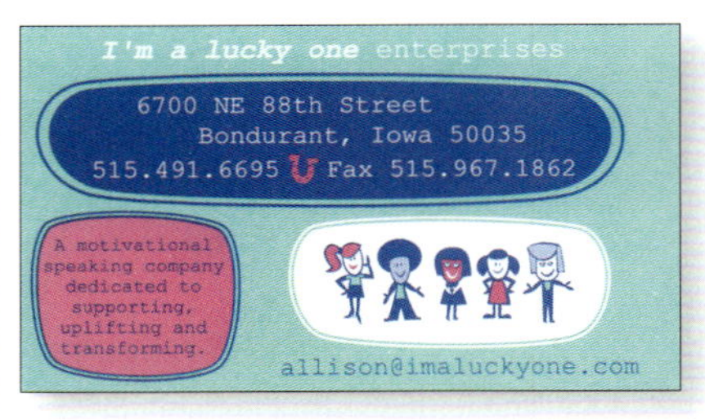

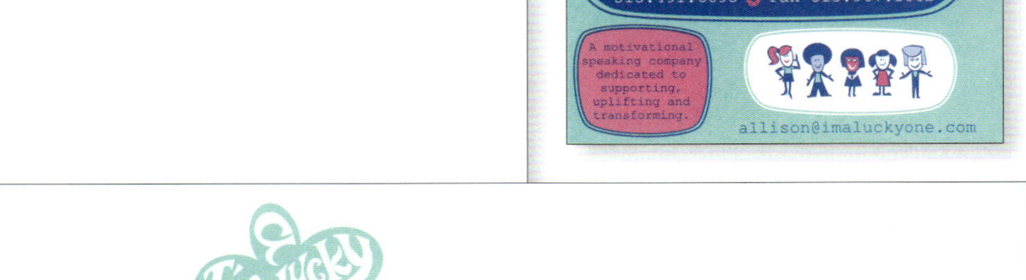

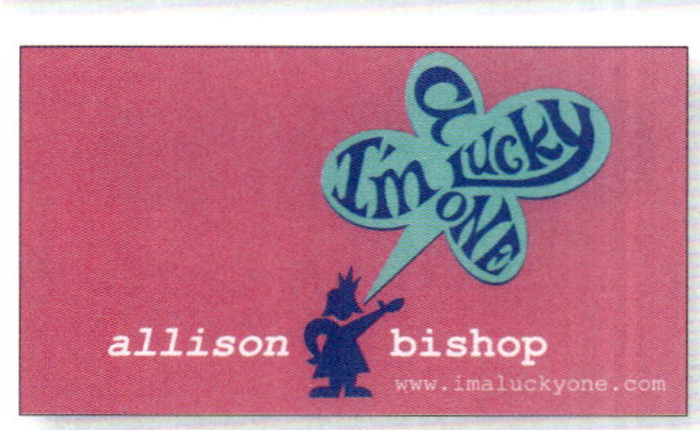

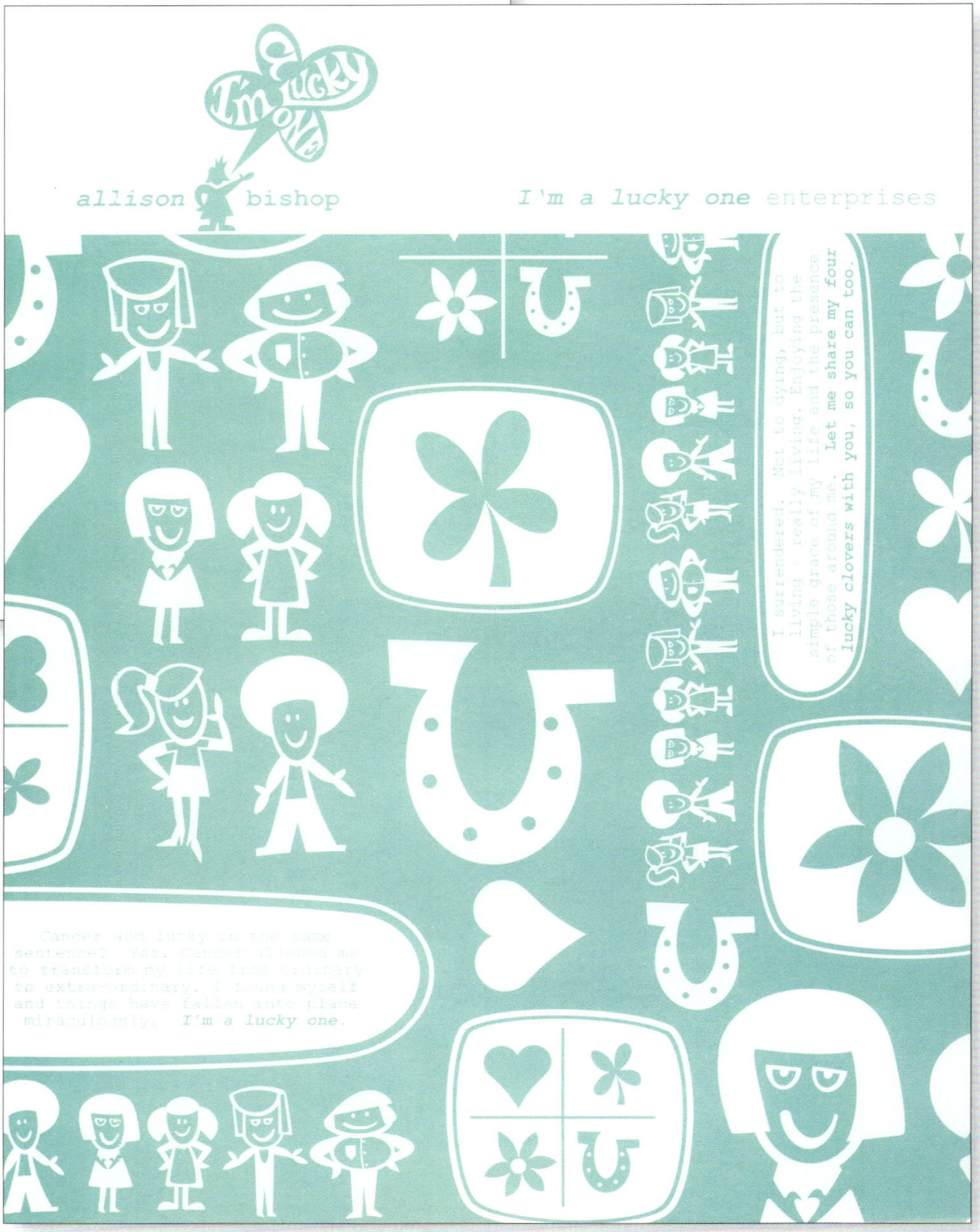

DESIGN FIRM
Sayles Graphic Design
Des Moines, (IA) USA
CLIENT
I'm A Lucky One
DESIGNER, ILLUSTRATOR
John Sayles

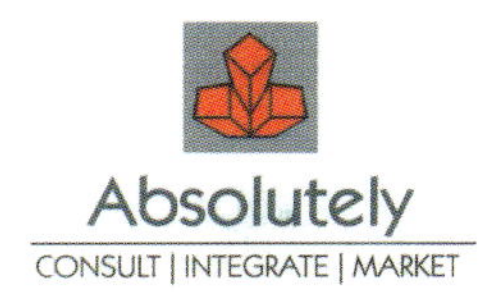

phone (415) 348-6397 ■ fax (415) 541-8589 ■ www.ablyinc.com
275 Fifth Street, San Francisco, CA 94103-4120 USA

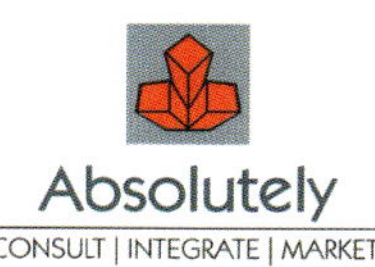

275 Fifth Street
San Francisco, CA
94103-4120 USA

www.ablyinc.com

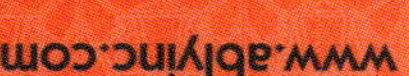

CONSULT | INTEGRATE | MARKET

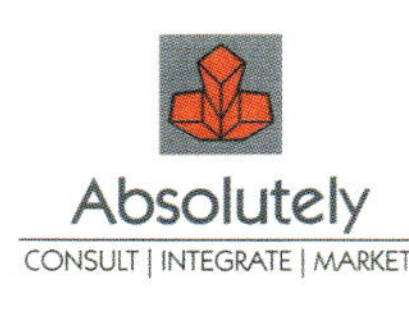

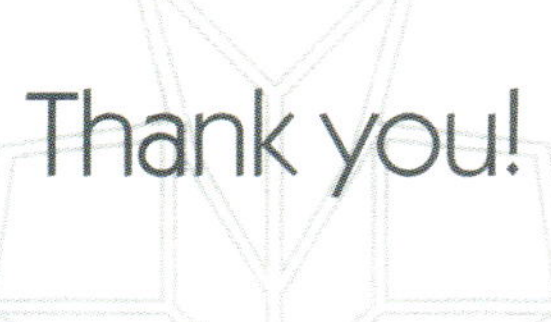

DESIGN FIRM
elf design
Belmont, (CA) USA
PROJECT
Absolutely stationery
ART DIRECTOR, DESIGNER
Erin Ferree

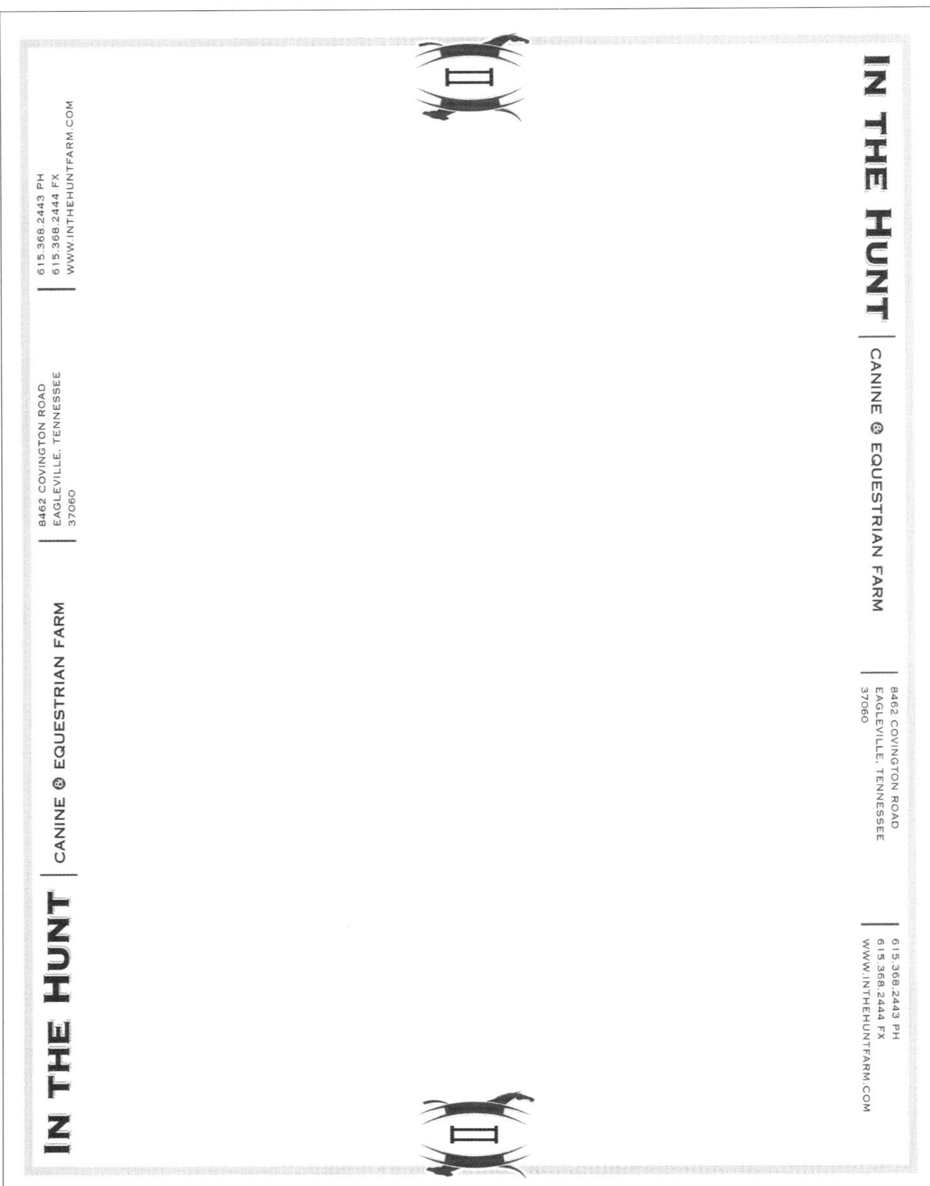

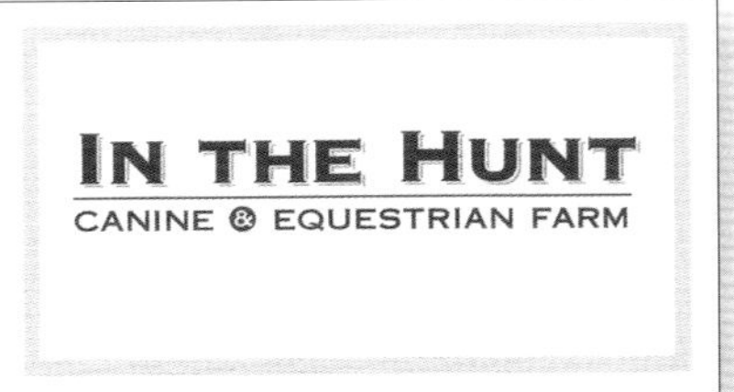

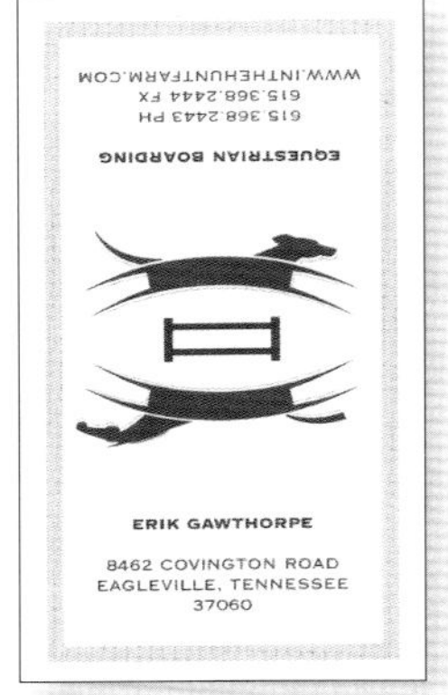

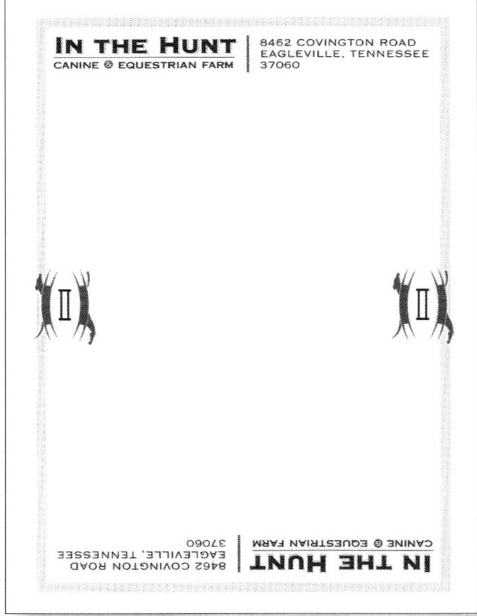

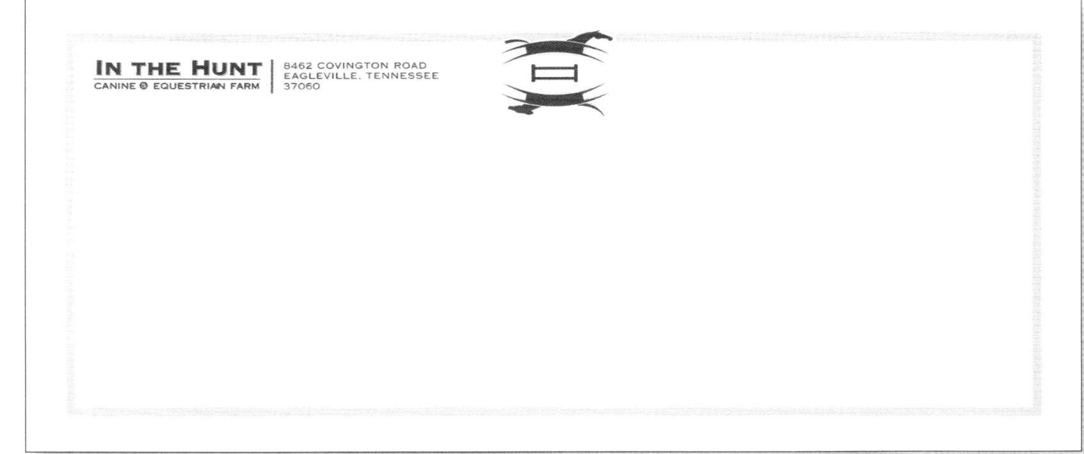

DESIGN FIRM
Hubbell Design Works
Orange, (CA) USA
PROJECT
In The Hunt
ART DIRECTOR, DESIGNER
Leighton Hubbell

BEYOND

20 Prospect Avenue, Suite 902 | Hackensack, NJ 07601 | Tel 201-996-4500 | Fax 201-996-4006

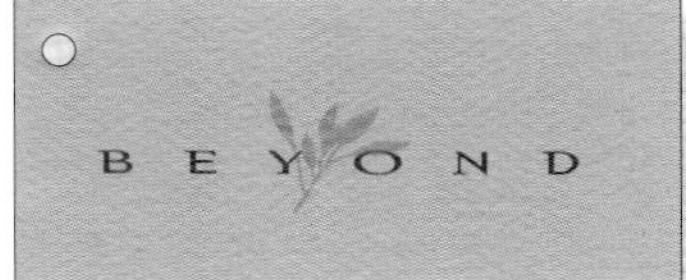

B E Y O N D

DESIGN FIRM
John Kneapler Design
New York, (NY) USA

PROJECT
Beyond Spa

DESIGNERS
John Kneapler,
Colleen Shea

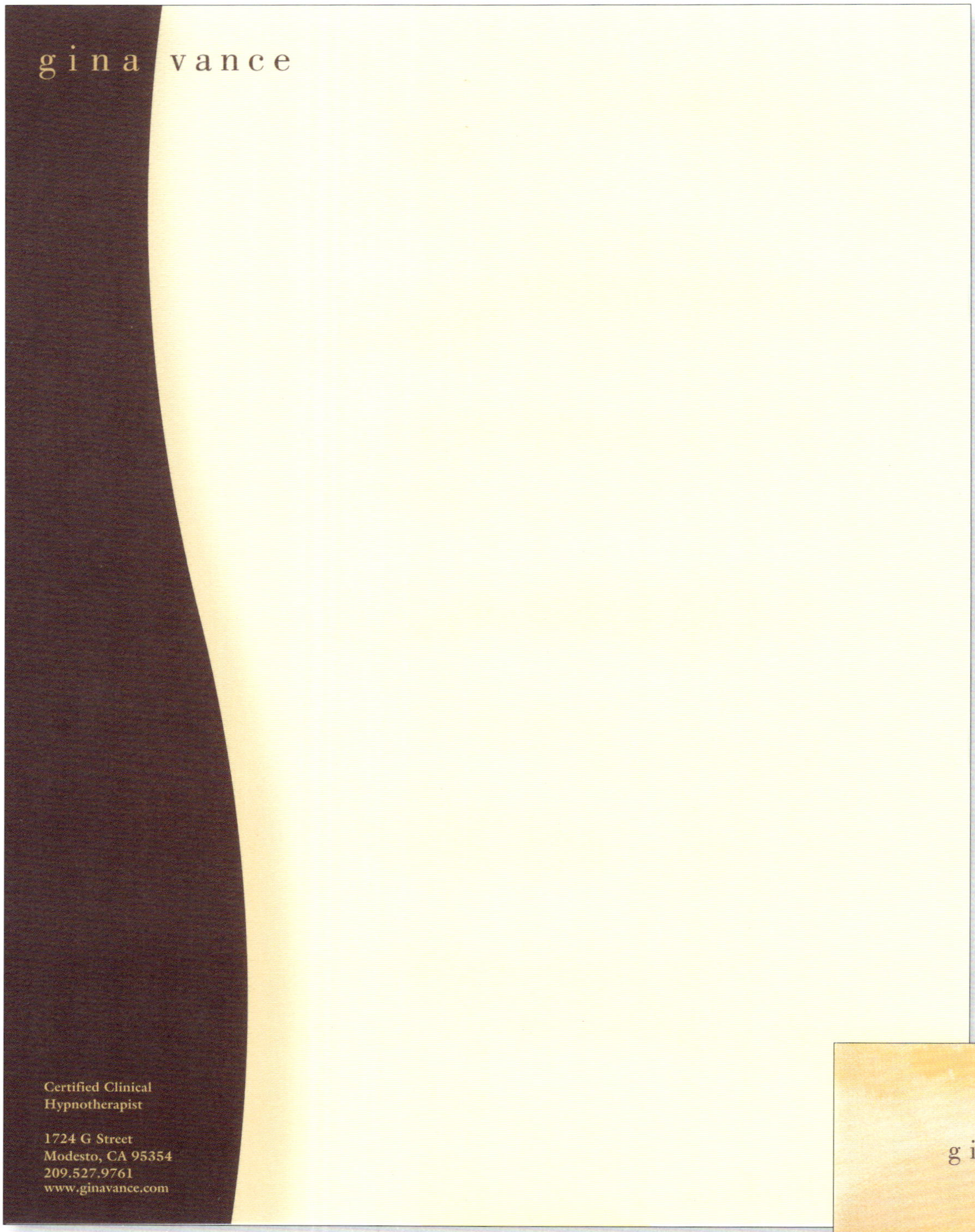

gina vance

Certified Clinical
Hypnotherapist

1724 G Street
Modesto, CA 95354
209.527.9761
www.ginavance.com

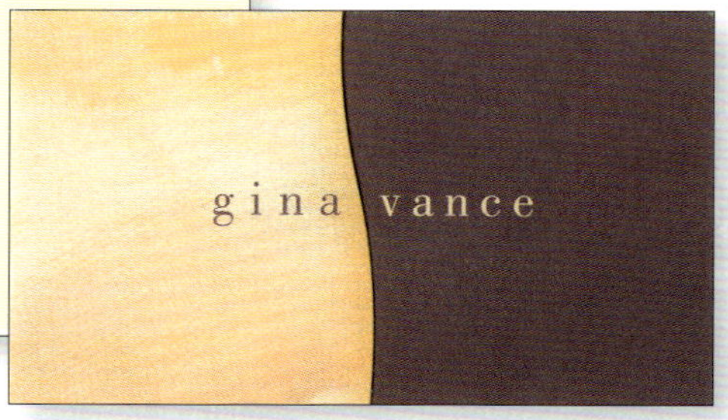

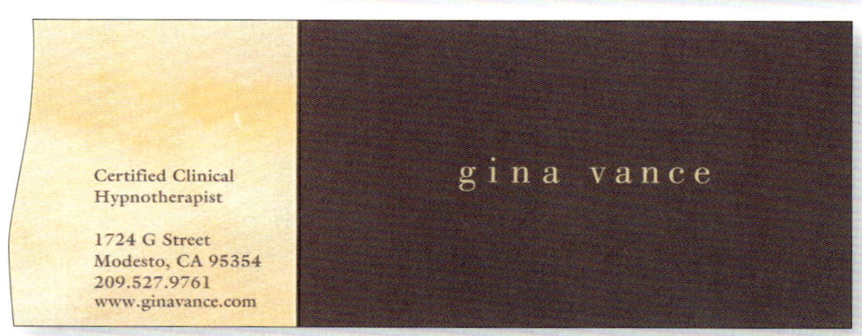

DESIGN FIRM
Never Boring Design Associates
Modesto, (CA) USA

PROJECT
Gina Vance

DESIGNERS
Julie Orona

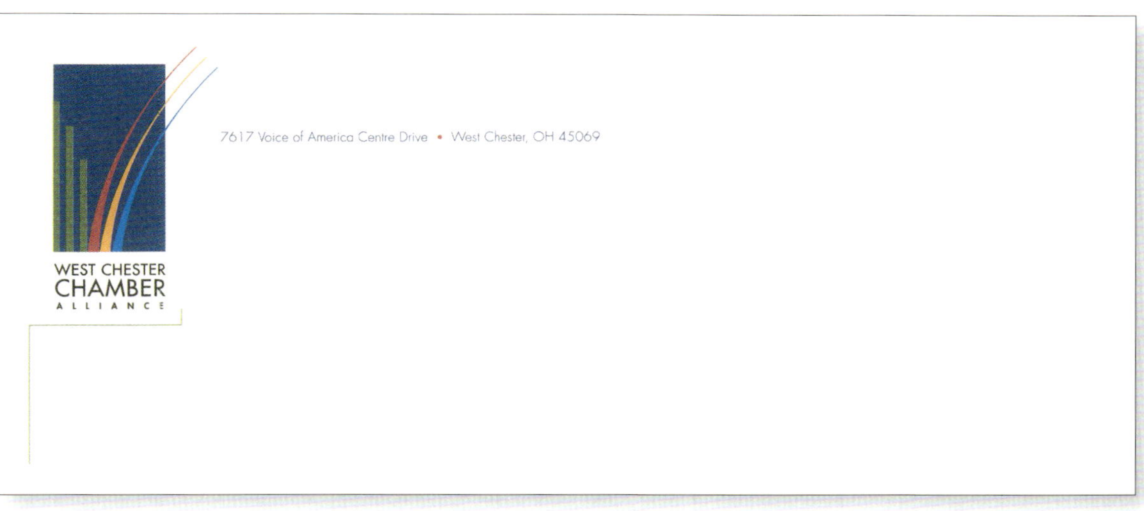

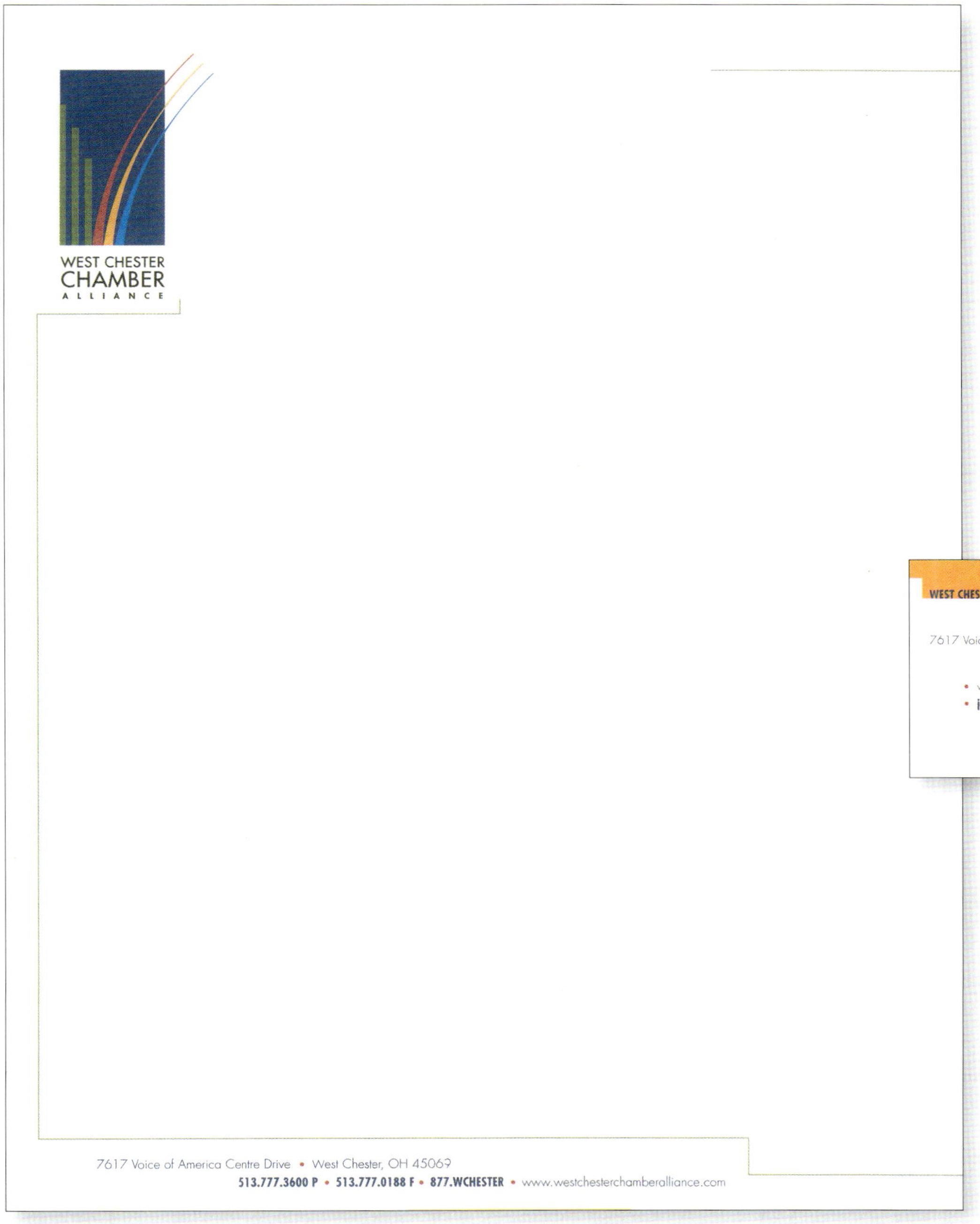

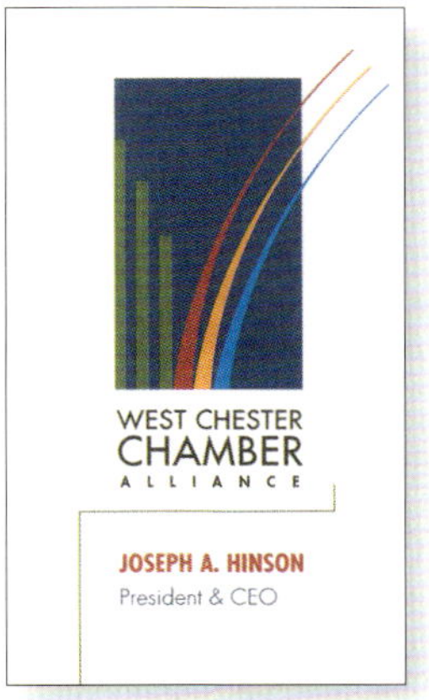

WEST CHESTER
CHAMBER
ALLIANCE

7617 Voice of America Centre Drive • West Chester, OH 45069
513.777.3600 P • 513.777.0188 F • 877.WCHESTER • www.westchesterchamberalliance.com

WEST CHESTER
CHAMBER
ALLIANCE

JOSEPH A. HINSON
President & CEO

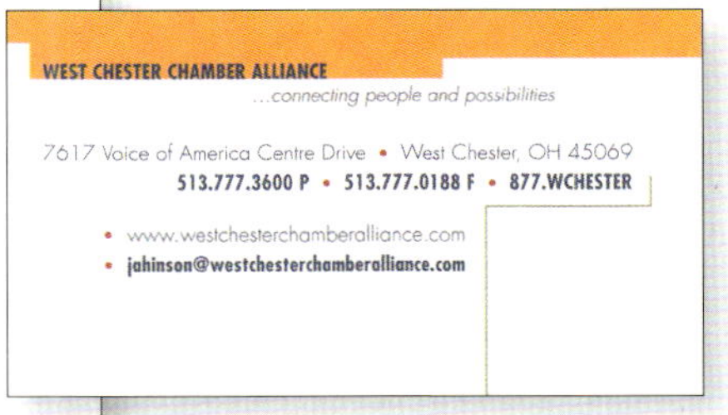

WEST CHESTER CHAMBER ALLIANCE
...connecting people and possibilities

7617 Voice of America Centre Drive • West Chester, OH 45069
513.777.3600 P • 513.777.0188 F • 877.WCHESTER

• www.westchesterchamberalliance.com
• jahinson@westchesterchamberalliance.com

DESIGN FIRM
Five Visual Communication & Design
West Chester, (OH) USA

PROJECT
West Chester Chamber Alliance

DESIGNER
Rondi Tschopp

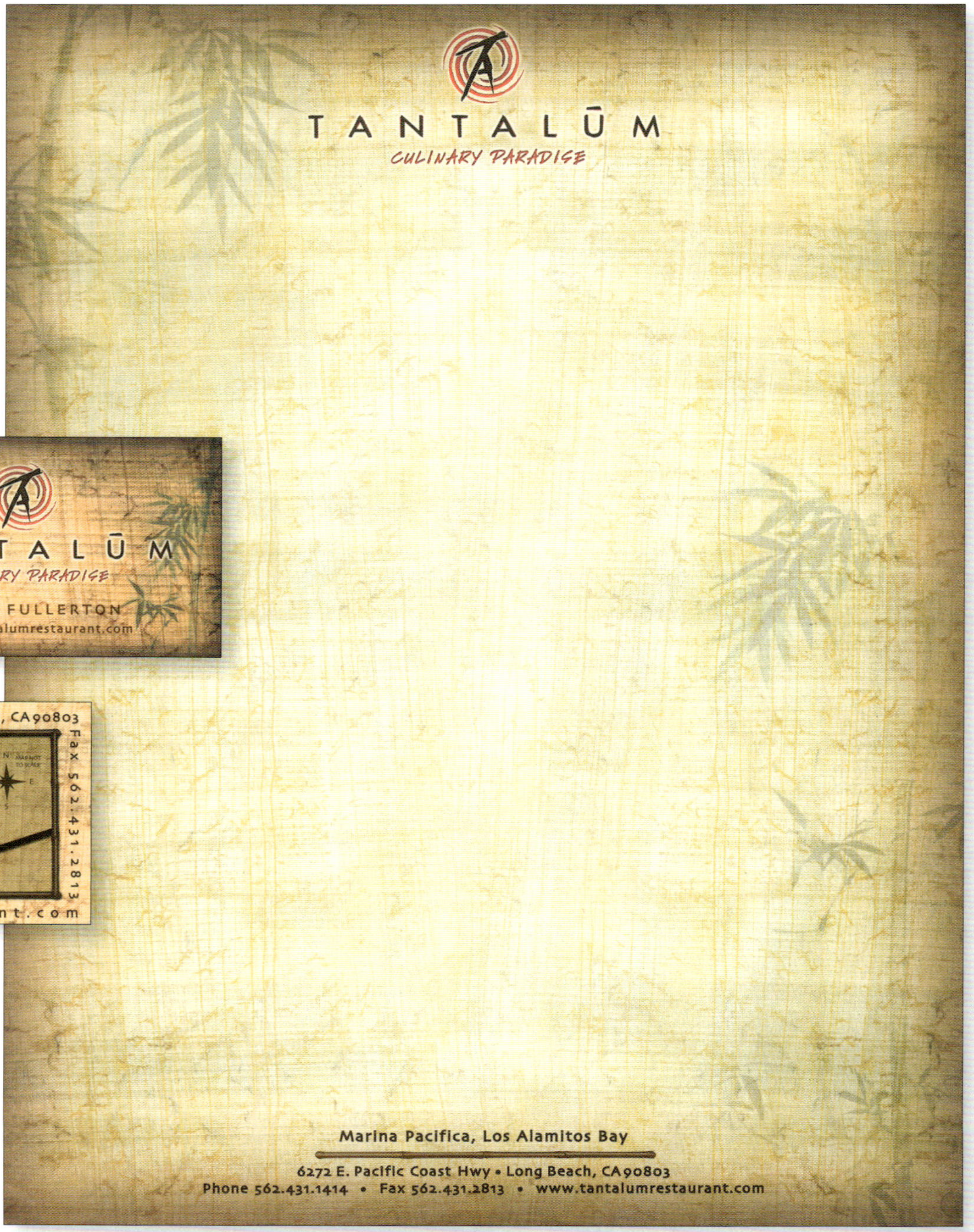

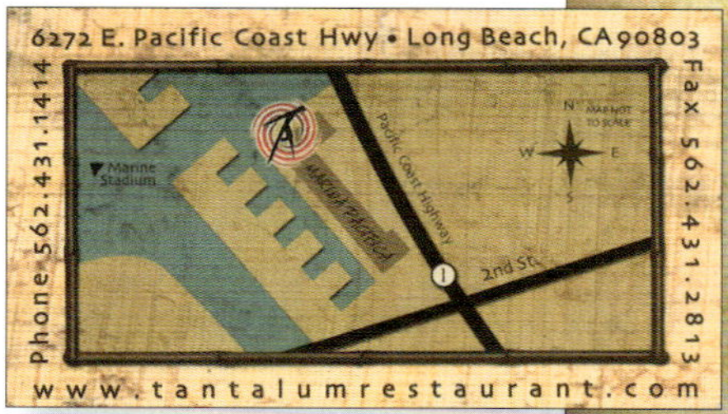

TANTALŪM
CULINARY PARADISE

Marina Pacifica, Los Alamitos Bay

6272 E. Pacific Coast Hwy • Long Beach, CA 90803
Phone 562.431.1414 • Fax 562.431.2813 • www.tantalumrestaurant.com

TANTALŪM
CULINARY PARADISE
CURTIS FULLERTON
curtis@tantalumrestaurant.com

6272 E. Pacific Coast Hwy • Long Beach, CA 90803
Phone 562.431.1414
Fax 562.431.2813
2nd St.
Pacific Coast Highway
www.tantalumrestaurant.com

DESIGN FIRM
On The Edge Design
Newport Beach, (CA) USA
PROJECT
Tantalum Restaurant
DESIGNER
Gina Mims

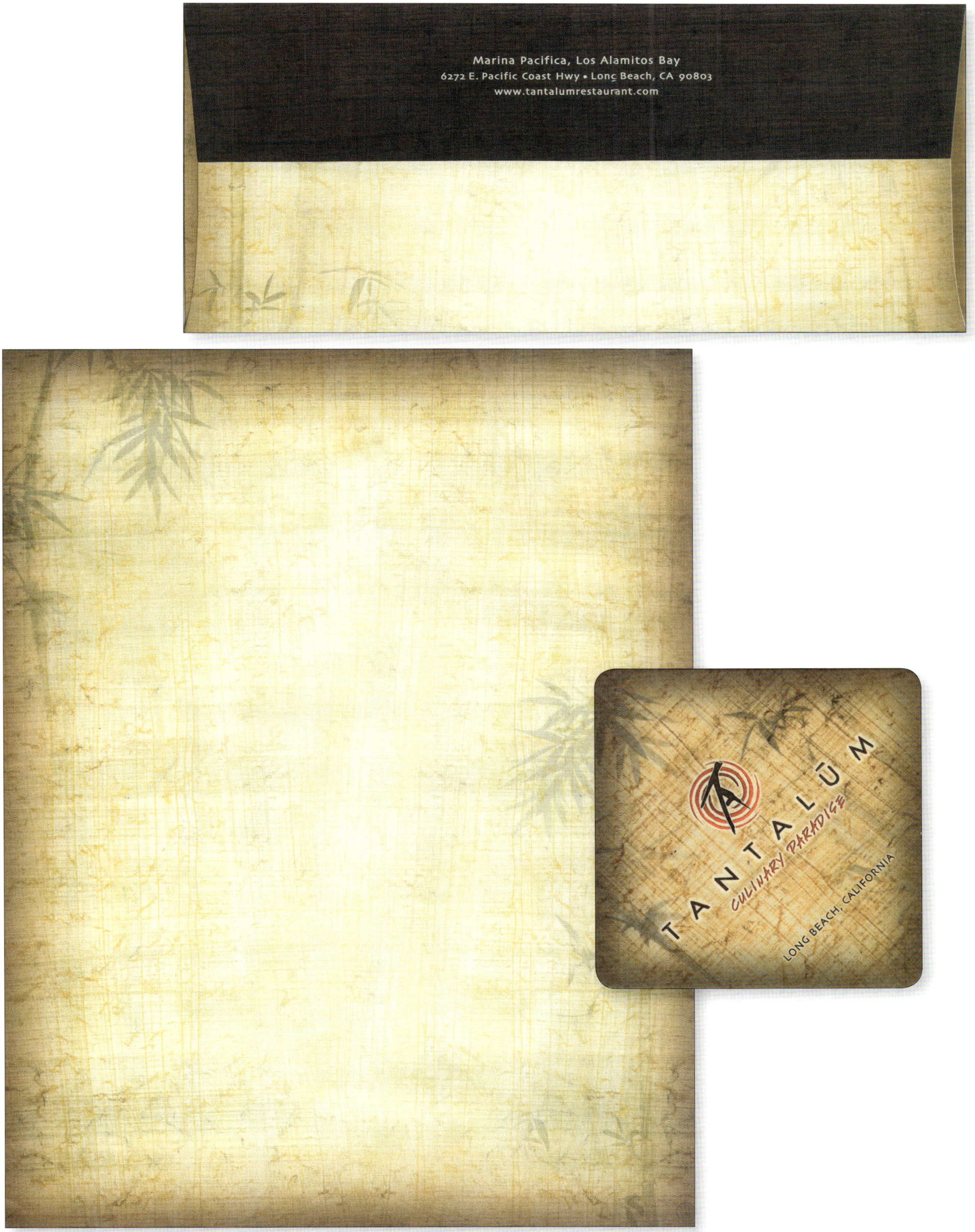

TANTALŪM
CULINARY PARADISE
LONG BEACH, CALIFORNIA

The COMMENCEMENT

THECOMMENCEMENT.COM T (800) 681.VIEW
5219 N SHIRLEY STREET • RUSTON WA 98407

The COMMENCEMENT

The COMMENCEMENT

The COMMENCEMENT

The COMMENCEMENT

THECOMMENCEMENT.COM T (800) 681.VIEW
5219 N SHIRLEY STREET • RUSTON WA 98407

DESIGN FIRM
BCRA
Tacoma, (WA) USA
PROJECT
The Commencement Stationery
DESIGNERS
Kristine Nims,
Lance Kagey

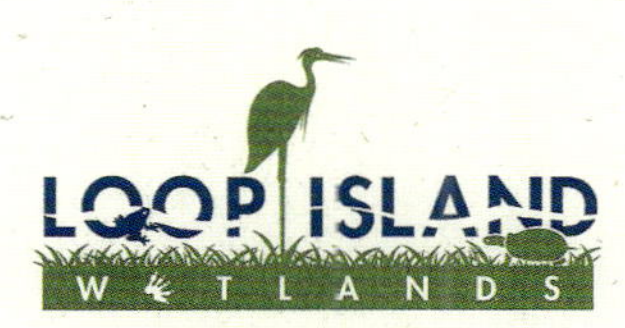

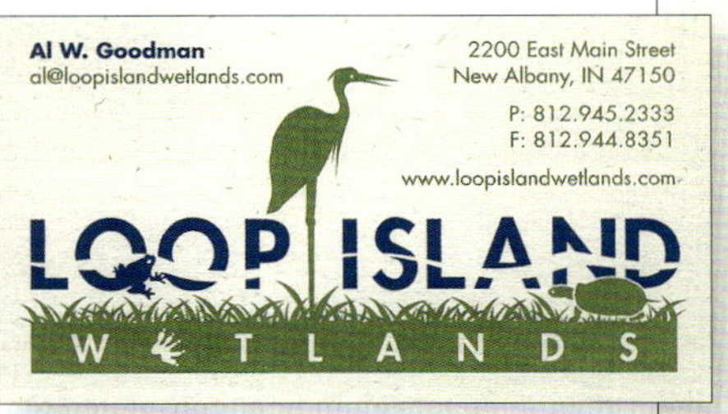

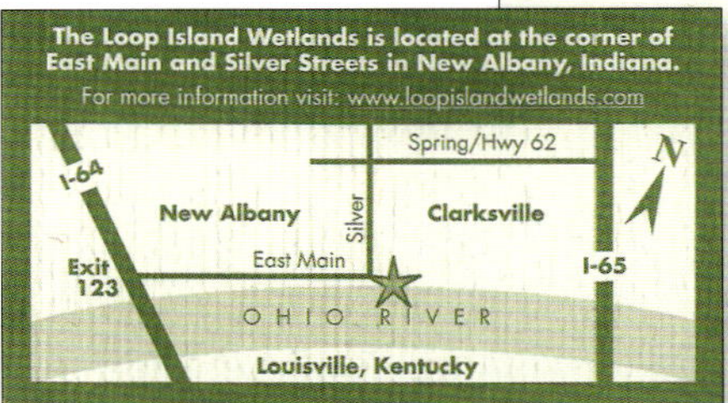

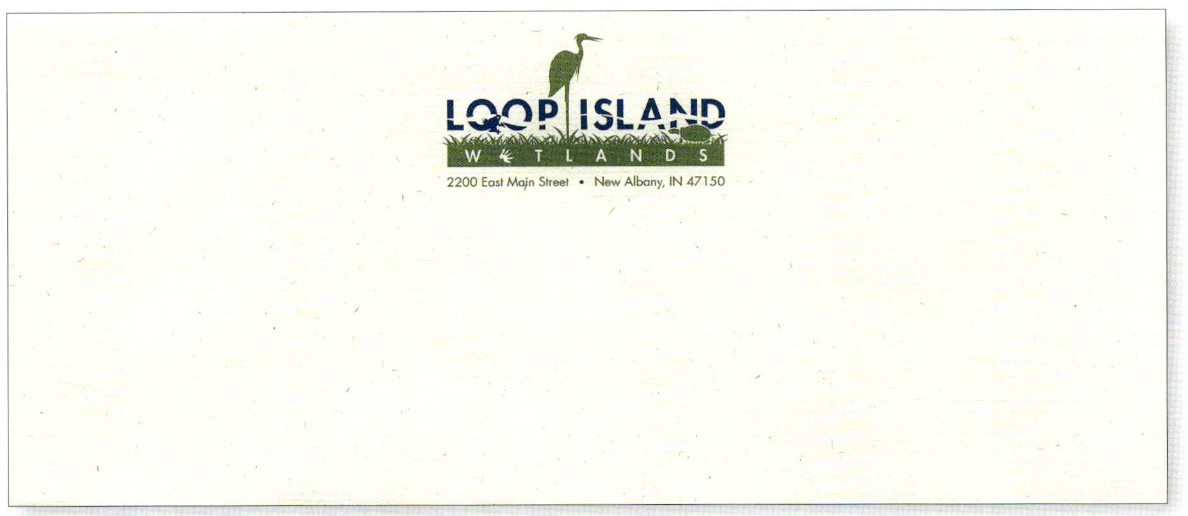

DESIGN FIRM
Mind's Eye Creative
New Albany, (IN) USA
CLIENT
Loop Island Wetlands
DESIGNER
Stephen Brown

DESIGN FIRM
Sommese Design
Port Matilda, (PA) USA
PROJECT
Savannah Hill
ART DIRECTORS
Kristin Sommese,
Lanny Sommese
DESIGNERS
Kristin Sommese,
Ryan Russell
ILLUSTRATOR
Lanny Sommese

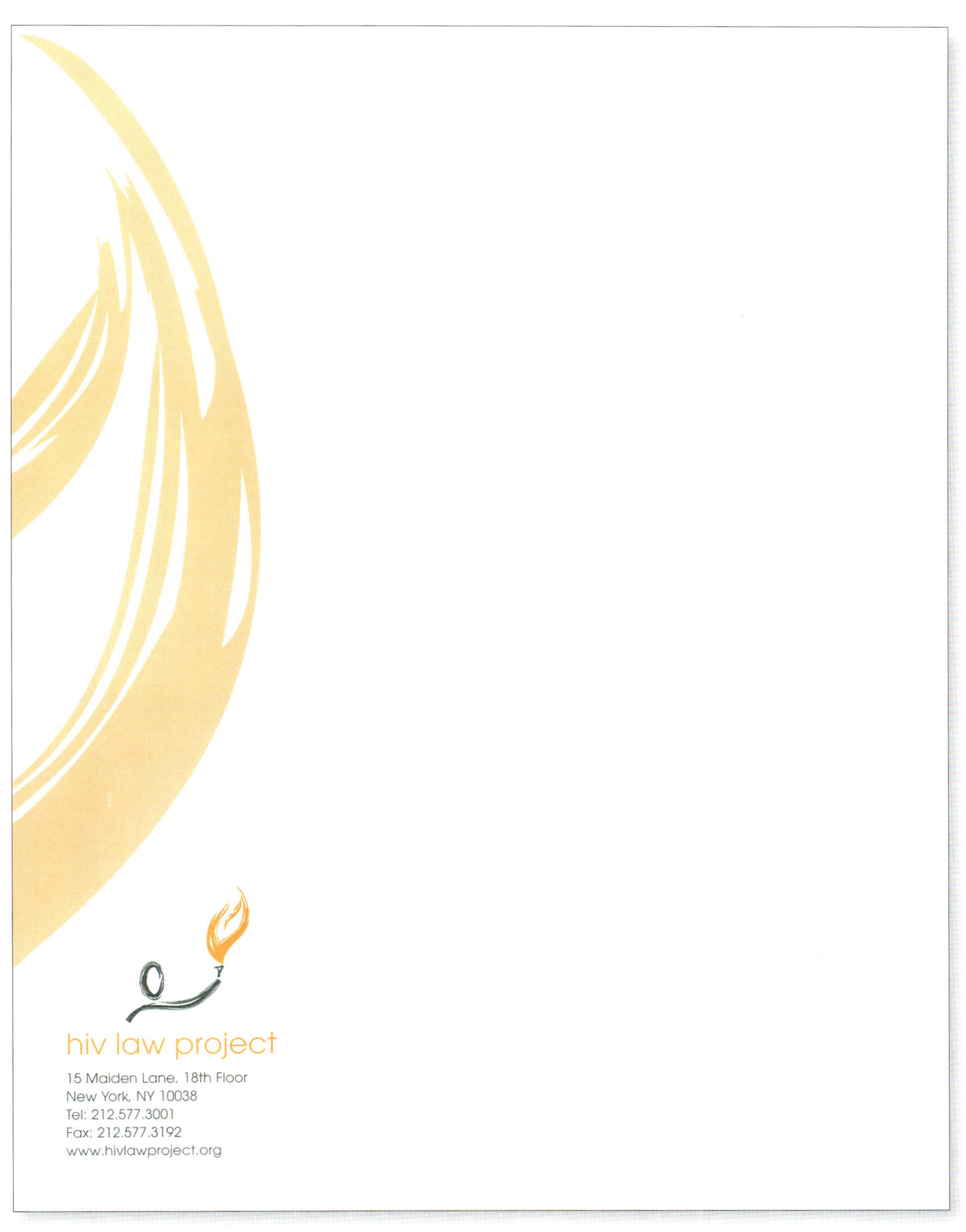

DESIGN FIRM
Chip Tolaney
New York, (NY) USA
PROJECT
hiv law project
ART DIRECTOR, DESIGNER
Chip Tolaney

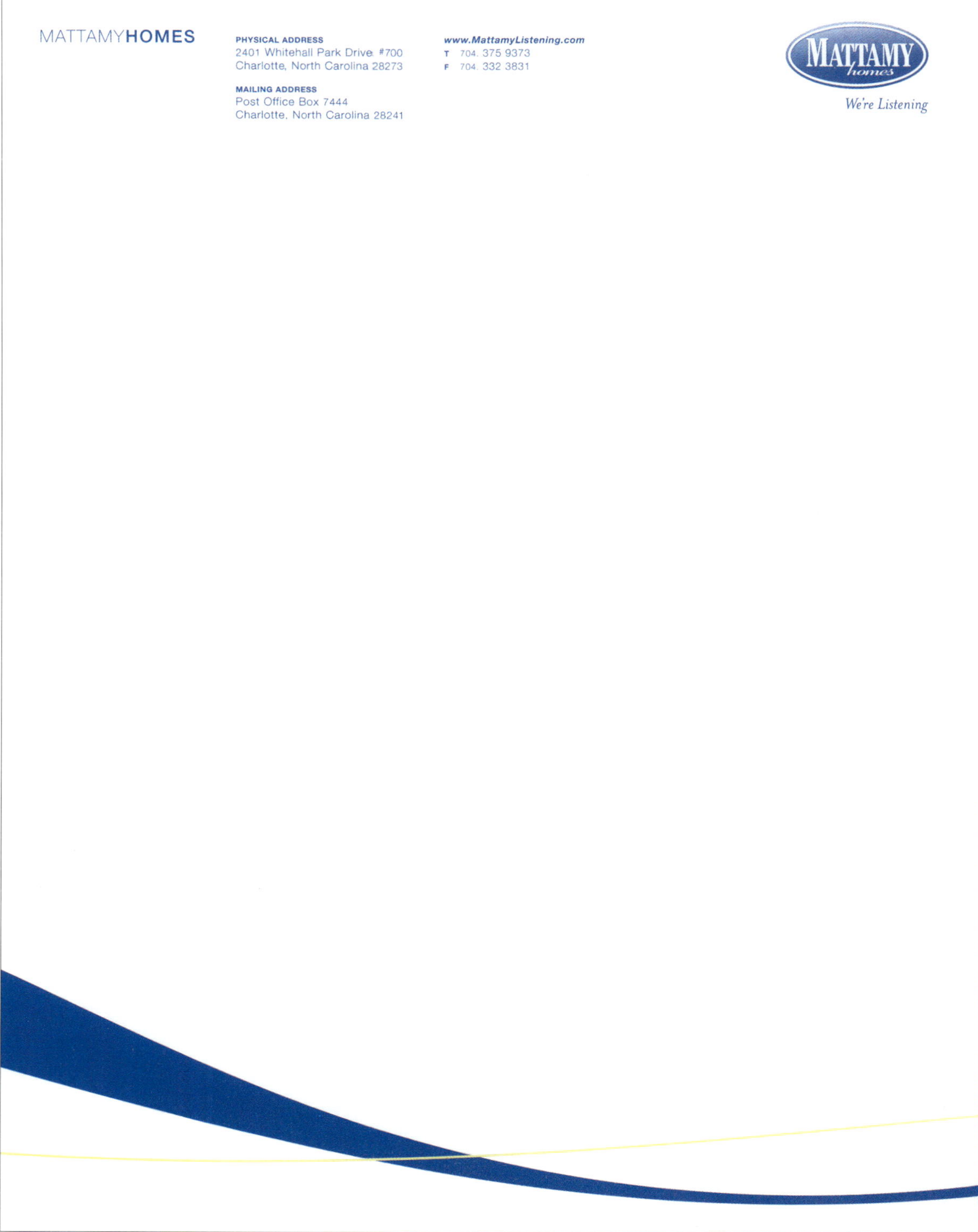

DESIGN FIRM
A3 Design
Charlotte, (NC) USA
CLIENT
Mattamy Homes
ART DIRECTOR
Amanda Altman
DESIGNER
Alan Altman

DESIGN FIRM
GOLD & Associates, Inc.
Ponte Vedra Beach, (FL) USA
PROJECT
Ponte Vedra Wine Fest
CREATIVE DIRECTOR
Keith Gold
DESIGNER
Jan Hanak

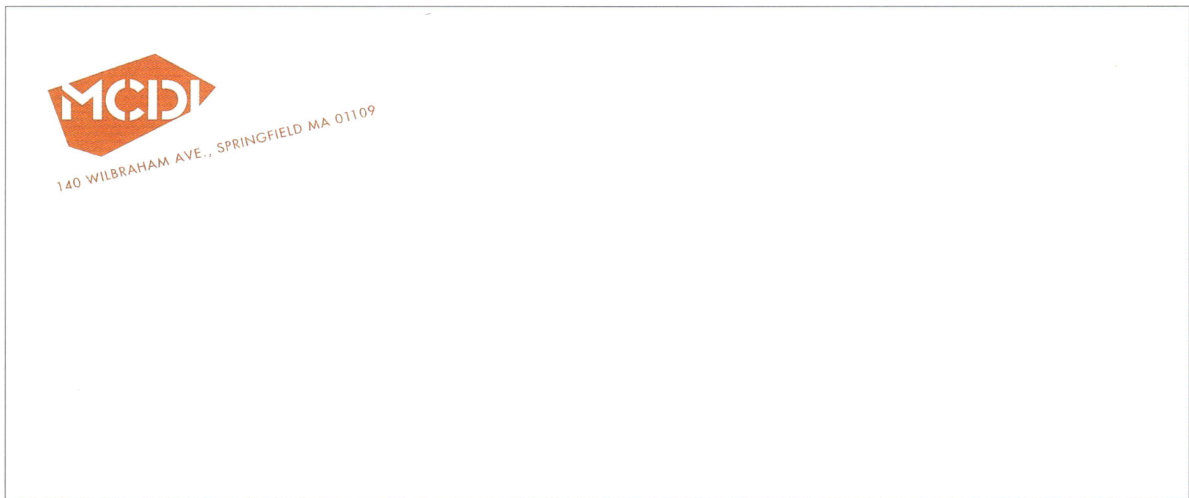

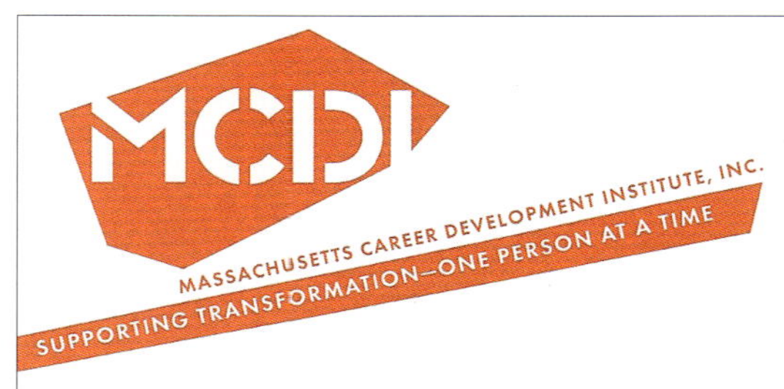

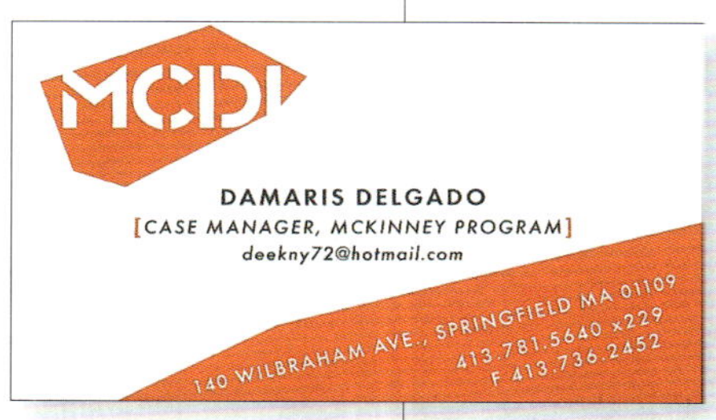

MASSACHUSETTS CAREER DEVELOPMENT INSTITUTE, INC.

SUPPORTING TRANSFORMATION
ONE PERSON AT A TIME

140 WILBRAHAM AVE.
SPRINGFIELD MA 01109
413.781.5640 F 413.736.2452
(TTD) 413.746.5227

DESIGN FIRM
TSM Design
Springfield, (MA) USA
PROJECT
MCDI
DESIGNER
Marisa Filippone

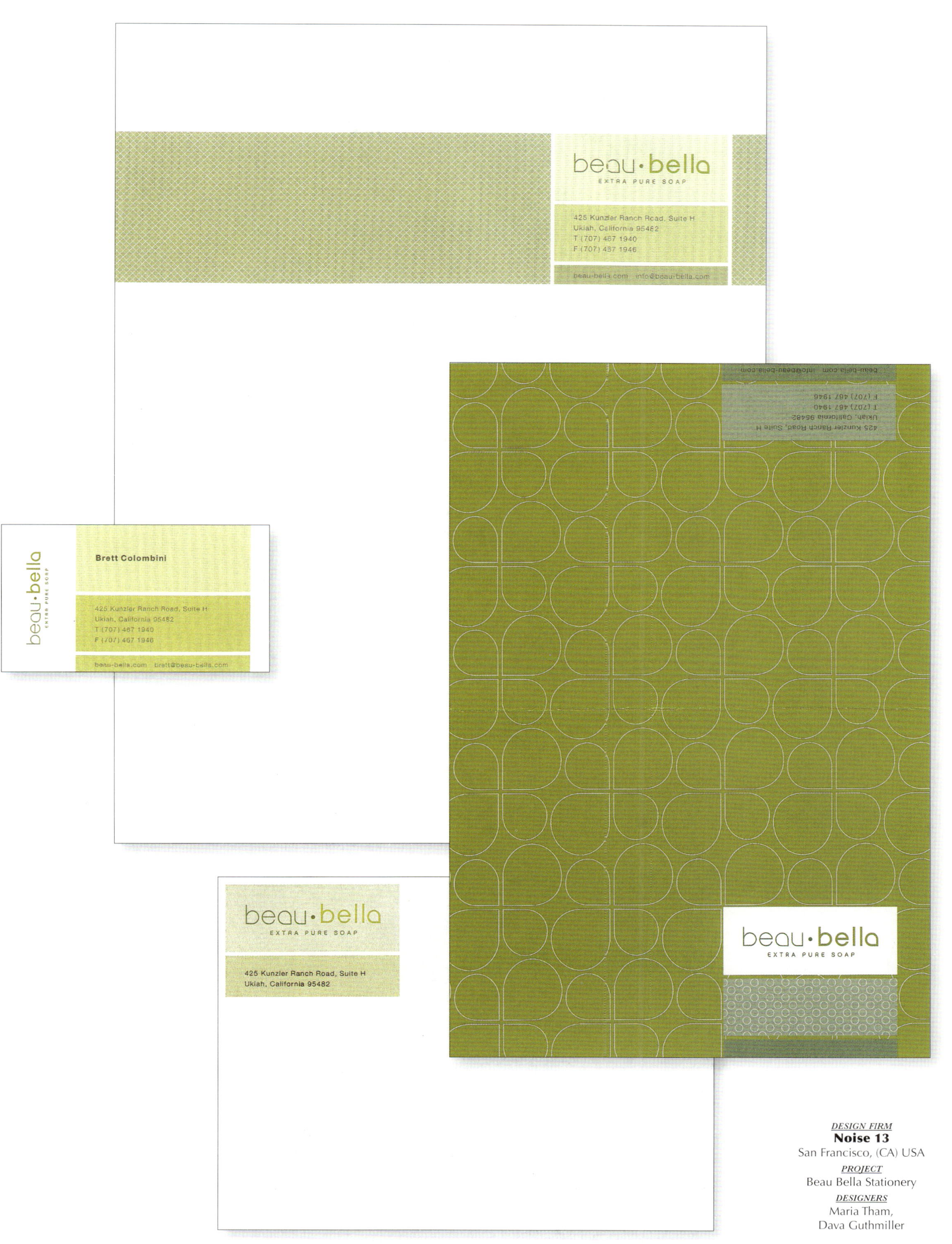

DESIGN FIRM
Noise 13
San Francisco, (CA) USA
PROJECT
Beau Bella Stationery
DESIGNERS
Maria Tham,
Dava Guthmiller

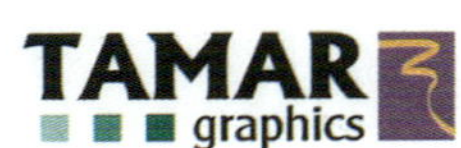

512.291.9200 austin // 978.290.3030 boston // 866.291.9643 fax // 738 main street, #222 // waltham, ma 02451 // www.tamargraphics.com // admin@tamargraphics.com

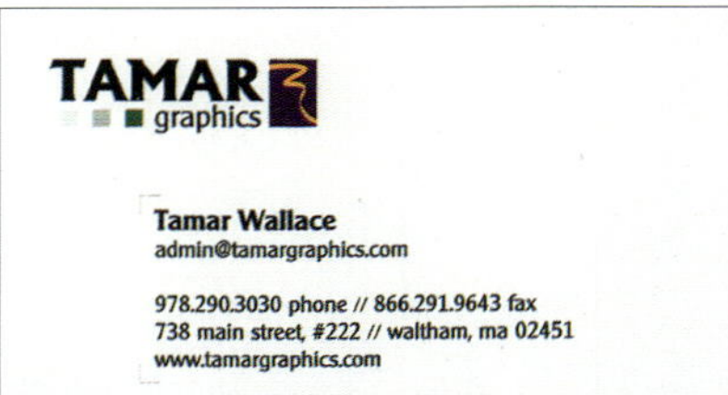

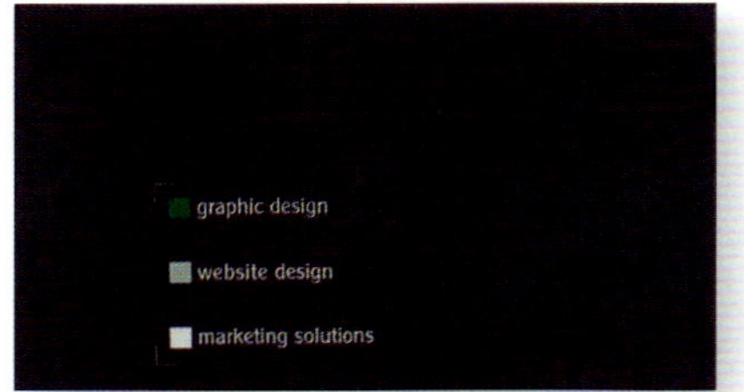

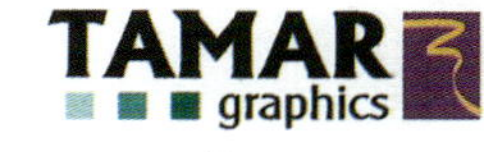

738 main street, #222
waltham, ma 02451
www.tamargraphics.com

DESIGN FIRM
TAMAR Graphics
Waltham, (MA) USA

CLIENT
TAMAR Graphics

DESIGNER
Tamar Wallace

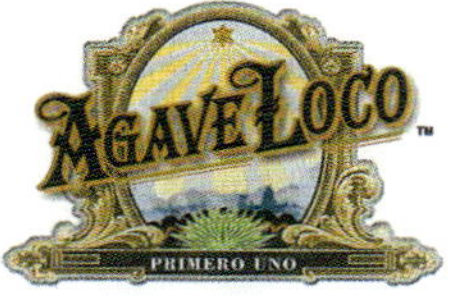

AGAVE LOCO LLC

400 N. MAY ST. • SUITE #201 • CHICAGO, IL 60622 • PHONE: 312.226.7445 • WWW.AGAVELOCO.COM

DESIGN FIRM
Di Donato Associates
Chicago, (IL) USA
CLIENT
Agave Loco LLC
CREATIVE DIRECTOR
Peter Di Donato
DESIGNER
Doug Miller

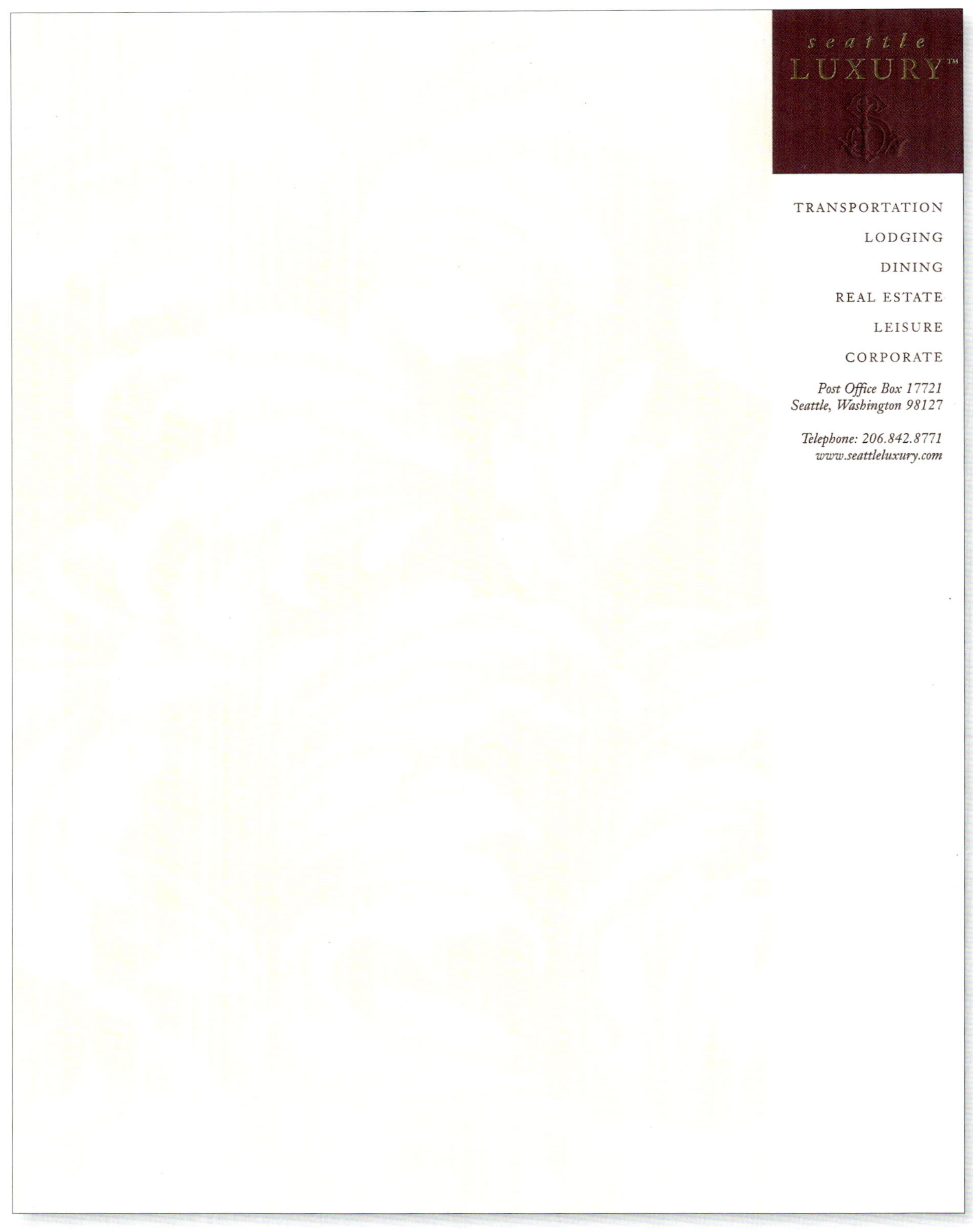

DESIGN FIRM
Sungrafx, Inc.
Silverdale, (WA) USA
CLIENT
Seattle Luxury
CREATIVE DIRECTOR
Vicky Koningisor
DESIGNER
Laura Zander

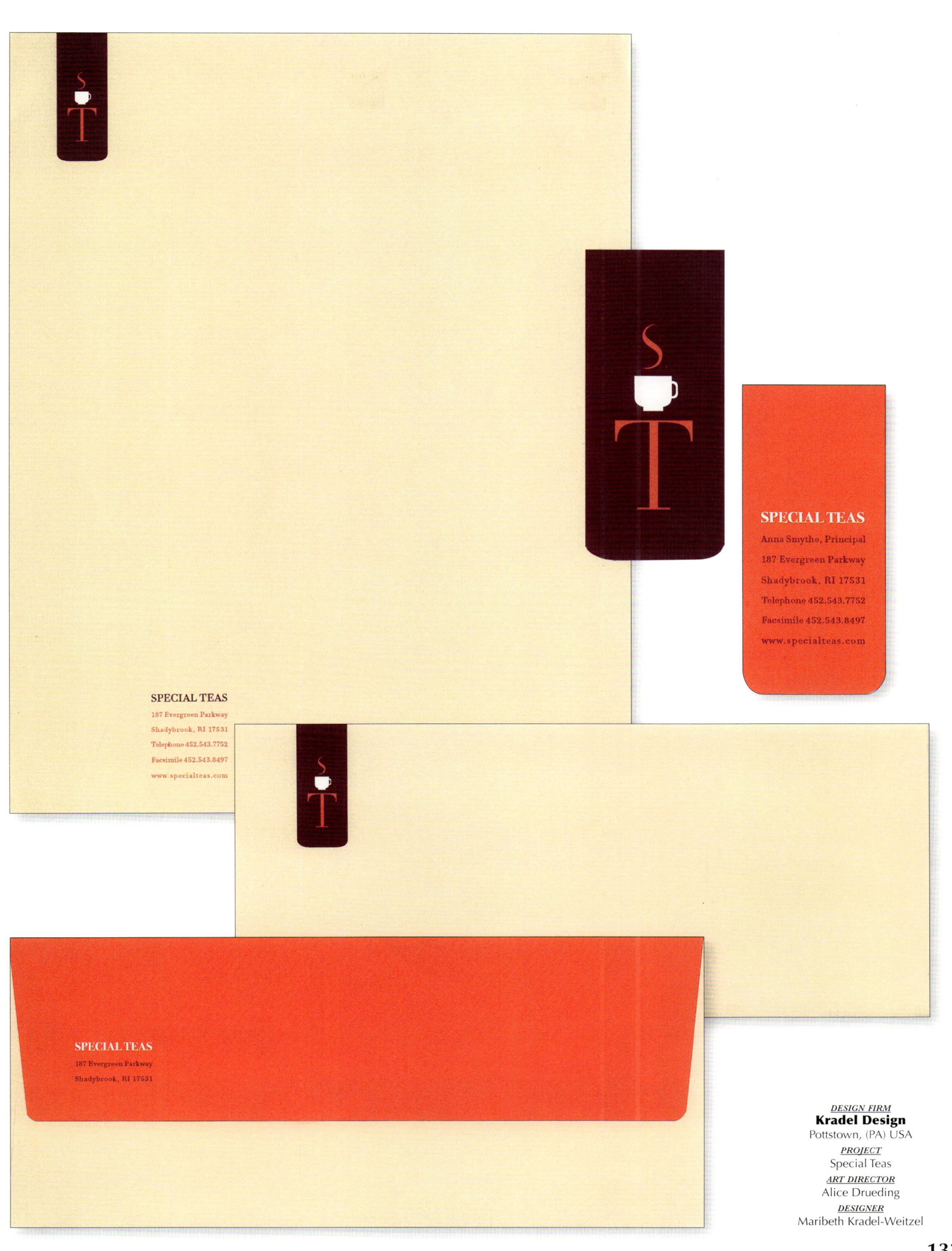

DESIGN FIRM
Kradel Design
Pottstown, (PA) USA
PROJECT
Special Teas
ART DIRECTOR
Alice Drueding
DESIGNER
Maribeth Kradel-Weitzel

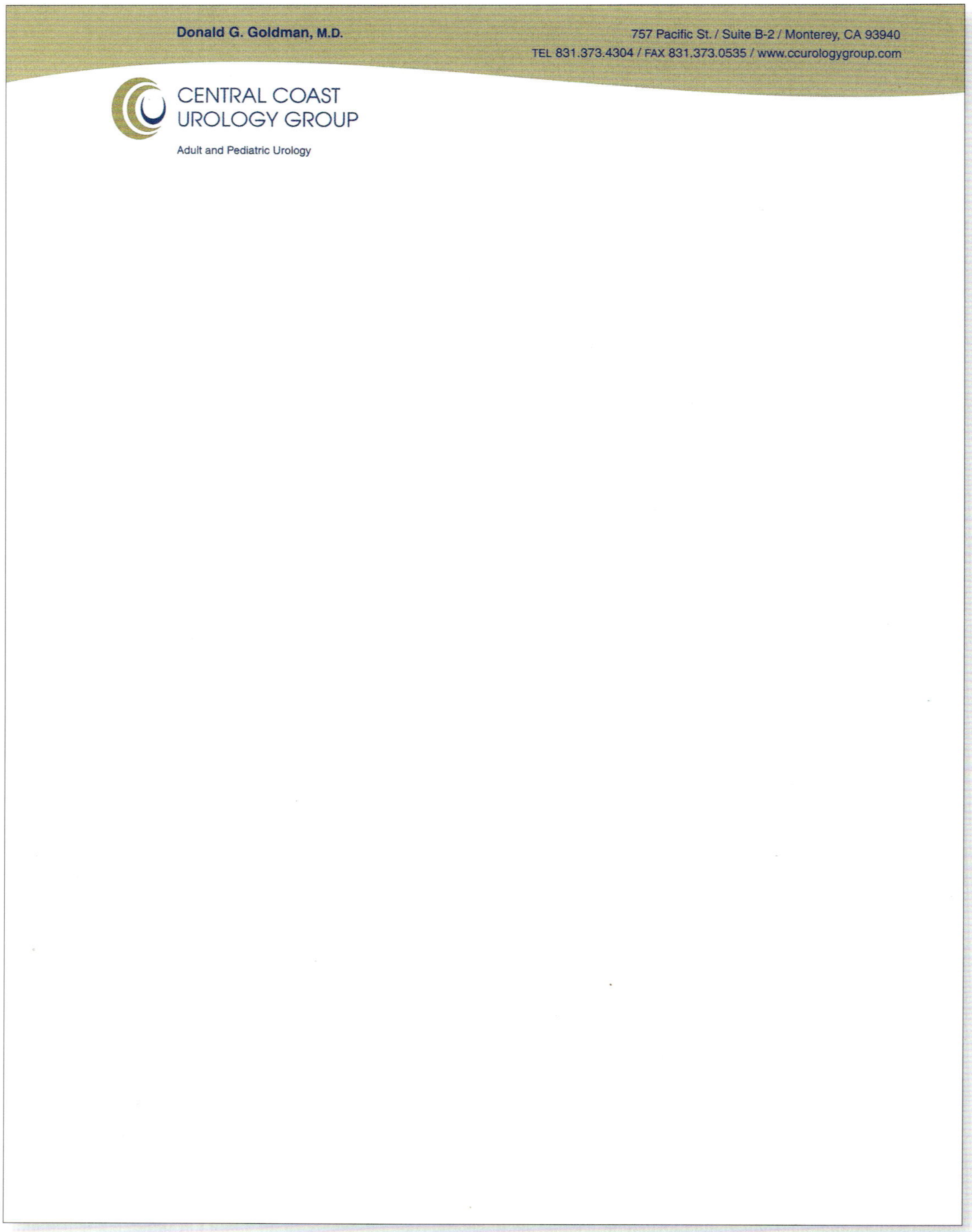

Donald G. Goldman, M.D.

757 Pacific St. / Suite B-2 / Monterey, CA 93940
TEL 831.373.4304 / FAX 831.373.0535 / www.ccurologygroup.com

CENTRAL COAST
UROLOGY GROUP

Adult and Pediatric Urology

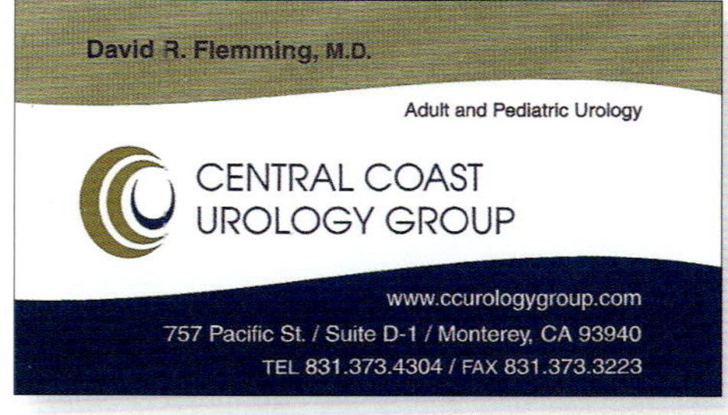

DESIGN FIRM
The Wecker Group
Monterey, (CA) USA
PROJECT
Central Coast Urology Group
DESIGNER
Robert Wecker

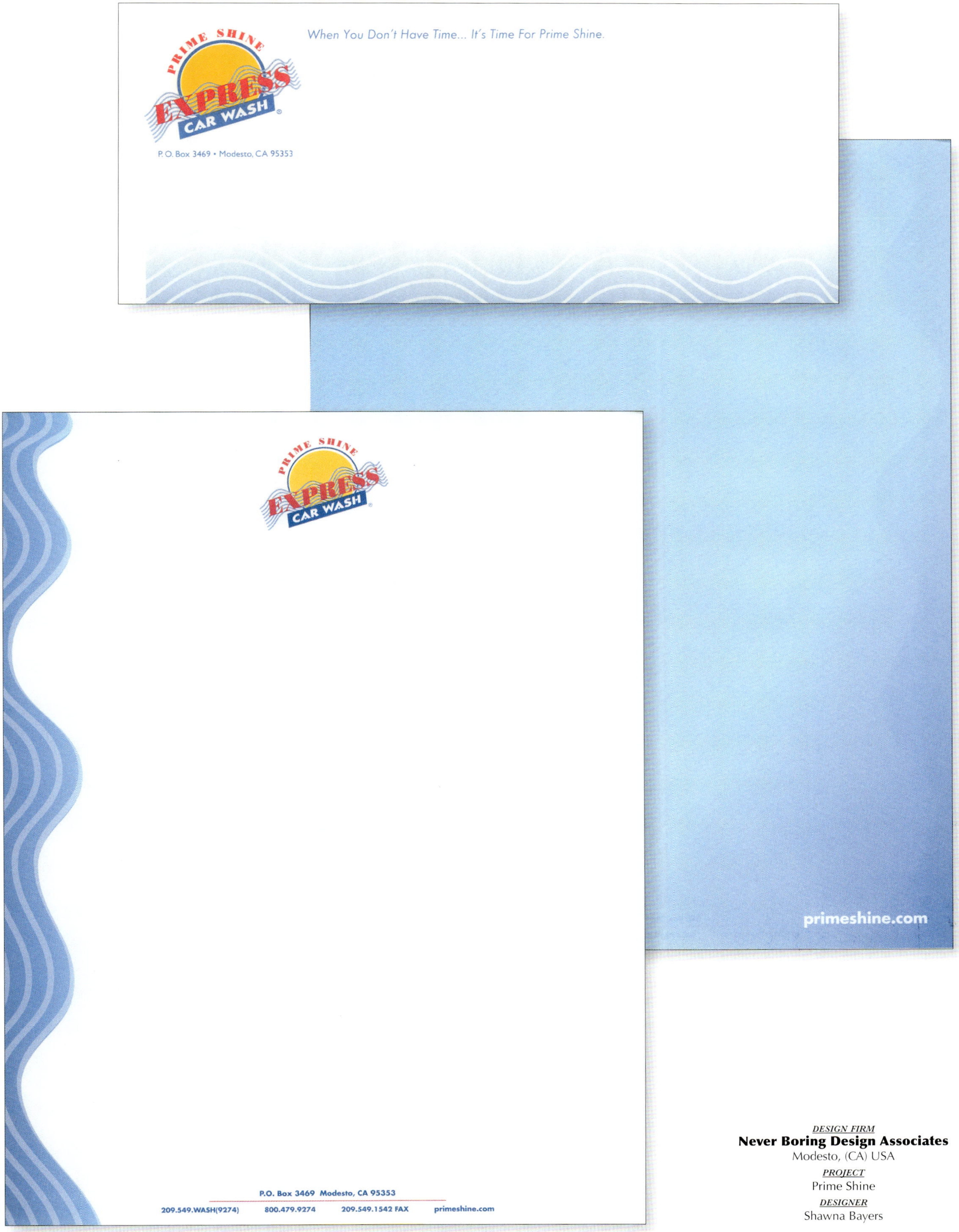

PRIME SHINE
EXPRESS
CAR WASH

P.O. Box 3469 Modesto, CA 95353
209.549.WASH(9274) 800.479.9274 209.549.1542 FAX primeshine.com

primeshine.com

DESIGN FIRM
Never Boring Design Associates
Modesto, (CA) USA

PROJECT
Prime Shine

DESIGNER
Shawna Bayers

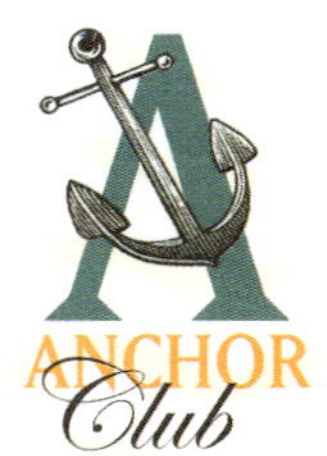

THE ANCHOR CLUB AT GRAND HARBOR

325 C.R. 380, BOX L003, COUNCE, TN 38326
ph: 731.689.2500 www.theanchorclub.com

DESIGN FIRM
Gouthier Design: a brand collective
Fort Lauderdale, (FL) USA

CLIENT
Tull Brothers, Inc.

CREATIVE DIRECTOR
Jonathan Gouthier

DESIGNER
Marina Larenz

PRINTER
APPI

DESIGN FIRM
Klündt Hosmer
Spokane, (WA) USA
PROJECT
Lloyd Charles Estates
ART DIRECTOR
Darin Klündt
DESIGNERS
Lorri Johnston,
Judy Heggem-Davis

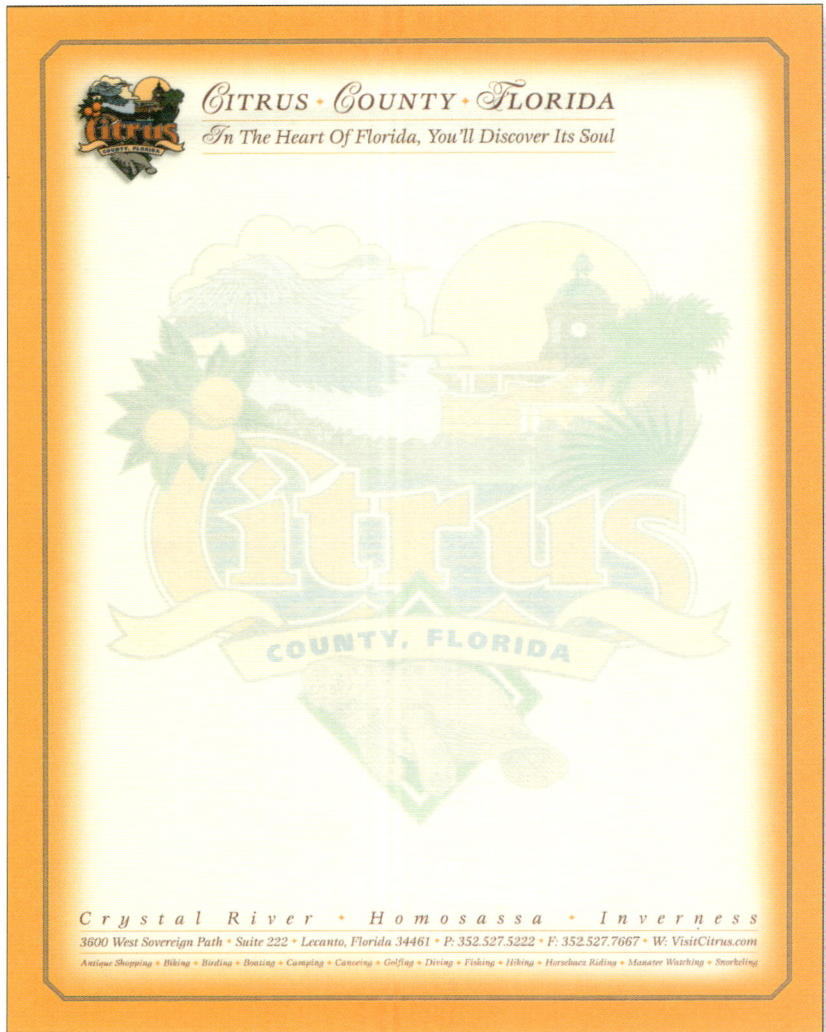

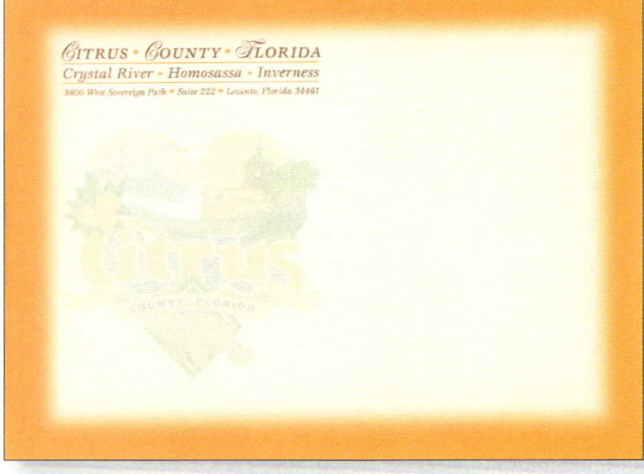

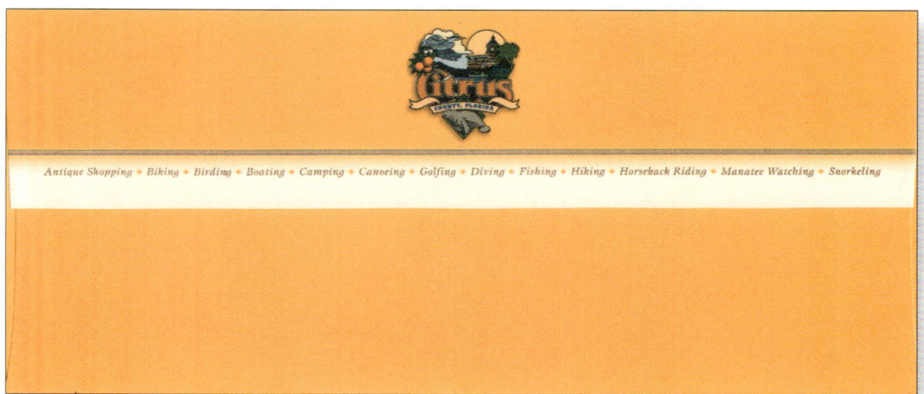

DESIGN FIRM
GOLD & Associates, Inc.
Ponte Vedra Beach, (FL) USA
PROJECT
Citrus Country, Florida
Visitors & Convention Bureau
DESIGNER
Peter Butcavage

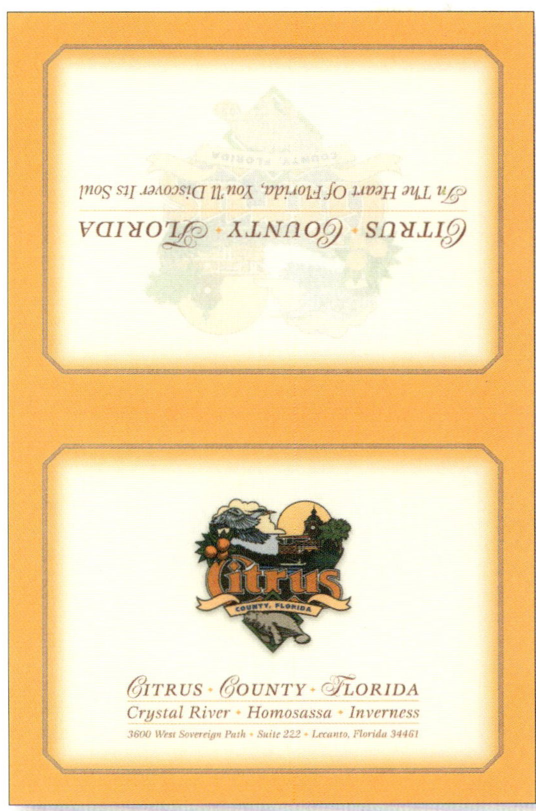
Citrus • County • Florida
In The Heart Of Florida, You'll Discover Its Soul
Citrus • County • Florida
Crystal River • Homosassa • Inverness
3600 West Sovereign Path • Suite 222 • Lecanto, Florida 34461

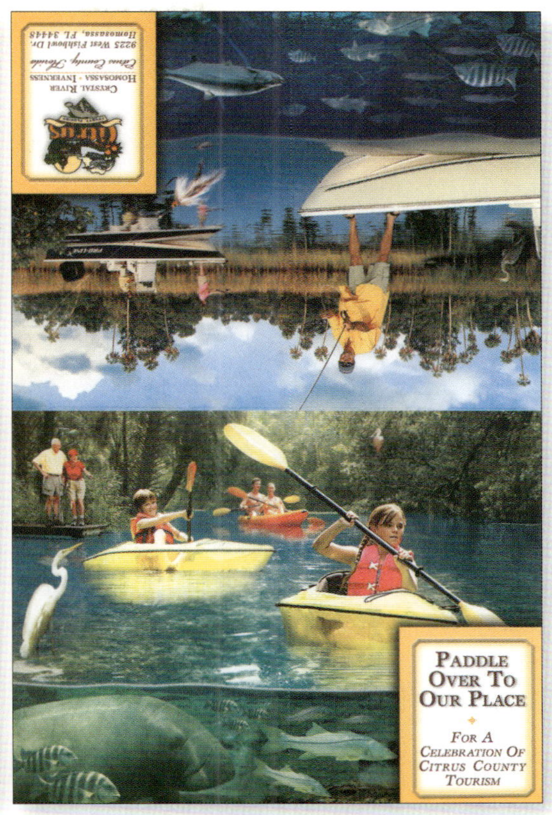
Crystal River
Homosassa • Inverness
9225 West Fishbowl Dr.
Homosassa, FL 34448
Paddle Over To Our Place
For A Celebration Of Citrus County Tourism

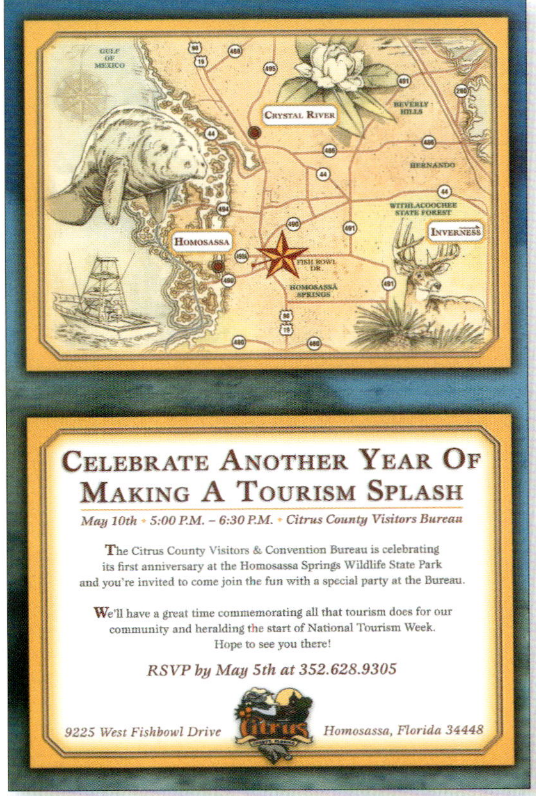
Crystal River
Homosassa
Inverness
Celebrate Another Year Of Making A Tourism Splash
May 10th • 5:00 P.M. – 6:30 P.M. • Citrus County Visitors Bureau
The Citrus County Visitors & Convention Bureau is celebrating its first anniversary at the Homosassa Springs Wildlife State Park and you're invited to come join the fun with a special party at the Bureau.
We'll have a great time commemorating all that tourism does for our community and heralding the start of National Tourism Week.
Hope to see you there!
RSVP by May 5th at 352.628.9305
9225 West Fishbowl Drive
Homosassa, Florida 34448

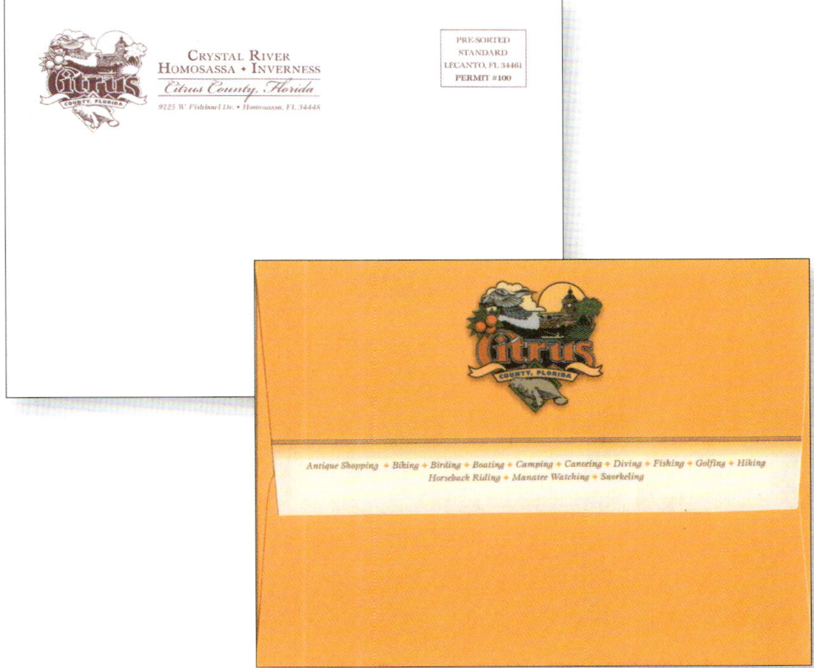
Crystal River
Homosassa • Inverness
Citrus County, Florida
Antique Shopping • Biking • Birding • Boating • Camping • Canoeing • Diving • Fishing • Golfing • Hiking
Horseback Riding • Manatee Watching • Snorkeling

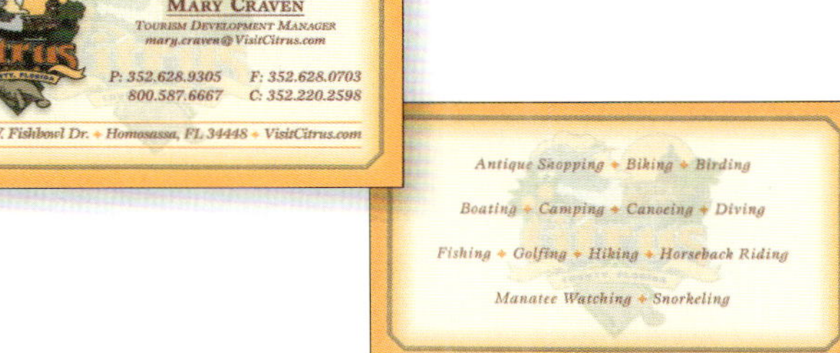
Citrus • County Visitors & Convention Bureau
Mary Craven
Tourism Development Manager
mary.craven@VisitCitrus.com
P: 352.628.9305
F: 352.628.0703
800.587.6667
C: 352.220.2598
9225 W. Fishbowl Dr. • Homosassa, FL 34448 • VisitCitrus.com
Antique Shopping • Biking • Birding
Boating • Camping • Canoeing • Diving
Fishing • Golfing • Hiking • Horseback Riding
Manatee Watching • Snorkeling

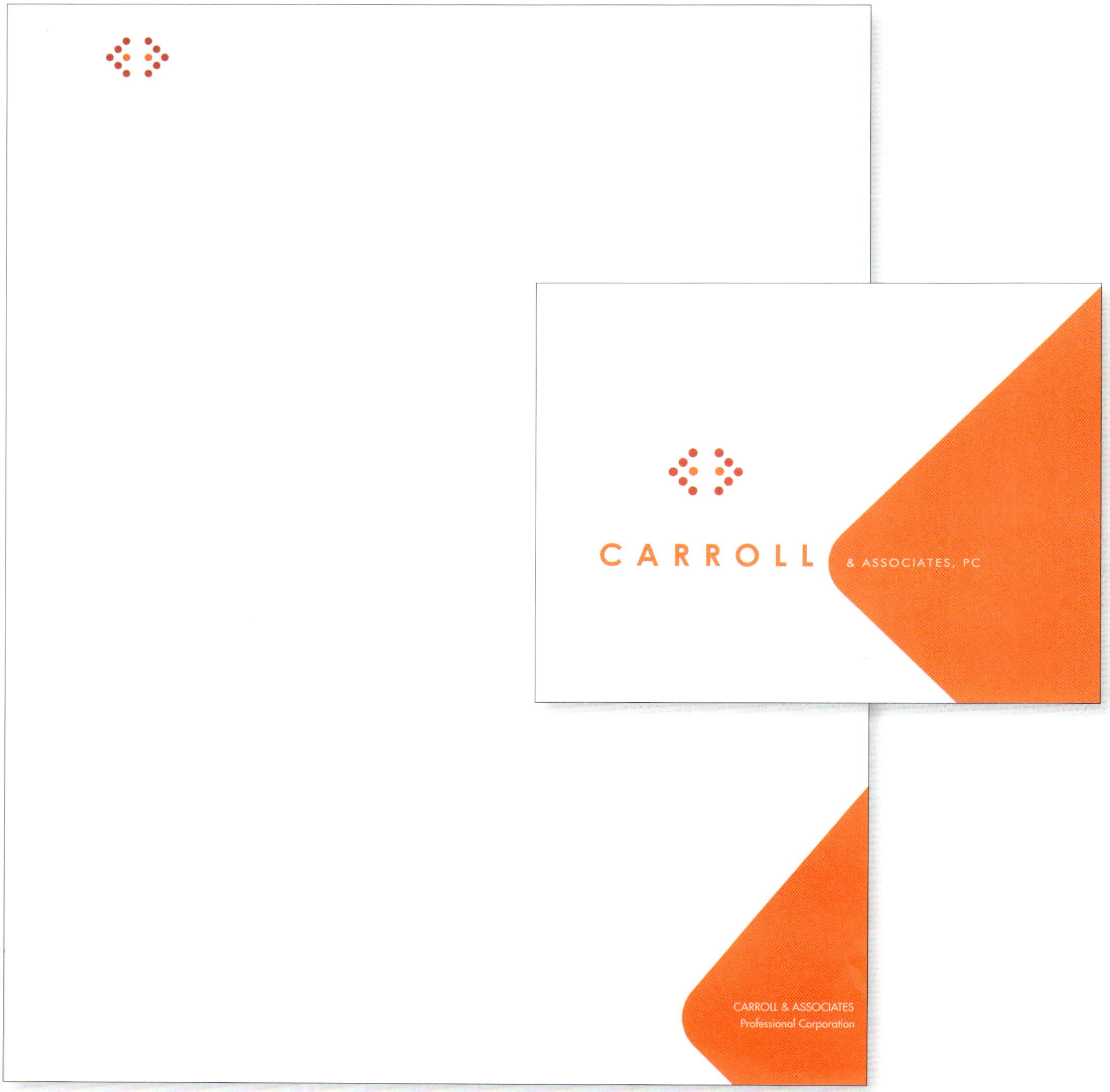

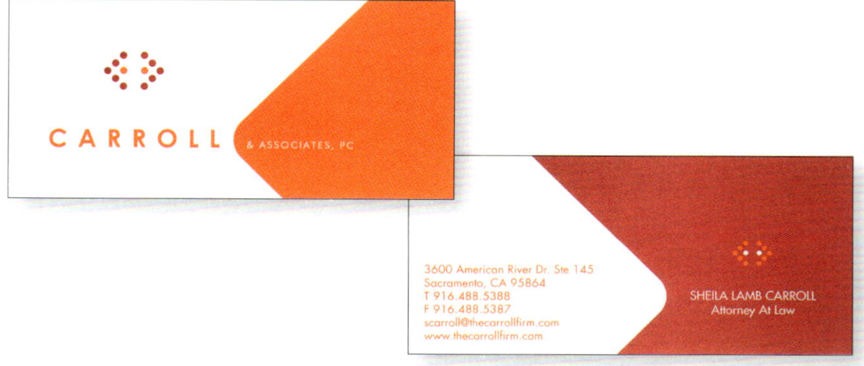

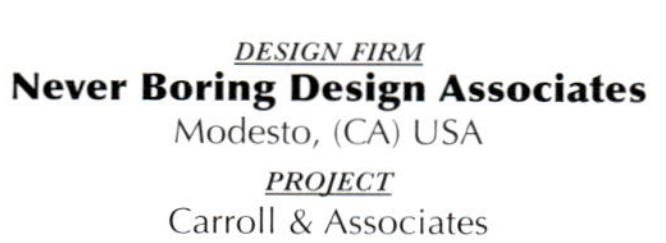

DESIGN FIRM
Never Boring Design Associates
Modesto, (CA) USA
PROJECT
Carroll & Associates
DESIGNER
Julia Orona

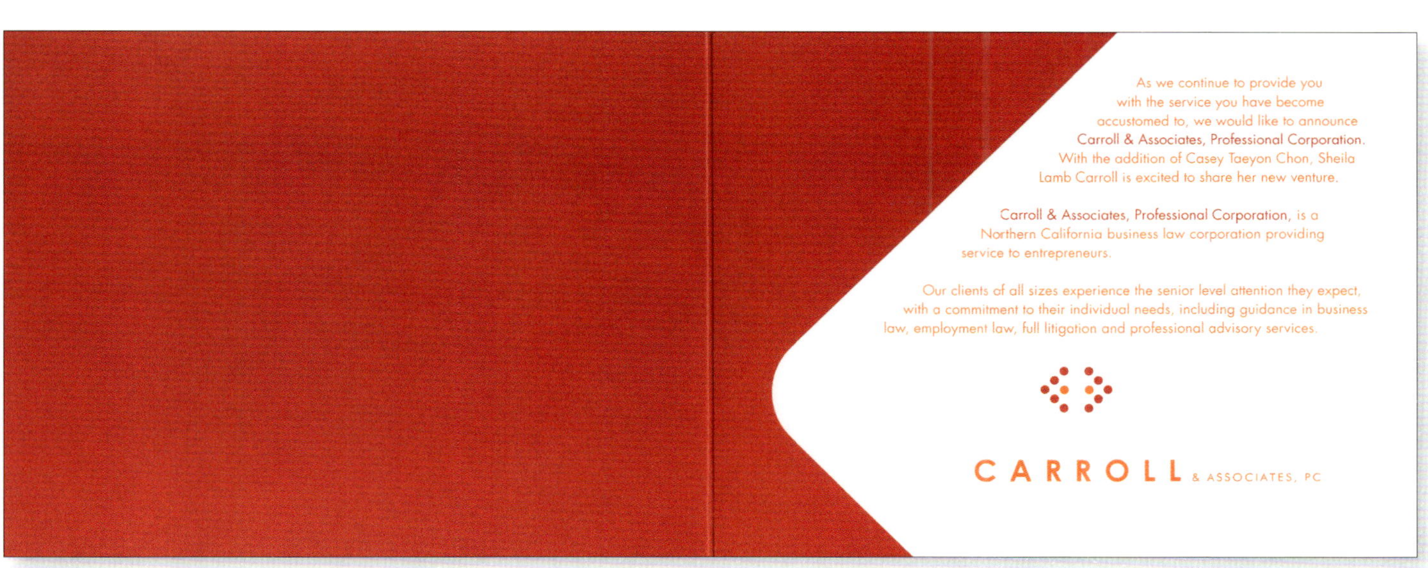
As we continue to provide you
with the service you have become
accustomed to, we would like to announce
Carroll & Associates, Professional Corporation.
With the addition of Casey Taeyon Chon, Sheila
Lamb Carroll is excited to share her new venture.
Carroll & Associates, Professional Corporation, is a
Northern California business law corporation providing
service to entrepreneurs.
Our clients of all sizes experience the senior level attention they expect,
with a commitment to their individual needs, including guidance in business
law, employment law, full litigation and professional advisory services.
CARROLL & ASSOCIATES, PC

CARROLL & ASSOCIATES, PC
3600 American River Dr. Ste 145
Sacramento, CA 95864

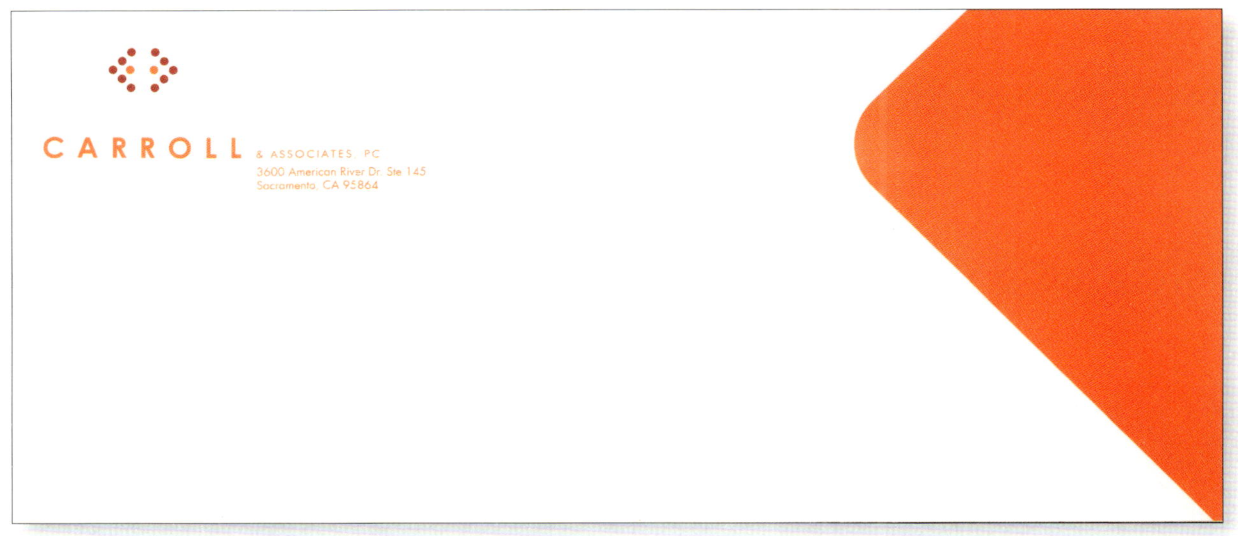
CARROLL & ASSOCIATES, PC
3600 American River Dr. Ste 145
Sacramento, CA 95864

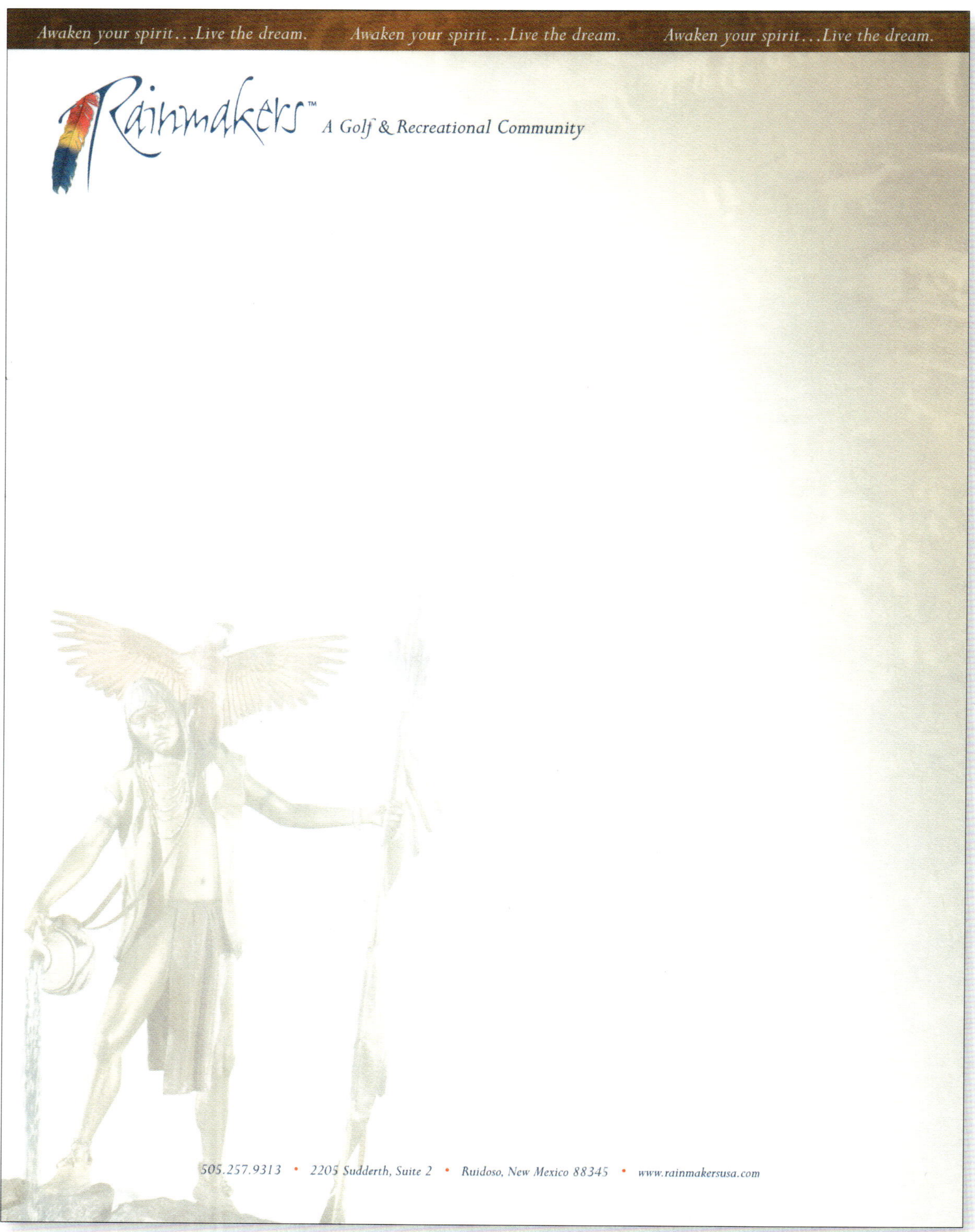

DESIGN FIRM
MDVC Creative
Dallas, (TX) USA
PROJECT
Rainmakers
CREATIVE DIRECTOR
Molly DeVoss

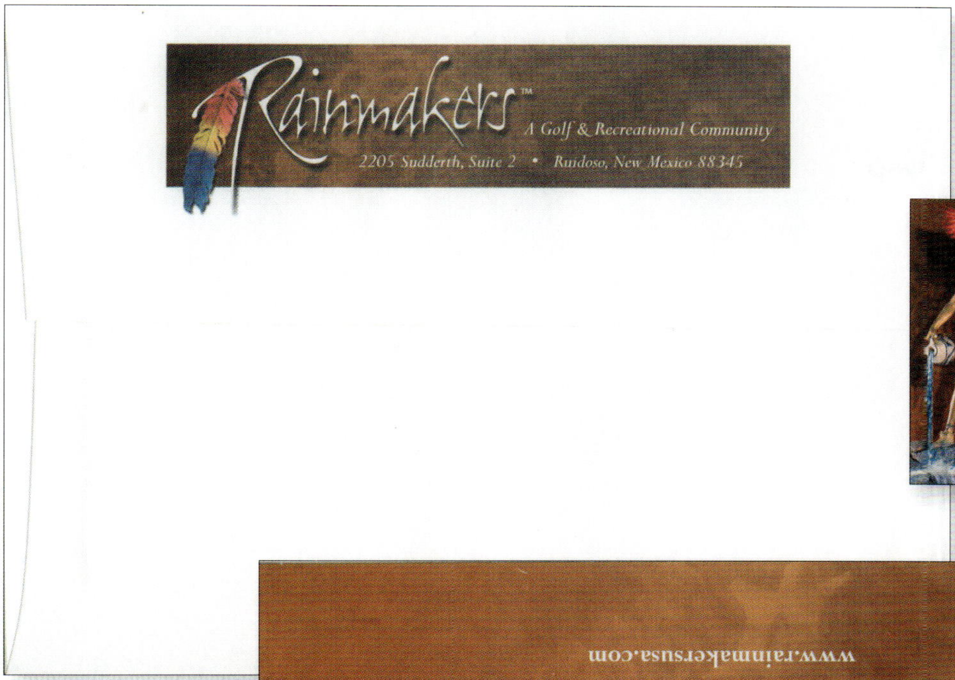

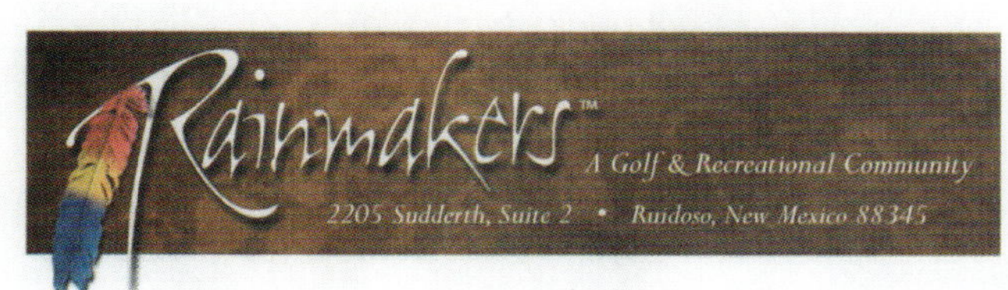

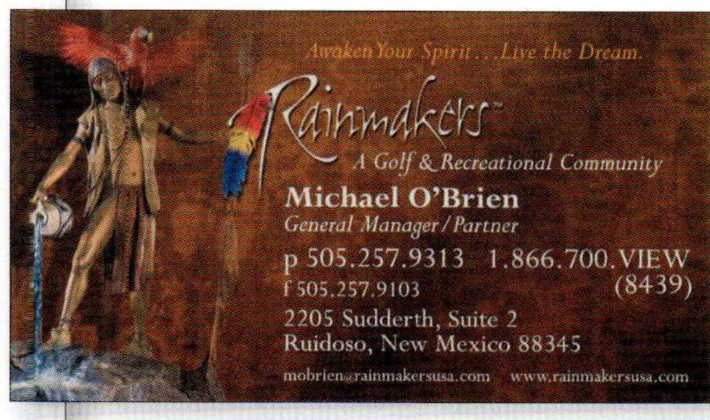

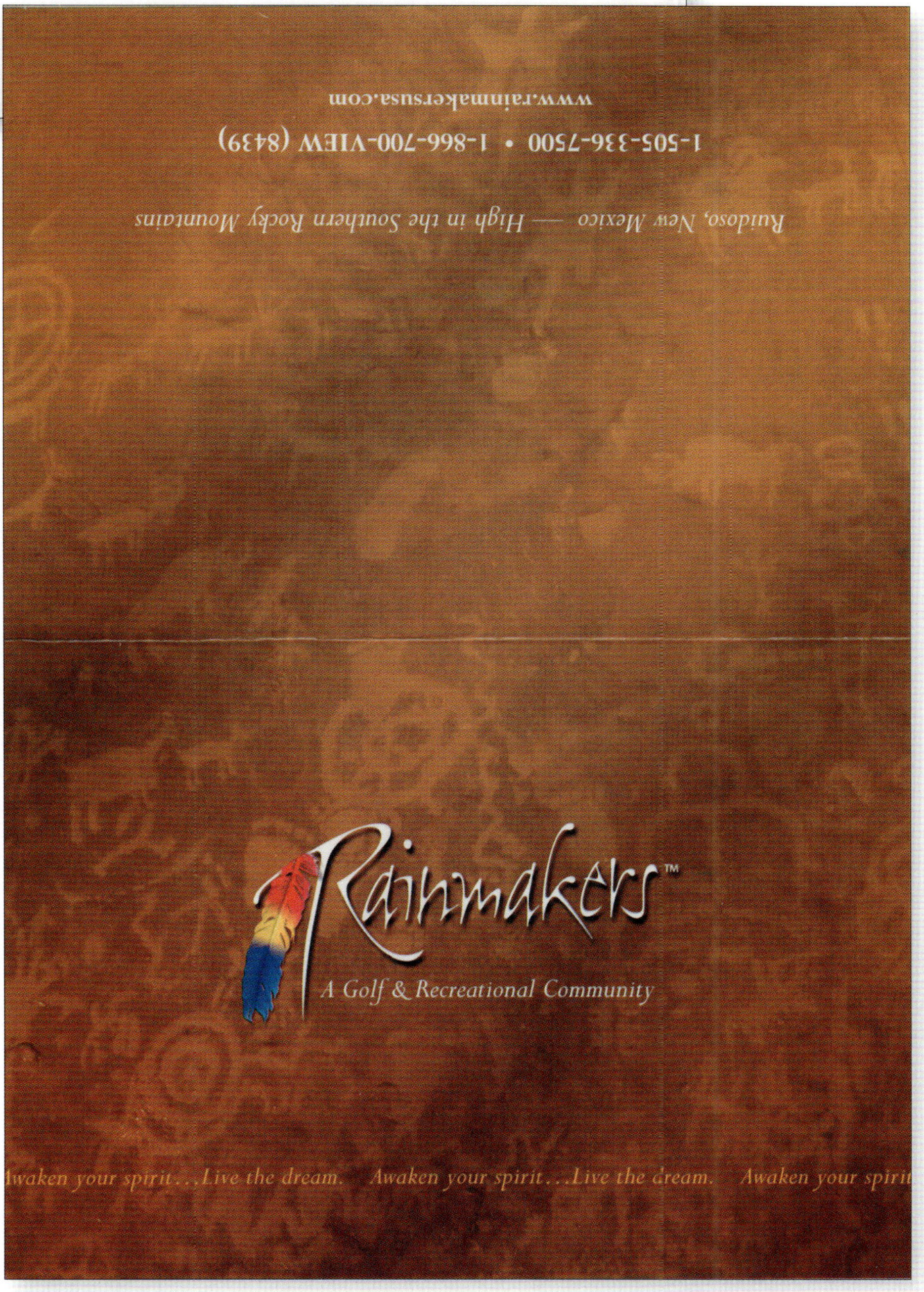

www.rainmakersusa.com

1-505-336-7500 • 1-866-700-VIEW (8439)

Ruidoso, New Mexico — High in the Southern Rocky Mountains

Rainmakers™

A Golf & Recreational Community

Awaken your spirit…Live the dream.

OPTIM audio

THE PENINSULA'S
PREMIER PRO AUDIO
SPECIALISTS
abn 55 841 685 021

Factory One, 34 Cumberland Drive
(P.O.Box 2174) Seaford VIC 3198
phone +61 3 8796 3954 **fax** +61 3 8796 3957
email info@optimaudio.com.au **web** www.optimaudio.com.au

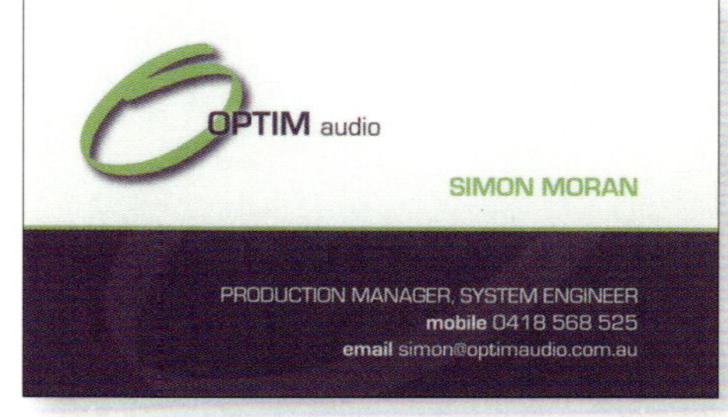

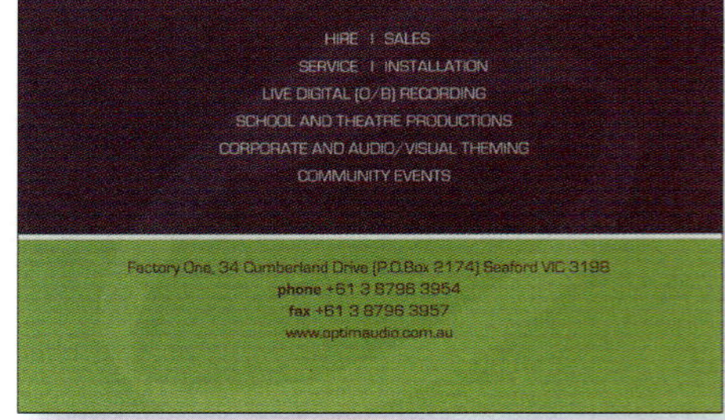

DESIGN FIRM
At First Sight
Ormond, Australia
CREATIVE DIRECTOR
Olivia Brown
DESIGNER
Barry Selleck

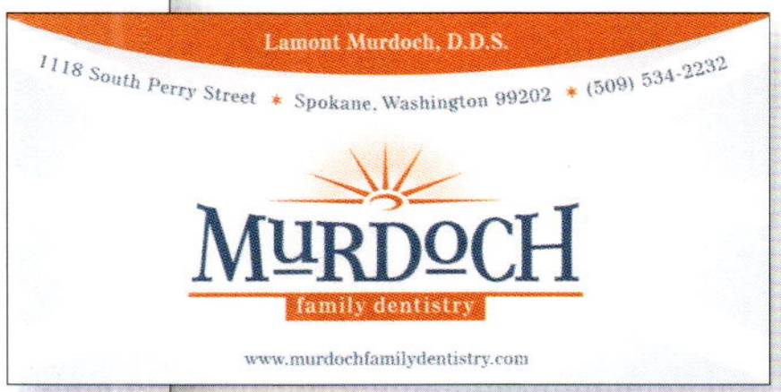

1118 South Perry Street • Spokane, Washington 99202 • (509) 534-2232 • www.murdochfamilydentistry.com

MURDOCH
family dentistry

Lamont Murdoch, D.D.S.
1118 South Perry Street • Spokane, Washington 99202 • (509) 534-2232

MURDOCH
family dentistry

www.murdochfamilydentistry.com

DESIGN FIRM
Kländt Hosmer
Spokane, (WA) USA

PROJECT
Murdoch Family Dentistry

ART DIRECTOR
Darin Kländt

DESIGNERS
Lorri Johnston,
Henry Ortega

DESIGN FIRM
Entermotion Design Studio
Wichita, (KS) USA
PROJECT
Aikins Appraisals Stationery
DESIGNER
Lea Carmichael

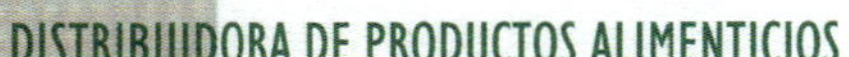

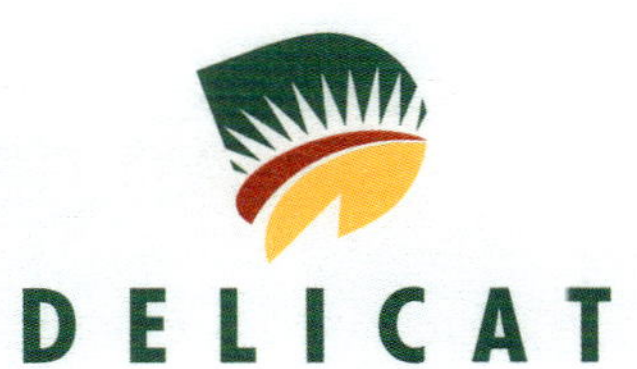

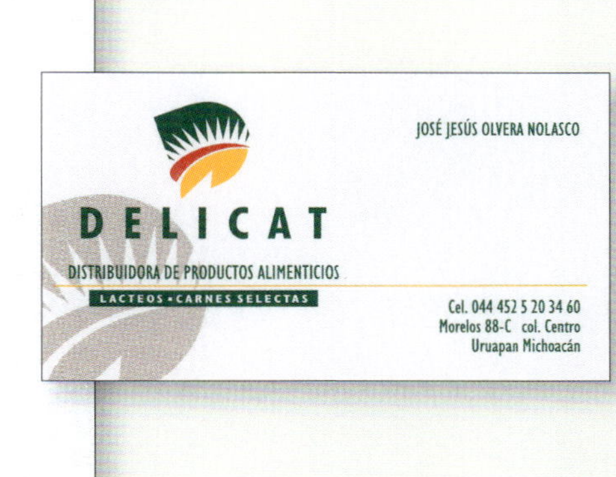

DESIGN FIRM
Kenneth Diseño
Uruapan, Mexico

PROJECT
Delicat

DESIGNERS
Kenneth Treviño,
Minerva Galván

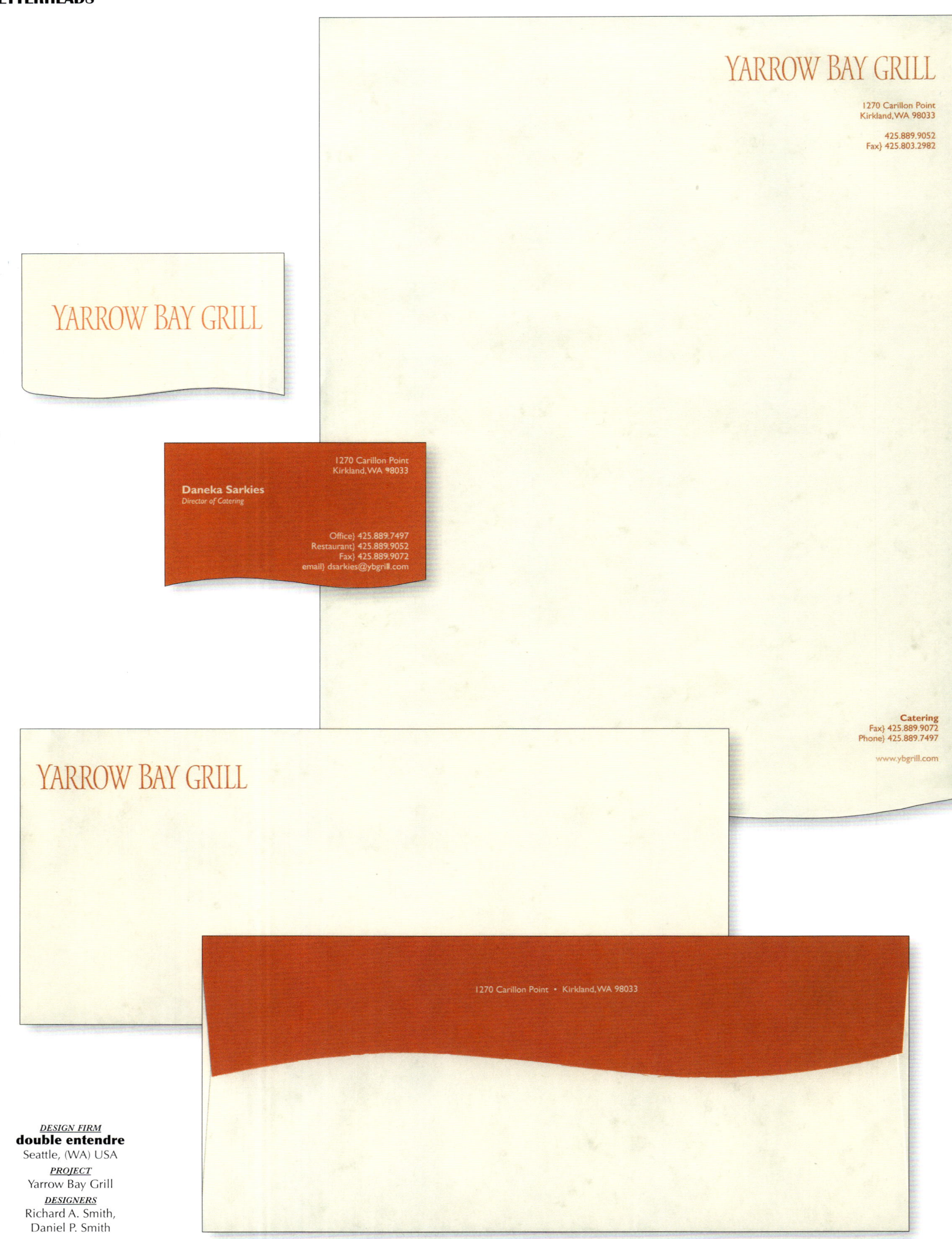

DESIGN FIRM
double entendre
Seattle, (WA) USA
PROJECT
Yarrow Bay Grill
DESIGNERS
Richard A. Smith,
Daniel P. Smith

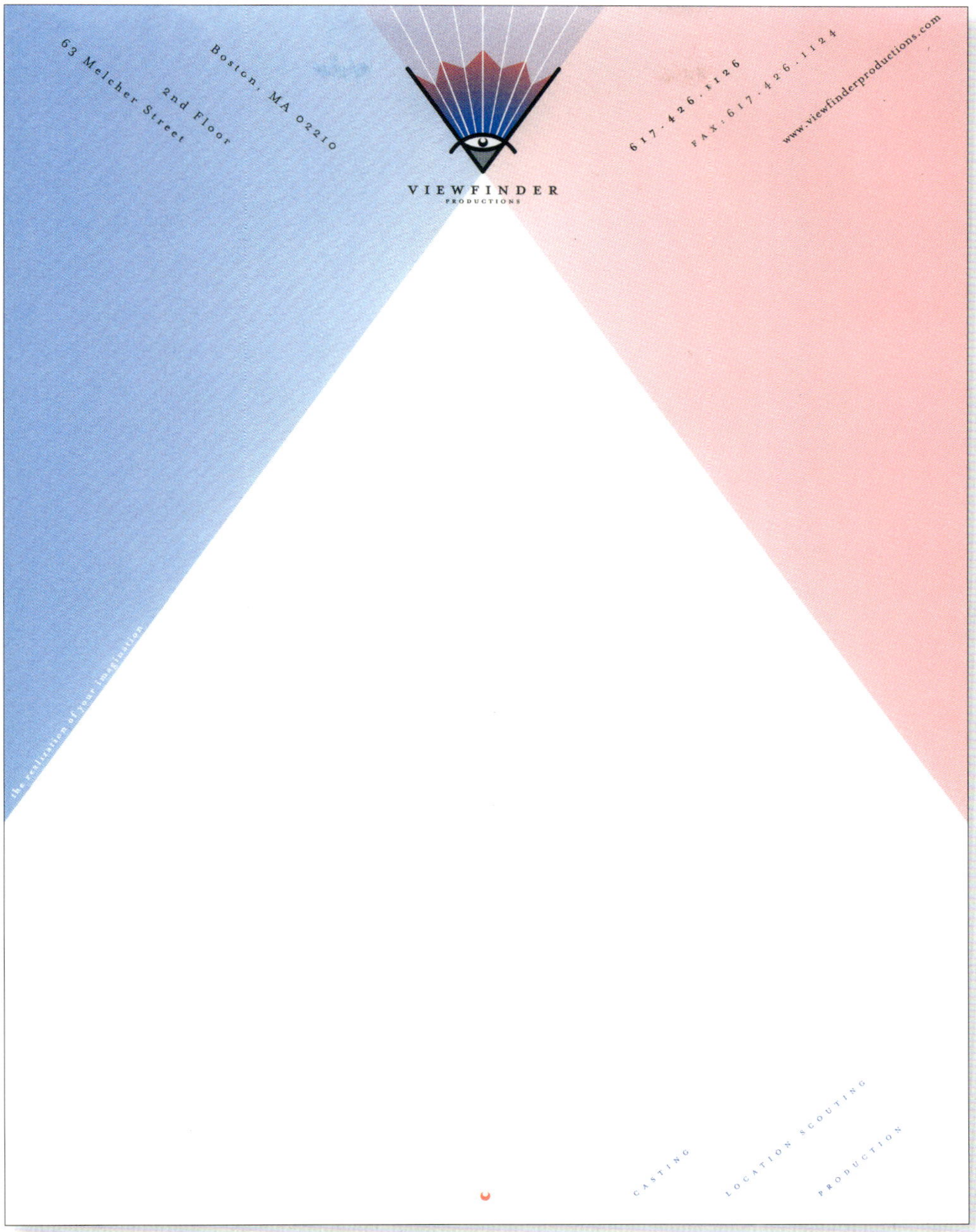

63 Melcher Street
2nd Floor
Boston, MA 02210

VIEWFINDER
PRODUCTIONS

617.426.1126
FAX: 617.426.1124
www.viewfinderproductions.com

the realization of your imagination

CASTING
LOCATION SCOUTING
PRODUCTION

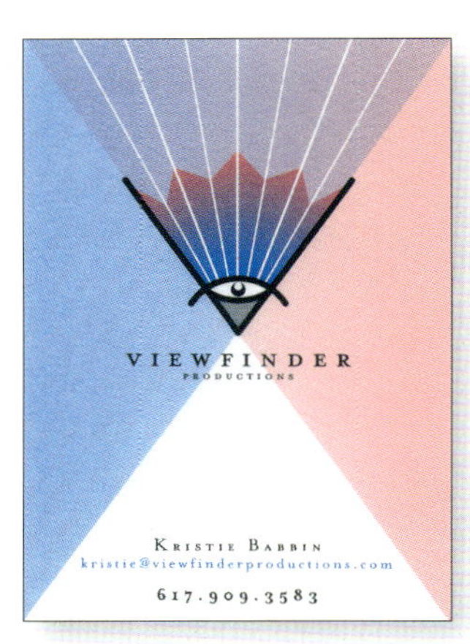

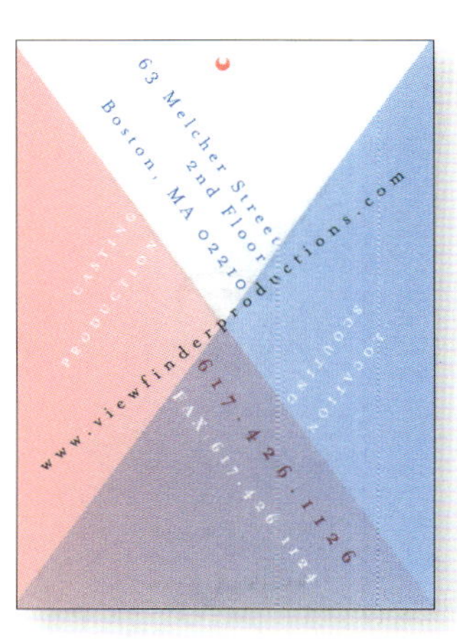

DESIGN FIRM
Interrobang Design Collaborative, Inc.
Richmond, (VT) USA
PROJECT
Viewfinder Productions
CREATIVE DIRECTOR, DESIGNER
Mark D. Sylvester

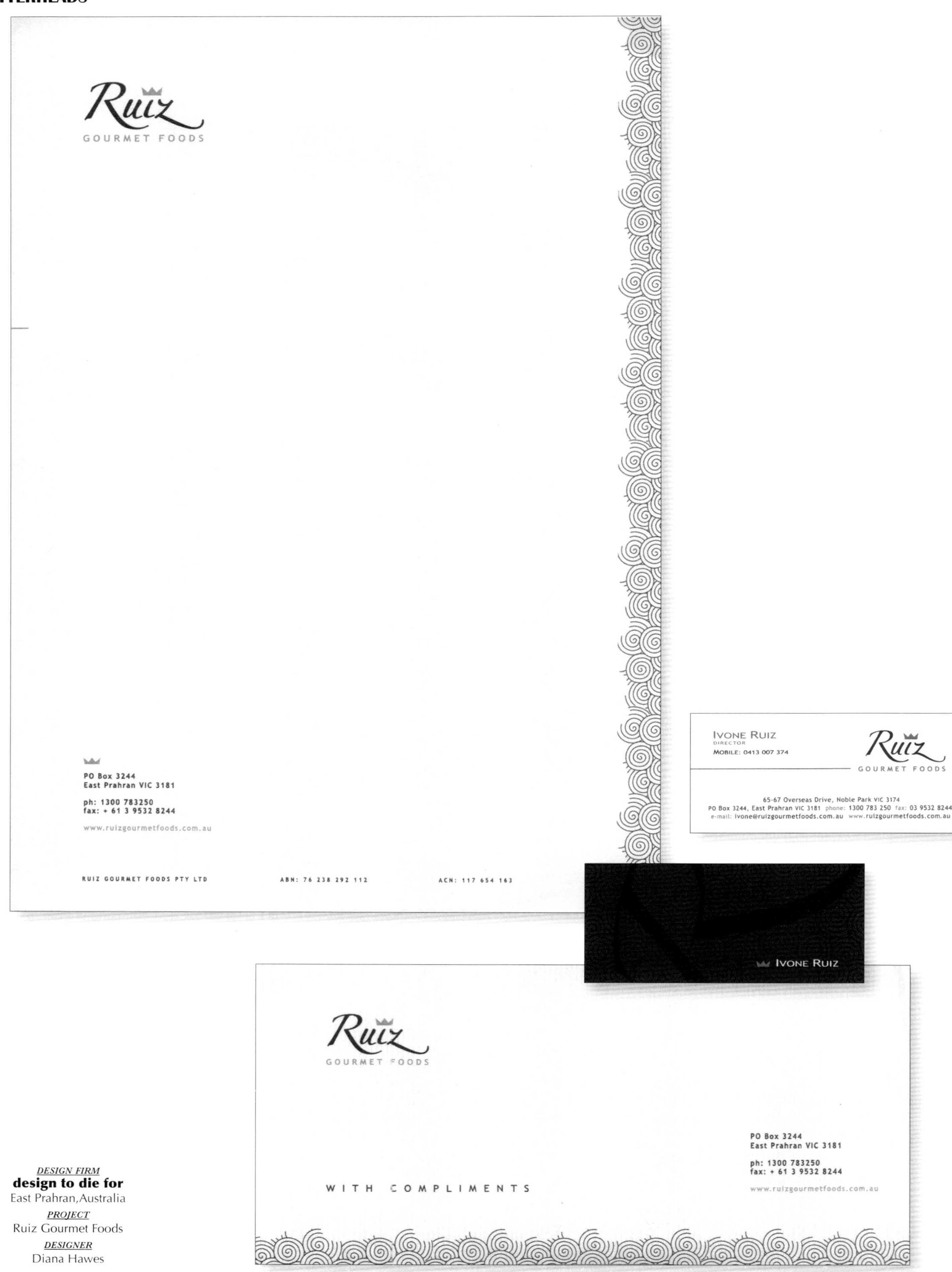

DESIGN FIRM
design to die for
East Prahran, Australia

PROJECT
Ruiz Gourmet Foods

DESIGNER
Diana Hawes

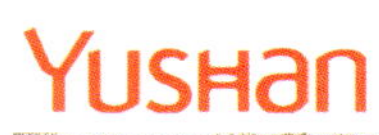

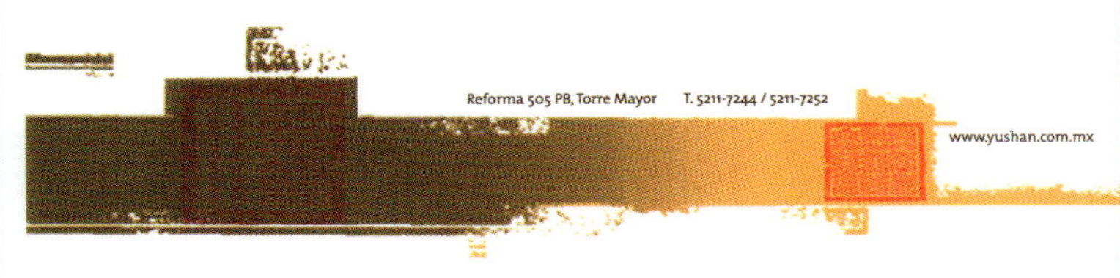

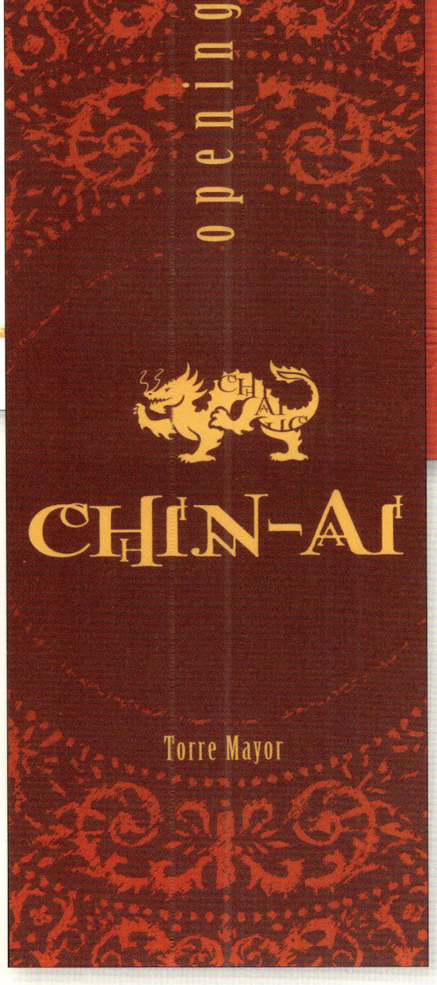

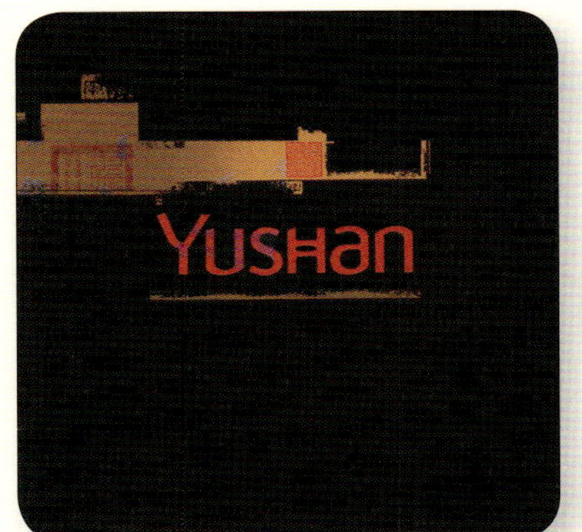

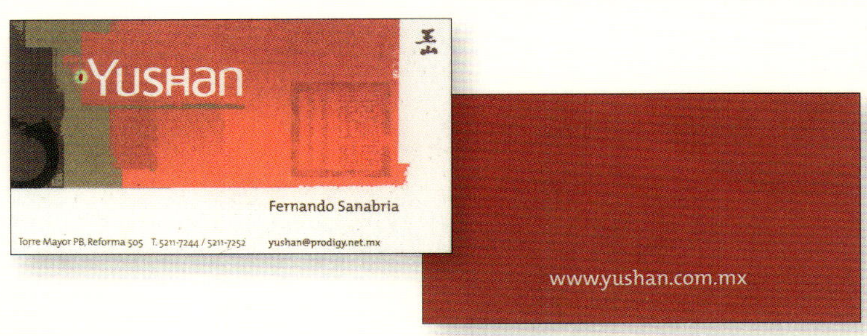

DESIGN FIRM
TD2
Mexico City, Mexico
CLIENT
Yushan Restaurant
DESIGNERS
R. Rodrigo Cordova, Gabriela Zamora

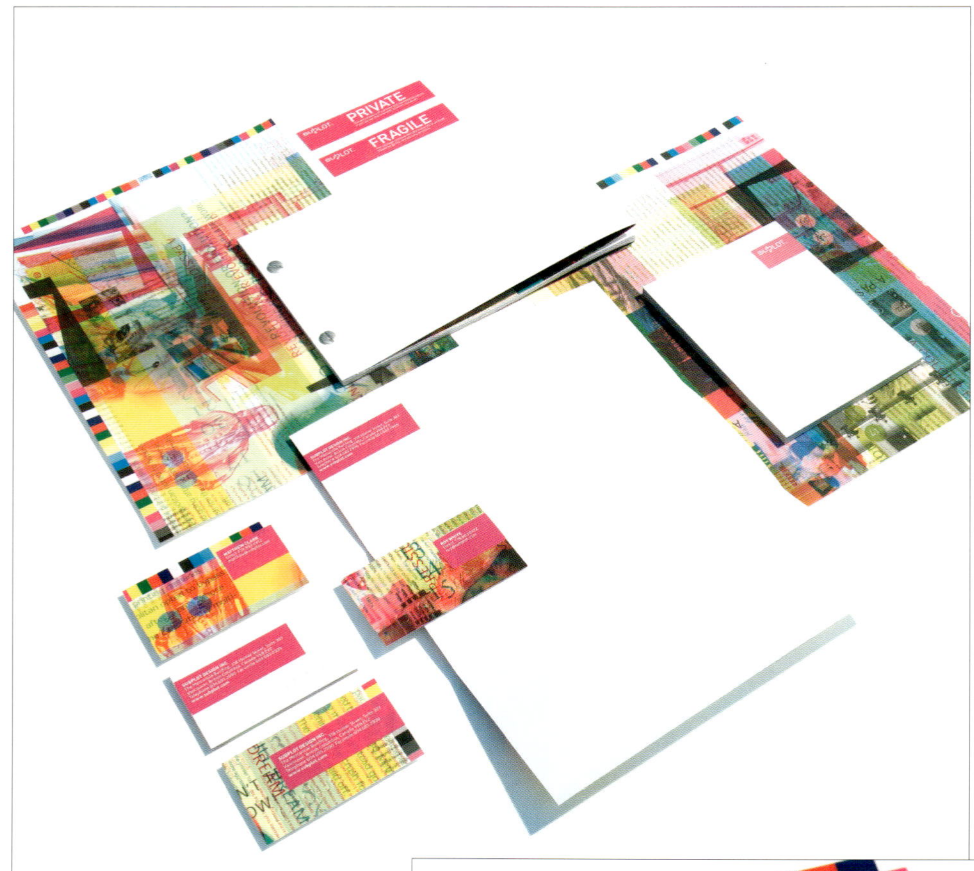

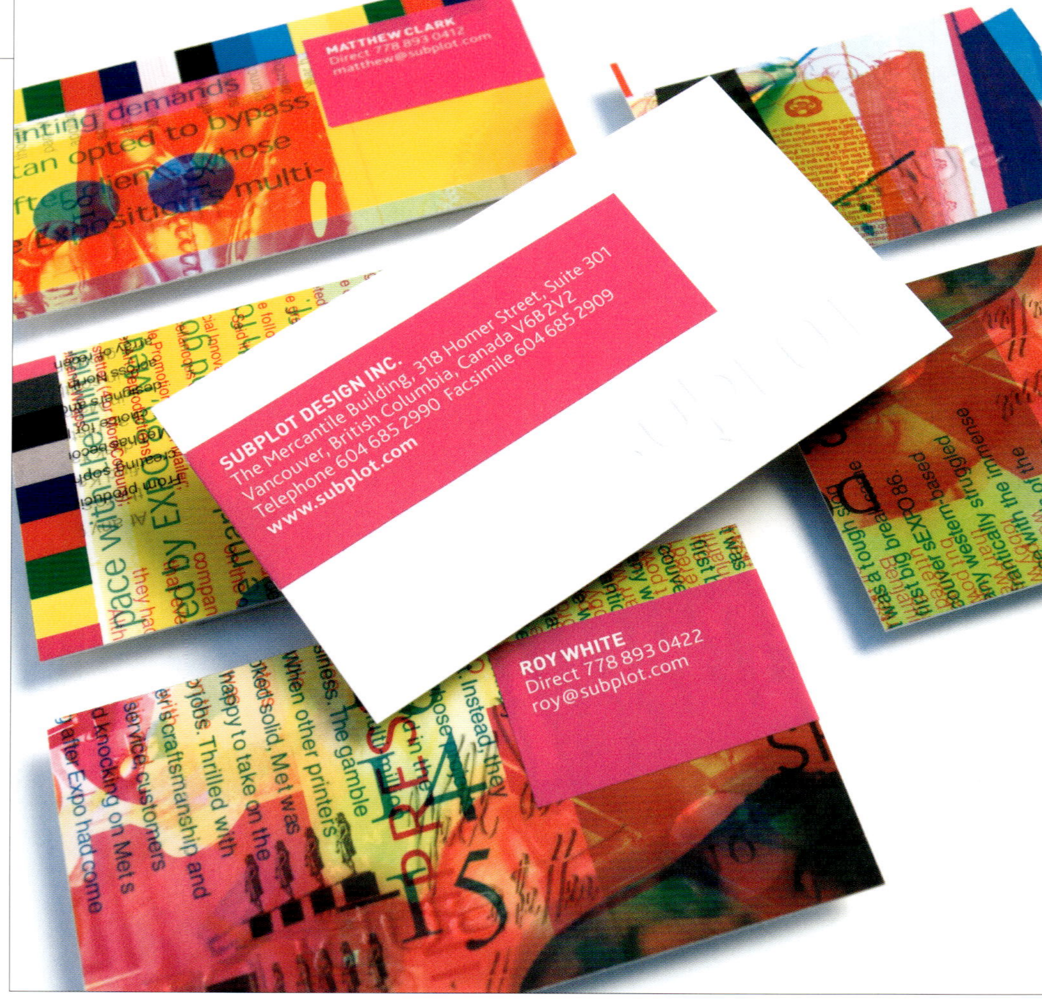

DESIGN FIRM
Subplot Design Inc.
Vancouver, Canada
PROJECT
Subplot

DESIGN FIRM
Sayles Graphic Design
Des Moines, (IA) USA
CLIENT
Beaverdale Village
DESIGNER, ILLUSTRATOR
John Sayles

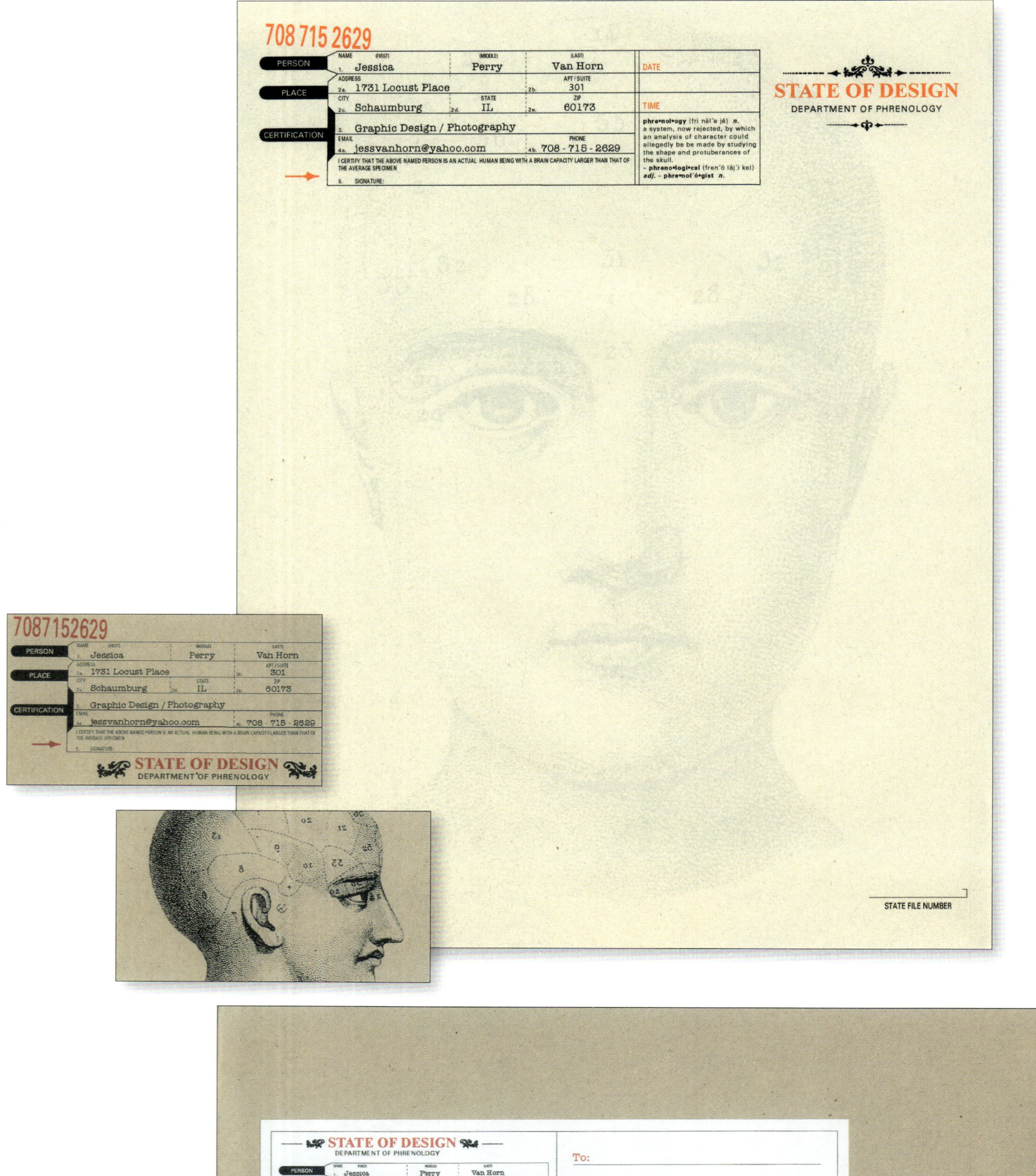

DESIGN FIRM
Jessica Van Horn
Schaumburg, (IL) USA
PROJECT
State of Design
DESIGNER
Jessica Van Horn

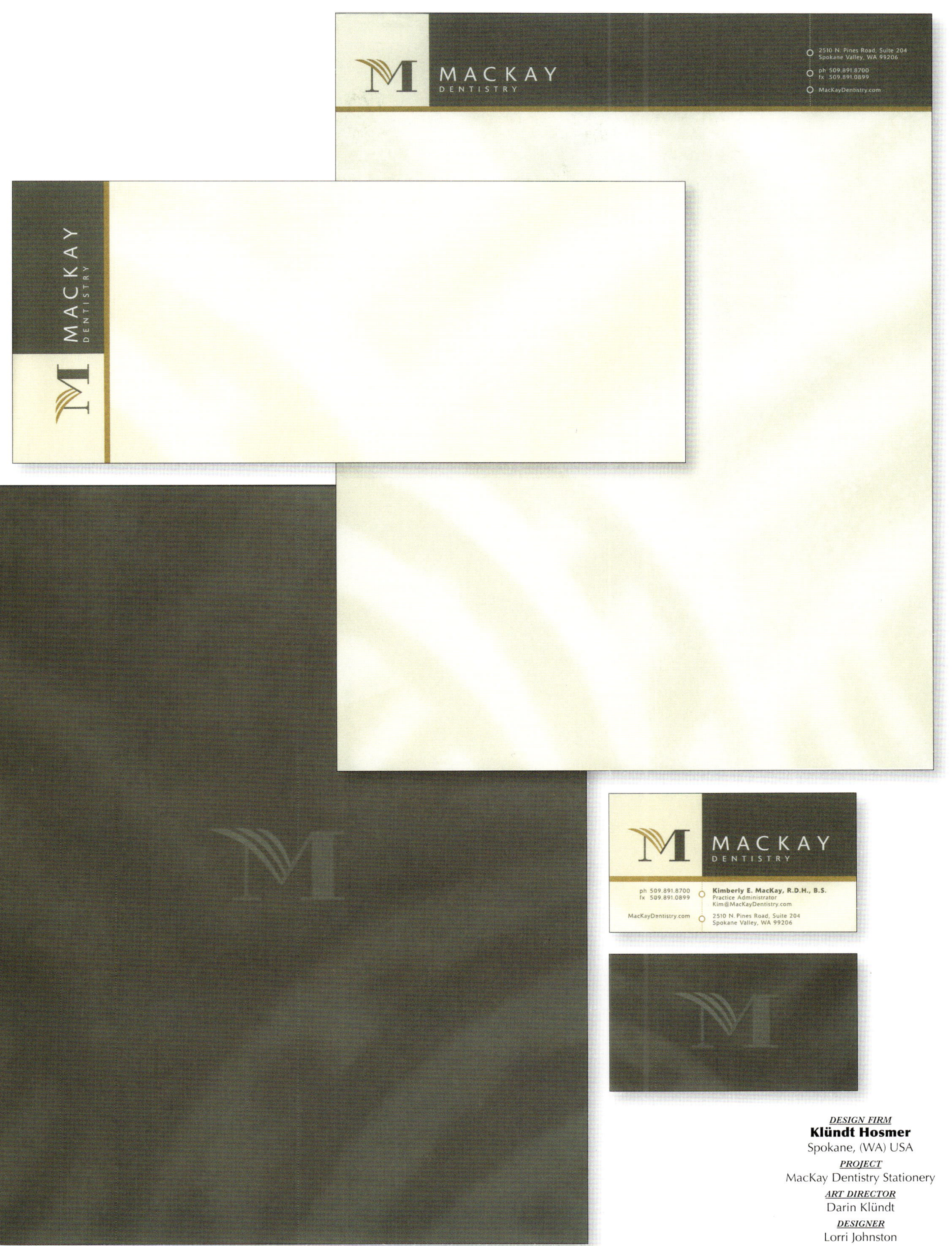

DESIGN FIRM
Kländt Hosmer
Spokane, (WA) USA
PROJECT
MacKay Dentistry Stationery
ART DIRECTOR
Darin Kländt
DESIGNER
Lorri Johnston

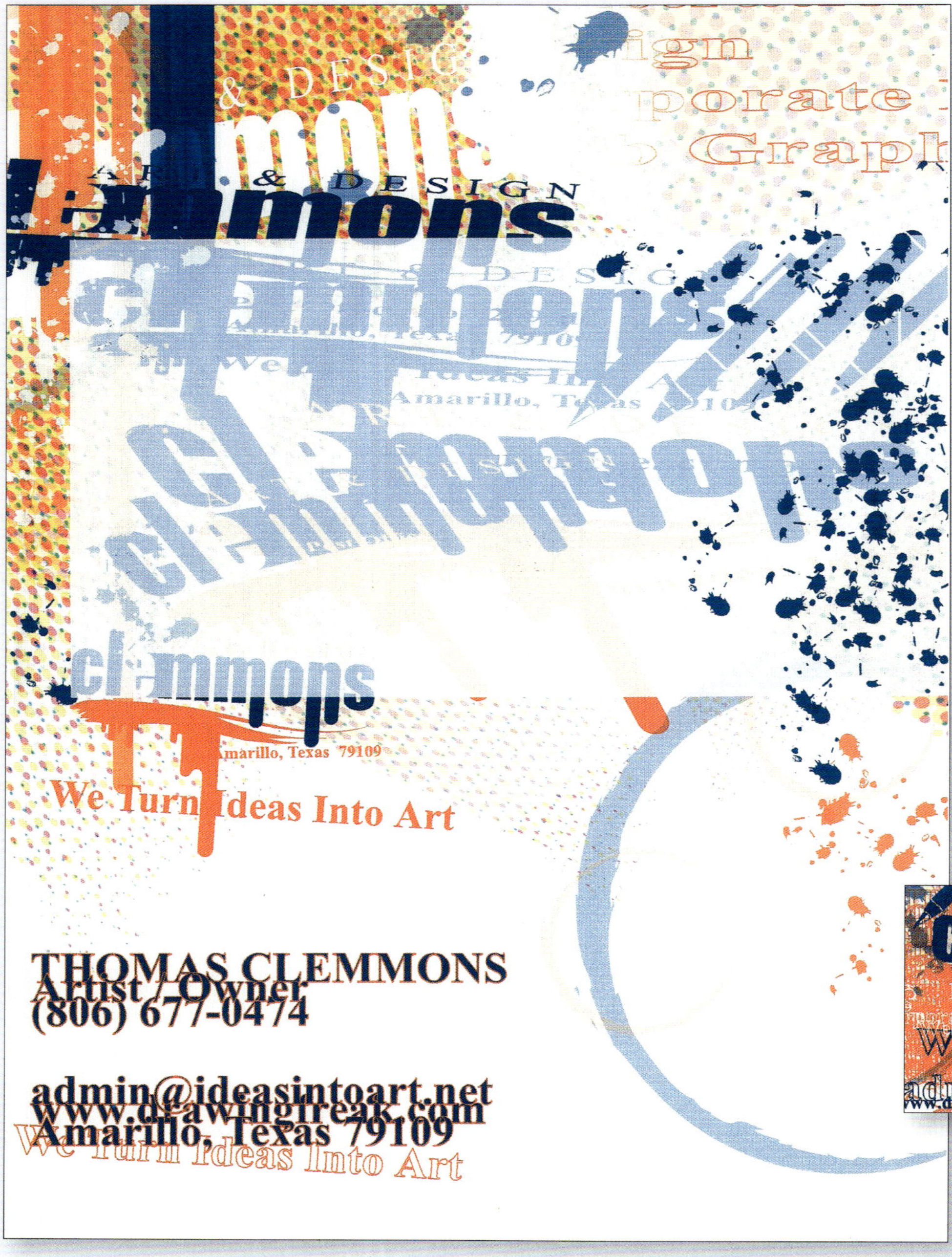

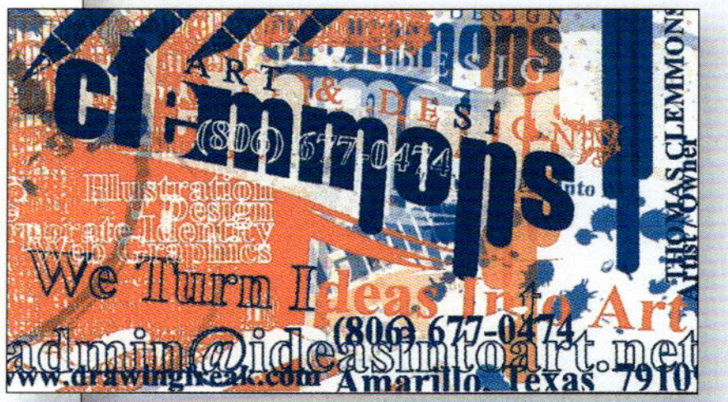

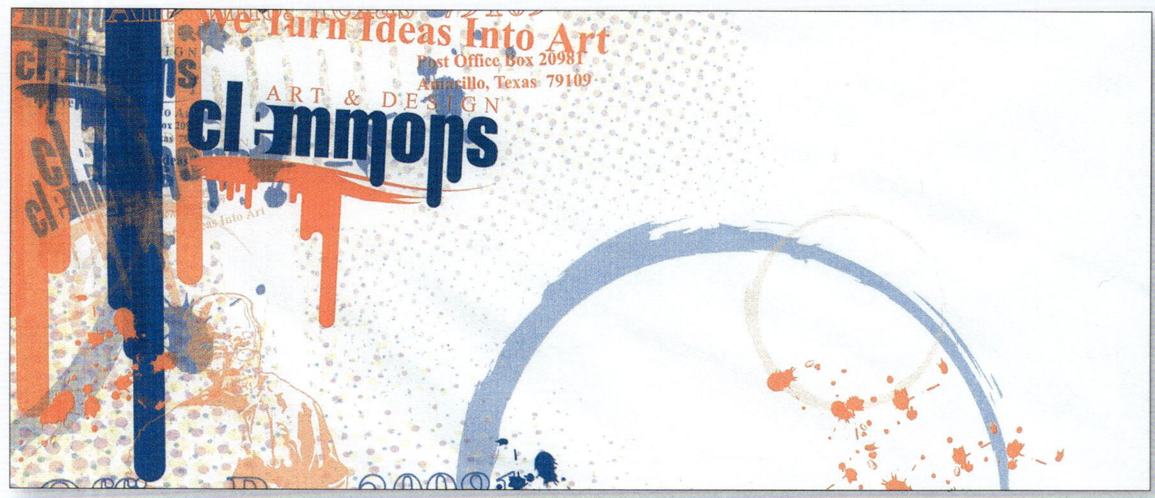

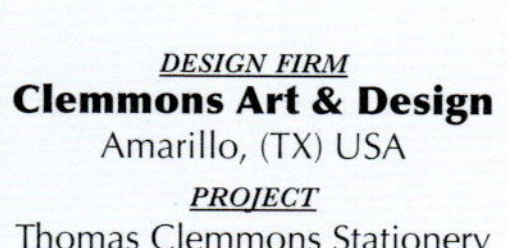

DESIGN FIRM
Clemmons Art & Design
Amarillo, (TX) USA
PROJECT
Thomas Clemmons Stationery
DESIGNER
Thomas G. Clemmons

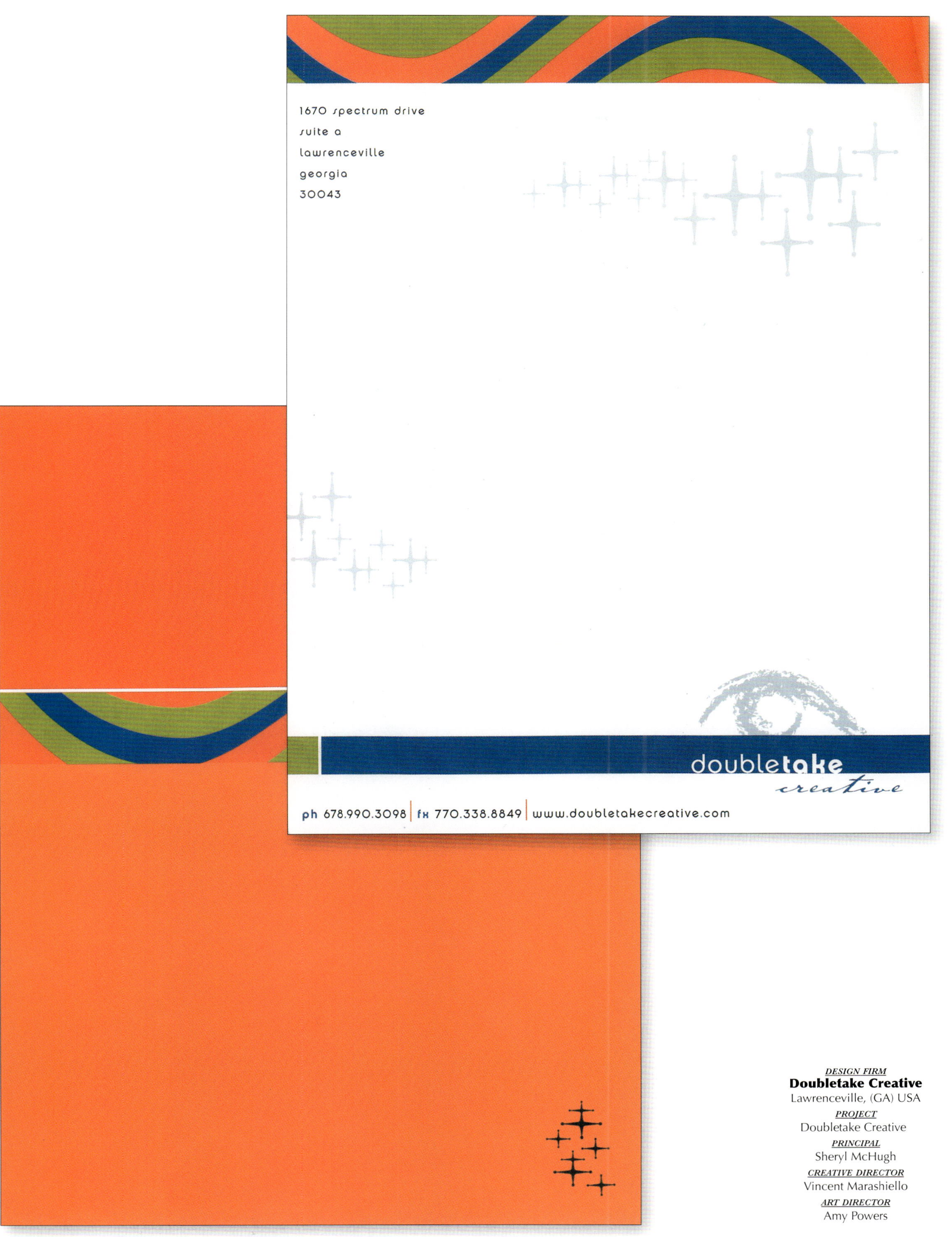

DESIGN FIRM
Doubletake Creative
Lawrenceville, (GA) USA
PROJECT
Doubletake Creative
PRINCIPAL
Sheryl McHugh
CREATIVE DIRECTOR
Vincent Marashiello
ART DIRECTOR
Amy Powers

1750 Peachtree Road NW
Atlanta, Georgia 30309

(404) 644–0260
(888) 242–6485 FAX

www.commercialrep.net

COMMERCIAL
REAL ESTATE PARTNERS, INC.
A FULL SERVICE RETAIL REAL ESTATE COMPANY

TENANT REPRESENTATION LEASING MANAGEMENT LAND BROKERAGE

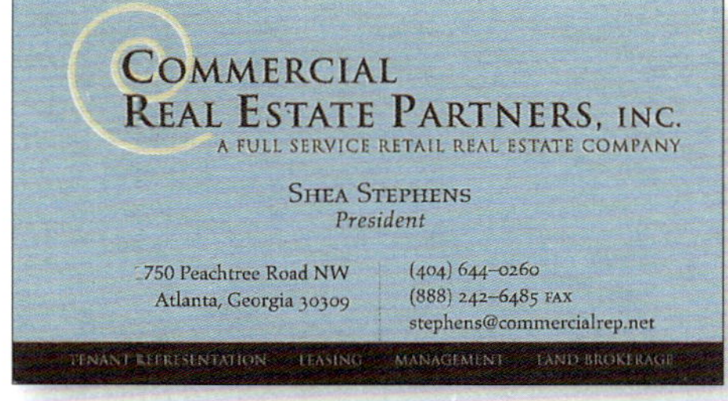

DESIGN FIRM
Jill Lynn Design
Jersey City, (NJ) USA
PROJECT
Commercial Real Estate Partners, Inc.

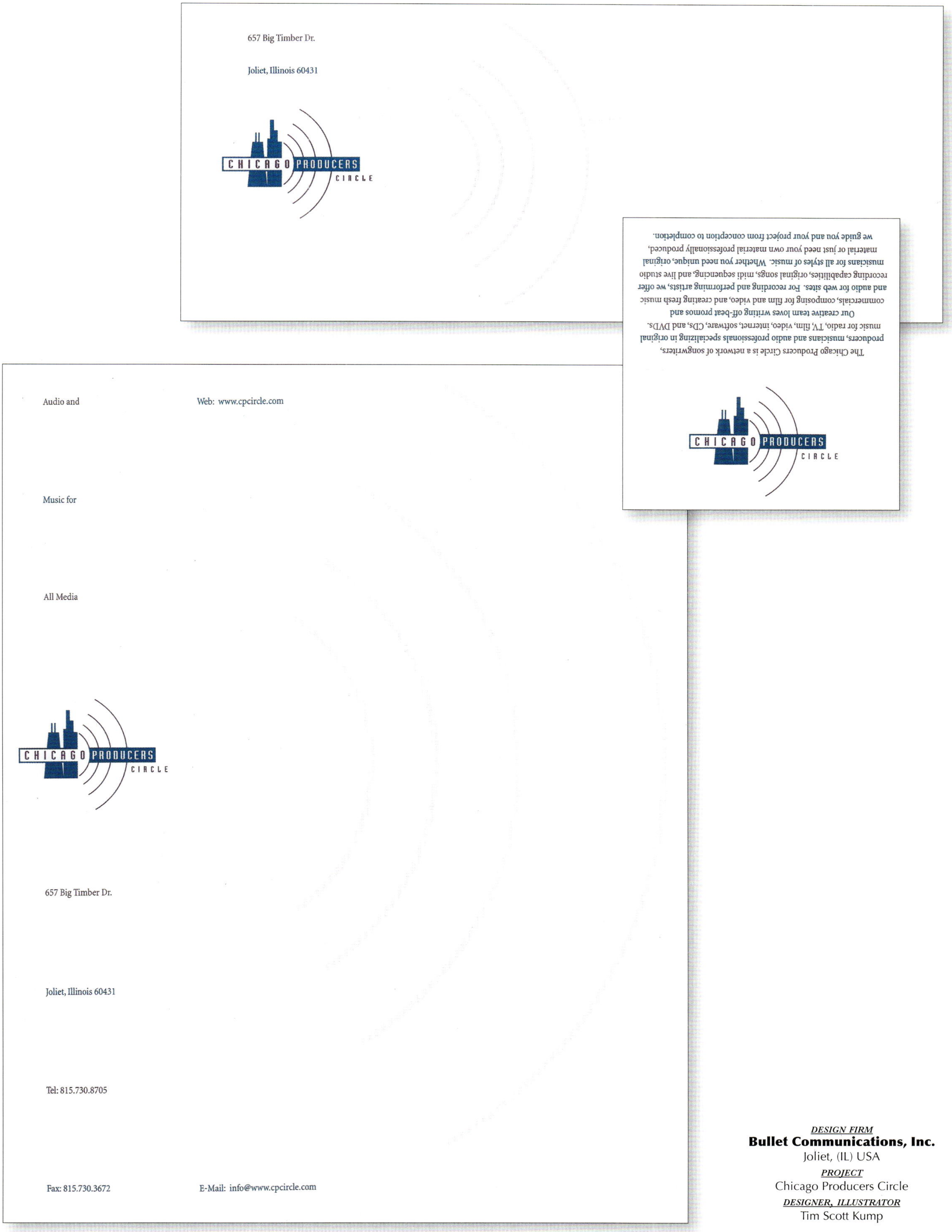

657 Big Timber Dr.

Joliet, Illinois 60431

CHICAGO PRODUCERS CIRCLE

The Chicago Producers Circle is a network of songwriters, producers, musicians and audio professionals specializing in original music for radio, TV, film, video, internet, software, CDs, and DVDs. Our creative team loves writing off-beat promos and commercials, composing for film and video, and creating fresh music and audio for web sites. For recording and performing artists, we offer recording capabilities, original songs, midi sequencing, and live studio musicians for all styles of music. Whether you need unique, original material or just need your own material professionally produced, we guide you and your project from conception to completion.

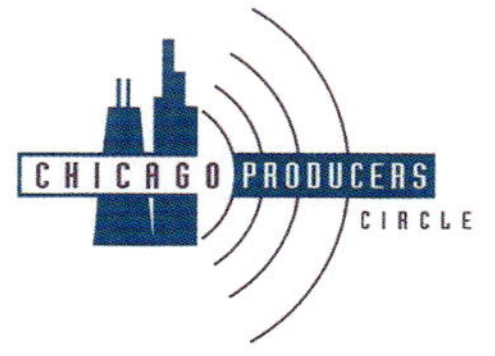

Audio and

Web: www.cpcircle.com

Music for

All Media

CHICAGO PRODUCERS CIRCLE

657 Big Timber Dr.

Joliet, Illinois 60431

Tel: 815.730.8705

Fax: 815.730.3672

E-Mail: info@www.cpcircle.com

DESIGN FIRM
Bullet Communications, Inc.
Joliet, (IL) USA

PROJECT
Chicago Producers Circle

DESIGNER, ILLUSTRATOR
Tim Scott Kump

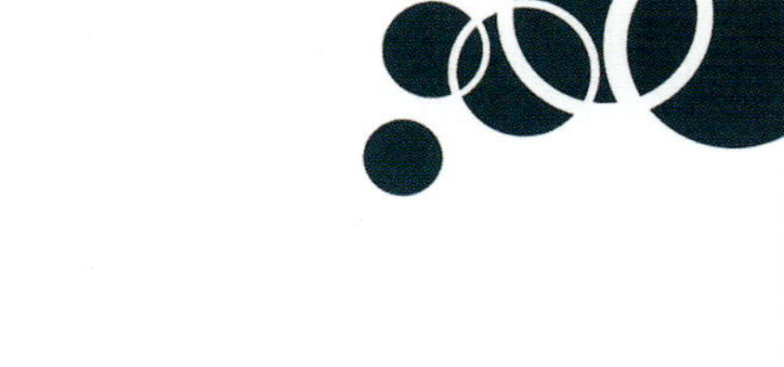

A 187 Lafayette Street, New York, NY 10013 P 212.431.7508 F 212.431.6793 URL www.expansionteam.org

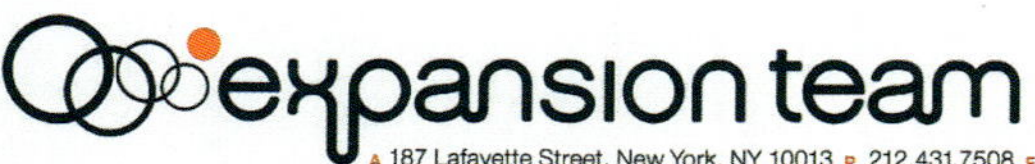

A 187 Lafayette Street, New York, NY 10013 P 212.431.7508 F 212.431.6793 URL www.expansionteam.org

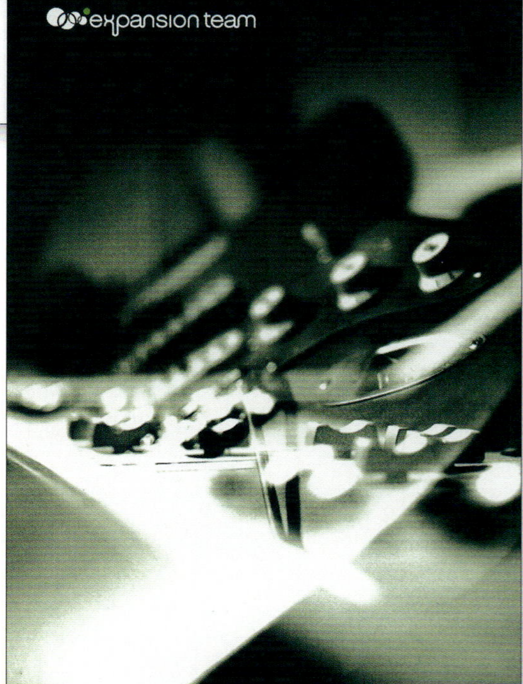

DESIGN FIRM
Studio Five
New York, (NY) USA
CLIENT
Expansion Team—EyeballNYC
DESIGNERS
Melissa Gorman
Tatiana Arocha

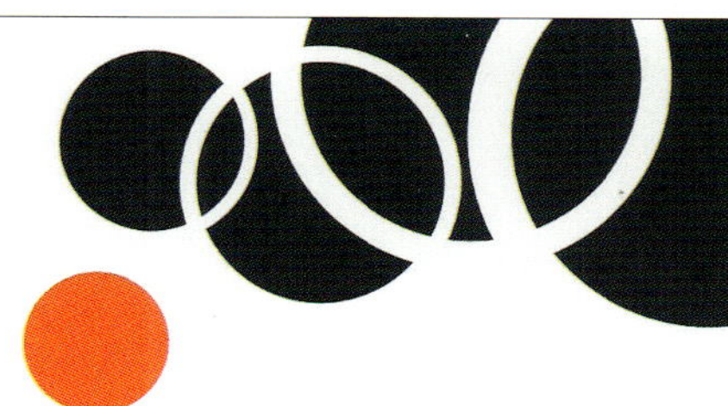

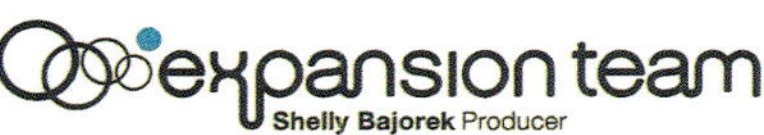

Shelly Bajorek Producer

E shelly@expansionteam.org
P 212.431.7508 F 212.431.6793
A 187 Lafayette Street, New York, NY 10013
URL www.expansionteam.org

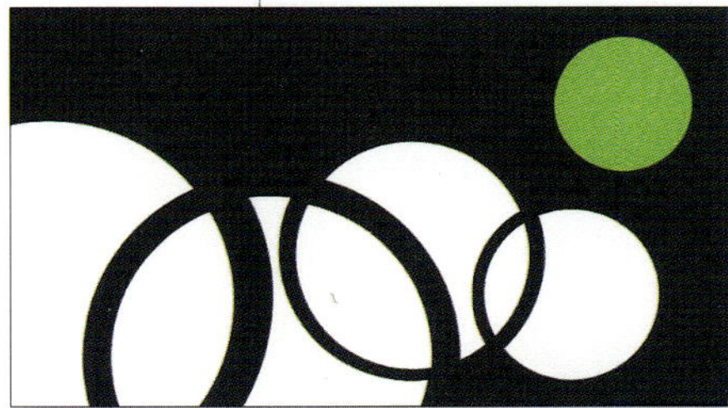

expansion team
ORIGINAL MUSIC SOUND DESIGN LICENSING

2006 DVD Reel Vol.4

Available Now
EMAIL US: info@expansionteam.org
OR CALL: 212.431.7508

COMMERCIAL REPRESENTATION:
EAST: Peter Ziegler 212.243.6364
WEST: Kelley Class 310.823.9808
MIDWEST: Liz Laine 312.329.1111
JAPAN: Mitsu Hagiwara 212.255.6116

URL: www.expansionteam.org

A 187 Lafayette Street, New York, NY 10013
RETURN SERVICE REQUESTED

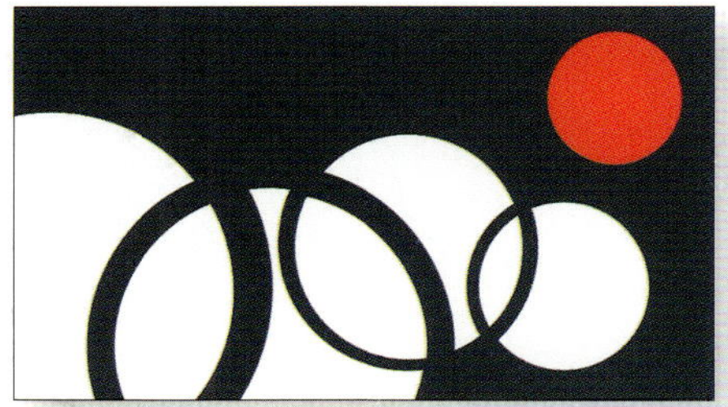

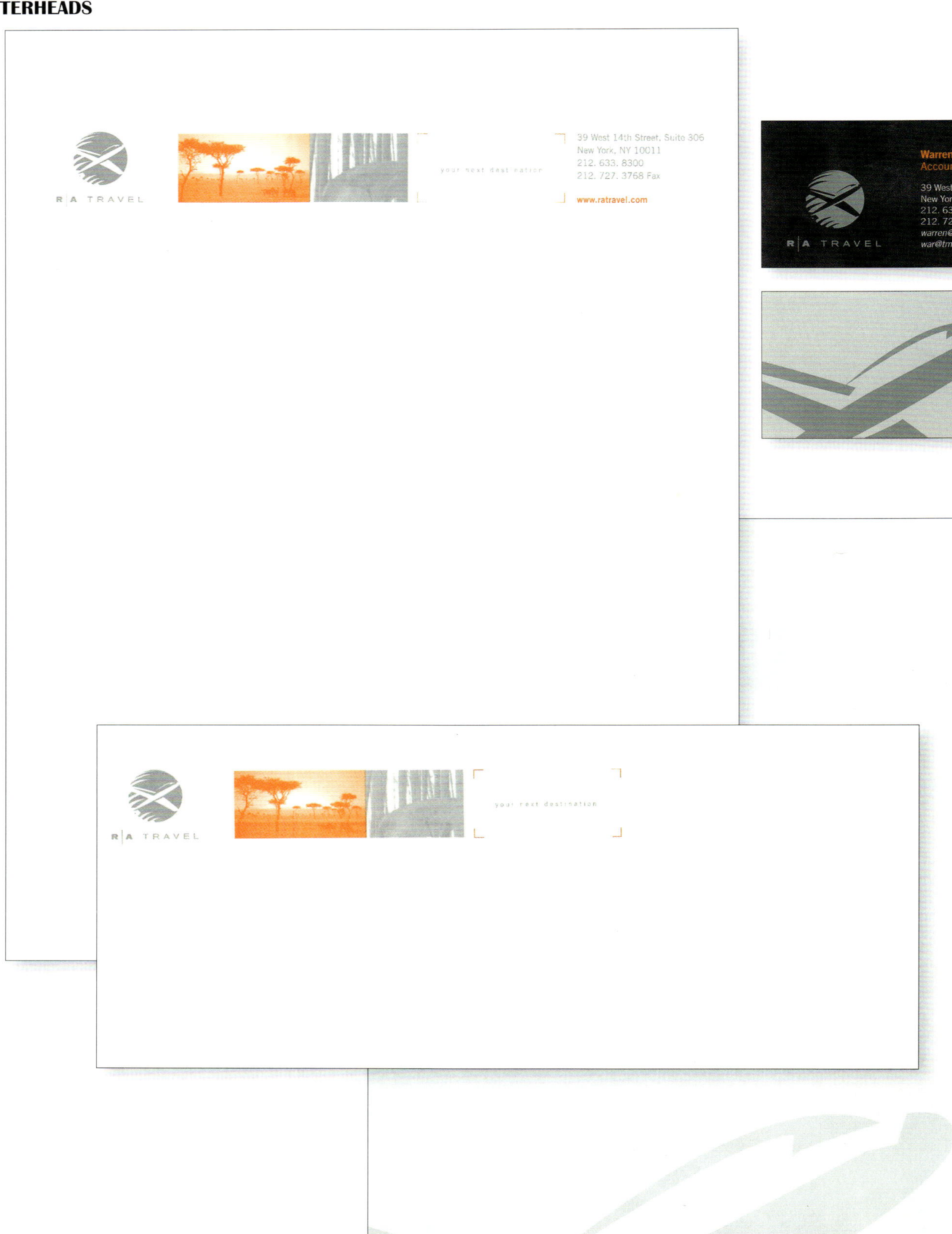

DESIGN FIRM
3rd Edge Communications
Jersey City, (NJ) USA

PROJECT
R | A Travel

ART DIRECTOR
Frankie Gonzalez

DESIGNER
Melissa Medina Mackin

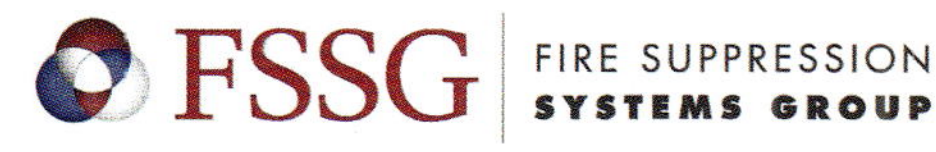

24 HOUR EMERGENCY SERVICE
1.800.799.6491

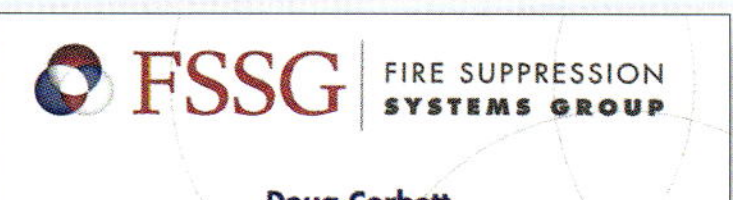

Doug Corbett
FIRE SERVICE MANAGER
mobile: 401.265.4756
dcorbett@firesuppression.com

24 HOUR SERVICE 1.800.799.6491 • tel: 401.723.7300 • fax: 401.724.0879
70 BACON STREET • PAWTUCKET, RI 02860 • WWW.FIRESUPPRESSION.COM

70 BACON STREET • PAWTUCKET, RI 02860 • 401.723.7300
A CINTAS COMPANY

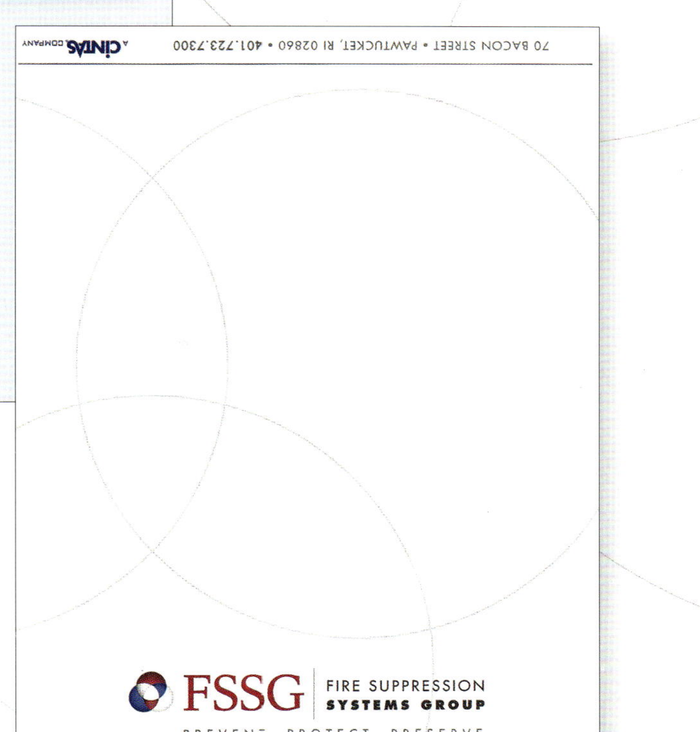

FSSG
FIRE SUPPRESSION
SYSTEMS GROUP
70 Bacon Street
Pawtucket, RI 02860

FSSG
FIRE SUPPRESSION
SYSTEMS GROUP
PREVENT. PROTECT. PRESERVE.

.234.2223 • fax: 508.234.7977 • www.firesuppression.com
SPECIAL HAZARDS INSPECTIONS A CINTAS COMPANY

DESIGN FIRM
Im-aj Communications & Design, Inc.
West Kingston, (RI) USA
CLIENT
FSSG
CREATIVE DIRECTOR
Jami Ouellette
ART DIRECTOR, SENIOR DESIGNER
Leslie Emert

DESIGN FIRM
Sungrafx, Inc.
Silverdale, (WA) USA
CLIENT
Silverdale Autoworks
CREATIVE DIRECTOR
Vicky Koningisor
DESIGNER
Laura Zander

DESIGN FIRM
Octavo Designs
Frederick, (MD) USA
CLIENT
Associated Credit Services, Inc.
ART DIRECTOR, DESIGNER
Sue Hough

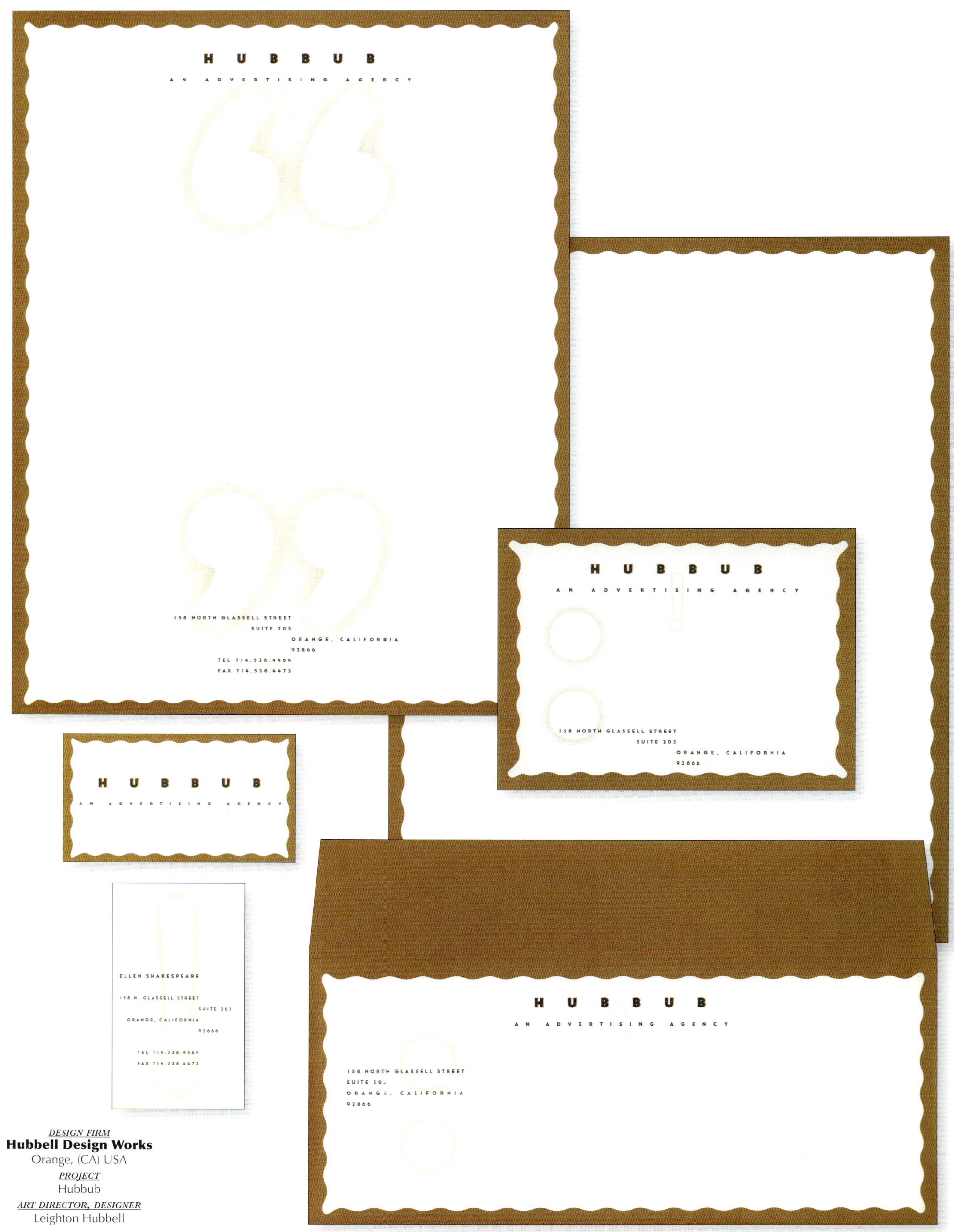

DESIGN FIRM
Hubbell Design Works
Orange, (CA) USA

PROJECT
Hubbub

ART DIRECTOR, DESIGNER
Leighton Hubbell

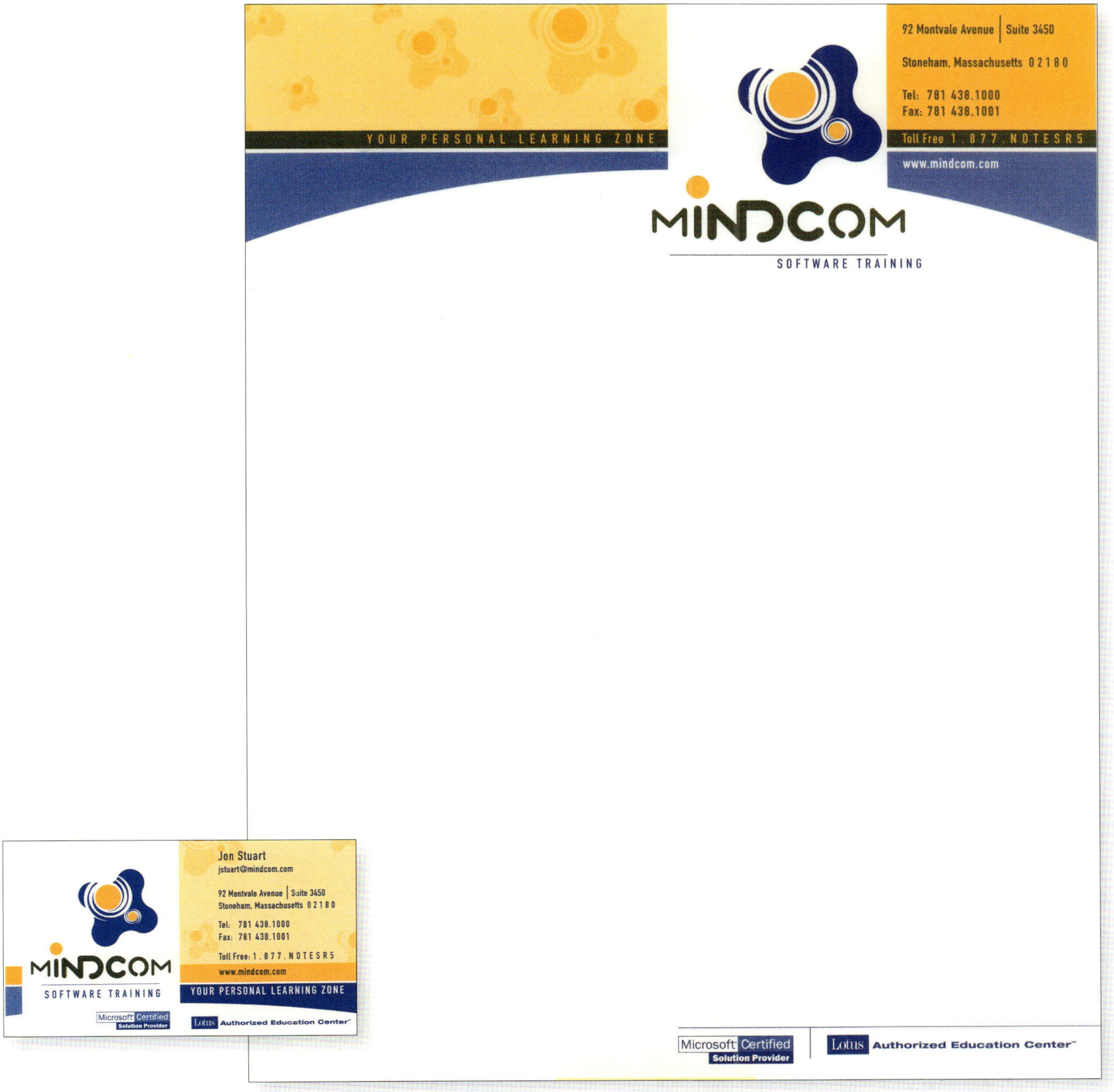

YOUR PERSONAL LEARNING ZONE

92 Montvale Avenue | Suite 3450
Stoneham, Massachusetts 02180
Tel: 781 438.1000
Fax: 781 438.1001
Toll Free 1.877.NOTESR5
www.mindcom.com

MINDCOM
SOFTWARE TRAINING

Microsoft Certified Solution Provider
Lotus Authorized Education Center

Jon Stuart
jstuart@mindcom.com
92 Montvale Avenue | Suite 3450
Stoneham, Massachusetts 02180
Tel: 781 438.1000
Fax: 781 438.1001
Toll Free: 1.877.NOTESR5
www.mindcom.com
YOUR PERSONAL LEARNING ZONE
MINDCOM
SOFTWARE TRAINING
Microsoft Certified Solution Provider
Lotus Authorized Education Center

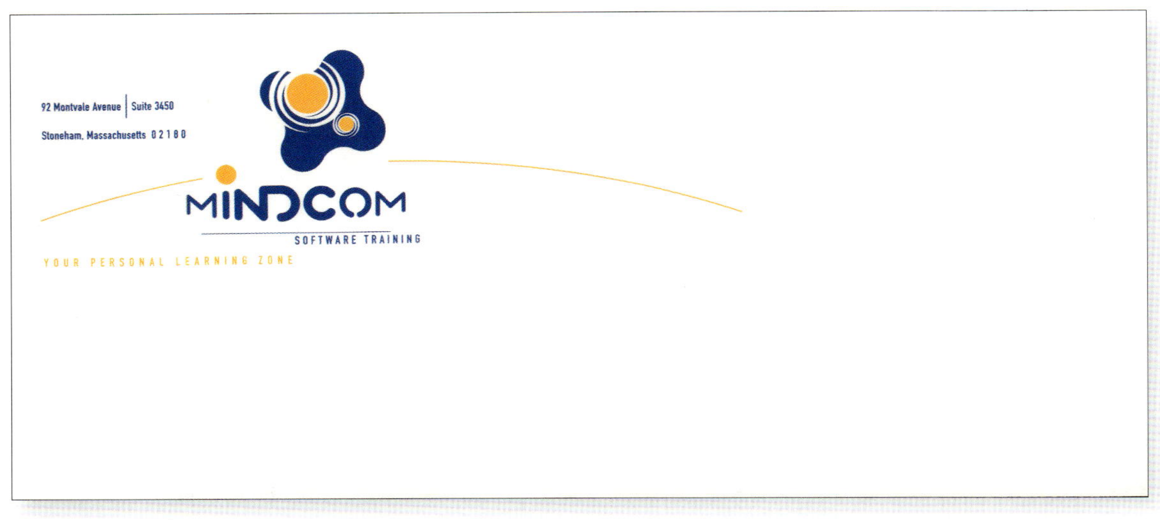

DESIGN FIRM
Interrobang Design Collaborative, Inc.
Richmond, (VT) USA
PROJECT
Mindcom Stationery
CREATIVE DIRECTOR, DESIGNER
Mark D. Sylvester

DESIGN FIRM
Market Street Marketing
Redding, (CA) USA
PROJECT
Avalon Medical Rejuvenation
PRINCIPAL
Kathleen Downs

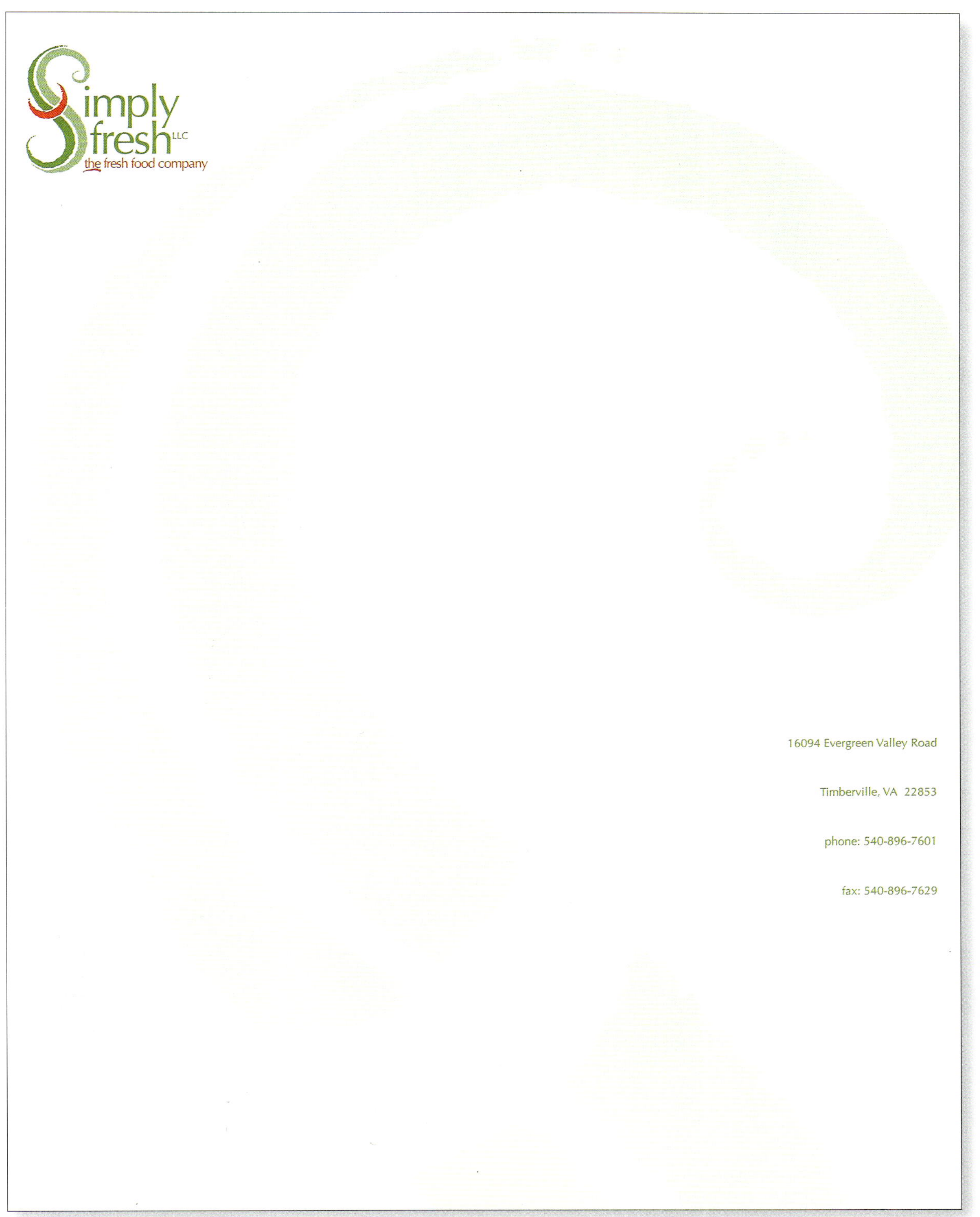

DESIGN FIRM
Mind's Eye Creative
New Albany, (IN) USA
CLIENT
Simply Fresh
DESIGNER
Stephen Brown

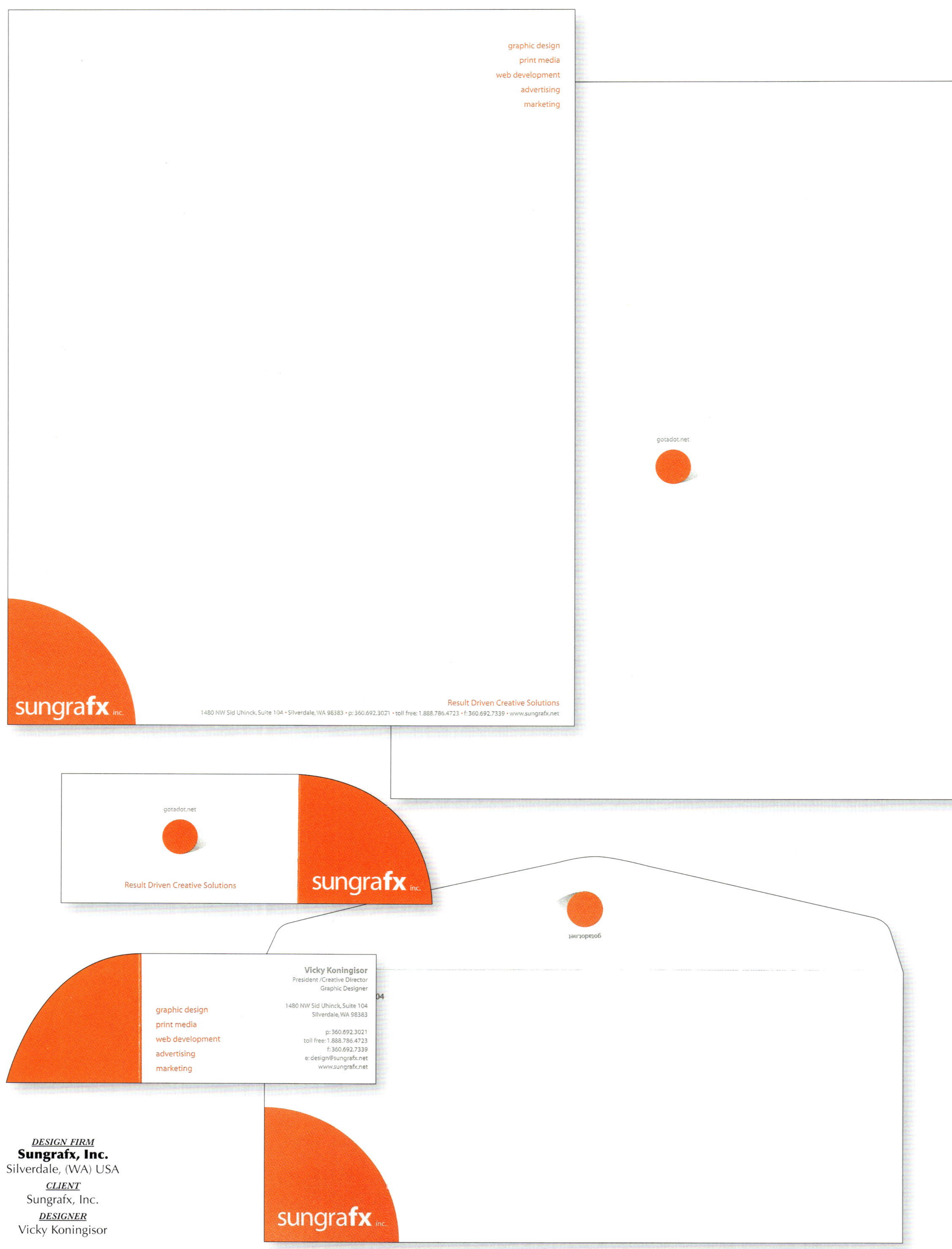

DESIGN FIRM
Sungrafx, Inc.
Silverdale, (WA) USA

CLIENT
Sungrafx, Inc.

DESIGNER
Vicky Koningisor

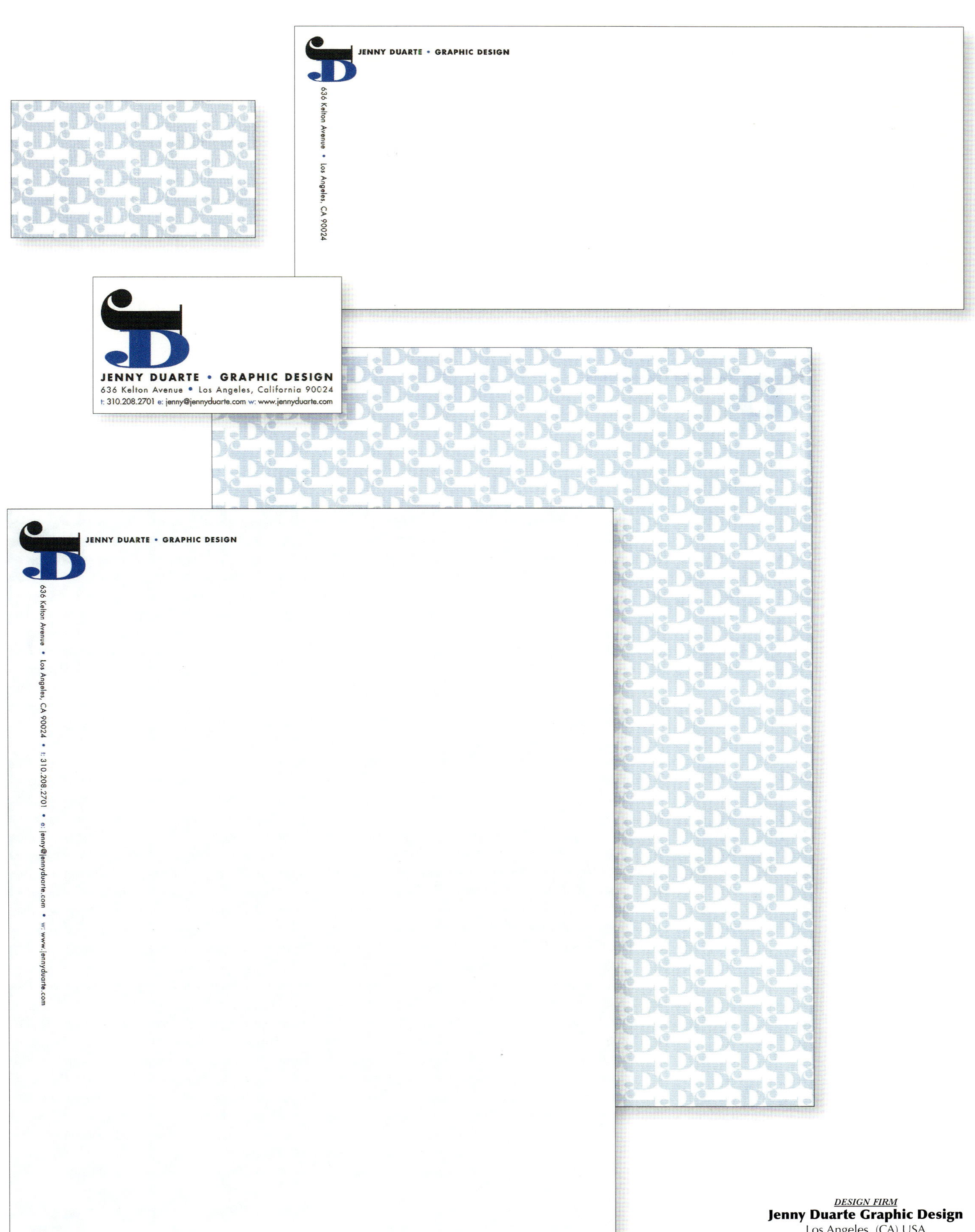

DESIGN FIRM
Jenny Duarte Graphic Design
Los Angeles, (CA) USA
PROJECT
Jenny Duarte Graphic Design

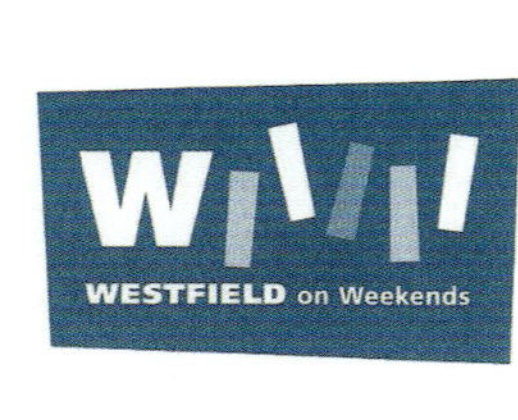

Westfield on Weekends P.O. Box 154, Westfield, MA 01036 www.westfieldonweekends.org Phone 41

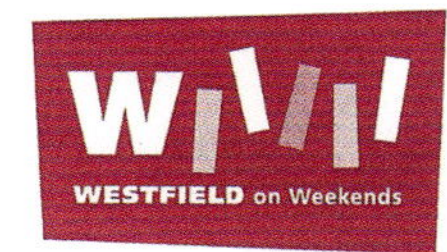

P.O. Box 154, Westfield, MA 01086
phone 413.562.2277
www.westfieldonweekends.org

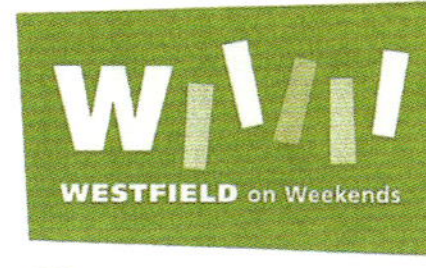

P.O. Box 154, Westfield, MA 01086

DESIGN FIRM
TSM Design
Springfield, (MA) USA
PROJECT
Westfield on Weekends
DESIGNER
Noël Szado

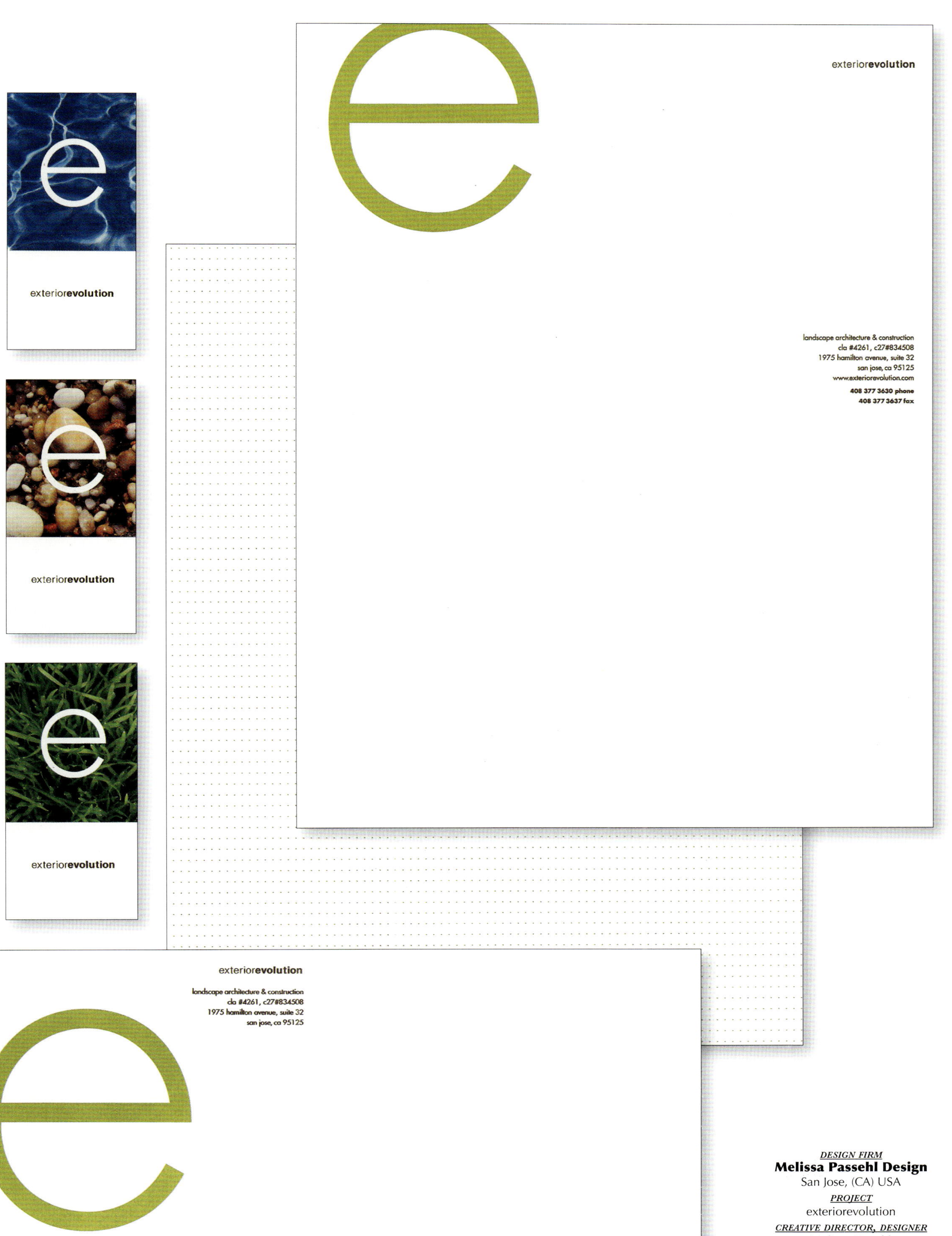

DESIGN FIRM
Melissa Passehl Design
San Jose, (CA) USA
PROJECT
exteriorevolution
CREATIVE DIRECTOR, DESIGNER
Melissa Passehl

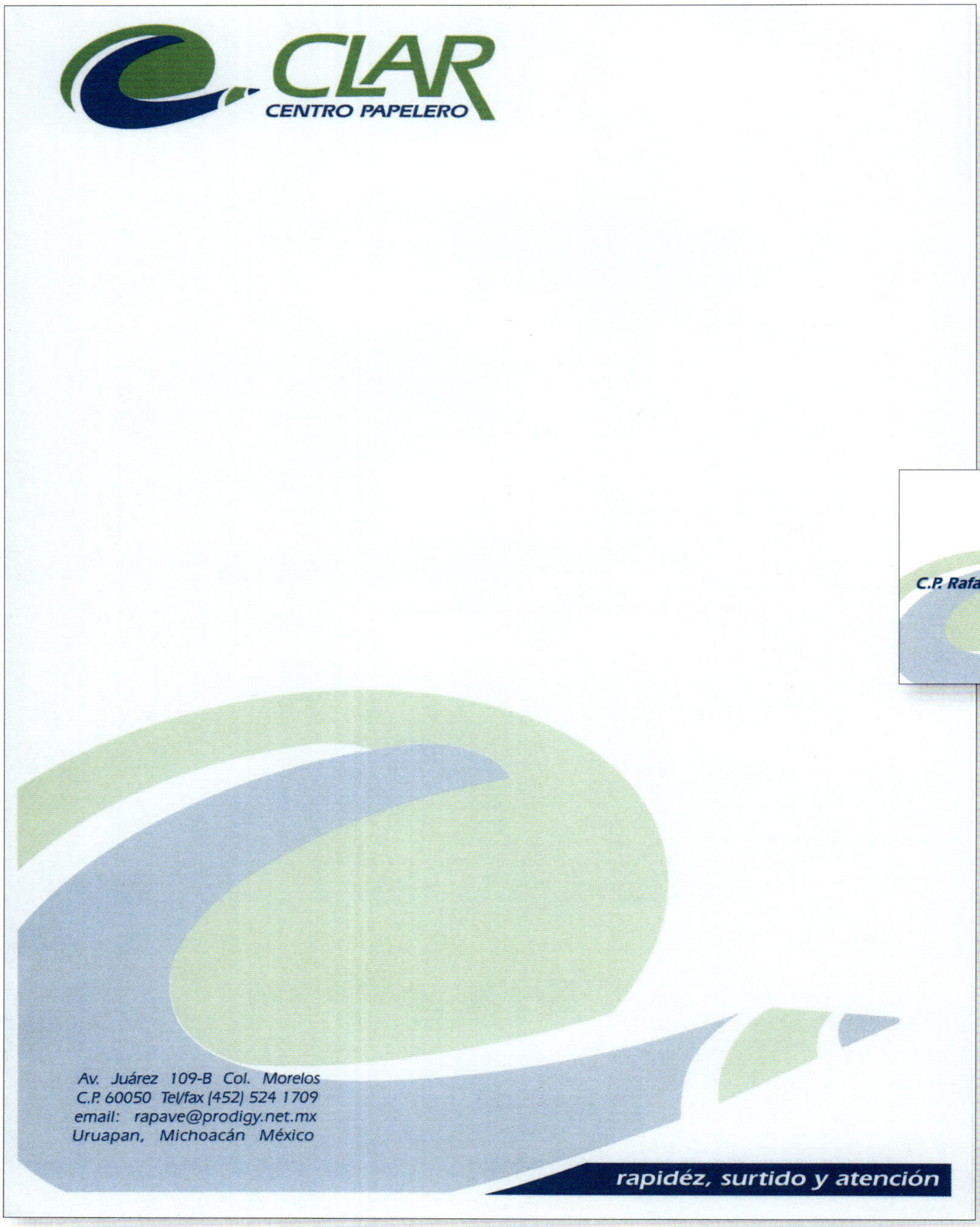

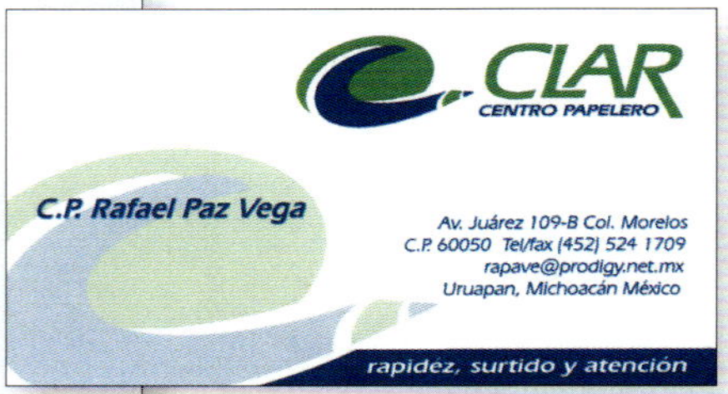

CLAR
CENTRO PAPELERO

Av. Juárez 109-B Col. Morelos
C.P. 60050 Tel/fax (452) 524 1709
email: rapave@prodigy.net.mx
Uruapan, Michoacán México

rapidéz, surtido y atención

CLAR
CENTRO PAPELERO

C.P. Rafael Paz Vega

Av. Juárez 109-B Col. Morelos
C.P. 60050 Tel/fax (452) 524 1709
rapave@prodigy.net.mx
Uruapan, Michoacán México

rapidéz, surtido y atención

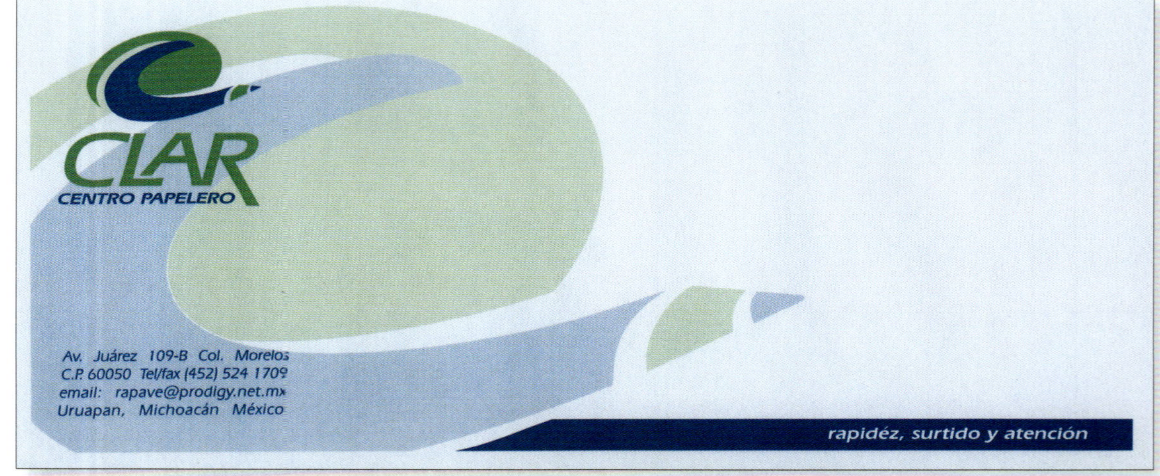

DESIGN FIRM
Kenneth Diseño
Uruapan, Mexico
PROJECT
CLAR
DESIGNERS
Kenneth Treviño,
Minerva Galván

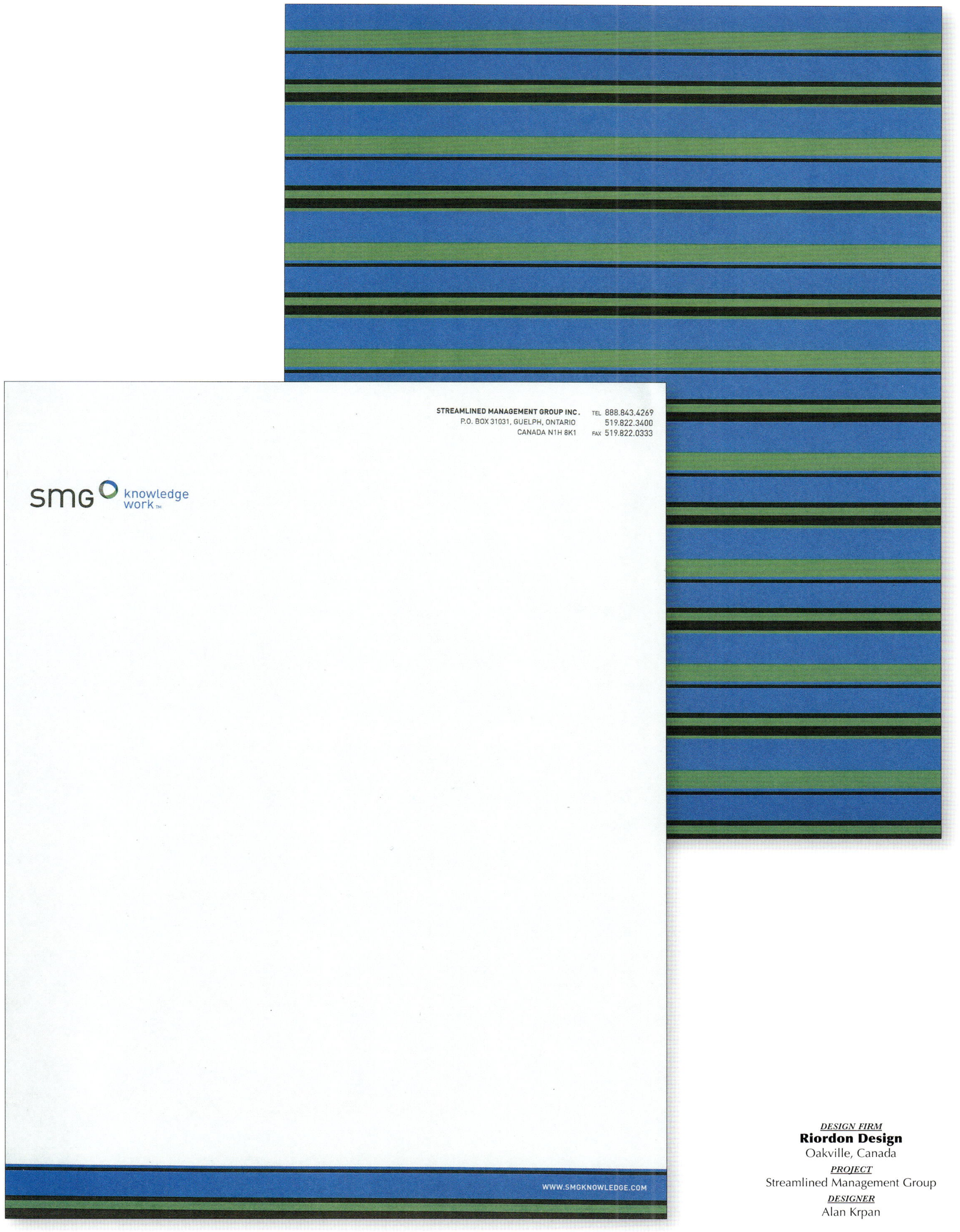

DESIGN FIRM
Riordon Design
Oakville, Canada
PROJECT
Streamlined Management Group
DESIGNER
Alan Krpan

DESIGN FIRM
Graphic Advance
Palisades Park, (NJ) USA
PROJECT
Apart From the Crowd
DESIGNER
Aviad Stark

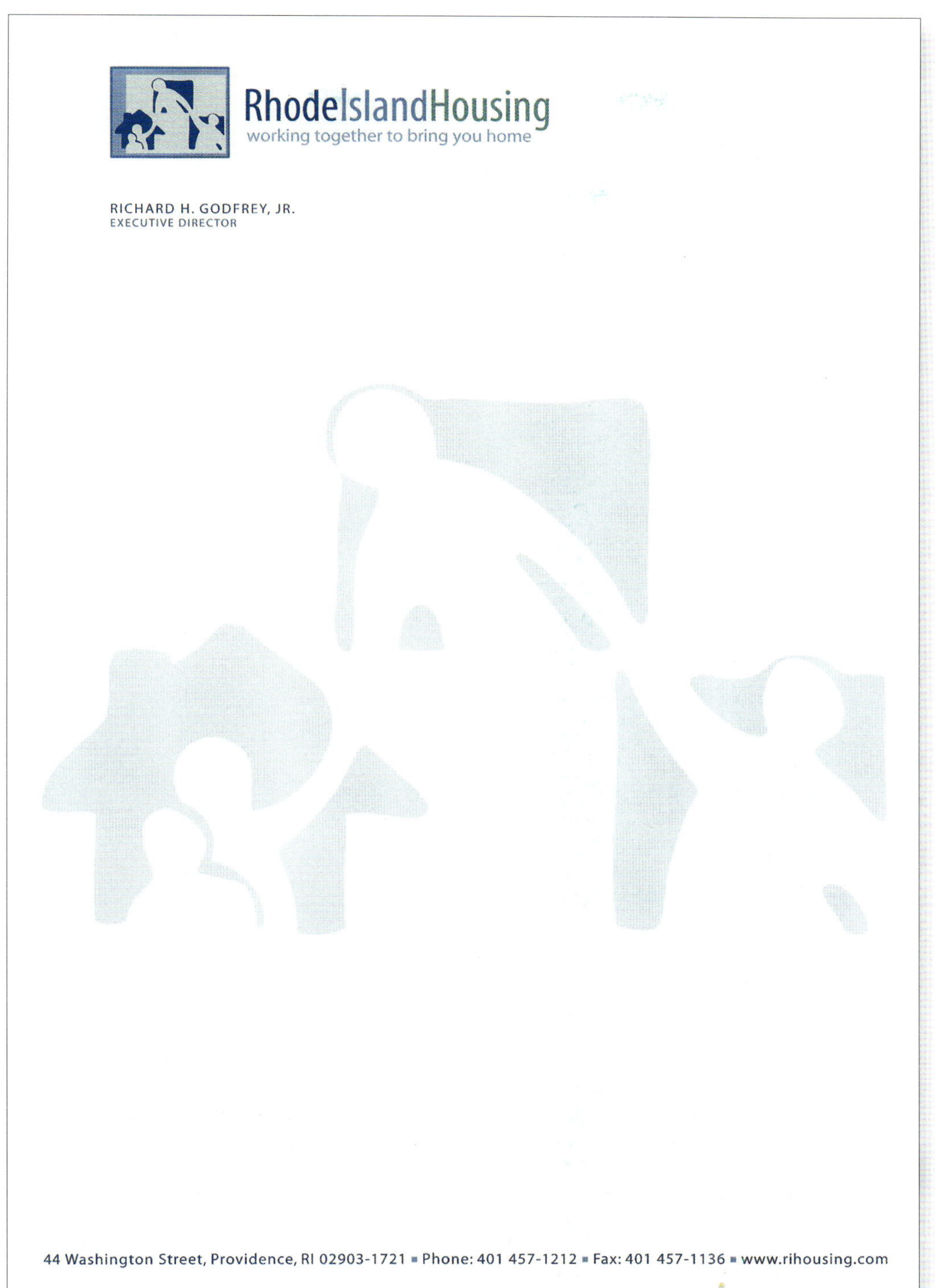

DESIGN FIRM
Im-aj Communications & Design, Inc.
West Kingston, (RI) USA
CLIENT
Rhode Island Housing
CREATIVE DIRECTOR
Jami Ouellette
ART DIRECTOR
Leslie Emert
SENIOR DESIGNERS
Amy Marie Madina,
Katie Wetherby

DESIGN FIRM
Red Circle Agency
Minneapolis, (MN) USA
PROJECT
Red Circle Agency Letterhead
DESIGNER
David Maloney

red·circle
agency

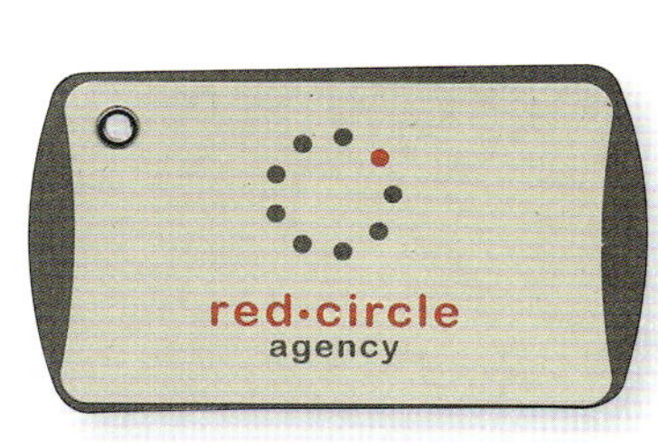
red·circle
agency

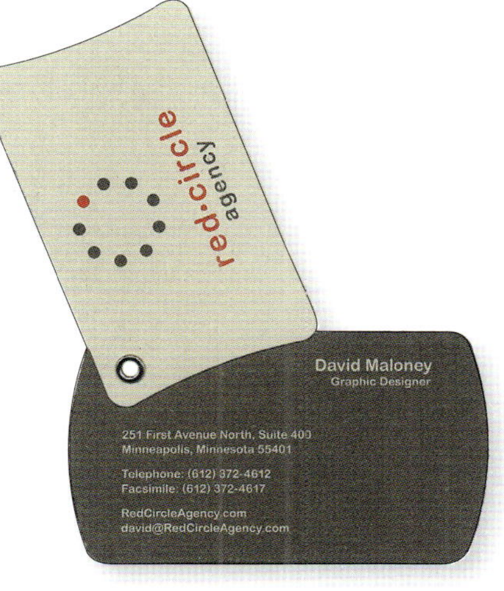
red·circle
agency
David Maloney
Graphic Designer
251 First Avenue North, Suite 400
Minneapolis, Minnesota 55401
Telephone: (612) 372-4612
Facsimile: (612) 372-4617
RedCircleAgency.com
david@RedCircleAgency.com

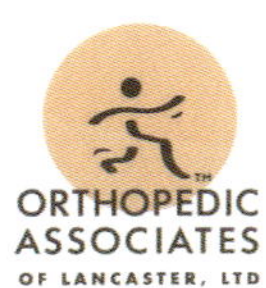

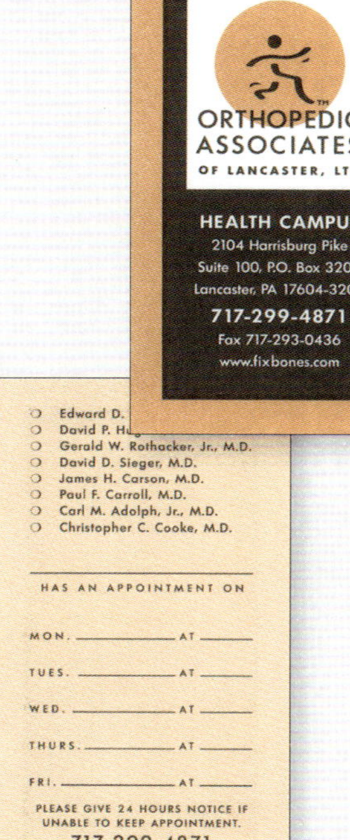

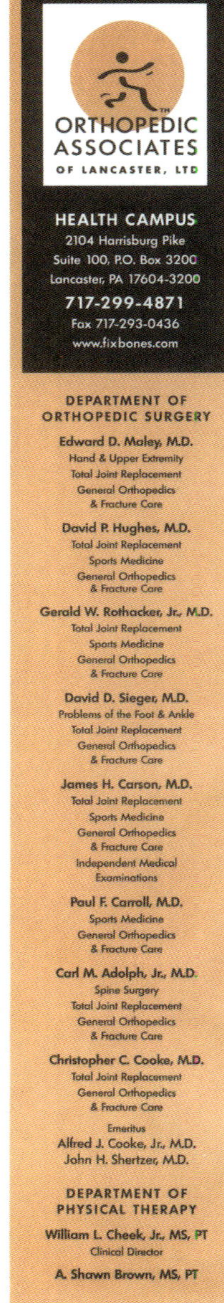

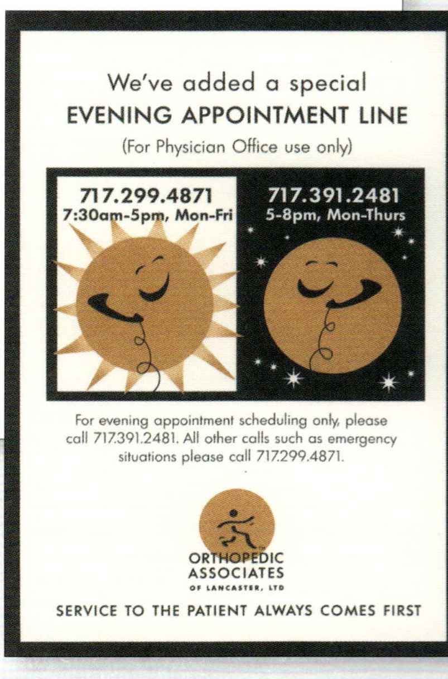

DESIGN FIRM
Dean Design/ Marketing Group, Inc.
Lancaster, (PA) USA

PROJECT
Orthopedic Associates of Lancaster

SENIOR DESIGNER
Lori Hess

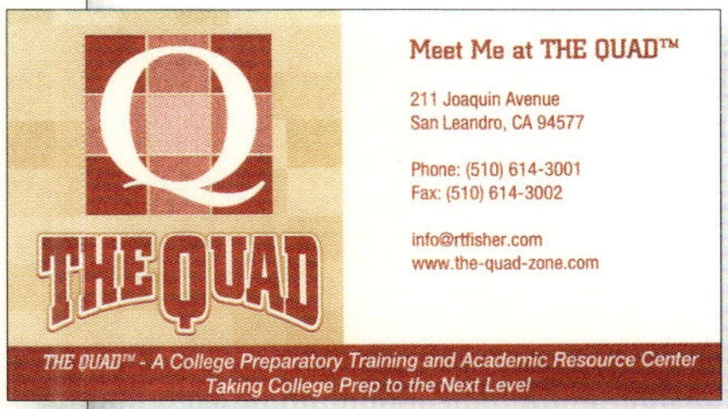

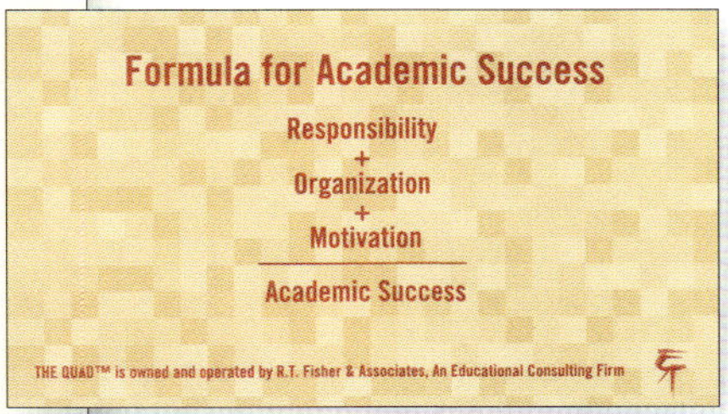

THE QUAD

211 Joaquin Avenue • San Leandro, CA 94577 • Phone: (510) 614-3001 • Fax: (510) 614-3002

THE QUAD™ - A College Preparatory Training and Academic Resource Center
Taking College Prep to the Next Level

THE QUAD

Meet Me at THE QUAD™

211 Joaquin Avenue
San Leandro, CA 94577

Phone: (510) 614-3001
Fax: (510) 614-3002

info@rtfisher.com
www.the-quad-zone.com

THE QUAD™ - A College Preparatory Training and Academic Resource Center
Taking College Prep to the Next Level

Formula for Academic Success

Responsibility
+
Organization
+
Motivation

Academic Success

THE QUAD™ is owned and operated by R.T. Fisher & Associates, An Educational Consulting Firm

DESIGN FIRM
Ontarget Marketing
Merced, (CA) USA
CLIENT
The Quad
ART DIRECTOR
Julie Rivard
DESIGNER
Jesse Bloodworth

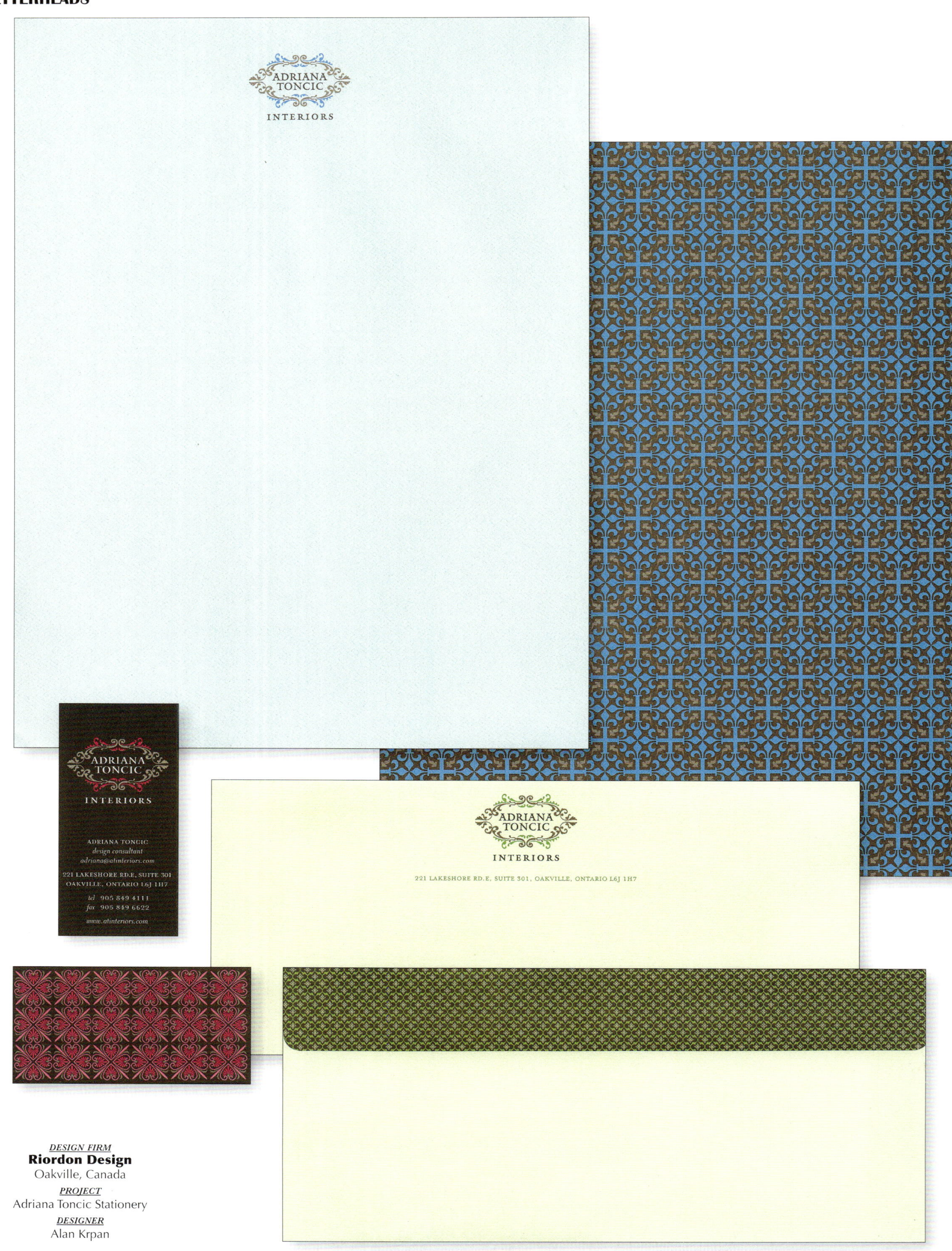

DESIGN FIRM
Riordon Design
Oakville, Canada
PROJECT
Adriana Toncic Stationery
DESIGNER
Alan Krpan

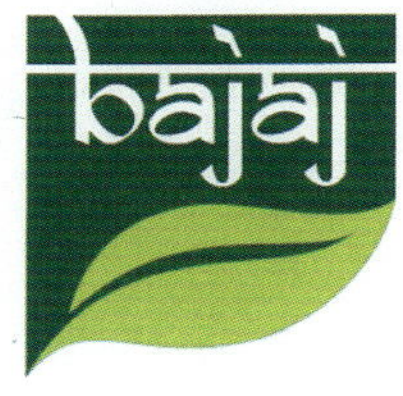

باجاج هربالزش.م.ح.

BAJAJ HERBALS FZE

P.O. Box: 8383, SAIF Zone, Sharjah, U.A.E.,
Tel: +971 6 5574063, Fax: +971 6 5574064, E mail: bajajfze@eim.ae, www.bajajgroups.com

India Office: 444, Ashwamegh Estate, Opp. M. N. Desai Petrol Pump, Changodar-Bawla Highway. Ahmedabad-382210
Tel: +91 2717 250184/250185/251822, Fax: +91 2717 251821/251020

DESIGN FIRM
Inca Tanvir Advertising LLC
Sharjah, UAE
PROJECT
Bajaj Herbals Fze
ART DIRECTOR
Suresh Pawar

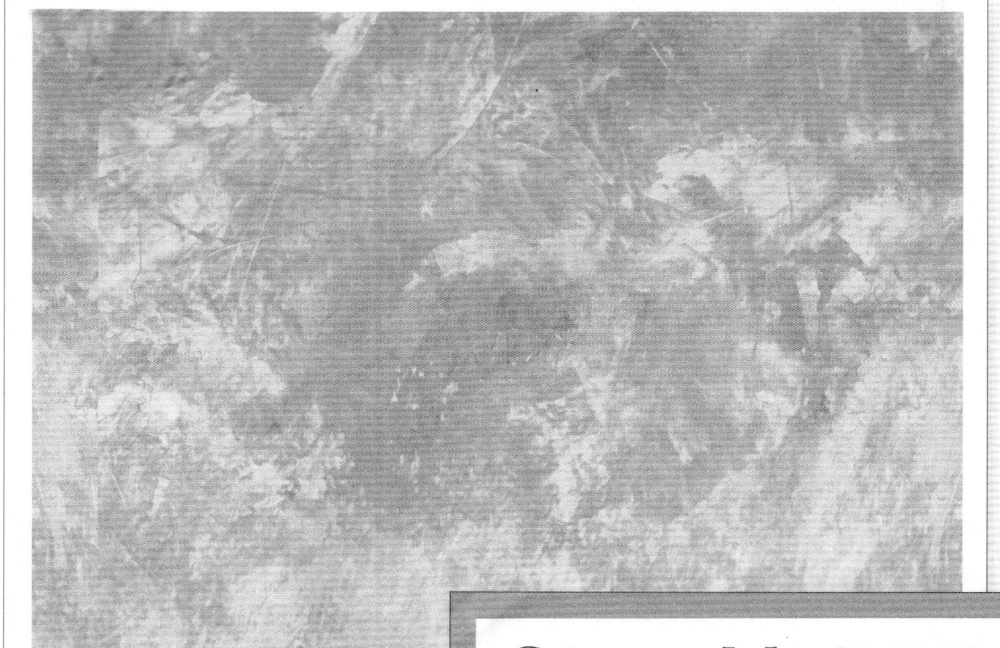

COLIN MAGNUSON CREATIVE

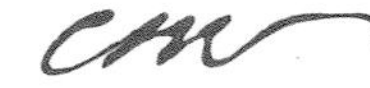

Tel . 253.964.5338 Fax . 253.964.5346 . 10320 91st Street Court Southwest . Tacoma, Washington 98498 . www.cmcreative.com

DESIGN FIRM
Colin Magnuson Creative
Lakewood, (WA) USA

CLIENT
Colin Magnuson Creative

DESIGNER
Colin Magnuson

DATE. ______________________________

CLIENT. ______________________________

PROJECT DESCRIPTION. ______________________________

____

PROGRAM USED. ______________________________

CONTENTS. ______________________________

SPECIFIED INK. ______________________________

PAPER STOCK. ______________________________

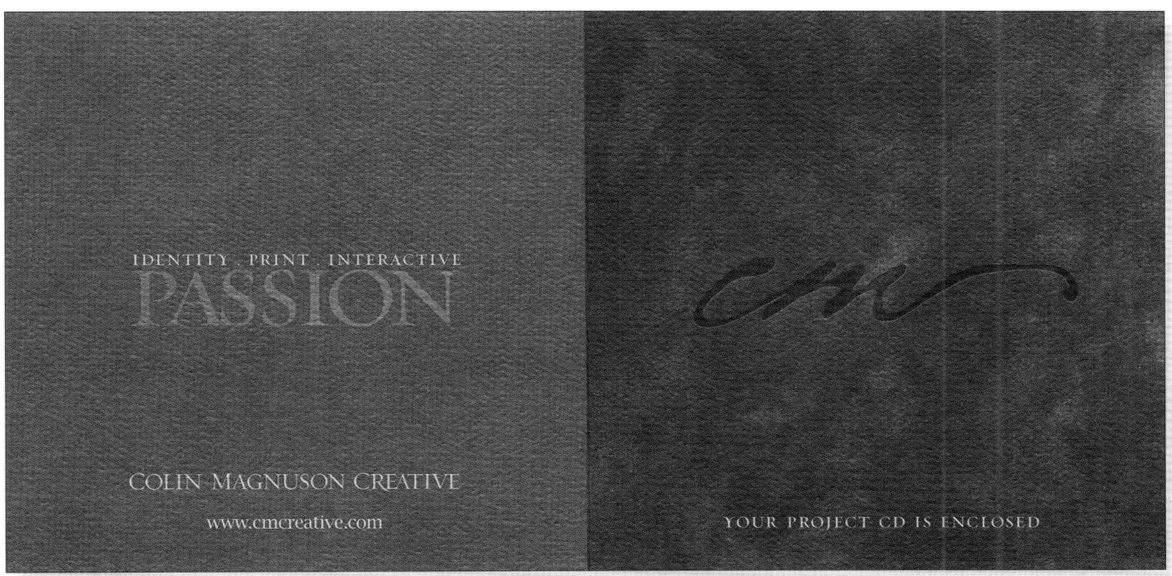

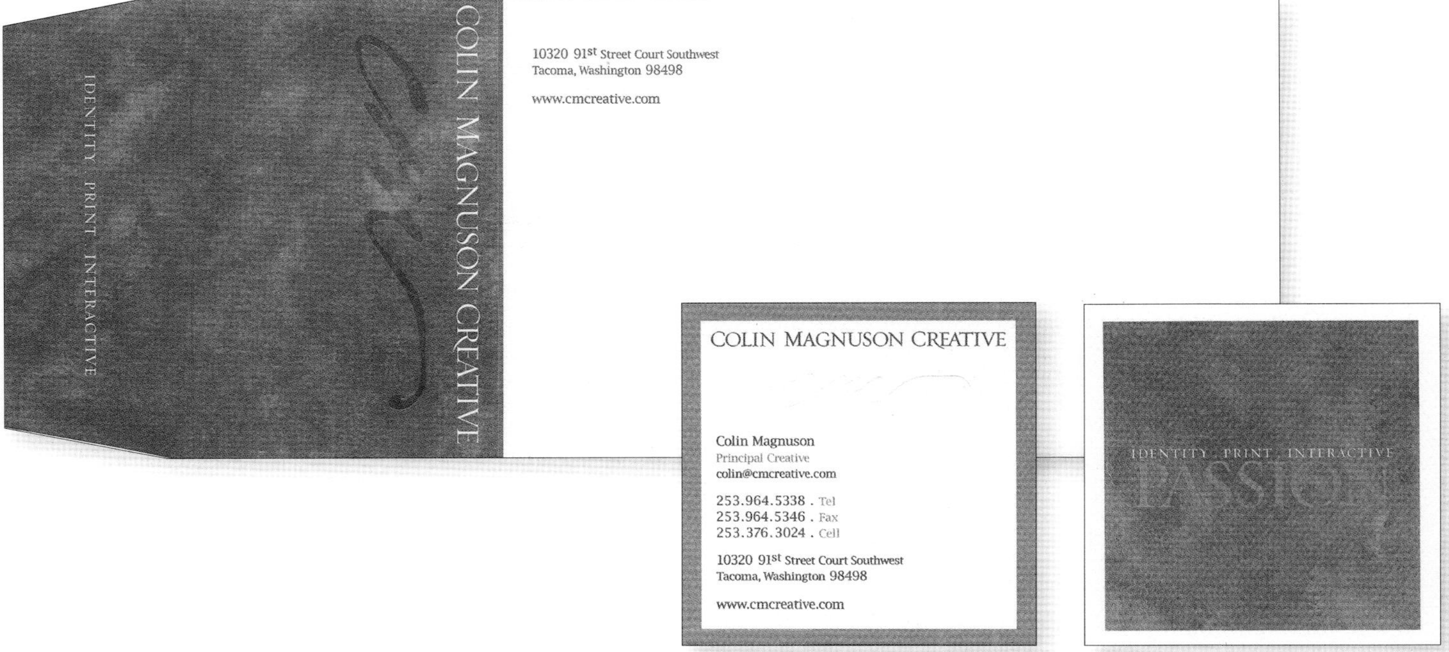

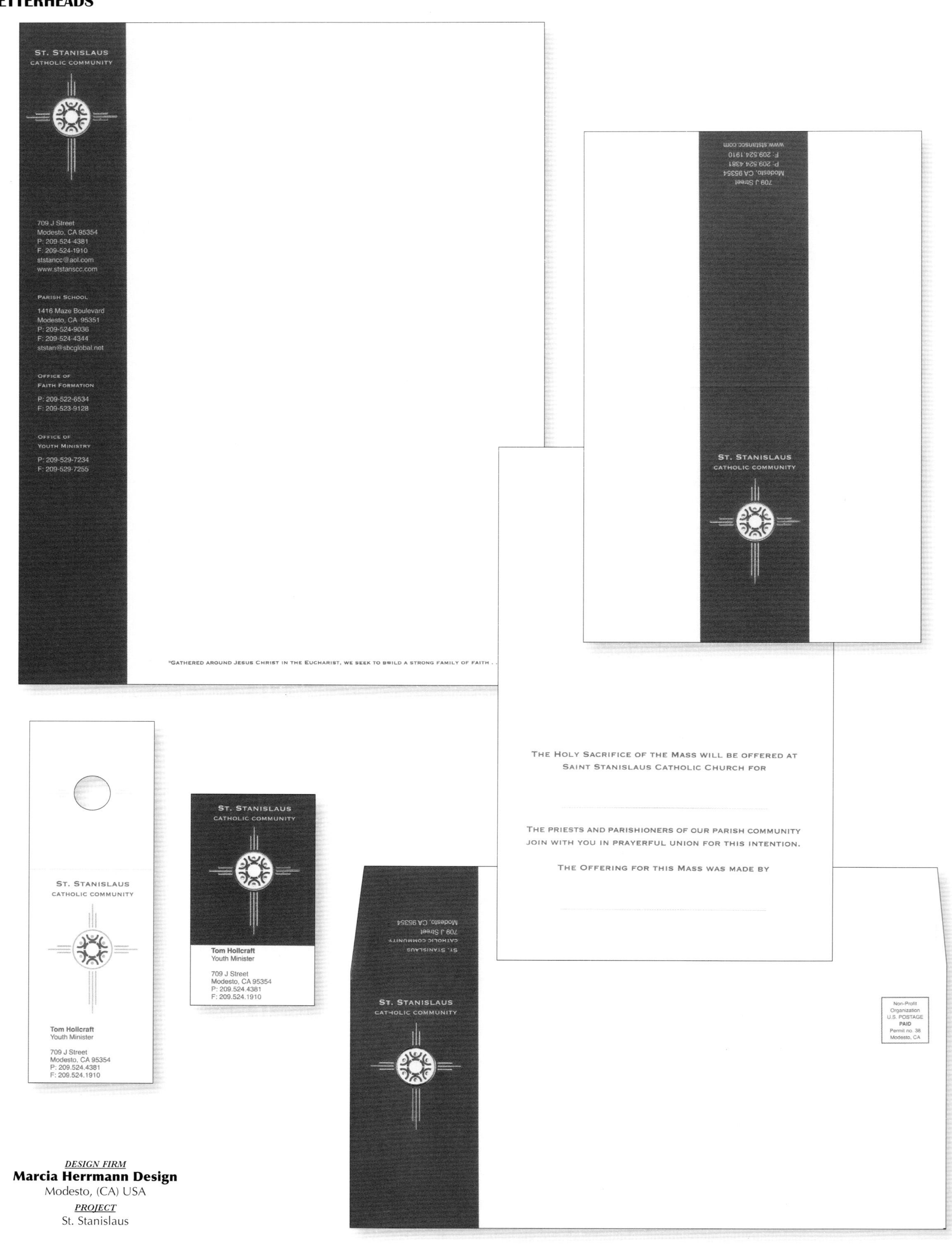

DESIGN FIRM
Marcia Herrmann Design
Modesto, (CA) USA
PROJECT
St. Stanislaus

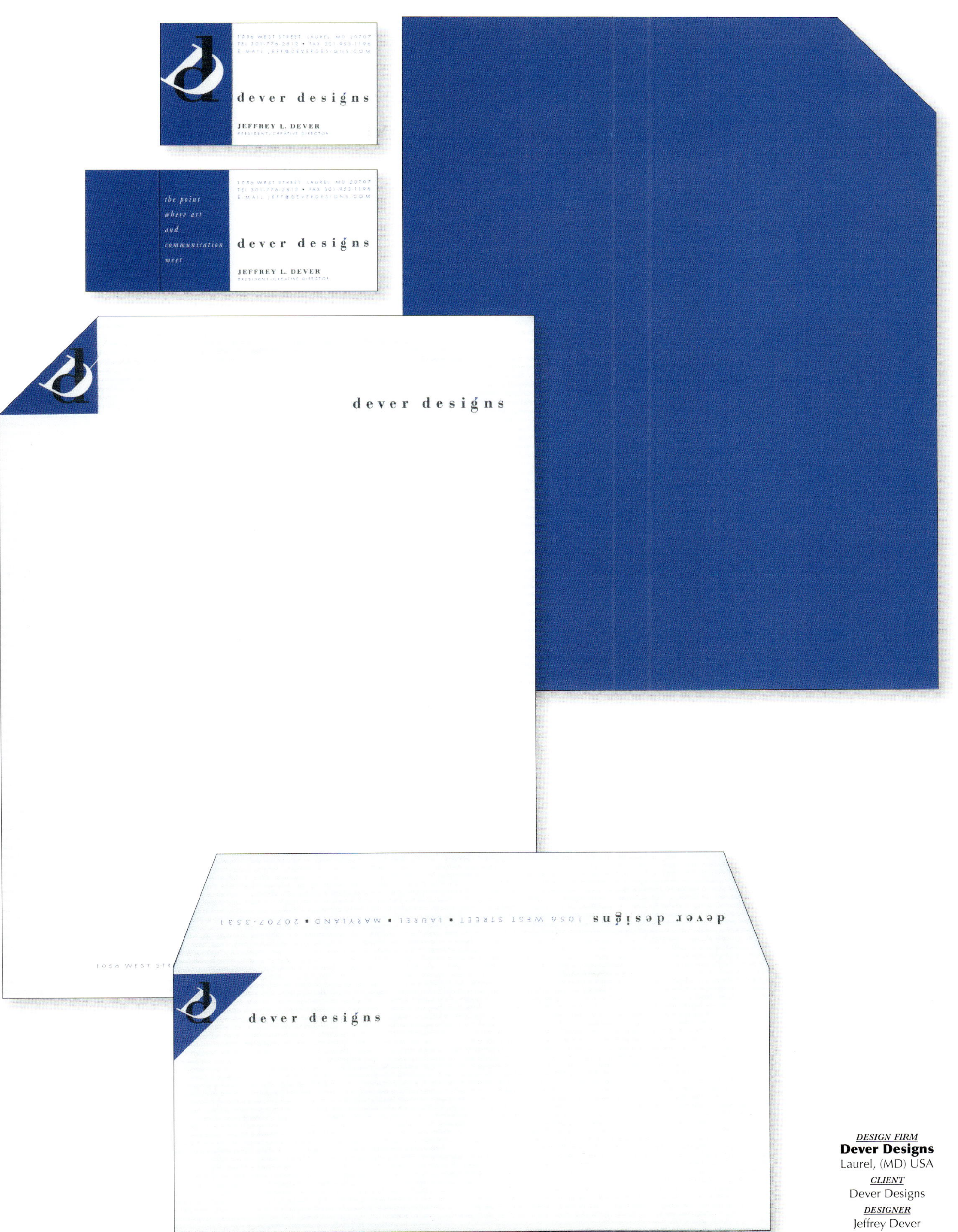

DESIGN FIRM
Dever Designs
Laurel, (MD) USA
CLIENT
Dever Designs
DESIGNER
Jeffrey Dever

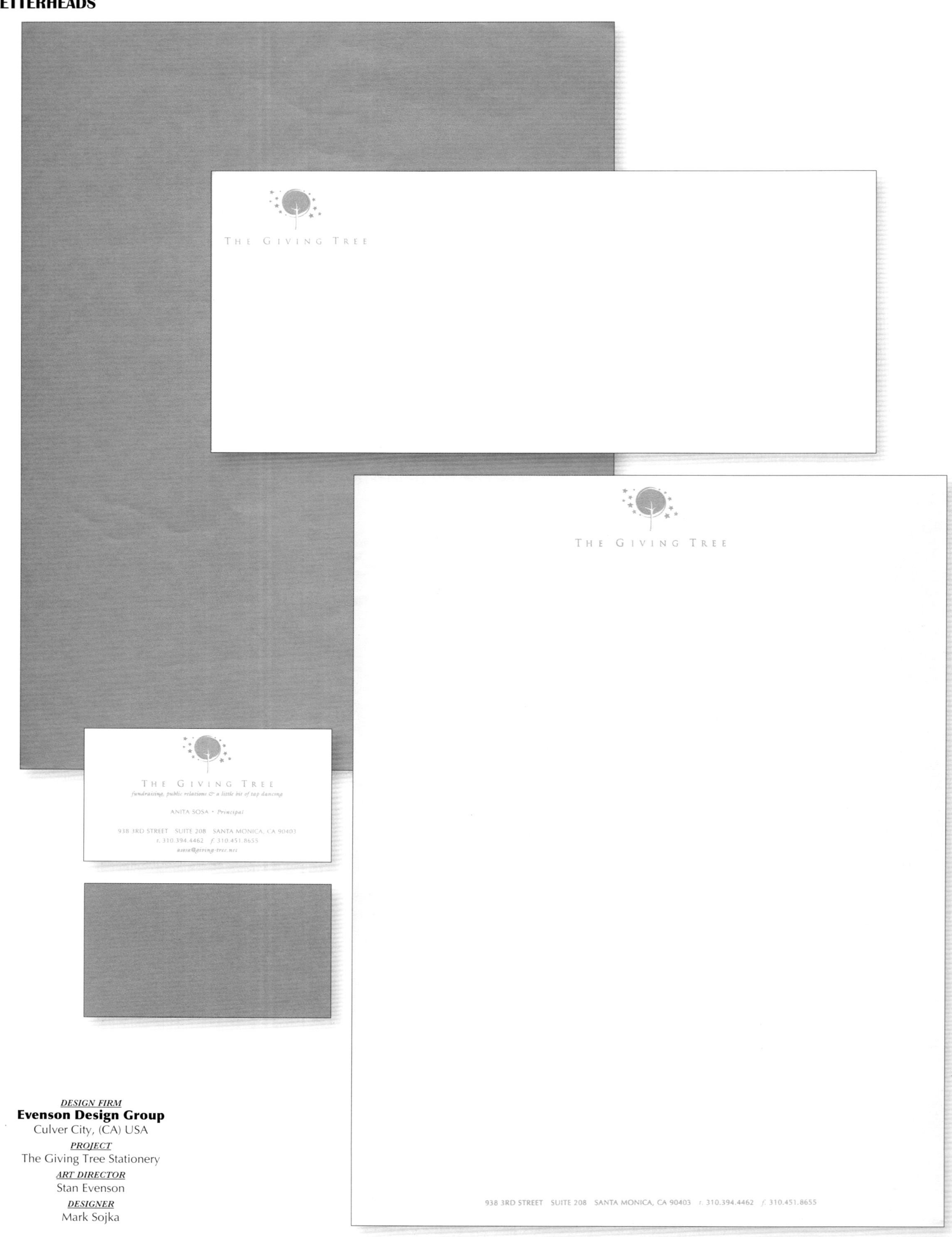

DESIGN FIRM
Evenson Design Group
Culver City, (CA) USA
PROJECT
The Giving Tree Stationery
ART DIRECTOR
Stan Evenson
DESIGNER
Mark Sojka

DESIGN FIRM
Market Street Marketing
Redding, (CA) USA
PROJECT
Ken Murray
PRINCIPAL
Kathleen Downs

P.O. BOX 1274
PONTE VEDRA BEACH • FL 32004
P: 904.273.4795 • F: 904.273.4899
www.womenspartnership.org
info@womenspartnership.org

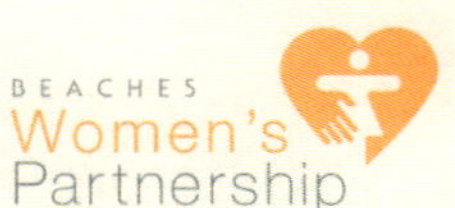

BOARD OF DIRECTORS
Wendy Roberts
President
Alice Stratton
Vice President & Secretary
Susan Tucker
Treasurer
Ginny Alexander
Janice Cobb
Rena Coughlin
Bea Goldsmith
Sharon Roberts Henderson, Esquire
Kristine King
Scott McGehee
Patricia L. Newell
Casimira (Cas) Pittman
Sharon Qualls
Muriel Sandiford
E. Dayan Sandler, M.D.

ADVISORY BOARD
Kathy A. Chinoy, Esquire
Laura A. D'Alisera
Theresa Greene Hazel
Wanda Lanier
Dawn Lockhart
Lorraine Meighan
Dr. LaWanda R
Sylvia Simmons

P.O. BOX 1274
PONTE VEDRA BEACH • FL 32004
P: 904.273.4795 • F: 904.273.4899
www.womenspartnership.org
info@womenspartnership.org
BEACHES
Women's
Partnership
Bea Goldsmith
BOARD OF DIRECTORS

P.O. BOX 1274
PONTE VEDRA BEACH • FL 32004
P: 904.273.4795 • F: 904.273.4899
BEACHES
Women's
Partnership

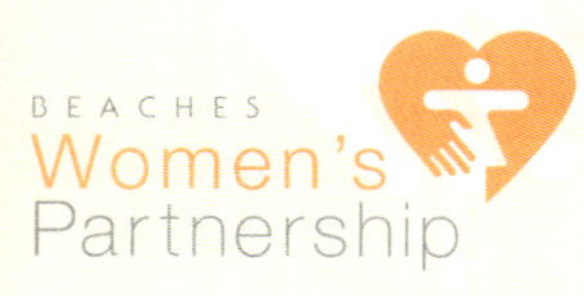

DESIGN FIRM
GOLD & Associates, Inc.
Ponte Vedra Beach, (FL) USA
PROJECT
Beaches Women's Partnership
CREATIVE DIRECTOR
Keith Gold
DESIGNER
Noone Savage

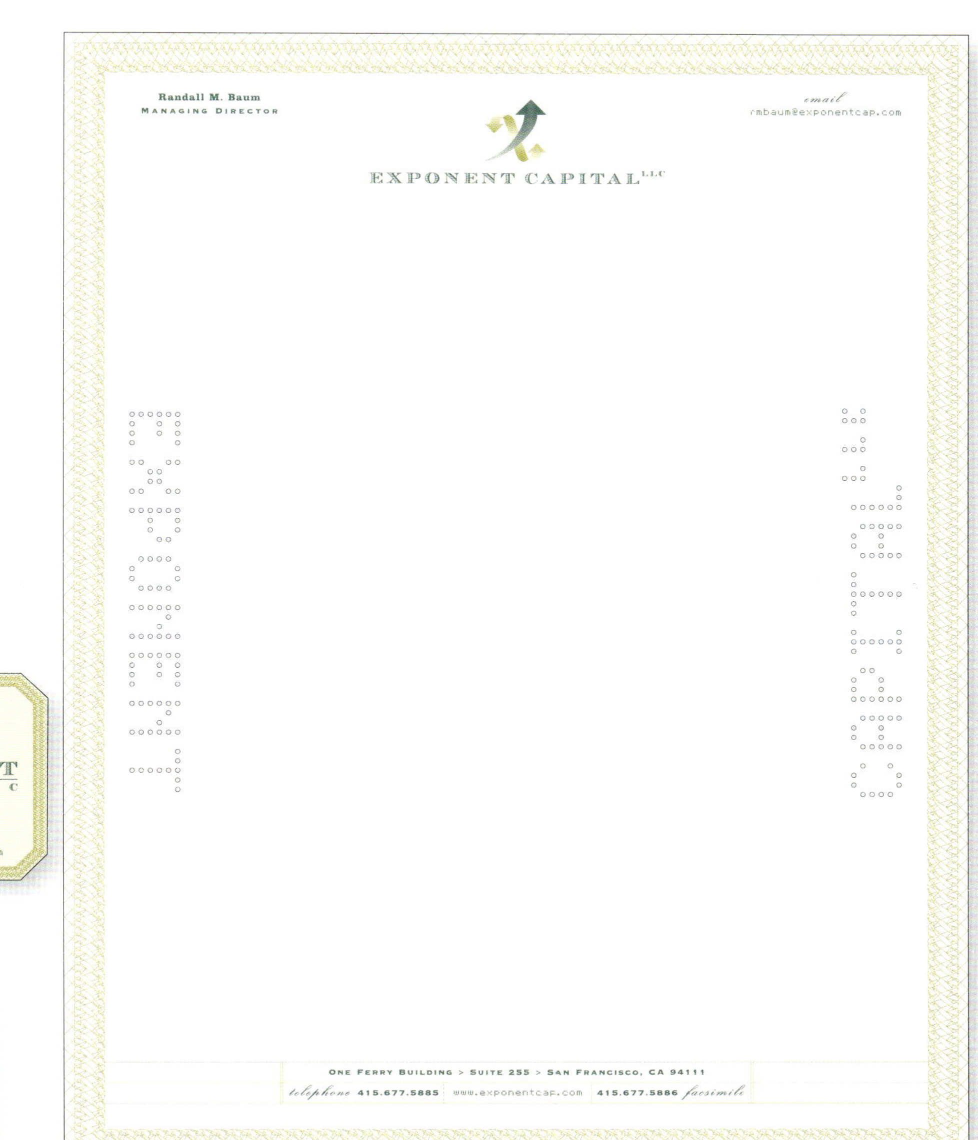

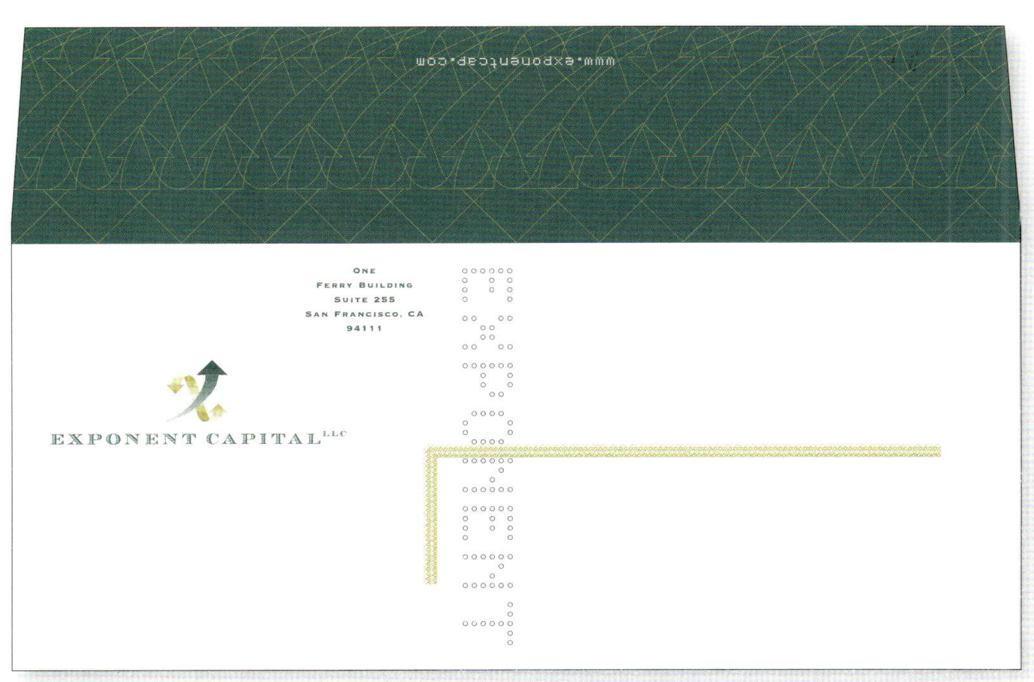

DESIGN FIRM
Gee + Chung Design
San Francisco, (CA) USA
PROJECT
Exponent Capital, LLC
ART DIRECTOR, DESIGNER, ILLUSTRATOR
Earl Gee

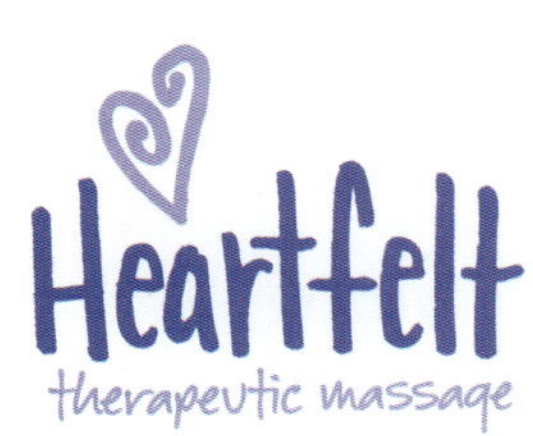

3939 E. ARAPAHOE RD.
SUITE #115
CENTENNIAL, CO 80122

303.319.3541

LESLIE@HEARTFELTMASSAGEDENVER.COM
WWW.HEARTFELTMASSAGEDENVER.COM

Leslie A. Pearce
CERTIFIED MASSAGE THERAPIST

3939 E. ARAPAHOE RD.
SUITE #115
CENTENNIAL, CO 80122

303.319.3541

Heartfelt
therapeutic massage

LESLIE@HEARTFELTMASSAGEDENVER.COM
WWW.HEARTFELTMASSAGEDENVER.COM

Heartfelt
STRONG AND SINCERE EMOTION

Therapeutic
WORK DONE TO RESTORE OR MAINTAIN ONE'S HEALTH

Massage
TREATMENT THAT INVOLVES RUBBING OR KNEADING THE MUSCLES FOR THERAPEUTIC PURPOSES

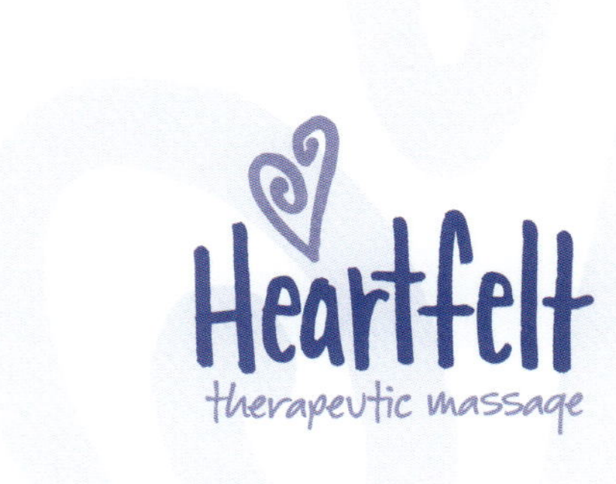

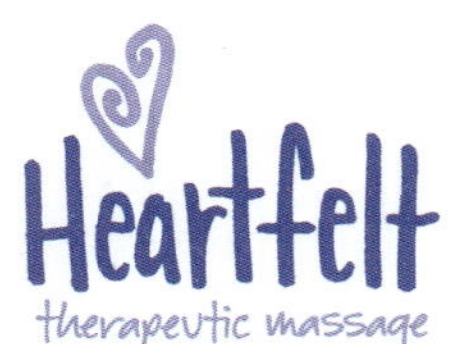

3939 E. ARAPAHOE RD.
SUITE #115
CENTENNIAL, CO 80122

303.319.3541

DESIGN FIRM
CATALYST creative, inc.
Denver, (CO) USA
PROJECT
Heartfelt
ART DIRECTOR, DESIGNER
Jeanna Pool

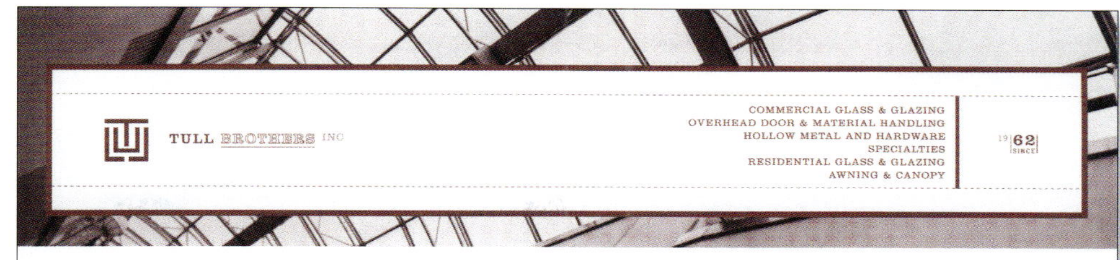

THE RUNG OF A LADDER WAS NEVER MEANT TO REST UPON, BUT ONLY TO HOLD A MAN'S FOOT LONG ENOUGH TO ENABLE HIM TO PUT THE OTHER SOMEWHAT HIGHER.

DESIGN FIRM
Gouthier Design: a brand collective
Fort Lauderdale, (FL) USA

CLIENT
Tull Brothers, Inc.

CREATIVE DIRECTOR
Jonathan Gouthier

DESIGNER
Kiley del Valle

PRINTER
Ritter's Printing

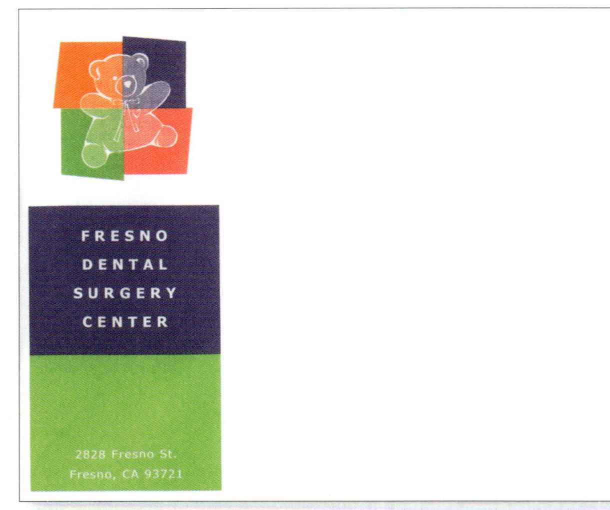

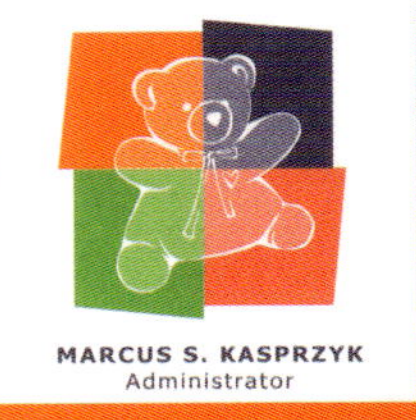

FRESNO DENTAL
SURGERY CENTER

2828 Fresno St.
Fresno, CA 93721
T 559.263.9648

MARCUS S. KASPRZYK
Administrator

marcus@fresnodentalsurgerycenter.com

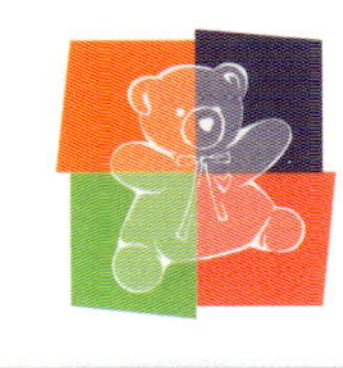

FRESNO
DENTAL
SURGERY
CENTER

2828 Fresno St.
Fresno, CA 93721
T 559.263.9648

DESIGN FIRM
Never Boring Design Associates
Modesto, (CA) USA
PROJECT
Fresno Dental Surgery Center
DESIGNER
Julie Orona

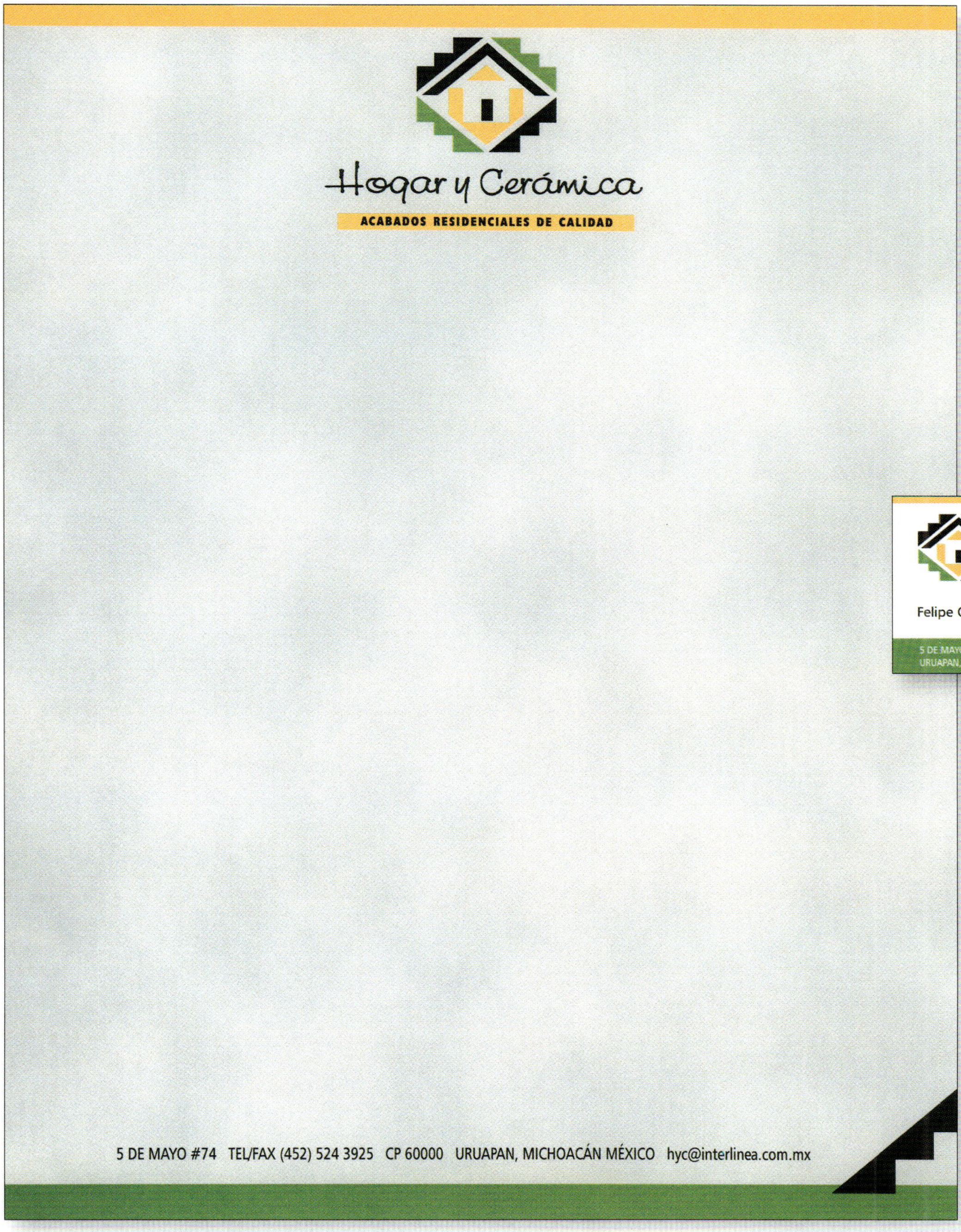

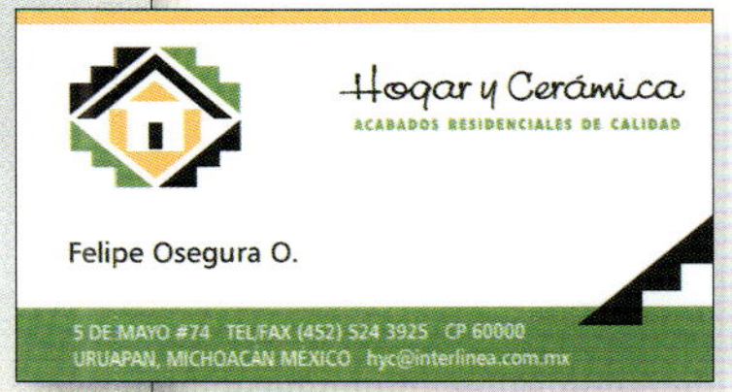

Hogar y Cerámica
ACABADOS RESIDENCIALES DE CALIDAD
5 DE MAYO #74 TEL/FAX (452) 524 3925 CP 60000 URUAPAN, MICHOACÁN MÉXICO hyc@interlinea.com.mx

Hogar y Cerámica
ACABADOS RESIDENCIALES DE CALIDAD
Felipe Osegura O.
5 DE MAYO #74 TEL/FAX (452) 524 3925 CP 60000
URUAPAN, MICHOACÁN MÉXICO hyc@interlinea.com.mx

DESIGN FIRM
Kenneth Diseño
Uruapan, Mexico
PROJECT
Hogar Y Cerámica
DESIGNERS
Kenneth Treviño,
Minerva Galván

Kevershan Testerman

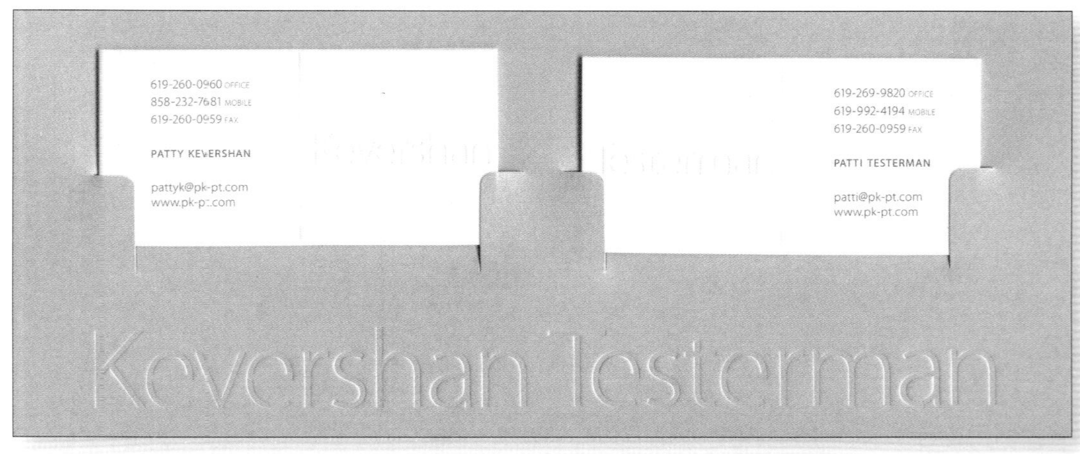

DESIGN FIRM
Kevershan Testerman
San Diego, (CA) USA
PROJECT
Kevershan Testerman Stationery
DESIGNERS
Patty Kevershan,
Patti Testerman

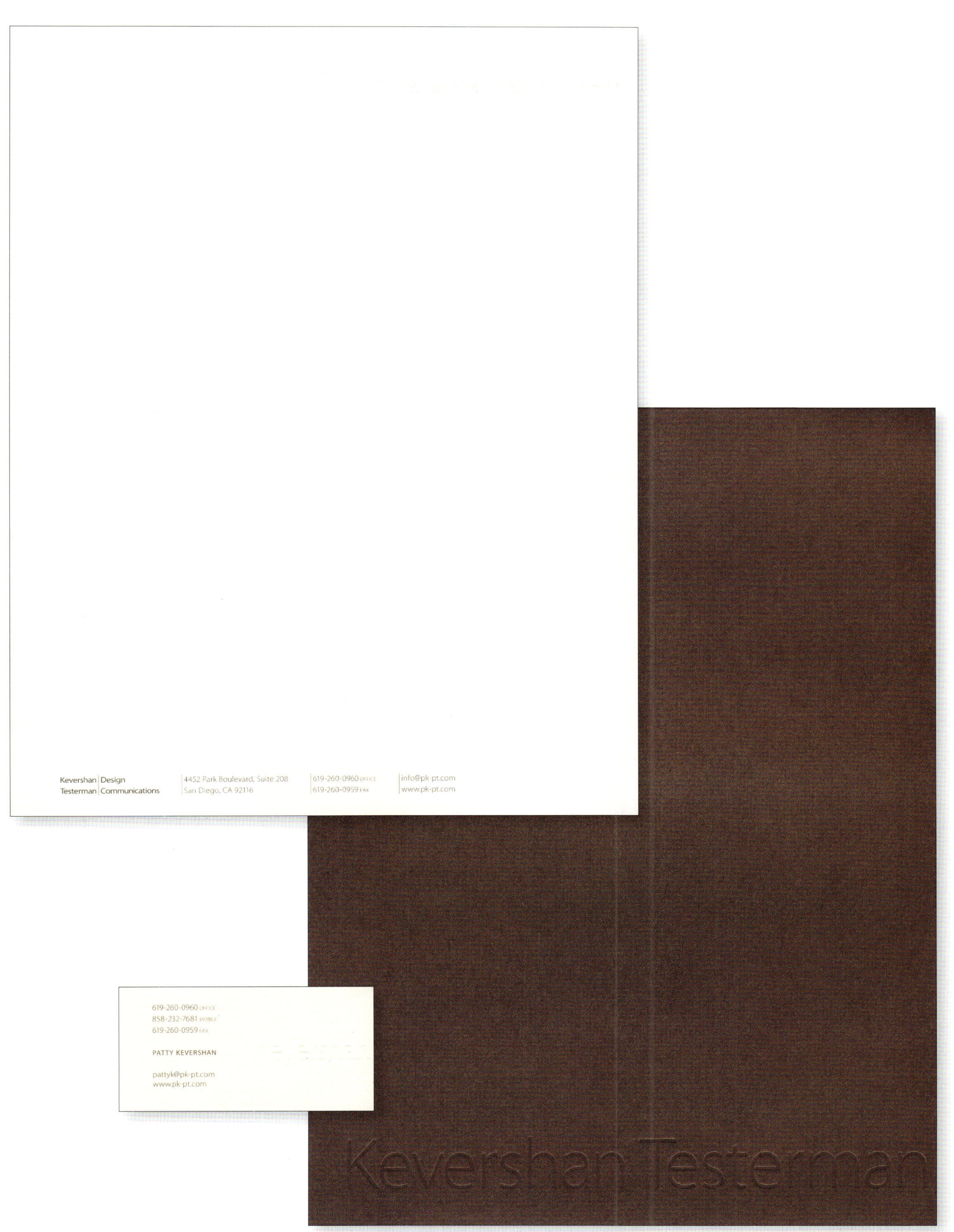
Kevershan | Design
Testerman | Communications
4452 Park Boulevard, Suite 208
San Diego, CA 92116
619-260-0960 OFFICE
619-260-0959 FAX
info@pk-pt.com
www.pk-pt.com
619-260-0960 OFFICE
858-232-7681 MOBILE
619-260-0959 FAX
PATTY KEVERSHAN
pattyk@pk-pt.com
www.pk-pt.com
Kevershan Testerman

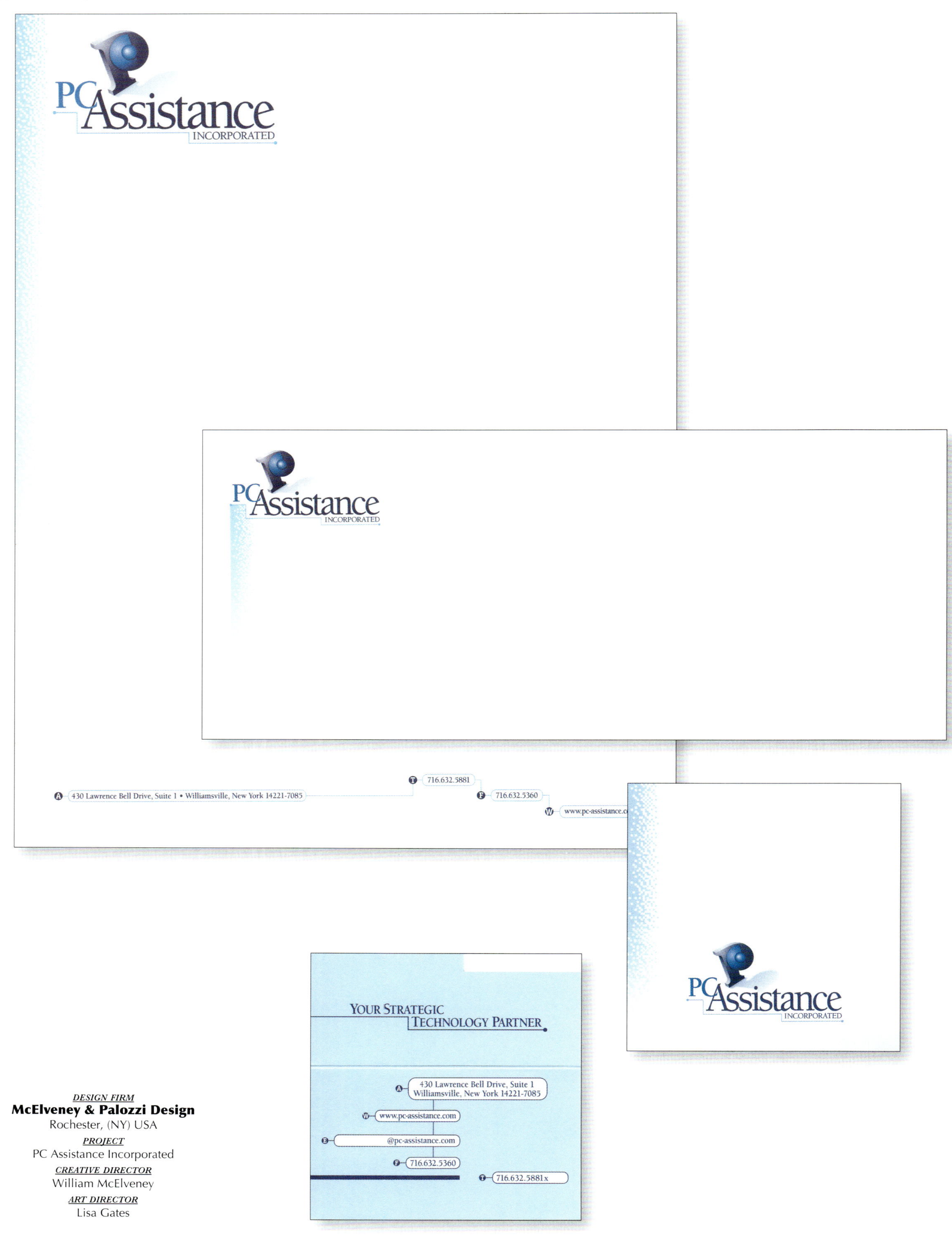

DESIGN FIRM
McElveney & Palozzi Design
Rochester, (NY) USA
PROJECT
PC Assistance Incorporated
CREATIVE DIRECTOR
William McElveney
ART DIRECTOR
Lisa Gates

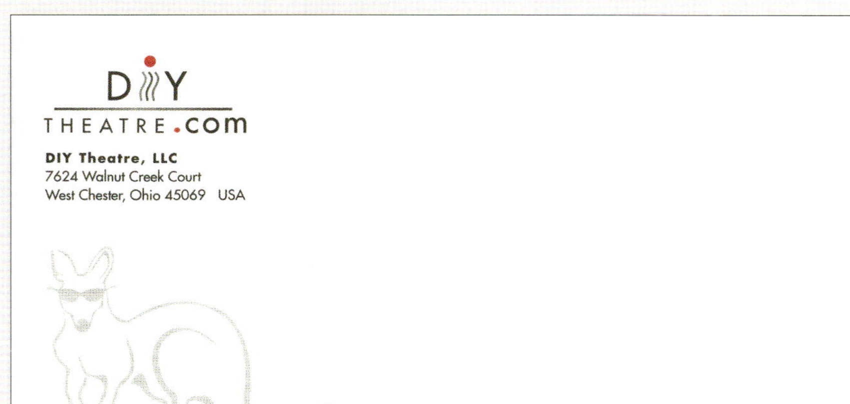

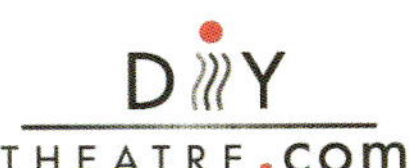

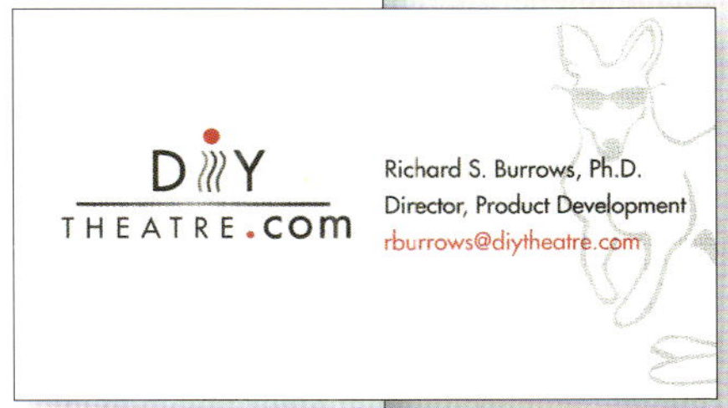

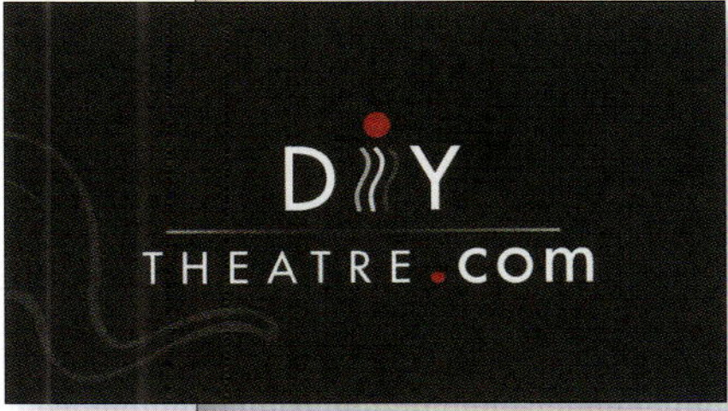

DESIGN FIRM
Five Visual Communication & Design
West Chester, (OH) USA

PROJECT
DIY Theatre.com

DESIGNER
Rondi Tschopp

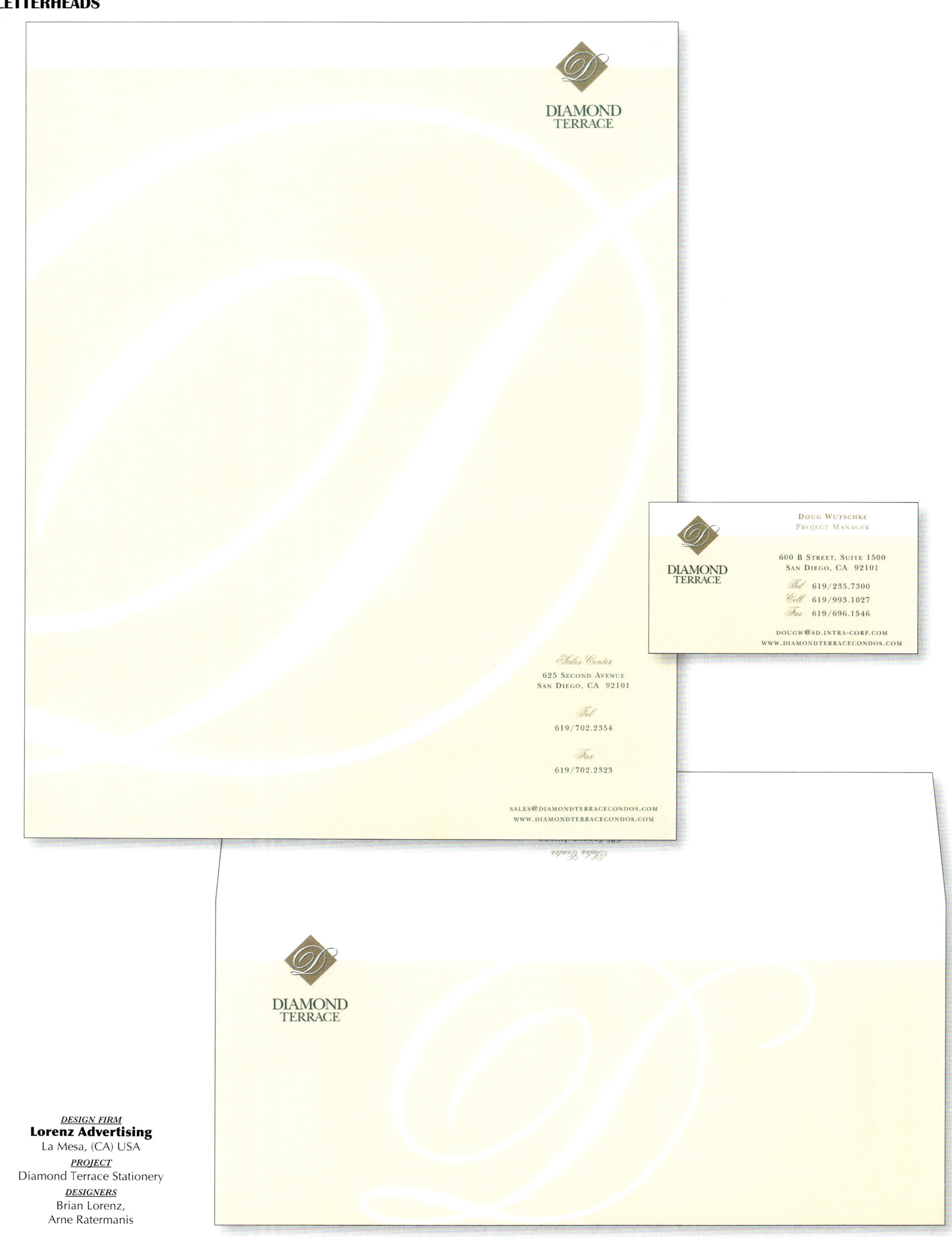

DESIGN FIRM
Lorenz Advertising
La Mesa, (CA) USA
PROJECT
Diamond Terrace Stationery
DESIGNERS
Brian Lorenz,
Arne Ratermanis

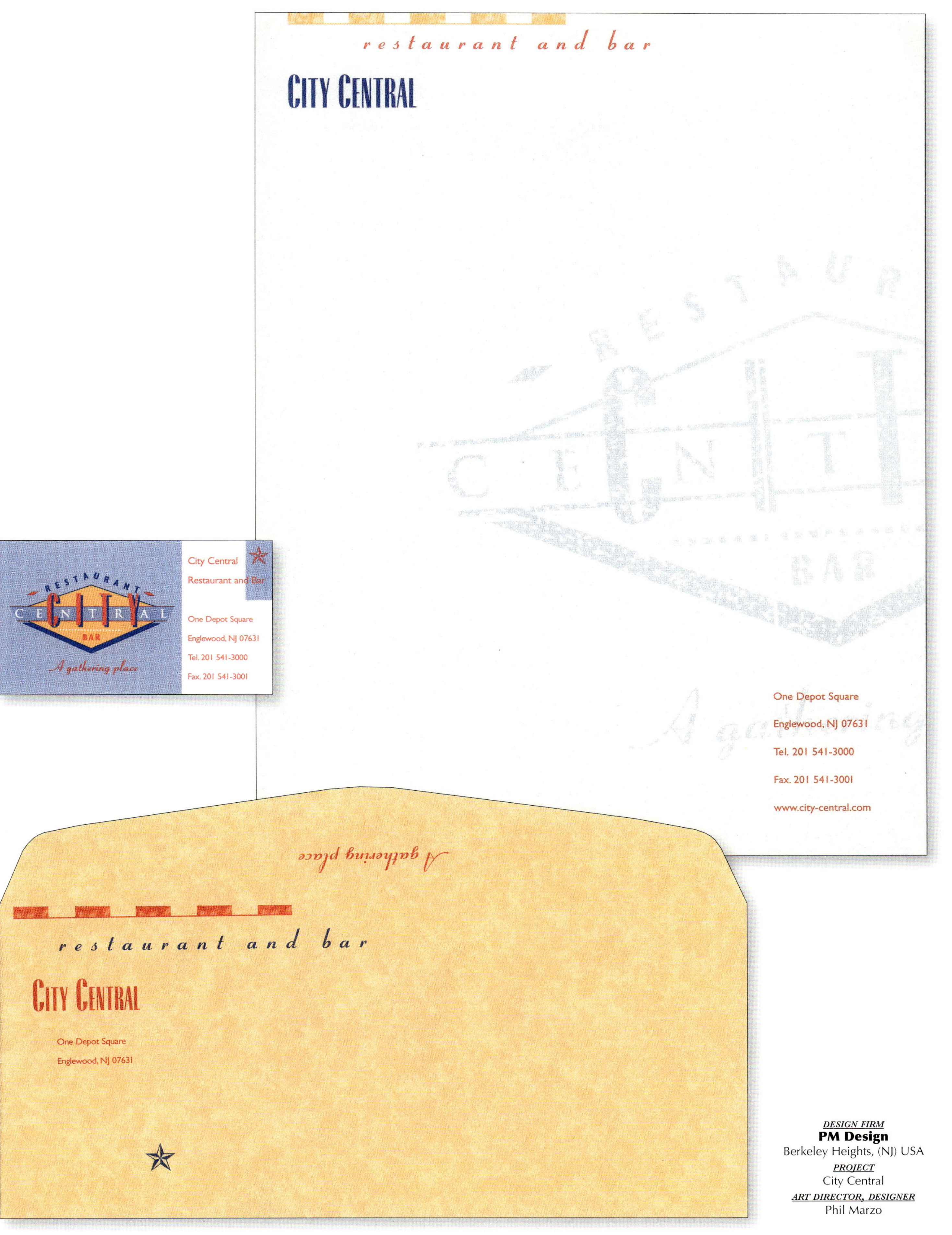

DESIGN FIRM
PM Design
Berkeley Heights, (NJ) USA
PROJECT
City Central
ART DIRECTOR, DESIGNER
Phil Marzo

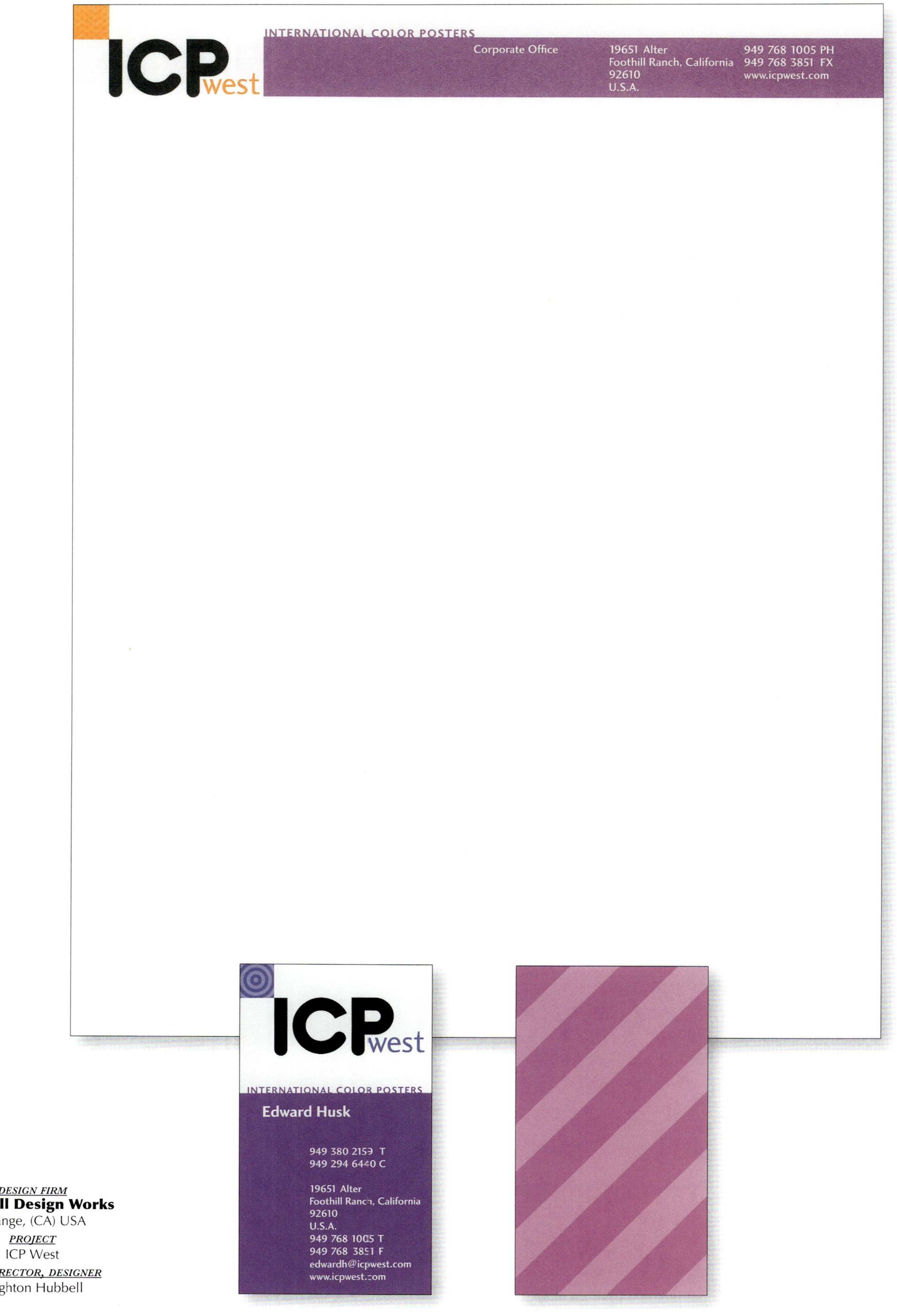

DESIGN FIRM
Hubbell Design Works
Orange, (CA) USA
PROJECT
ICP West
ART DIRECTOR, DESIGNER
Leighton Hubbell

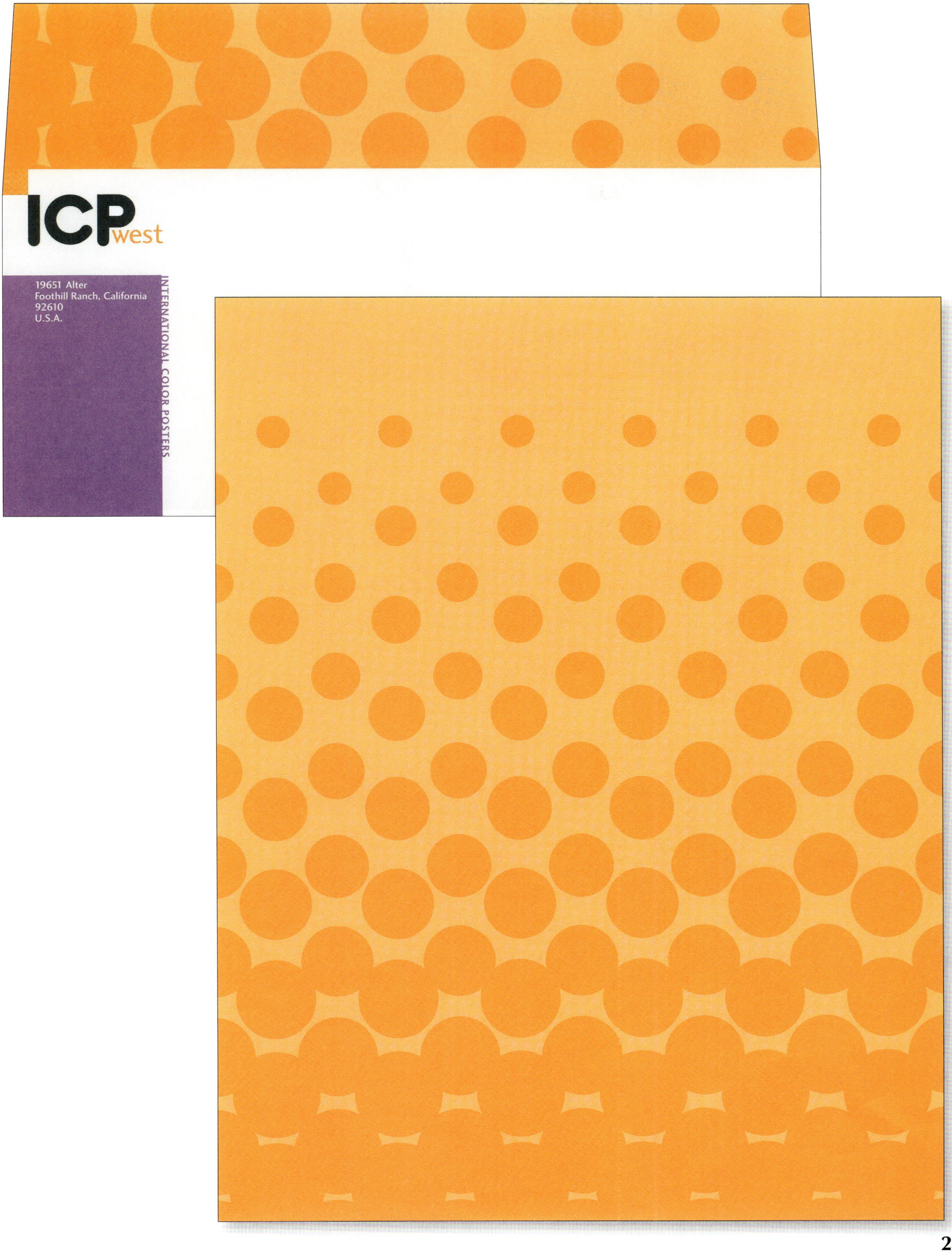

ICP west
19651 Alter
Foothill Ranch, California
92610
U.S.A.
INTERNATIONAL COLOR POSTERS

DESIGN FIRM
stressdesign
Syracuse, (NY) USA
PROJECT
Clayscapes Pottery Inc.
CREATIVE DIRECTOR
Marc Stress
DESIGNER
Christine Walker

MOJO

mojo pictures + sound

film : video : docu-info-com-mercials
strategy : writing : branded entertainment
experiential marketing : storytelling : problem solving

800 NW Sixth Avenue SUITE 313 Portland Oregon 97209
telephone 503.493.2242 facsimile 503.493.2246

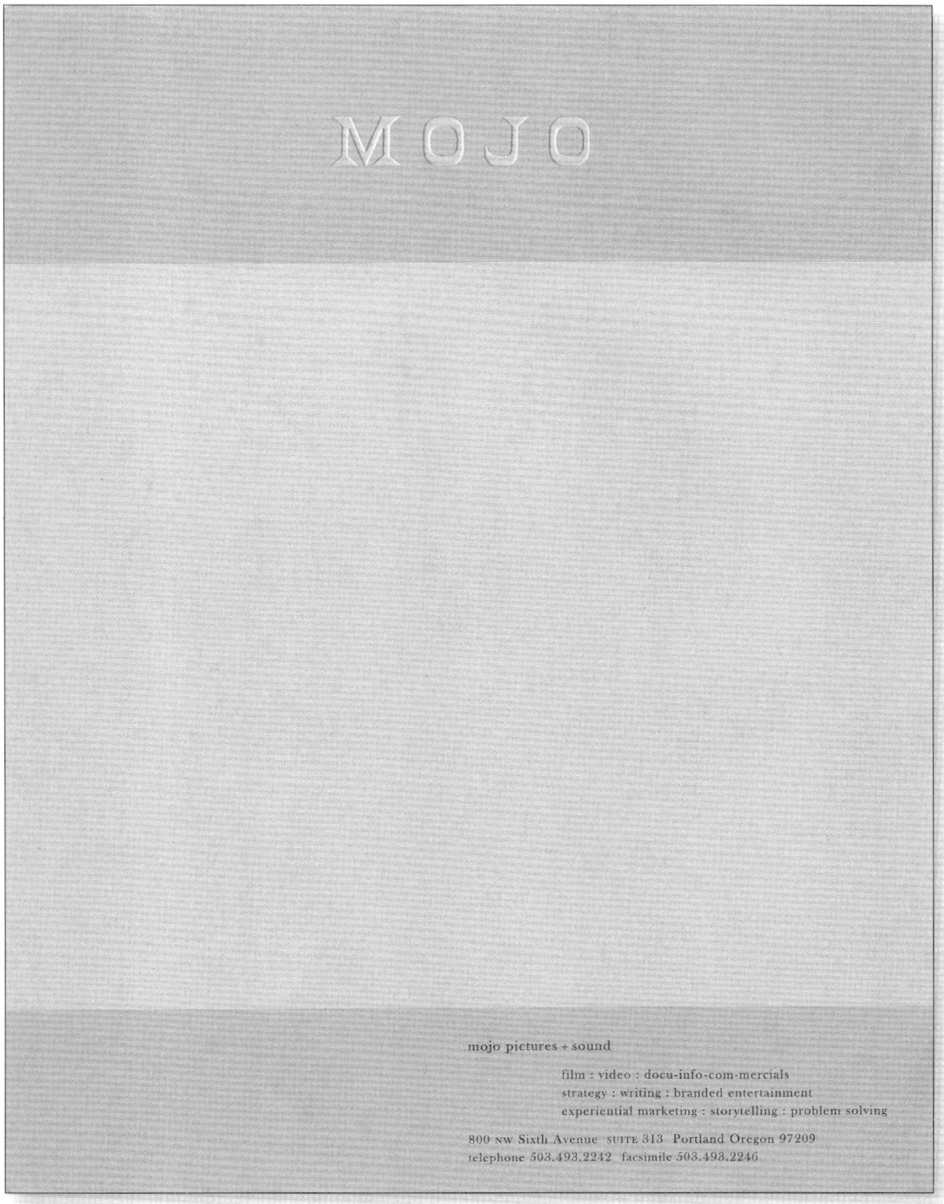

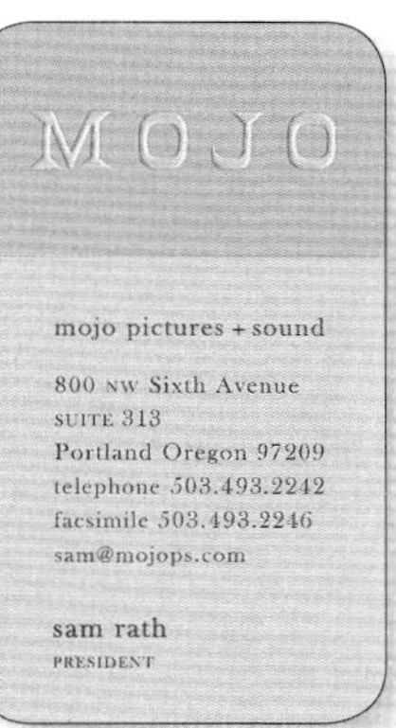

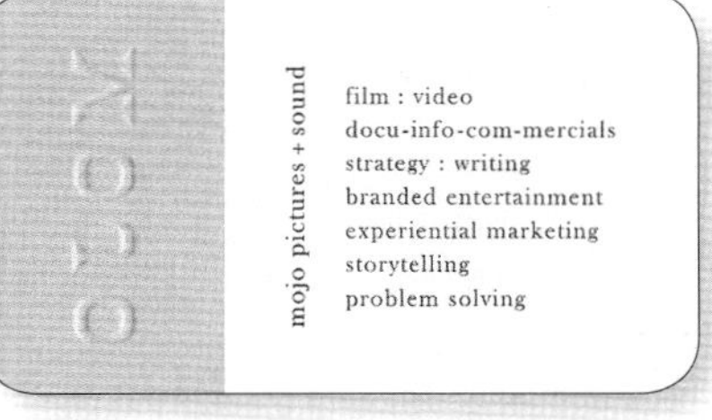

DESIGN FIRM
Sandstrom Design
Portland, (OR) USA
CLIENT
Mojo Pictures + Sound
ART DIRECTOR
Sally Morrow
DESIGNERS
Sally Morrow,
Shanin Andrew
COPYWRITER
David Brooks
PROJECT MANAGER
Spike Selby

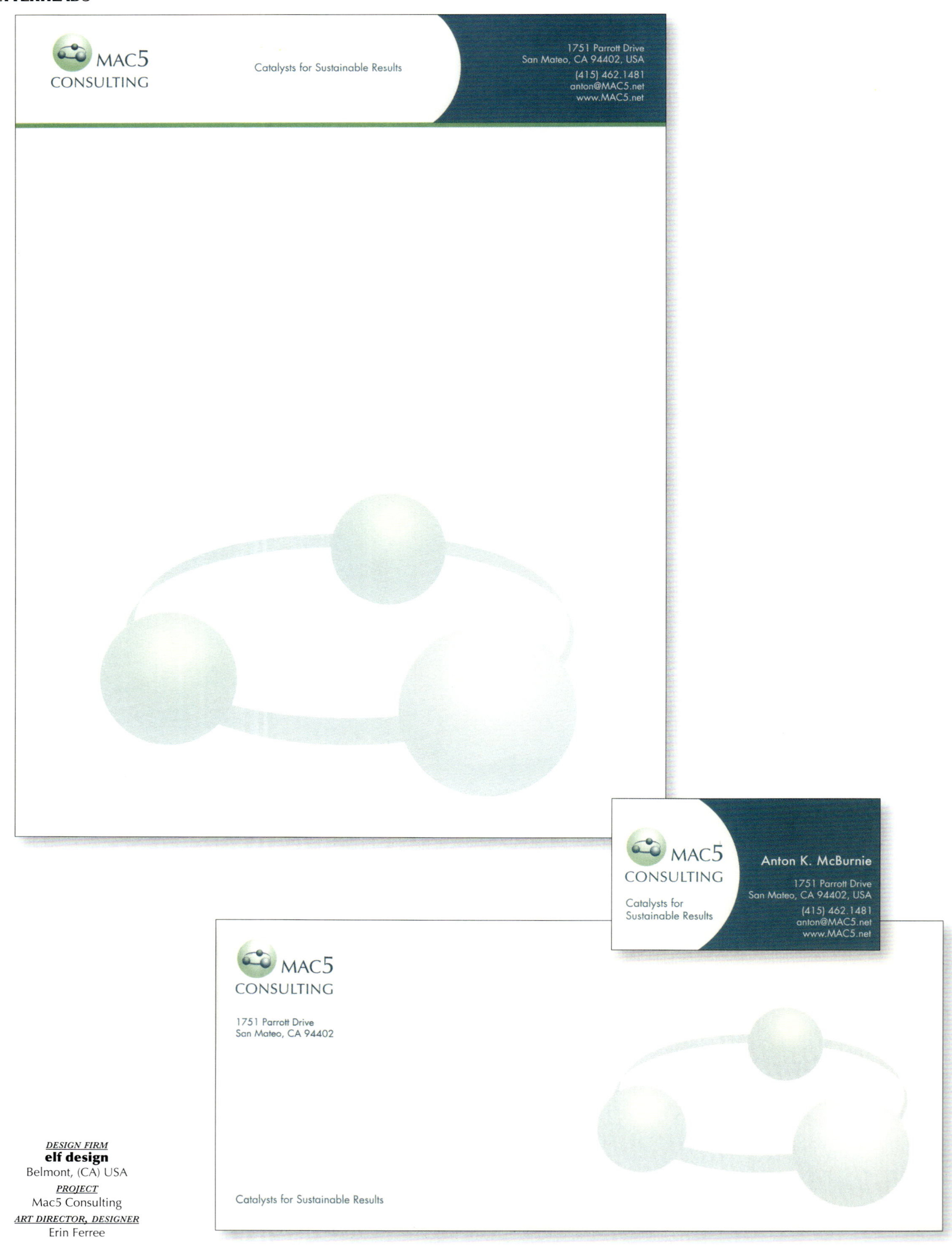

DESIGN FIRM
elf design
Belmont, (CA) USA

PROJECT
Mac5 Consulting

ART DIRECTOR, DESIGNER
Erin Ferree

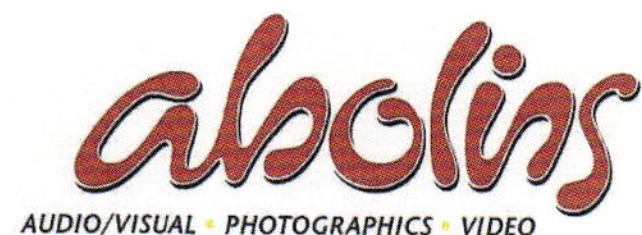

Specializing in Digital Imaging Produ

abolins
DIGITAL IMAGING PRODUCTS

• AUDIO/VISUAL
• PHOTOGRAPHICS
• VIDEO

David H. Senner
President
david@abolins.com

2811 South 12th Street
Tacoma, WA 98405

Local Tel 253.272.9898
Fax 253.272.9090
Toll Free 800.562.2200
www.abolins.com

abolins
AUDIO/VISUAL • PHOTOGRAPHICS • VIDEO

2811 South 12th Street
Tacoma, WA 98405
www.abolins.com

DESIGN FIRM
Colin Magnuson Creative
Lakewood, (WA) USA
CLIENT
Abolins Audio/Visual
DESIGNER
Colin Magnuson

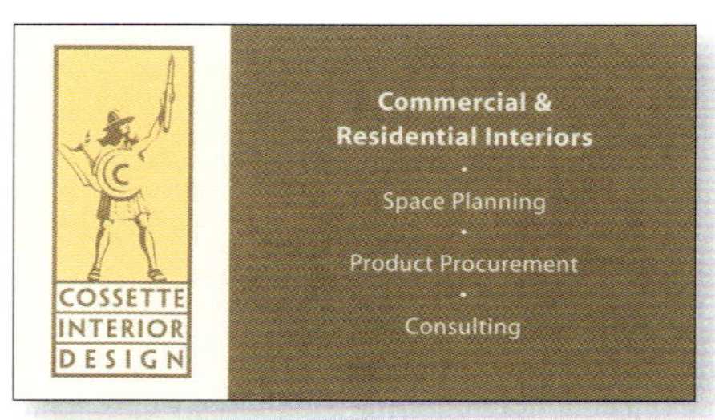

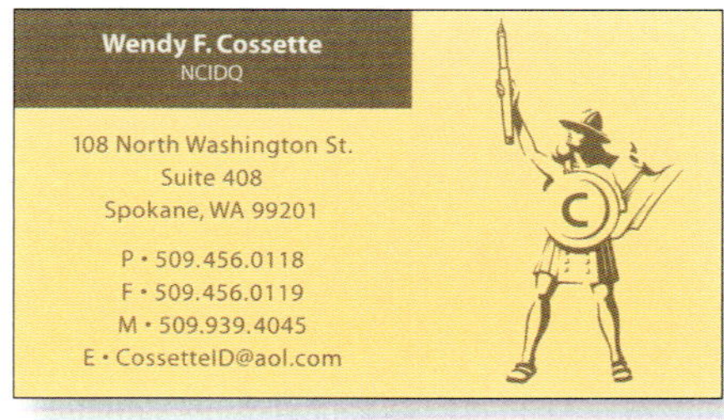

DESIGN FIRM
double entendre
Seattle, (WA) USA
PROJECT
Cossette Interior Design
DESIGNERS
Richard A. Smith,
Daniel P. Smith

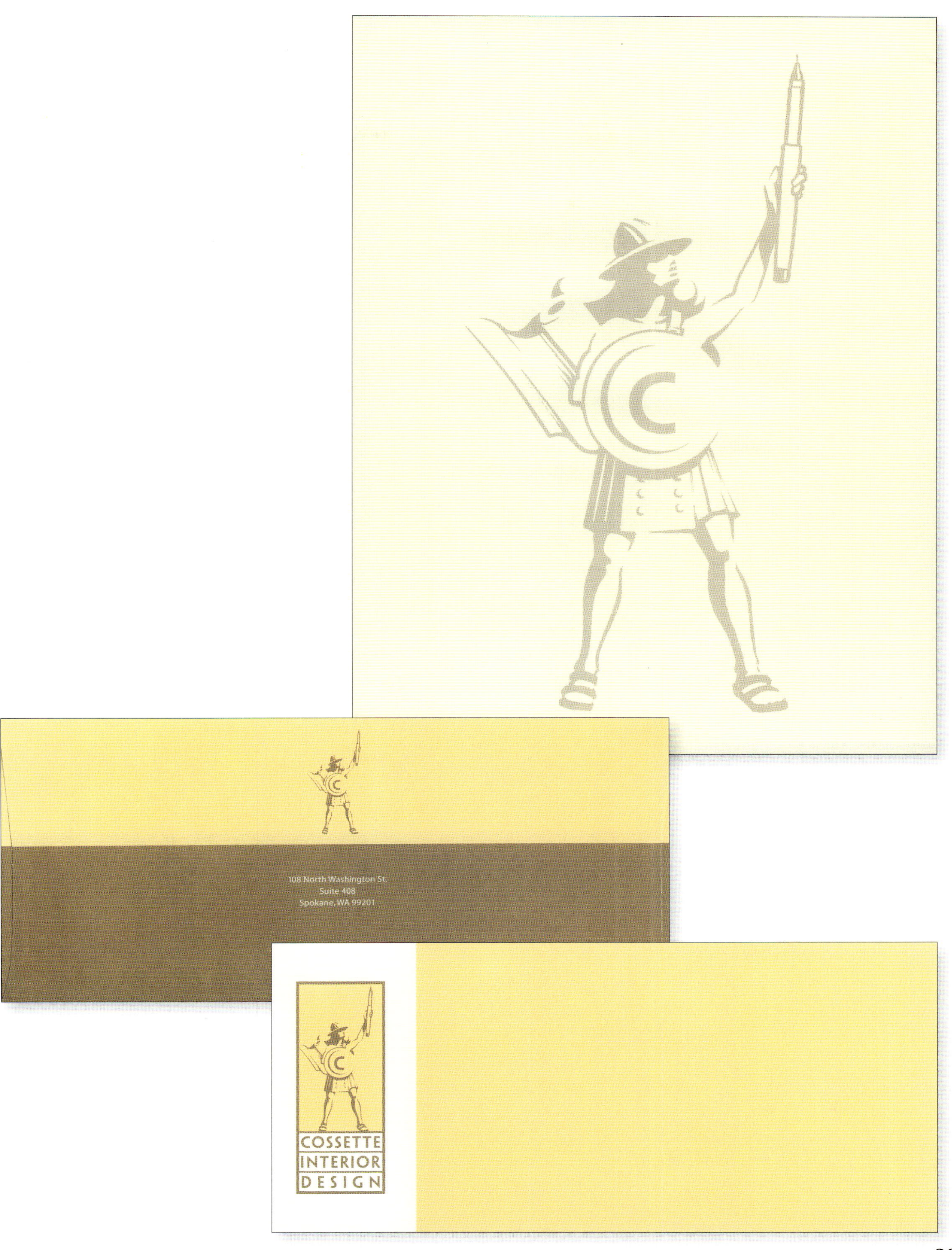
108 North Washington St.
Suite 408
Spokane, WA 99201
COSSETTE
INTERIOR
DESIGN

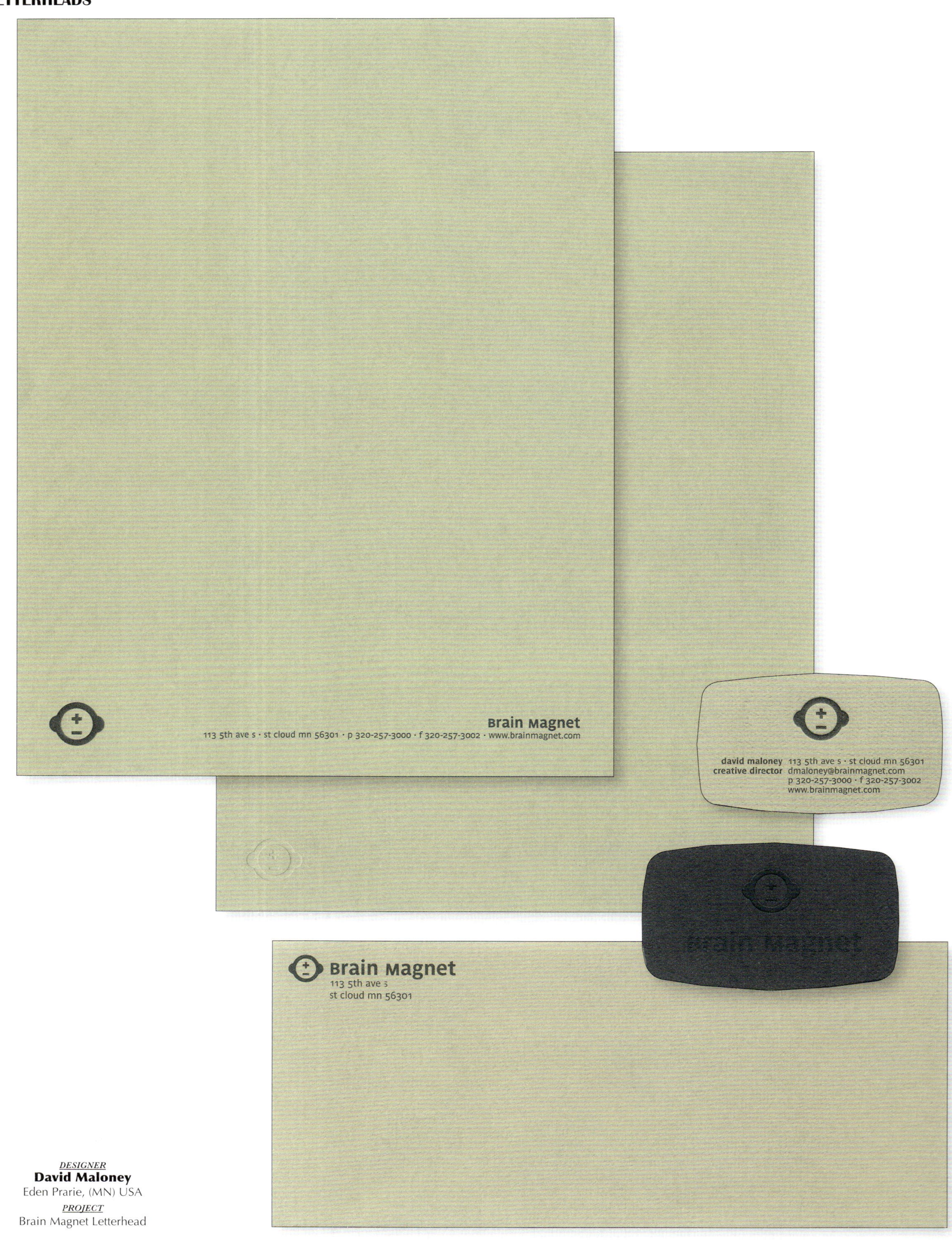

DESIGNER
David Maloney
Eden Prarie, (MN) USA
PROJECT
Brain Magnet Letterhead

DESIGN FIRM
Lidia Varesco Design
Chicago, (IL) USA
PROJECT
Osage Stationery
DESIGNER
Lidia Varesco

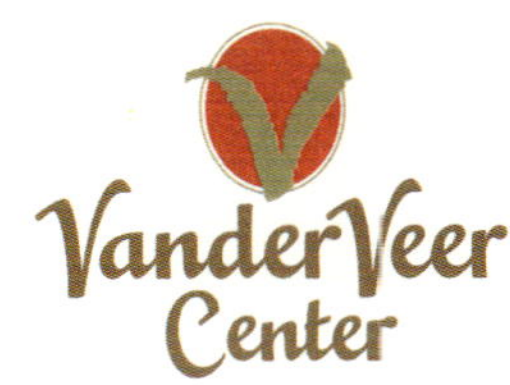

The Art & Science of Image Enhancement℠

6650 S.W. Redwood Lane • Portland, OR 97224 • www.VanderVeerCenter.com • P: (5

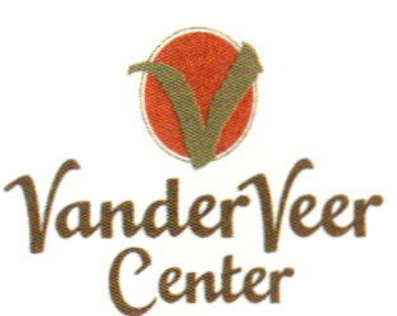

6650 S.W. Redwood Lane
Portland, OR 97224

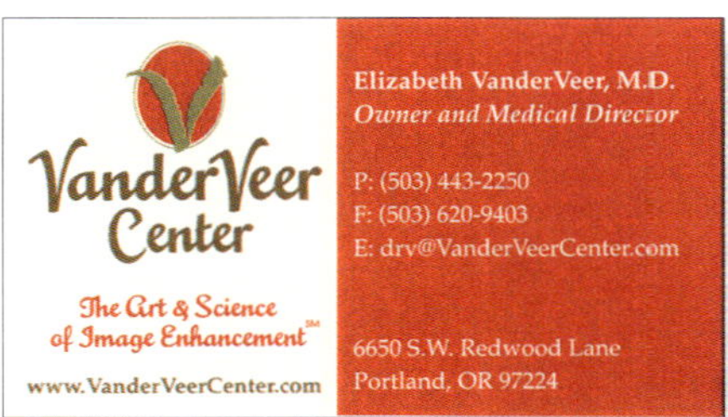

The Art & Science of Image Enhancement℠
6650 S.W. Redwood Lane • Portland, OR 97224
info@VanderVeerCenter.com • www.VanderVeerCenter.com
P: 503.443.2250 • F: 503.620.9403

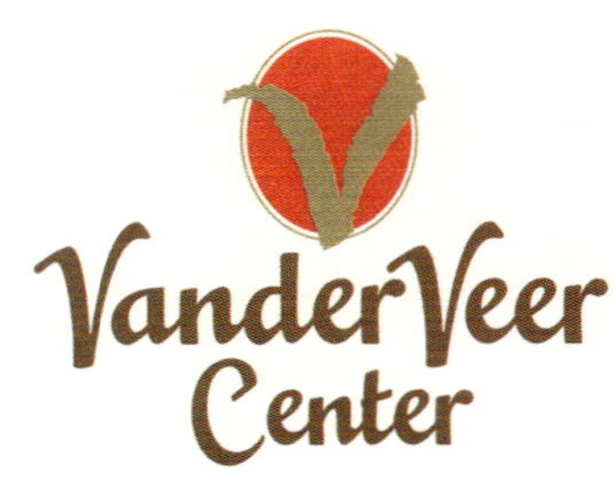

DESIGN FIRM
Jeff Fisher LogoMotives
Portland, (OR) USA
CLIENT
VanderVeer Center
ART DIRECTOR, DESIGNER
Jeff Fisher

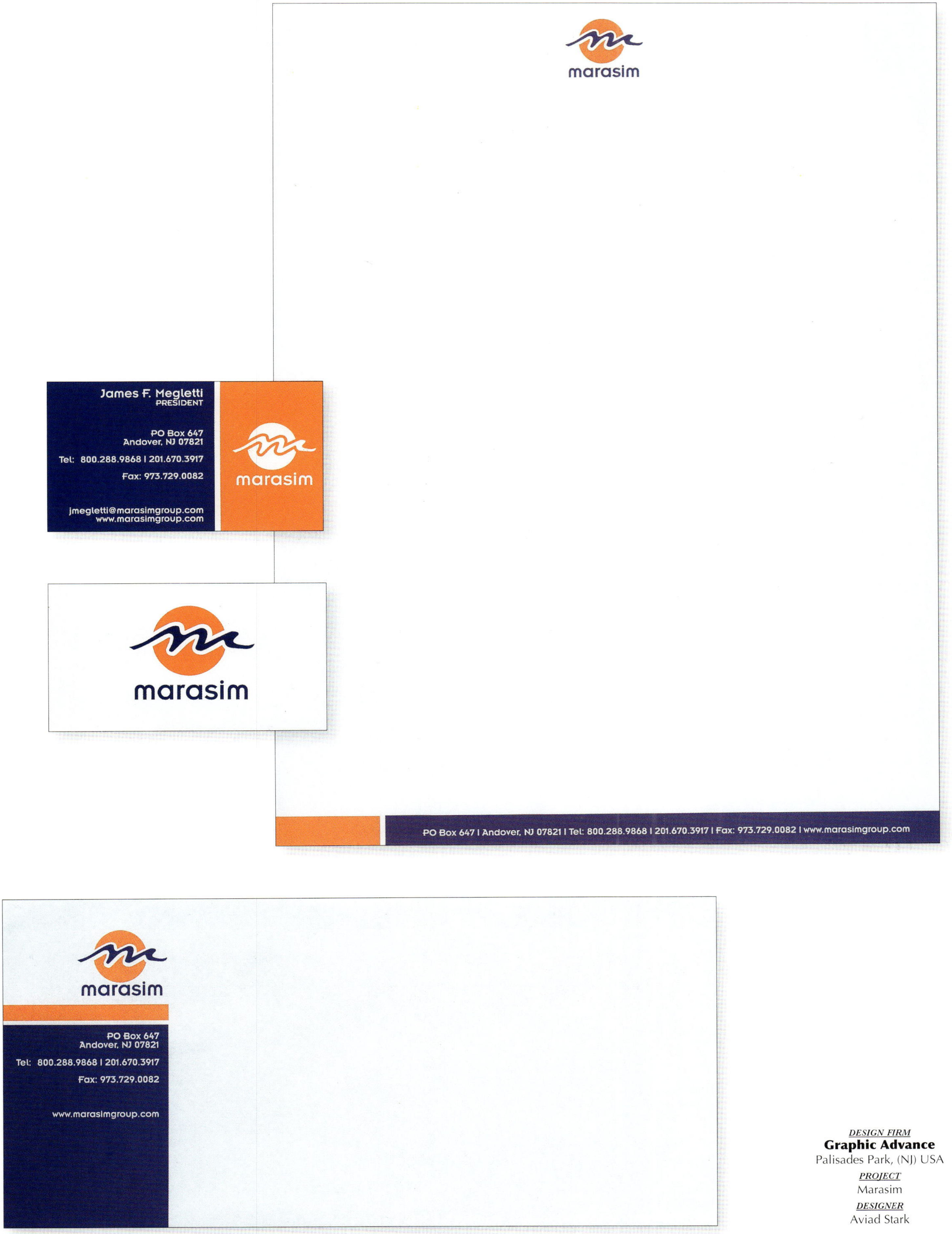

marasim

PO Box 647 I Andover, NJ 07821 I Tel: 800.288.9868 I 201.670.3917 I Fax: 973.729.0082 I www.marasimgroup.com

James F. Megletti
PRESIDENT

PO Box 647
Andover, NJ 07821

Tel: 800.288.9868 I 201.670.3917

Fax: 973.729.0082

jmegletti@marasimgroup.com
www.marasimgroup.com

marasim

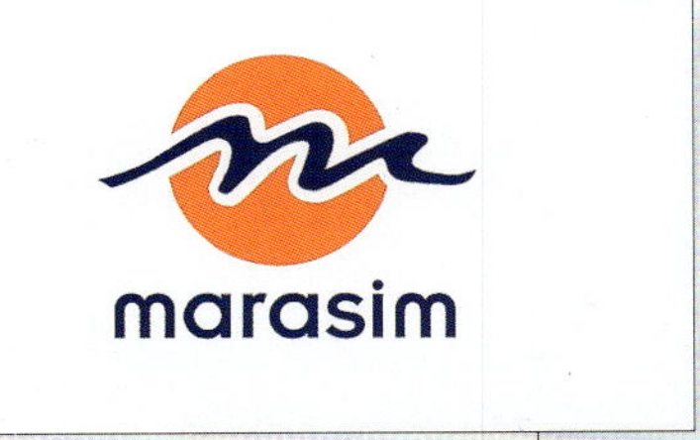

DESIGN FIRM
Graphic Advance
Palisades Park, (NJ) USA

PROJECT
Marasim

DESIGNER
Aviad Stark

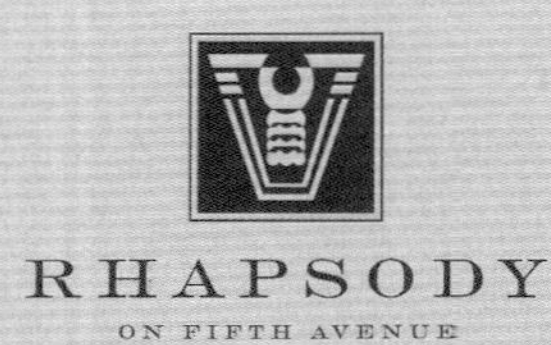

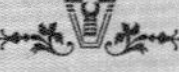

1 West 125th Street, New York, NY 10027
Tel: (212) 828-5556
Fax: (212) 426-5555
www.rhapsodyonfifth.com

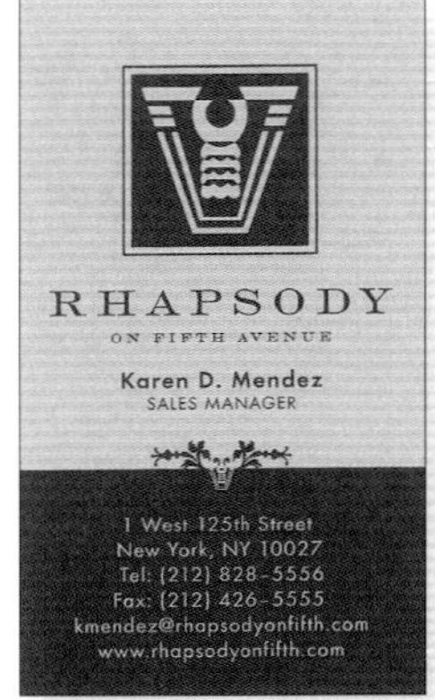

1 West 125th Street, New York, NY 10027
Tel: (212) 828-5556 Fax: (212) 426-5555
www.rhapsodyonfifth.com

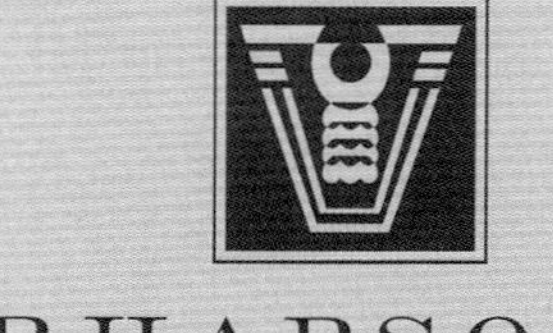

RHAPSODY
ON FIFTH AVENUE

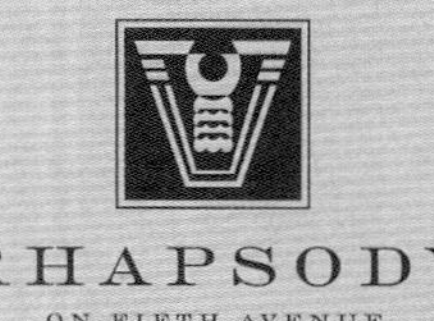

1 West 125th Street
New York, NY 10027

DESIGN FIRM
The Mixx
New York, (NY) USA
PROJECT
Rhapsody on Fifth Avenue

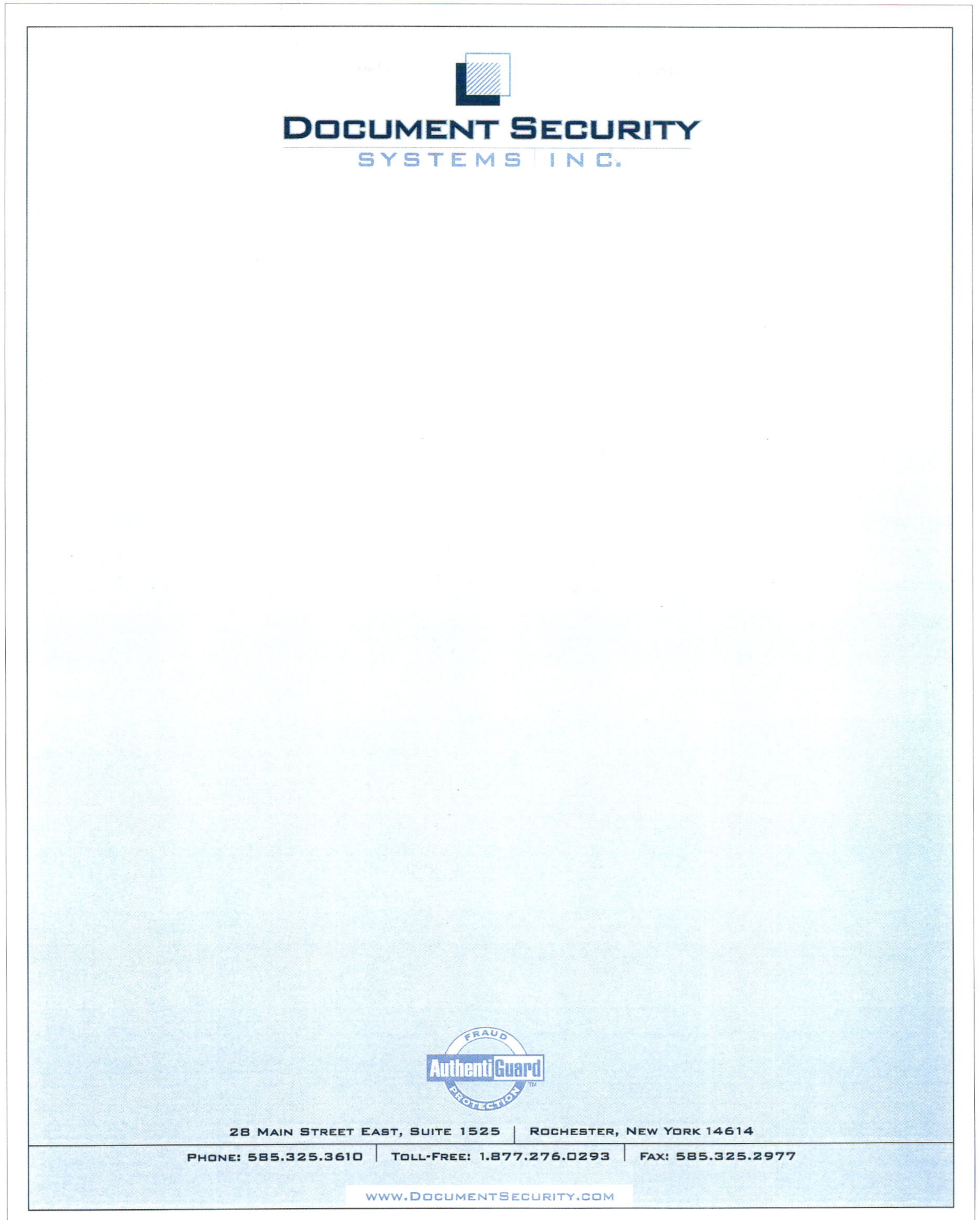

DESIGN FIRM
McElveney & Palozzi Design Group
Rochester, (NY) USA
PROJECT
Document Security Systems
CREATIVE DIRECTOR
Bill McElveney
ART DIRECTOR, DESIGNER
Lisa Gates

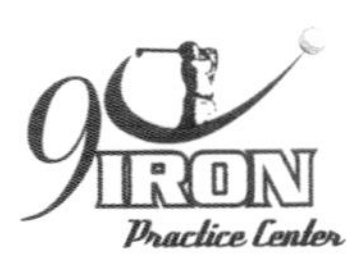

3536 N. Santa Fe Drive
Merced, CA 95340

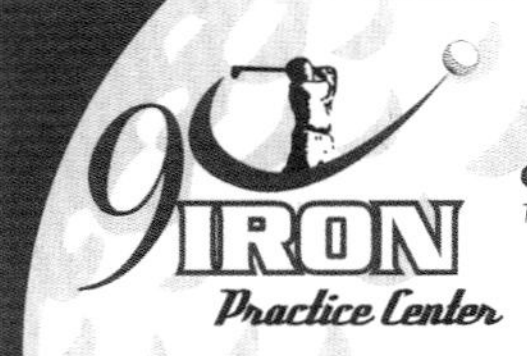

Chris Martineson
Teaching Professional

3536 N. Santa Fe Drive
Merced, CA 95340

Phone: (209) 726-7740
Mobile: (209) 535-5728

9 IRON Practice Center

3536 N. Santa Fe Drive • Merced, CA 95340 • Phone: (209) 726-7740

DESIGN FIRM
Ontarget Marketing
Merced, (CA) USA
CLIENT
9 Iron Practice Center
ART DIRECTOR
Jesse Bloodworth
DESIGNER
Scott Slown

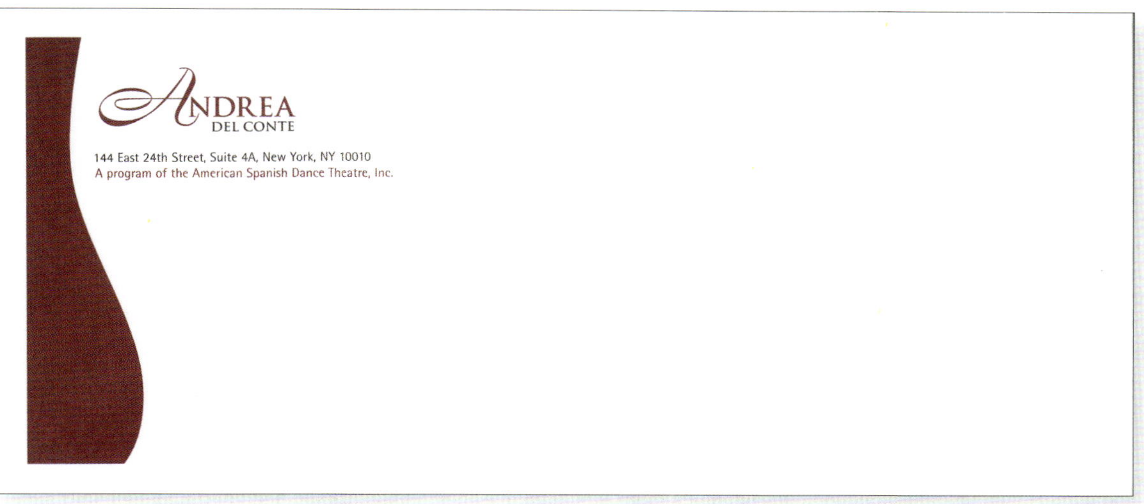

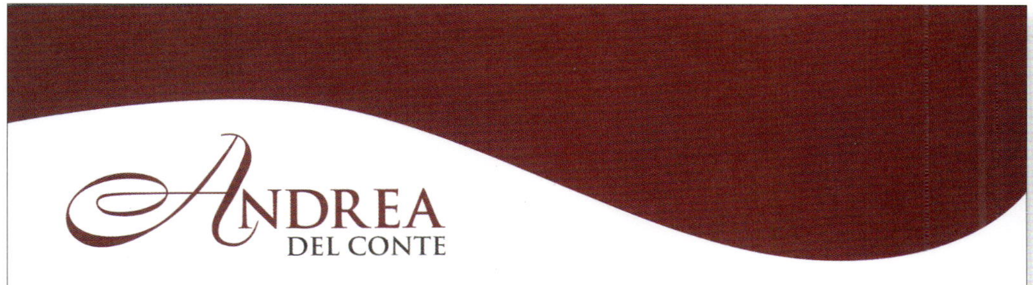

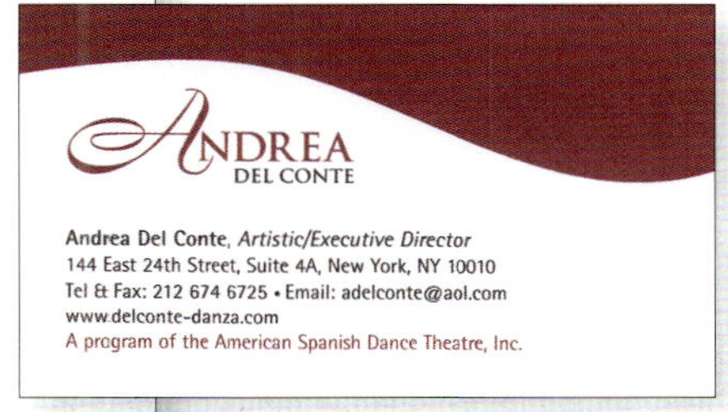

144 East 24th Street, Suite 4A, New York, NY 10010 • Tel & Fax: 212 674 6725 • www.delconte-danza.com
A program of the American Spanish Dance Theatre, Inc.

DESIGN FIRM
WestGroup Creative
New York, (NY) USA
PROJECT
Andrea Del Conte
CREATIVE DIRECTOR
Marvin Berk
ART DIRECTOR, DESIGNER
Chip Tolaney

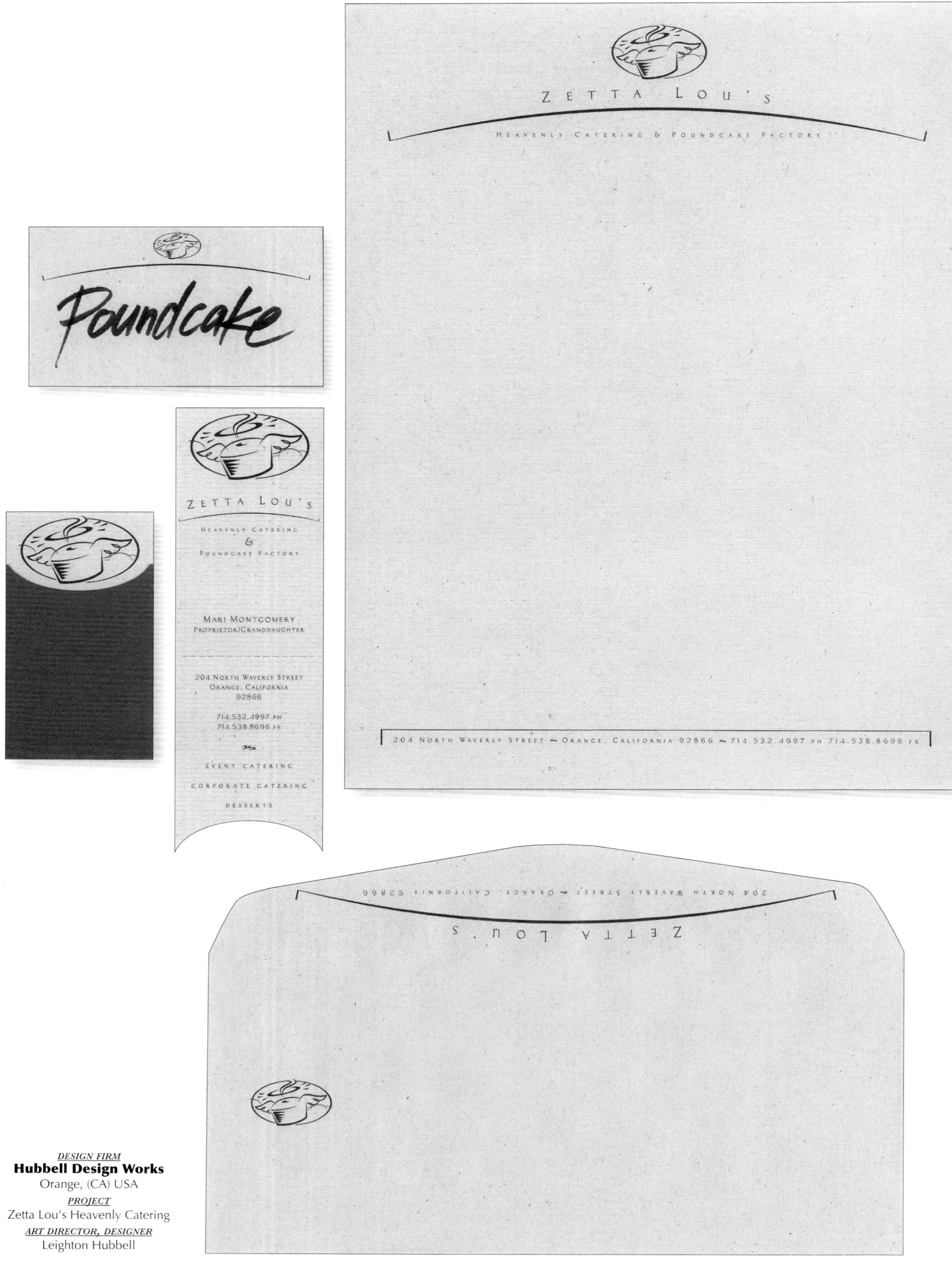

DESIGN FIRM
Hubbell Design Works
Orange, (CA) USA
PROJECT
Zetta Lou's Heavenly Catering
ART DIRECTOR, DESIGNER
Leighton Hubbell

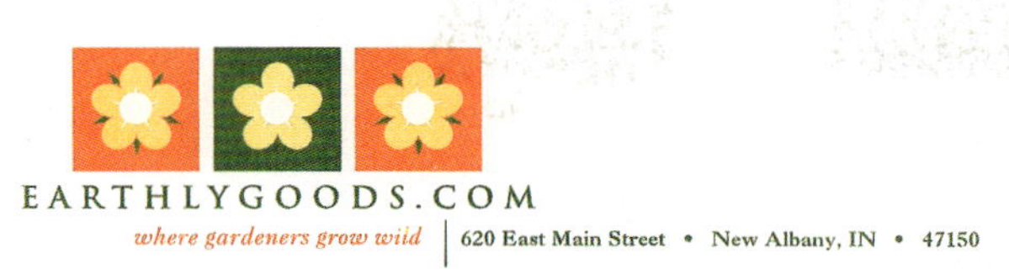

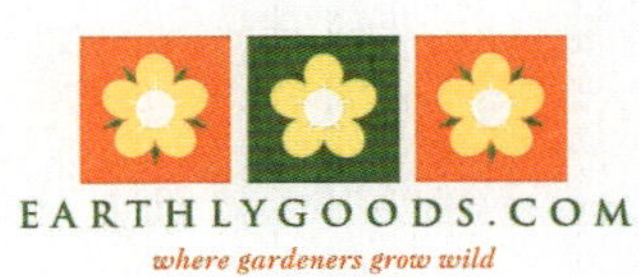

620 East Main Street • New Albany, IN • 47150
P: 812.944.3283 • F: 812.944.2903 • E: info@earthlygoods.com • W: www.earthlygoods.com

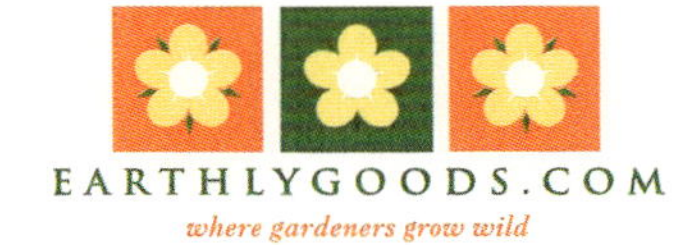

Ann Streckfus

620 East Main Street • New Albany, IN • 47150
P: 812.944.3283 • F: 812.944.2903 • E: info@earthlygoods.com
W: www.earthlygoods.com

EARTHLYGOODS.COM

Your online source for:

- Personalized and custom seed packets
- Wildflower seed for weddings and other special events
- Paper-That-Grows *(invitations, announcements, memorials)*
- Over 100 species of wildflower, native grass and herb seeds
- Over 50 wildflower seed mixes
- Unique gifts for gardeners
- Free gardening e-newsletter

DESIGN FIRM
Mind's Eye Creative
New Albany, (IN) USA
CLIENT
EarthlyGoods.com
DESIGNER
Stephen Brown

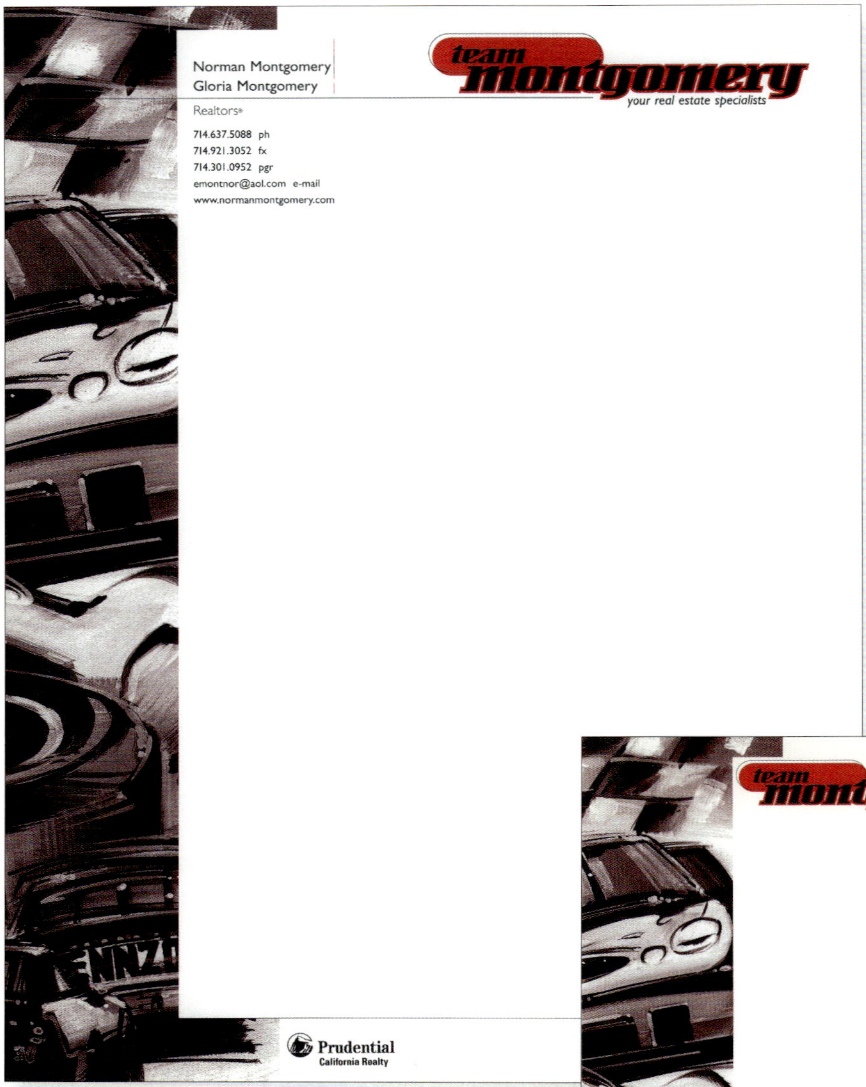

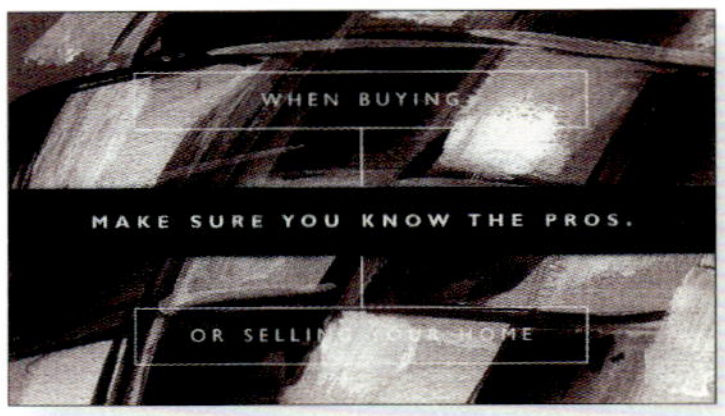

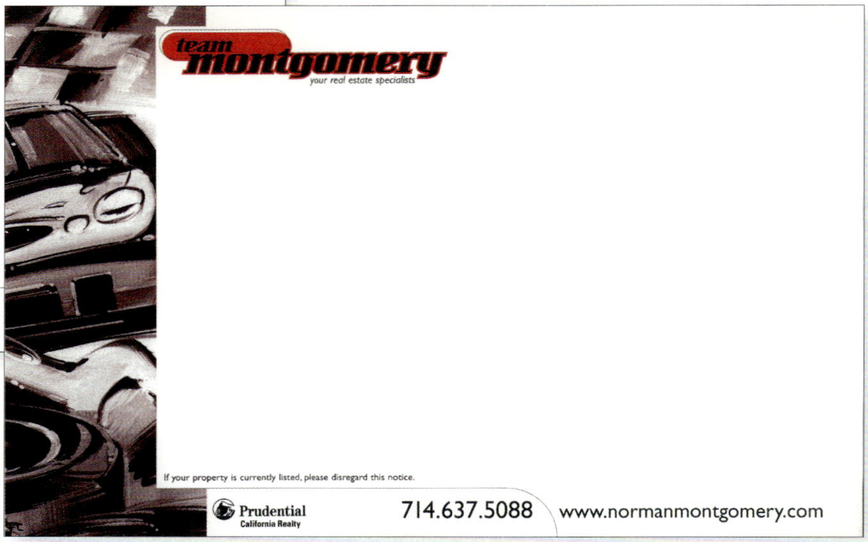

Norman Montgomery
Gloria Montgomery
Realtors®
714.637.5088 ph
714.921.3052 fx
714.301.0952 pgr
emontnor@aol.com e-mail
www.normanmontgomery.com

team montgomery
your real estate specialists

Prudential
California Realty

WHEN BUYING
MAKE SURE YOU KNOW THE PROS.
OR SELLING YOUR HOME

team montgomery
your real estate specialists

Norman Montgomery
Gloria Montgomery
Realtors®

714.637.5088 ph
714.921.3052 fx
714.301.0952 pgr
emontnor@aol.com e-mail
www.normanmontgomery.com

Prudential
California Realty

team montgomery
your real estate specialists

If your property is currently listed, please disregard this notice.

Prudential
California Realty

714.637.5088 www.normanmontgomery.com

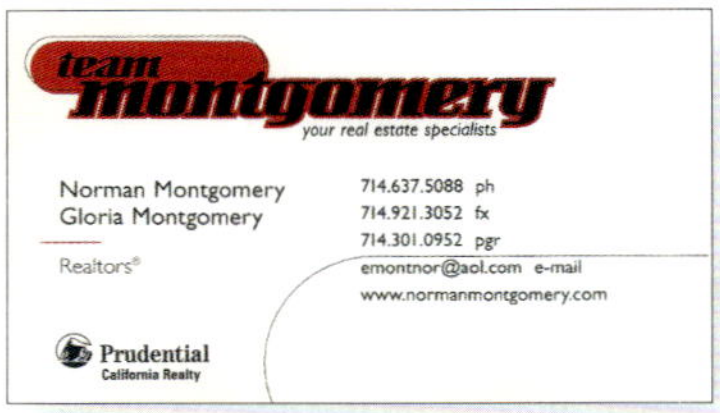

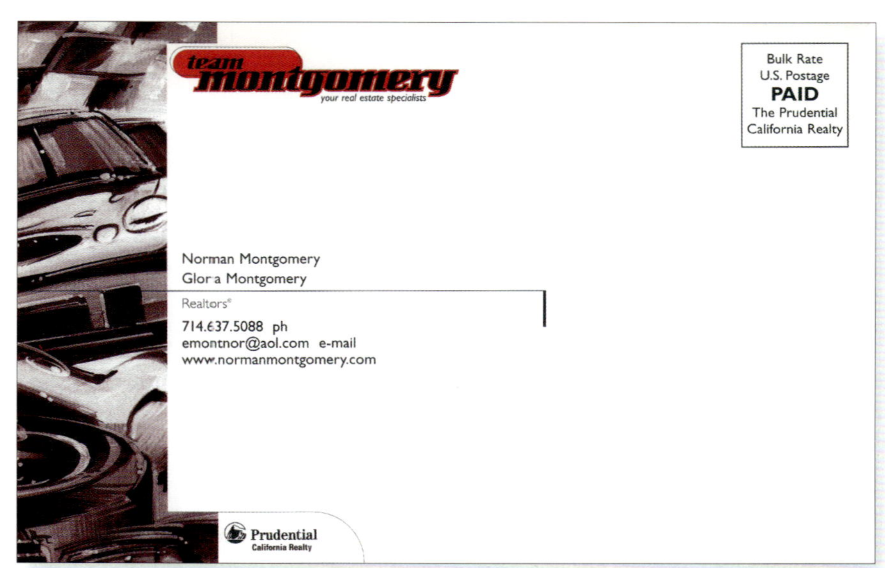

DESIGN FIRM
Hubbell Design Works
Orange, (CA) USA

PROJECT
Team Montgomery

ART DIRECTOR, DESIGNER, ILLUSTRATOR
Leighton Hubbell

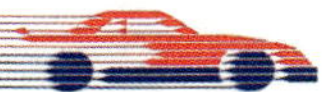

Exeter Oak Racing
Liberty Lane
Hampton, NH 03842
603.926.5911

Mike Dingman
Driver

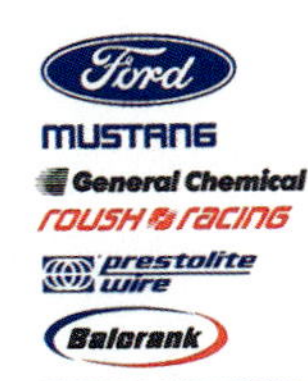

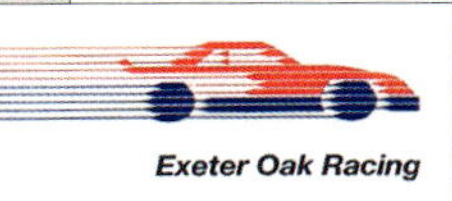

Exeter Oak Racing

Ford
MUSTANG
General Chemical
ROUSH RACING
prestolite wire
Balcrank
TOLEDO STAMPING

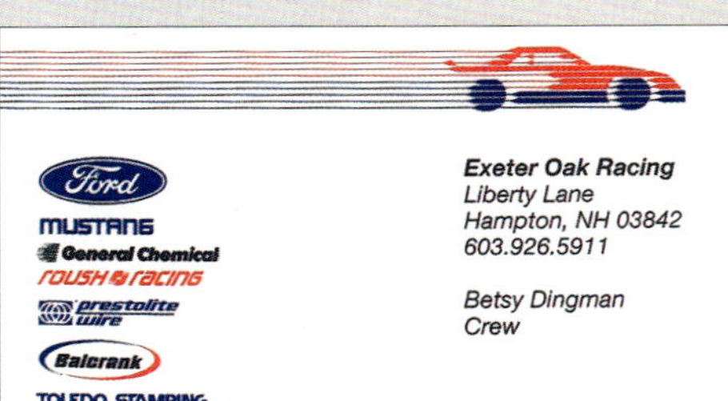

DESIGN FIRM
Arnold Saks Associates, Inc.
New York, (NY) USA
PROJECT
Exeter Oak Racing
ART DIRECTOR
Arnold Saks
DESIGNER
Ingo Scharrenbroich

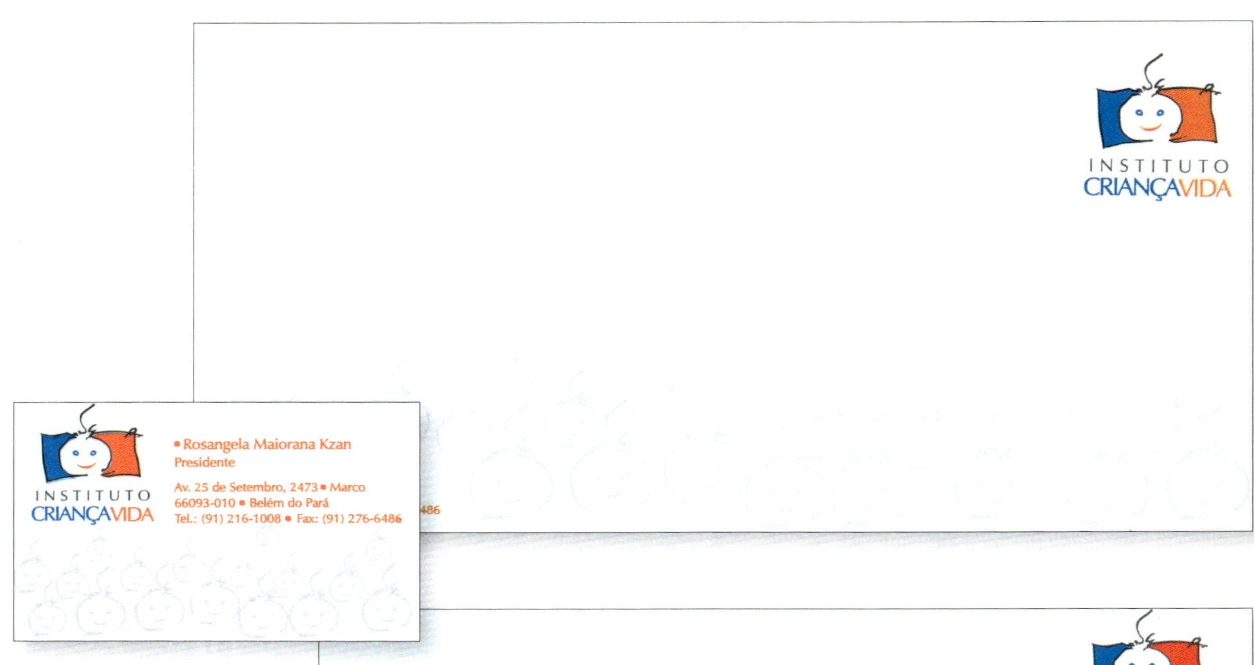

INSTITUTO
CRIANÇAVIDA

Av. 25 de Setembro, 2473 • Marco
66093-010 • Belém do Pará
Tel.: (91) 216-1008 • Fax: (91) 276-6486

DESIGN FIRM
Mendes Publicidade
Belém, Brazil
PROJECT
Instituto Criança Vida
DESIGNERS
Oswaldo Mendes,
Maria Alice Pena

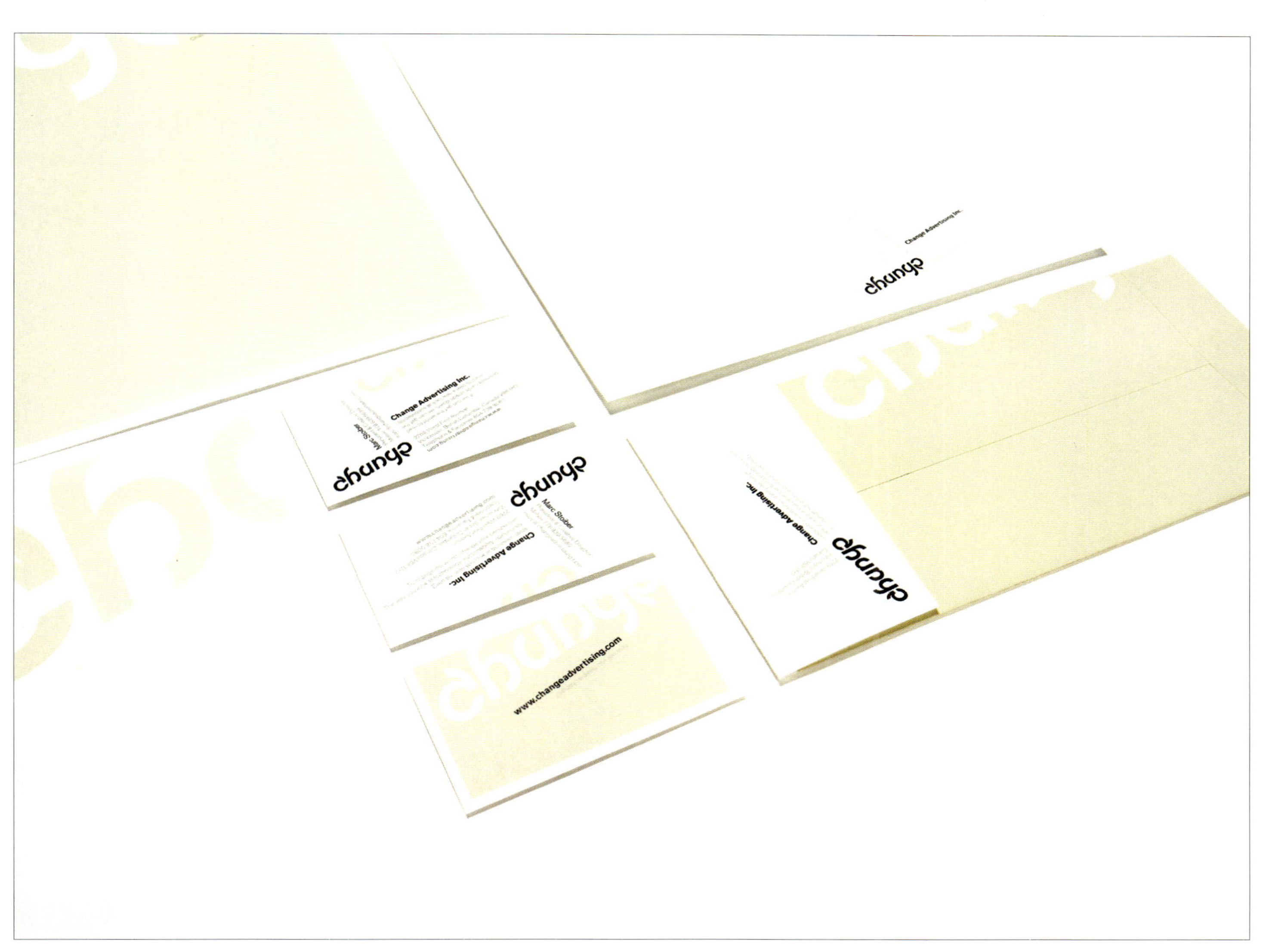

DESIGN FIRM
Subplot Design Inc.
Vancouver, Canada
PROJECT
Change Advertising

Dessirée Hernández Locutora

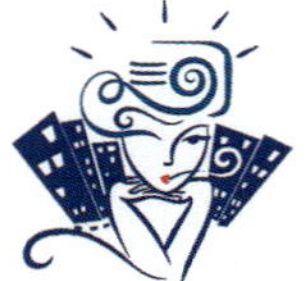

T. 5342-1261
F. 5396-5591
C. 04455-2247-4055
dessiree_h@yahoo.com

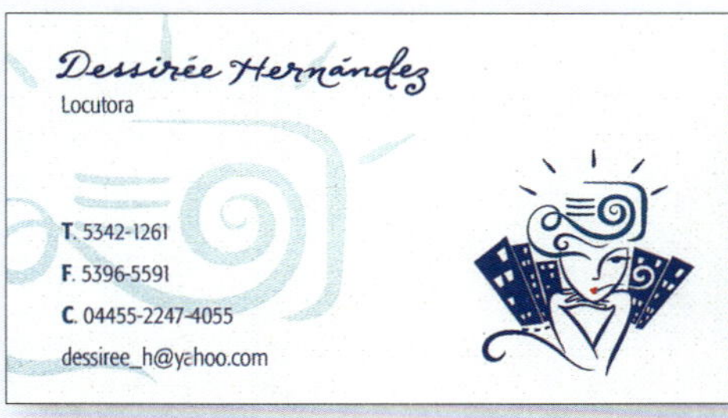

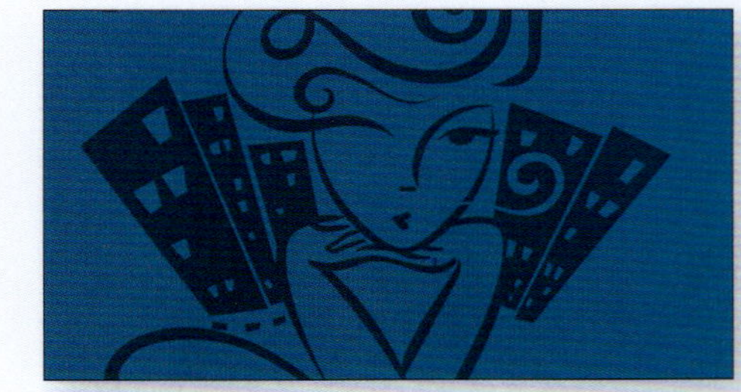

DESIGN FIRM
TD2
Mexico City, Mexico
CLIENT
Desiree Hernandez/Locutora
DESIGNERS
R. Rodrigo Cordova,
Ana Rodriguez

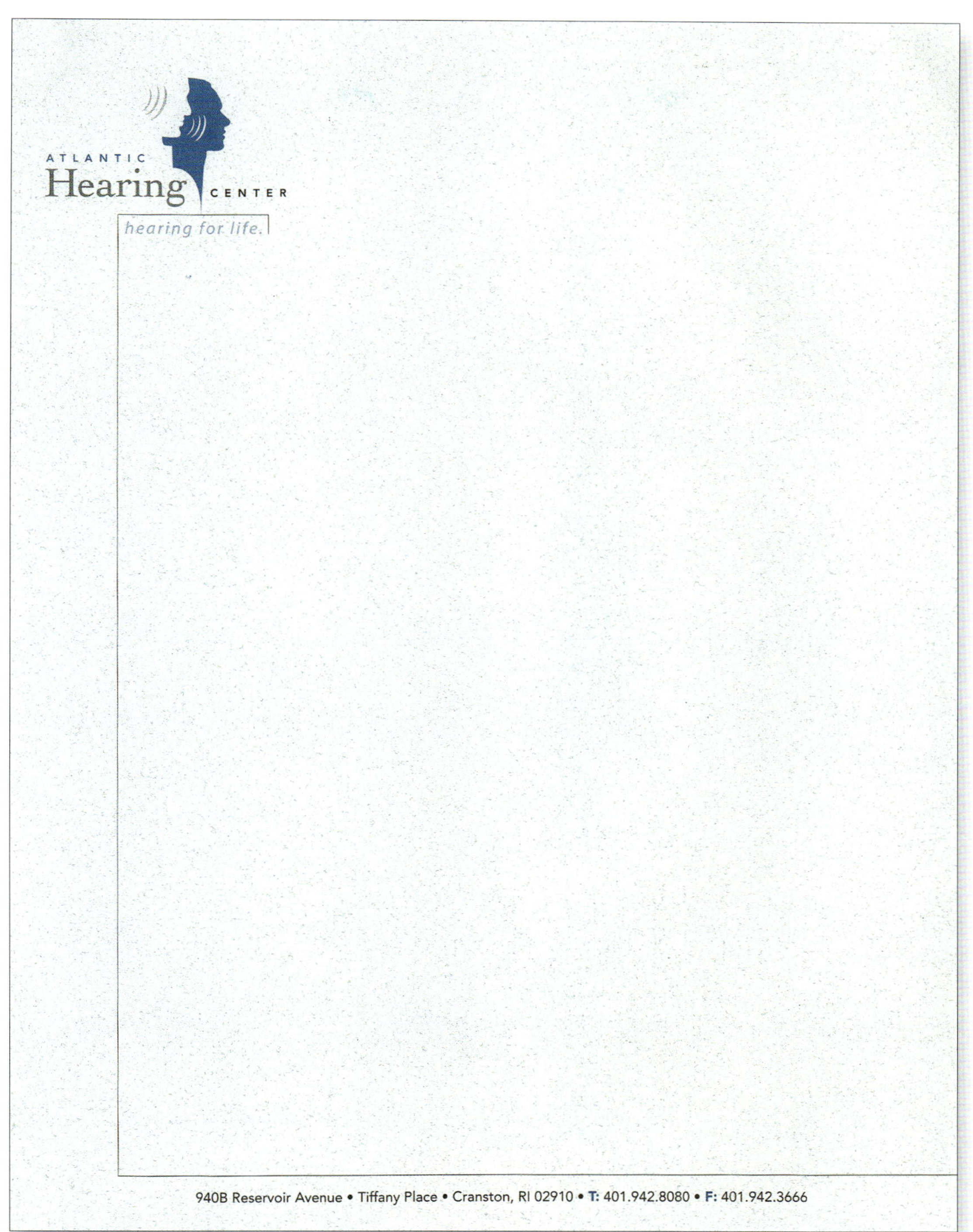

DESIGN FIRM
Im-aj Communications & Design, Inc.
West Kingston, (RI) USA
CLIENT
Atlantic Hearing
CREATIVE DIRECTOR
Jami Ouellette
SENIOR DESIGNER
Amy Marie Madina

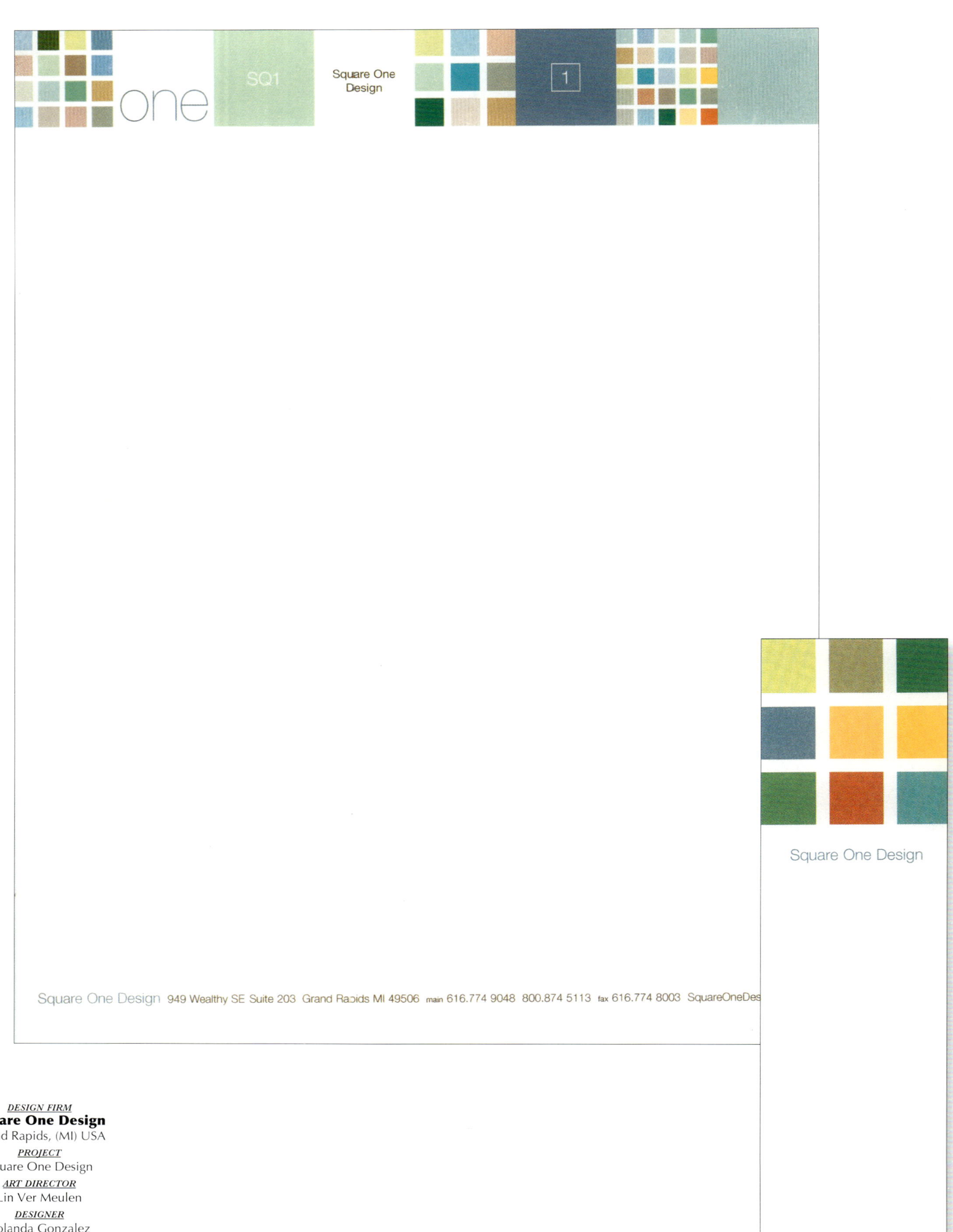

DESIGN FIRM
Square One Design
Grand Rapids, (MI) USA
PROJECT
Square One Design
ART DIRECTOR
Lin Ver Meulen
DESIGNER
Yolanda Gonzalez

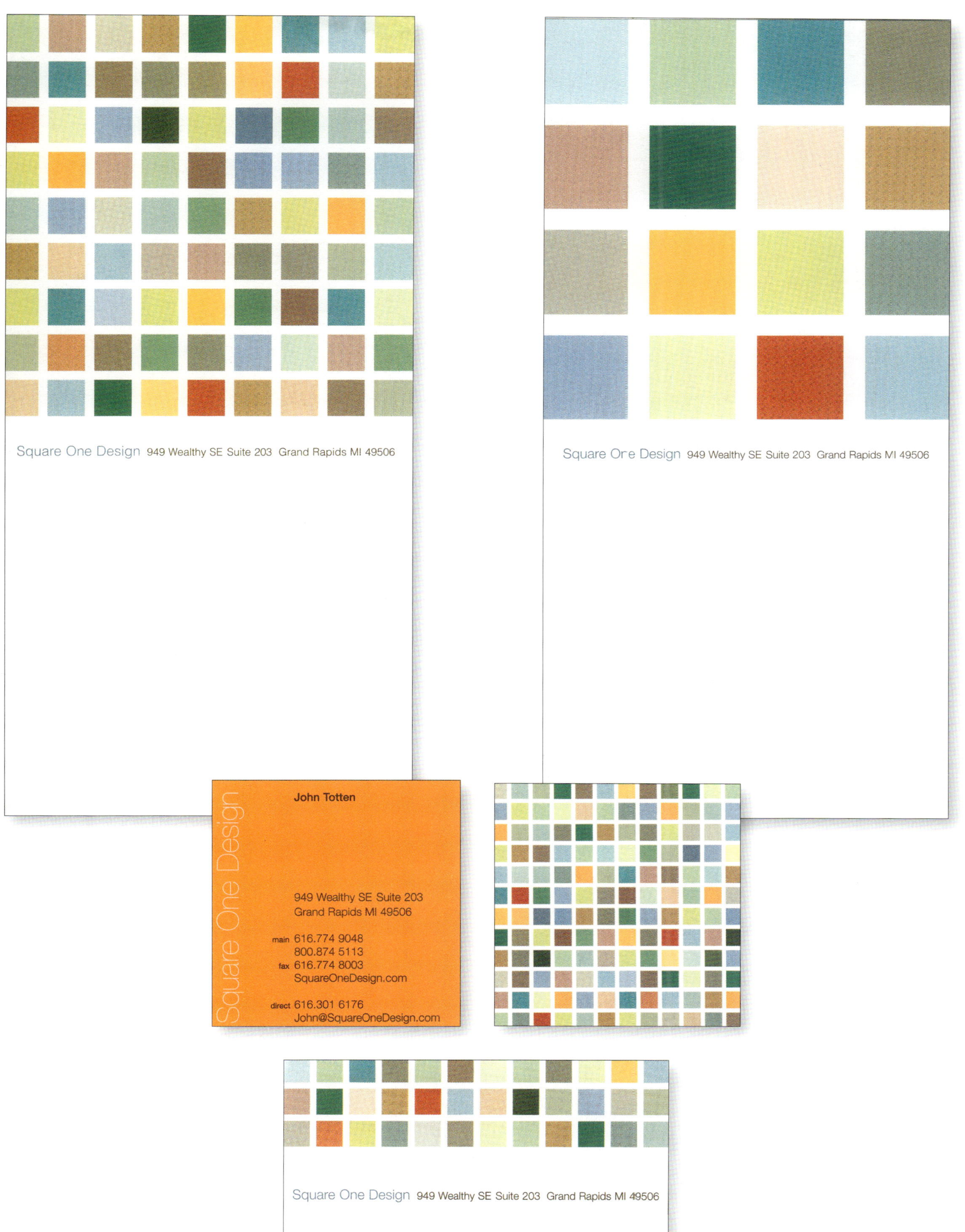
Square One Design 949 Wealthy SE Suite 203 Grand Rapids MI 49506
Square One Design 949 Wealthy SE Suite 203 Grand Rapids MI 49506
Square One Design
John Totten
949 Wealthy SE Suite 203
Grand Rapids MI 49506
main 616.774 9048
800.874 5113
fax 616.774 8003
SquareOneDesign.com
direct 616.301 6176
John@SquareOneDesign.com
Square One Design 949 Wealthy SE Suite 203 Grand Rapids MI 49506

DESIGN FIRM
Colin Magnuson Creative
Lakewood, (WA) USA
PROJECT
Chatelain Property Management
DESIGNERS
Colin Magnuson,
Rachael Costner

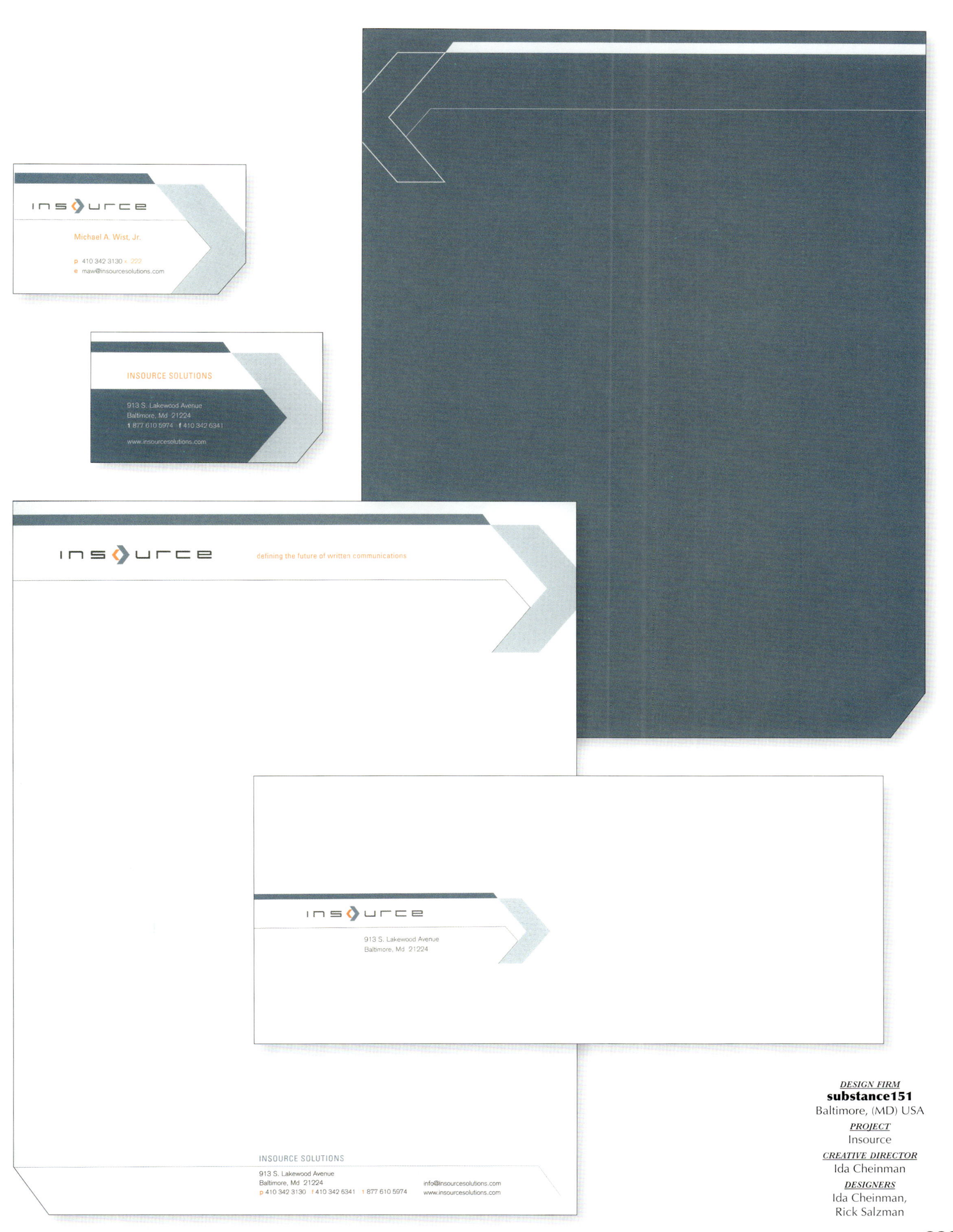

DESIGN FIRM
substance151
Baltimore, (MD) USA

PROJECT
Insource

CREATIVE DIRECTOR
Ida Cheinman

DESIGNERS
Ida Cheinman,
Rick Salzman

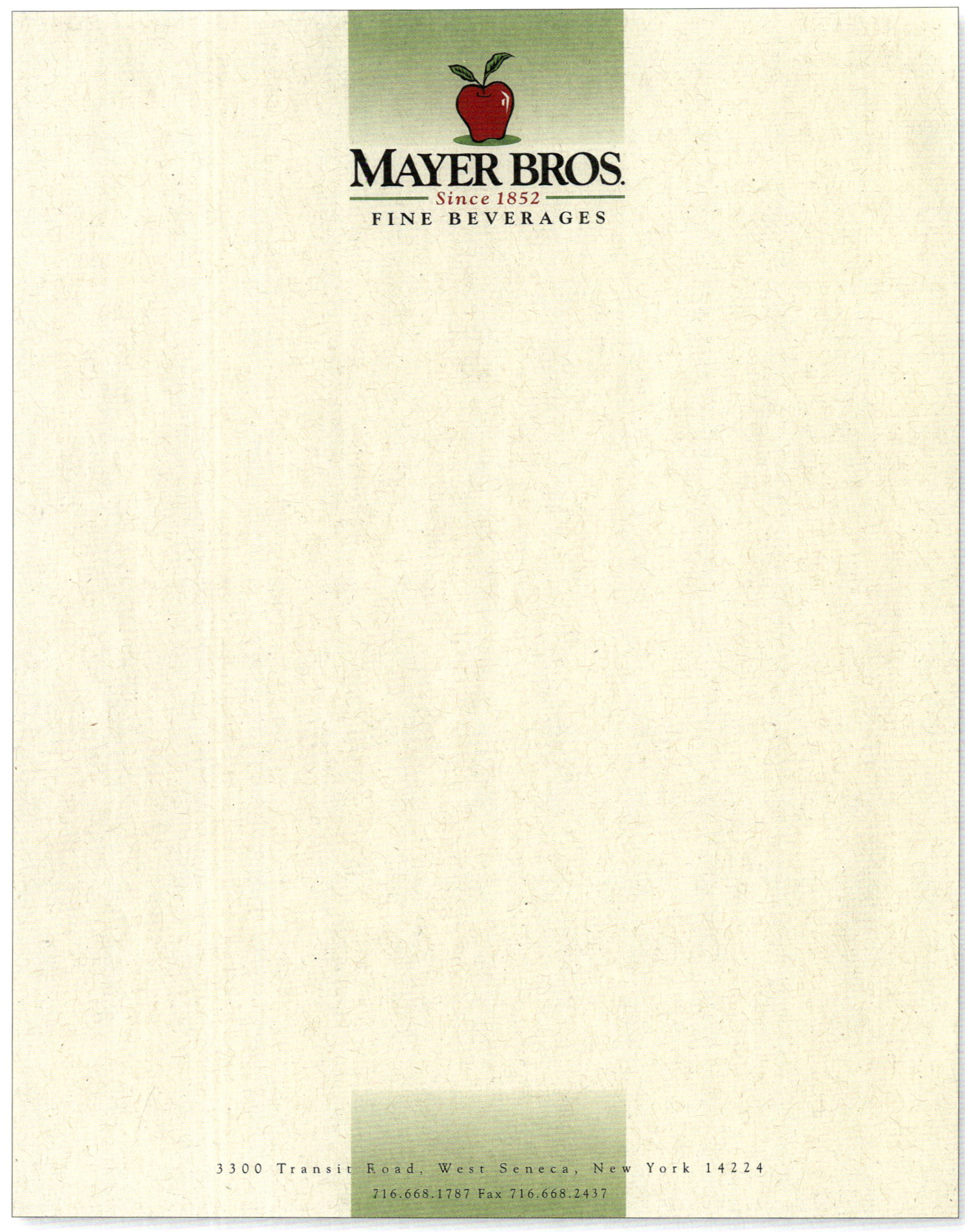

DESIGN FIRM
McElveney & Palozzi Design Group
Rochester, (NY) USA
PROJECT
Mayer Bros.
CREATIVE DIRECTOR
Bill McElveney
ART DIRECTOR
Lisa Parenti

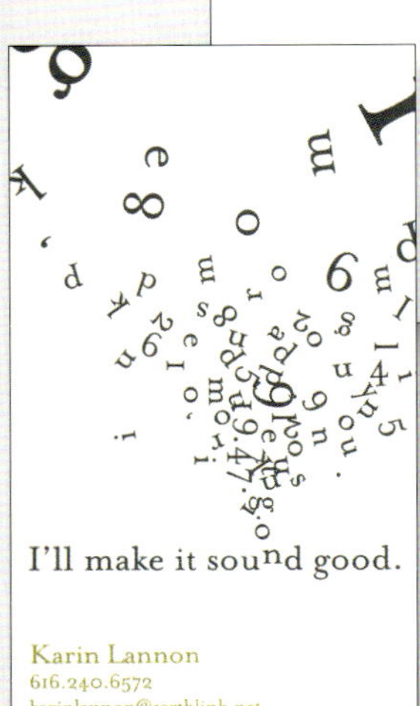

DESIGN FIRM
Square One Design
Grand Rapids, (MI) USA
PROJECT
Karin Lannon
ART DIRECTOR
Lin Ver Meulen
DESIGNER
Anna Huddleston

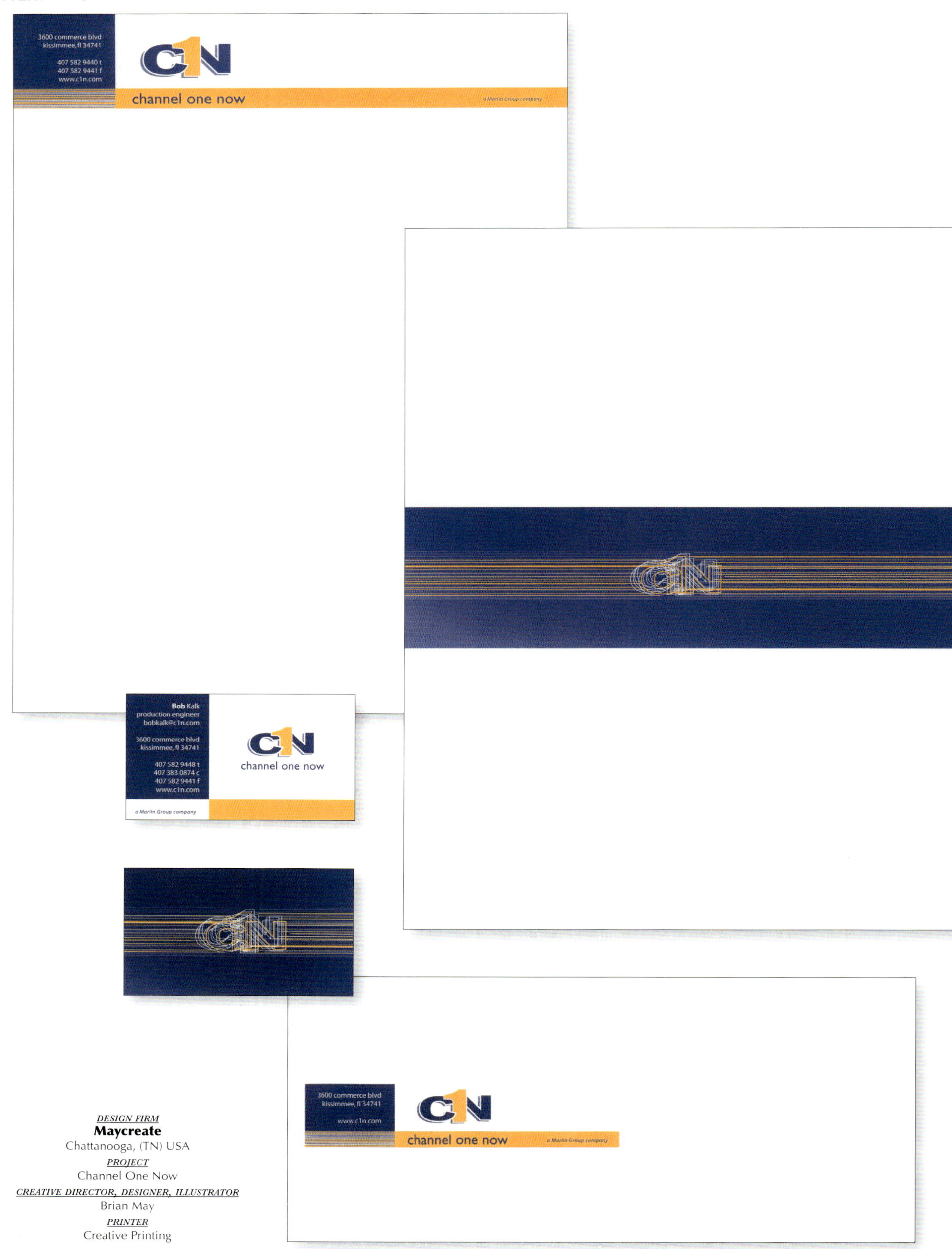

DESIGN FIRM
Maycreate
Chattanooga, (TN) USA
PROJECT
Channel One Now
CREATIVE DIRECTOR, DESIGNER, ILLUSTRATOR
Brian May
PRINTER
Creative Printing

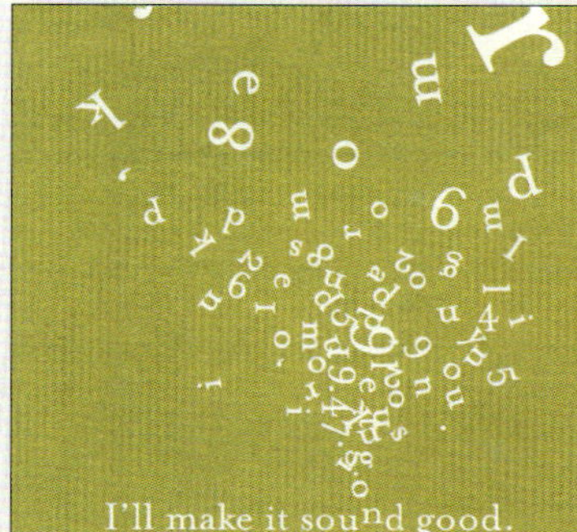

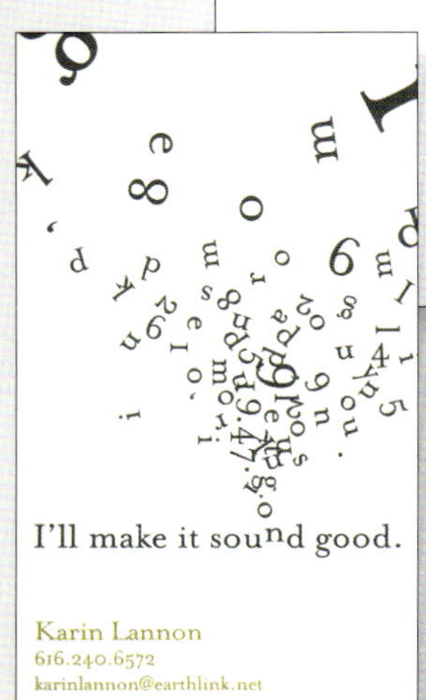

DESIGN FIRM
Square One Design
Grand Rapids, (MI) USA
PROJECT
Karin Lannon
ART DIRECTOR
Lin Ver Meulen
DESIGNER
Anna Huddleston

DESIGN FIRM
Ontarget Marketing
Merced, (CA) USA
CLIENT
Livingston Court Theater Project
ART DIRECTOR
Jesse Bloodworth
DESIGNER
Dusty Dahlgren

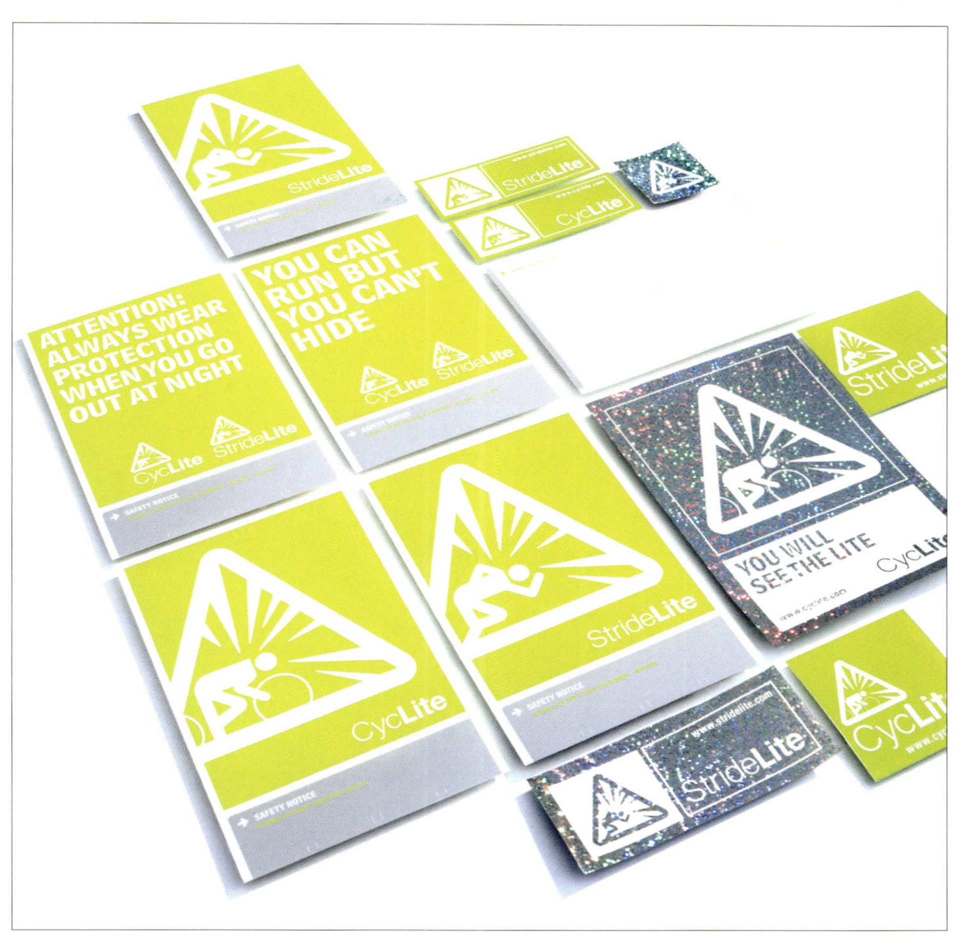

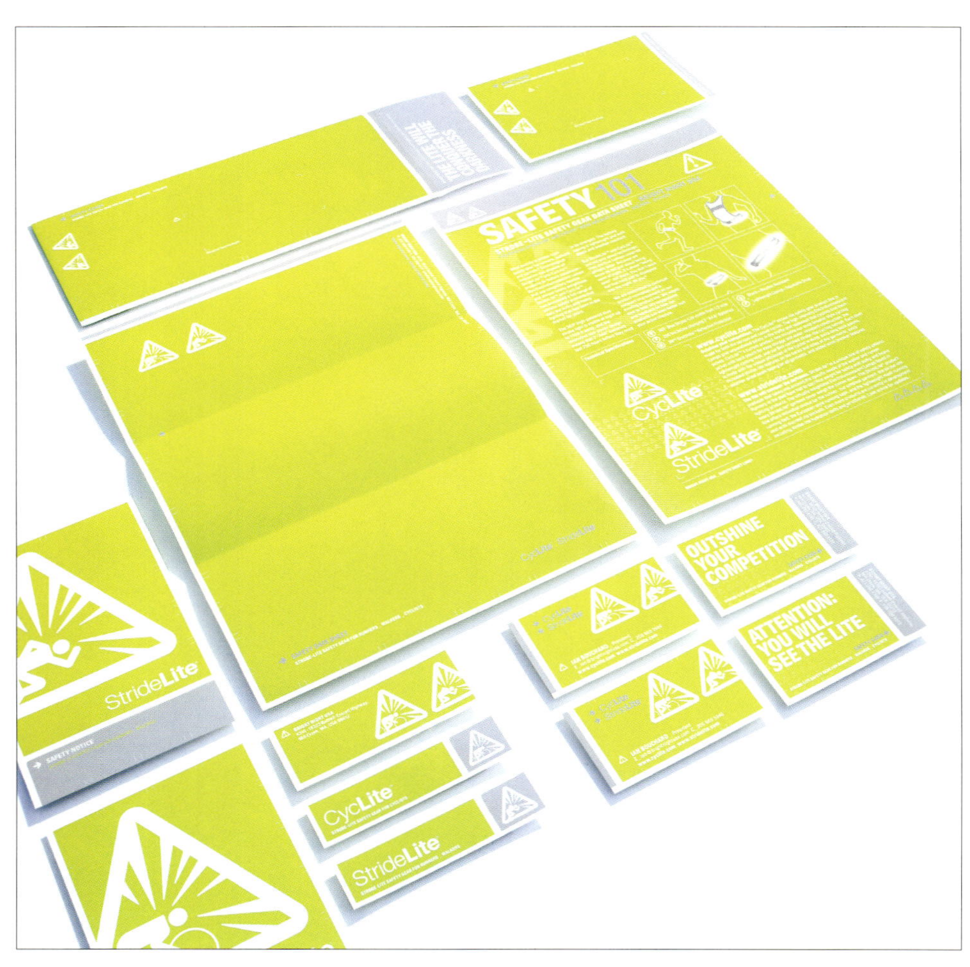

DESIGN FIRM
Subplot Design Inc.
Vancouver, Canada
PROJECT
Stridelite

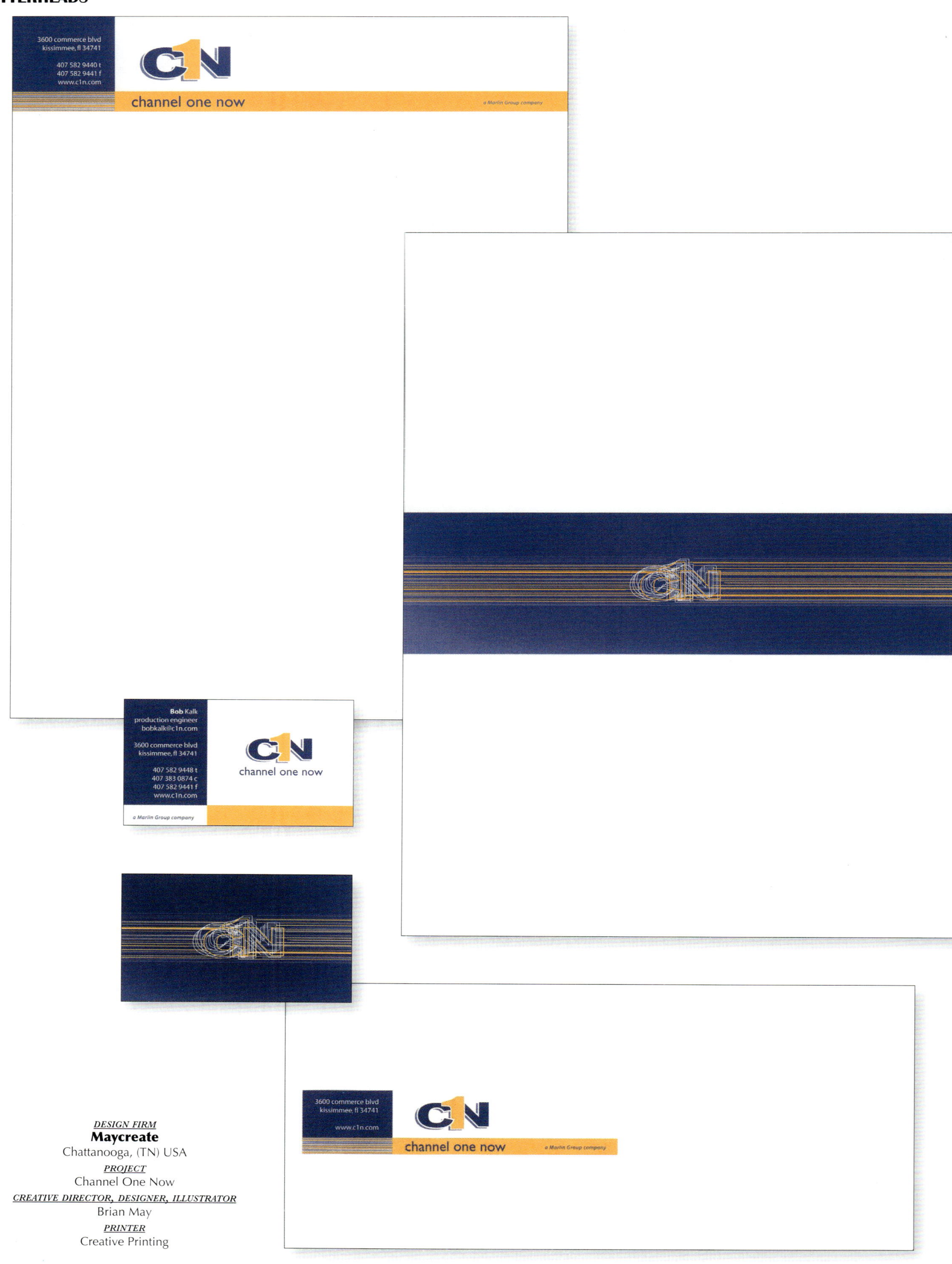

DESIGN FIRM
Maycreate
Chattanooga, (TN) USA
PROJECT
Channel One Now
CREATIVE DIRECTOR, DESIGNER, ILLUSTRATOR
Brian May
PRINTER
Creative Printing

DESIGN FIRM
Market Street Marketing
Redding, (CA) USA
PROJECT
Cardiovascular Associates of Redding
PRINCIPAL
Kathleen Downs

CAUGHT FRESH SERVED FRESH
KING'S
FISH HOUSE
1945

WWW.KINGSFISHHOUSE.COM

CORONA
THE CROSSINGS
2530 TUSCANY ROAD, CORONA, CALIFORNIA 92881 PHONE: 951-284-7900 FAX: 951-284-7908

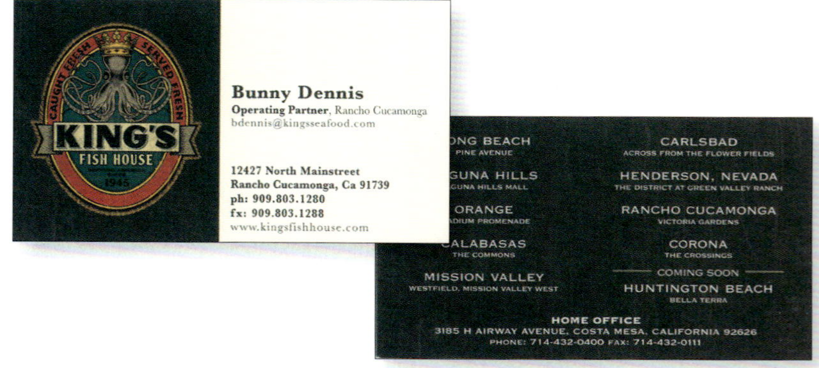

DESIGN FIRM
30sixty Advertising+Design
Los Angeles, (CA) USA
CLIENT
King's Seafood Company
CREATIVE DIRECTOR
Henry Vizcarra
ART DIRECTOR
David Fuscellaro

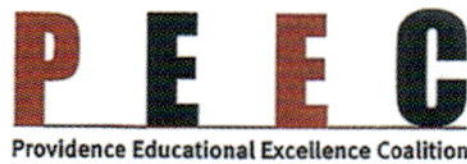

Rhode Island Children's Crusade 134 Thurbers Avenue, Suite 111, Providence, RI 02905

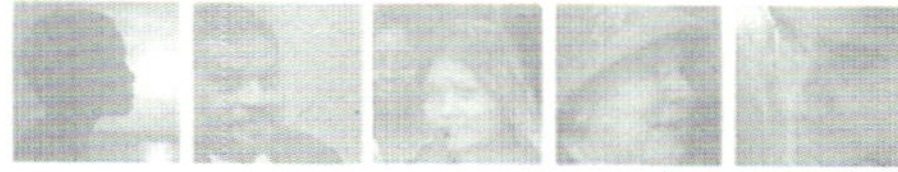

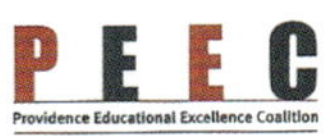

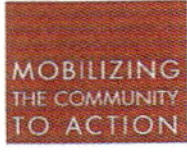

Reza C. Clifton
Community Organizer

Rhode Island Children's Crusade
134 Thurbers Avenue, Suite 111
Providence, RI 02905

t **401.854.5506 x 142**
f **401.854.5511**
reza@childrenscrusade.org

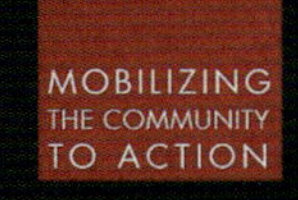

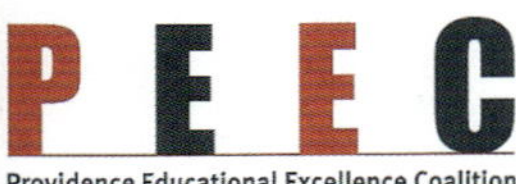

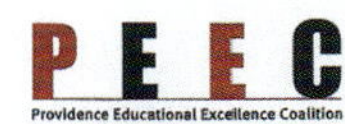

Rhode Island Children's Crusade
134 Thurbers Avenue, Suite 111
Providence, RI 02905

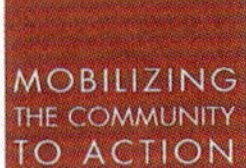

Rhode Island Children's Crusade
134 Thurbers Avenue, Suite 111
Providence, RI 02905
401.854.5506 x 141

PROVIDENCE EDUCATIONAL EXCELLENCE COALITION

DESIGN FIRM
Im-aj Communications & Design, Inc.
West Kingston, (RI) USA

CLIENT
PEEC

CREATIVE DIRECTOR
Jami Ouellette

ART DIRECTOR
Leslie Emert

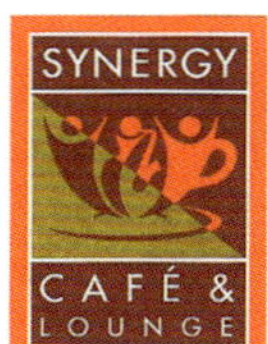

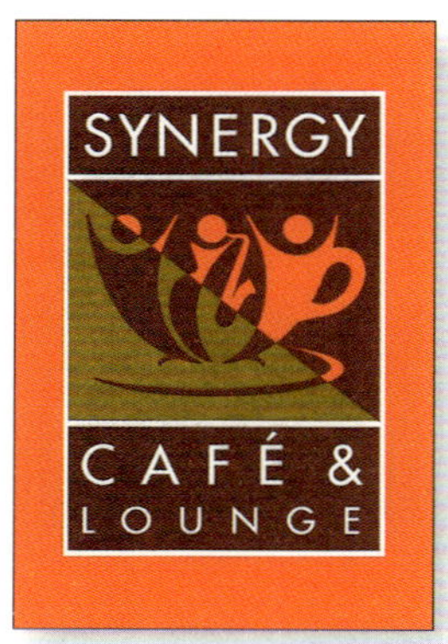

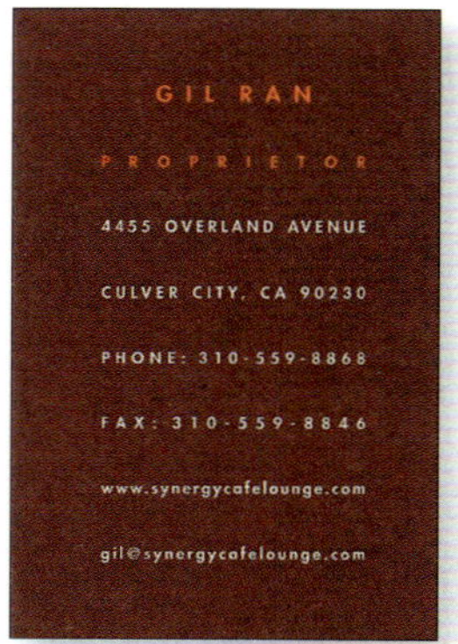

4455 OVERLAND AVENUE
CULVER CITY, CA 90230
PHONE: 310-559-8868
FAX: 310-559-8846
info@synergycafelounge.com

DESIGN FIRM
Evenson Design Group
Culver City, (CA) USA

PROJECT
Synergy

ART DIRECTOR
Stan Evenson

DESIGNER
Katja Loesch

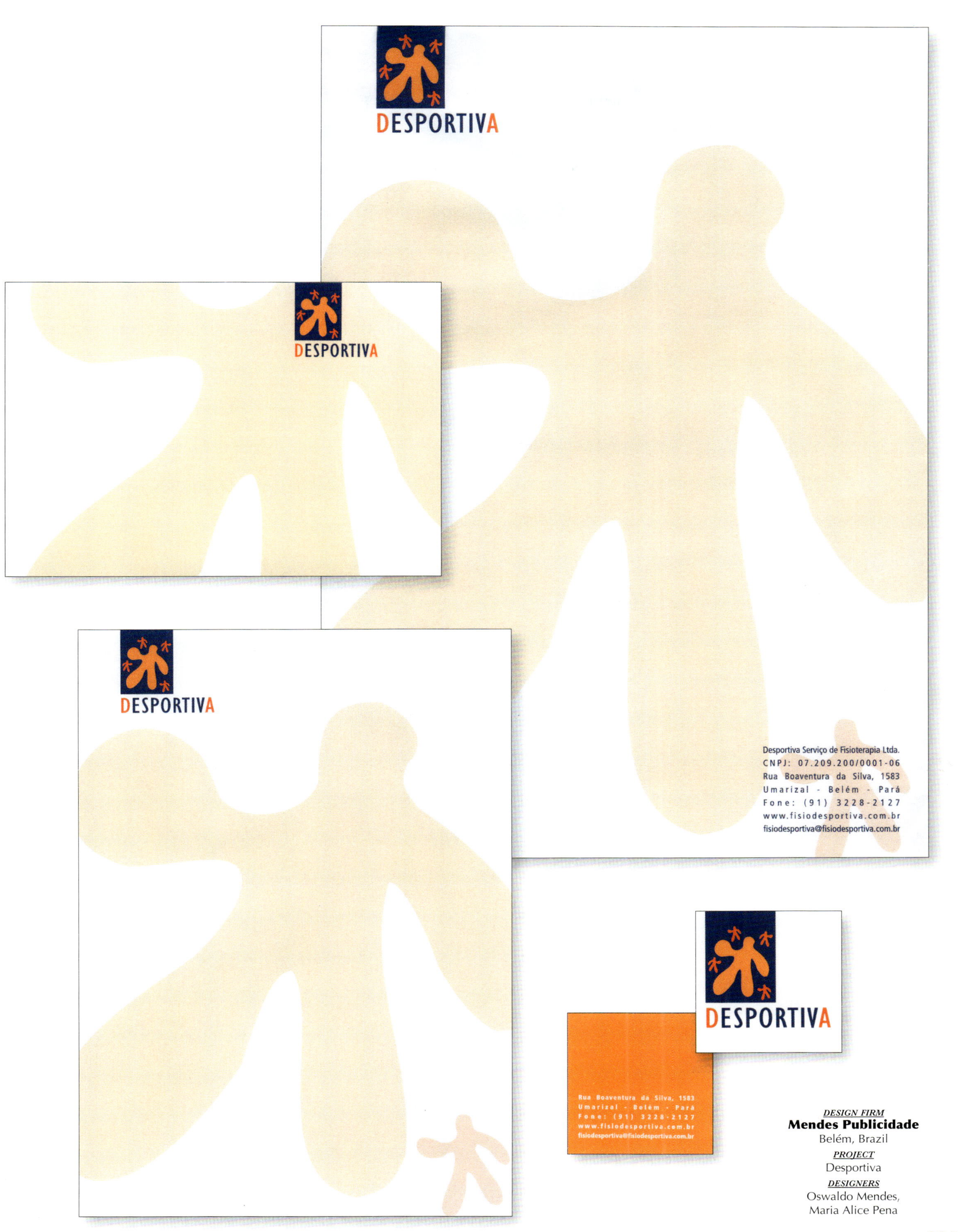

DESIGN FIRM
Mendes Publicidade
Belém, Brazil
PROJECT
Desportiva
DESIGNERS
Oswaldo Mendes,
Maria Alice Pena

DESIGN FIRM
TrueFACES Creation Sdn. Bhd.
Selangor, Malaysia
PROJECT
ABRIC
DESIGNERS
TrueFACES Creative Team

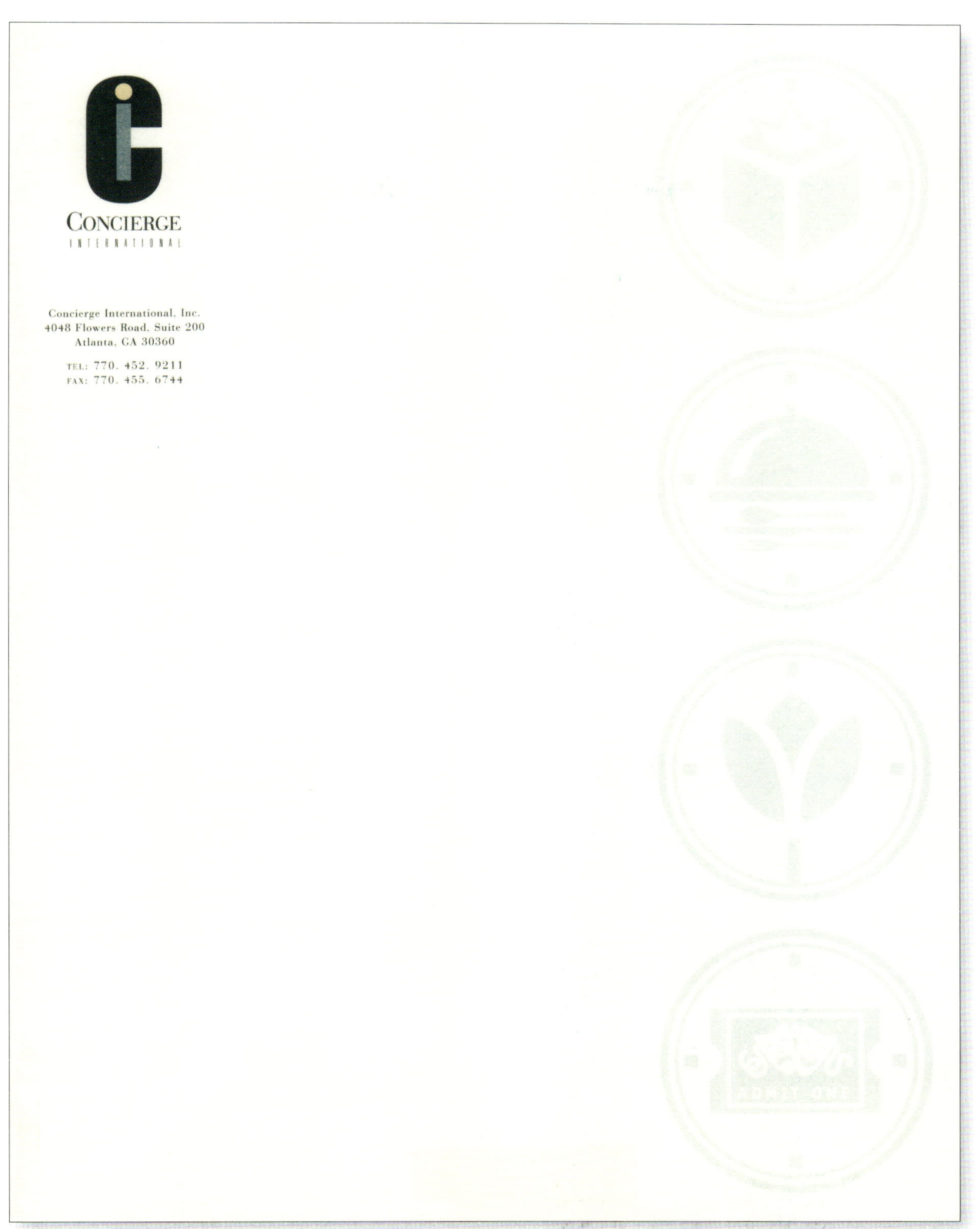

DESIGN FIRM
Young & Martin Design
Atlanta, (GA) USA
PROJECT
Concierge International
DESIGNERS
Connie Herrell,
Ed Young

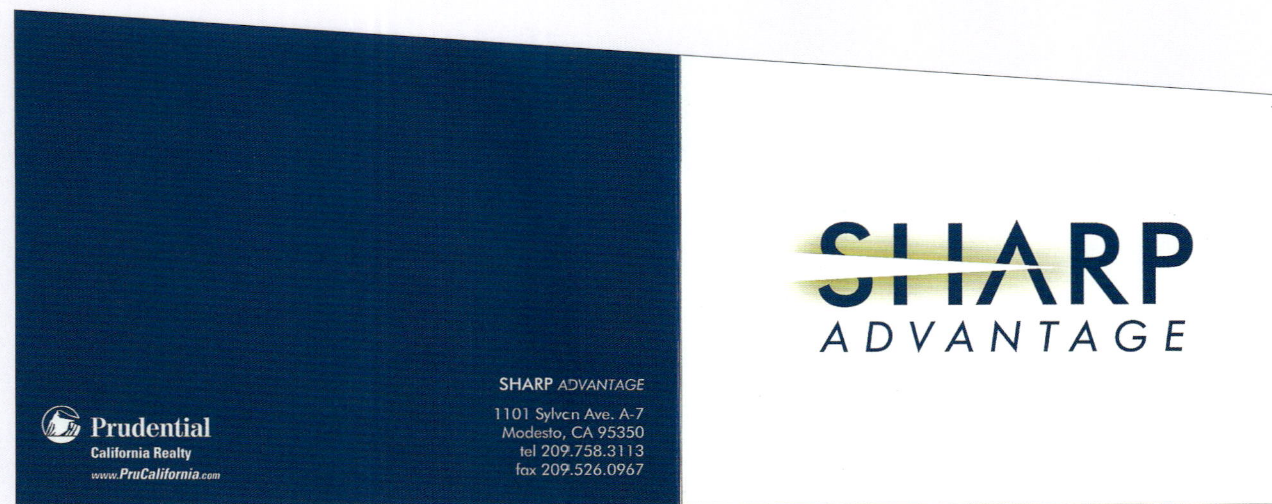

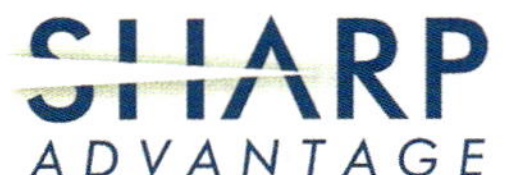

As Real Estate Consultants, we have made a conscious decision to run our business different than "traditional sales people." Rather than rush you into a home that doesn't fit your needs, we review all the options and help you select the right home for your situation. You will not find us cold calling in the evenings and knocking doors on the weekends because our business comes from referrals – not traditional sales tactics. Our goal is to provide a level of service that makes it easy for you to refer people you care about to us. Your personal endorsement is the greatest compliment we could ever receive.

1101 Sylvan Ave. A-7
Modesto, CA 95350
fax 209.526.0967

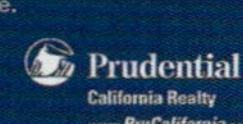

SHARP
ADVANTAGE

Carl R. Sharp
REAL ESTATE CONSULTANT
tel 209.758.3113
csharp@prucalifornia.com

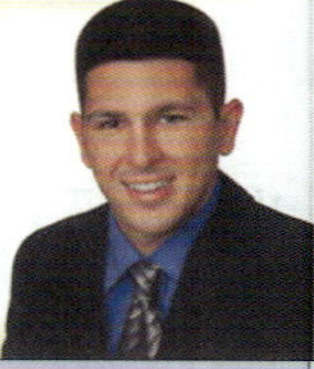

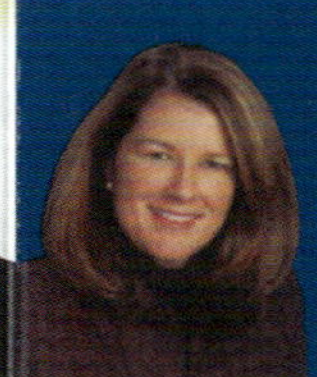

Sharon Sharp-Knox
REAL ESTATE CONSULTANT
tel 209.758.3113
ssknox@prucalifornia.com

1101 Sylvan Ave. A-7
Modesto, CA 95350
tel 209.758.3113
fax 209.526.0967

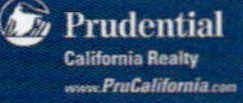

DESIGN FIRM
Never Boring Design Associates
Modesto, (CA) USA
PROJECT
Sharp Advantage
DESIGNER
Julie Orona

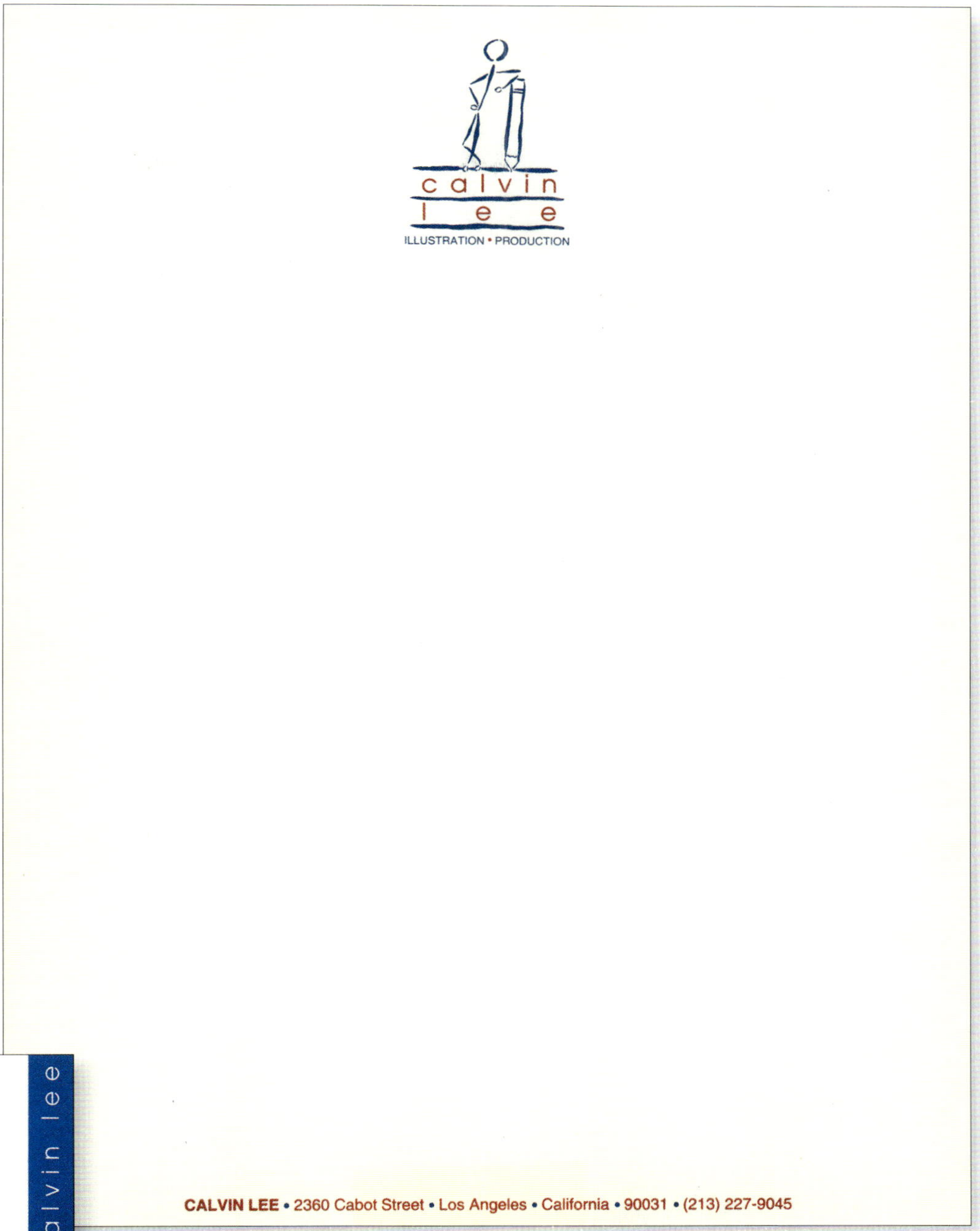

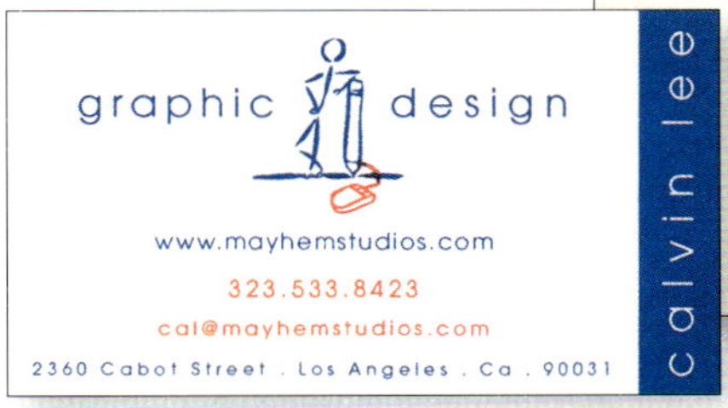

calvin lee

ILLUSTRATION • PRODUCTION

CALVIN LEE • 2360 Cabot Street • Los Angeles • California • 90031 • (213) 227-9045

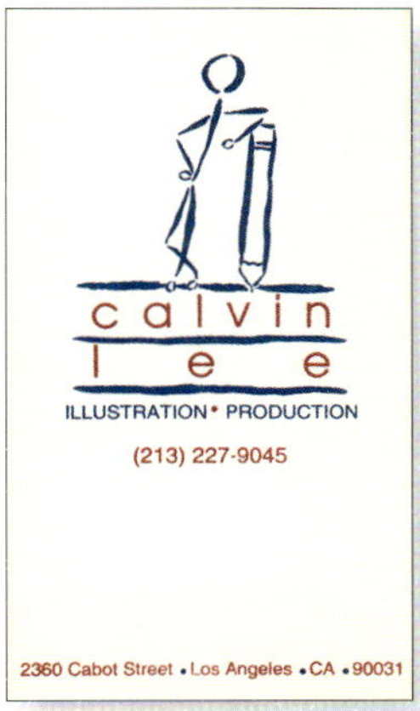

calvin lee

ILLUSTRATION • PRODUCTION

(213) 227-9045

2360 Cabot Street • Los Angeles • CA • 90031

graphic design

www.mayhemstudios.com

323.533.8423

cal@mayhemstudios.com

2360 Cabot Street . Los Angeles . Ca . 90031

calvin lee

DESIGN FIRM
Mayhem Studios
Los Angeles, (CA) USA
PROJECT
Calvin Lee Stationery
DESIGNER
Calvin Lee

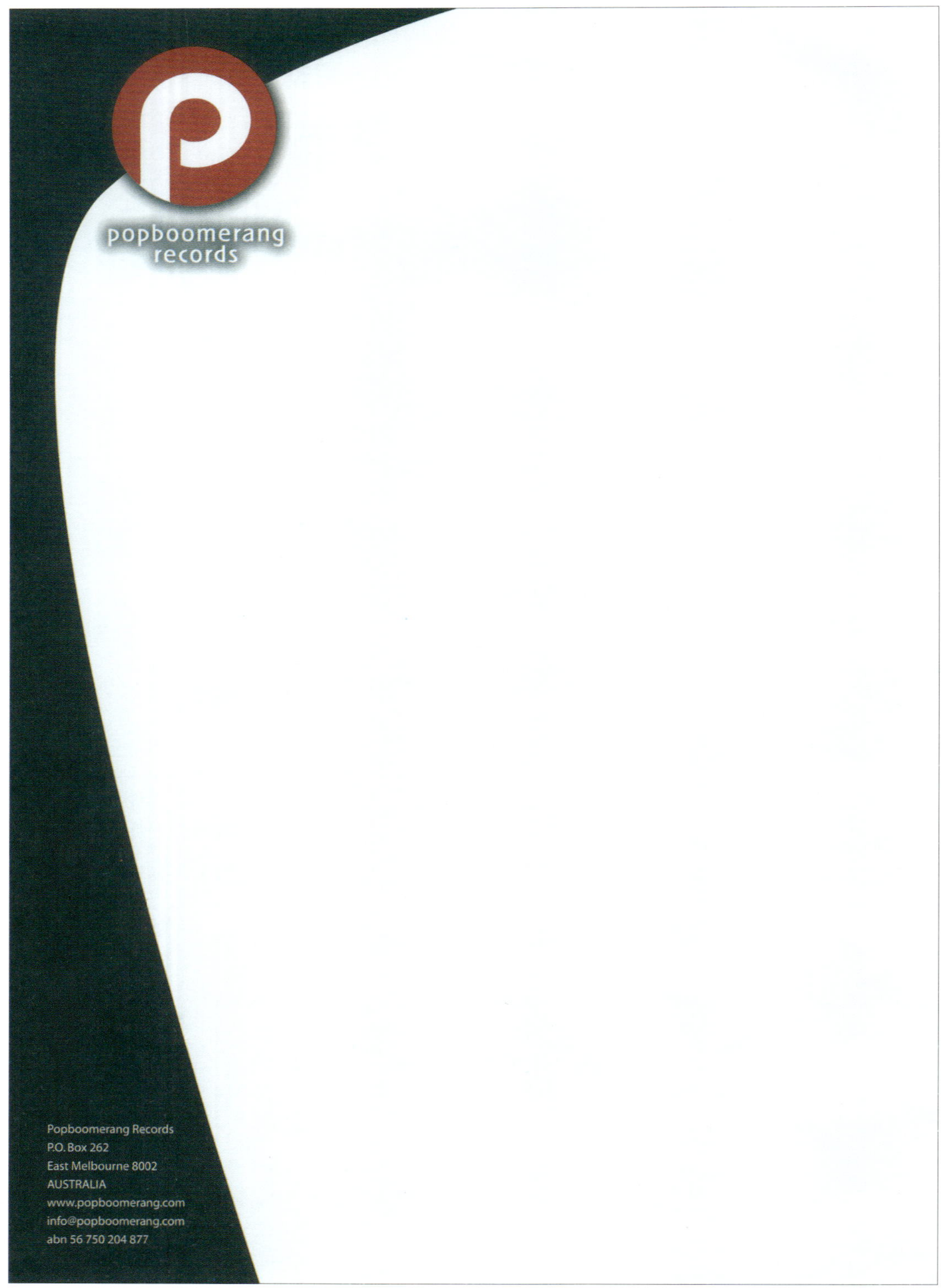

DESIGN FIRM
At First Sight
Ormond, Australia
CREATIVE DIRECTOR
Olivia Brown
DESIGNER
Barry Selleck

Finger Lakes Tourism
309 Lake Street
Penn Yan, New York 14527

Phone: 315.536.7488 Fax: 315.536.1237
E-mail: info@fingerlakes.org
www.fingerlakes.org

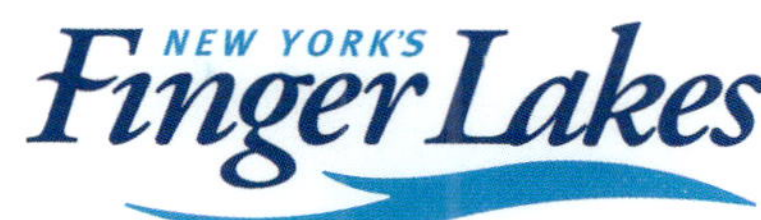

DESIGN FIRM
McElveney & Palozzi Design
Rochester, (NY) USA
PROJECT
New York's Finger Lakes
CREATIVE DIRECTOR
William McElveney
ART DIRECTORS
Lisa Gates,
Matt Nowicki

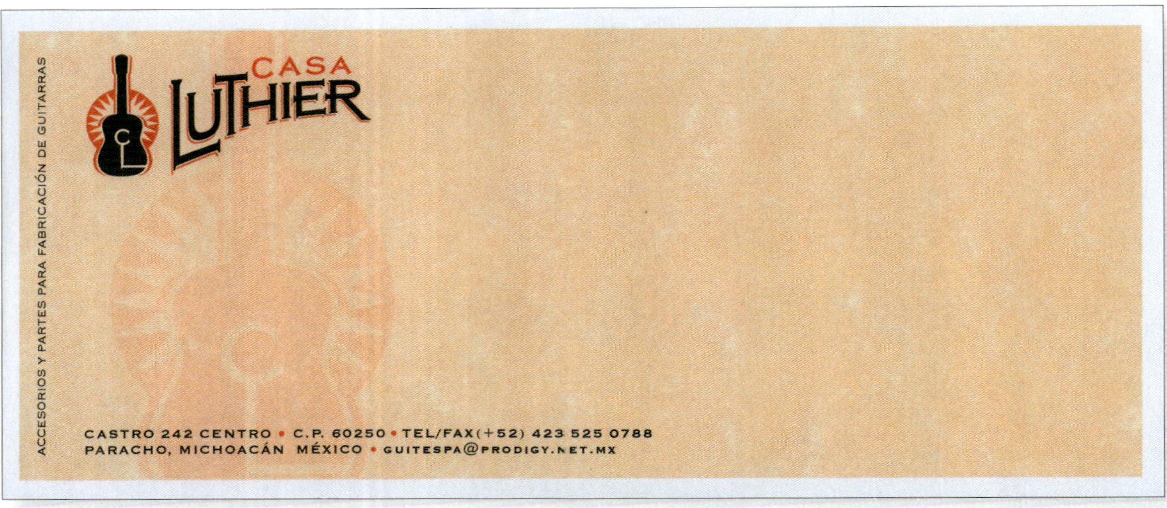

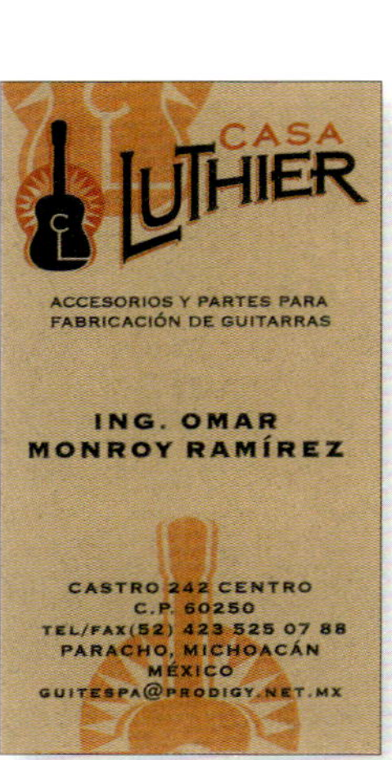

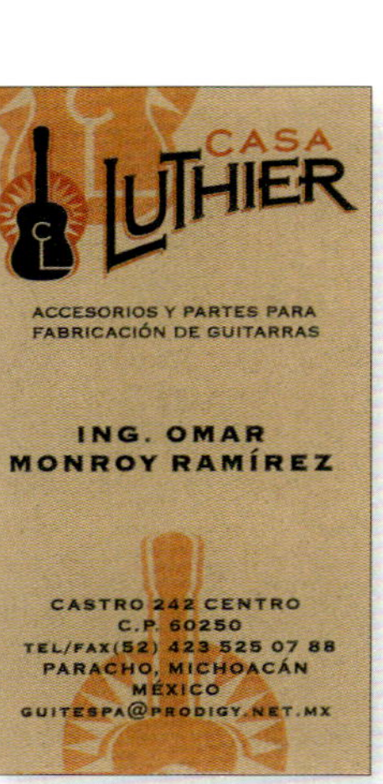

ACCESORIOS Y PARTES PARA FABRICACIÓN DE GUITARRAS

CASA
LUTHIER

CASTRO 242 CENTRO • C.P. 60250 • TEL/FAX(+52) 423 525 0788
PARACHO, MICHOACÁN MÉXICO • GUITESPA@PRODIGY.NET.MX

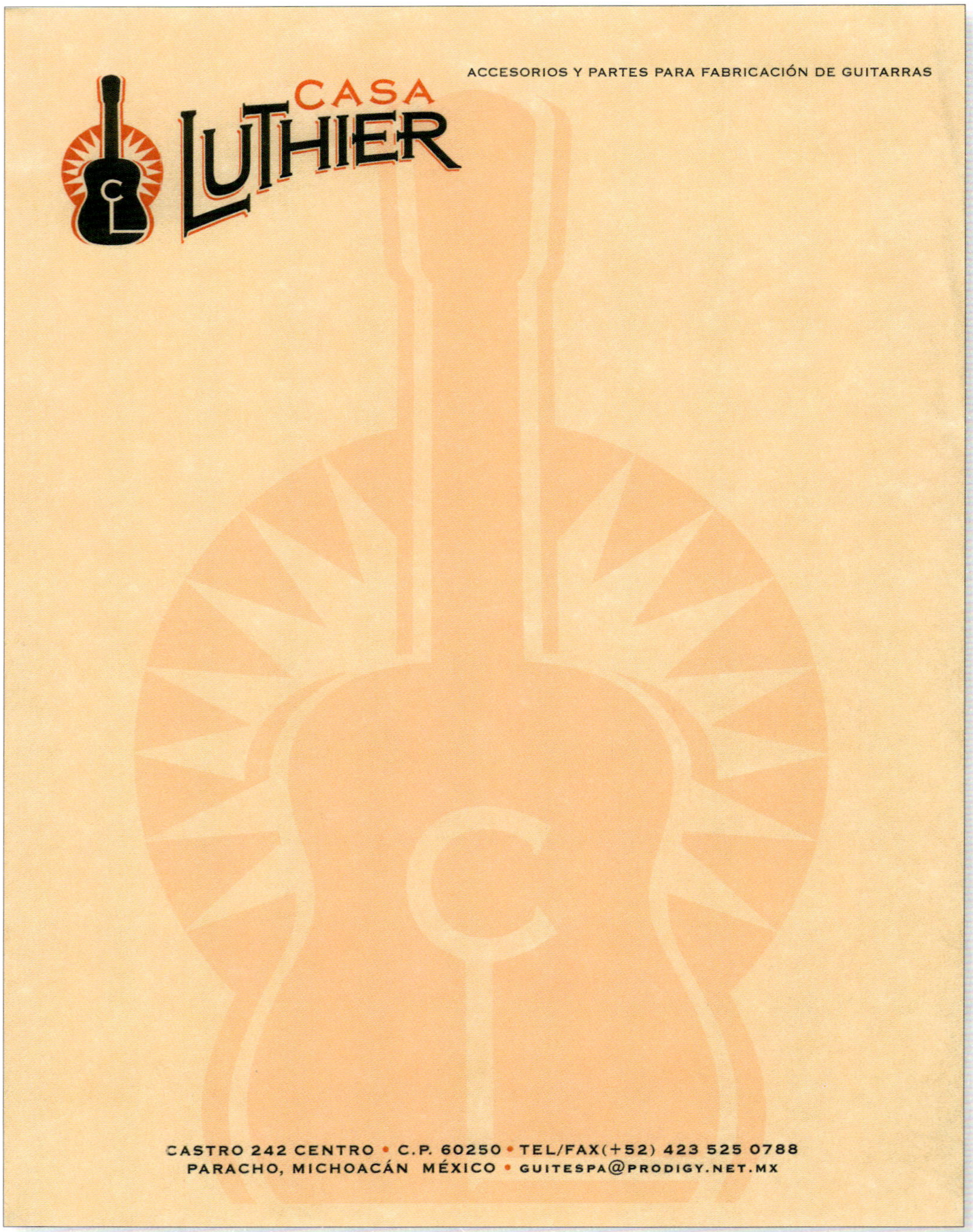

DESIGN FIRM
Kenneth Diseño
Uruapan, Mexico
PROJECT
Casa Luthier
DESIGNERS
Kenneth Treviño,
Minerva Galván

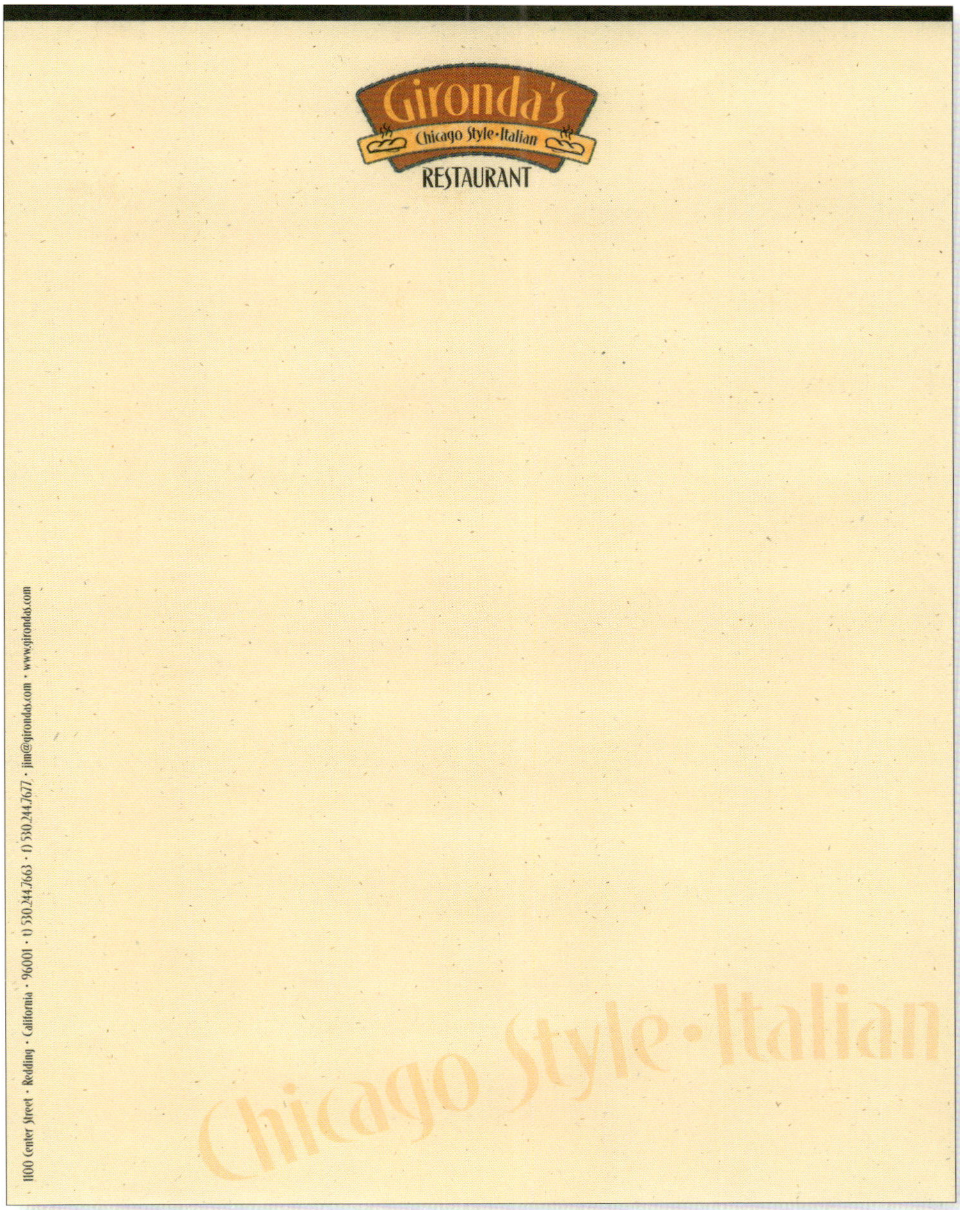

Gironda's
Chicago Style • Italian
RESTAURANT

1100 Center Street • Redding • California • 96001 • t) 530.244.7663 • f) 530.244.7677 • jim@girondas.com • www.girondas.com

Chicago Style • Italian

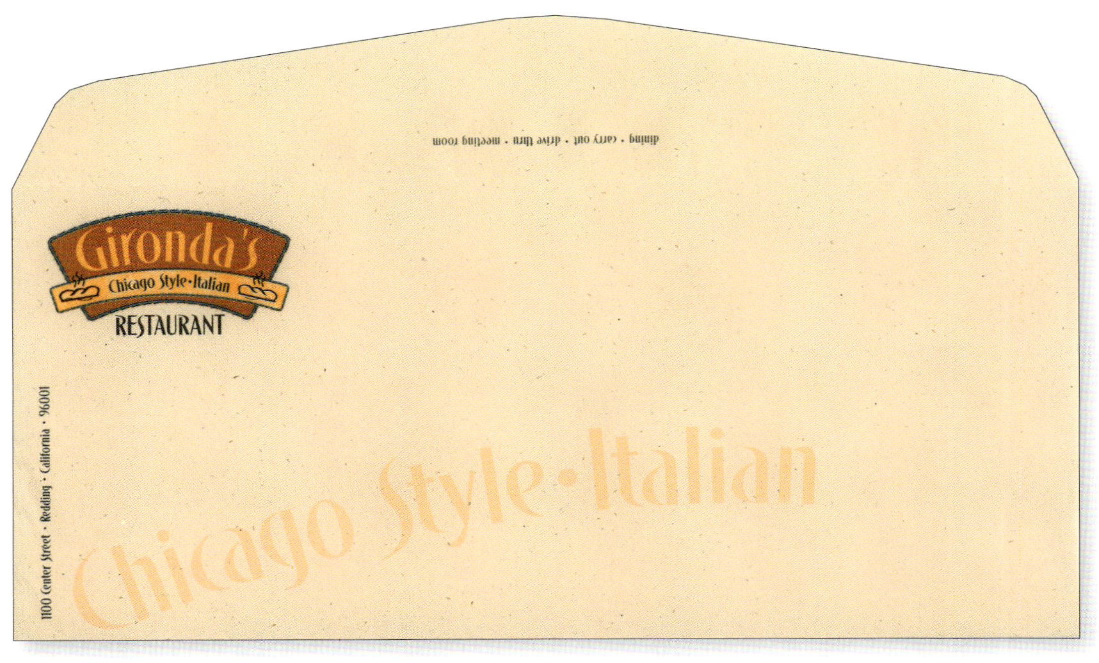

DESIGN FIRM
Market Street Marketing
Redding, (CA) USA
PROJECT
Gironda's
DESIGNER
Kathleen Downs

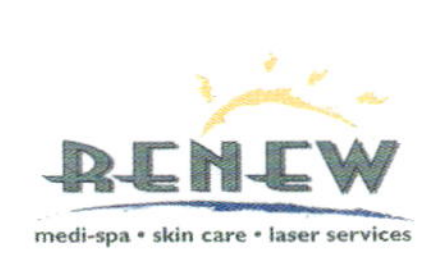

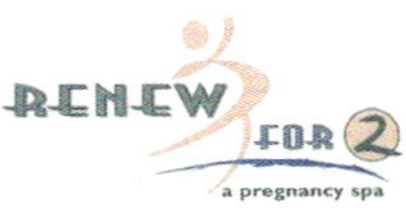

2626 Edith Ave. Suite D · Redding, CA 96001

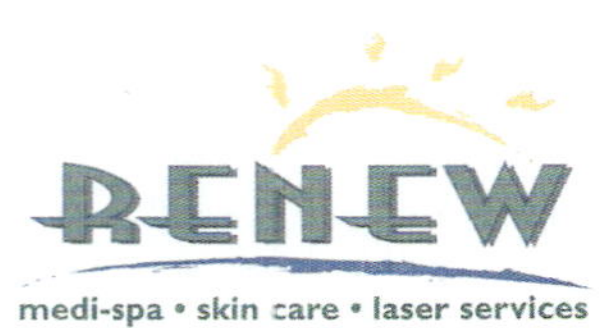

RENEW FOR 2
a pregnancy spa

2626 Edith Ave. Suite D
Redding, CA 96001

T. 530.241.7772
F. 530.241.7786

w w w . r e n e w l a s e r s k i n c a r e . c o m

DESIGN FIRM
Market Street Marketing
Redding, (CA) USA

PROJECT
Renew for 2

PRINCIPAL
Kathleen Downs

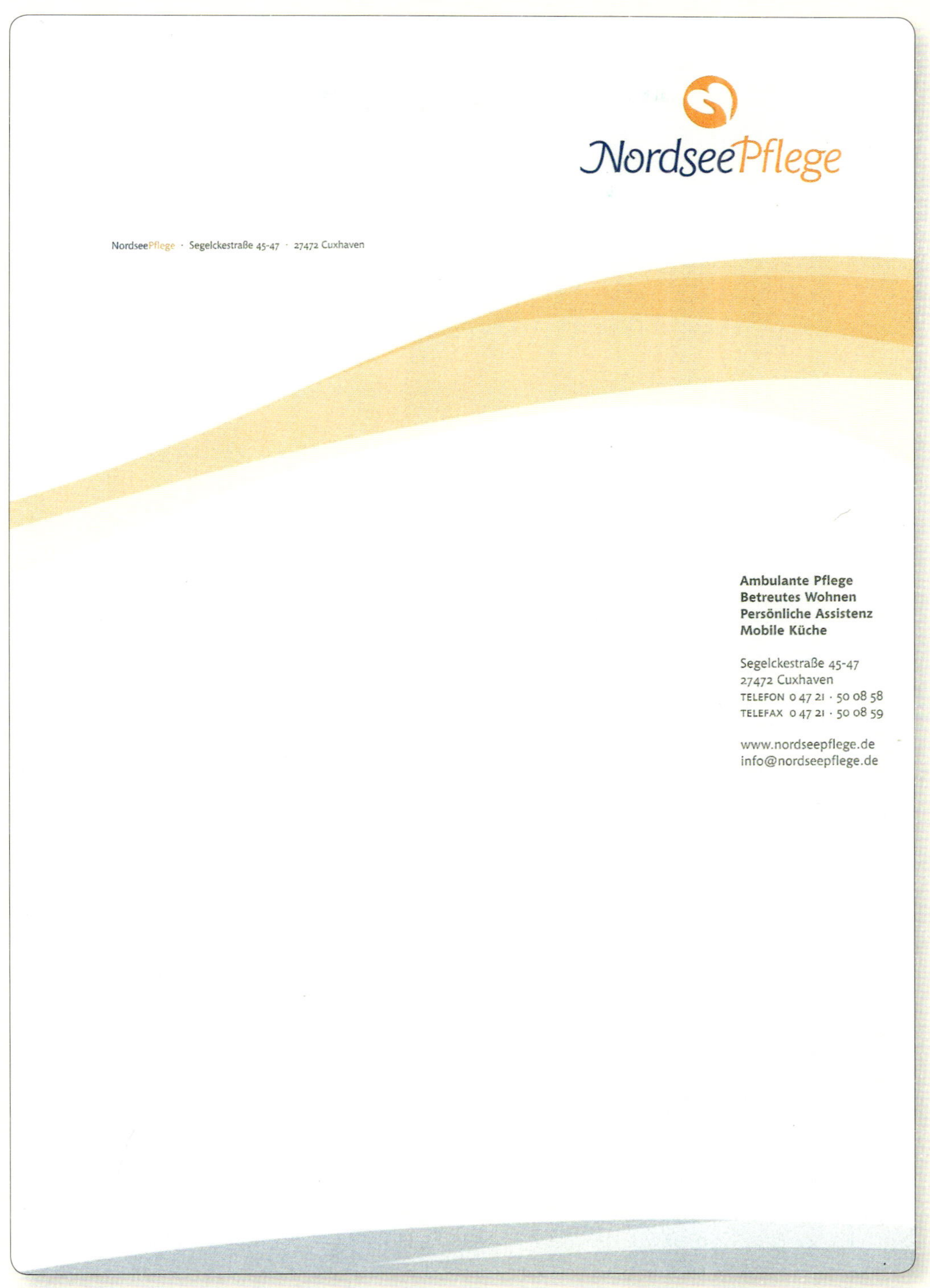

DESIGN FIRM
Braue: Branding & Corporate Design
Bremerhaven, Germany
CLIENT
NordseePflege
CREATIVE DIRECTOR
Kai Braue
ART DIRECTOR
Marcel Robbers
DESIGNERS
Marcel Robbers,
Annika Schmidt

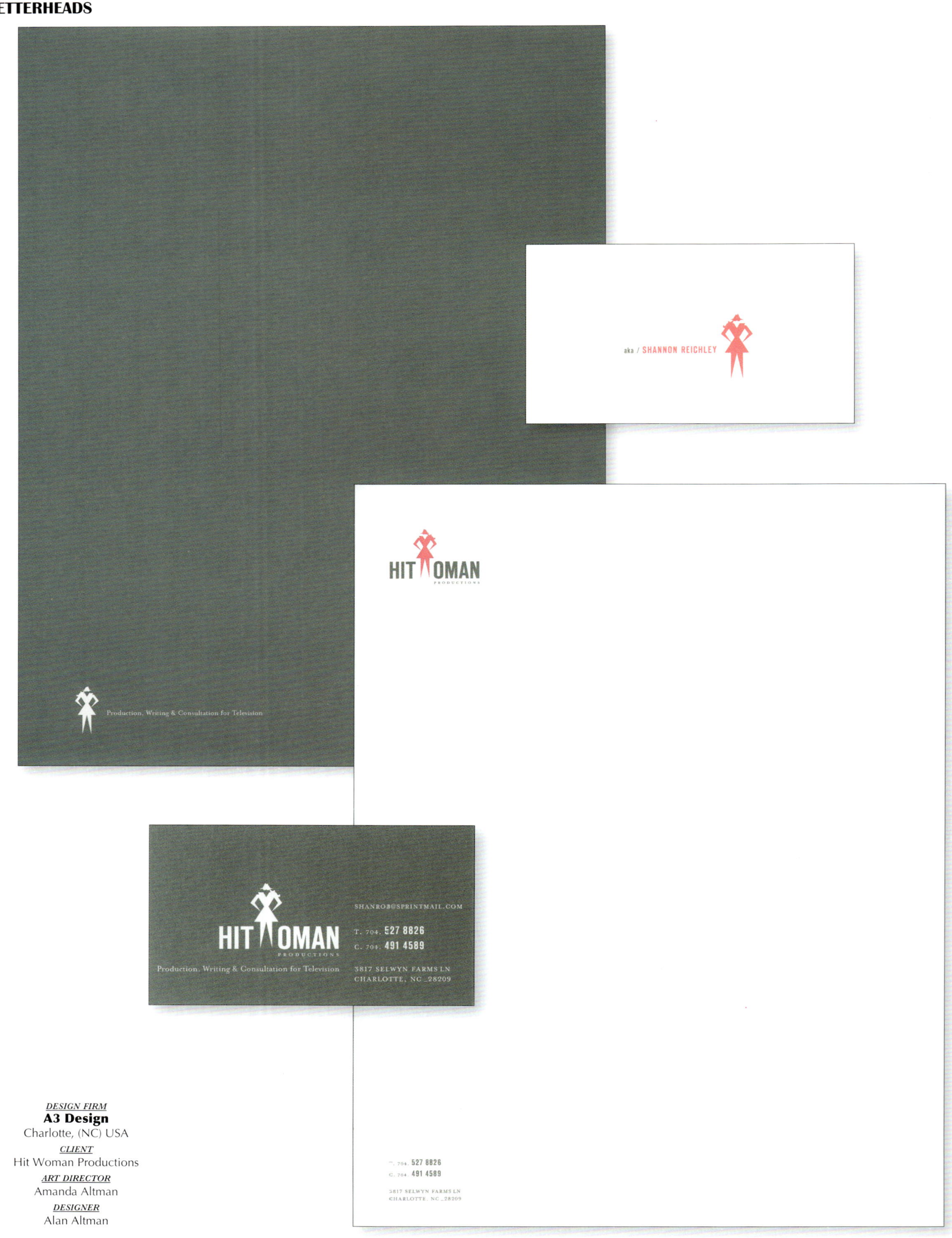

DESIGN FIRM
A3 Design
Charlotte, (NC) USA
CLIENT
Hit Woman Productions
ART DIRECTOR
Amanda Altman
DESIGNER
Alan Altman

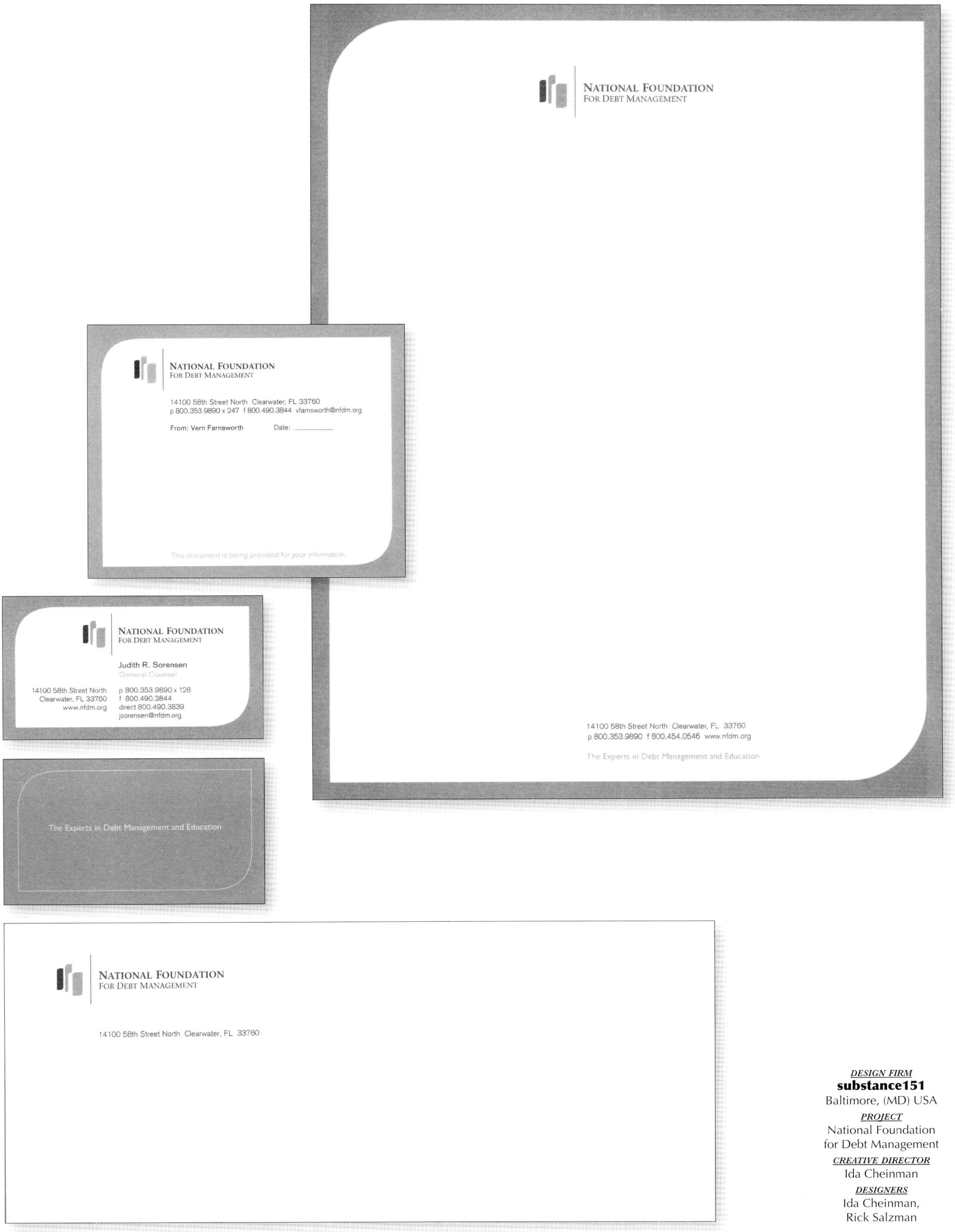

NATIONAL FOUNDATION
FOR DEBT MANAGEMENT

14100 58th Street North Clearwater, FL 33760
p 800.353.9890 f 800.454.0546 www.nfdm.org

The Experts in Debt Management and Education

NATIONAL FOUNDATION
FOR DEBT MANAGEMENT

14100 58th Street North Clearwater, FL 33760
p 800.353.9890 x 247 f 800.490.3844 vfarnsworth@nfdm.org

From: Vern Farnsworth Date: ____________

This document is being provided for your information.

NATIONAL FOUNDATION
FOR DEBT MANAGEMENT

Judith R. Sorensen
General Counsel

14100 58th Street North
Clearwater, FL 33760
www.nfdm.org

p 800.353.9890 x 128
f 800.490.3844
direct 800.490.3839
jsorensen@nfdm.org

The Experts in Debt Management and Education

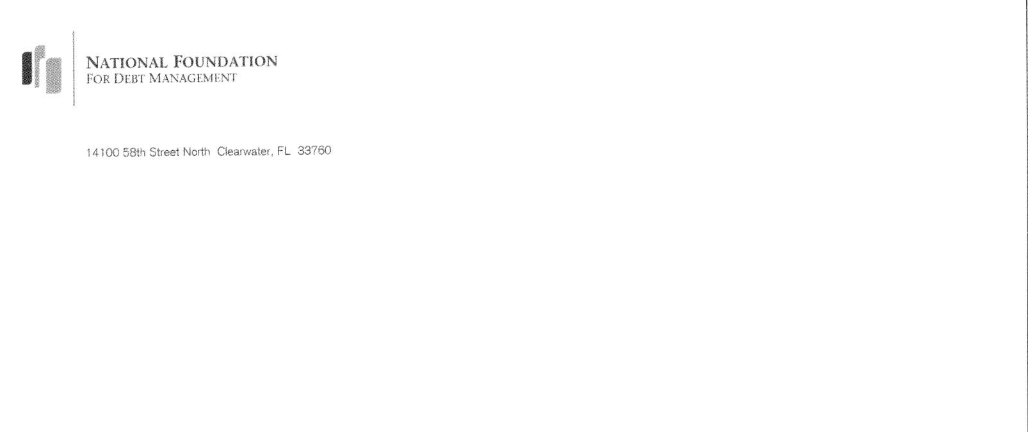

DESIGN FIRM
substance151
Baltimore, (MD) USA
PROJECT
National Foundation
for Debt Management
CREATIVE DIRECTOR
Ida Cheinman
DESIGNERS
Ida Cheinman,
Rick Salzman

DESIGN FIRM
Entermotion Design Studio
Wichita, (KS) USA
PROJECT
Life Sizing
DESIGNER
Melissa Carr

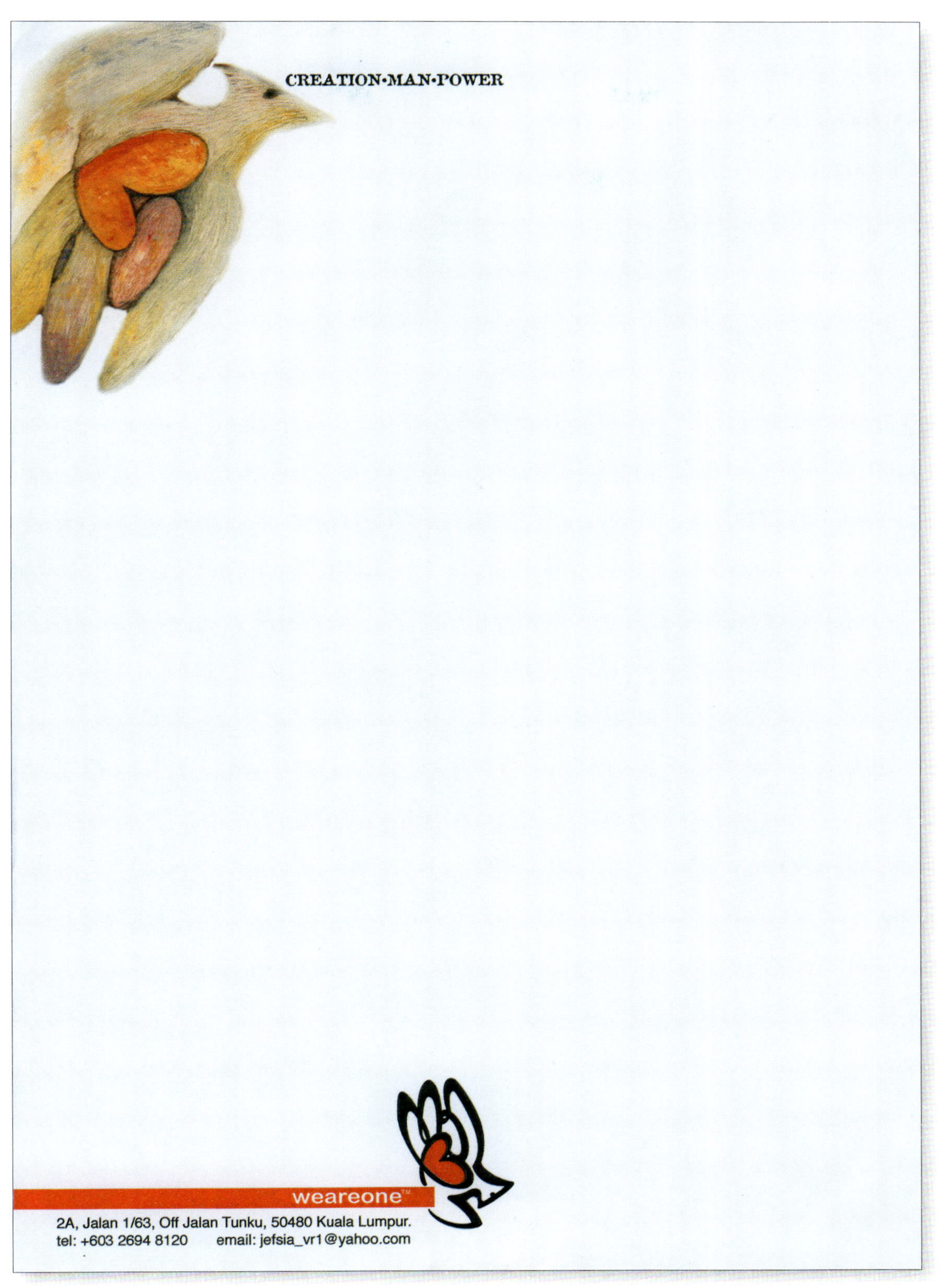

DESIGN FIRM
TrueFACES Creation Sdn. Bhd.
Selangor, Malaysia
PROJECT
weareone
DESIGNERS
TrueFACES Creative Team

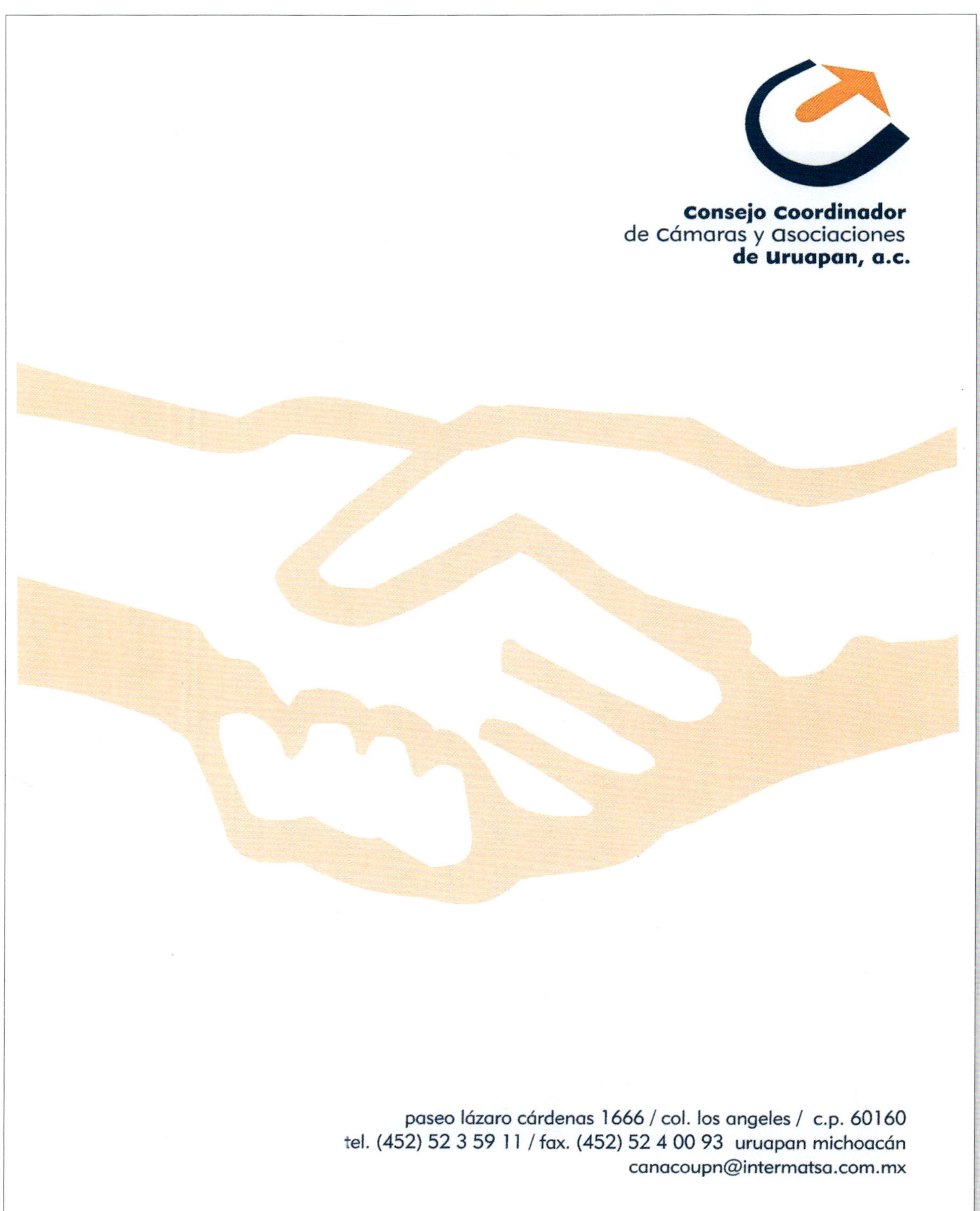

DESIGN FIRM
Kenneth Diseño
Uruapan, Mexico
PROJECT
Coordinadora De Cámaras Uruapan
DESIGNERS
Kenneth Treviño,
Minerva Galván

da vinci

4397 NW 124 Avenue, Coral Springs, FL 33065 USA
Tel 954.688.5600 Fax 954.575.5936

www.davsys.com

da vinci

Neil Kempt
Regional Vice President, Western United States

7625 Hayvenhurst Avenue, Unit #25, Van Nuys, CA 91406 USA
Tel 661.268.0074 Fax 661.268.7480
Email neilhk@davsys.com, neilhk@aol.com
Pager 818.712.7655
www.davsys.com

www.davsys.com

4397 NW 124 Avenue, Coral Springs, FL 33065 USA

da vinci

www.davsys.com

4397 NW 124 Avenue, Coral Springs, FL 33065 USA

da vinci

DESIGN FIRM
Gouthier Design: a brand collective
Fort Lauderdale, (FL) USA

CLIENT
daVinci Systems, Inc.

CREATIVE DIRECTOR
Jonathan Gouthier

DESIGNER
Kiley del Valle

PRINTER
Ritter's Printing

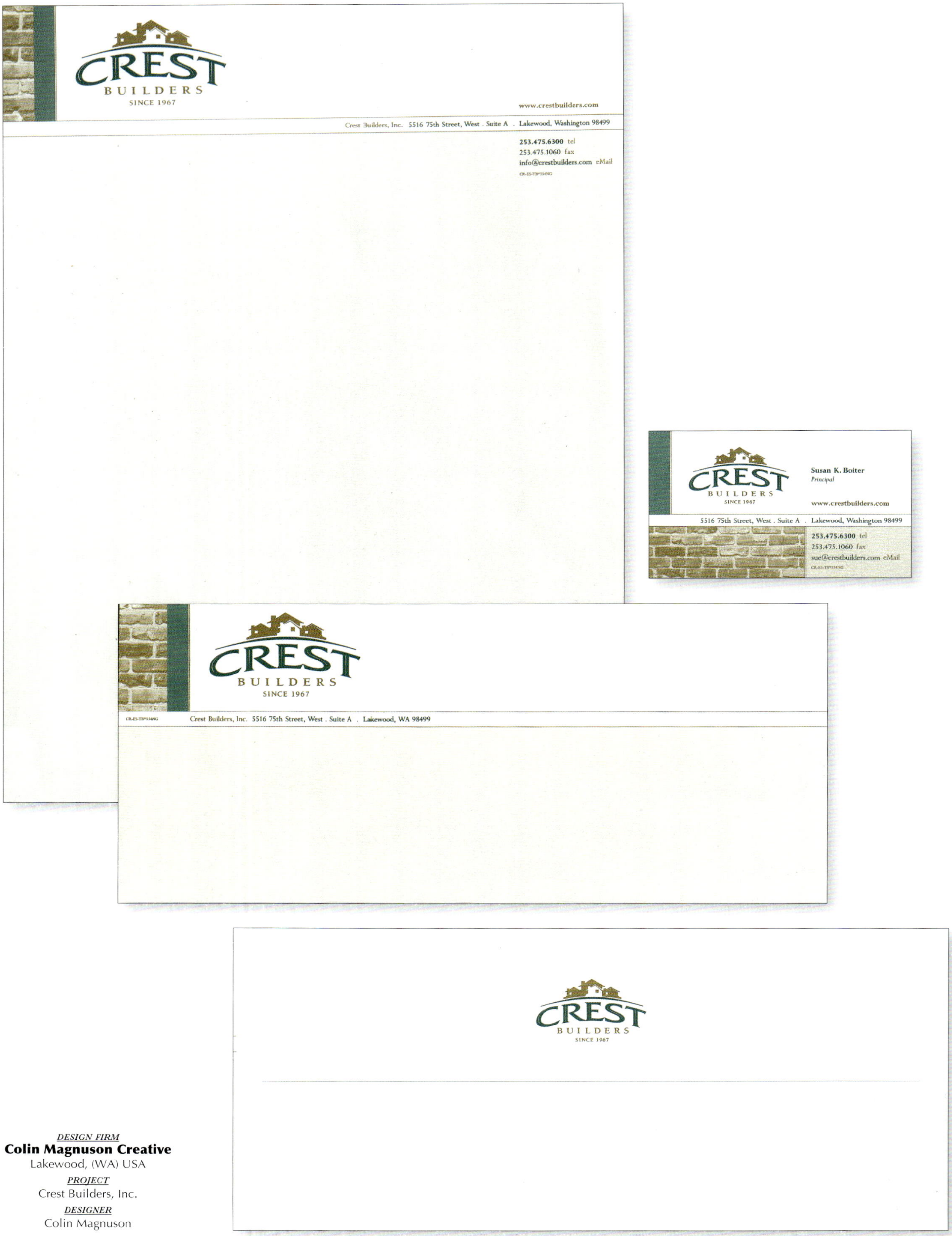

CREST
BUILDERS
SINCE 1967

www.crestbuilders.com

Crest Builders, Inc. 5516 75th Street, West . Suite A . Lakewood, Washington 98499

253.475.6300 tel
253.475.1060 fax
info@crestbuilders.com eMail

CREST
BUILDERS
SINCE 1967

Susan K. Boiter
Principal

www.crestbuilders.com

5516 75th Street, West . Suite A . Lakewood, Washington 98499

253.475.6300 tel
253.475.1060 fax
sue@crestbuilders.com eMail

CREST
BUILDERS
SINCE 1967

Crest Builders, Inc. 5516 75th Street, West . Suite A . Lakewood, WA 98499

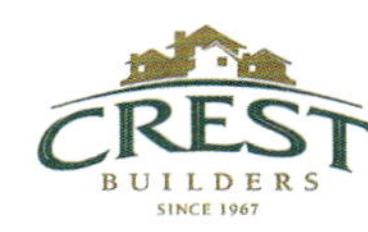

DESIGN FIRM
Colin Magnuson Creative
Lakewood, (WA) USA
PROJECT
Crest Builders, Inc.
DESIGNER
Colin Magnuson

helping ► everyone ► live ► proudly

help
is here

2655 N. Ocean Drive, Suite 300, Singer Island, Riviera Beach, FL 33404 Phone 561 842 5662 Fax 561 842 6360

DESIGN FIRM
Longwater & Company, Inc.
Savannah, (GA) USA
CLIENT
Help Is Here
CREATIVE DIRECTOR
Elaine Longwater
DESIGNER
Kitty Strozier

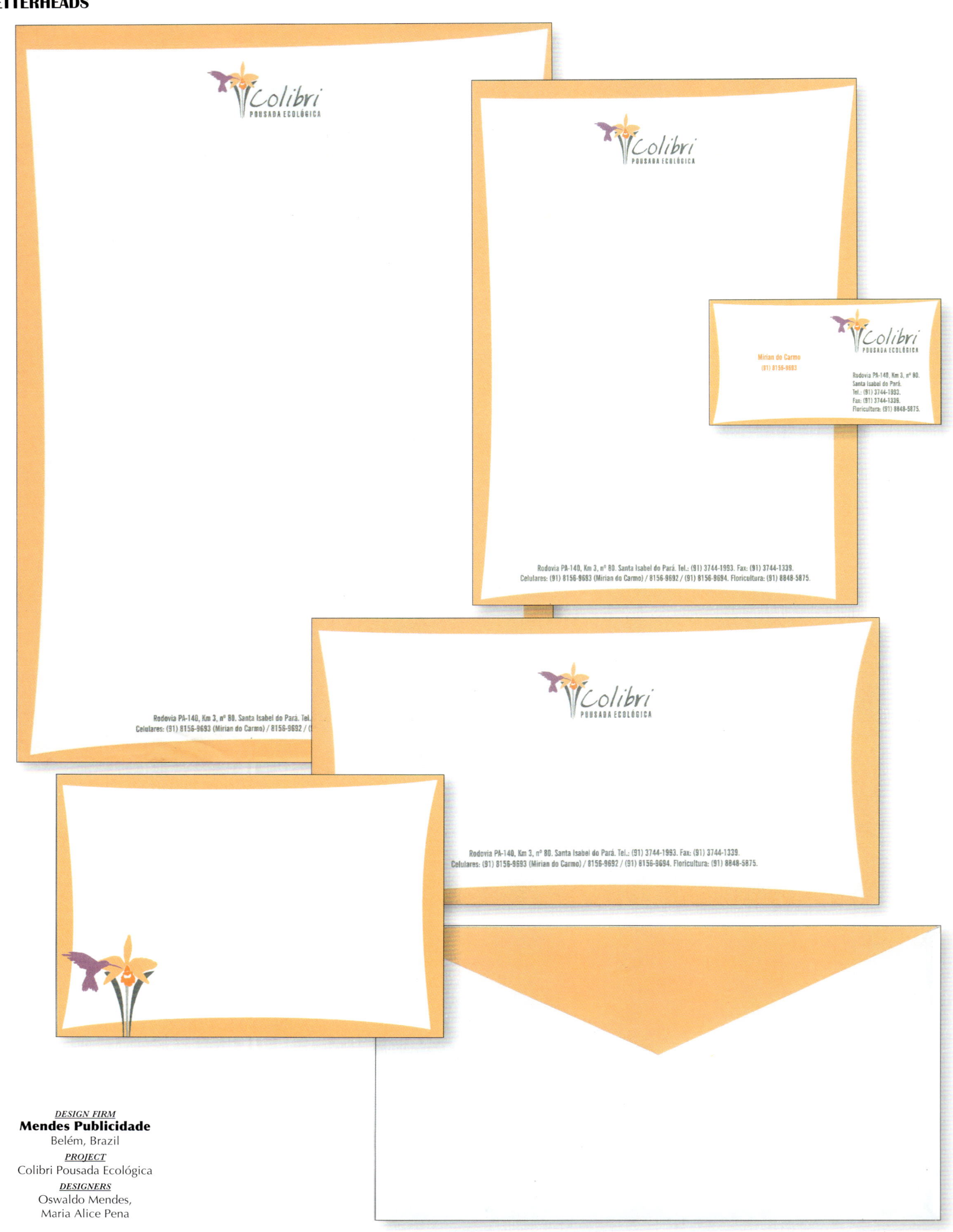

DESIGN FIRM
Mendes Publicidade
Belém, Brazil

PROJECT
Colibri Pousada Ecológica

DESIGNERS
Oswaldo Mendes,
Maria Alice Pena

1270 Carillon Point, Kirkland, WA 98033 F: 425.803.2982 Reservations: 425.889.0303

Banquets & Catering F: 425.889.9072 P: 425.889.7497

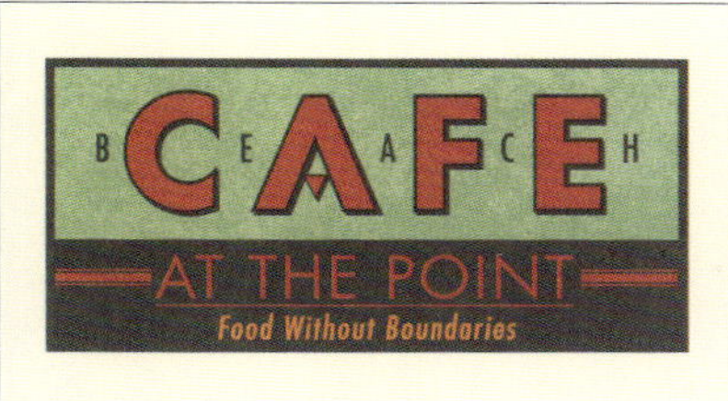

Cameon Orel
Head Chef

1270 Carillon Point
Kirkland, WA 98033

Restaurant: 425.889.0303
Fax: 425.803.2982
Kitchen: 425.889.0791
cafeinfo@ybbeachcafe.com

DESIGN FIRM
double entendre
Seattle, (WA) USA
PROJECT
Cafe at the Point
DESIGNERS
Richard A. Smith,
Daniel P. Smith

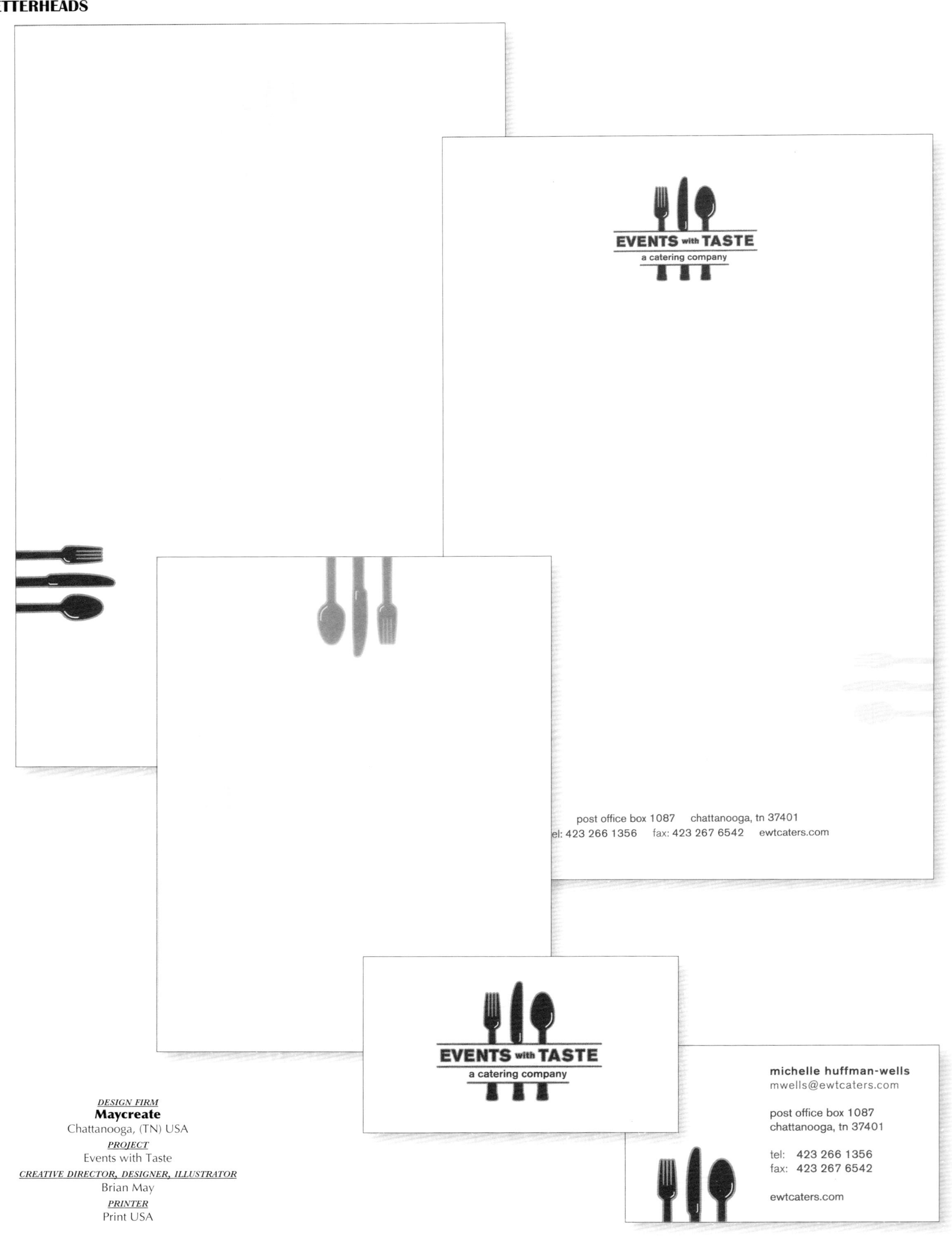

DESIGN FIRM
Maycreate
Chattanooga, (TN) USA

PROJECT
Events with Taste

CREATIVE DIRECTOR, DESIGNER, ILLUSTRATOR
Brian May

PRINTER
Print USA

DESIGN FIRM
elf design
Belmont, (CA) USA
PROJECT
Dropwise Essentials
ART DIRECTOR, DESIGNER
Erin Ferree

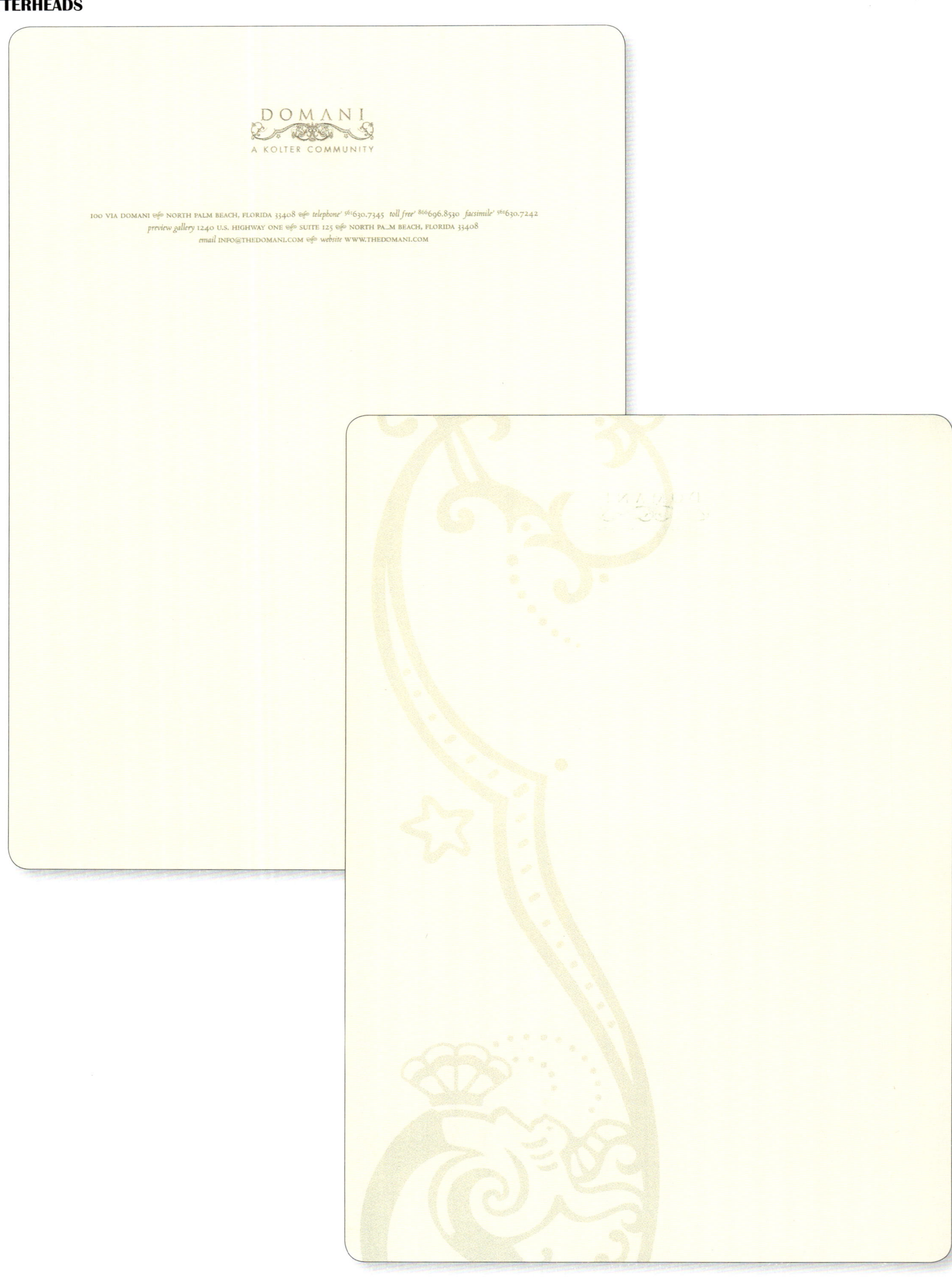
DOMANI
A KOLTER COMMUNITY
100 VIA DOMANI NORTH PALM BEACH, FLORIDA 33408 telephone' 561 630.7345 toll free' 866 696.8530 facsimile' 561 630.7242
preview gallery 1240 U.S. HIGHWAY ONE SUITE 125 NORTH PA_M BEACH, FLORIDA 33408
email INFO@THEDOMANI.COM website WWW.THEDOMANI.COM

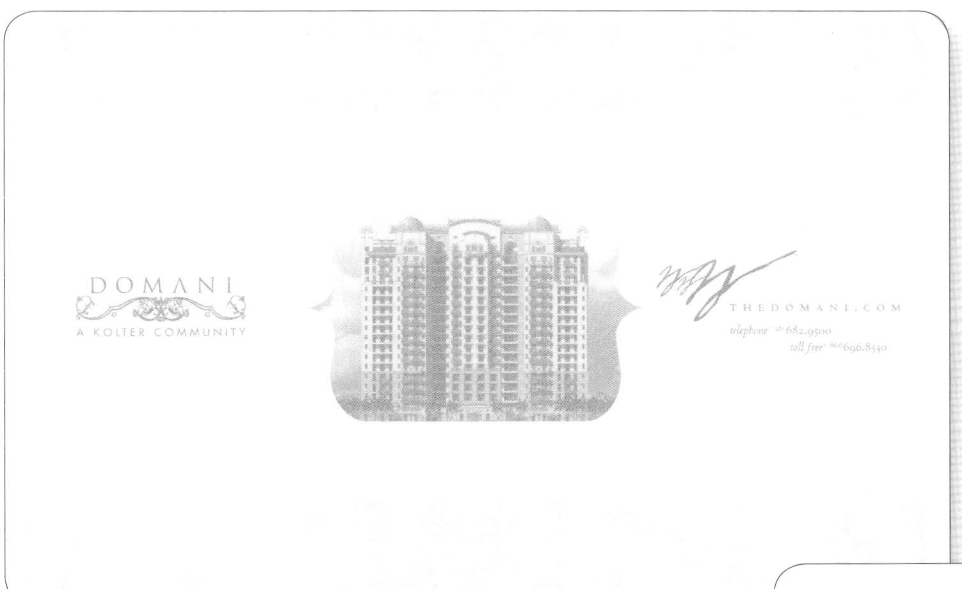

DESIGN FIRM
Gouthier Design: a brand collective
Fort Lauderdale, (FL) USA

CLIENT
Kolter Communities

CREATIVE DIRECTOR
Jonathan Gouthier

DESIGNER
Kiley del Valle

PRINTER
Pfaffco, Inc.

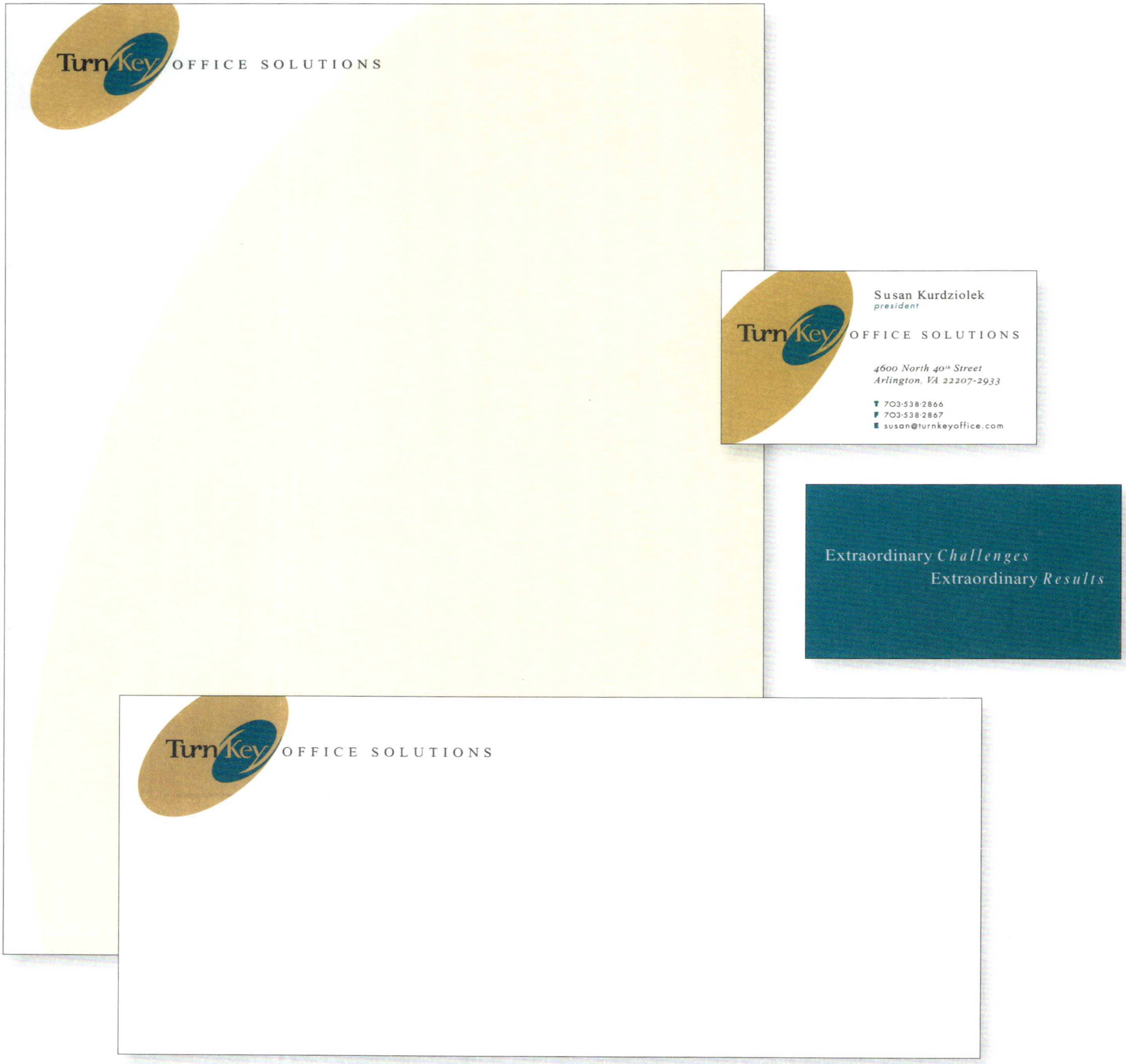

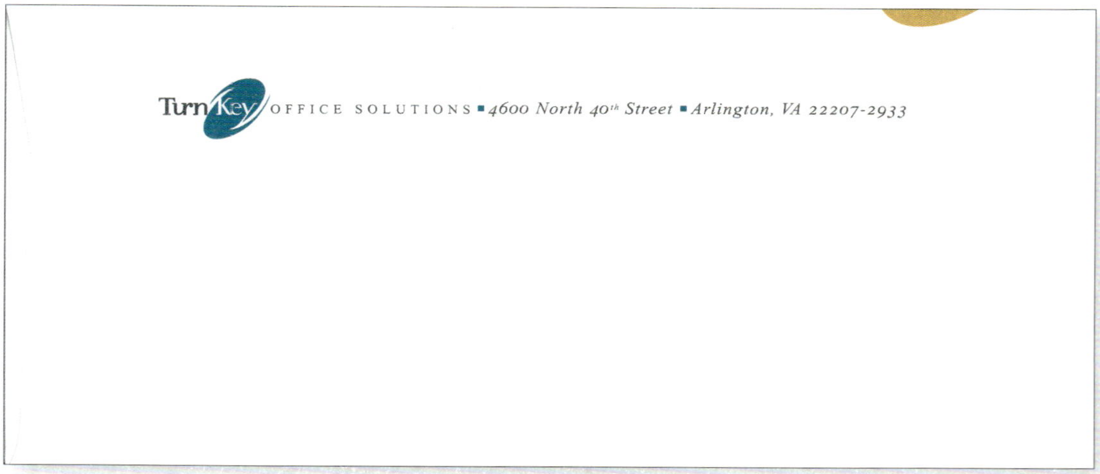

TurnKey OFFICE SOLUTIONS

Susan Kurdziolek
president
TurnKey OFFICE SOLUTIONS
4600 North 40th Street
Arlington, VA 22207-2933
T 703-538-2866
F 703-538-2867
E susan@turnkeyoffice.com

Extraordinary *Challenges*
Extraordinary *Results*

TurnKey OFFICE SOLUTIONS

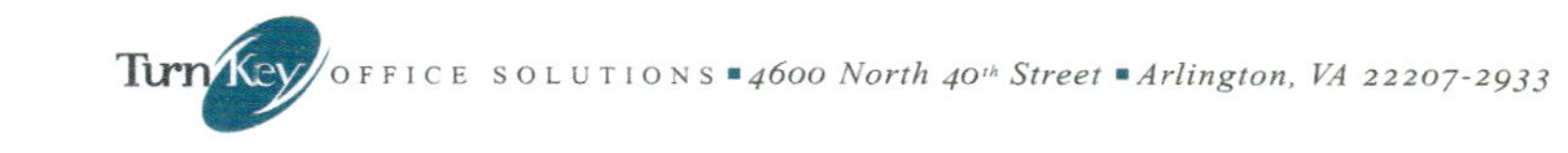

DESIGN FIRM
Dever Designs
Laurel, (MD) USA
PROJECT
TurnKey Office Solutions
DESIGNER
Jeffrey Dever

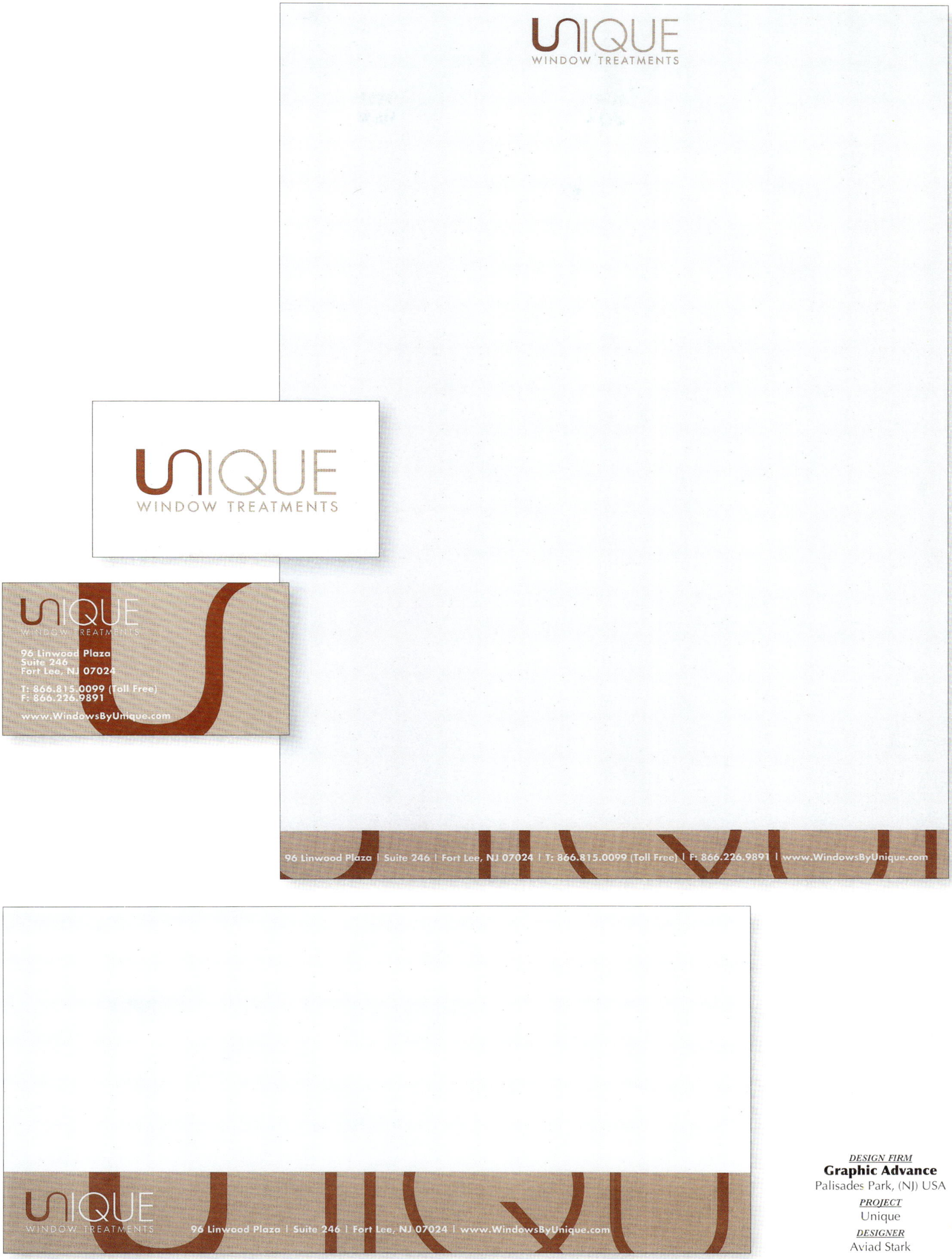

UNIQUE
WINDOW TREATMENTS

96 Linwood Plaza | Suite 246 | Fort Lee, NJ 07024 | T: 866.815.0099 (Toll Free) | F: 866.226.9891 | www.WindowsByUnique.com

UNIQUE
WINDOW TREATMENTS

UNIQUE
WINDOW TREATMENTS
96 Linwood Plaza
Suite 246
Fort Lee, NJ 07024
T: 866.815.0099 (Toll Free)
F: 866.226.9891
www.WindowsByUnique.com

DESIGN FIRM
Graphic Advance
Palisades Park, (NJ) USA
PROJECT
Unique
DESIGNER
Aviad Stark

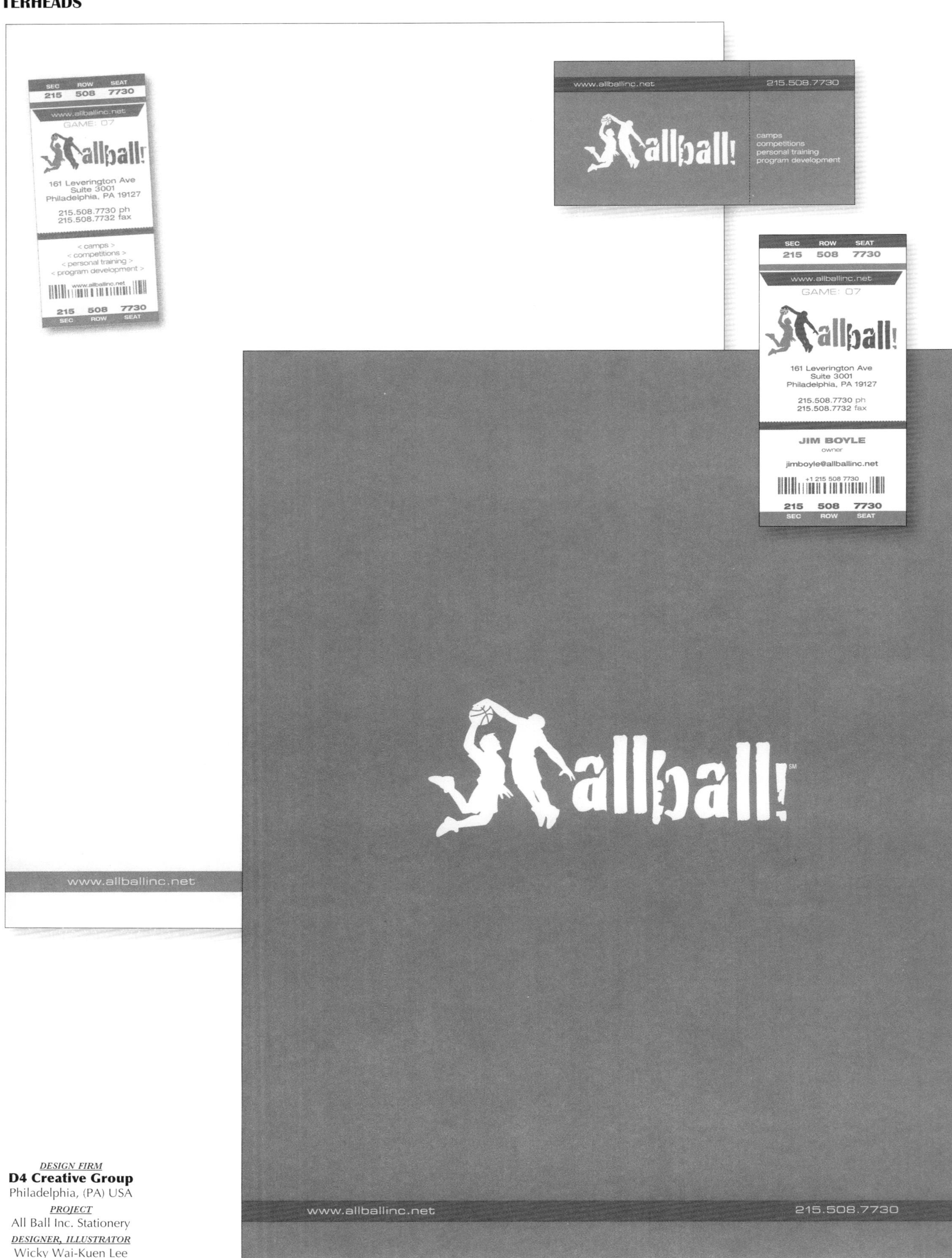

DESIGN FIRM
D4 Creative Group
Philadelphia, (PA) USA
PROJECT
All Ball Inc. Stationery
DESIGNER, ILLUSTRATOR
Wicky Wai-Kuen Lee

DESIGN FIRM
Kenneth Diseño
Uruapan, Mexico
PROJECT
La Bodega
DESIGNERS
Kenneth Treviño,
Minerva Galván

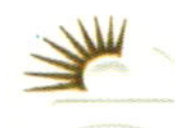

Longwater & Company

Marketing
Advertising
and Public
Relations

619 Tattnall
Street
Savannah, GA
U.S.A. 31401

Phone:
912 233 9200
Fax:
912 233 1663

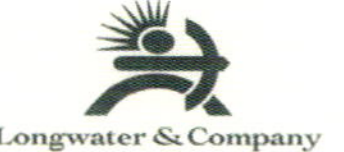

Longwater & Company

Marketing
Advertising
and Public
Relations

619 Tattnall
Street
Savannah, GA
U.S.A. 31401

Phone:
912 233 9200
Fax:
912 233 1663

DESIGN FIRM
Longwater & Company, Inc.
Savannah, (GA) USA

CLIENT
Longwater & Co., Inc.

CREATIVE DIRECTOR
Elaine Longwater

DESIGNER
Kitty Strozier

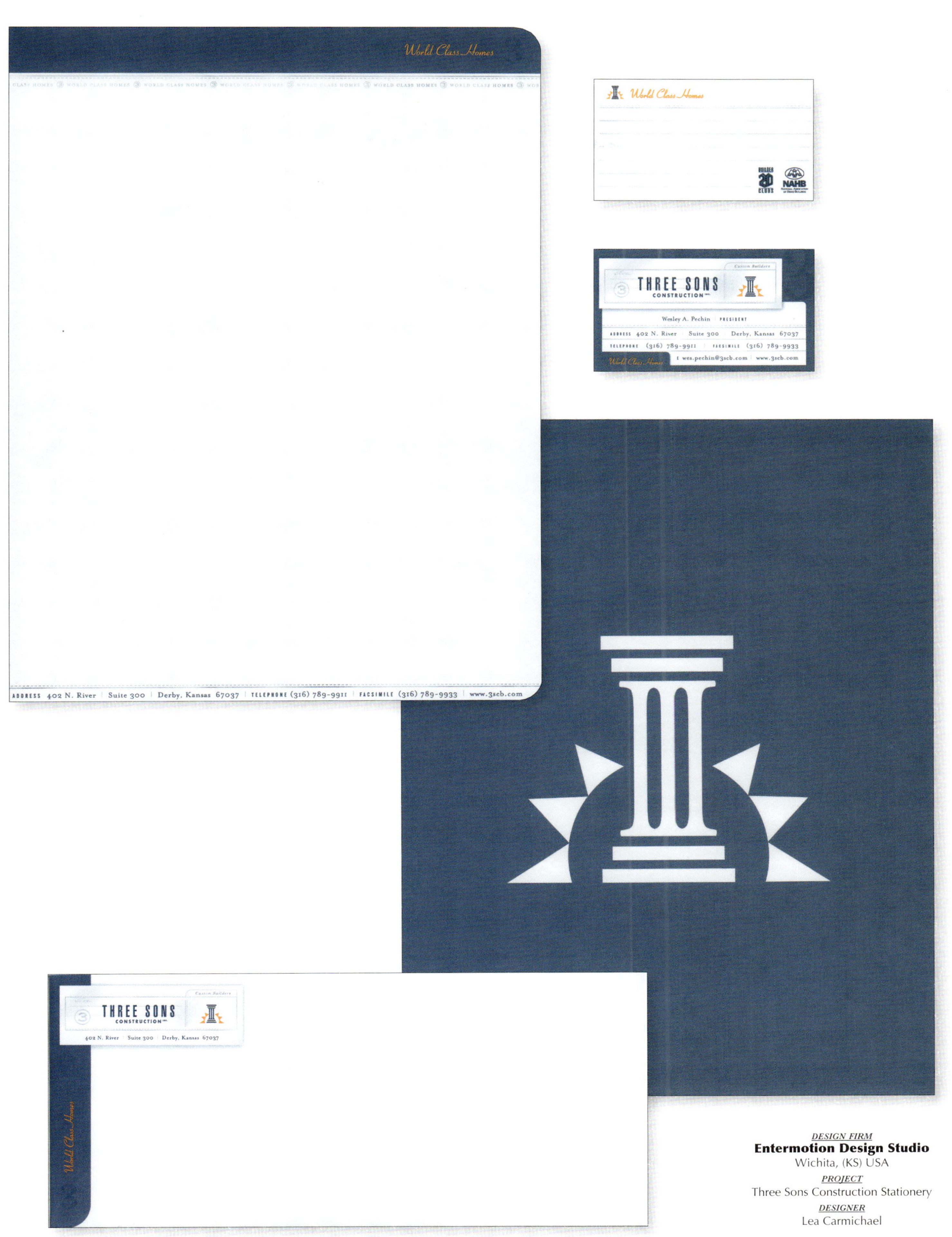

DESIGN FIRM
Entermotion Design Studio
Wichita, (KS) USA
PROJECT
Three Sons Construction Stationery
DESIGNER
Lea Carmichael

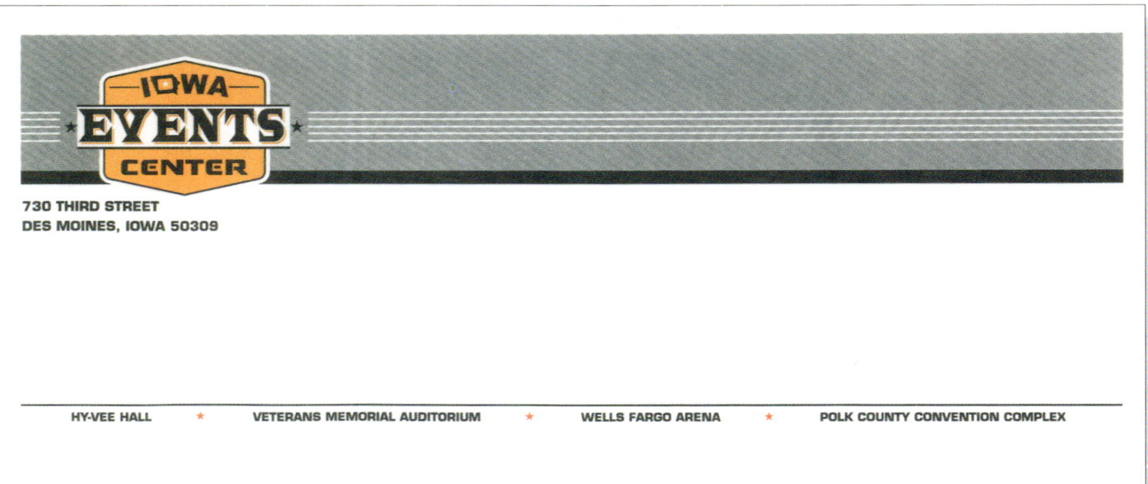

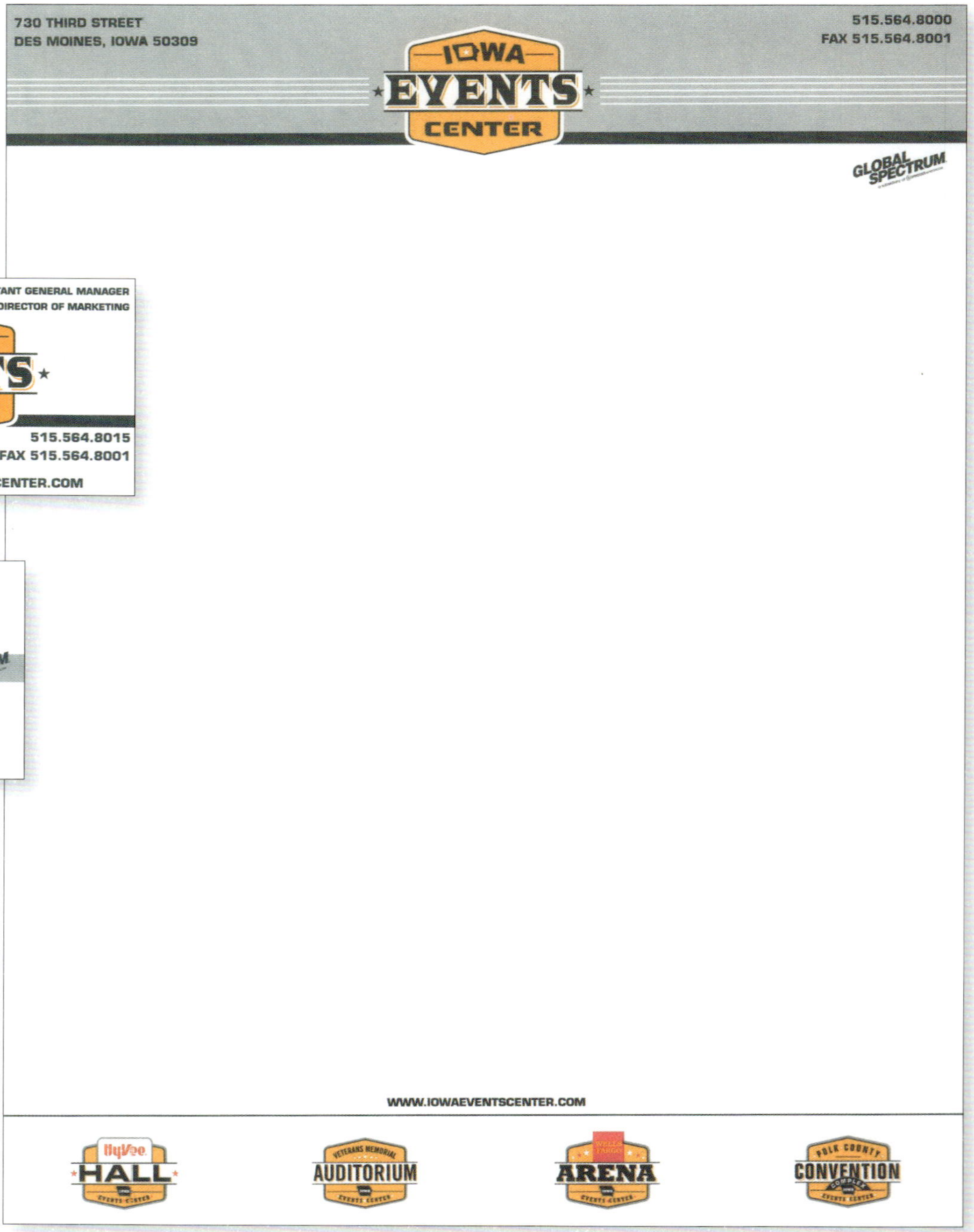

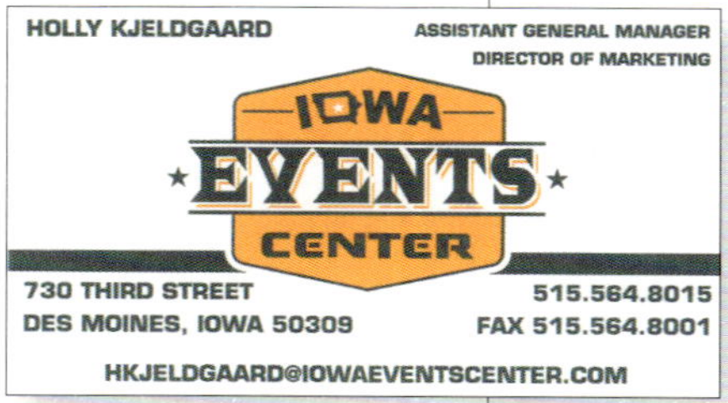

730 THIRD STREET
DES MOINES, IOWA 50309

IOWA EVENTS CENTER

515.564.8000
FAX 515.564.8001

GLOBAL SPECTRUM

HOLLY KJELDGAARD

ASSISTANT GENERAL MANAGER
DIRECTOR OF MARKETING

IOWA EVENTS CENTER

730 THIRD STREET
DES MOINES, IOWA 50309

515.564.8015
FAX 515.564.8001

HKJELDGAARD@IOWAEVENTSCENTER.COM

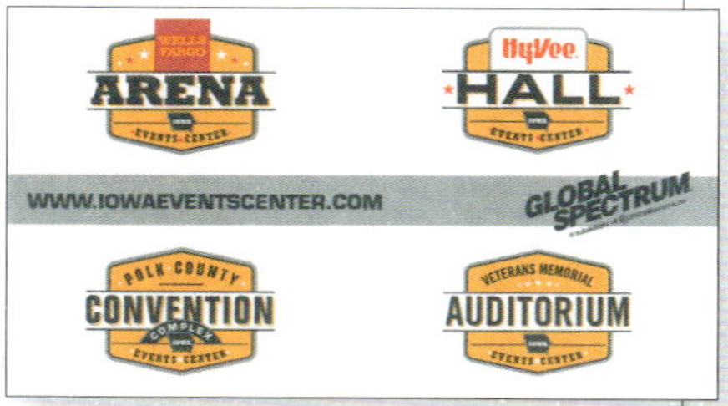

ARENA

HyVee HALL

WWW.IOWAEVENTSCENTER.COM

GLOBAL SPECTRUM

POLK COUNTY CONVENTION

VETERANS MEMORIAL AUDITORIUM

WWW.IOWAEVENTSCENTER.COM

HyVee HALL

VETERANS MEMORIAL AUDITORIUM

ARENA

POLK COUNTY CONVENTION

DESIGN FIRM
Sayles Graphic Design
Des Moines, (IA) USA

CLIENT
Iowa Events Center

DESIGNER, ILLUSTRATOR
John Sayles

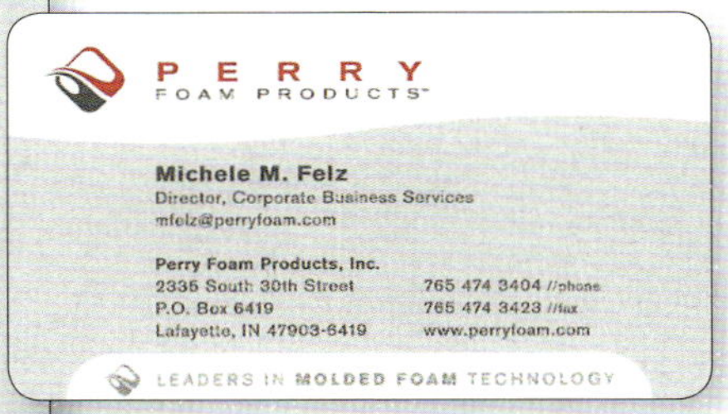

PERRY
FOAM PRODUCTS™

Perry Foam Products, Inc.
2335 South 30th Street
P.O. Box 6419
Lafayette, IN 47903-6419

765 474 3404 //phone
765 474 3423 //fax
800 592 6614 //toll-free
www.perryfoam.com

LEADERS IN MOLDED FOAM TECHNOLOGY

PERRY
FOAM PRODUCTS™

Michele M. Felz
Director, Corporate Business Services
mfelz@perryfoam.com

Perry Foam Products, Inc.
2335 South 30th Street
P.O. Box 6419
Lafayette, IN 47903-6419

765 474 3404 //phone
765 474 3423 //fax
www.perryfoam.com

LEADERS IN MOLDED FOAM TECHNOLOGY

DESIGN FIRM
Indiana Design Consortium, Inc.
Lafayette, (IN) USA
CLIENT
Perry Foam Products, Inc.
DESIGNER
Andrew R. Schwint

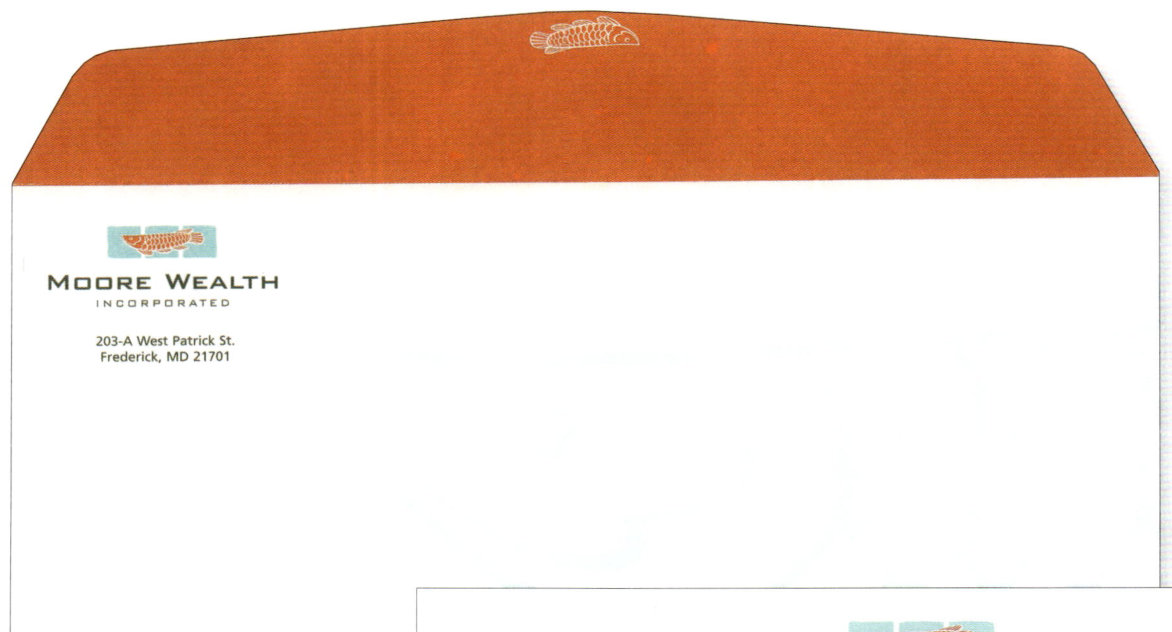

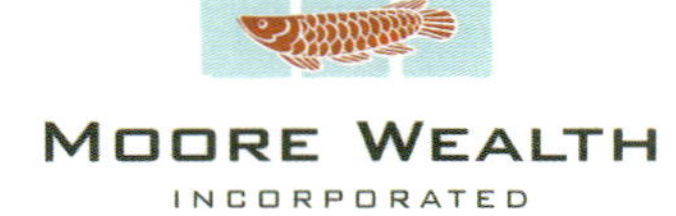

DESIGN FIRM
Octavo Designs
Frederick, (MD) USA
CLIENT
Moore Wealth Incorporated
ART DIRECTOR, DESIGNER
Sue Hough

Rapidac
Machine Corporation®

750 St. Paul Street Rochester, New York 14605 585-546-8868 1-800-799-8868 Fax: 585-546-4918 Web: www.rapidac.com

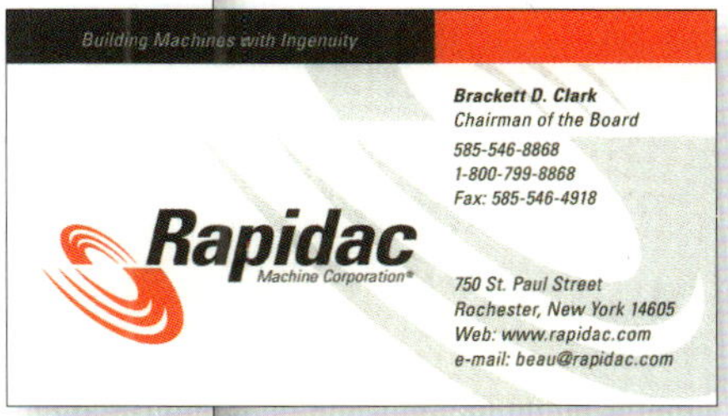

Building Machines with Ingenuity

Brackett D. Clark
Chairman of the Board
585-546-8868
1-800-799-8868
Fax: 585-546-4918

Rapidac
Machine Corporation®

750 St. Paul Street
Rochester, New York 14605
Web: www.rapidac.com
e-mail: beau@rapidac.com

DESIGN FIRM
McElveney & Palozzi Design
Rochester, (NY) USA
PROJECT
Rapidac Machine Corporation®
ART DIRECTORS
Lisa Gates,
Matt Nowicki

MAYHEM [M+S] STUDIOS

[M+S]

Where

Design

Form &

Function

Converge

[www.mayhemstudios.com]

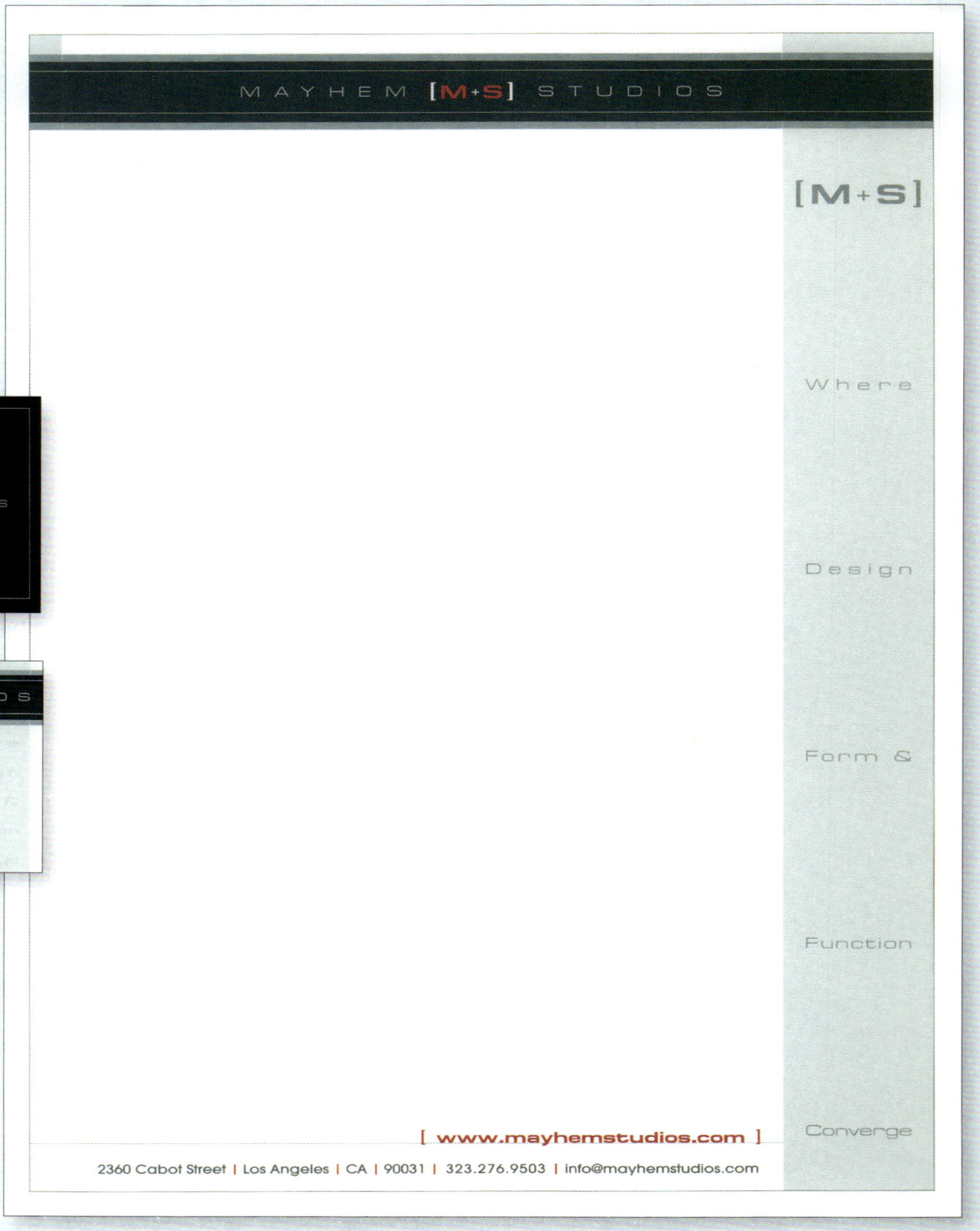

2360 Cabot Street | Los Angeles | CA | 90031 | 323.276.9503 | info@mayhemstudios.com

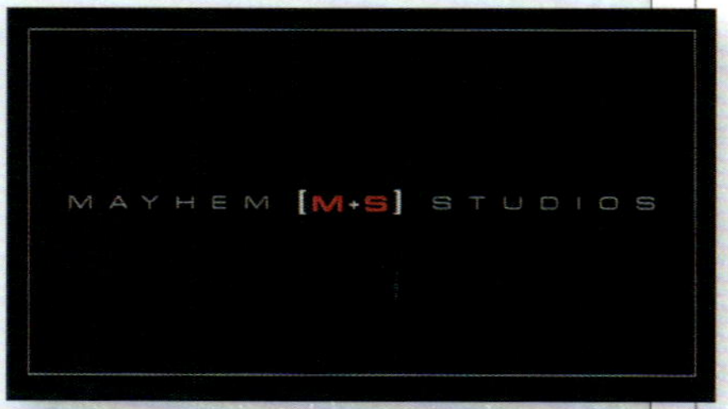

MAYHEM [M+S] STUDIOS

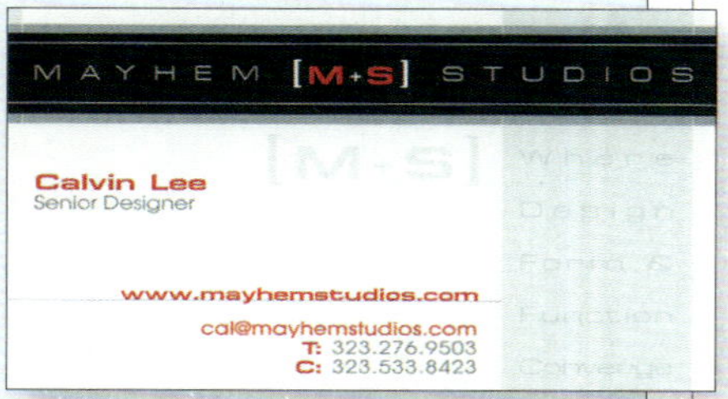

MAYHEM [M+S] STUDIOS

Calvin Lee
Senior Designer

www.mayhemstudios.com

cal@mayhemstudios.com
T: 323.276.9503
C: 323.533.8423

DESIGN FIRM
Mayhem Studios
Los Angeles, (CA) USA
PROJECT
Mayhem Studios Stationery
DESIGNER
Calvin Lee

DESIGN FIRM
Dezainwerkz
Singapore
CLIENT
Splendor
CREATIVE DIRECTOR
Xavier Sanjiman

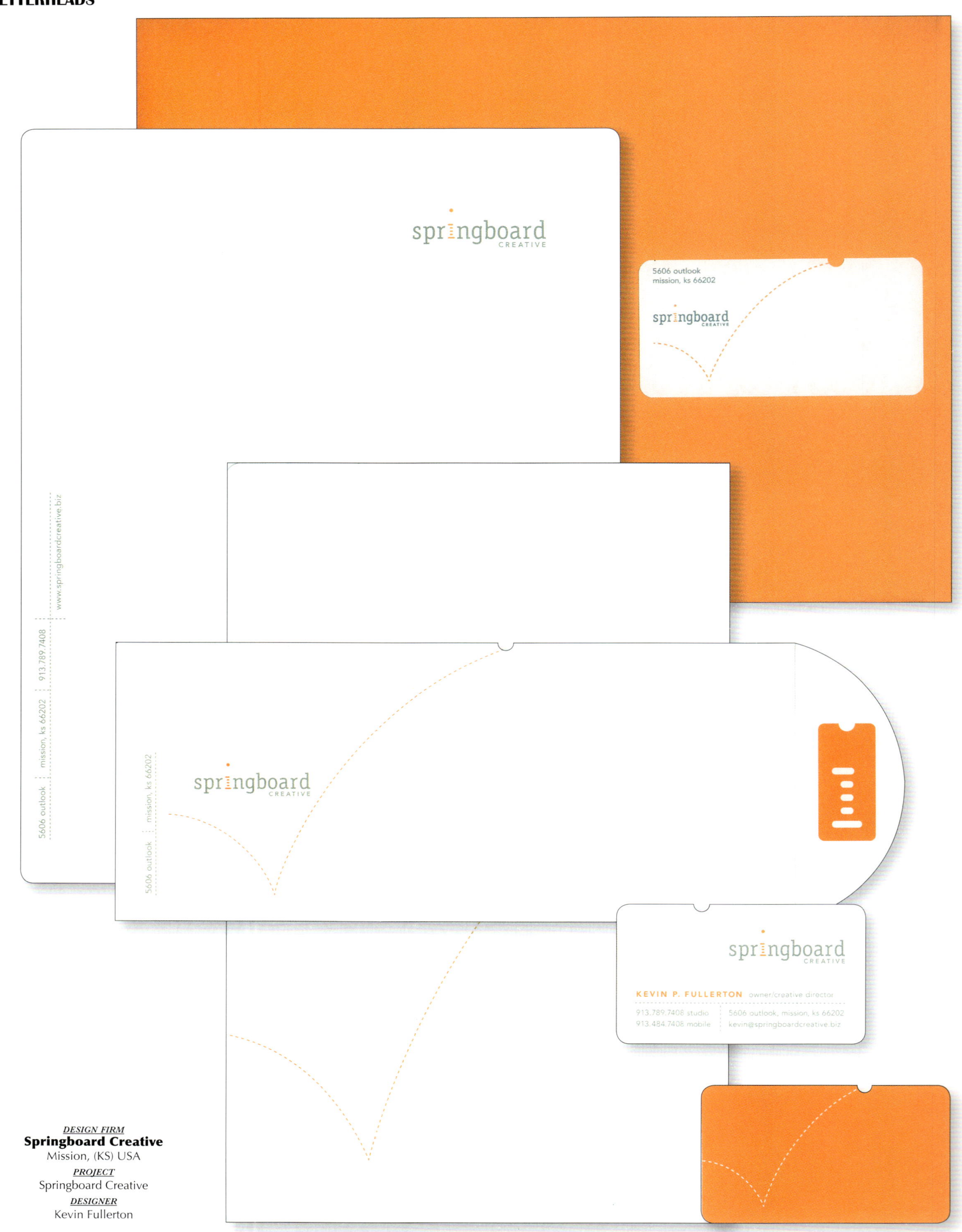

DESIGN FIRM
Springboard Creative
Mission, (KS) USA
PROJECT
Springboard Creative
DESIGNER
Kevin Fullerton

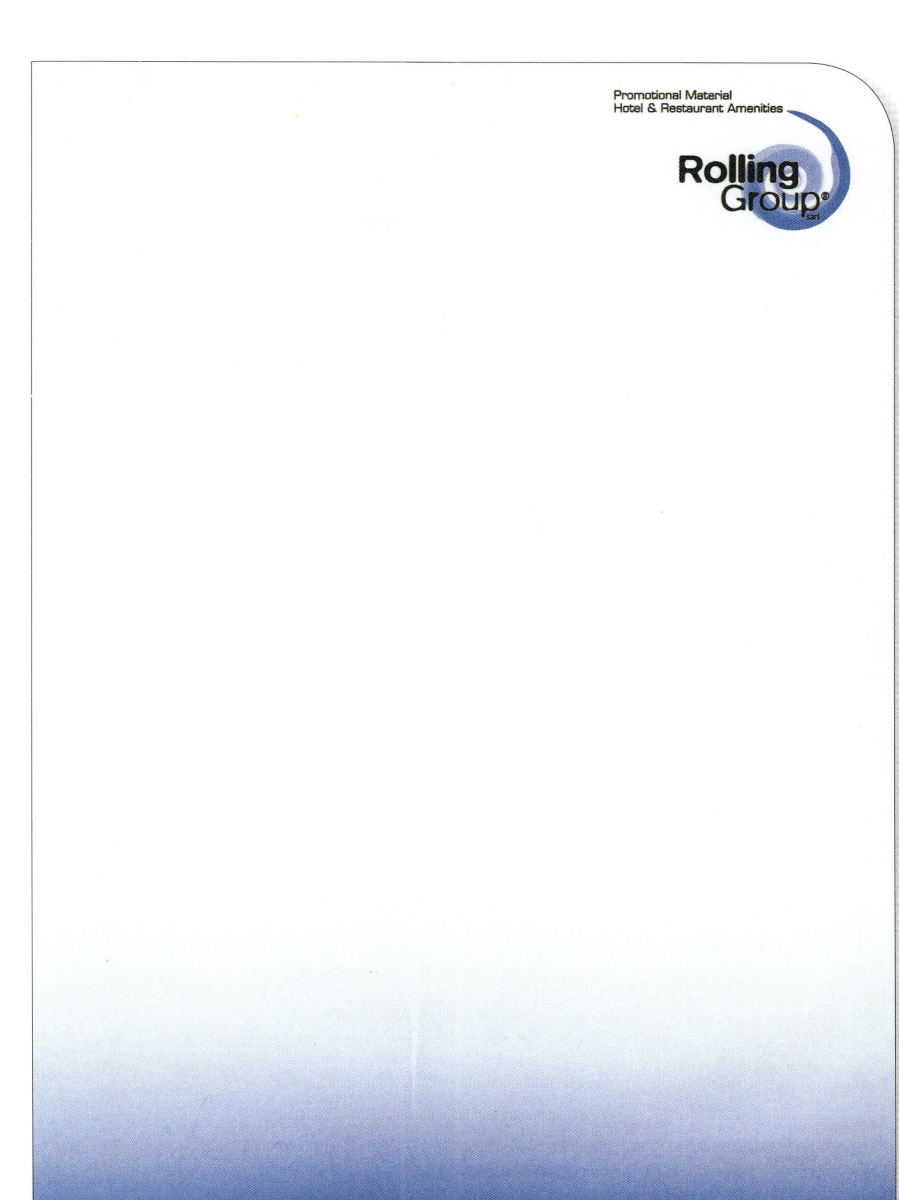

DESIGN FIRM
Go Graphic
Beirut, Lebanon
CLIENT
Rolling Group
CREATIVE DIRECTOR, DESIGNER
Maria Assi

SCIENCE of RACING™
EXPLORE IT. LIVE IT. IT'S YOUR FUTURE.™
One Research Court, Suite 450, Rockville, MD 20850
TEL 301.515.9113 FAX 866.269.5618
www.scienceofracing.com

YOUR

EXPLORE
IT.
LIVE
IT.
IT'S
YOUR
FUTURE.™
www.scienceofracing.com

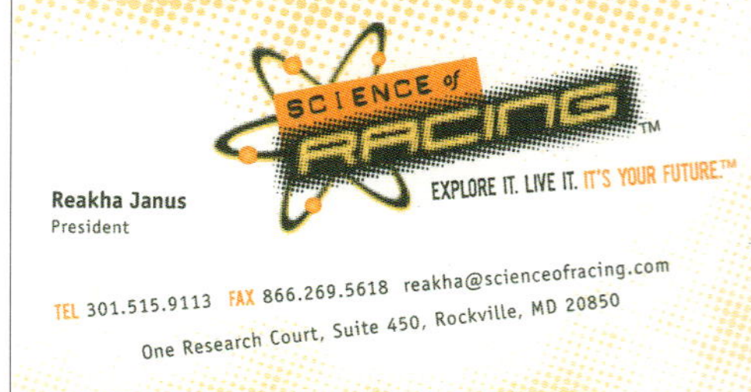

DESIGN FIRM
Jill Tanenbaum
Graphic Design & Advertising Inc.
Bethesda, (MD) USA
CLIENT
Science of Racing
DESIGNER
Jennifer Prophet

DESIGN FIRM
The Wecker Group
Monterey, (CA) USA
PROJECT
Manzoni
DESIGNER
Robert Wecker

417 SECOND STREET SW   ALBUQUERQUE, NEW MEXICO 87102
505.242.8300   FAX 505.242.2585   www.studiohilldesign.com

STUDiO HiLL

HILL

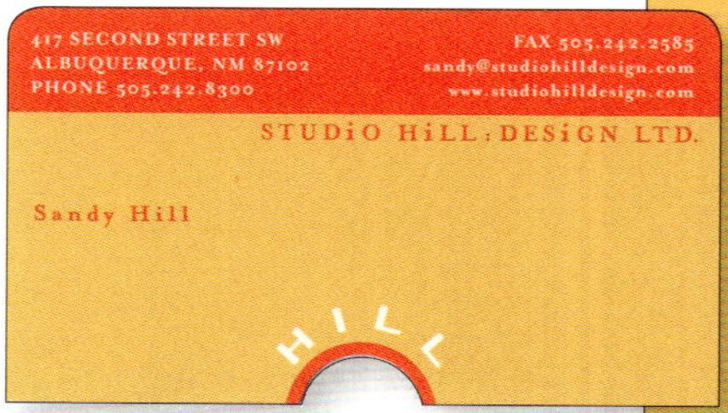

417 SECOND STREET SW
ALBUQUERQUE, NM 87102
PHONE 505.242.8300

FAX 505.242.2585
sandy@studiohilldesign.com
www.studiohilldesign.com

STUDiO HiLL : DESiGN LTD.

Sandy Hill

HILL

DESIGN FIRM
Studio Hill Design
Albuquerque, (NM) USA
PROJECT
Studio Hill Design
ART DIRECTOR
Sandy Hill
DESIGNERS
Sean M. Chavez,
Sandy Hill

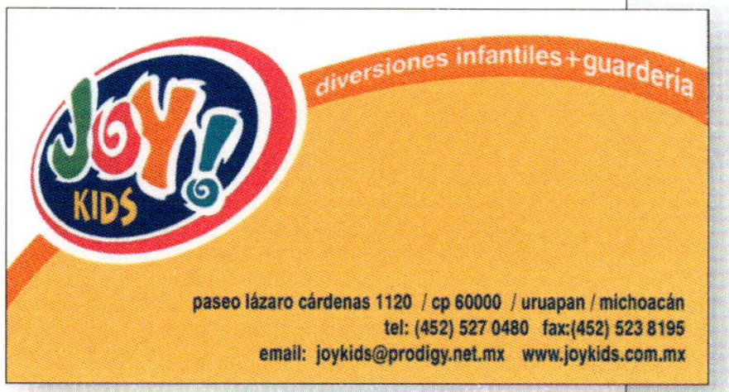

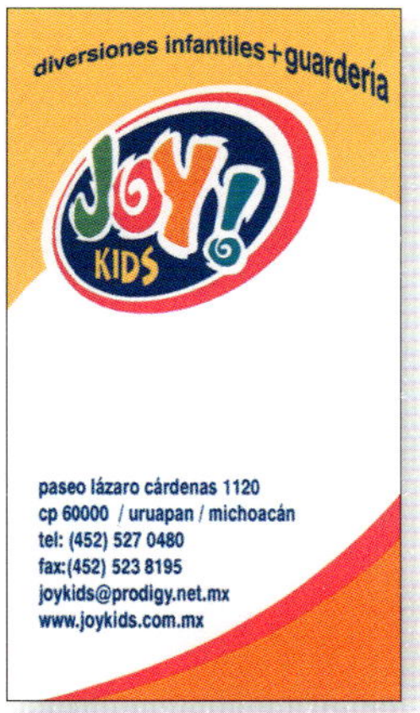

diversiones infantiles+guardería

JOY! KIDS

paseo lázaro cárdenas 1120
cp 60000 / uruapan / michoacán
tel: (452) 527 0480 fax:(452) 523 8195
email: joykids@prodigy.net.mx www.joykids.com.mx

diversiones infantiles+guardería

JOY! KIDS

paseo lázaro cárdenas 1120 / cp 60000 / uruapan / michoacán
tel: (452) 527 0480 fax:(452) 523 8195
email: joykids@prodigy.net.mx www.joykids.com.mx

diversiones infantiles+guardería

JOY! KIDS

paseo lázaro cárdenas 1120
cp 60000 / uruapan / michoacán
tel: (452) 527 0480
fax:(452) 523 8195
joykids@prodigy.net.mx
www.joykids.com.mx

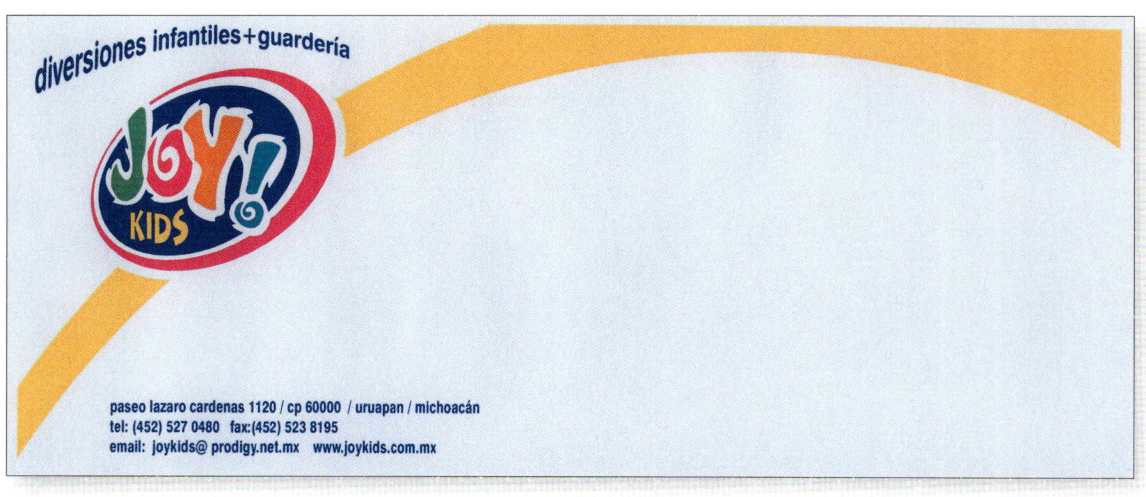

DESIGN FIRM
Kenneth Diseño
Uruapan, Mexico
PROJECT
Joy! Kids
DESIGNERS
Kenneth Treviño,
Minerva Galván

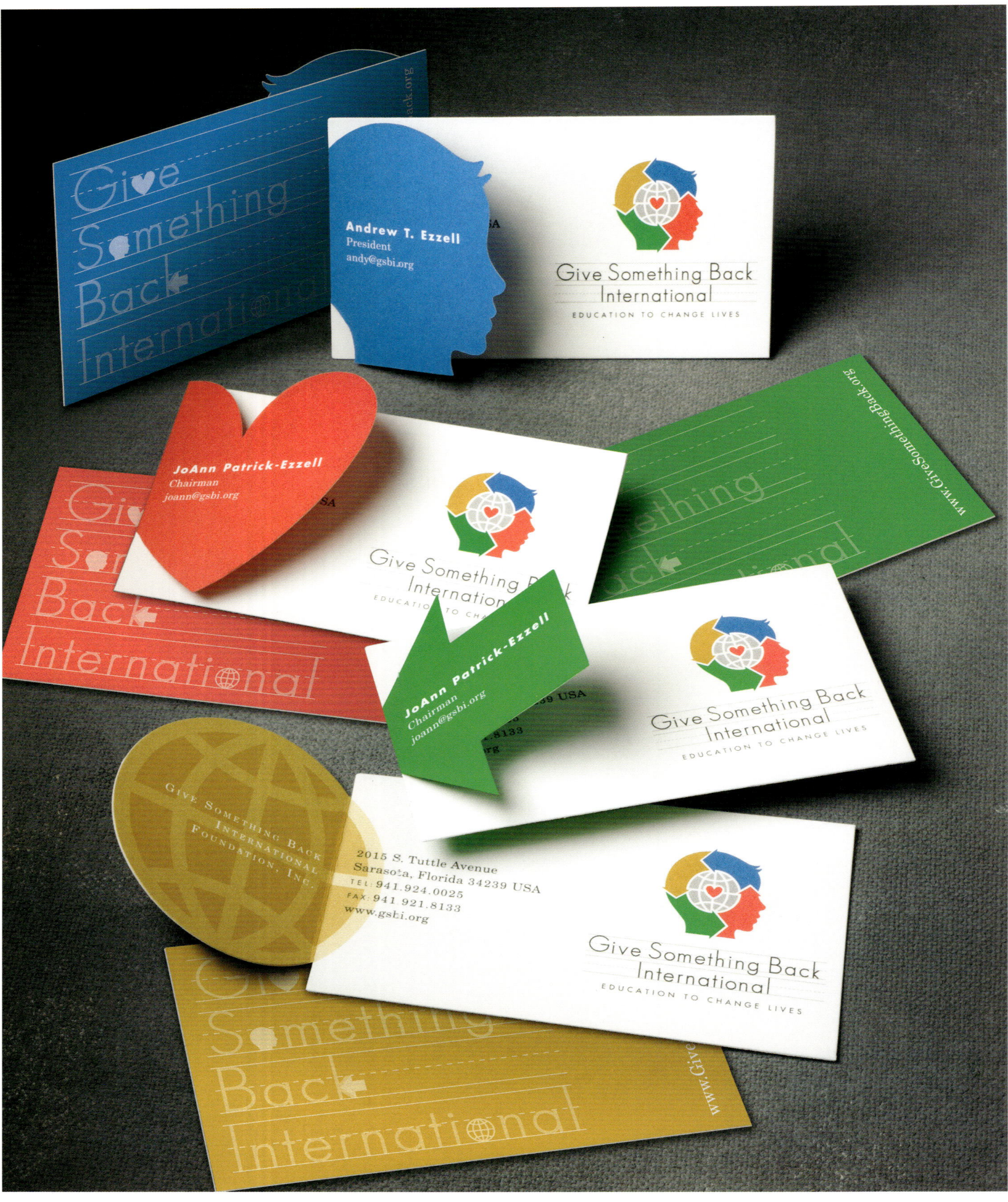
Give Something Back International
Andrew T. Ezzell
President
andy@gsbi.org
Give Something Back
International
EDUCATION TO CHANGE LIVES
JoAnn Patrick-Ezzell
Chairman
joann@gsbi.org
www.GiveSomethingBack.org
Give Something Back International Foundation, Inc.
2015 S. Tuttle Avenue
Sarasota, Florida 34239 USA
TEL: 941.924.0025
FAX: 941 921.8133
www.gsbi.org

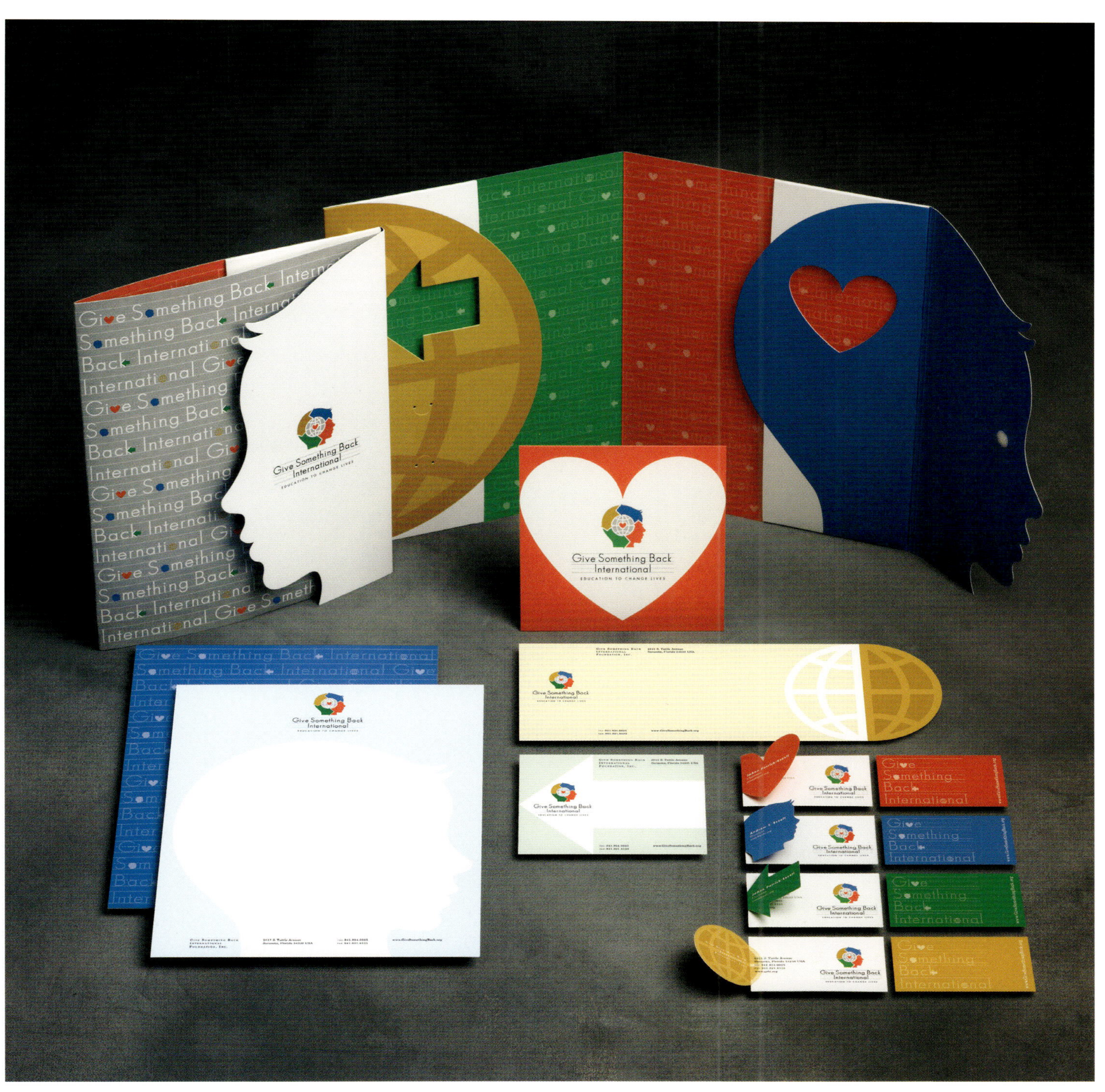

DESIGN FIRM
Gee + Chung Design
San Francisco, (CA) USA
PROJECT
Give Something Back International
ART DIRECTOR, DESIGNER, ILLUSTRATOR
Earl Gee

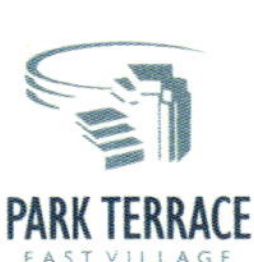

PARK TERRACE
EAST VILLAGE

SALES CENTER
625 SECOND AVENUE
SAN DIEGO, CA 92101

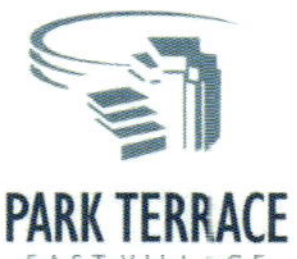

PARK TERRACE
EAST VILLAGE

SALES CENTER
625 SECOND AVENUE
SAN DIEGO, CA 92101

TEL
619/702.2354

FAX
619/702.2323

sales@parkterracecondos.com
www.parkterracecondos.com

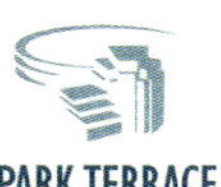

PARK TERRACE
EAST VILLAGE

SERGIO SANDOVAL
PROJECT MANAGER

600 B STREET, SUITE 1500, SAN DIEGO, CA 92101
TEL 619.544.6966 FAX 619.696.1546
sergios@sd.intra-corp.com www.parkterracecondos.com

DESIGN FIRM
Lorenz Advertising
La Mesa, (CA) USA
DESIGNERS
Brian Lorenz,
Arne Ratermanis

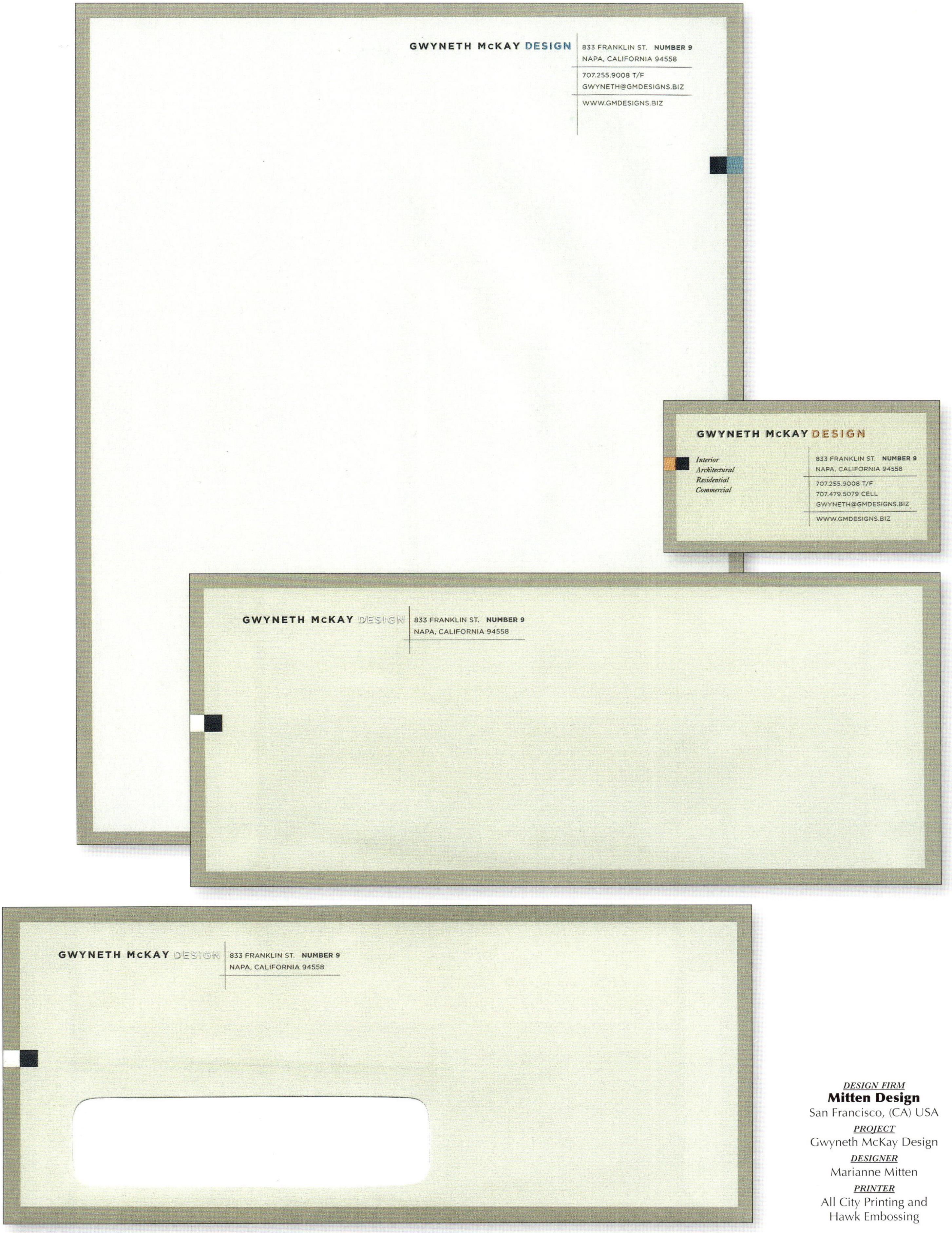

GWYNETH McKAY DESIGN

833 FRANKLIN ST. **NUMBER 9**
NAPA, CALIFORNIA 94558

707.255.9008 T/F
GWYNETH@GMDESIGNS.BIZ

WWW.GMDESIGNS.BIZ

GWYNETH McKAY DESIGN

Interior
Architectural
Residential
Commercial

833 FRANKLIN ST. **NUMBER 9**
NAPA, CALIFORNIA 94558

707.255.9008 T/F
707.479.5079 CELL
GWYNETH@GMDESIGNS.BIZ

WWW.GMDESIGNS.BIZ

GWYNETH McKAY DESIGN

833 FRANKLIN ST. **NUMBER 9**
NAPA, CALIFORNIA 94558

DESIGN FIRM
Mitten Design
San Francisco, (CA) USA
PROJECT
Gwyneth McKay Design
DESIGNER
Marianne Mitten
PRINTER
All City Printing and
Hawk Embossing

DESIGN FIRM
BCRA
Tacoma, (WA) USA
PROJECT
BCRA Stationery
DESIGNERS
Kristine Nims,
Lance Kagey

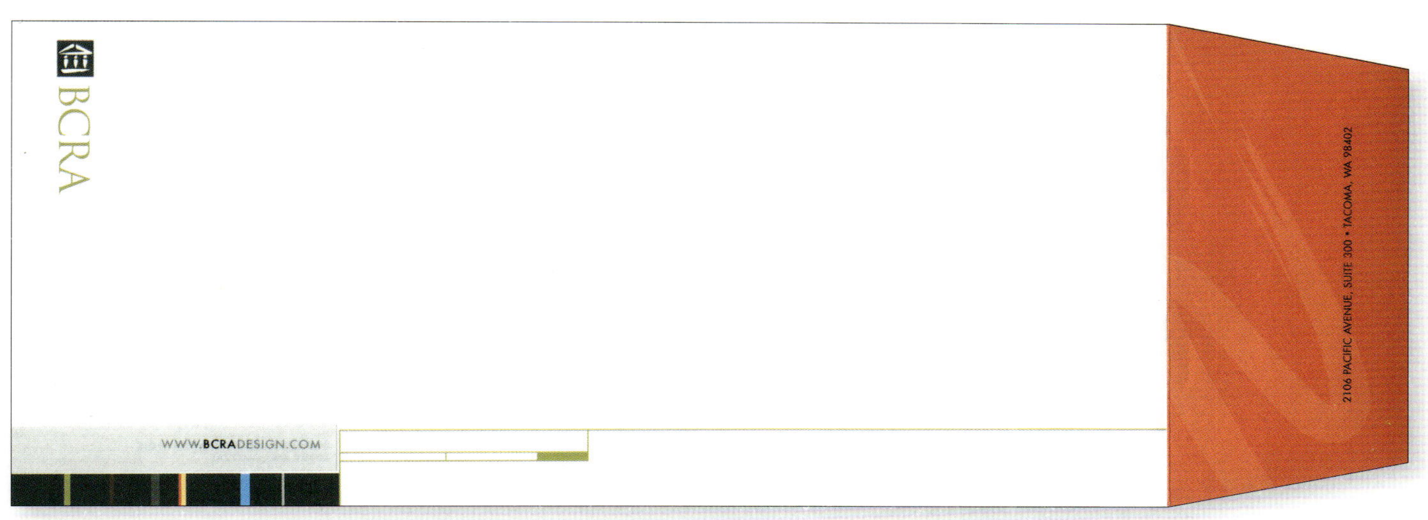
BCRA
WWW.BCRADESIGN.COM
2106 PACIFIC AVENUE, SUITE 300 • TACOMA, WA 98402

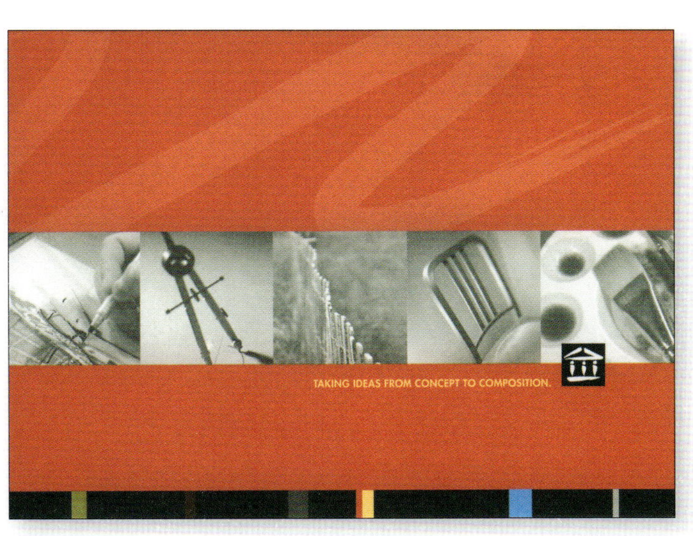
TAKING IDEAS FROM CONCEPT TO COMPOSITION.

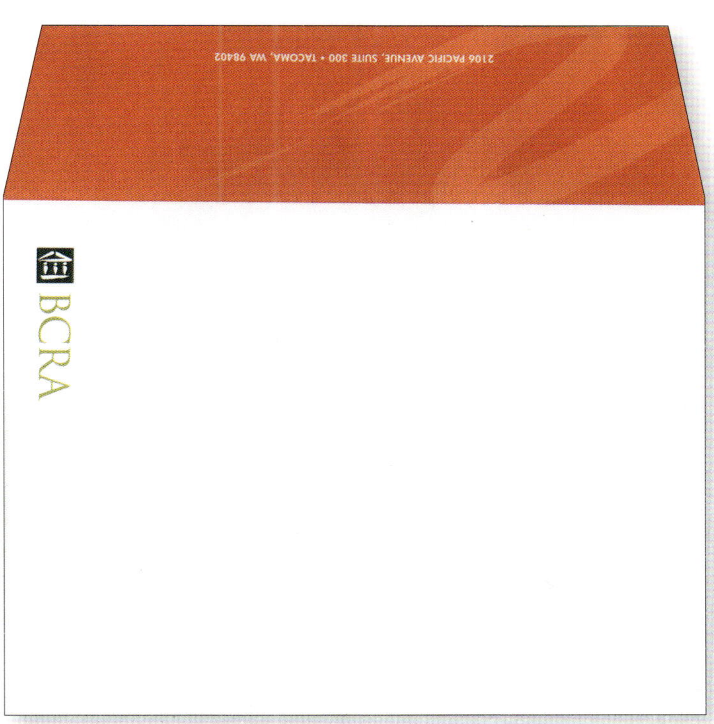
2106 PACIFIC AVENUE, SUITE 300 • TACOMA, WA 98402
BCRA

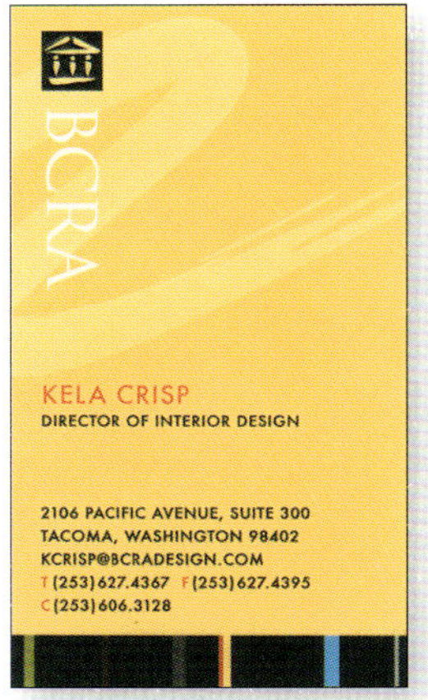
BCRA
KELA CRISP
DIRECTOR OF INTERIOR DESIGN
2106 PACIFIC AVENUE, SUITE 300
TACOMA, WASHINGTON 98402
KCRISP@BCRADESIGN.COM
T (253) 627.4367 F (253) 627.4395
C (253) 606.3128

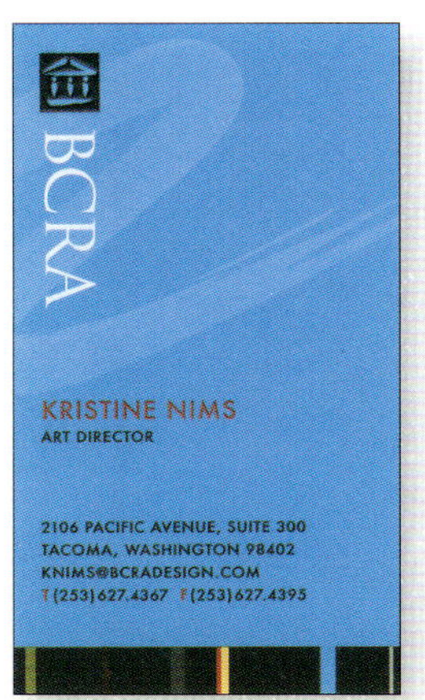
BCRA
KRISTINE NIMS
ART DIRECTOR
2106 PACIFIC AVENUE, SUITE 300
TACOMA, WASHINGTON 98402
KNIMS@BCRADESIGN.COM
T (253) 627.4367 F (253) 627.4395

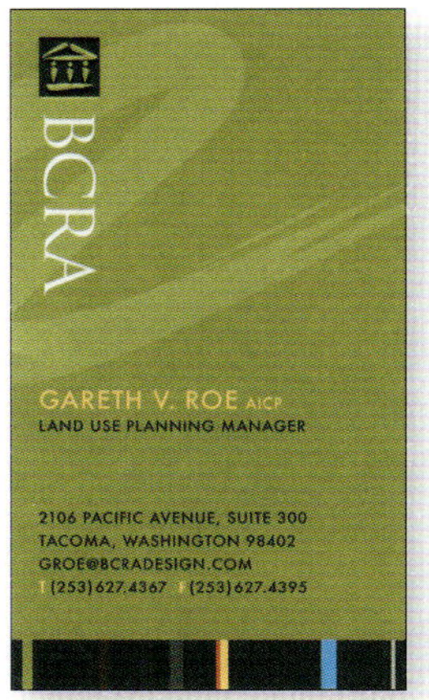
BCRA
GARETH V. ROE AICP
LAND USE PLANNING MANAGER
2106 PACIFIC AVENUE, SUITE 300
TACOMA, WASHINGTON 98402
GROE@BCRADESIGN.COM
T (253) 627.4367 F (253) 627.4395

monte vista
CHAPEL

P. 209.634.4935 • F. 209.634.5562
1619 E. Monte Vista Ave.
P.O. Box 1006, Turlock, CA 95381
www.montevistachapel.org

Real people. Real life. Real hope.

DESIGN FIRM
Never Boring Design Associates
Modesto, (CA) USA

PROJECT
Monte Vista

DESIGNER
Shawna Bayers

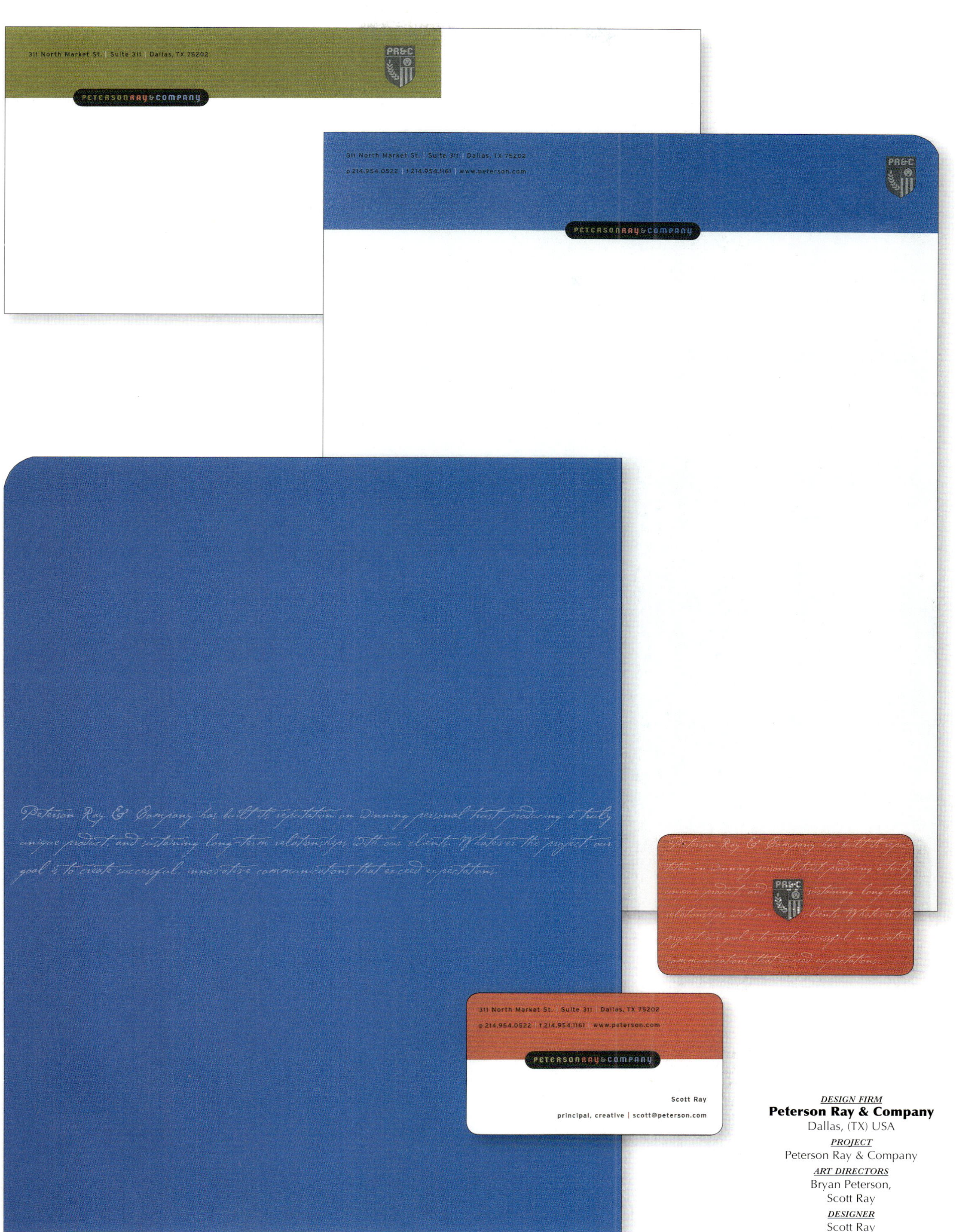

DESIGN FIRM
Peterson Ray & Company
Dallas, (TX) USA
PROJECT
Peterson Ray & Company
ART DIRECTORS
Bryan Peterson,
Scott Ray
DESIGNER
Scott Ray

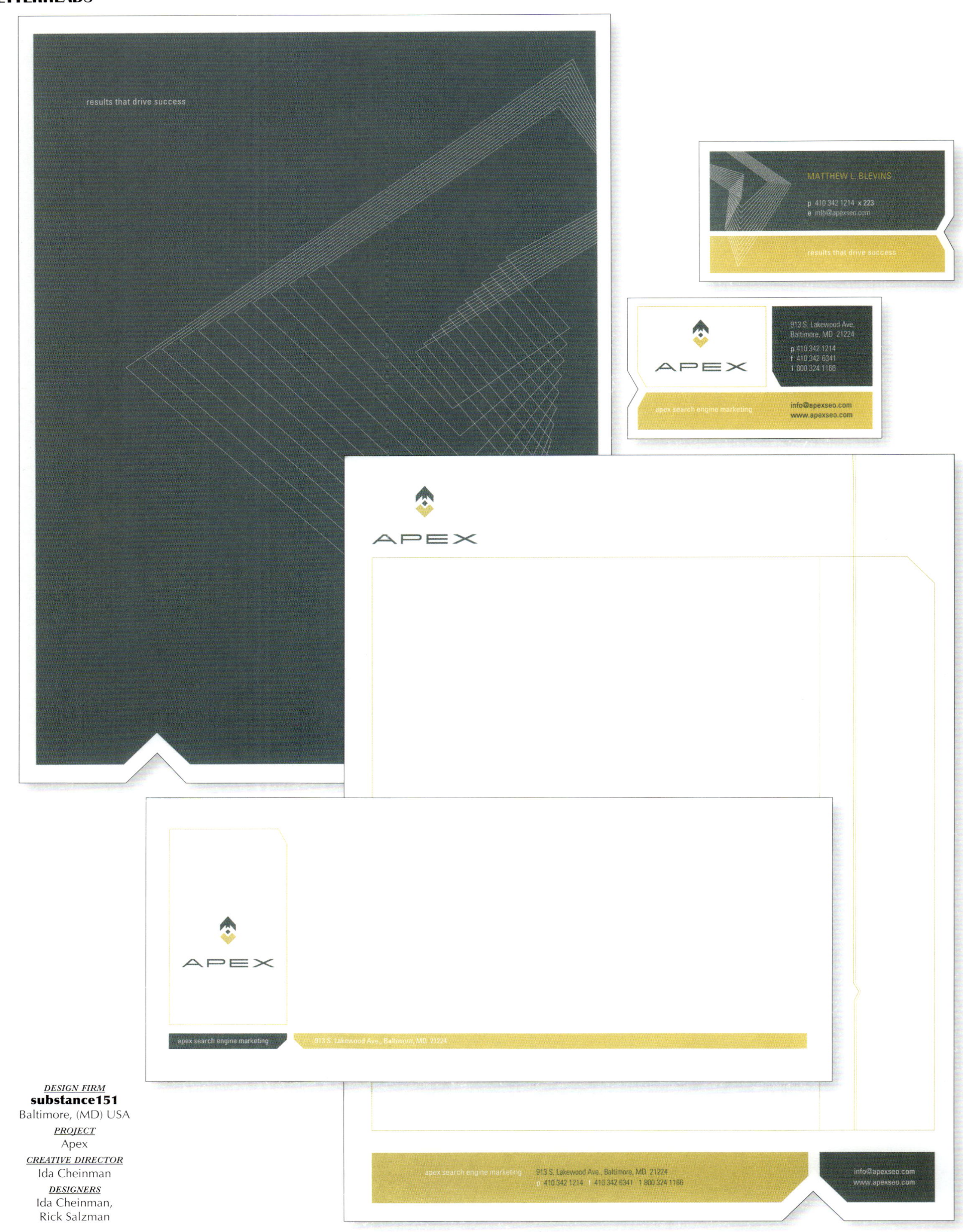

DESIGN FIRM
substance151
Baltimore, (MD) USA
PROJECT
Apex
CREATIVE DIRECTOR
Ida Cheinman
DESIGNERS
Ida Cheinman,
Rick Salzman

DESIGN FIRM
Braue: Branding & Corporate Design
Bremerhaven, Germany

CLIENT
Shin'Sei

CREATIVE DIRECTOR
Kai Braue

ART DIRECTOR
Marçel Robbers

DESIGNER
Annika Schmidt

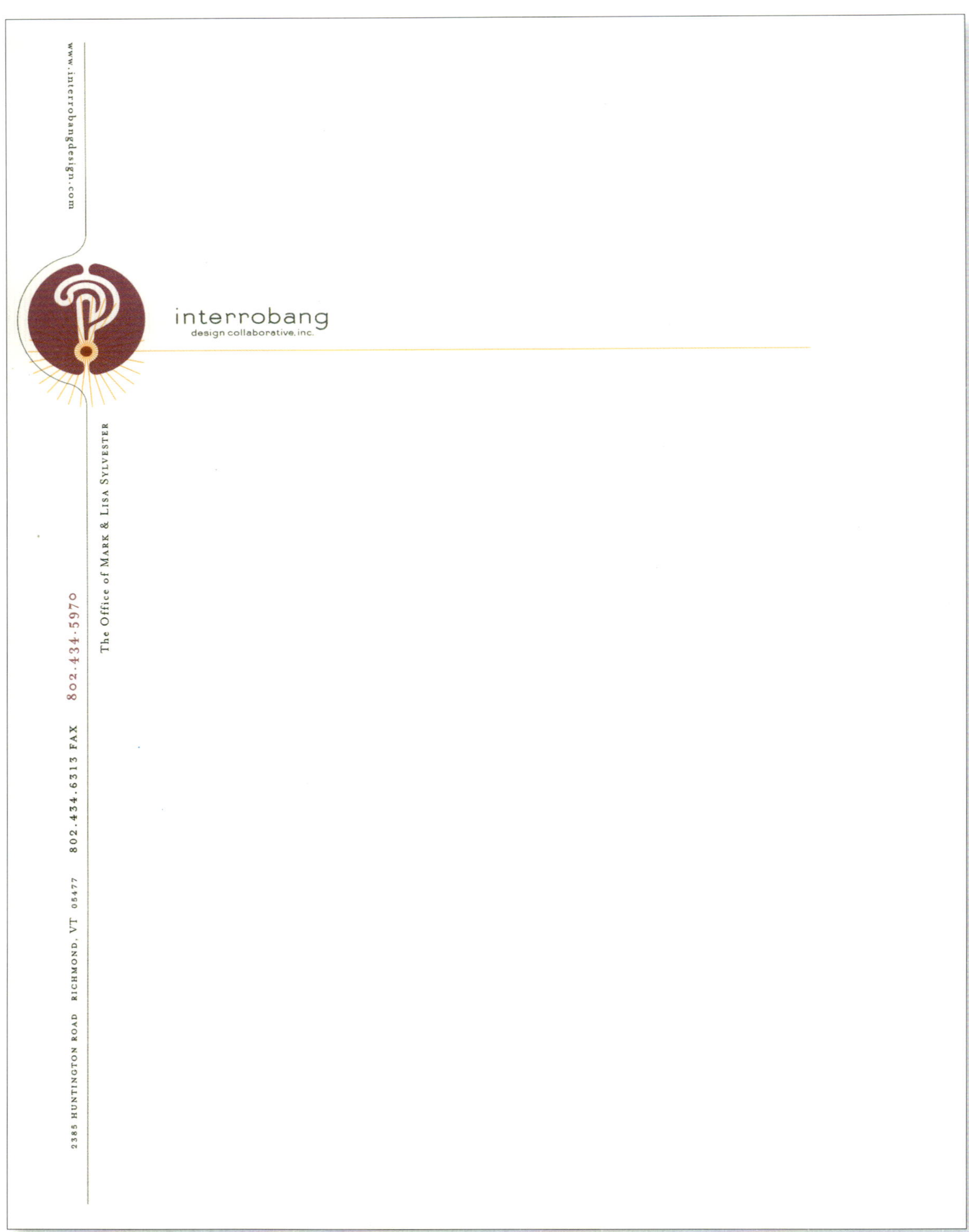

DESIGN FIRM
Interrobang Design Collaborative, Inc.
Richmond, (VT) USA

PROJECT
Interrobang Design Collaborative, Inc.

CREATIVE DIRECTOR
Mark D. Sylvester

DESIGNERS
Mark D. Sylvester,
Lisa Taft Sylvester

DESIGN FIRM
Funk/Levis & Associates
Eugene, (OR) USA
PROJECT
Inn of the Seventh Mountain
CREATIVE DIRECTOR
David Funk
DESIGNER
Chris Berner

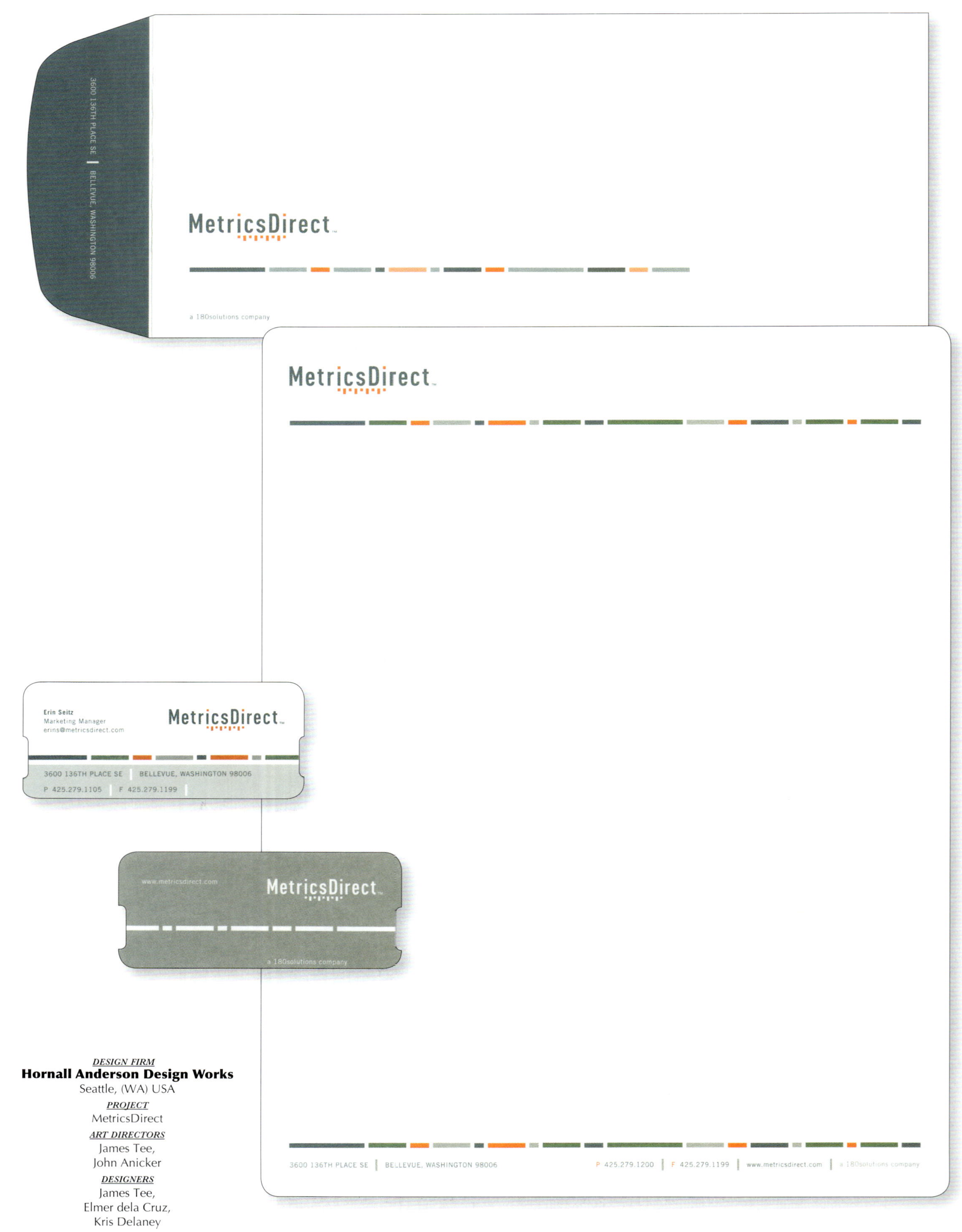

DESIGN FIRM
Hornall Anderson Design Works
Seattle, (WA) USA
PROJECT
MetricsDirect
ART DIRECTORS
James Tee,
John Anicker
DESIGNERS
James Tee,
Elmer dela Cruz,
Kris Delaney

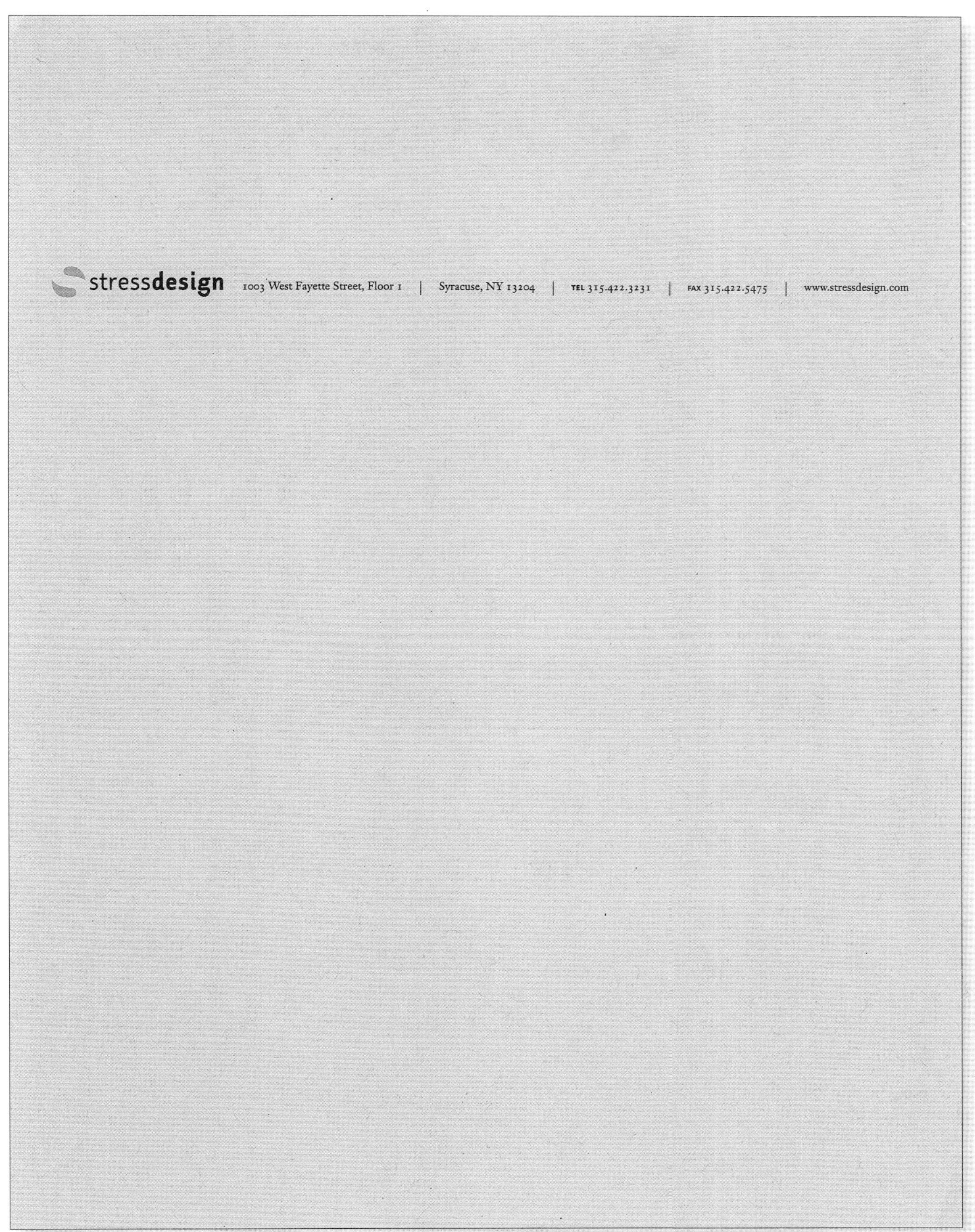

DESIGN FIRM
stressdesign
Syracuse, (NY) USA
PROJECT
stressdesign
DESIGNER
Marc Stress

DESIGN FIRM
Octavo Designs
Frederick, (MD) USA

CLIENT
Old Town Tea Company

ART DIRECTOR, DESIGNER
Sue Hough

DESIGN FIRM
On The Edge Design
Newport Beach, (CA) USA
PROJECT
Kantina
Modern Mexican Cuisine
DESIGNER
Melanie Fujita

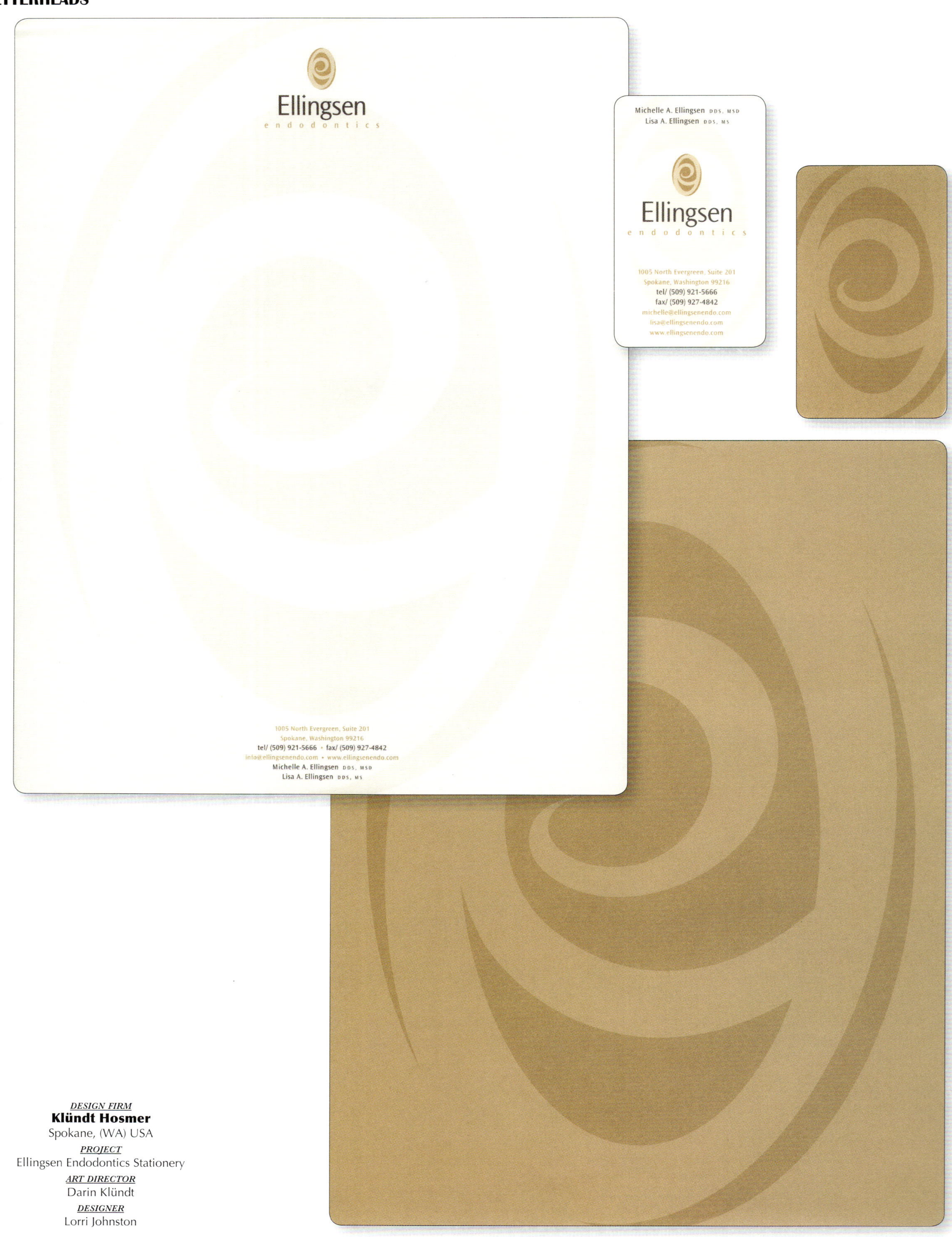

DESIGN FIRM
Kländt Hosmer
Spokane, (WA) USA
PROJECT
Ellingsen Endodontics Stationery
ART DIRECTOR
Darin Kländt
DESIGNER
Lorri Johnston

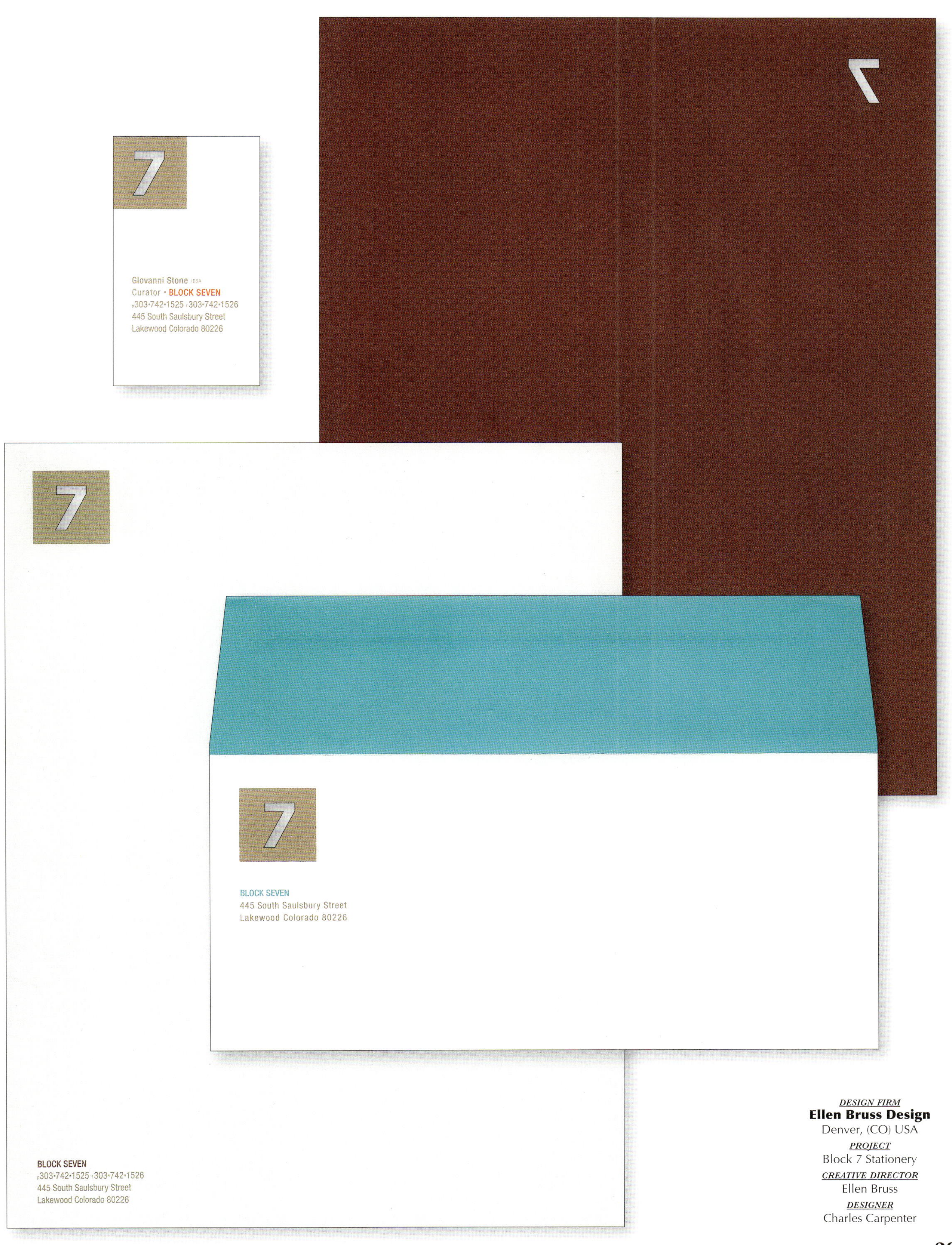

DESIGN FIRM
Ellen Bruss Design
Denver, (CO) USA
PROJECT
Block 7 Stationery
CREATIVE DIRECTOR
Ellen Bruss
DESIGNER
Charles Carpenter

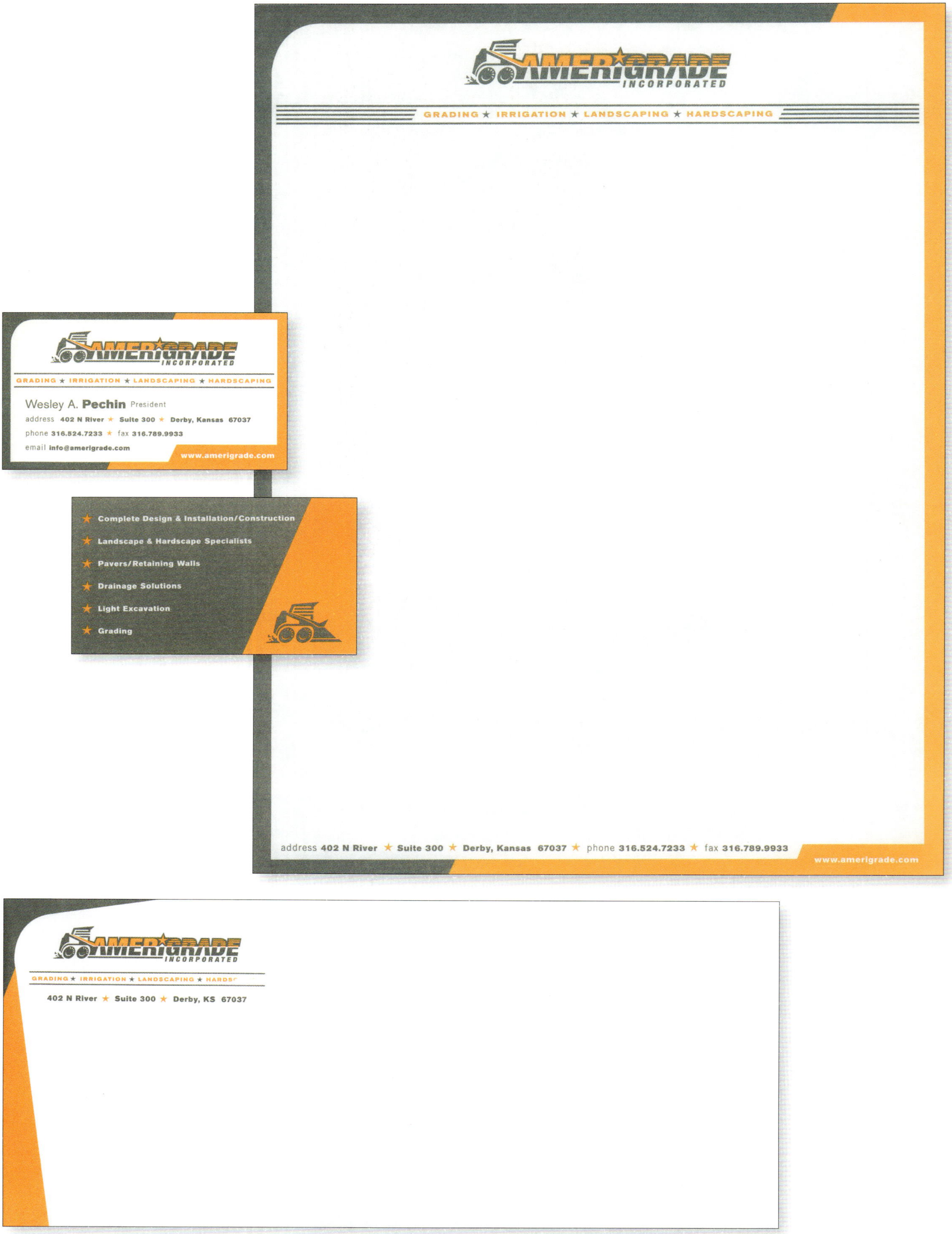

AMERIGRADE
INCORPORATED

GRADING ★ IRRIGATION ★ LANDSCAPING ★ HARDSCAPING

address 402 N River ★ Suite 300 ★ Derby, Kansas 67037 ★ phone 316.524.7233 ★ fax 316.789.9933

www.amerigrade.com

AMERIGRADE
INCORPORATED

GRADING ★ IRRIGATION ★ LANDSCAPING ★ HARDSCAPING

Wesley A. **Pechin** President

address 402 N River ★ Suite 300 ★ Derby, Kansas 67037

phone 316.524.7233 ★ fax 316.789.9933

email info@amerigrade.com

www.amerigrade.com

★ Complete Design & Installation/Construction

★ Landscape & Hardscape Specialists

★ Pavers/Retaining Walls

★ Drainage Solutions

★ Light Excavation

★ Grading

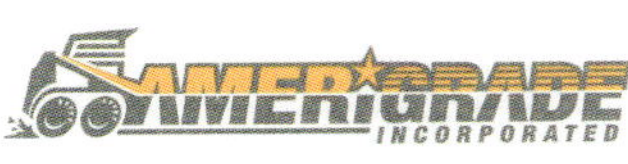

DESIGN FIRM
Entermotion Design Studio
Wichita, (KS) USA
PROJECT
Amerigrade Stationery
DESIGNER
Lea Carmichael

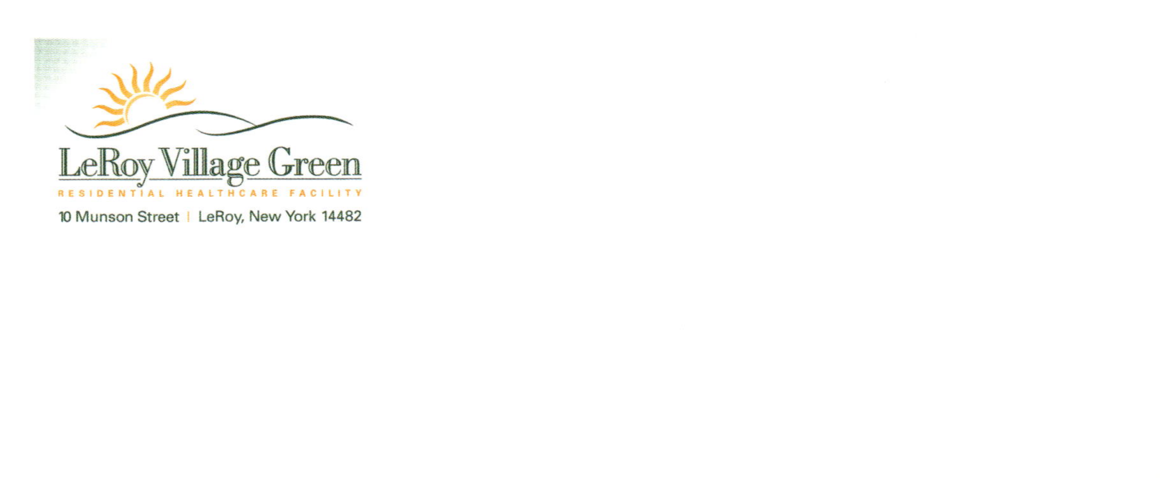

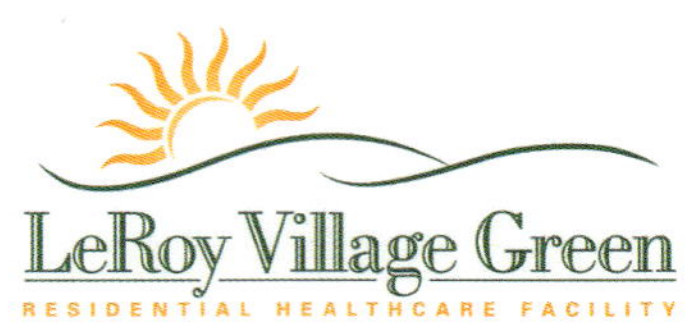

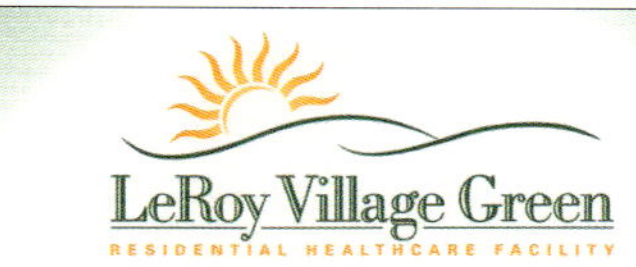

10 Munson Street
LeRoy, New York 14482
(716) 768-2561
Fax (716) 768-4335

Catherine M. Caito
Admissions Coordinator

10 Munson Street | LeRoy, New York 14482 | (716) 768-2561 | Fax (716) 247-7507

DESIGN FIRM
McElveney & Palozzi Design
Rochester, (NY) USA
PROJECT
LeRoy Village Green
CREATIVE DIRECTOR
William McElveney
ART DIRECTOR
Lisa Parenti

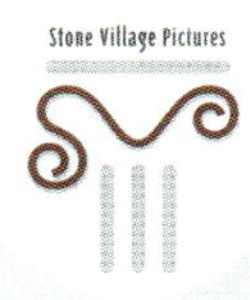

9200 Sunset Blvd. Suite 520
West Hollywood, CA 90069

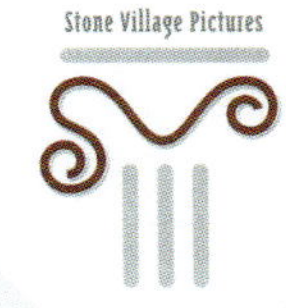

9200 Sunset Blvd. Suite 520
West Hollywood, CA 90069
t 310.777.2163
f 310.777.2150

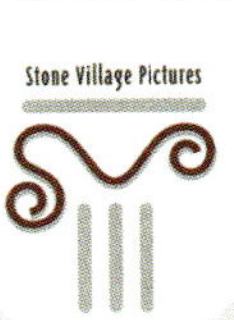

Scott Steindorff
president/producer

9200 Sunset Blvd. Suite 520
West Hollywood, CA 90069
t 310.402.5173
f 310.402.5172
scott@stonevillageprods.com

DESIGN FIRM
Greenspun Media Group
Henderson, (NV) USA

CLIENT
Stone Village Pictures

ART DIRECTOR
Mami Awamura

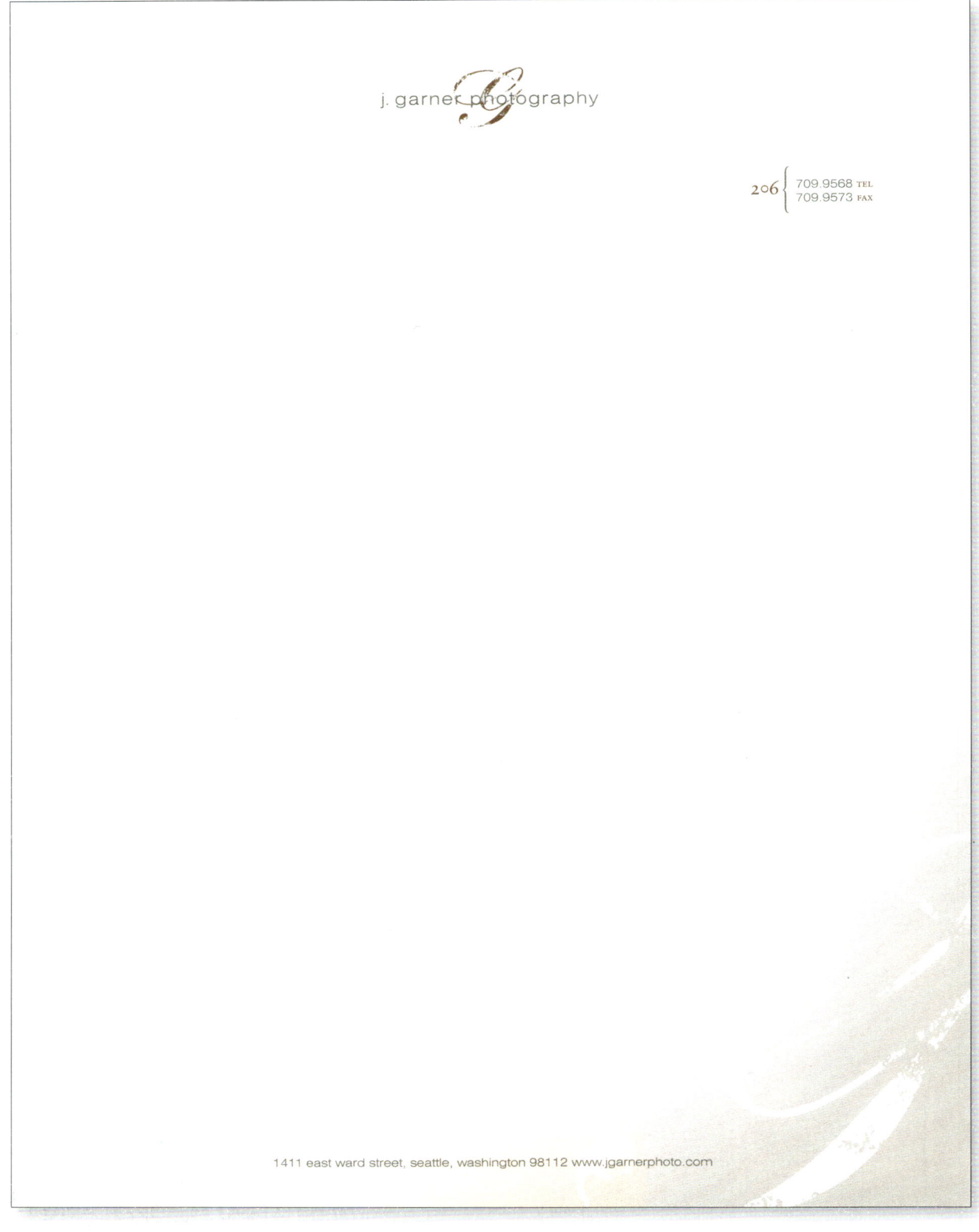

DESIGN FIRM
Eben Design
Seattle, (WA) USA
PROJECT
J. Garner Photography
ART DIRECTOR, DESIGNER
Dan Meehan

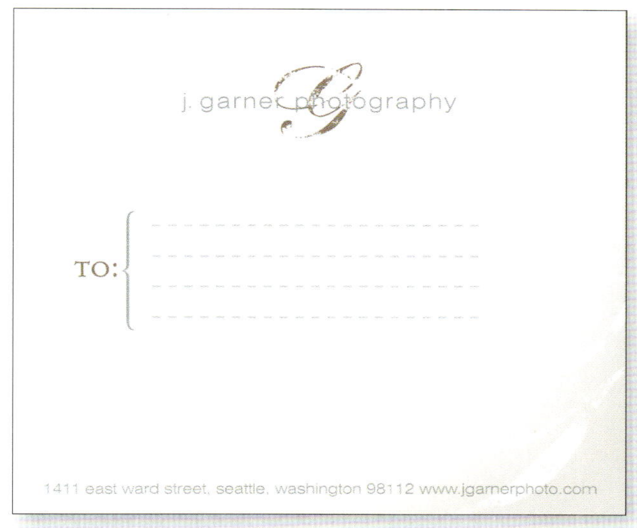
j. garner photography
TO:
1411 east ward street, seattle, washington 98112 www.jgarnerphoto.com

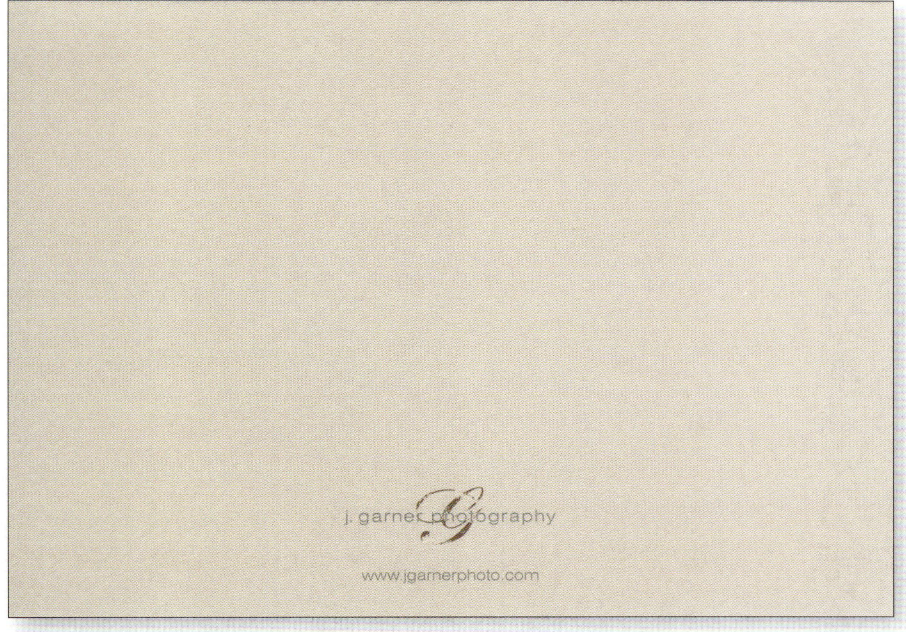
j. garner photography
www.jgarnerphoto.com

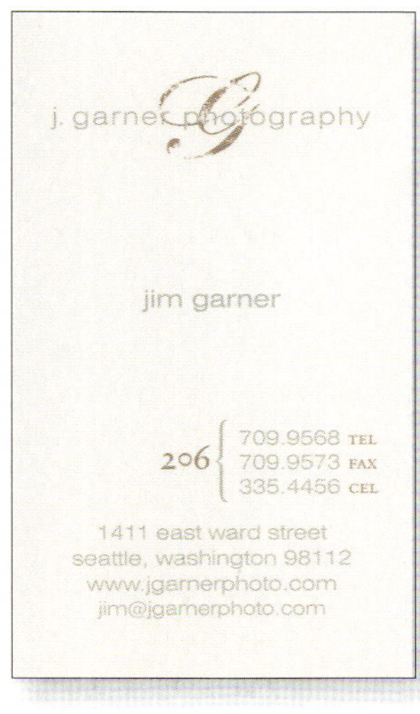
j. garner photography
jim garner
206
709.9568 TEL
709.9573 FAX
335.4456 CEL
1411 east ward street
seattle, washington 98112
www.jgarnerphoto.com
jim@jgarnerphoto.com

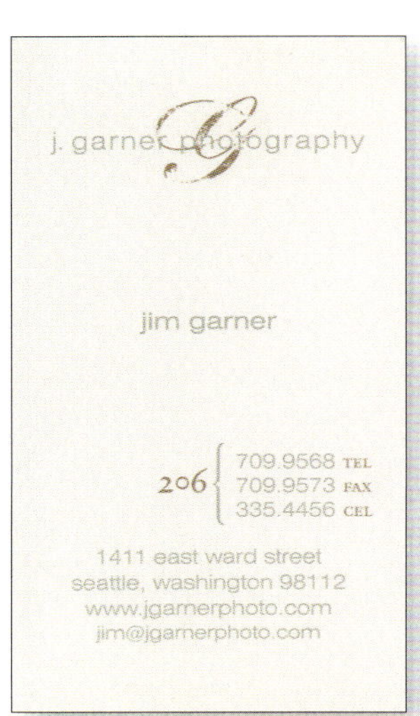
j. garner photography
jim garner
206
709.9568 TEL
709.9573 FAX
335.4456 CEL
1411 east ward street
seattle, washington 98112
www.jgarnerphoto.com
jim@jgarnerphoto.com

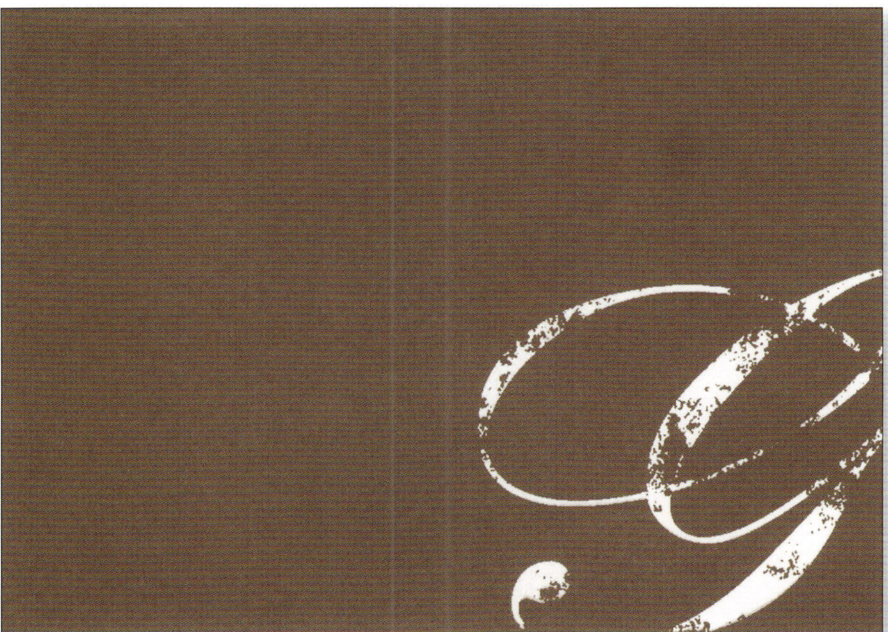

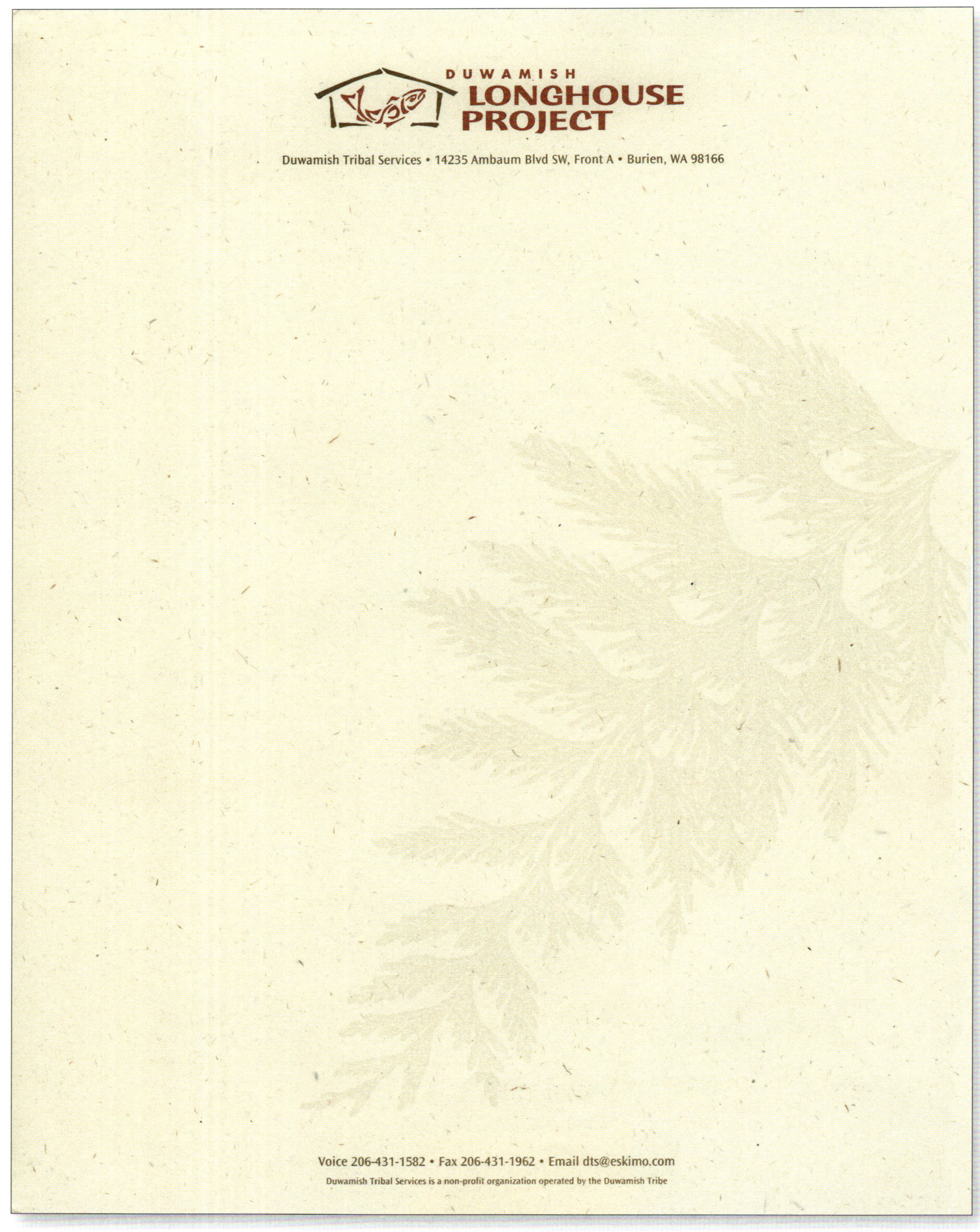

DESIGN FIRM
Ray Braun Design
Seattle, (WA) USA
CLIENT
Duwamish Tribal Services
DESIGNER
Ray Braun

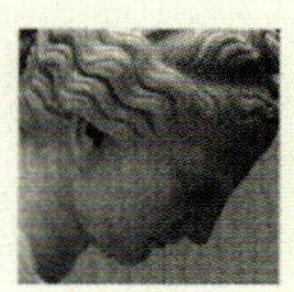

LATONA
ASSOCIATES

Paul M. Montrone
Managing Director

Liberty Lane
Hampton, NH 03842
Telephone: 603.929.2607
Facsimile: 603.926.1152
www.LatonaAssociates.com

DESIGN FIRM
Arnold Saks Associates, Inc.
New York, (NY) USA
PROJECT
Latona Associates
ART DIRECTOR
Arnold Saks
DESIGNER
Lisa Corcoran

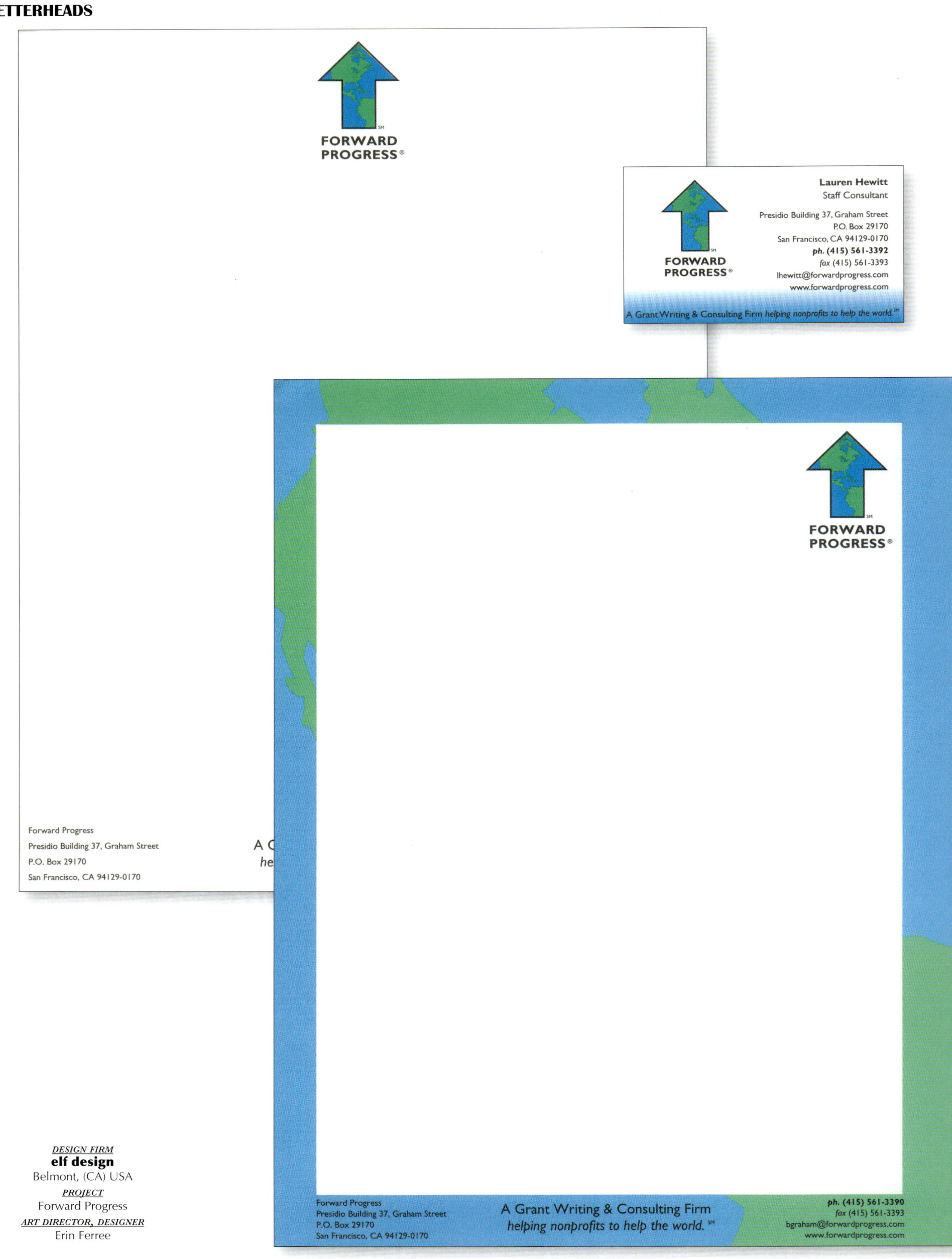

DESIGN FIRM
elf design
Belmont, (CA) USA
PROJECT
Forward Progress
ART DIRECTOR, DESIGNER
Erin Ferree

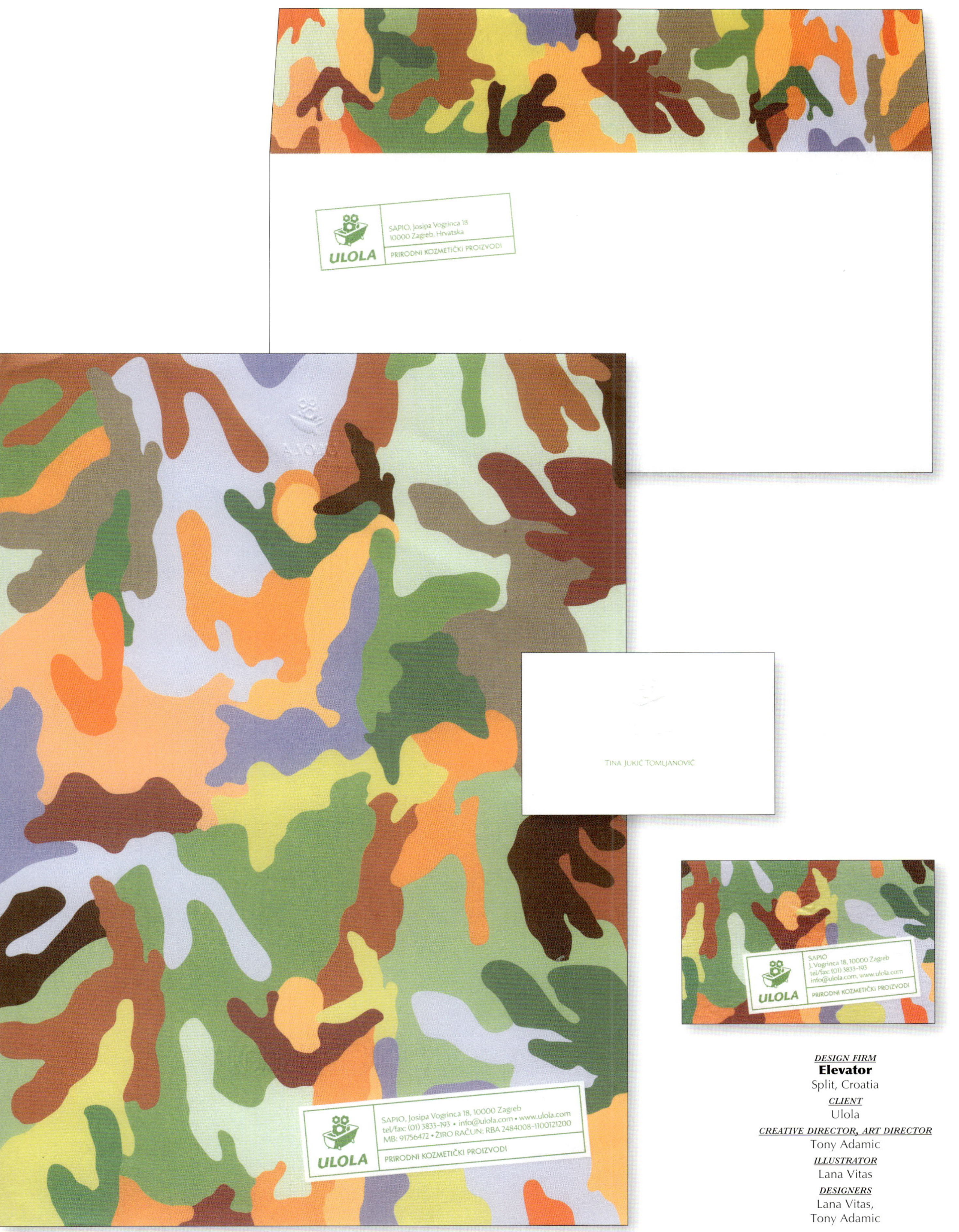

DESIGN FIRM
Elevator
Split, Croatia

CLIENT
Ulola

CREATIVE DIRECTOR, ART DIRECTOR
Tony Adamic

ILLUSTRATOR
Lana Vitas

DESIGNERS
Lana Vitas,
Tony Adamic

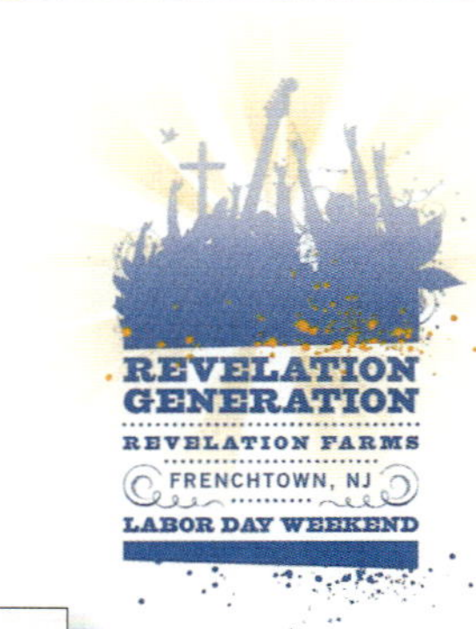

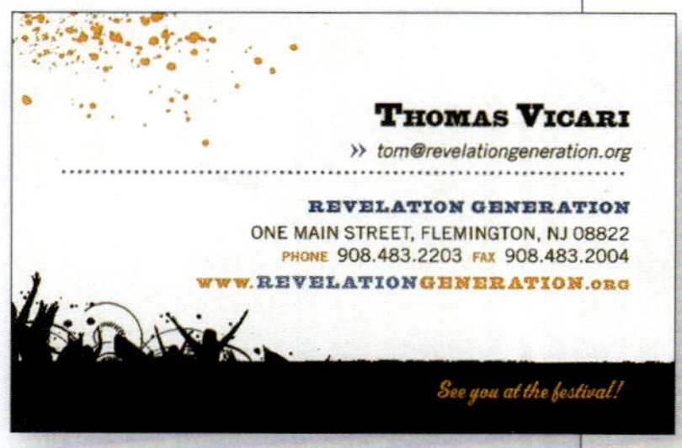

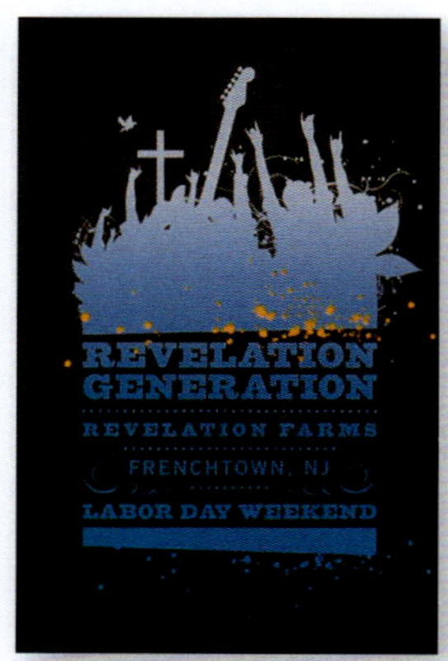

DESIGN FIRM
3rd Edge Communications
Jersey City, (NJ) USA
PROJECT
Revelation Generation
ART DIRECTOR
Frankie Gonzalez
DESIGNER
Melissa Medina Mackin

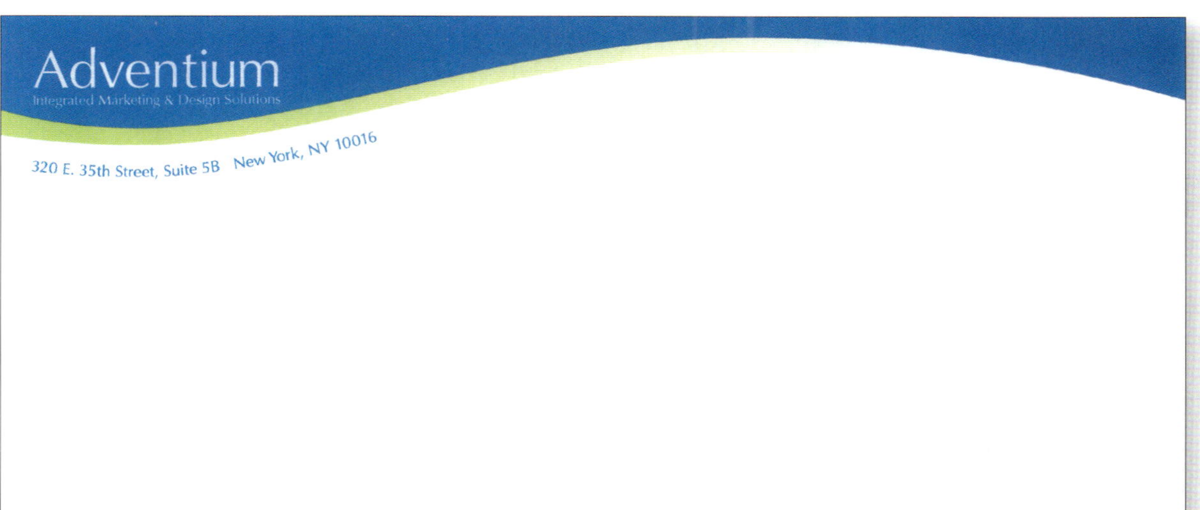

Adventium
Integrated Marketing & Design Solutions
320 E. 35th Street, Suite 5B New York, NY 10016 P:212•481•9576 F:501•325•3968 www.adventium.net

Adventium
Integrated Marketing & Design
Penny Chuang
President/Creative Director
320 East 35th Street, Suite 5B
New York, NY 10016
T: 212•481•9576
F: 501•325•3968
E: penny@adventium.net
www.adventium.net

Adventium Integrated Marketing & Design Solutions • Advertising • Direct Marketing • Collateral • Corporate Communications • Brand Development • Quality • Logo and Stationery Design • Sales Kits • Strategy Consulting • Brochures • Catalogs • Responsive • Event Planning • Invitations • Reliable • Media Kits • FSI • Newsletters • Signage • Fast • Outdoor • Product Launches • Web Design and Architecture • Annual Reports • Press Kits • Value • Poster Design • Promotional Videos • Packaging • Trade Show Exhibits • Broadcast Advertising • Web Banners • 212•481•9576 • www.adventium.net

DESIGN FIRM
Adventium Marketing & Design
New York, (NY) USA
PROJECT
Adventium Marketing & Design
CREATIVE DIRECTOR, DESIGNER
Penny Chuang

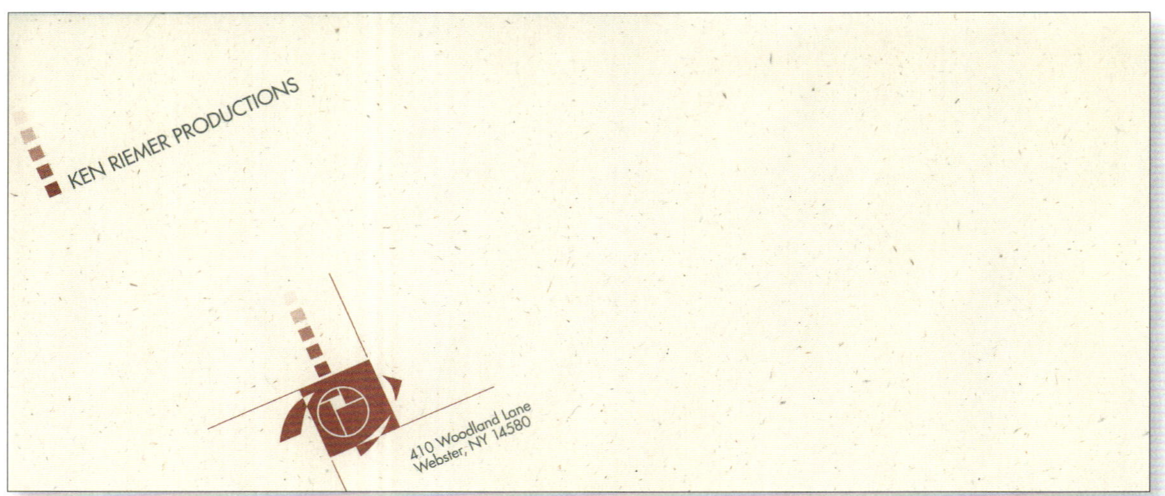

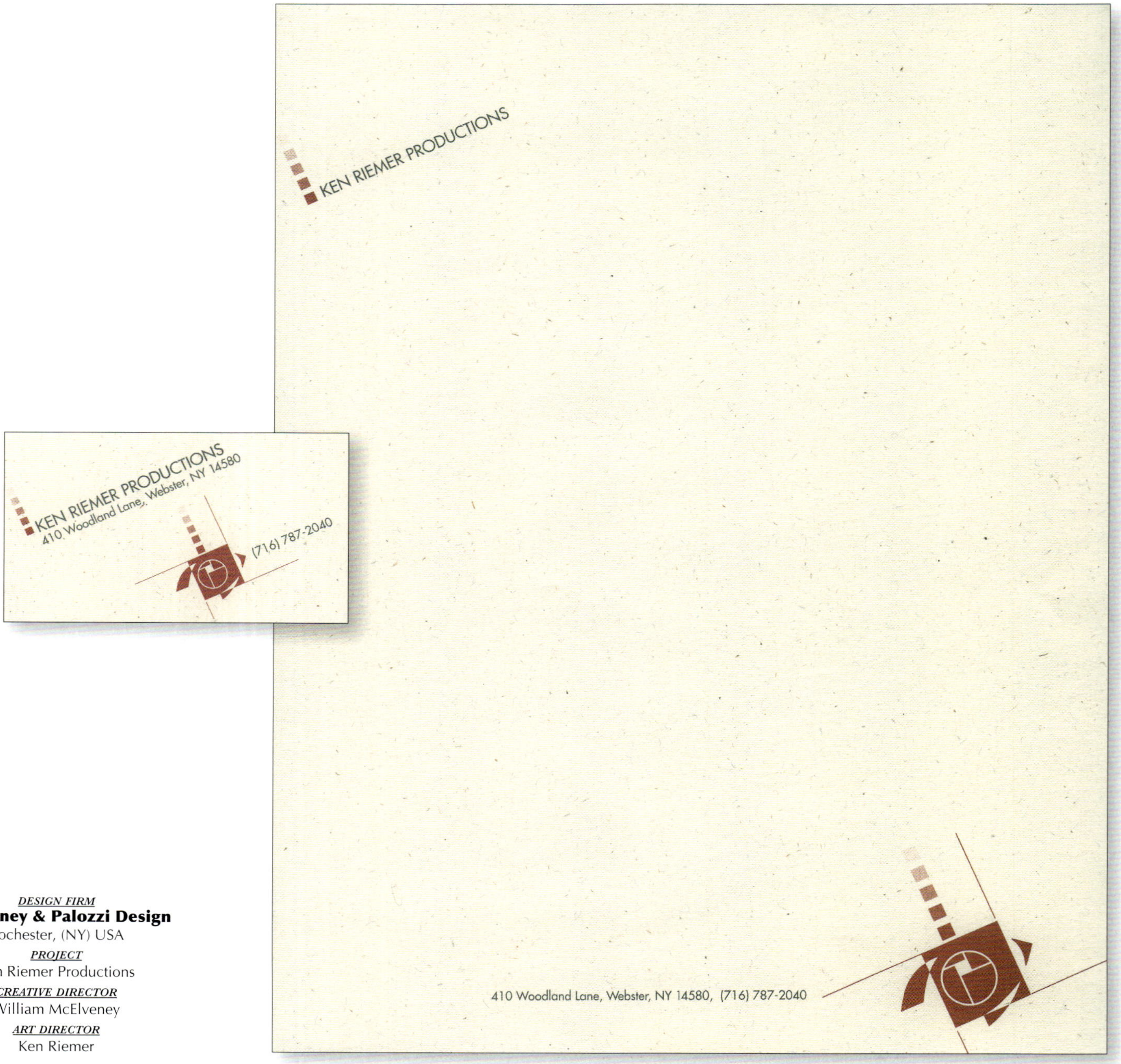

KEN RIEMER PRODUCTIONS

410 Woodland Lane, Webster, NY 14580, (716) 787-2040

KEN RIEMER PRODUCTIONS
410 Woodland Lane, Webster, NY 14580
(716) 787-2040

DESIGN FIRM
McElveney & Palozzi Design
Rochester, (NY) USA
PROJECT
Ken Riemer Productions
CREATIVE DIRECTOR
William McElveney
ART DIRECTOR
Ken Riemer

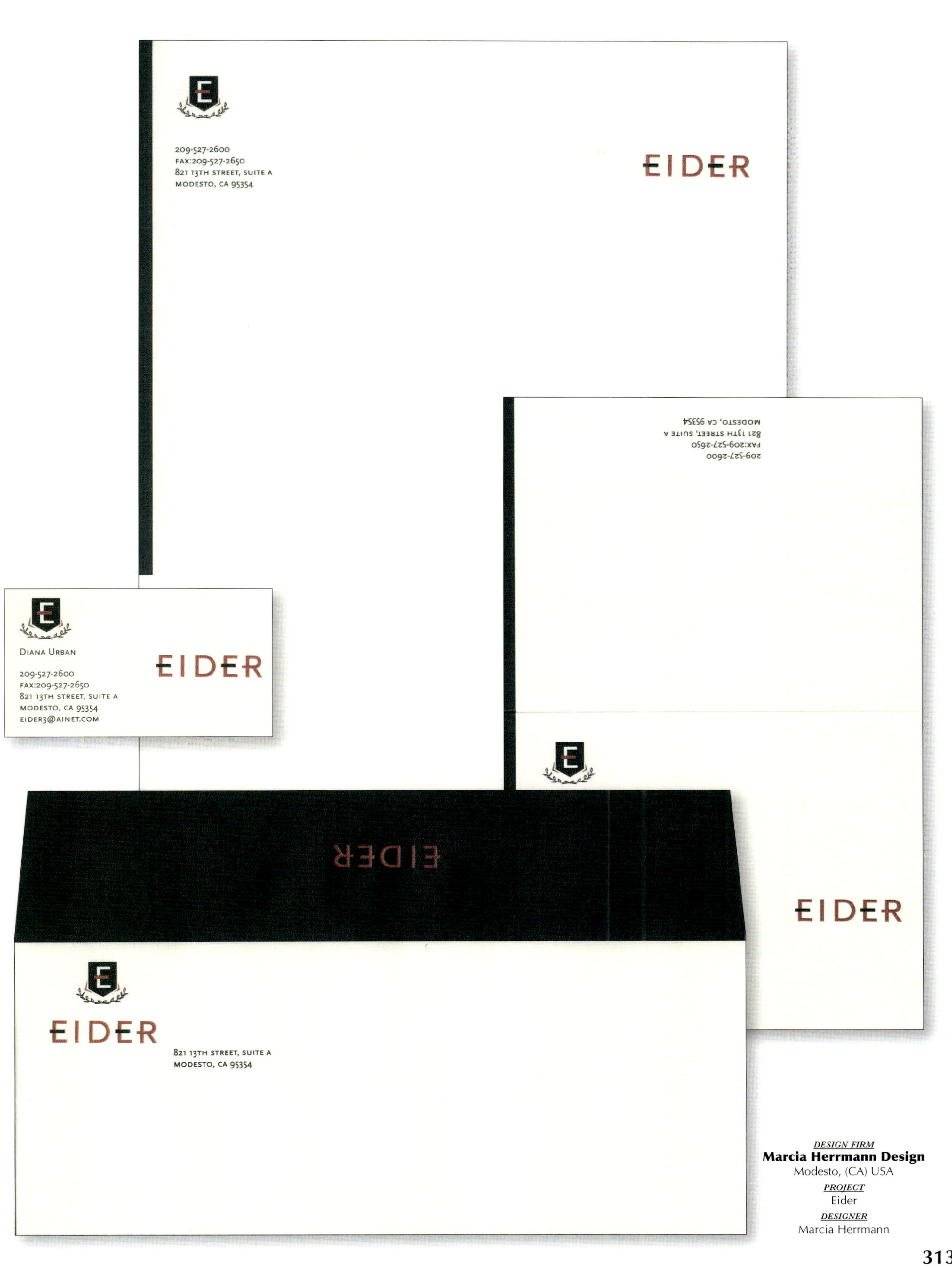

DESIGN FIRM
Marcia Herrmann Design
Modesto, (CA) USA
PROJECT
Eider
DESIGNER
Marcia Herrmann

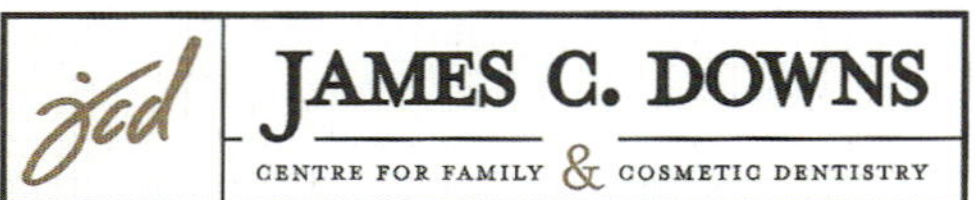
jcd
JAMES C. DOWNS
CENTRE FOR FAMILY & COSMETIC DENTISTRY

jcd
DENTISTRY FOR LIFE

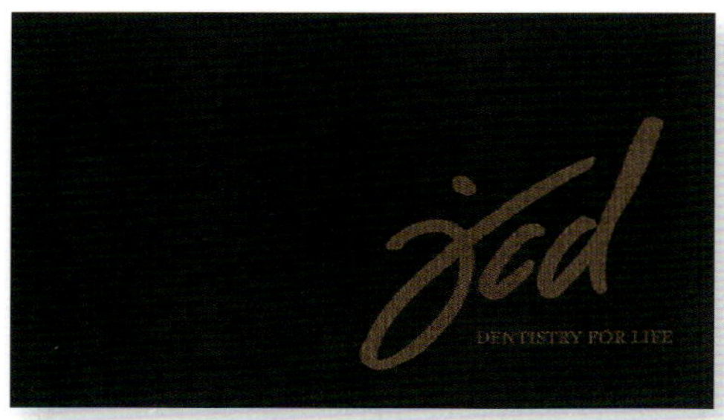
jcd
DENTISTRY FOR LIFE

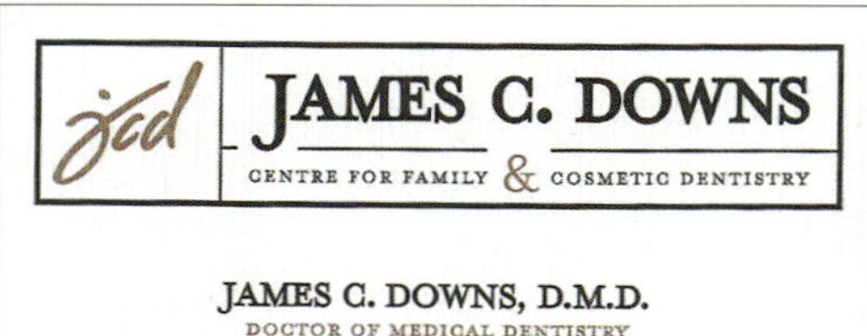
jcd
JAMES C. DOWNS
CENTRE FOR FAMILY & COSMETIC DENTISTRY
JAMES C. DOWNS, D.M.D.
DOCTOR OF MEDICAL DENTISTRY
820 CLERMONT ST., SUITE 310 DENVER, CO 80220
303.377.9278 WWW.JAMESCDOWNS.COM

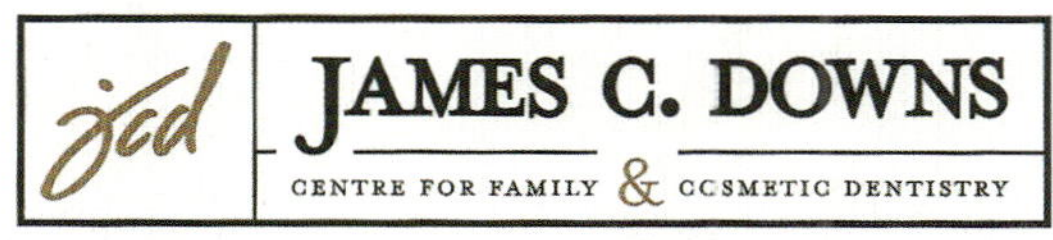

820 CLERMONT ST., SUITE 310 DENVER, CO 80220
303.377.9278 WWW.JAMESCDOWNS.COM

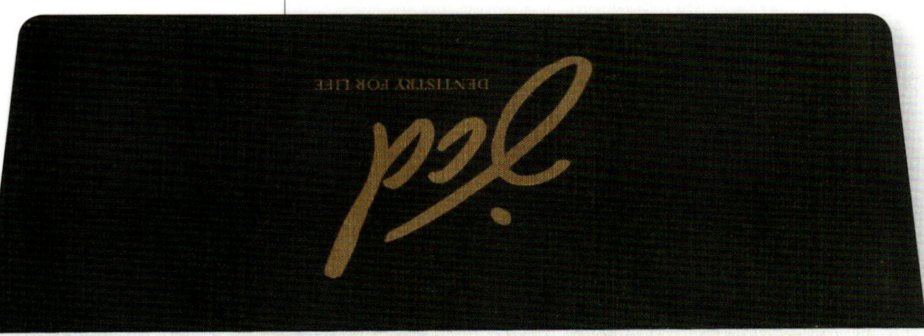

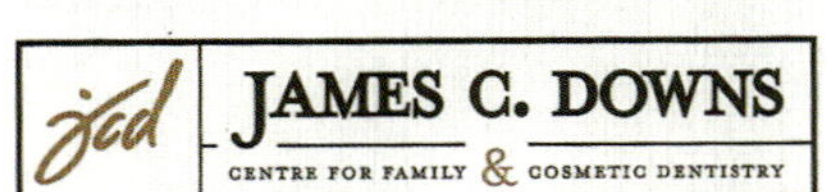

820 CLERMONT ST., SUITE 310 DENVER, CO 80220
303.377.9278 WWW.JAMESCDOWNS.COM

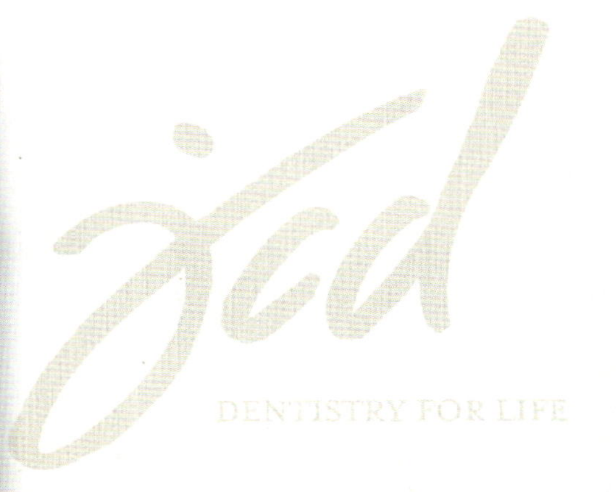

DESIGN FIRM
CATALYST creative, inc.
Denver, (CO) USA
PROJECT
James C. Downs
ART DIRECTOR, DESIGNER
Jeanna Pool

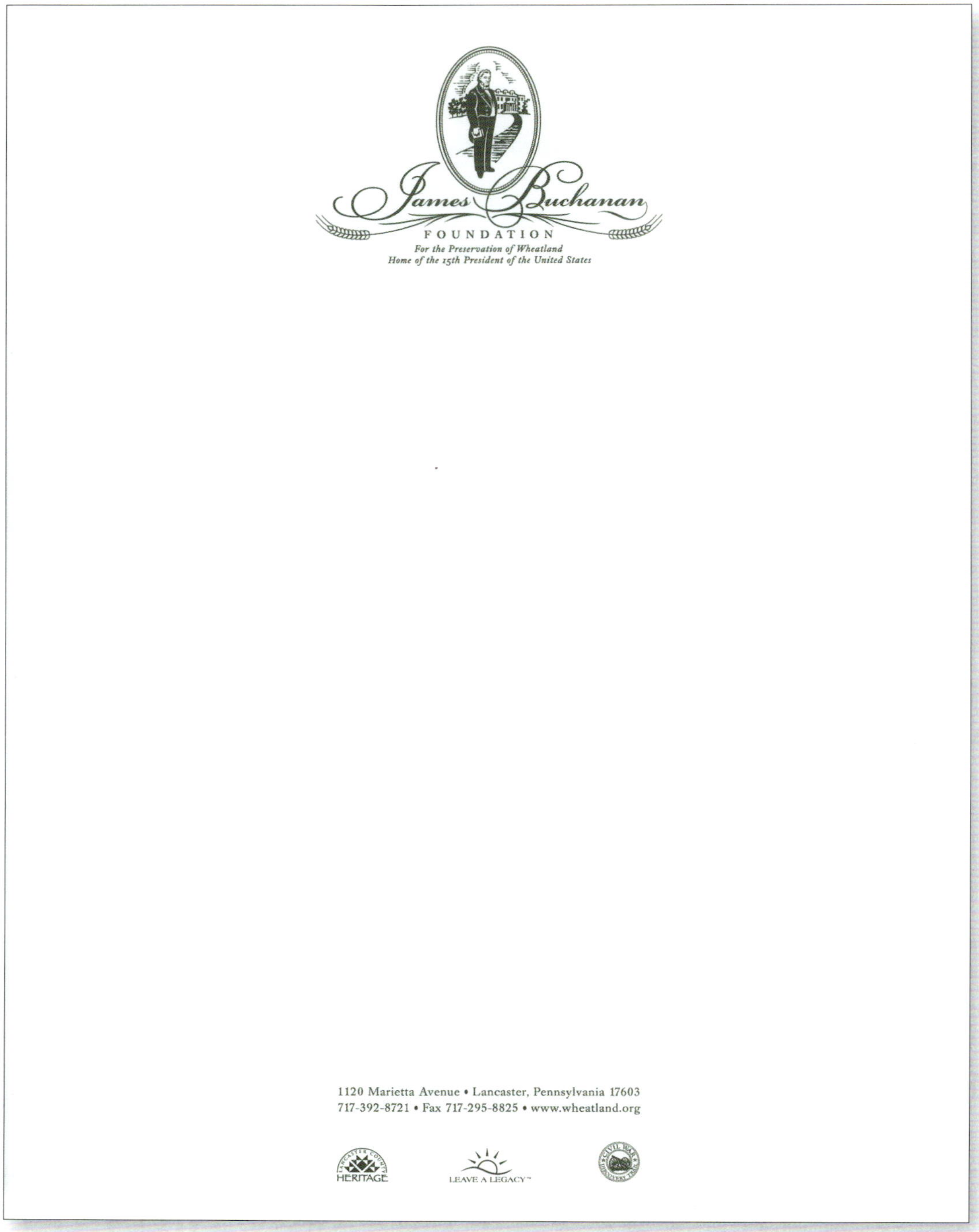

James Buchanan
FOUNDATION
For the Preservation of Wheatland
Home of the 15th President of the United States

1120 Marietta Avenue • Lancaster, Pennsylvania 17603
717-392-8721 • Fax 717-295-8825 • www.wheatland.org

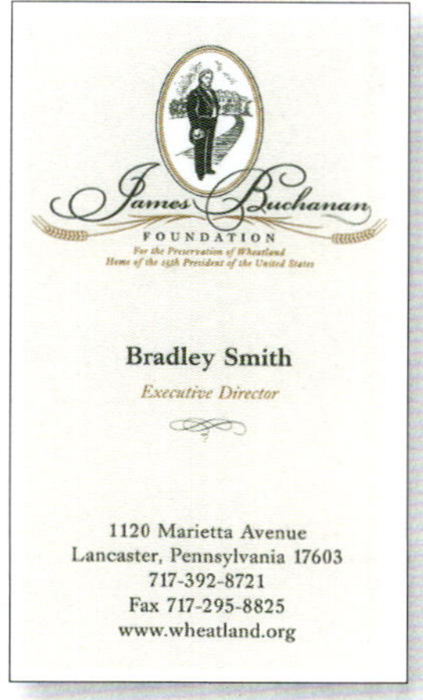

James Buchanan
FOUNDATION
For the Preservation of Wheatland
Home of the 15th President of the United States

Bradley Smith
Executive Director

1120 Marietta Avenue
Lancaster, Pennsylvania 17603
717-392-8721
Fax 717-295-8825
www.wheatland.org

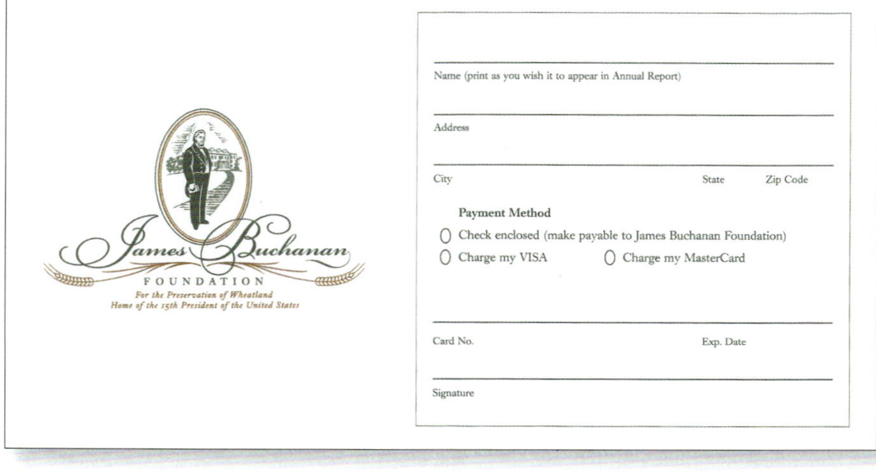

James Buchanan
FOUNDATION
For the Preservation of Wheatland
Home of the 15th President of the United States

Name (print as you wish it to appear in Annual Report)

Address

City State Zip Code

Payment Method

○ Check enclosed (make payable to James Buchanan Foundation)

○ Charge my VISA ○ Charge my MasterCard

Card No. Exp. Date

Signature

The Wilbur S. Smith Challenge Grant

A Special Giving Opportunity for Wheatland Members

Ms. Sally Smith Cahalan, former Executive Director of The James Buchanan Foundation, is a consistent and loyal supporter of restoration projects at President Buchanan's home. Ms. Cahalan recently gave the Foundation a generous grant of $4,500 in honor of her father, Wilbur S. Smith. The grant is intended to challenge everyone who cherishes Wheatland and wishes to see it preserved and maintained appropriately and accurately. Your matching gift to the Wilbur S. Smith Challenge Grant will be used to accomplish a major and much needed restoration project: the replacement of carpeting in Wheatland's family parlor, President Buchanan's library, and the stairway and upper halls of the house.

The goal for this challenge is $20,000.

◯ *Yes, I want to meet the Wilbur S. Smith Challenge. Enclosed is my matching gift of:*

◯ $25 ◯ $75 ◯ $100 ◯ $250

◯ $500 ◯ $1,000 ◯ $2,500 ◯ $5,000

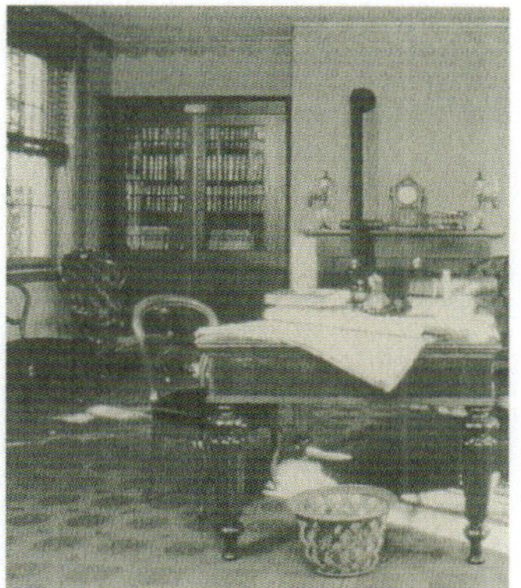

The library where Buchanan wrote his inaugural address and presidential memoirs.

Detach here and send the card in the enclosed envelope.

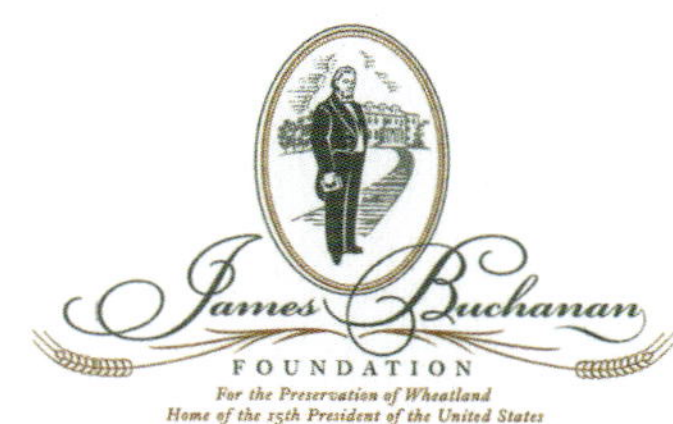

James Buchanan

FOUNDATION

For the Preservation of Wheatland
Home of the 15th President of the United States

1120 Marietta Avenue • Lancaster, Pennsylvania 17603
717-392-8721 • Fax 717-295-8825 • www.wheatland.org

HERITAGE   LEAVE A LEGACY™

DESIGN FIRM
Dean Design/Marketing Group, Inc.
Lancaster, (PA) USA

PROJECT
James Buchanan Foundation

SENIOR DESIGNER
Jeff Phillips

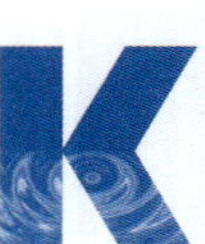

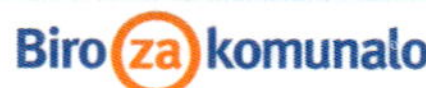
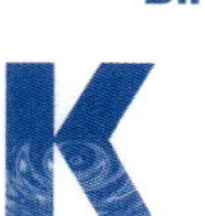

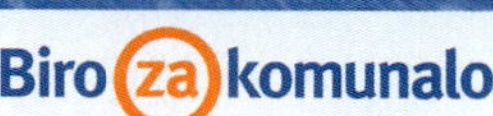

DESIGN FIRM
KROG, Ljubljana
Ljubljana, Slovenia
CLIENT
Biro za komunalo, Ljubljana
ART DIRECTOR, DESIGNER
Edi Berk

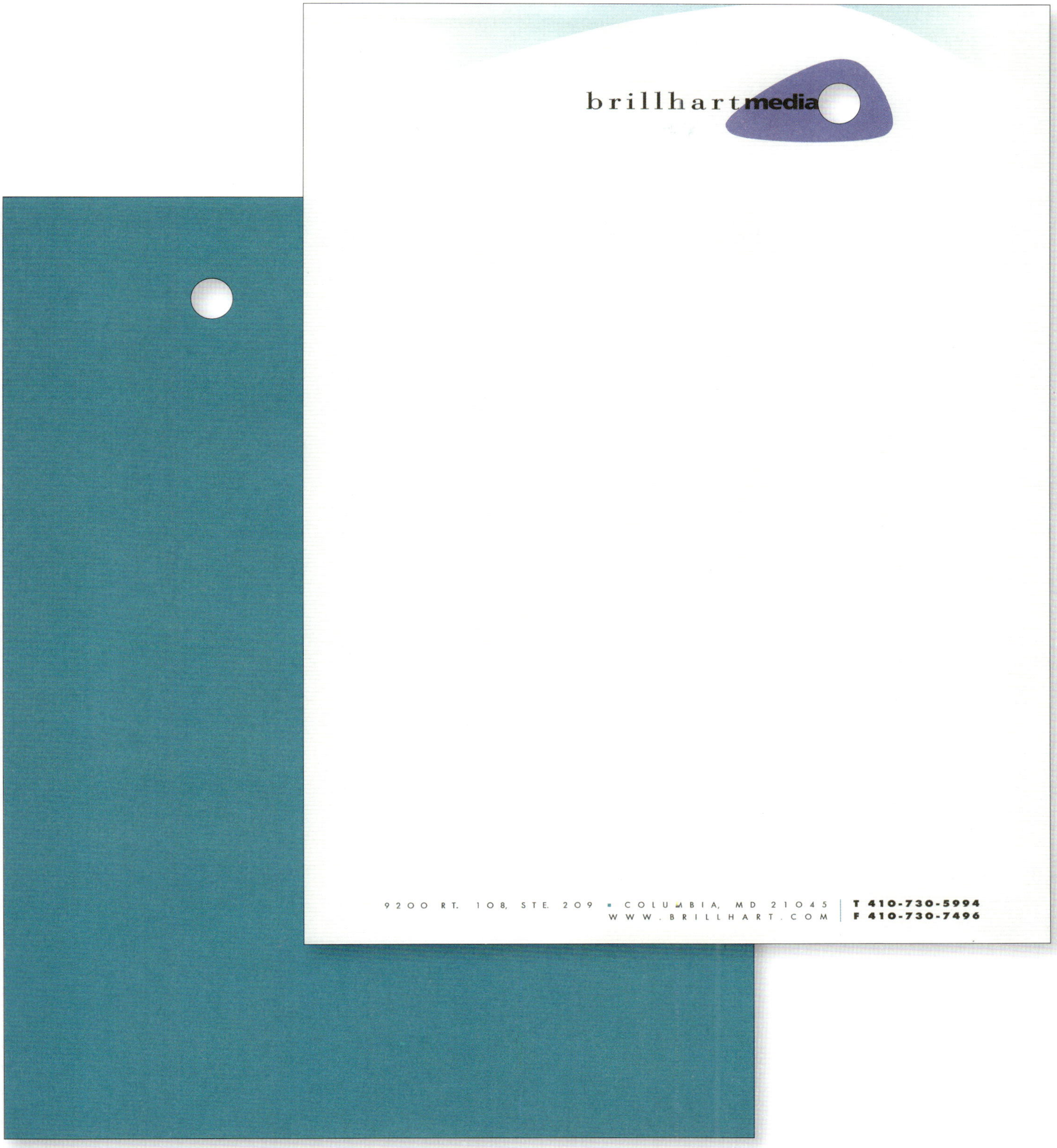

brillhartmedia

9200 RT. 108, STE. 209 • COLUMBIA, MD 21045 | T 410-730-5994
WWW.BRILLHART.COM | F 410-730-7496

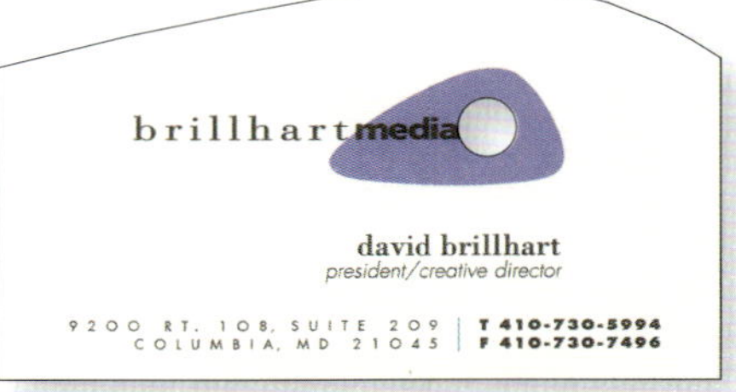

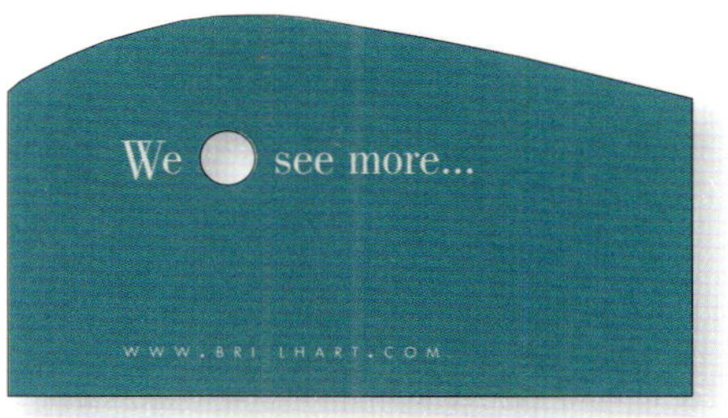

DESIGN FIRM
Dever Designs
Laurel, (MD) USA
PROJECT
Brillhart Media
DESIGNER
Jeffrey Dever

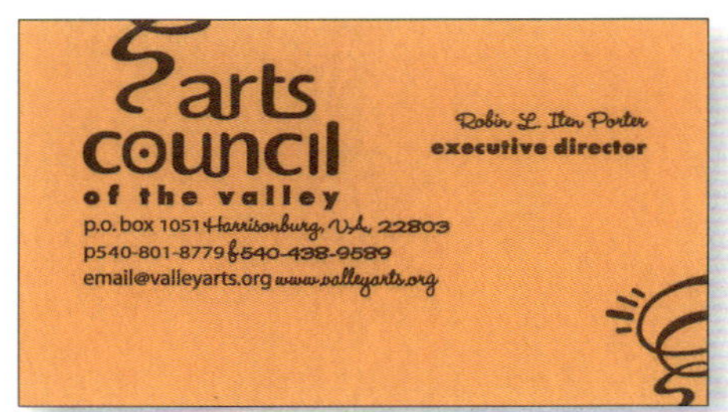

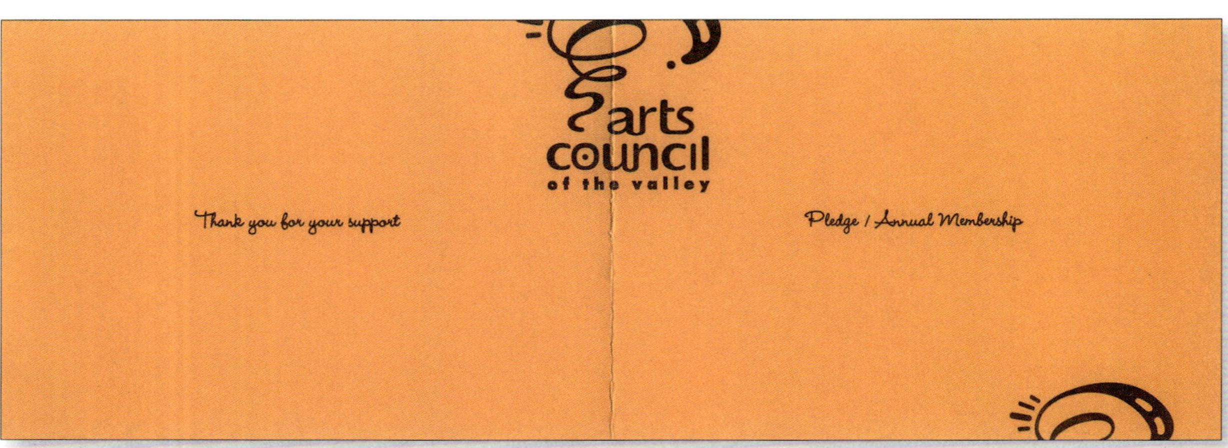

o make checks payable to *Arts Council of the Valley*

o please bill me in __ __ / __ __ (month/year)

please charge to my o mastercard o visa

____ ____ ____ ____ card #

__ __ / __ __ exp. date

________________ signature

arts council of the valley is a nonprofit, 501(c)3 organization
contributions are deductible for federal income tax purposes
for more information, please contact arts council of the valley
p.o. box 1051 Harrisonburg, VA 22803, p540-801-8779, f540-438-9589
email@valleyarts.org, www.valleyarts.org

name ________________________
(as it will apear in acknowledgements)

mailing address ________________________

____

city ________ state ____ zip ______

phone __ __ __ - __ __ __ - __ __ __

e-mail ________________________

o gift $ ________ (gifts of securities are also accepted)

o individual - *Arts Patron* ($25)

o individual - *Artist* ($25)

o organization - *Annual Budget* \$50,000 *and under* ($50)

o organization - *Annual Budget over* \$50,000 ($100)

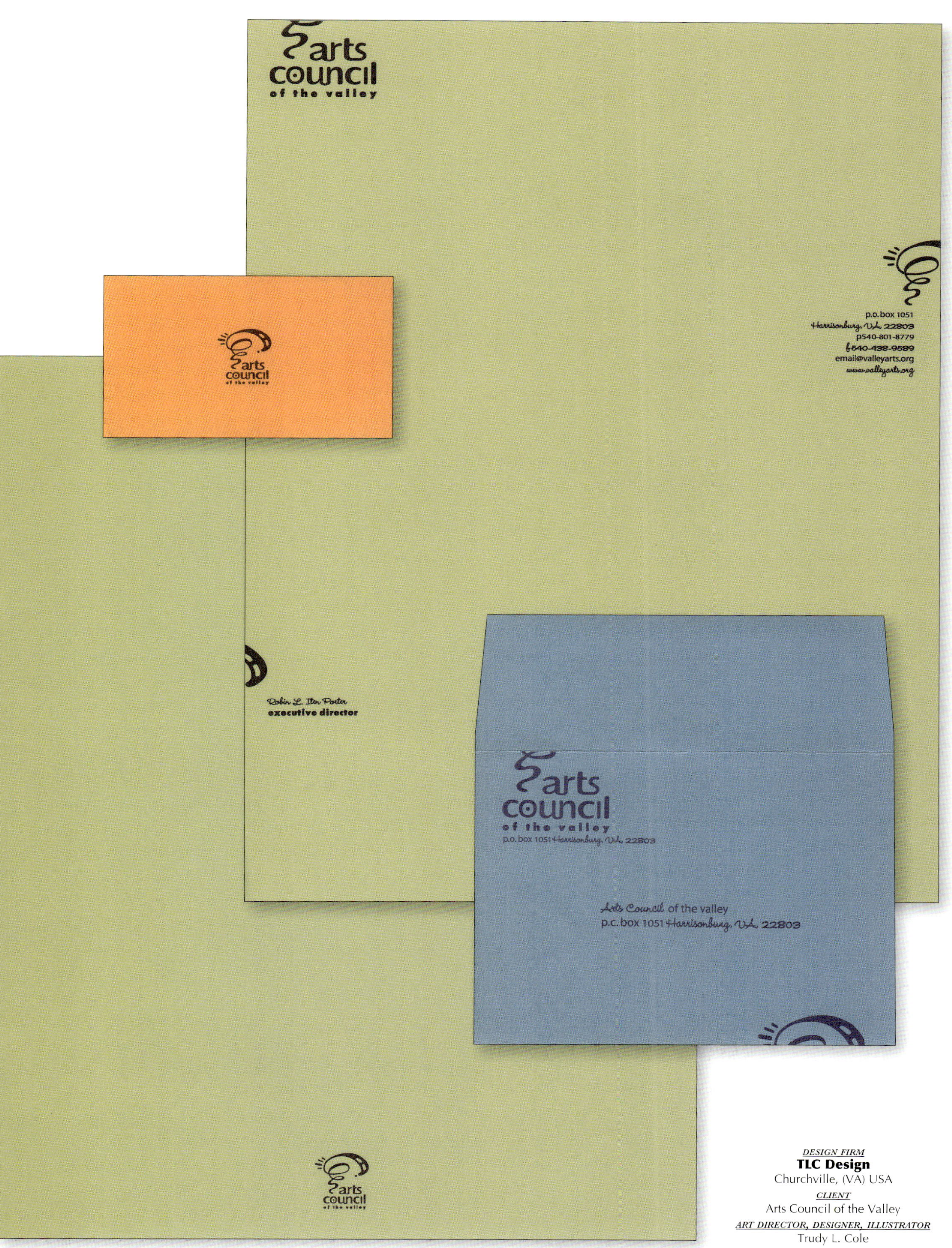

DESIGN FIRM
TLC Design
Churchville, (VA) USA
CLIENT
Arts Council of the Valley
ART DIRECTOR, DESIGNER, ILLUSTRATOR
Trudy L. Cole

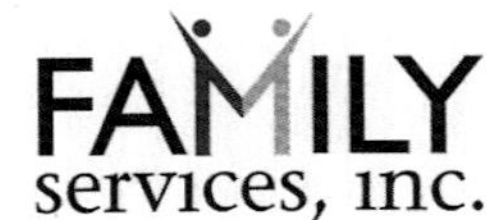

helping families help themselves since 1964

731 Main Street / Lafayette, IN 47901-1459
765.423.5361 / 800.875.5361 / fax 765.742.8272 / www.fsilafayette.org

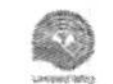
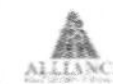

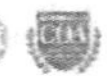

DESIGN FIRM
Indiana Design Consortium, Inc.
Lafayette, (IN) USA
CLIENT
Family Services, Inc.
DESIGNER
Kristy Blair

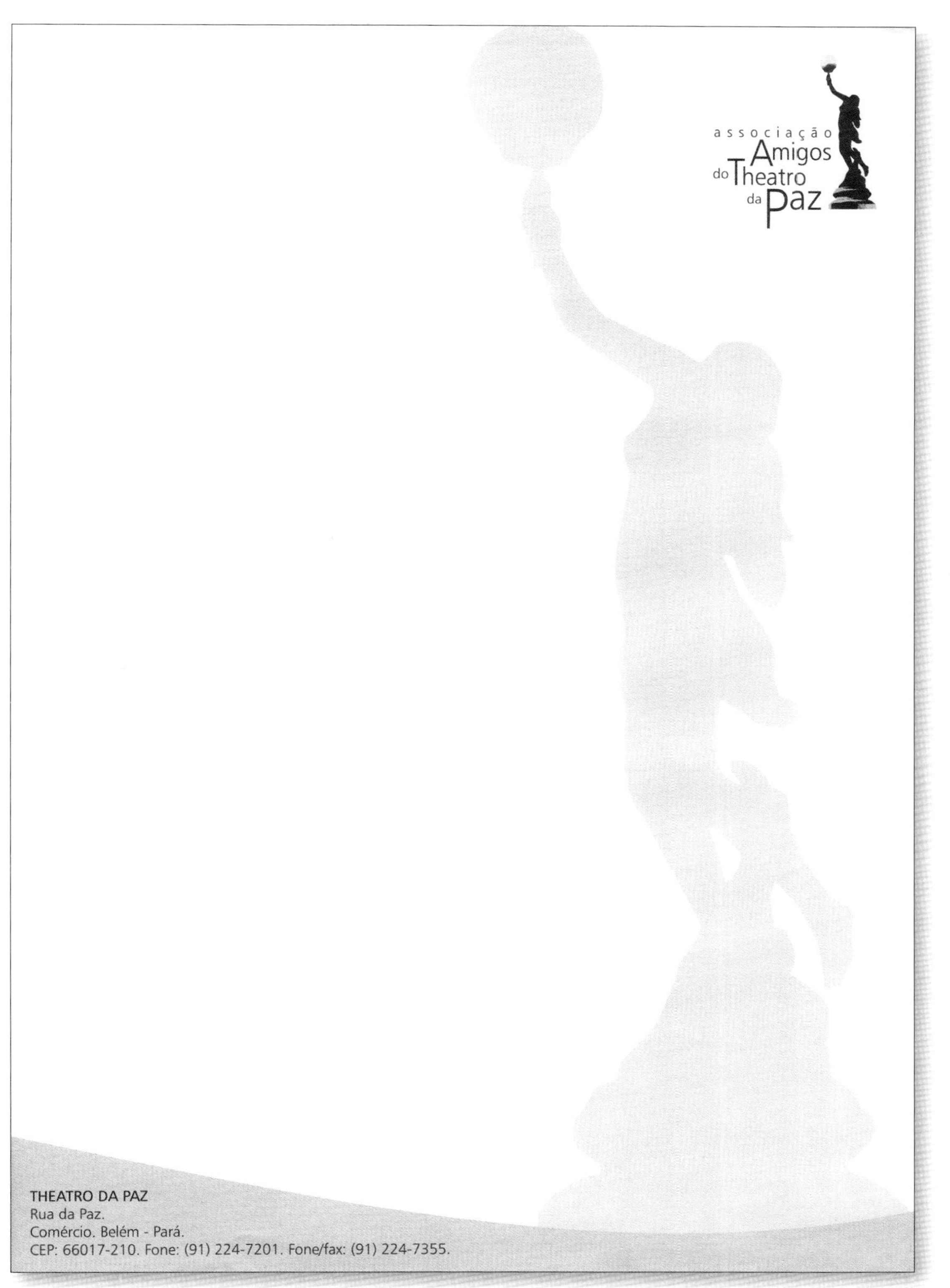

<u>*DESIGN FIRM*</u>
Mendes Publicidade
Belém, (Pará) Brazil
<u>*PROJECT*</u>
Associação Amigos do Theatro da Paz
<u>*DESIGNERS*</u>
Oswaldo Mendes, Maria Alice Pena

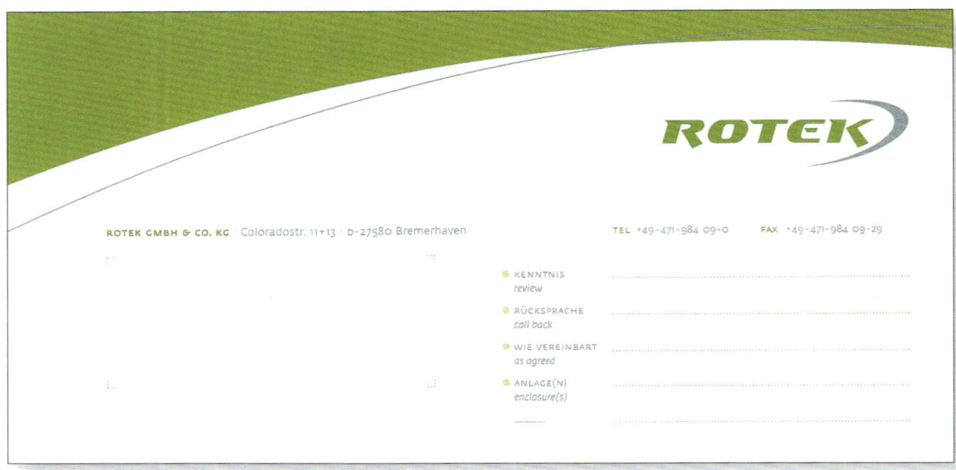

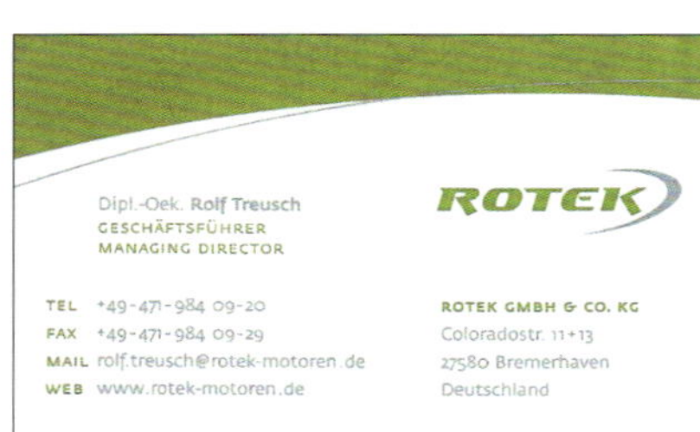

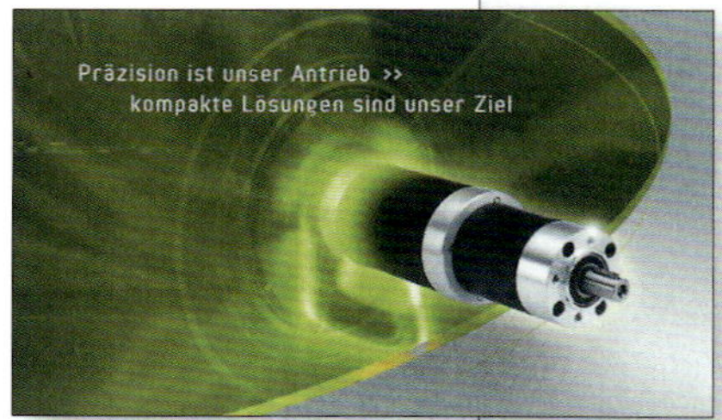

DESIGN FIRM
Braue: Branding & Corporate Design
Bremerhaven, Germany

CLIENT
Rotek

CREATIVE DIRECTOR
Kai Braue

ART DIRECTOR
Marçel Robbers

DESIGNERS
Marçel Robbers,
Sandra Blum

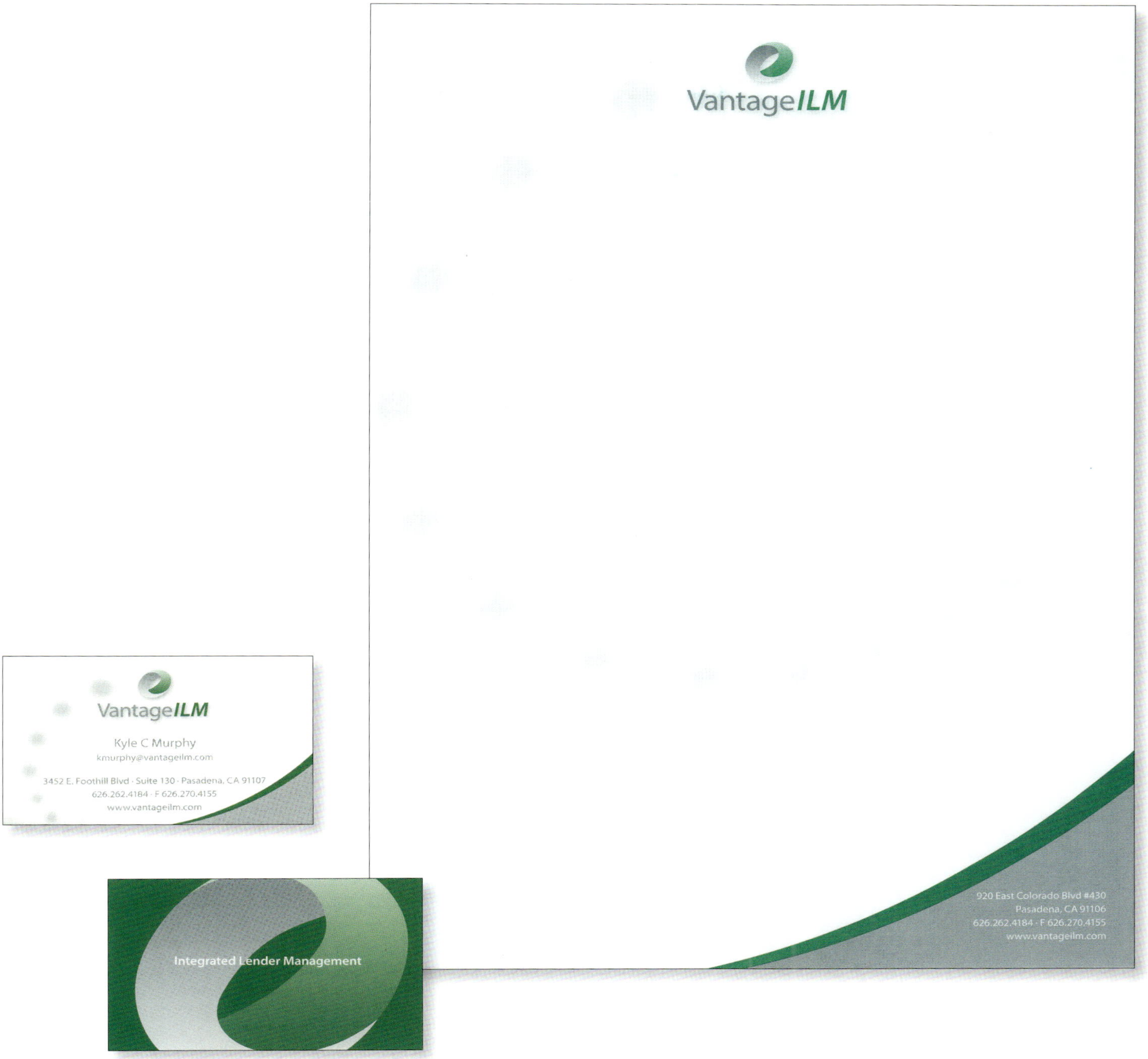

VantageILM

920 East Colorado Blvd #430
Pasadena, CA 91106
626.262.4184 · F 626.270.4155
www.vantageilm.com

VantageILM

Kyle C Murphy
kmurphy@vantageilm.com

3452 E. Foothill Blvd · Suite 130 · Pasadena, CA 91107
626.262.4184 · F 626.270.4155
www.vantageilm.com

Integrated Lender Management

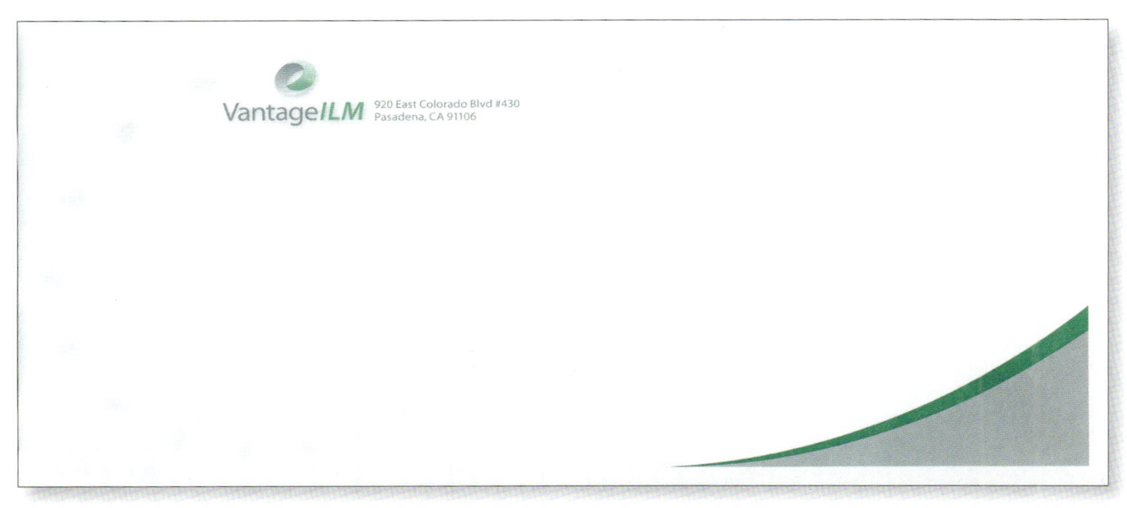

DESIGN FIRM
SwitchStream
Redondo Beach, (CA) USA
PROJECT
Vantage ILM
ART DIRECTOR
Kyle Murphy

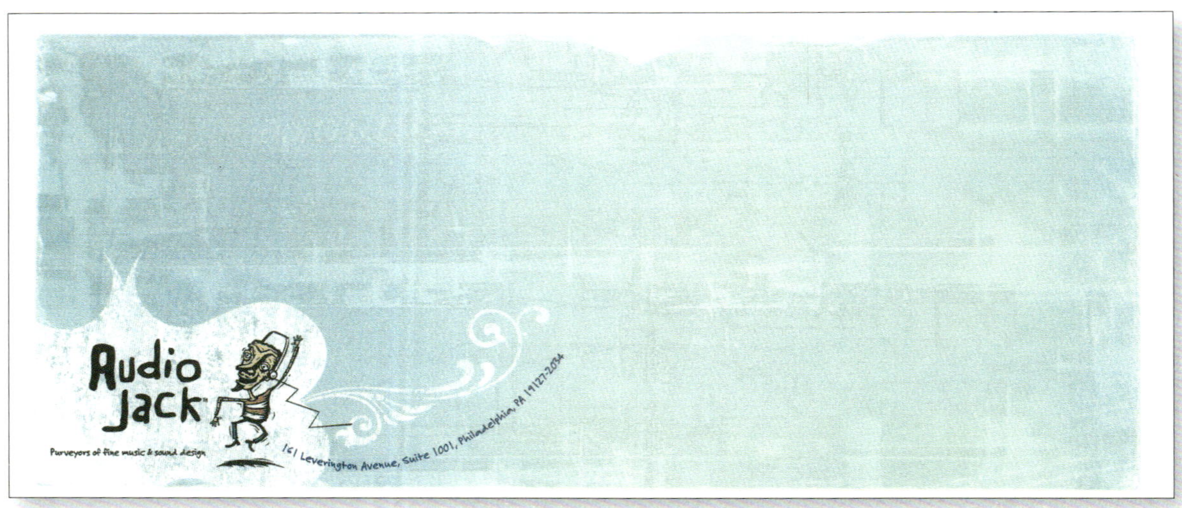

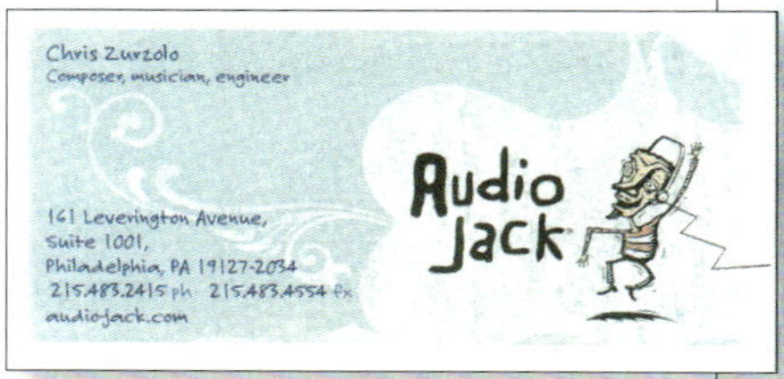

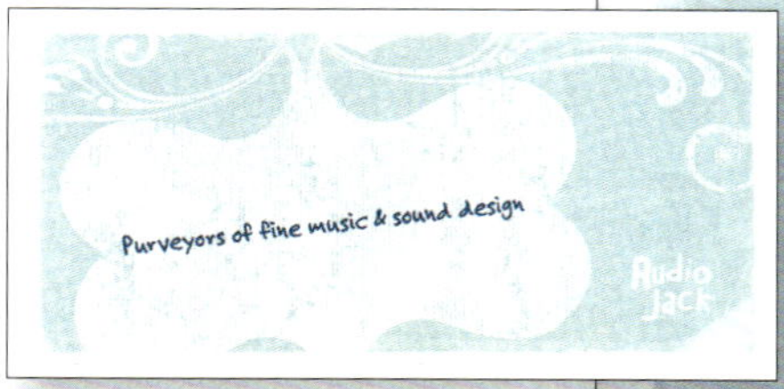

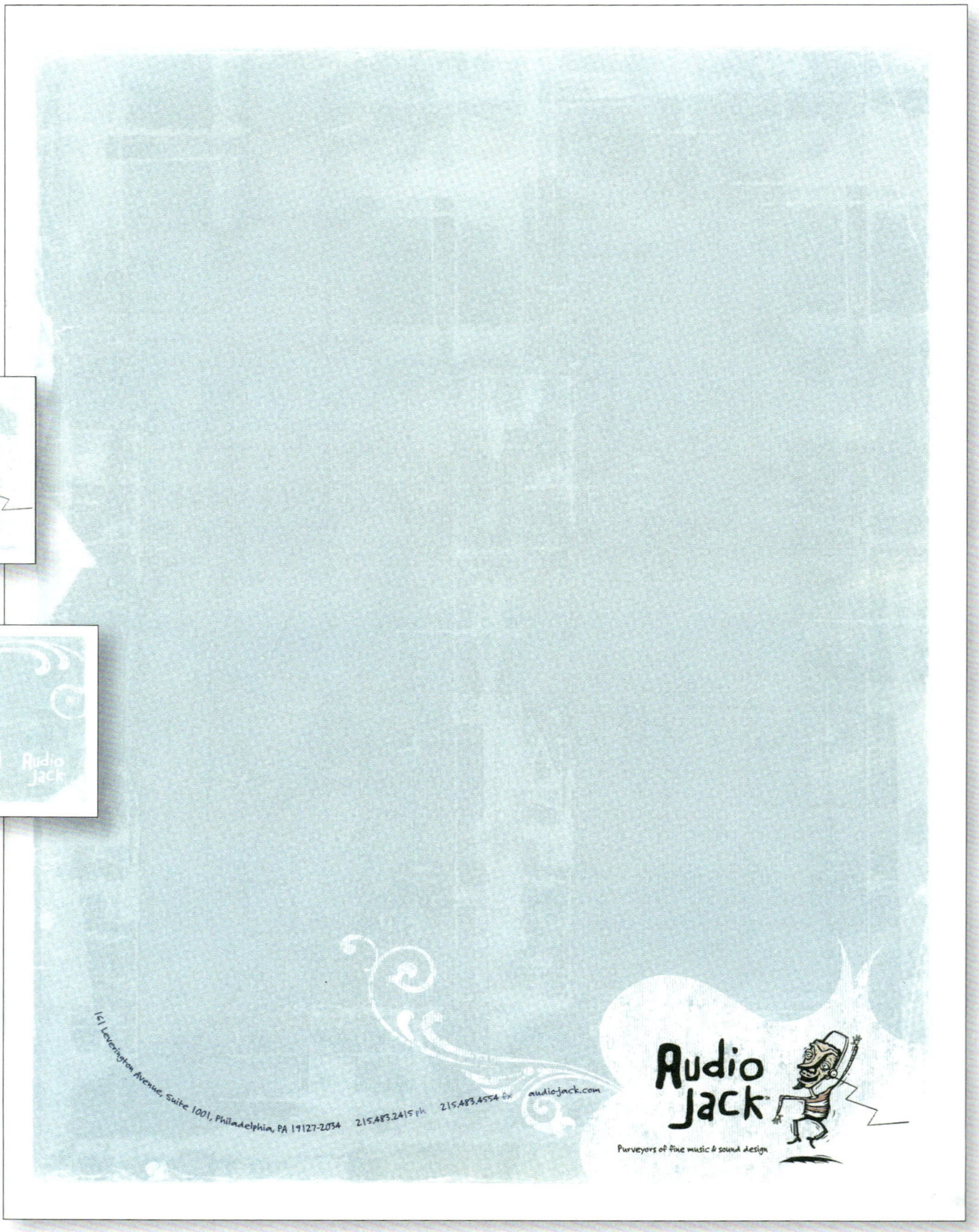

DESIGN FIRM
D4 Creative Group
Philadelphia, (PA) USA
PROJECT
Audio Jack Stationery
DESIGNER
Wicky Wai-Kuen Lee

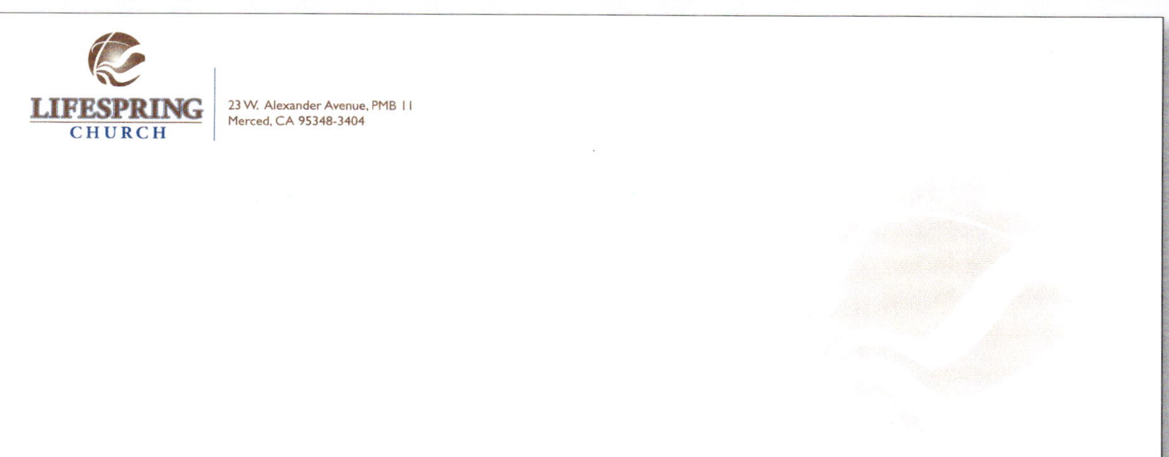

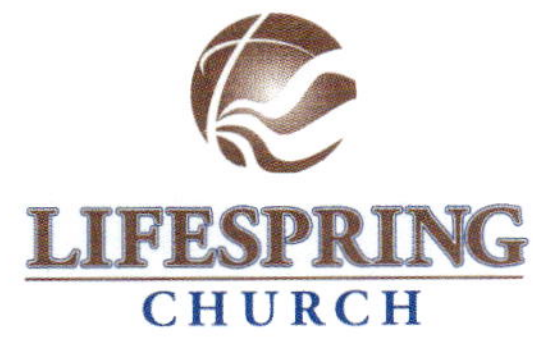

23 W. Alexander Avenue, PMB 11 • Merced, CA 95348-3404 • (209) 327-0308 (cell) • (209) 383-4257 (home) • bruce@lifespringchurch.net

WWW.LIFESPRINGCHURCH.NET

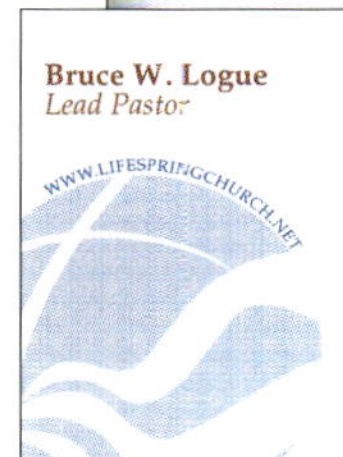

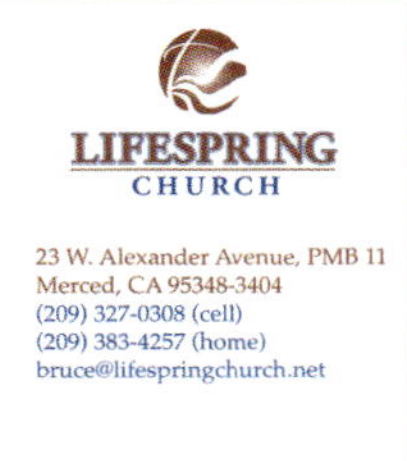

DESIGN FIRM
Ontarget Marketing
Merced, (CA) USA
CLIENT
Lifespring Church
ART DIRECTOR
Jesse Bloodworth
DESIGNER
Dusty Dahlgren

fresh thinking matters.

31.5 patten parkway chattanooga, tn 37402

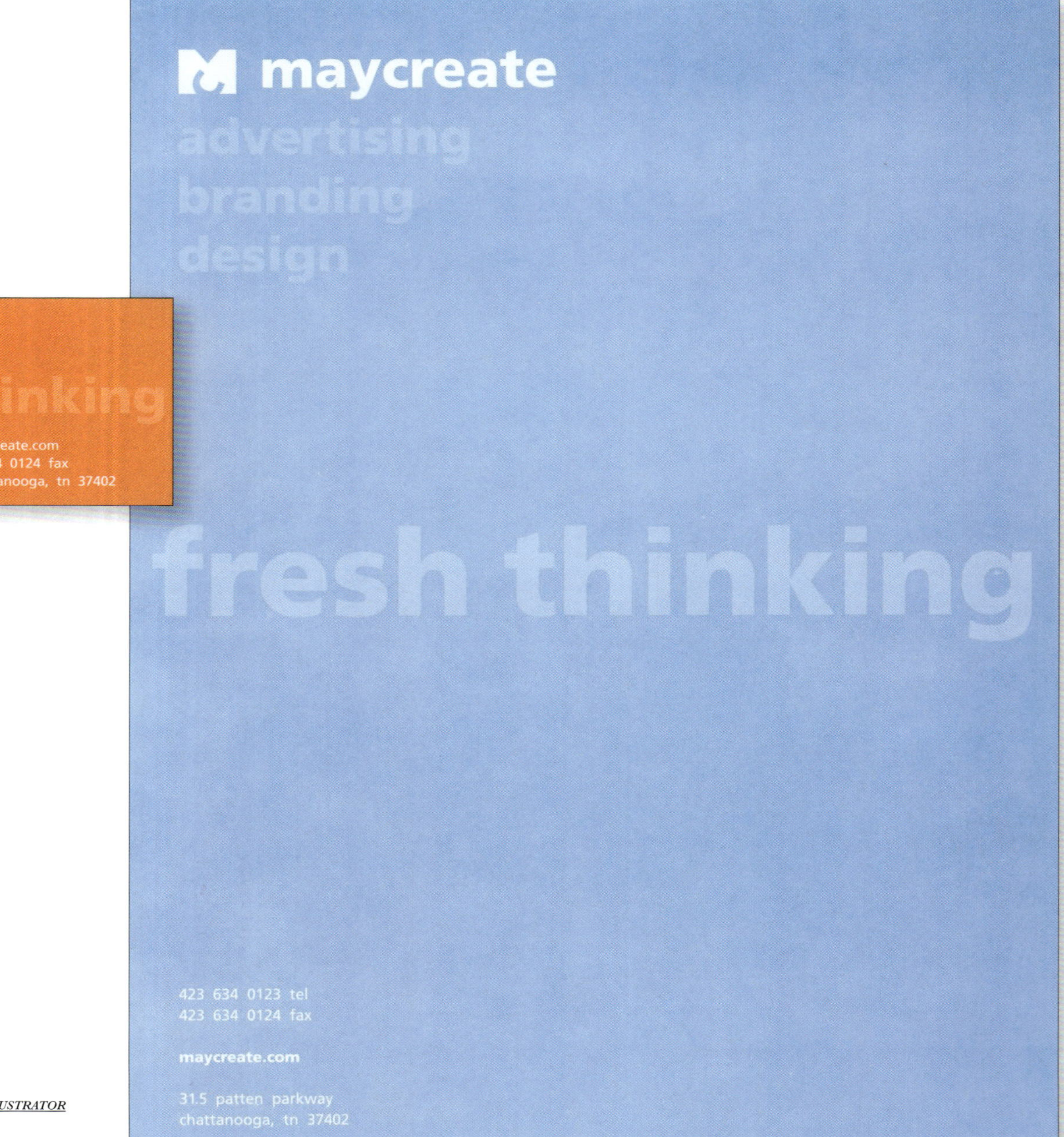

DESIGN FIRM
Maycreate
Chattanooga, (TN) USA
PROJECT
Maycreate
CREATIVE DIRECTOR, DESIGNER, ILLUSTRATOR
Brian May
PRINTER
Creative Printing

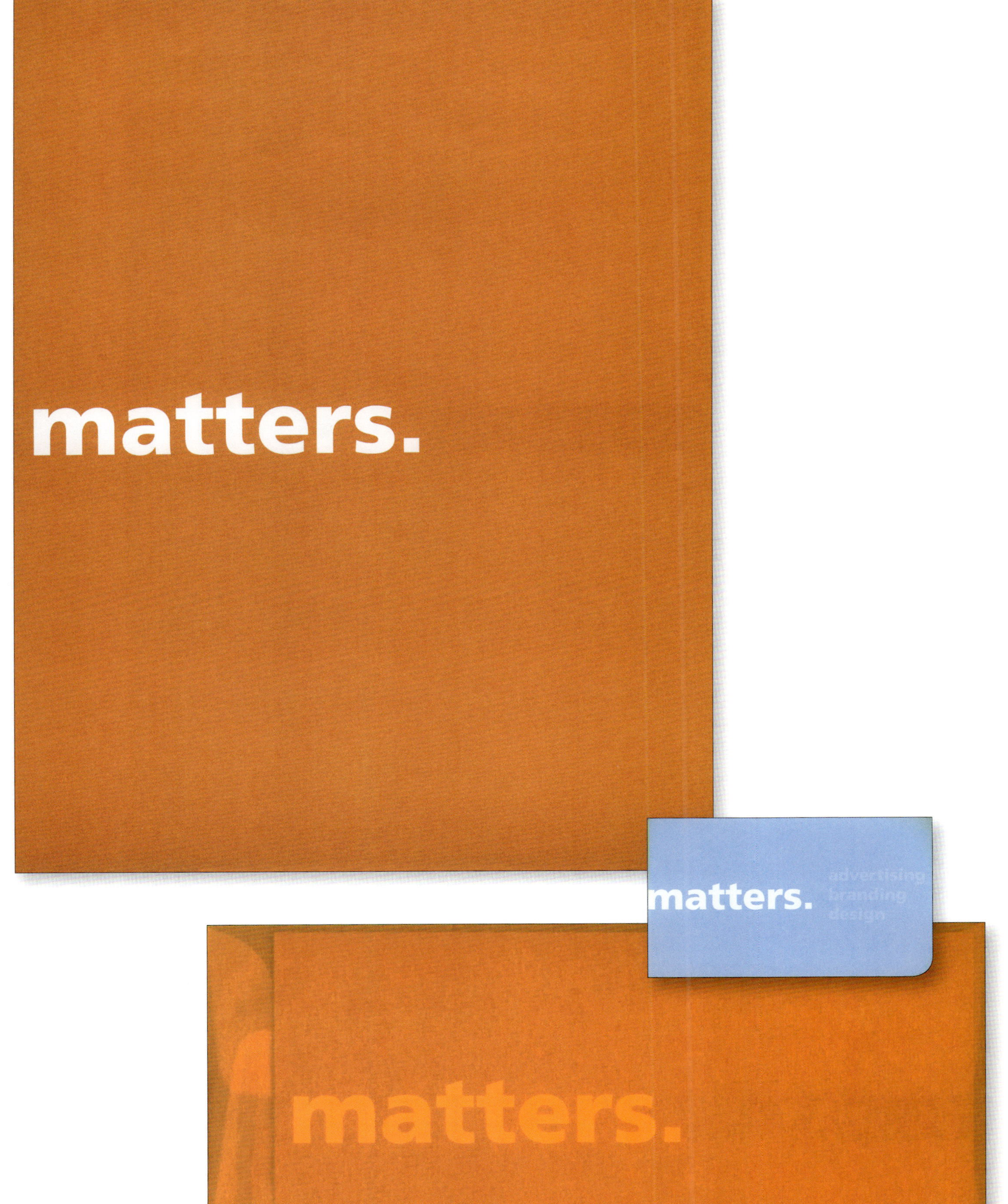
matters.
matters.
advertising
branding
design
matters.

DESIGN FIRM
Maycreate
Chattanooga, (TN) USA
PROJECT
The Ark
CREATIVE DIRECTOR, DESIGNER, ILLUSTRATOR
Brian May
PRINTER
Jakprints

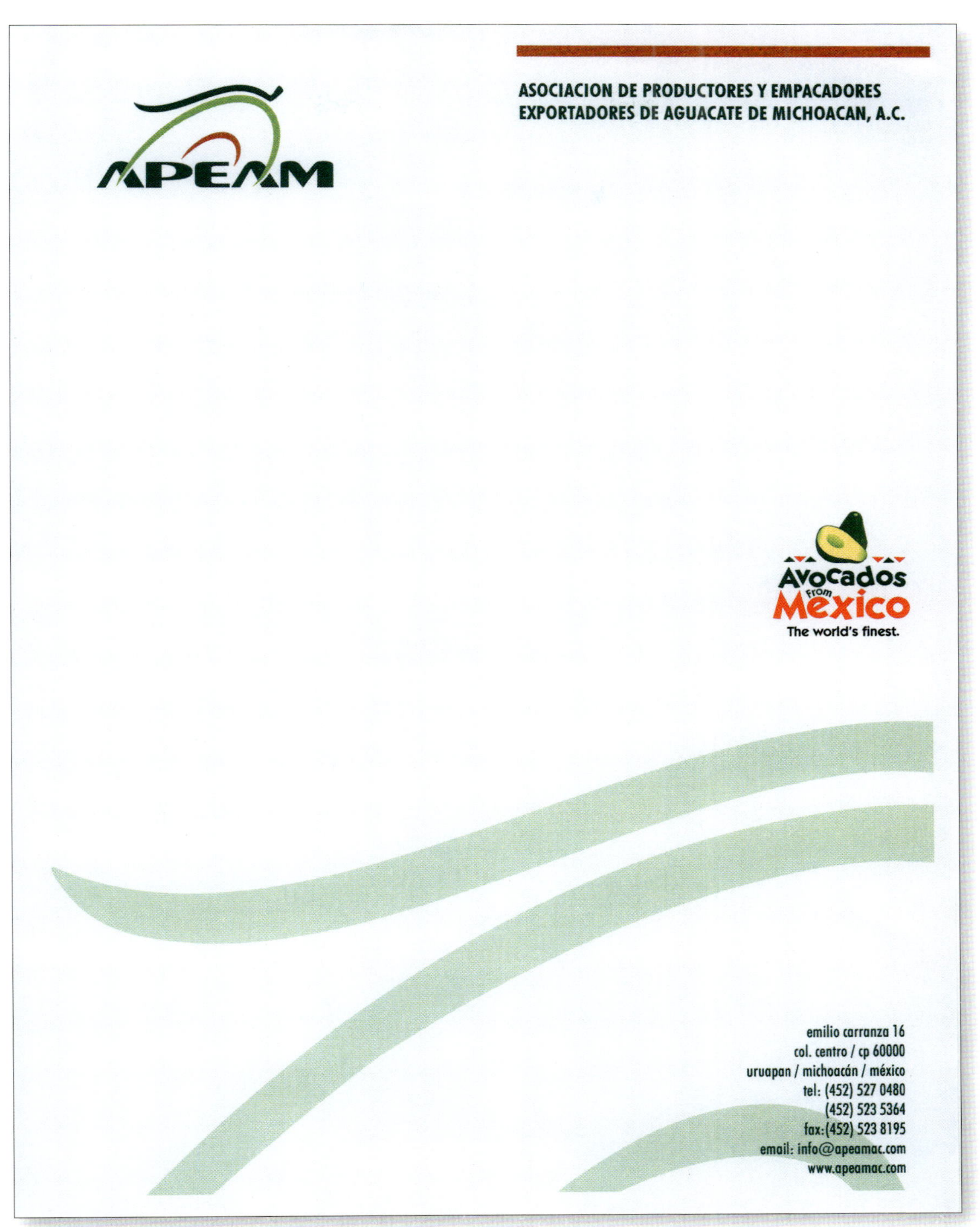

DESIGN FIRM
Kenneth Diseño
Uruapan, Mexico
PROJECT
Apeam
DESIGNERS
Kenneth Treviño,
Minerva Galván

DESIGN FIRM
Sungrafx, Inc.
Silverdale, (WA) USA
CLIENT
Puget Sound Naval Bases Association
DESIGNER
Vicky Koningisor

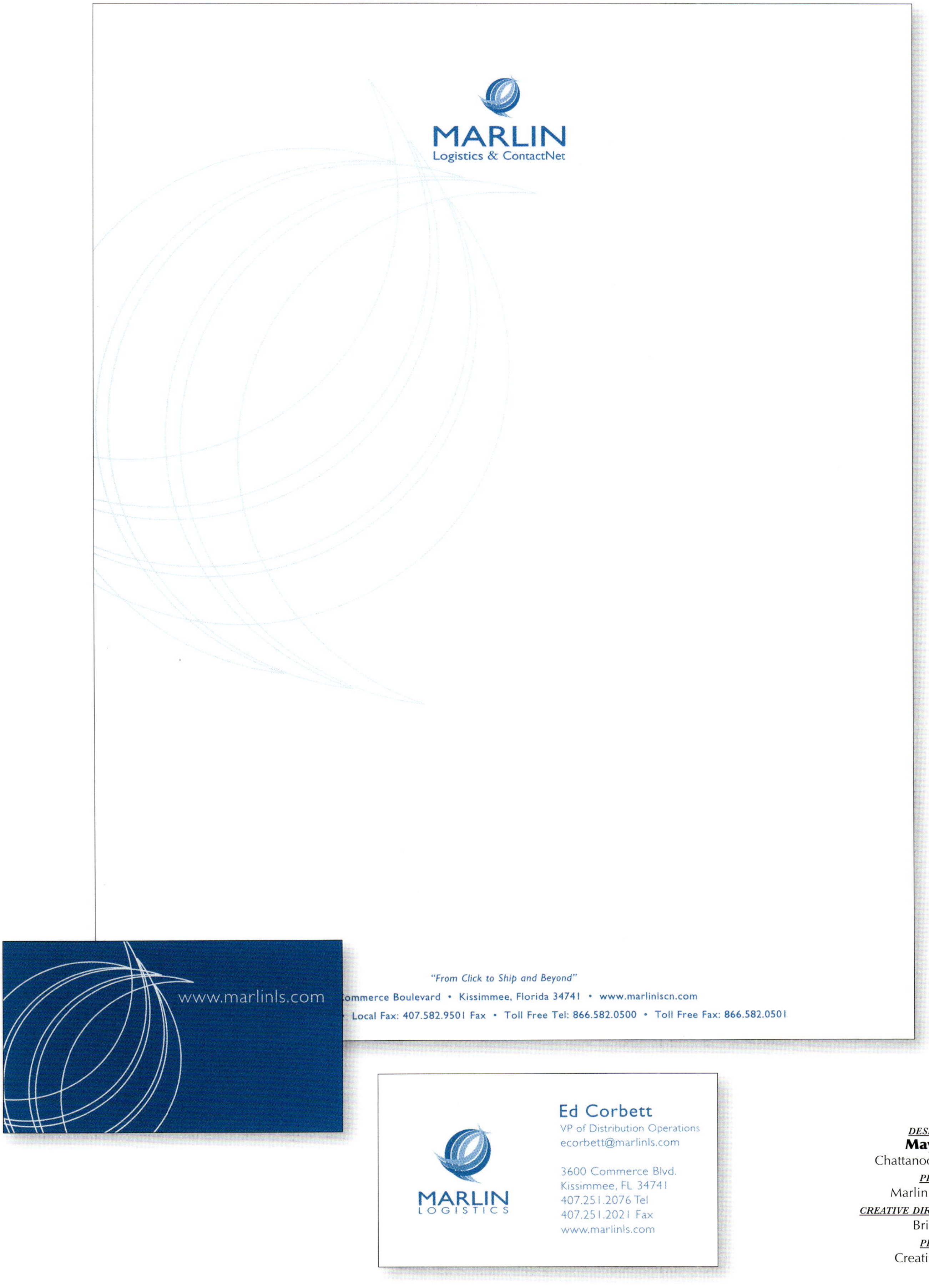

MARLIN
Logistics & ContactNet

"From Click to Ship and Beyond"
...ommerce Boulevard • Kissimmee, Florida 34741 • www.marlinlscn.com
• Local Fax: 407.582.9501 Fax • Toll Free Tel: 866.582.0500 • Toll Free Fax: 866.582.0501

www.marlinls.com

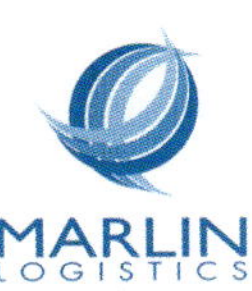

MARLIN
LOGISTICS

Ed Corbett
VP of Distribution Operations
ecorbett@marlinls.com

3600 Commerce Blvd.
Kissimmee, FL 34741
407.251.2076 Tel
407.251.2021 Fax
www.marlinls.com

DESIGN FIRM
Maycreate
Chattanooga, (TN) USA
PROJECT
Marlin Contactnet
CREATIVE DIRECTOR, DESIGNER
Brian May
PRINTER
Creative Printing

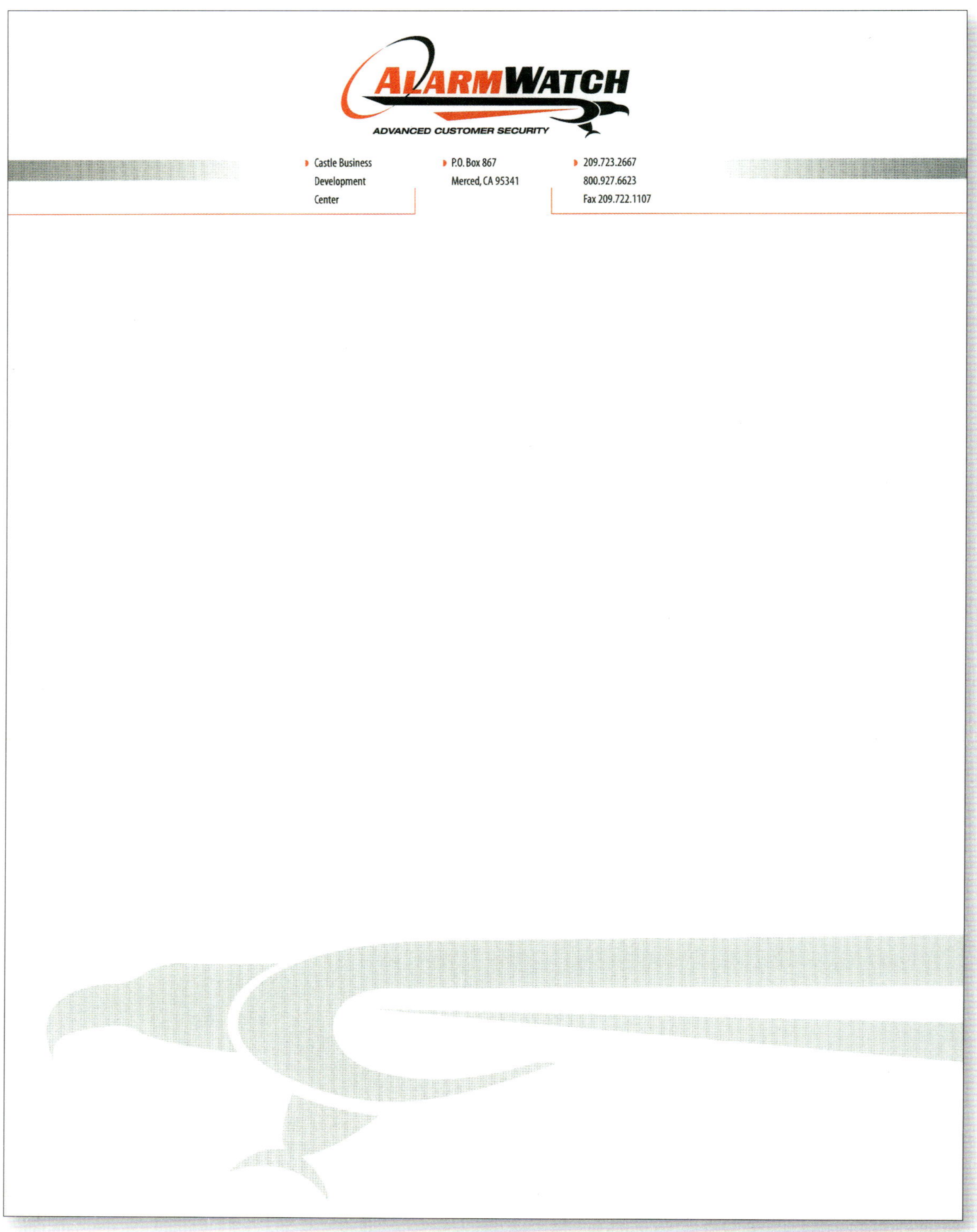

DESIGN FIRM
Ontarget Marketing
Merced, (CA) USA
CLIENT
Alarm Watch
ART DIRECTOR
Julie Rivard
DESIGNER
Juan Medina

DESIGN FIRM
Sandstrom Design
Portland, (OR) USA
CLIENT
Todd Eckleman Photography
ART DIRECTOR
Steve Sandstrom
DESIGNERS
Steve Sandstrom,
Kristy Adewumi
PROJECT MANAGER
Kirsten Cassidy

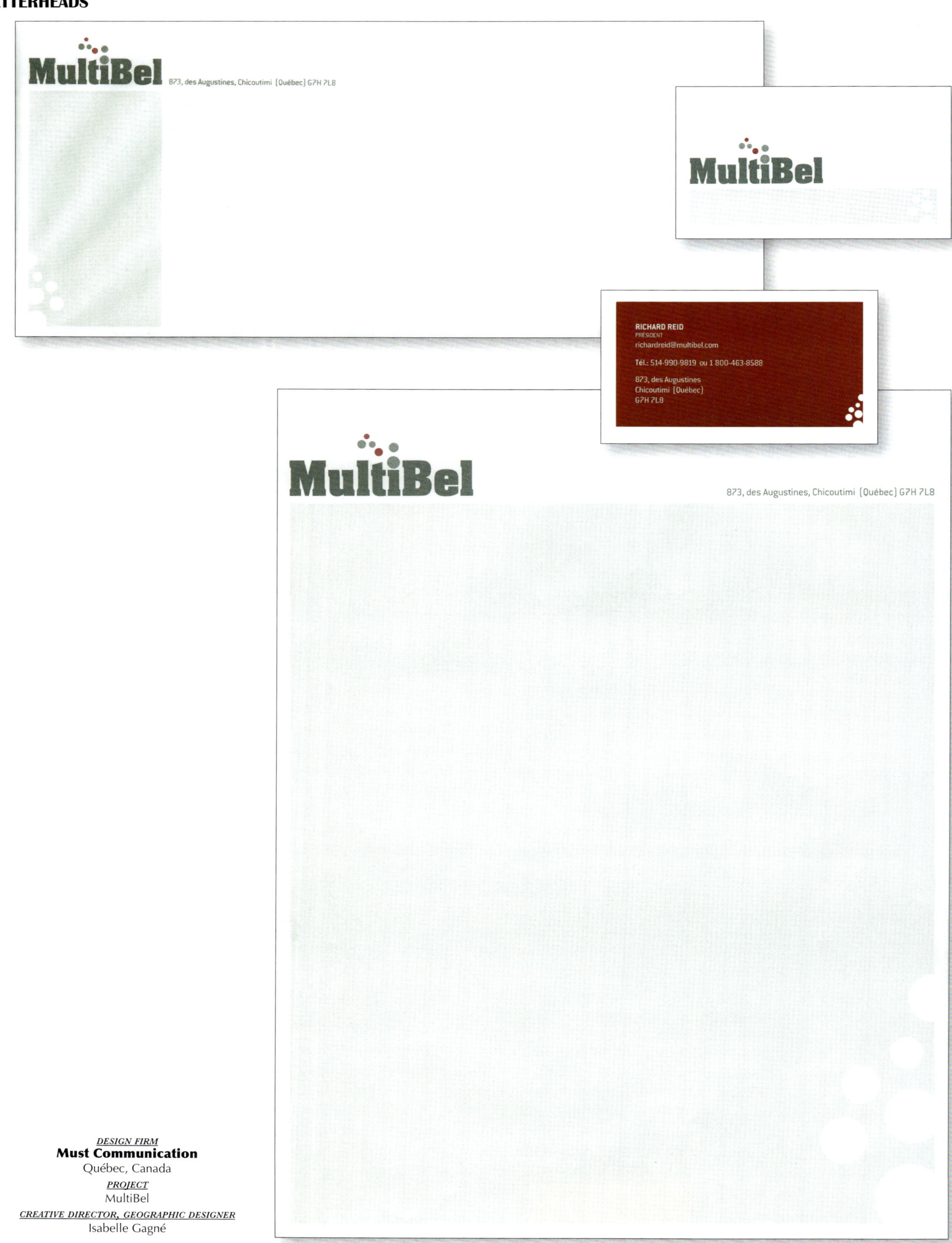

DESIGN FIRM
Must Communication
Québec, Canada
PROJECT
MultiBel
CREATIVE DIRECTOR, GEOGRAPHIC DESIGNER
Isabelle Gagné

DESIGN FIRM
TAMAR Graphics
Waltham, (MA) USA
CLIENT
Sakura Sushi Bar and Grill
DESIGNER
Tamar Wallace

DESIGN FIRM
McElveney & Palozzi Design
Rochester, (NY) USA
PROJECT
Impact Print Solutions
ART DIRECTOR
Matt Nowicki

DESIGN FIRM
Organ Donor Productions
Burbank, (CA) USA
CREATIVE PRODUCERS
Dorian J. Compo,
Michael Velasquez

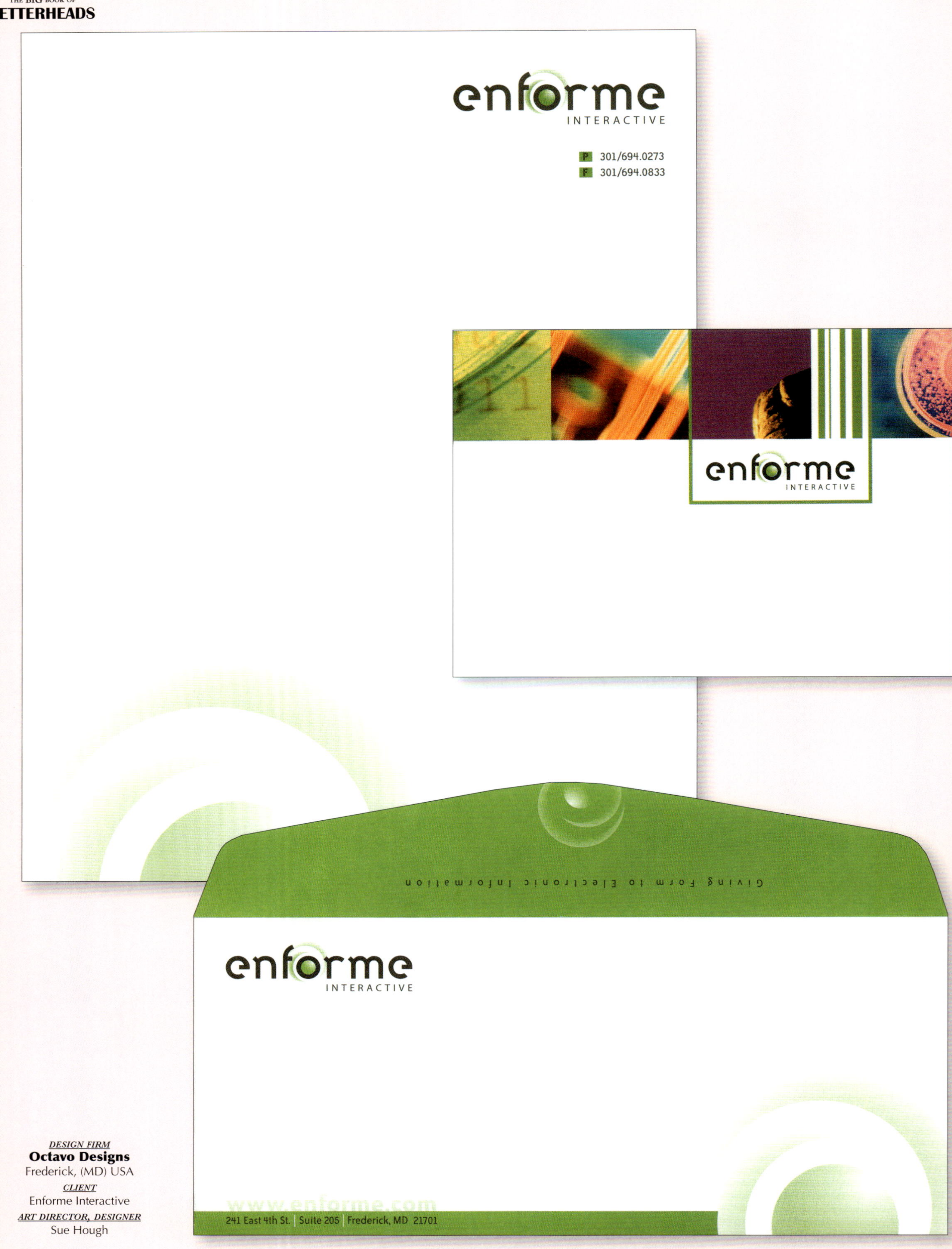

DESIGN FIRM
Octavo Designs
Frederick, (MD) USA
CLIENT
Enforme Interactive
ART DIRECTOR, DESIGNER
Sue Hough

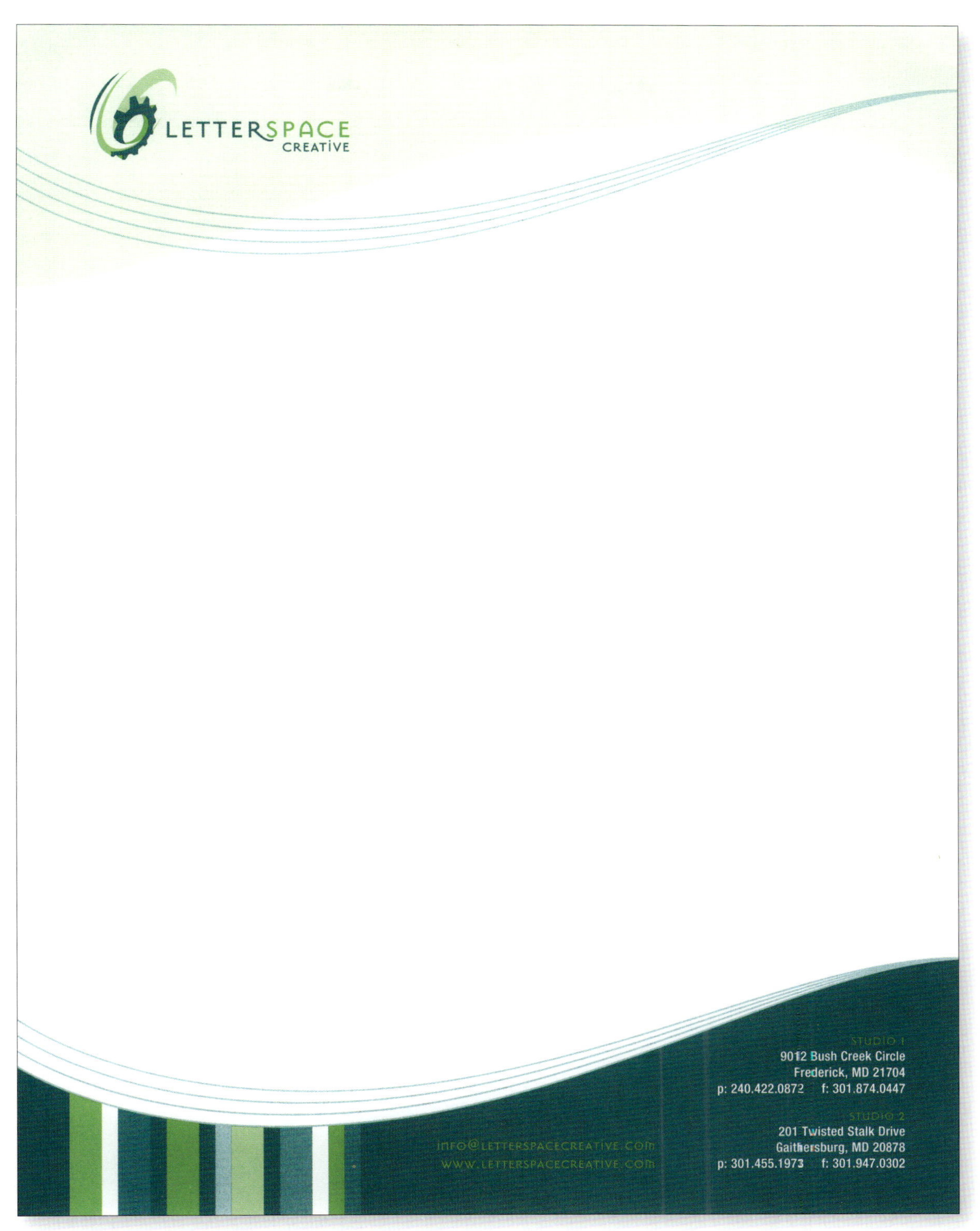

DESIGN FIRM
LetterSpace Creative, LLC
Gaithersburg, (MD) USA
CLIENT
LetterSpace Creative, LLC
ART DIRECTORS
Fredrik Hviid,
Laura Muncy

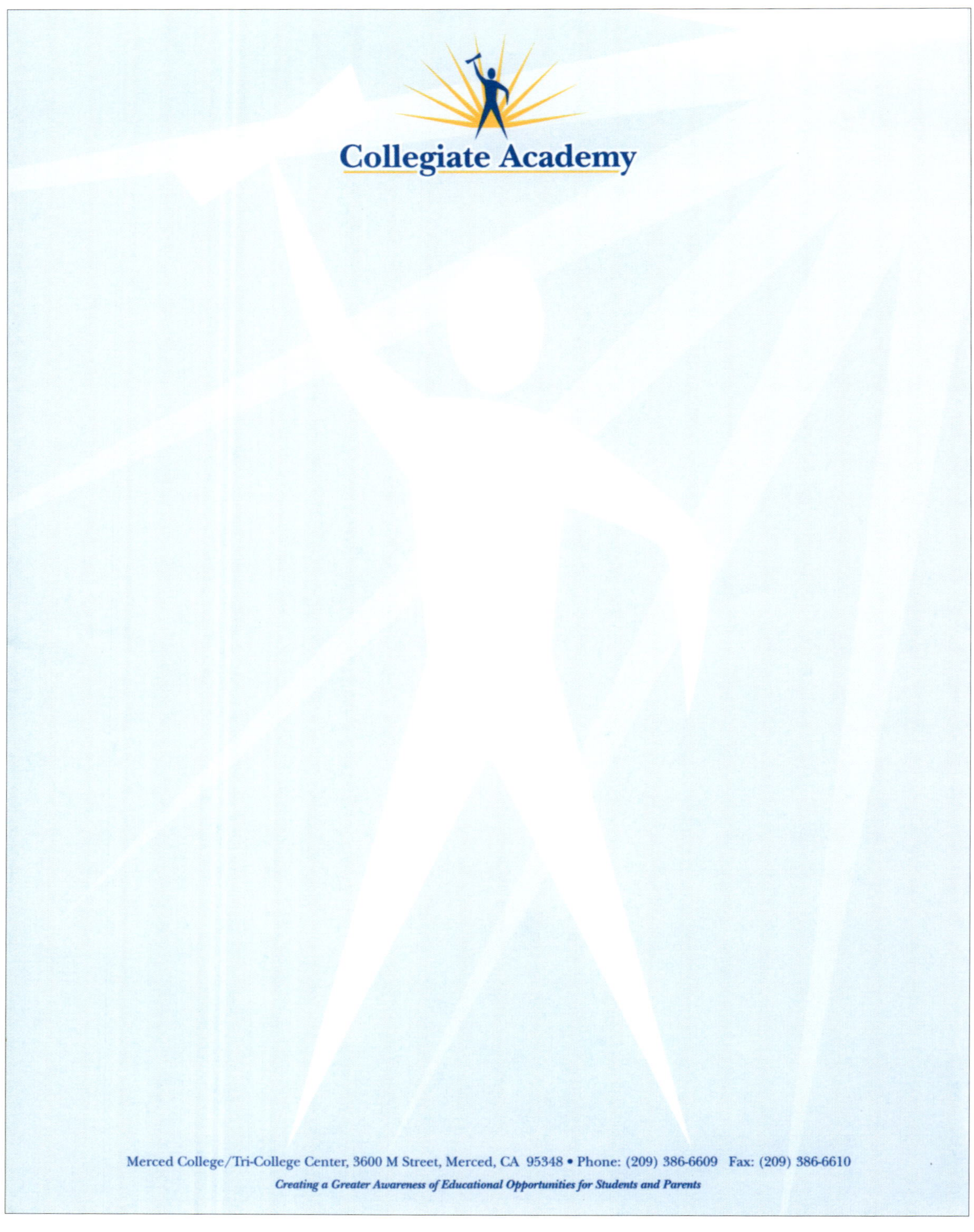

DESIGN FIRM
Ontarget Marketing
Merced, (CA) USA
CLIENT
Collegiate Academy
ART DIRECTOR
Julie Rivard
DESIGNER
Jesse Bloodworth

DESIGN FIRM
TrueFACES Creation Sdn. Bhd.
Selangor, Malaysia
DESIGNERS
TrueFACES Creative Team

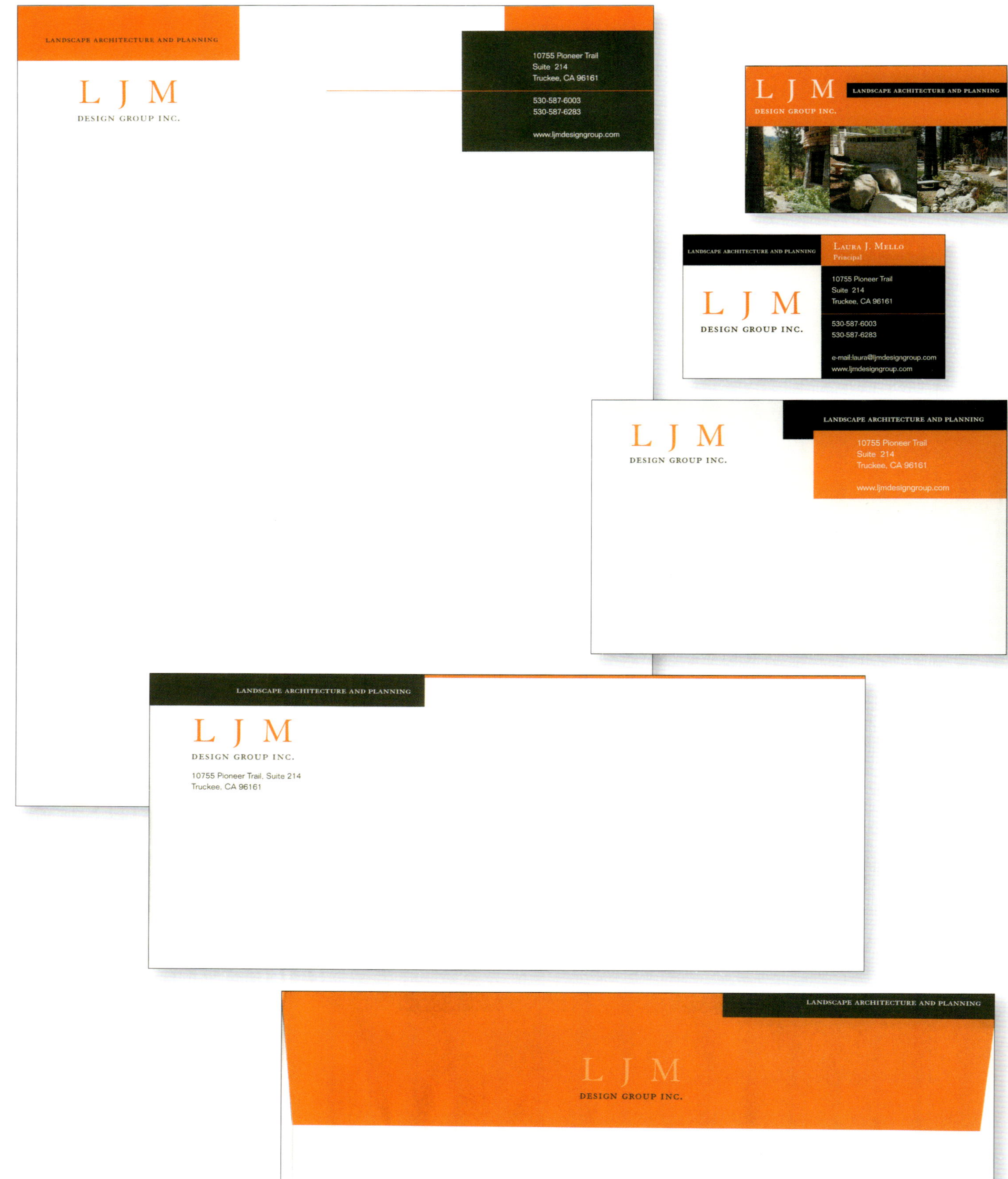

DESIGN FIRM
Marcia Herrmann Design
Modesto, (CA) USA
PROJECT
LJM Design Group
DESIGNER
Marcia Herrmann

SANDIA PREP

Sandia Preparatory School
532 Osuna Road NE Albuquerque NM 87113
P: 505.338.3000 F: 505.338.3099
www.sandiaprep.org

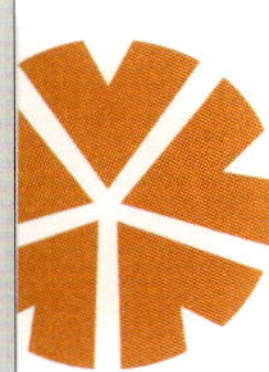

Sandia Preparatory School 532 Osuna Road NE Albuquerque NM 87113

SANDIA PREP

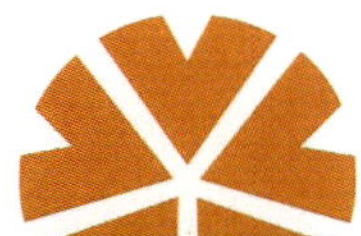

SANDIA PREP

Dibby Olson, 6th Grade Coordinator/Science
dolson@sandiaprep.org

Sandia Preparatory School
532 Osuna Road NE Albuquerque NM 87113
phone: 505.338.3000 direct: 505.338.3012
fax: 505.338.3099 www.sandiaprep.org

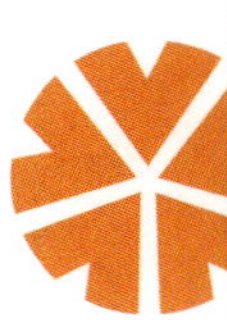

DESIGN FIRM
Studio Hill Design
Albuquerque, (NM) USA

PROJECT
Sandia Prep

ART DIRECTOR
Sandy Hill

DESIGNERS
Sean M. Chavez,
Sandy Hill

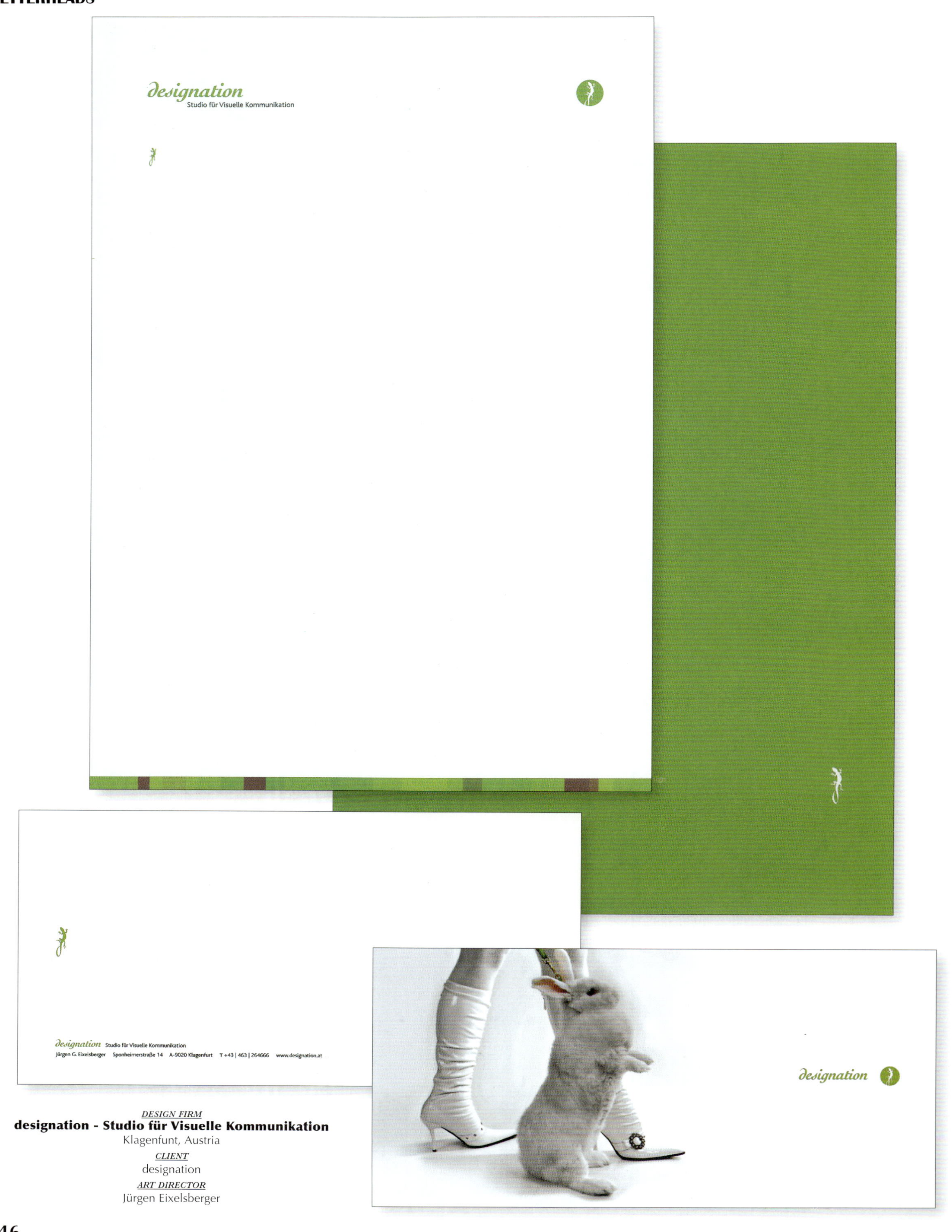

DESIGN FIRM
designation - Studio für Visuelle Kommunikation
Klagenfunt, Austria
CLIENT
designation
ART DIRECTOR
Jürgen Eixelsberger

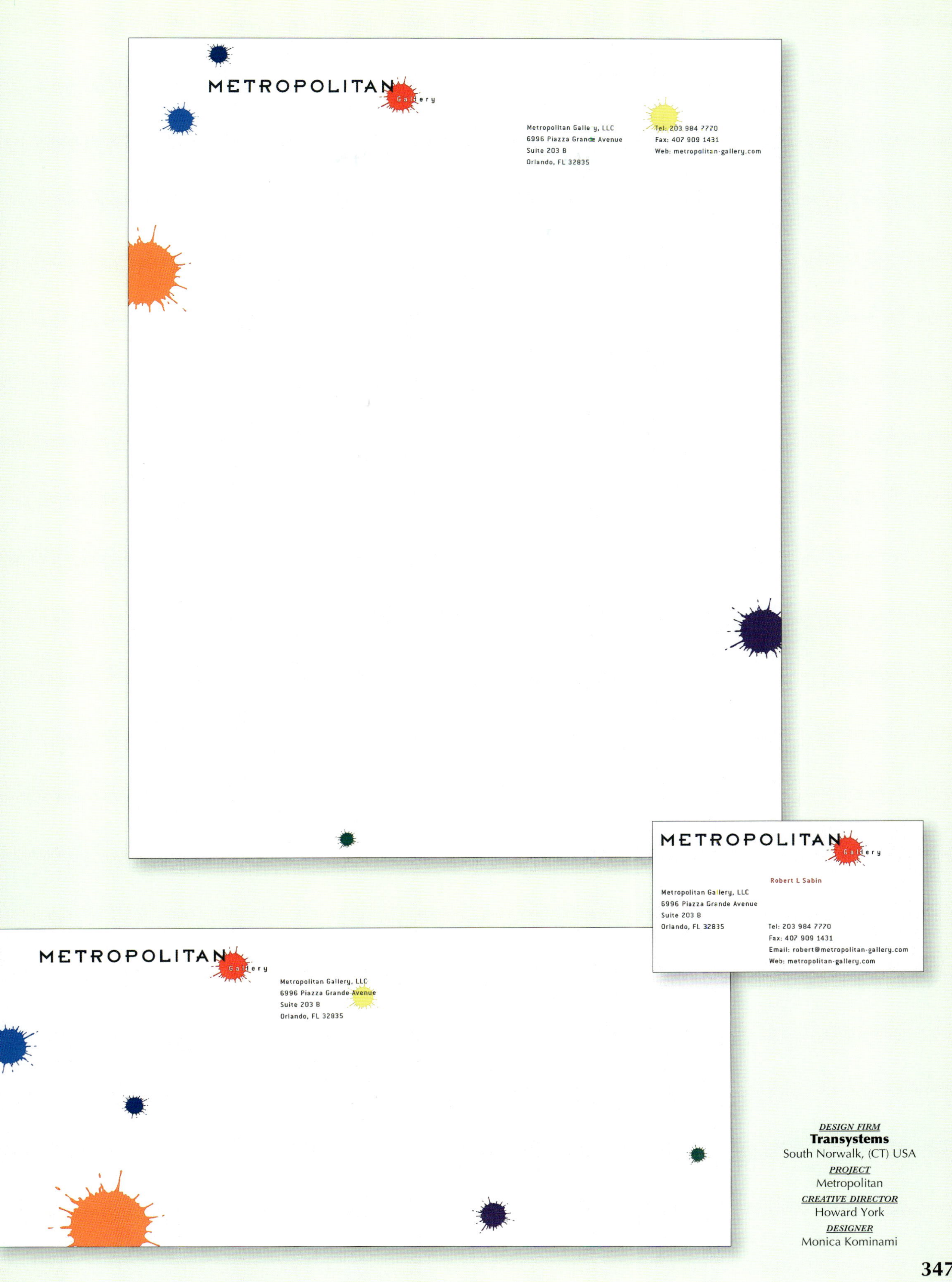

DESIGN FIRM
Transystems
South Norwalk, (CT) USA
PROJECT
Metropolitan
CREATIVE DIRECTOR
Howard York
DESIGNER
Monica Kominami

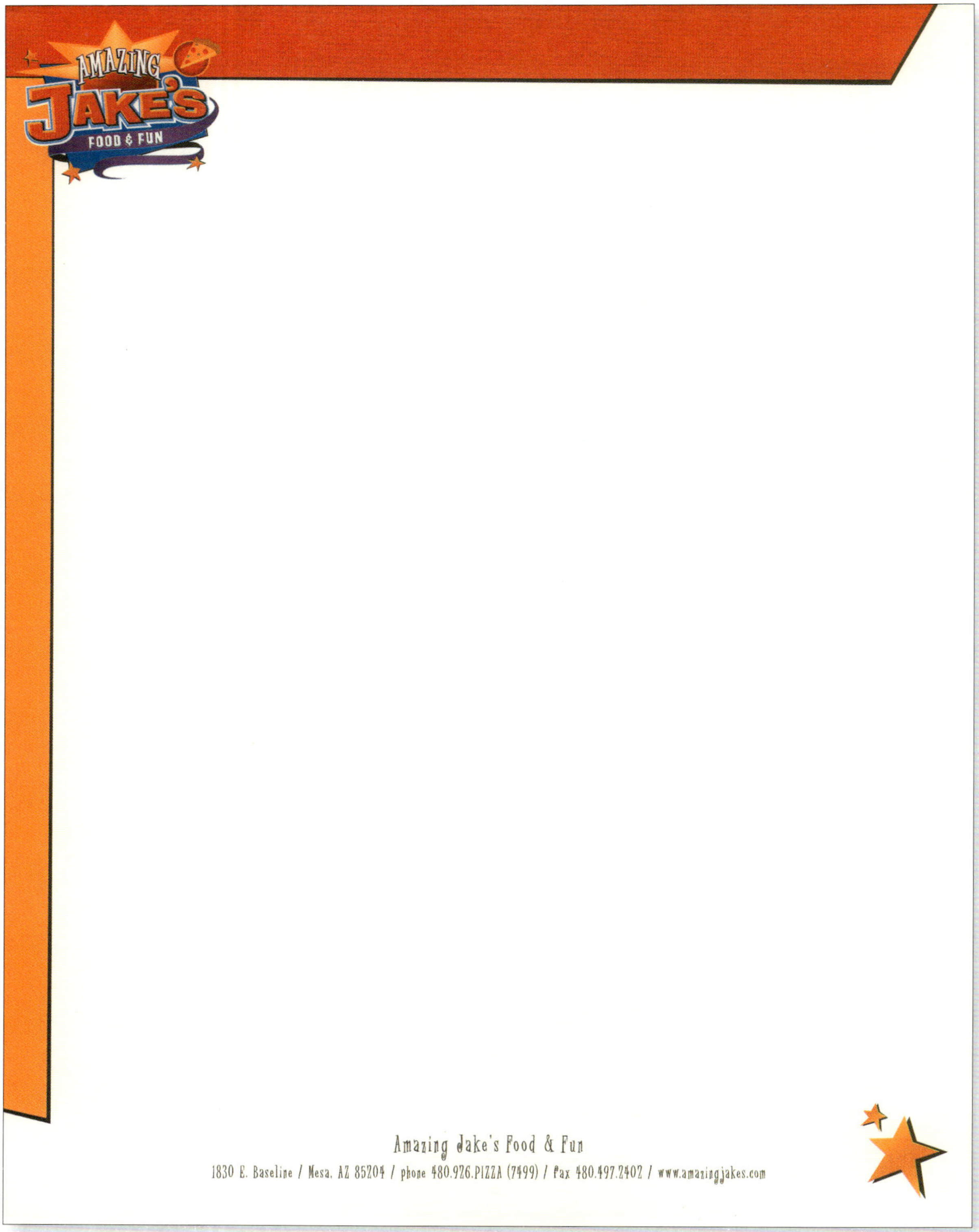

AMAZING JAKE'S
FOOD & FUN

Amazing Jake's Food & Fun

1830 E. Baseline / Mesa, AZ 85204 / phone 480.926.PIZZA (7499) / fax 480.497.2402 / www.amazingjakes.com

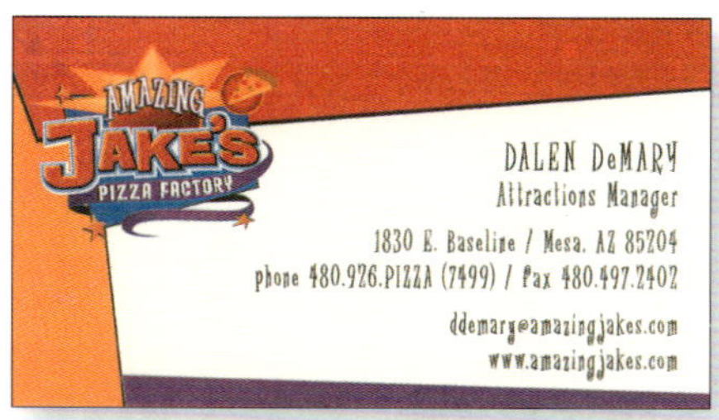

DESIGN FIRM
On The Edge Design
Newport Beach, (CA) USA
PROJECT
Amazing Jake's Pizza Factory
DESIGNER
Jonathan Corke

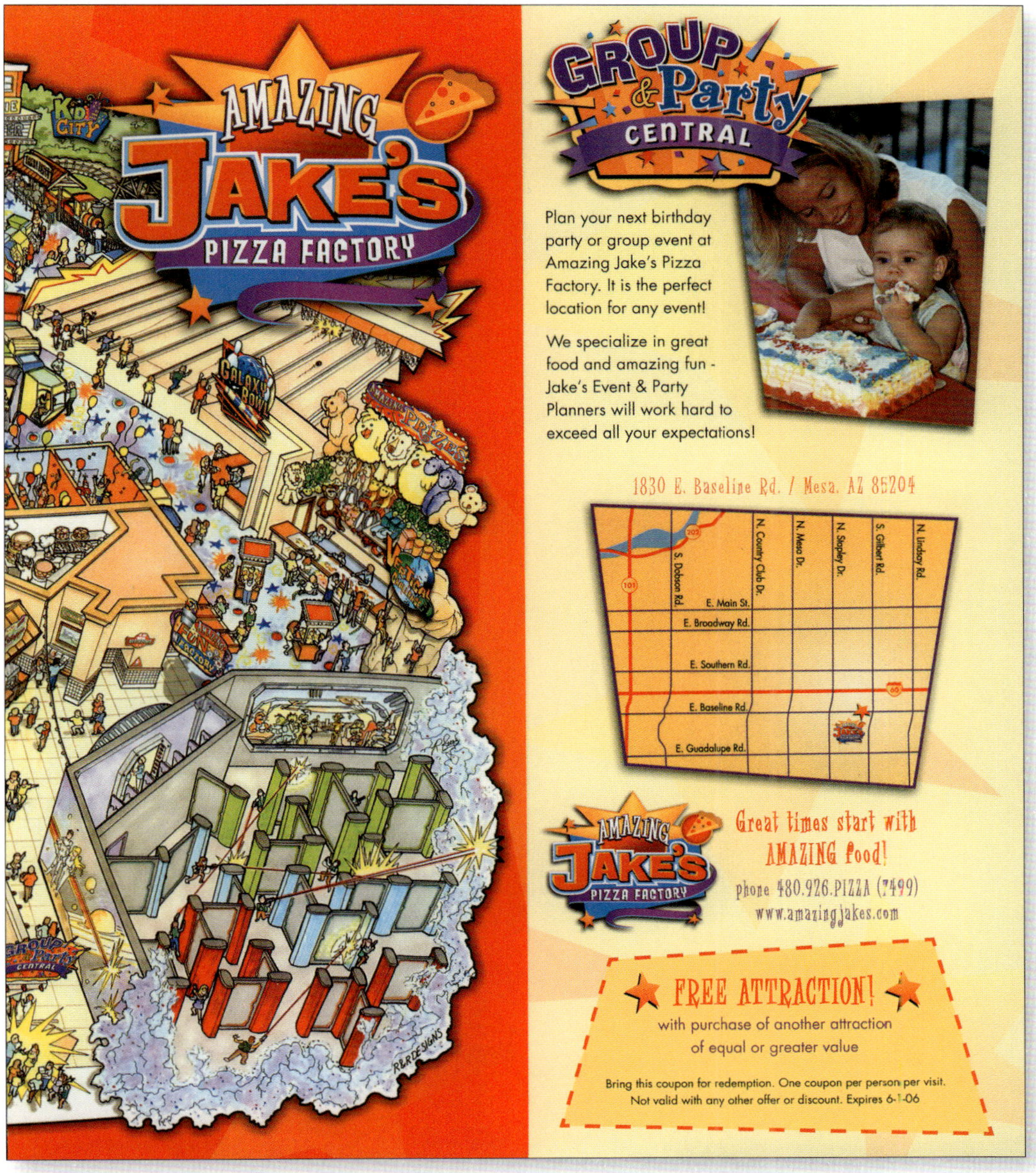

AMAZING JAKE'S PIZZA FACTORY

GROUP & Party CENTRAL

Plan your next birthday party or group event at Amazing Jake's Pizza Factory. It is the perfect location for any event!

We specialize in great food and amazing fun - Jake's Event & Party Planners will work hard to exceed all your expectations!

1830 E. Baseline Rd. / Mesa, AZ 85204

S. Dobson Rd.
N. Country Club Dr.
N. Mesa Dr.
N. Stapley Dr.
S. Gilbert Rd.
N. Lindsay Rd.
E. Main St.
E. Broadway Rd.
E. Southern Rd.
E. Baseline Rd.
E. Guadalupe Rd.

AMAZING JAKE'S PIZZA FACTORY

Great times start with AMAZING food!

phone 480.926.PIZZA (7499)
www.amazingjakes.com

FREE ATTRACTION!
with purchase of another attraction of equal or greater value

Bring this coupon for redemption. One coupon per person per visit. Not valid with any other offer or discount. Expires 6-1-06

www.fahrenheit.com

fs

fahrenheit studio

10303 Mississippi Avenue | Los Angeles | CA 90025
P 310 282 8422 | F 310 282 8522

fs

fahrenheit studio

DYLAN TRAN
dylan@fahrenheit.com

10303 Mississippi Avenue | Los Angeles | CA 90025
P 310 282 8422 | F 310 282 8522

www.fahrenheit.com

DESIGN
identity | web | print | environmental | motion

fs

fahrenheit studio

DESIGN FIRM

Fahrenheit Studio

Los Angeles, (CA) USA

PROJECT

Fahrenheit Studio

DESIGNERS

Dylan Tran,
Robert Weitz

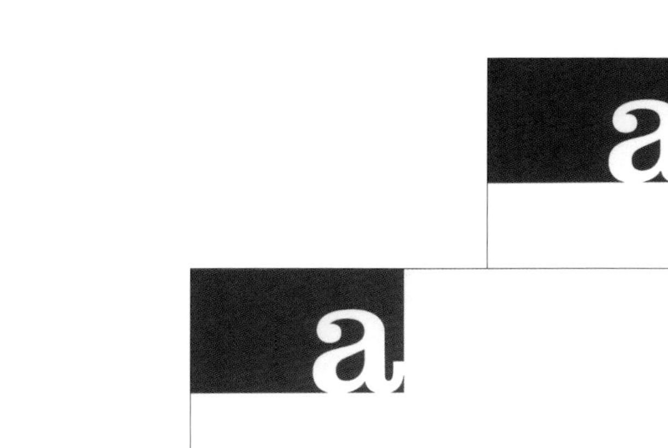

DESIGN FIRM
John Kneapler Design
New York, (NY) USA
PROJECT
Adam Raphael Photography, LLC
DESIGNERS
John Kneapler,
Colleen Shea

DESIGN FIRM
Never Boring Design Associates
Modesto, (CA) USA
PROJECT
Center Stage
DESIGNER
Shawna Bayers

DESIGN FIRM
Maycreate
Chattanooga, (TN) USA
PROJECT
Advantage Point Telecom
CREATIVE DIRECTOR, DESIGNER, ILLUSTRATOR
Brian May
PRINTER
Creative Printing

DESIGN FIRM
Ontarget Marketing
Merced, (CA) USA
CLIENT
Blue Moon Construction
ART DIRECTOR
Julie Rivard
DESIGNER
Quincy Adams

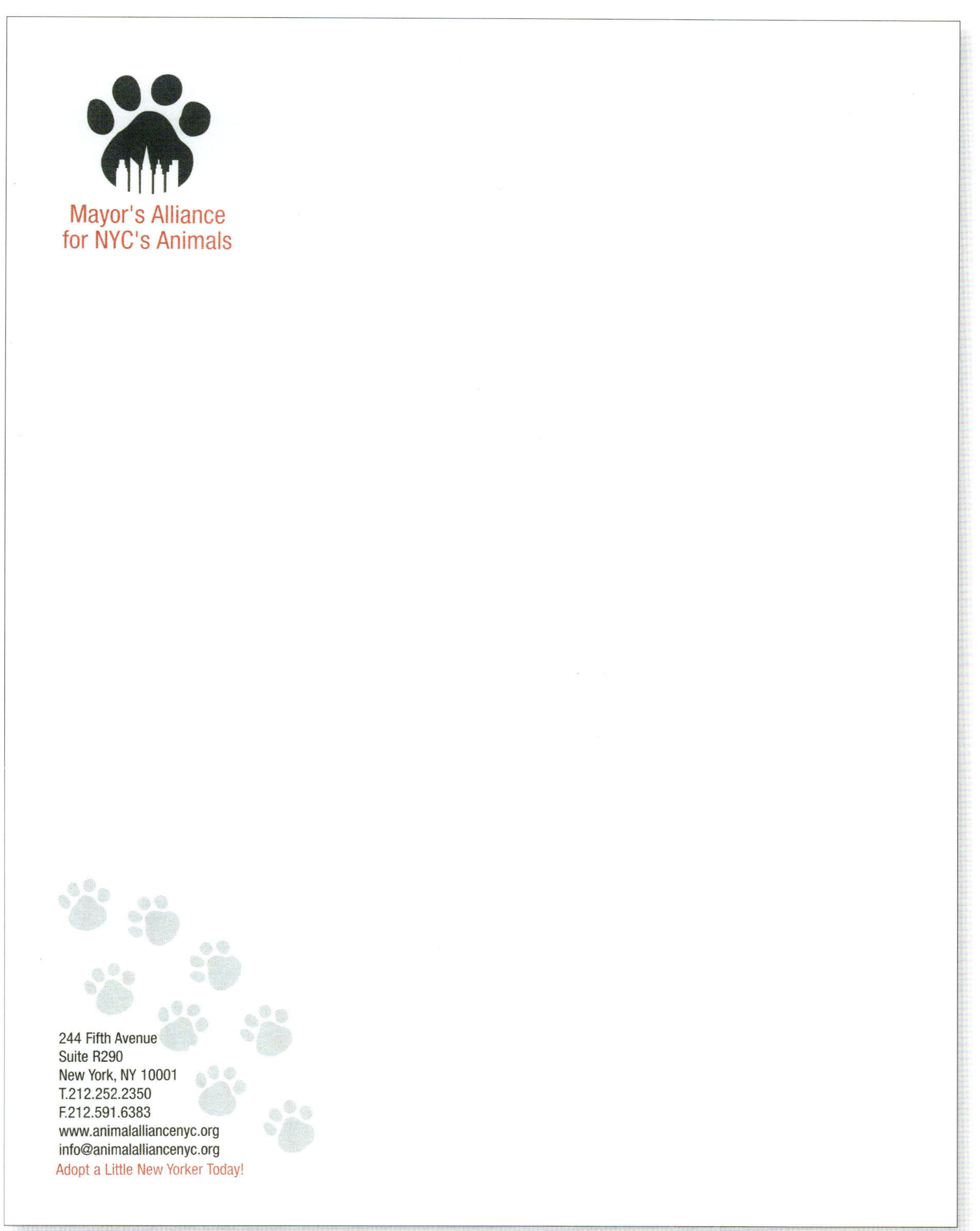

DESIGN FIRM
Chip Tolaney
New York, (NY) USA
PROJECT
Mayor's Alliance for NYC's Animals
ART DIRECTOR, DESIGNER
Chip Tolaney

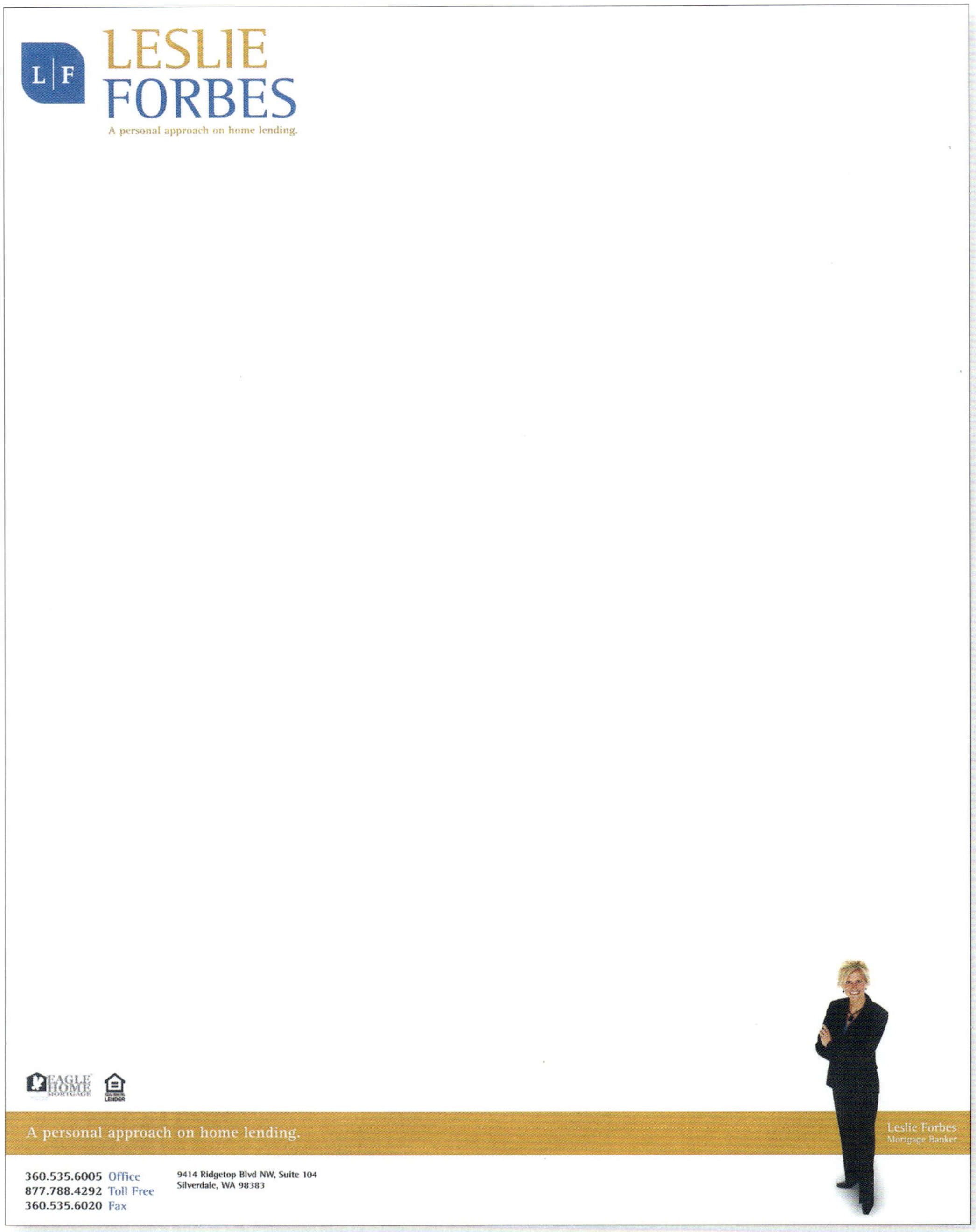

L | F LESLIE FORBES

A personal approach on home lending.

EAGLE HOME MORTGAGE

A personal approach on home lending.

Leslie Forbes
Mortgage Banker

360.535.6005 Office
877.788.4292 Toll Free
360.535.6020 Fax

9414 Ridgetop Blvd NW, Suite 104
Silverdale, WA 98383

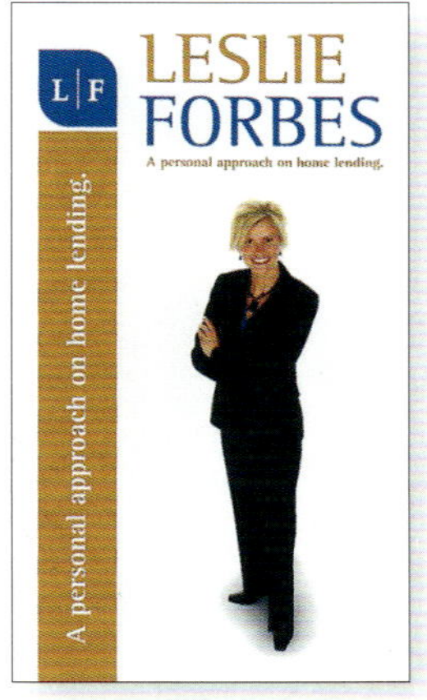

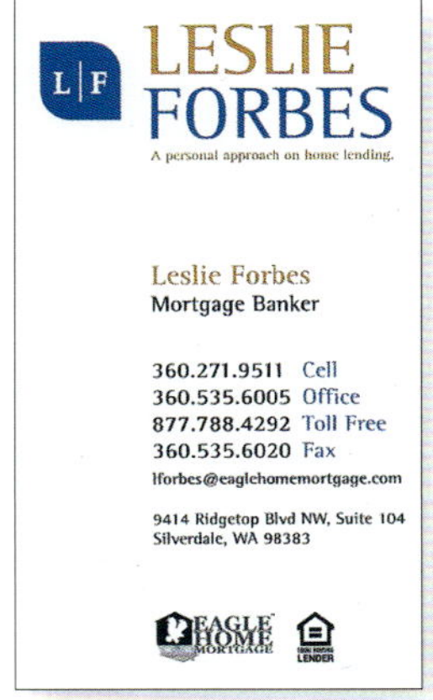

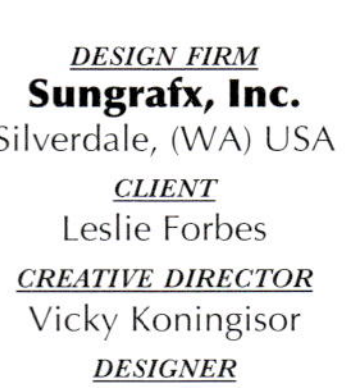

DESIGN FIRM
Sungrafx, Inc.
Silverdale, (WA) USA
CLIENT
Leslie Forbes
CREATIVE DIRECTOR
Vicky Koningisor
DESIGNER
Laura Zander

STUTT KITCHENS
& FINE CABINETRY

Stutt Kitchen
1140189 Ont

Showroom
& Factory
4635 Burgoyne St.
Unit One
Mississauga, ON
Canada L4W 1V9

Dreamkitchens.ca | STYLE. DETAIL. PASSION.

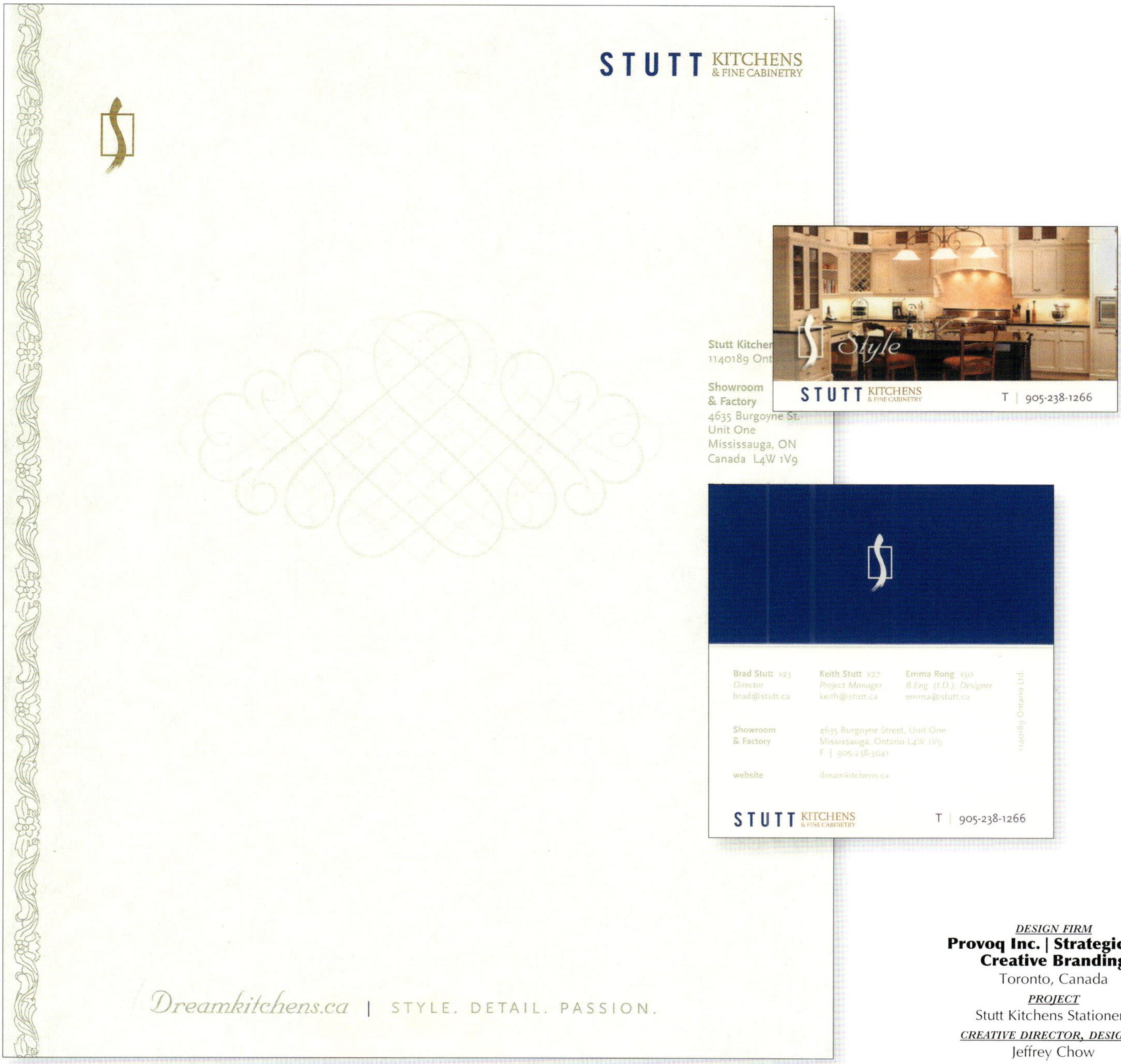

Style

STUTT KITCHENS & FINE CABINETRY T | 905-238-1266

STUTT KITCHENS & FINE CABINETRY T | 905-238-1266

DESIGN FIRM
Provoq Inc. | Strategic and Creative Branding
Toronto, Canada

PROJECT
Stutt Kitchens Stationery

CREATIVE DIRECTOR, DESIGNER
Jeffrey Chow

DESIGN FIRM
double entendre
Seattle, (WA) USA
PROJECT
Main Mercantile
DESIGNERS
Richard A. Smith,
Daniel P. Smith

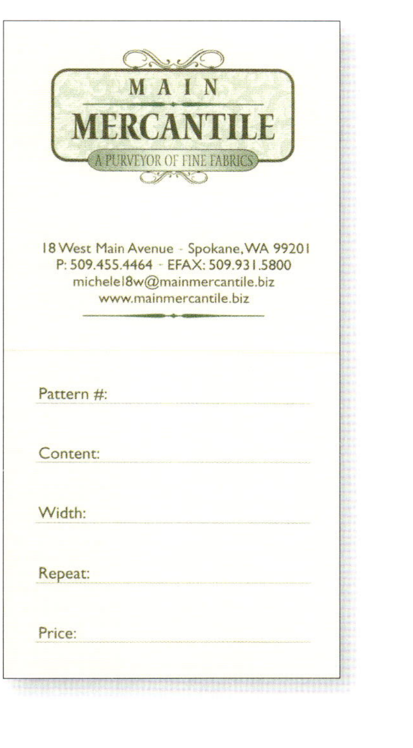

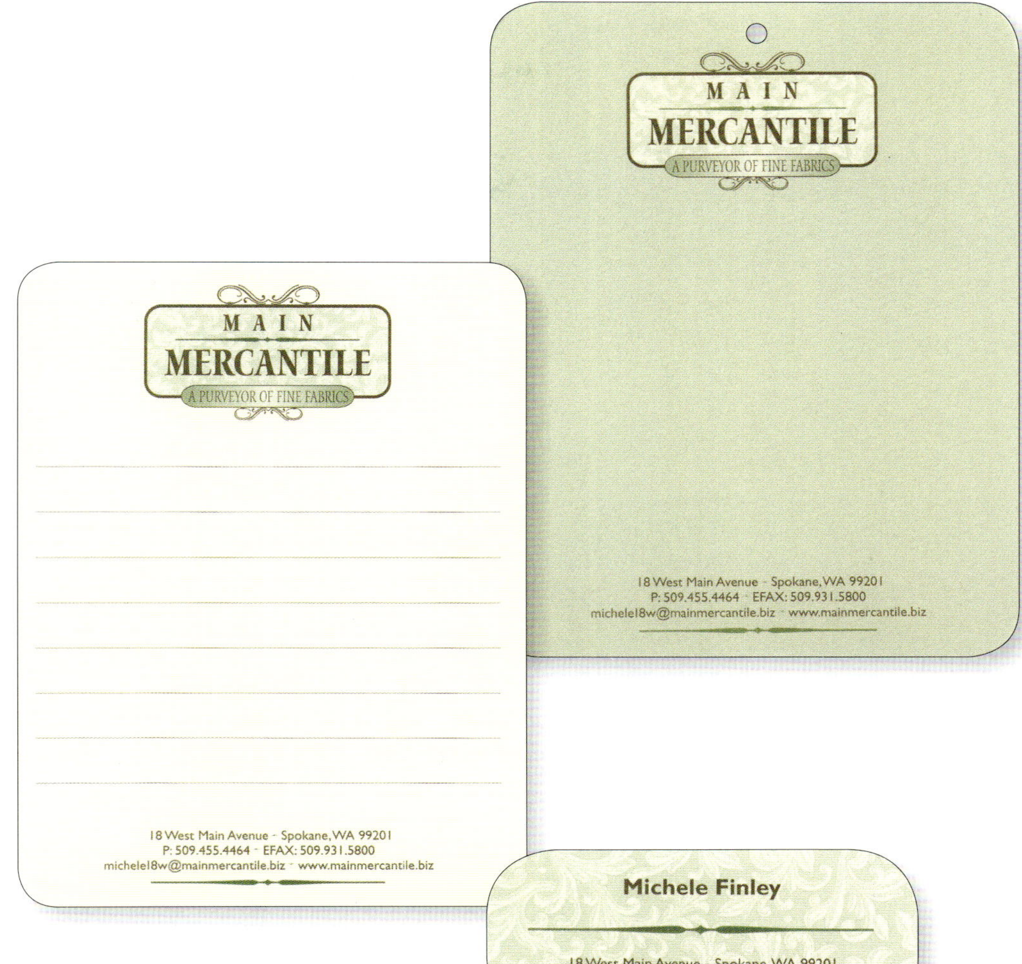

Michele Finley

18 West Main Avenue - Spokane, WA 99201
P: 509.455.4464 - EFAX: 509.931.5800
michele18w@mainmercantile.biz - www.mainmercantile.biz

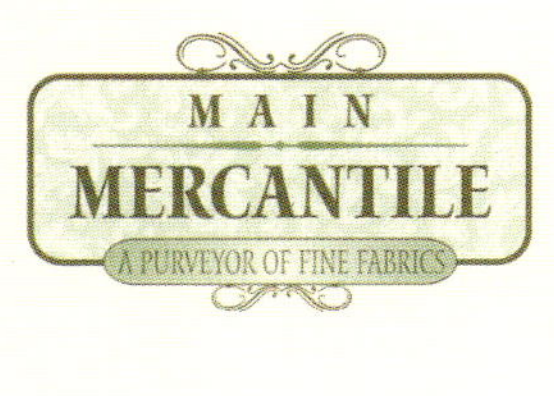

18 West Main Avenue - Spokane, WA 99201

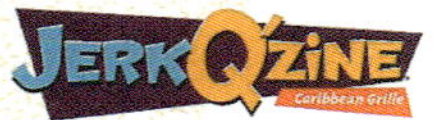

Caribbean Food Delights Grille, LLC

117 Route 303, Suite A
Tappan, NY 10983
T. 845 398 3000
F. 845 398 3001
www.jerkqzine.com

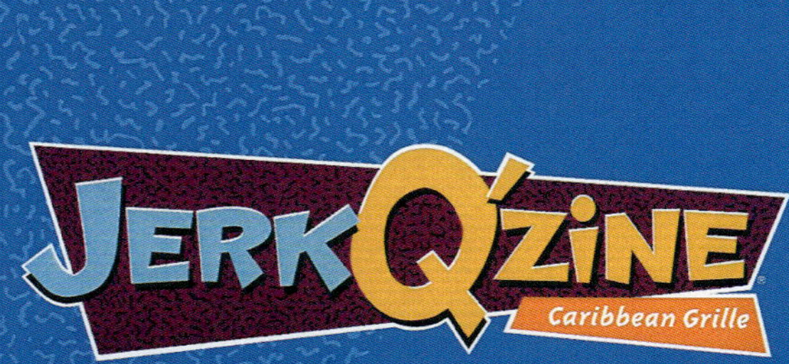

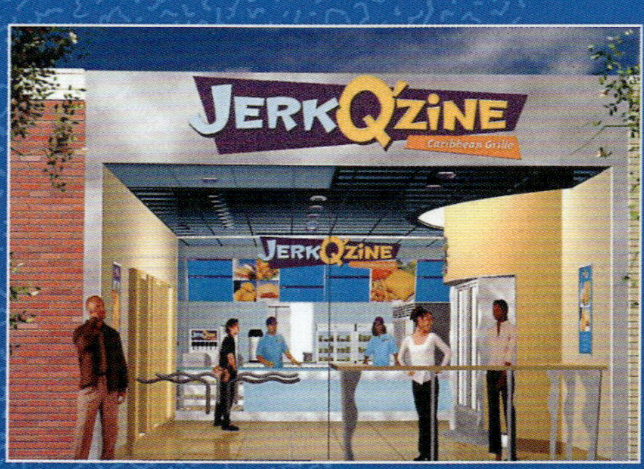

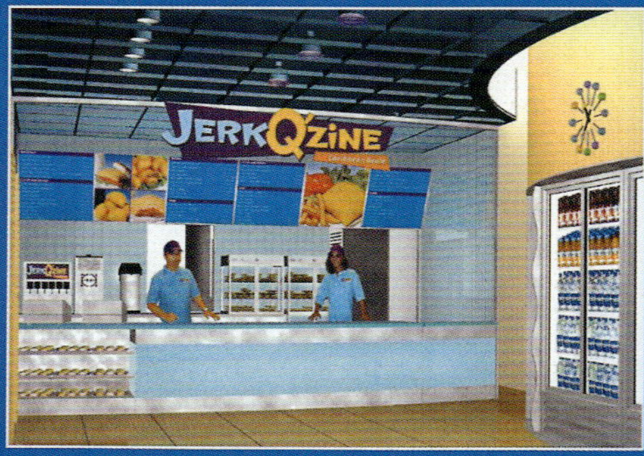

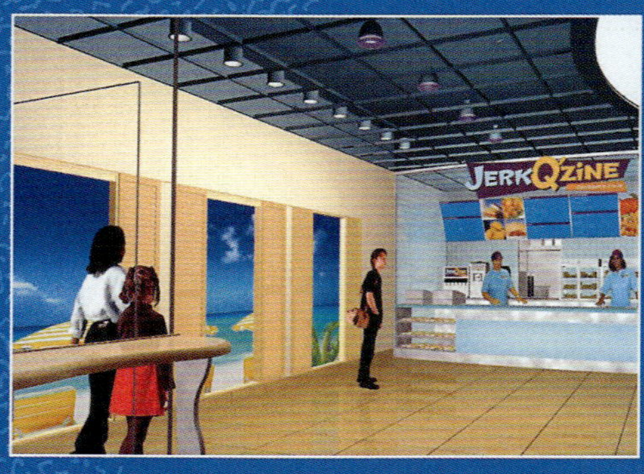

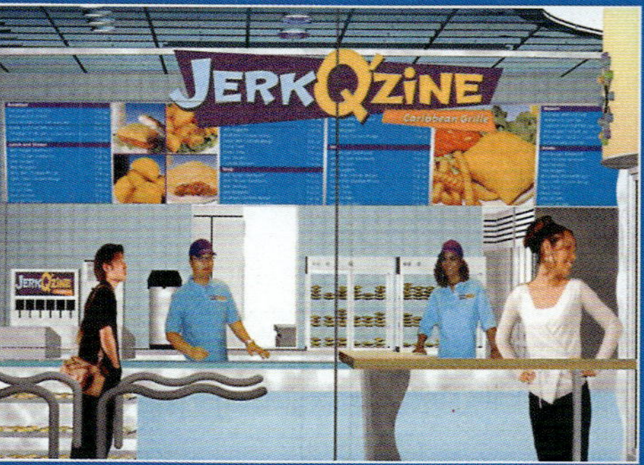

DESIGN FIRM
Transystems
South Norwalk, (CT) USA
CLIENT
Jerk Q'zine
CREATIVE DIRECTOR
Howard York
DESIGNER
Monica Kominami

DESIGN FIRM
On The Edge Design
Newport Beach, (CA) USA
PROJECT
Chat Noir Bistro & Jazz Lounge
DESIGNER
Tracey Lamberson

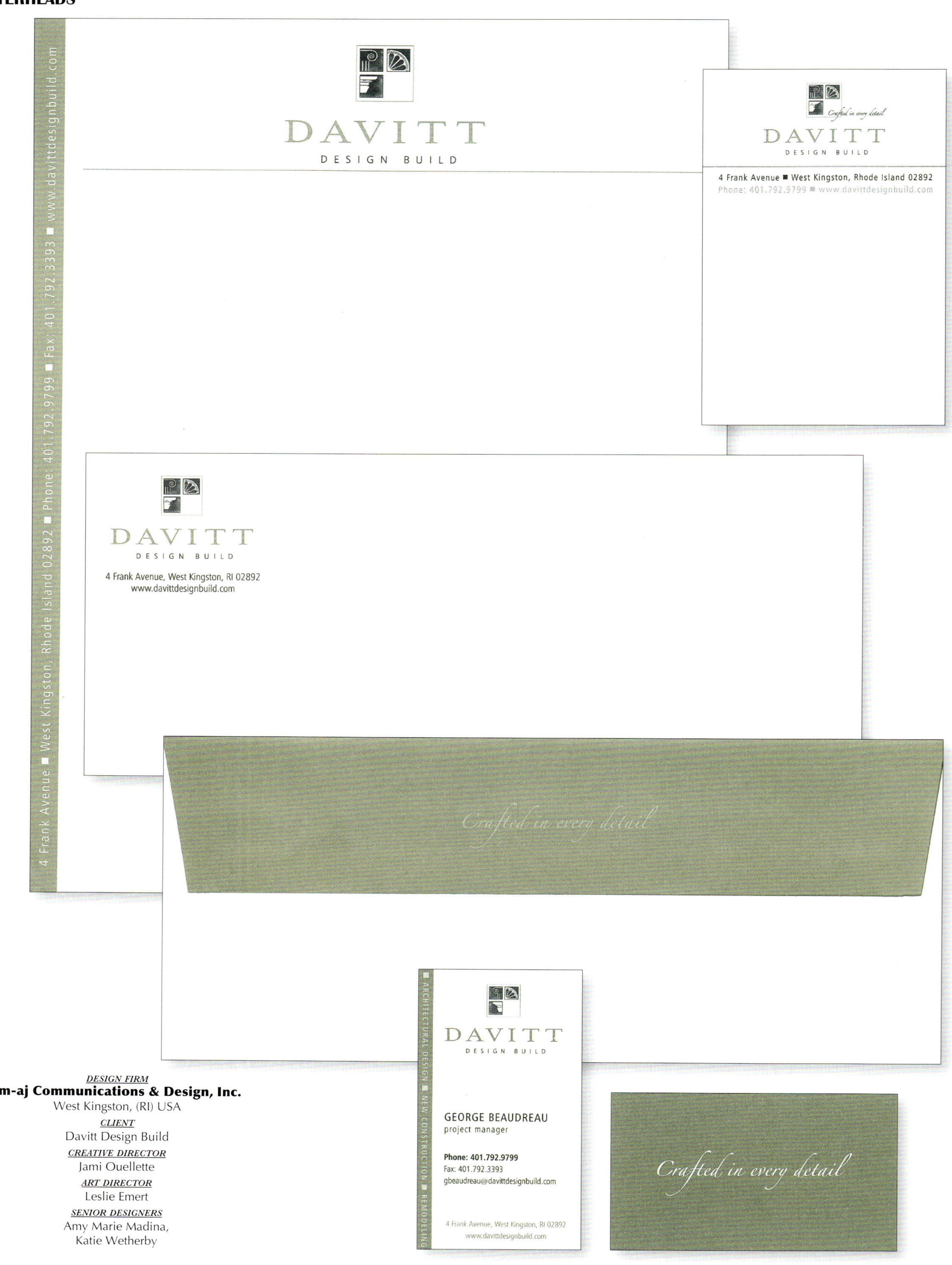

DESIGN FIRM
Im-aj Communications & Design, Inc.
West Kingston, (RI) USA
CLIENT
Davitt Design Build
CREATIVE DIRECTOR
Jami Ouellette
ART DIRECTOR
Leslie Emert
SENIOR DESIGNERS
Amy Marie Madina,
Katie Wetherby

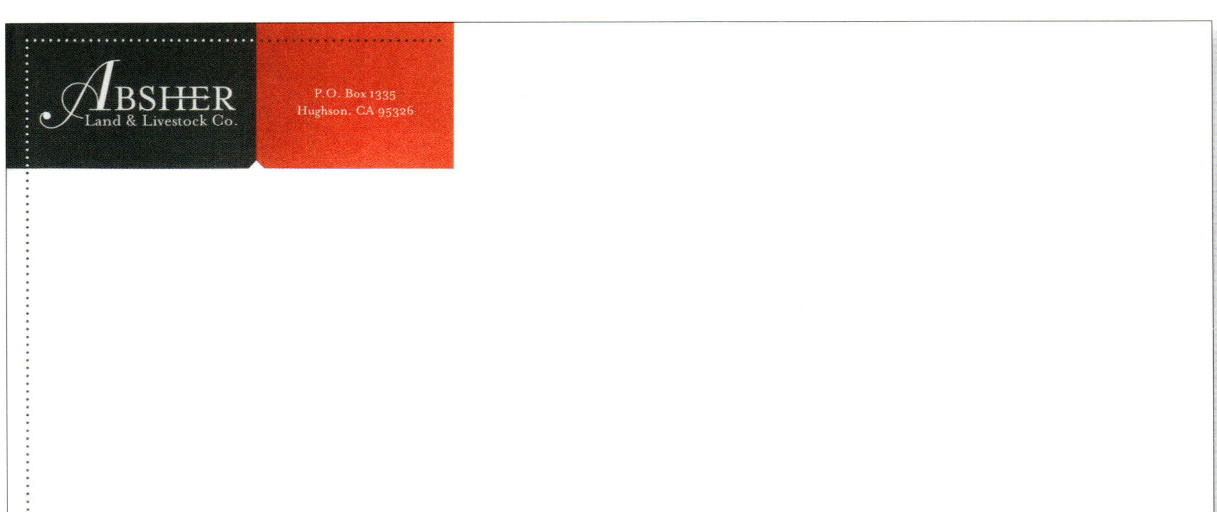

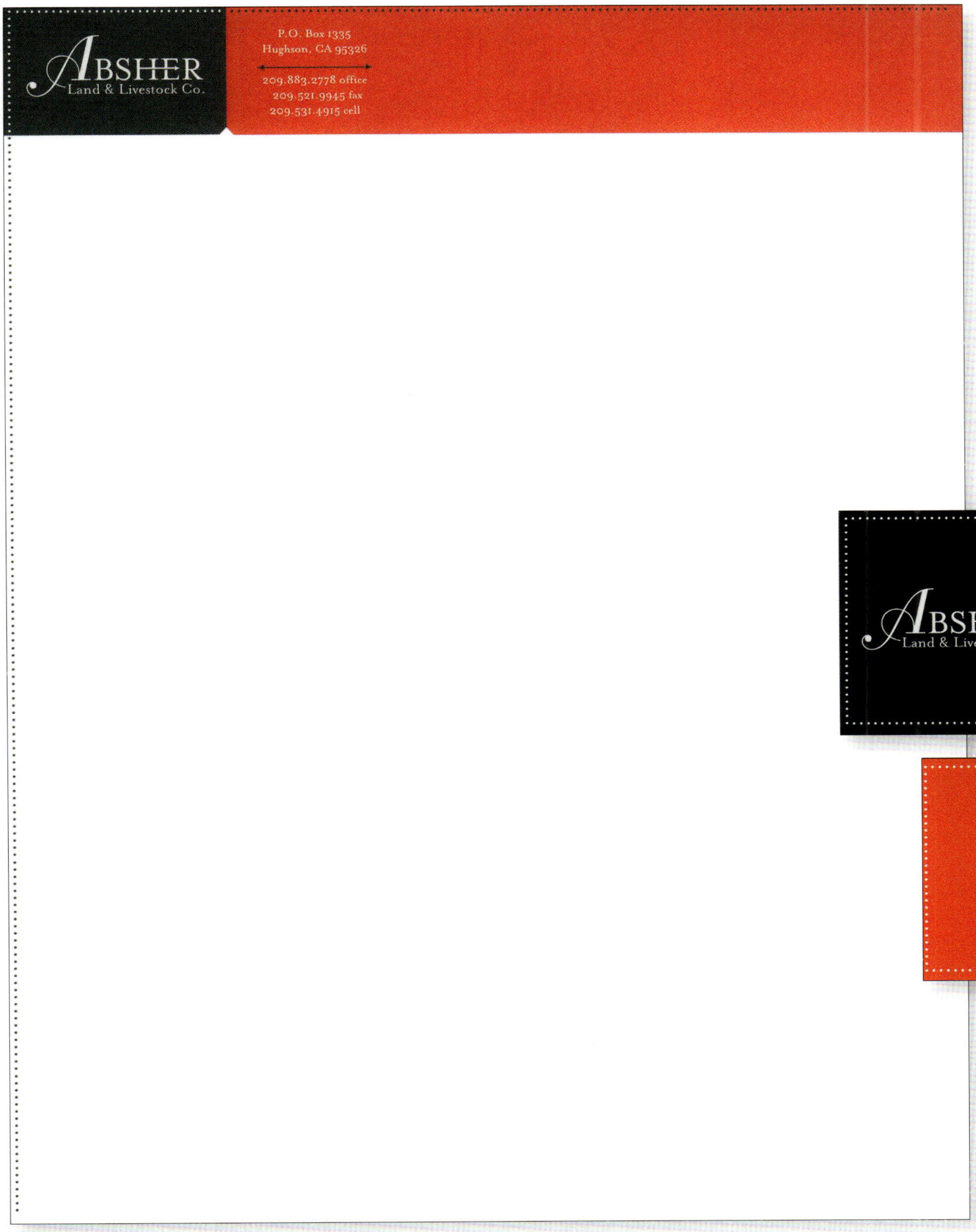

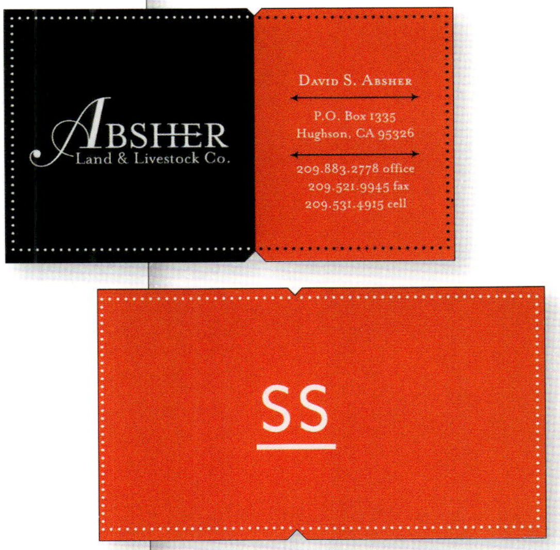

ABSHER
Land & Livestock Co.
P.O. Box 1335
Hughson, CA 95326
209.883.2778 office
209.521.9945 fax
209.531.4915 cell

ABSHER
Land & Livestock Co.
DAVID S. ABSHER
P.O. Box 1335
Hughson, CA 95326
209.883.2778 office
209.521.9945 fax
209.531.4915 cell

DESIGN FIRM
Never Boring Design Associates
Modesto, (CA) USA
PROJECT
Absher
DESIGNER
Katrina Furton

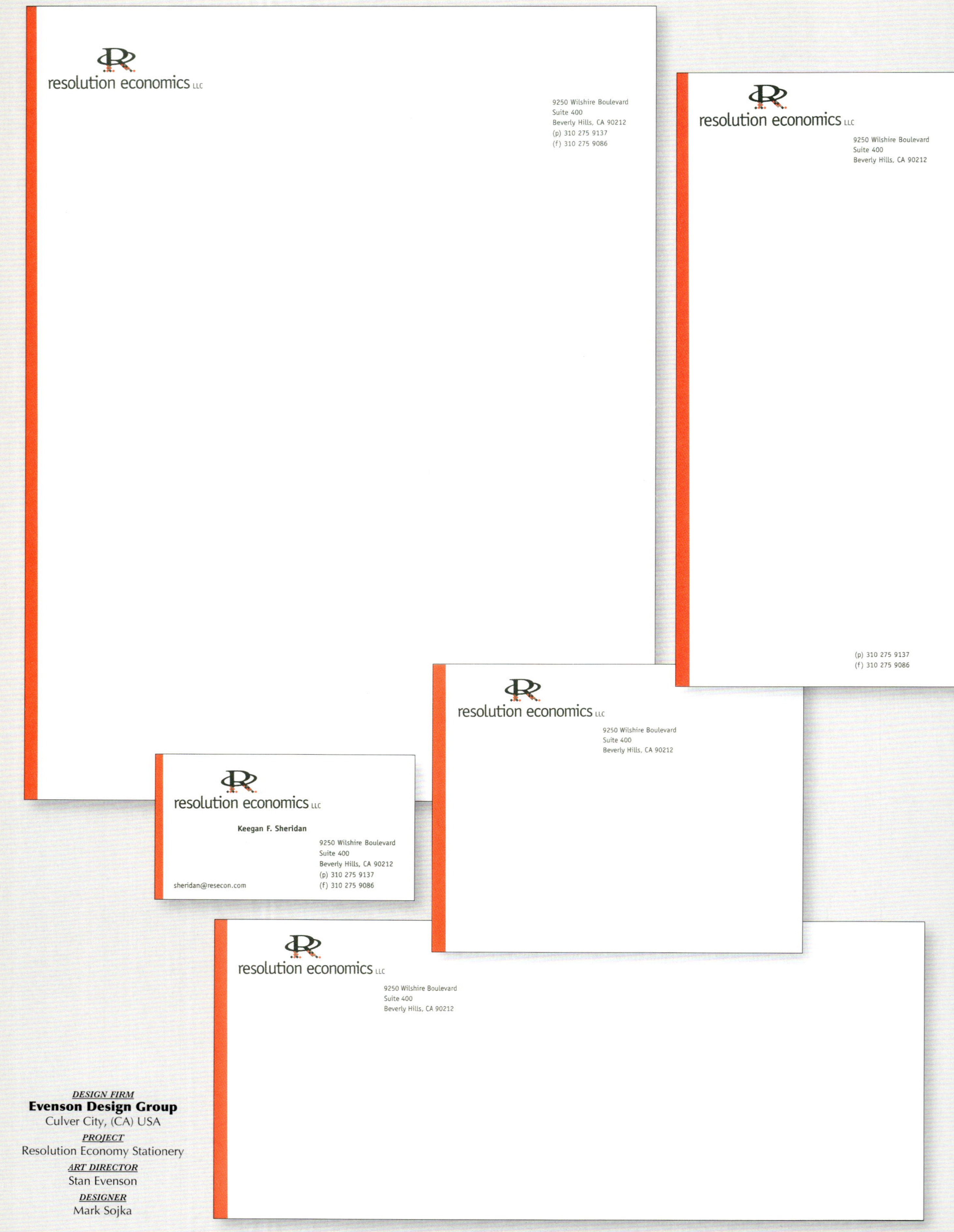

DESIGN FIRM
Evenson Design Group
Culver City, (CA) USA

PROJECT
Resolution Economy Stationery

ART DIRECTOR
Stan Evenson

DESIGNER
Mark Sojka

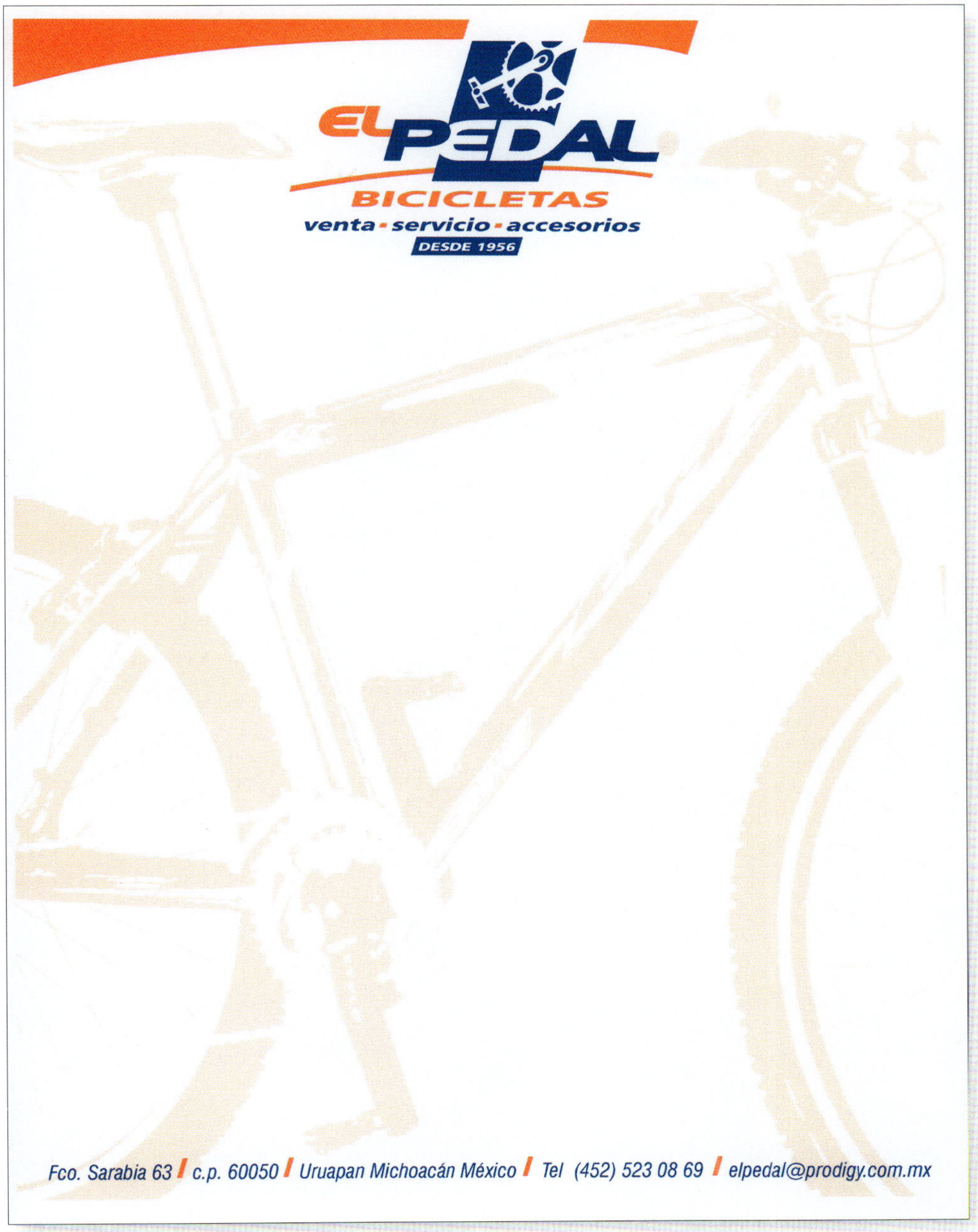

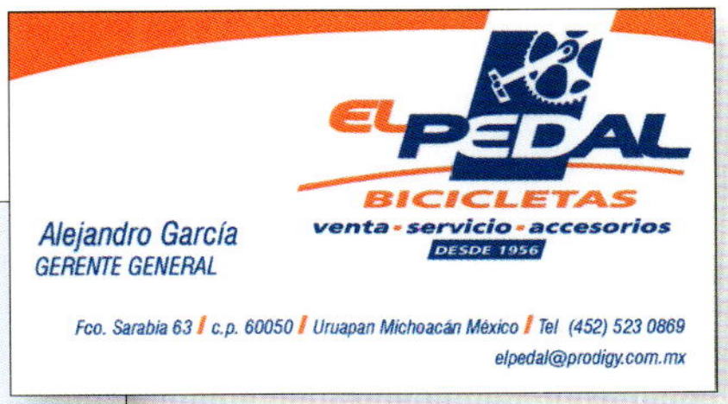

EL PEDAL
BICICLETAS
venta • servicio • accesorios
DESDE 1956

Fco. Sarabia 63 / c.p. 60050 / Uruapan Michoacán México / Tel (452) 523 08 69 / elpedal@prodigy.com.mx

EL PEDAL
BICICLETAS
venta • servicio • accesorios
DESDE 1956

Alejandro García
GERENTE GENERAL

Fco. Sarabia 63 / c.p. 60050 / Uruapan Michoacán México / Tel (452) 523 0869
elpedal@prodigy.com.mx

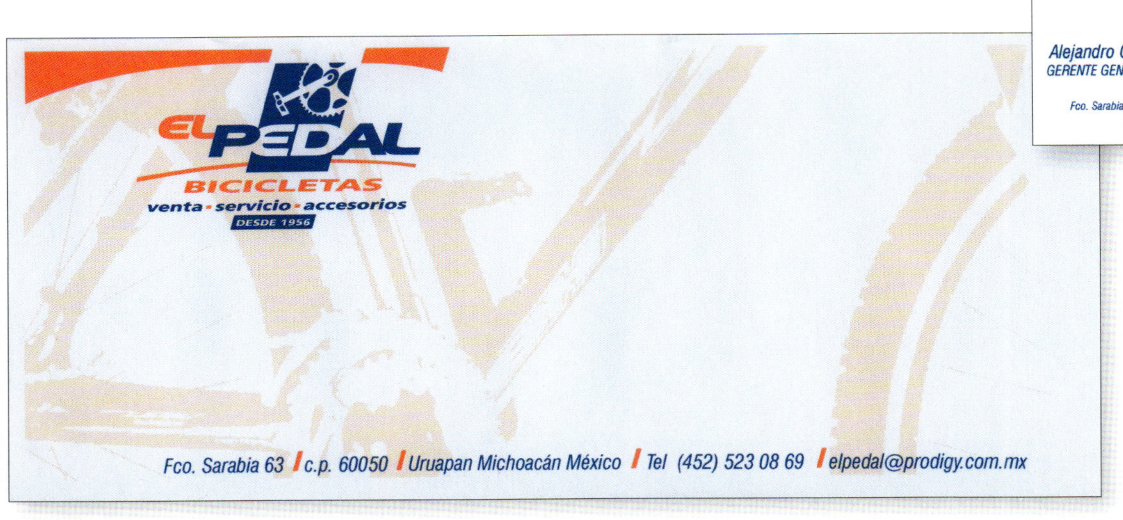

DESIGN FIRM
Kenneth Diseño
Uruapan, Mexico
PROJECT
El Pedal
DESIGNERS
Kenneth Treviño,
Minerva Galván

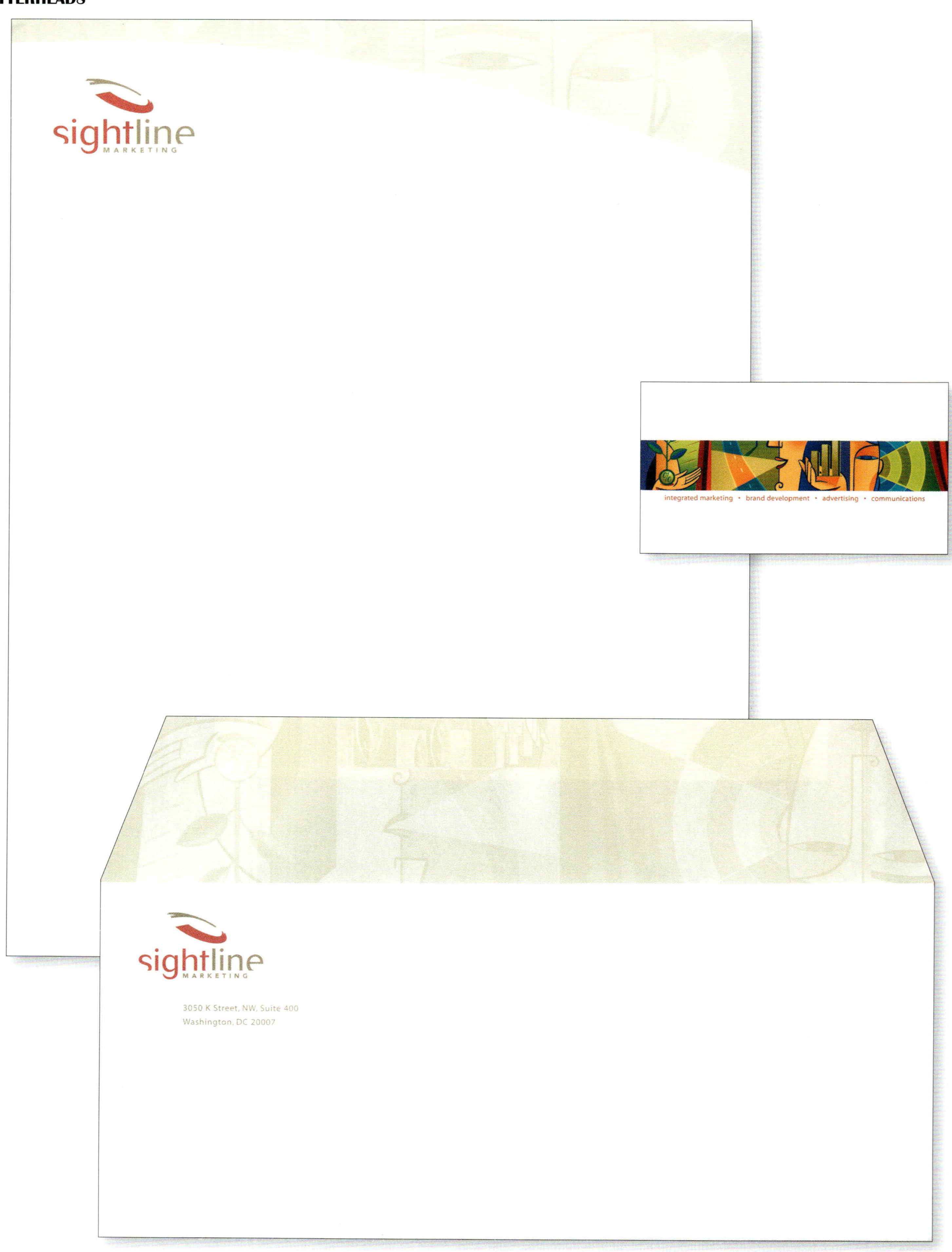
sightline
MARKETING
integrated marketing • brand development • advertising • communications
sightline
MARKETING
3050 K Street, NW, Suite 400
Washington, DC 20007

DESIGN FIRM
Sightline Marketing
Washington, (DC) USA
PROJECT
Sightline Marketing
DESIGNER
Robert McVearry

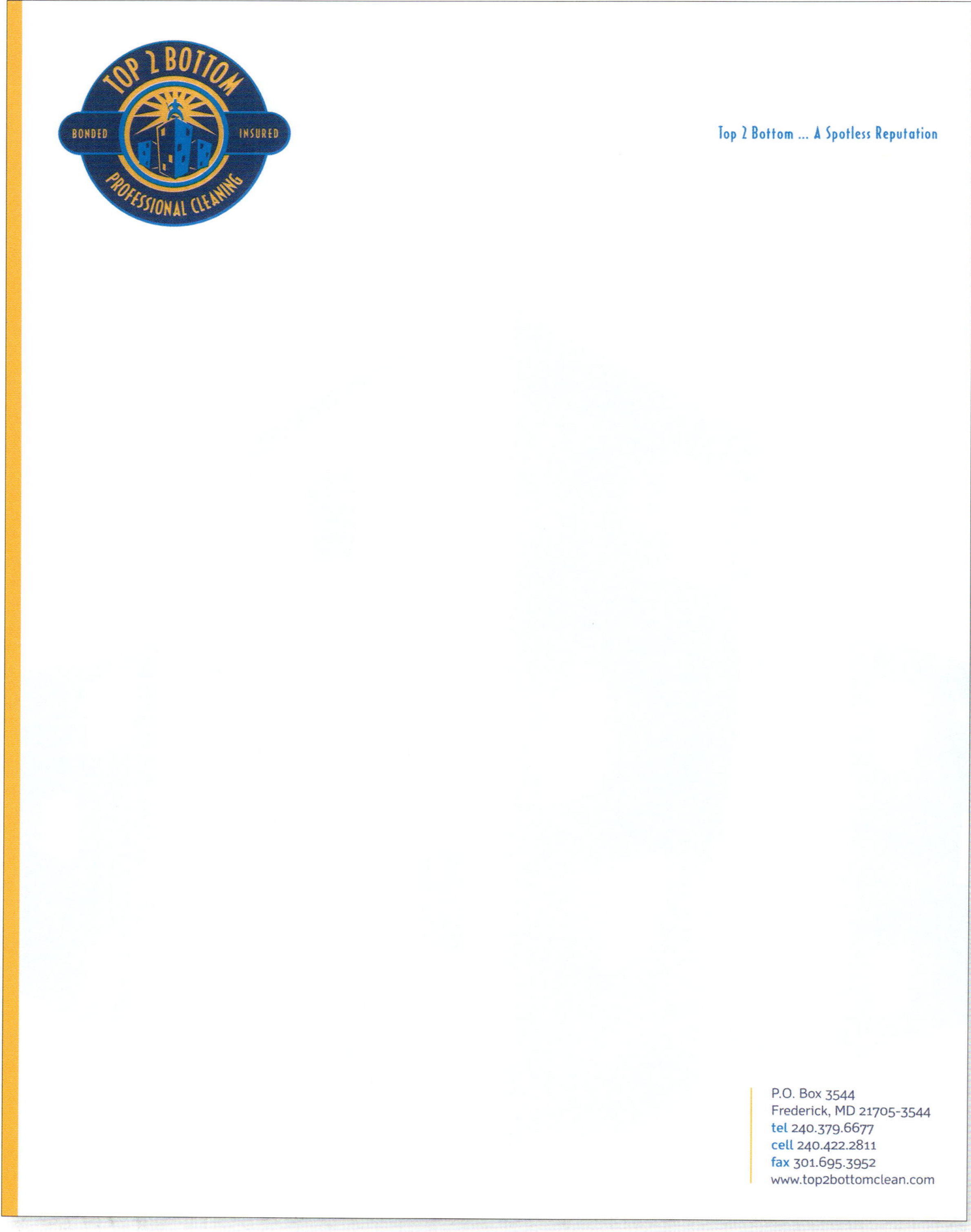

DESIGN FIRM
Octavo Designs
Frederick, (MD) USA
CLIENT
Top 2 Bottom Professional Cleaning
ART DIRECTOR, DESIGNER
Sue Hough

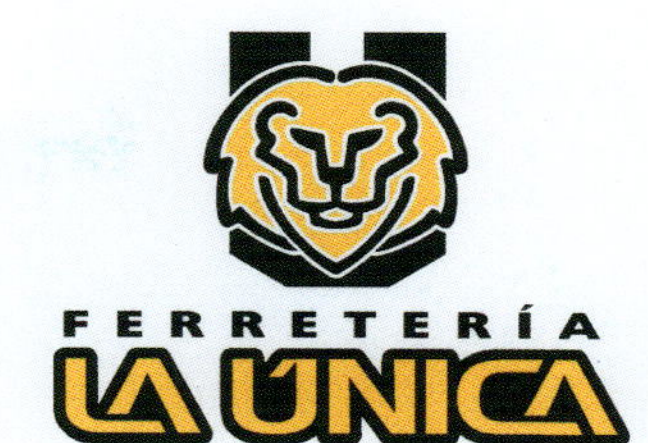

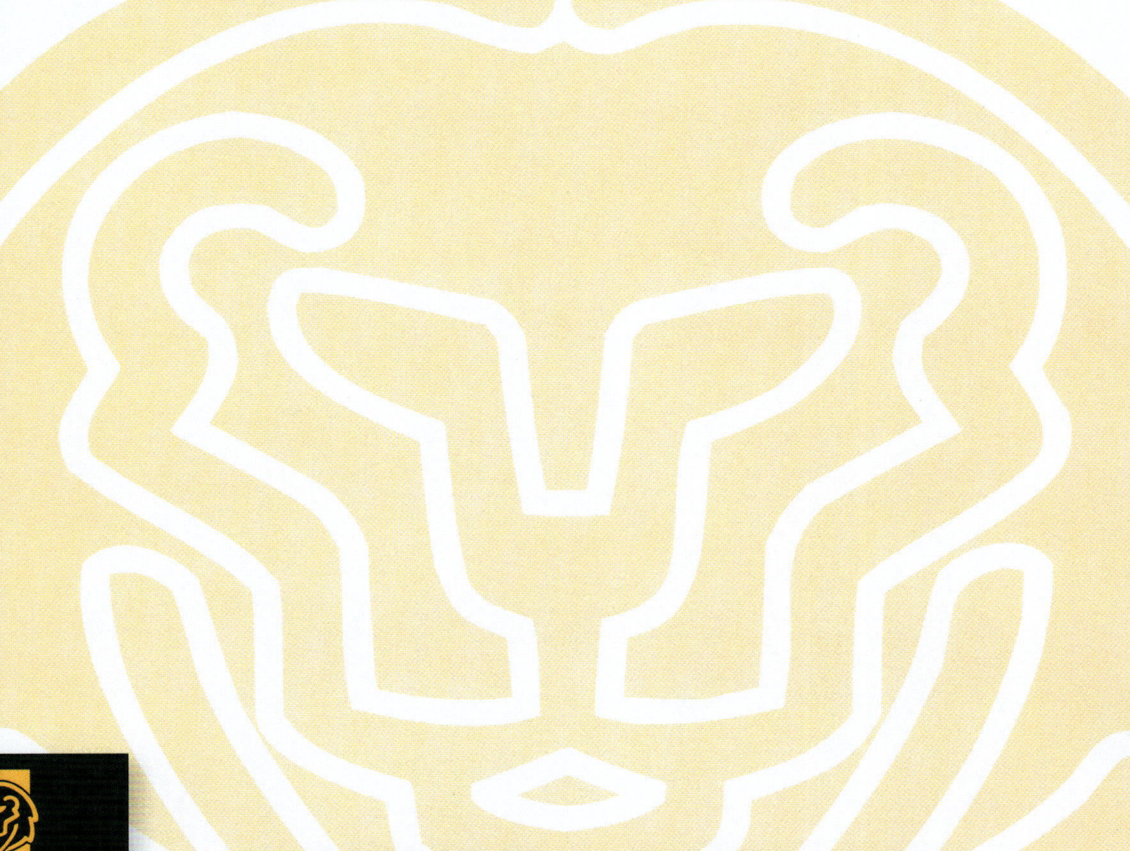

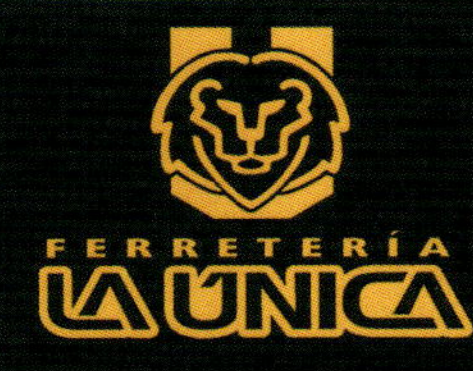

DESIGN FIRM
Kenneth Diseño
Uruapan, Mexico
PROJECT
La Unica
DESIGNERS
Kenneth Treviño,
Minerva Galván

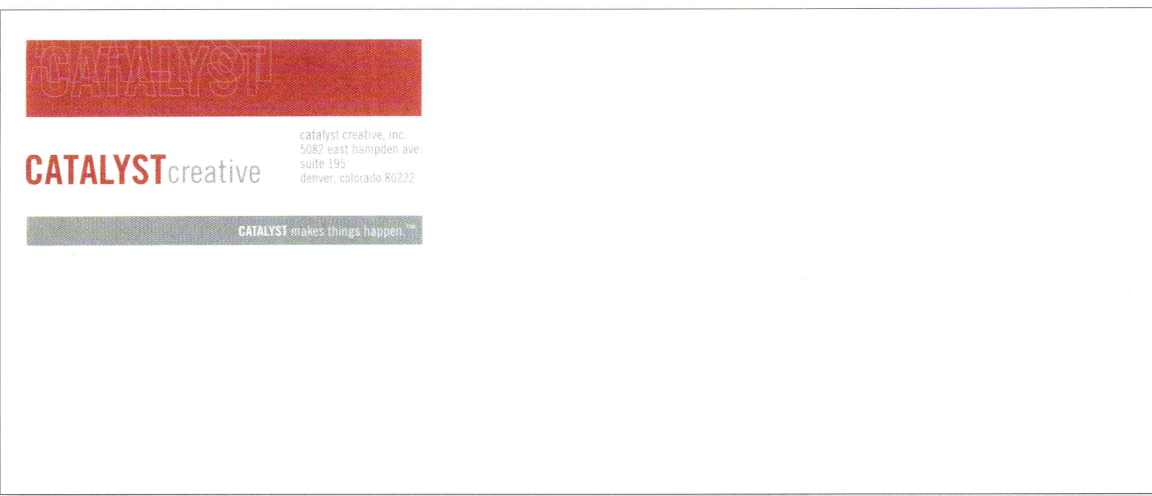

CATALYSTcreative

catalyst creative, inc.
5082 east hampden ave.
suite 195
denver, colorado 80222

303.380.9100 main
303.380.9111 fax

info@catalystcreativeinc.com
www.catalystcreativeinc.com

CATALYST makes things happen.™

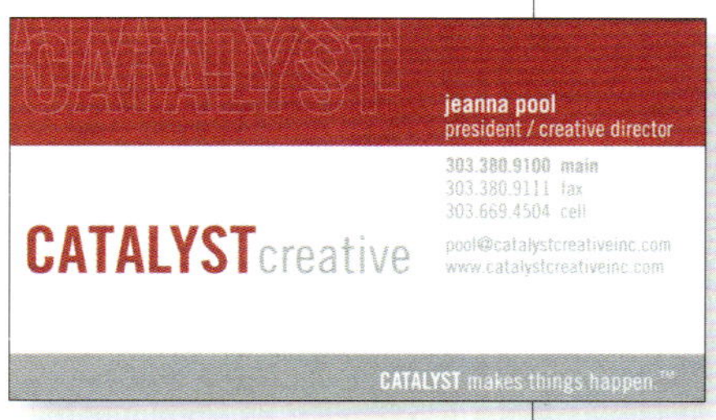

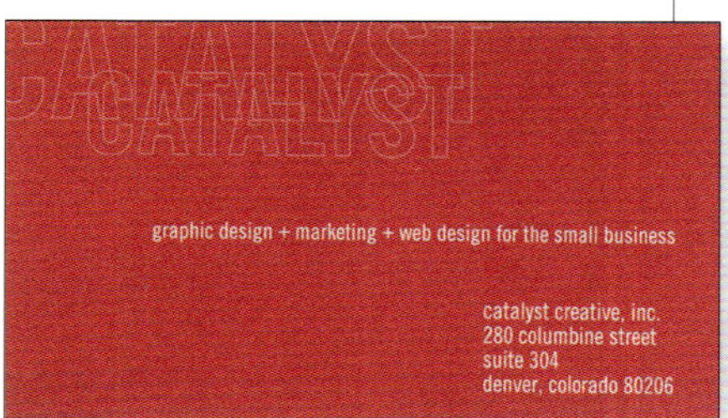

DESIGN FIRM
CATALYST creative, inc.
Denver, (CO) USA
PROJECT
CATALYST creative, inc.
ART DIRECTOR, DESIGNER
Jeanna Pool

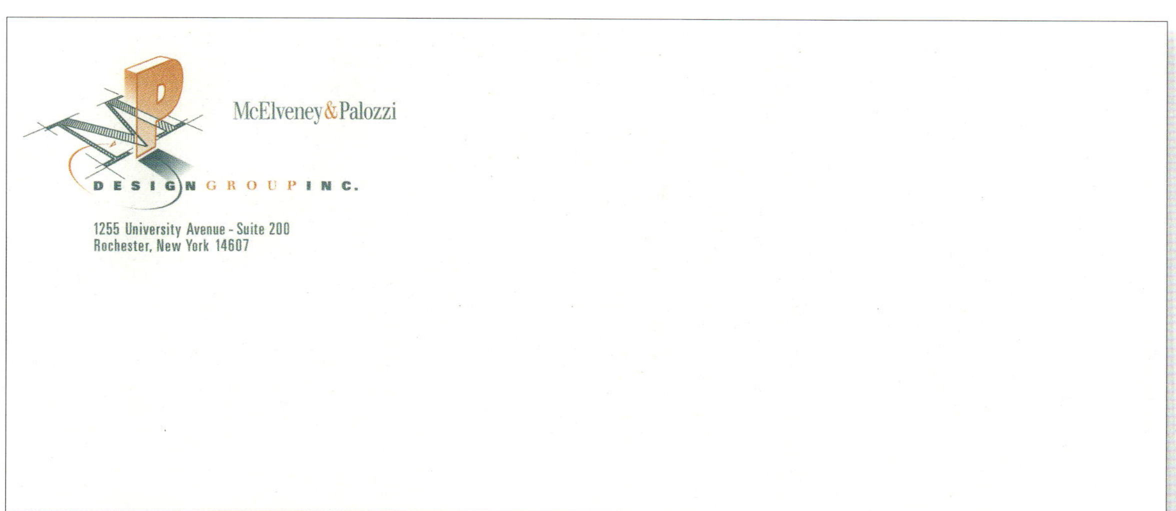

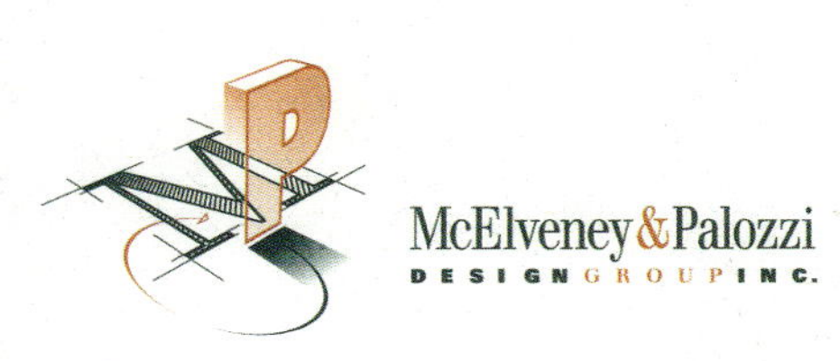

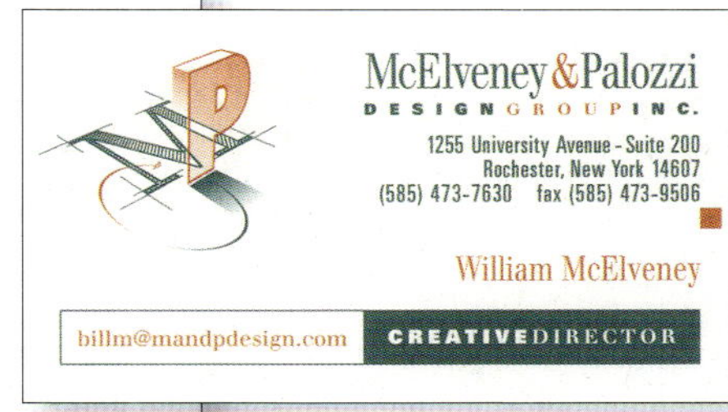

1255 University Avenue - Suite 200 . Rochester, New York 14607 . Phone (585) 473-7630 . Fax (585) 473-9506
www.mandpdesign.com

DESIGN FIRM
McElveney & Palozzi Design
Rochester, (NY) USA

PROJECT
McElveney & Palozzi Design

CREATIVE DIRECTORS
William McElveney,
Steve Palozzi

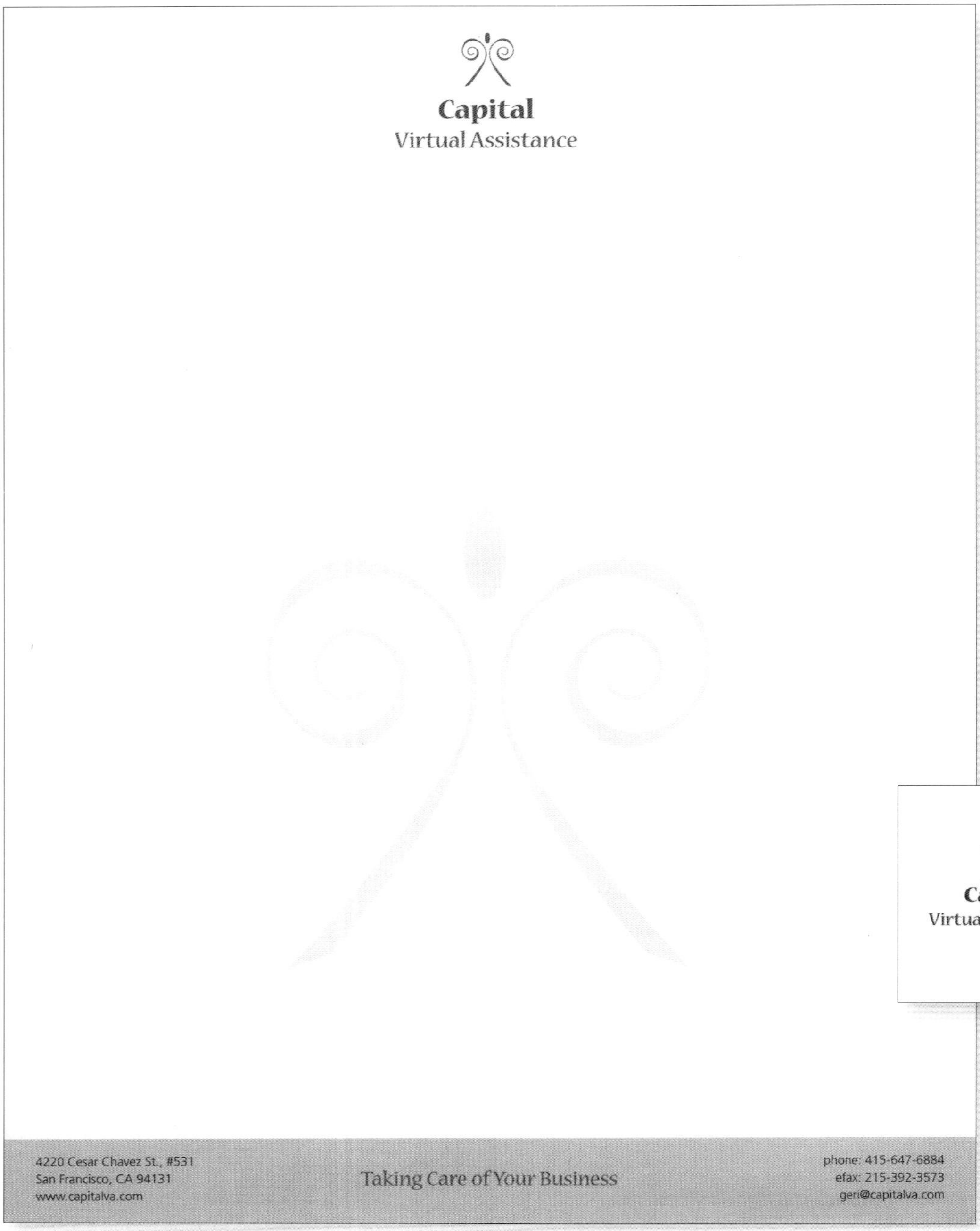

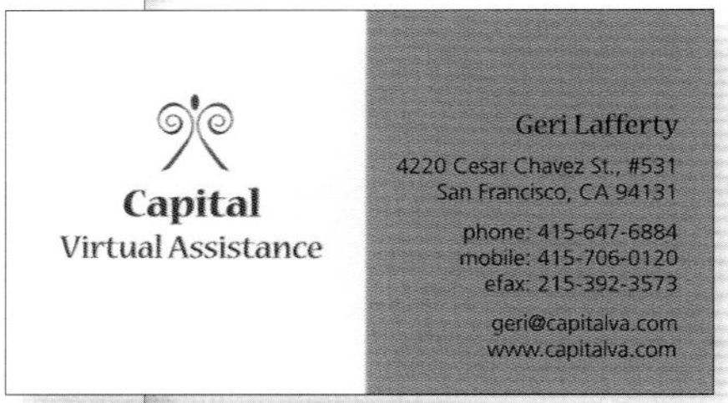

Capital
Virtual Assistance

4220 Cesar Chavez St., #531
San Francisco, CA 94131
www.capitalva.com

Taking Care of Your Business

phone: 415-647-6884
efax: 215-392-3573
geri@capitalva.com

Capital
Virtual Assistance

Geri Lafferty
4220 Cesar Chavez St., #531
San Francisco, CA 94131

phone: 415-647-6884
mobile: 415-706-0120
efax: 215-392-3573

geri@capitalva.com
www.capitalva.com

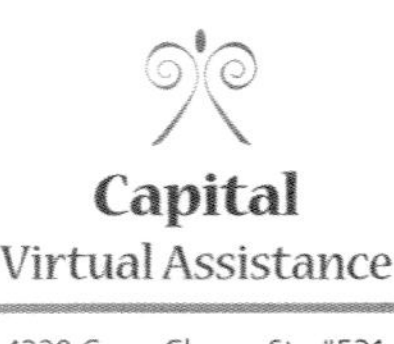

4220 Cesar Chavez St., #531
San Francisco, CA 94131

DESIGN FIRM
elf design
Belmont, (CA) USA
PROJECT
Capital Virtual Assistance
ART DIRECTOR, DESIGNER
Erin Ferree

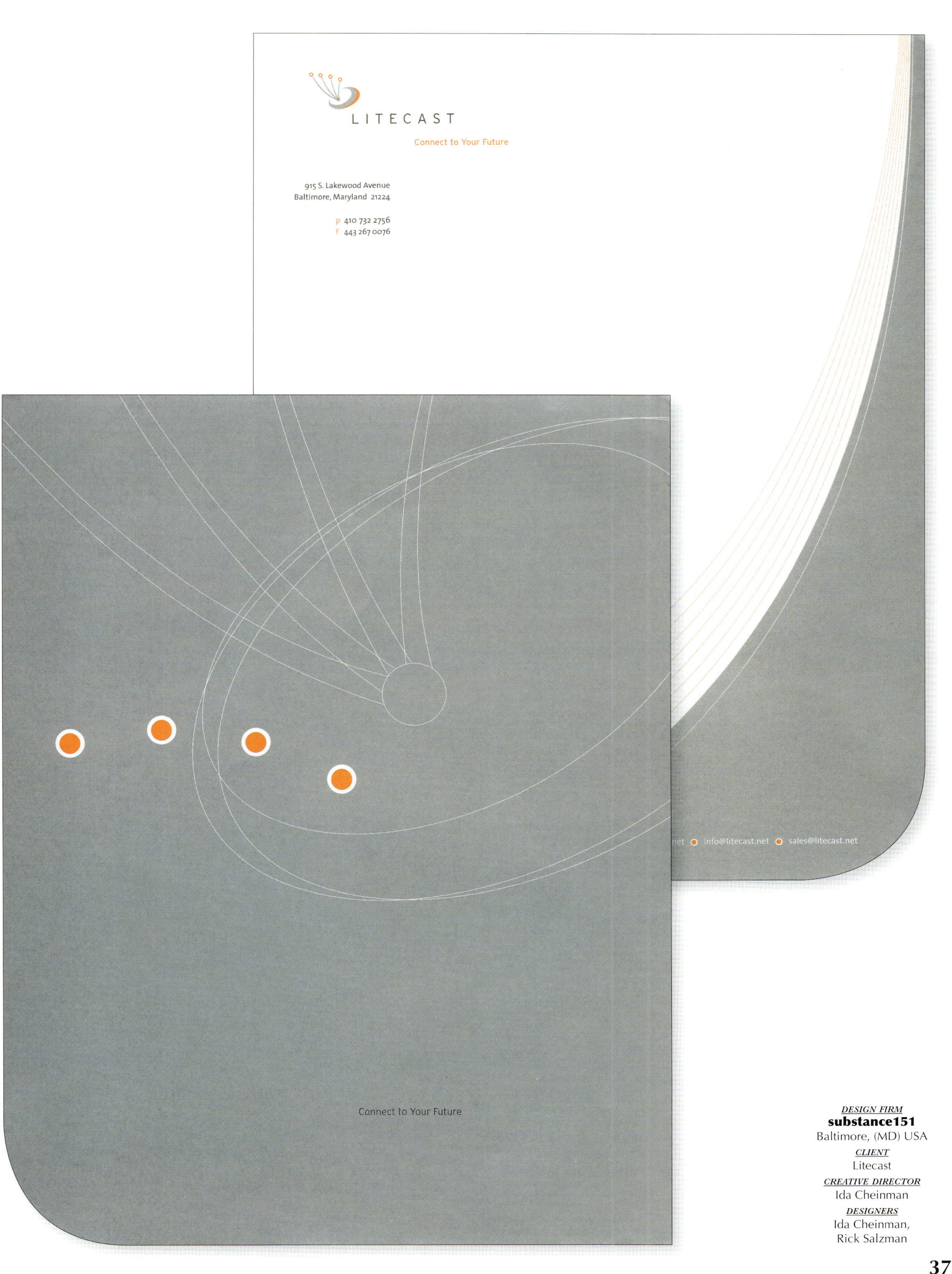

DESIGN FIRM
substance151
Baltimore, (MD) USA
CLIENT
Litecast
CREATIVE DIRECTOR
Ida Cheinman
DESIGNERS
Ida Cheinman,
Rick Salzman

andy kitchen photography

3039 Henrietta Avenue La Crescenta, California 91214 **T:** 818.957.4819 **F:** 818.957.5530 **E:** akitchen@earthlink.net

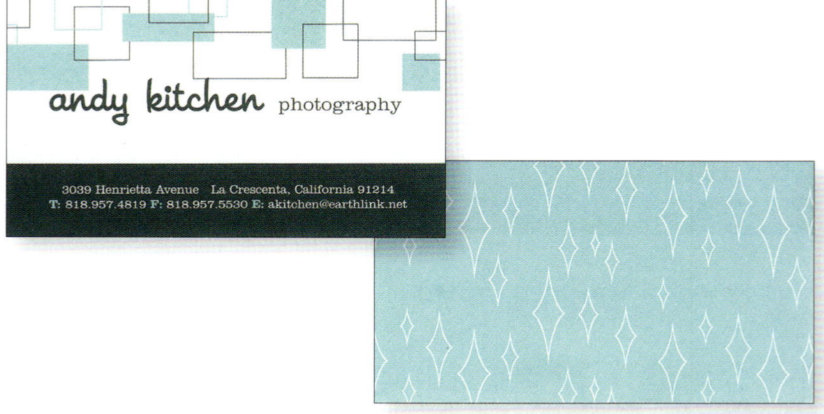

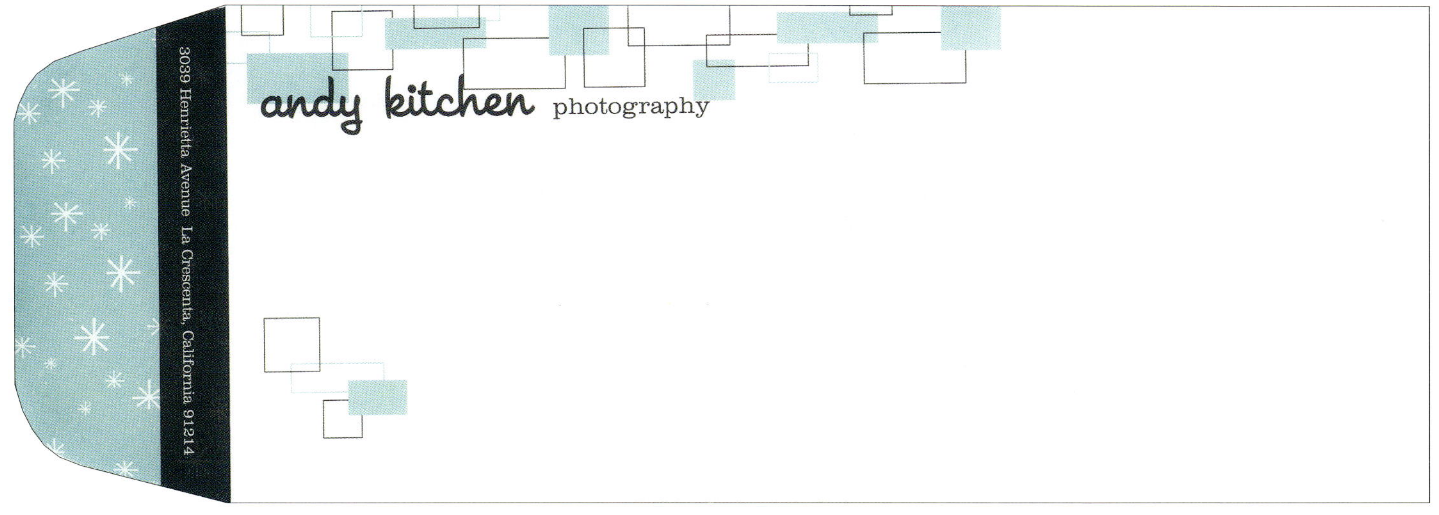

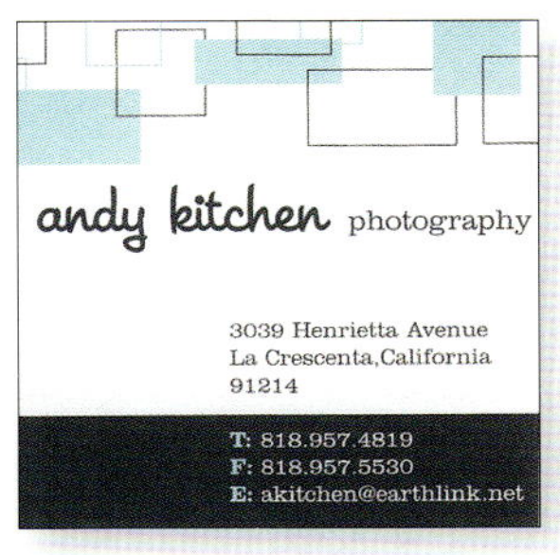

DESIGN FIRM
Hubbell Design Works
Orange, (CA) USA
PROJECT
Andy Kitchen Photography
ART DIRECTOR, DESIGNER
Leighton Hubbell

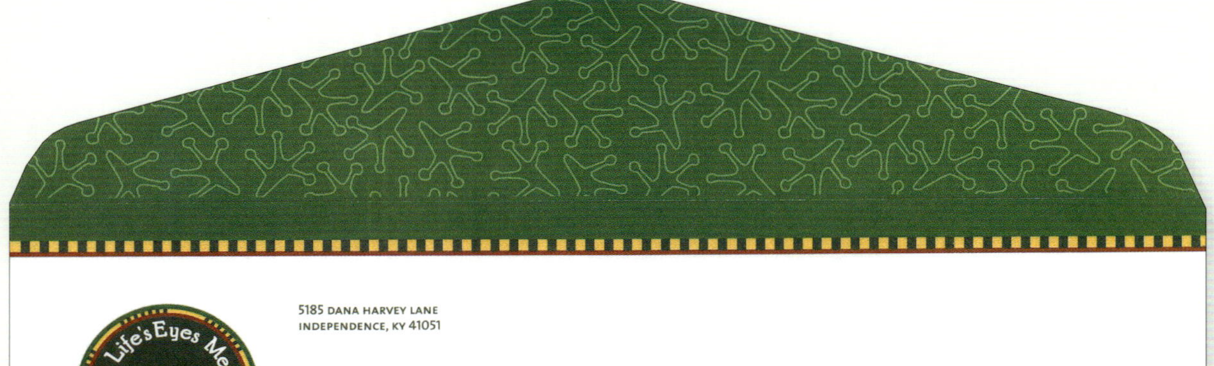

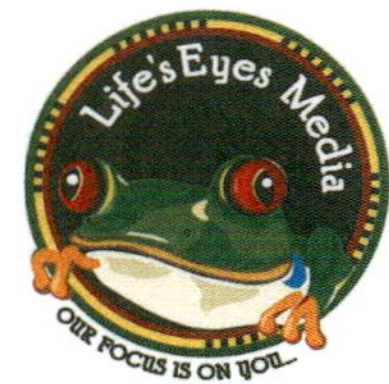

5185 DANA HARVEY LANE
INDEPENDENCE, KY 41051

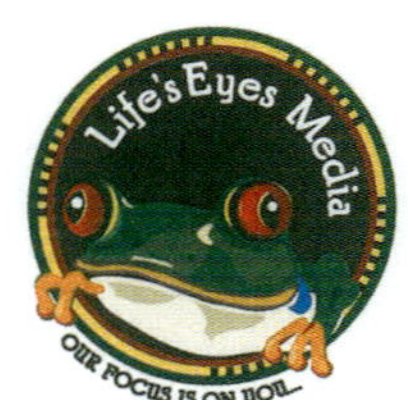

859 | 363.3916 PHONE/FAX

5185 DANA HARVEY LANE
INDEPENDENCE, KY 41051

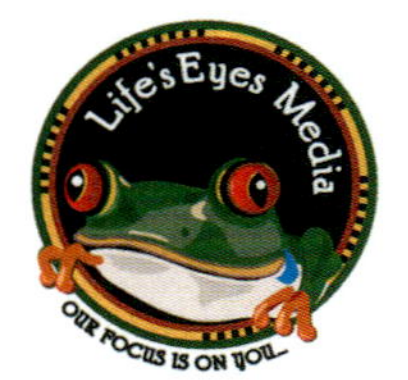

Kristan Getsy
CEO | PRESIDENT

859 | 363.3916 PHONE/FAX

KGETSY@LIFESEYESMEDIA.COM
WWW.LIFESEYESMEDIA.COM

5185 DANA HARVEY LANE
INDEPENDENCE, KY 41051

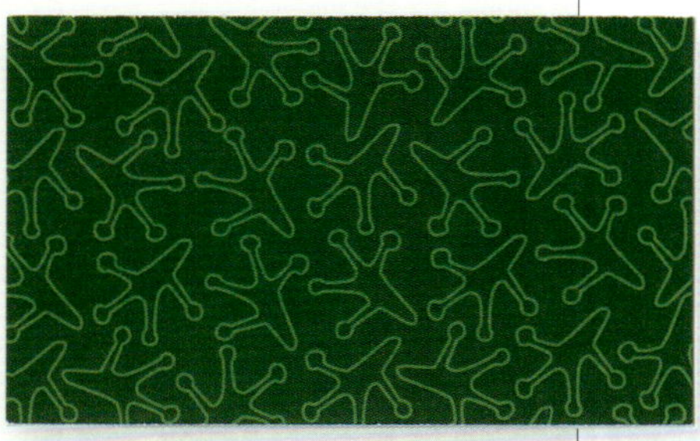

DESIGN FIRM
Five Visual Communication & Design
West Chester, (OH) USA

PROJECT
Life's Eyes Media

DESIGNER
Rondi Tschopp

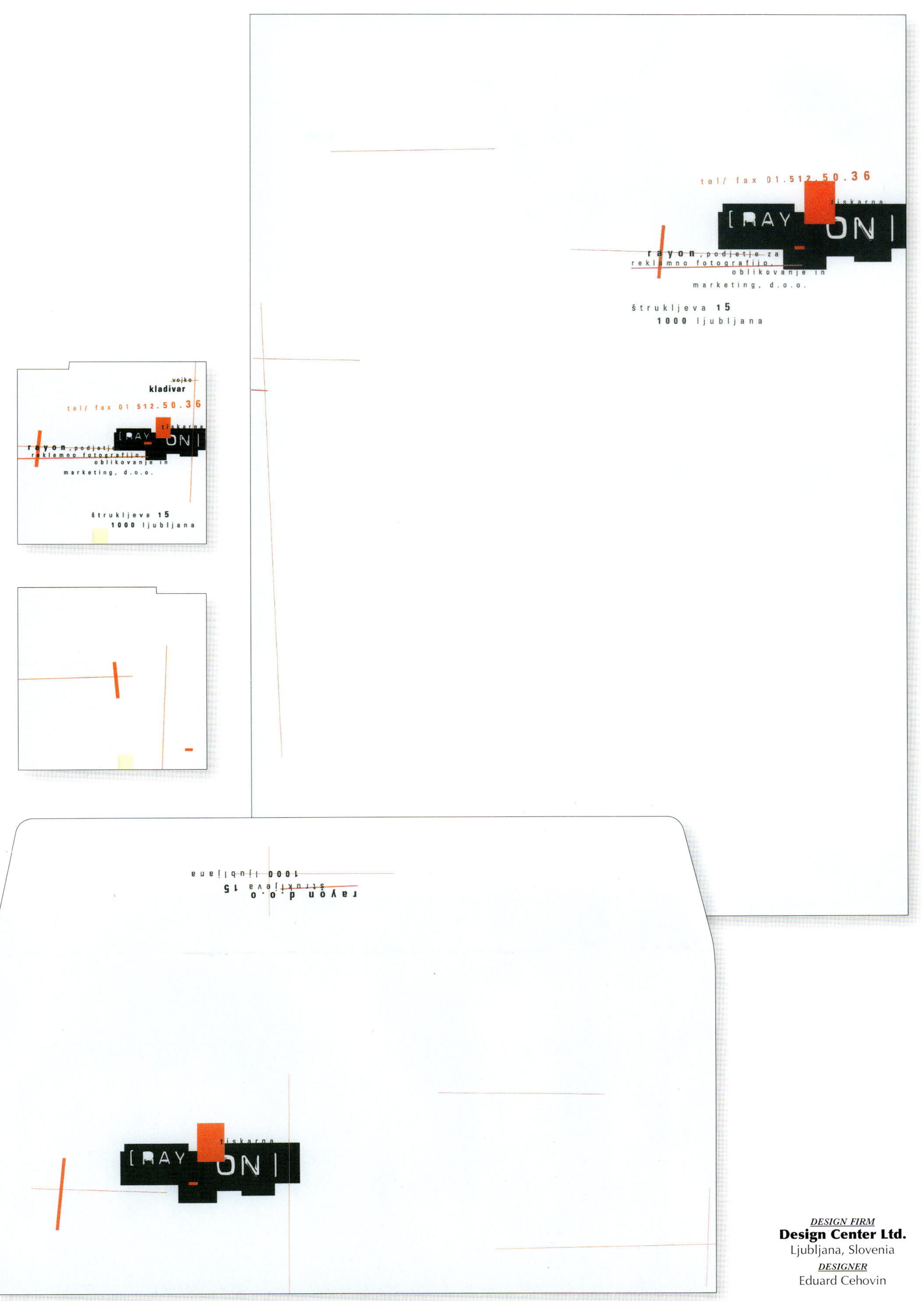

DESIGN FIRM
Design Center Ltd.
Ljubljana, Slovenia
DESIGNER
Eduard Cehovin

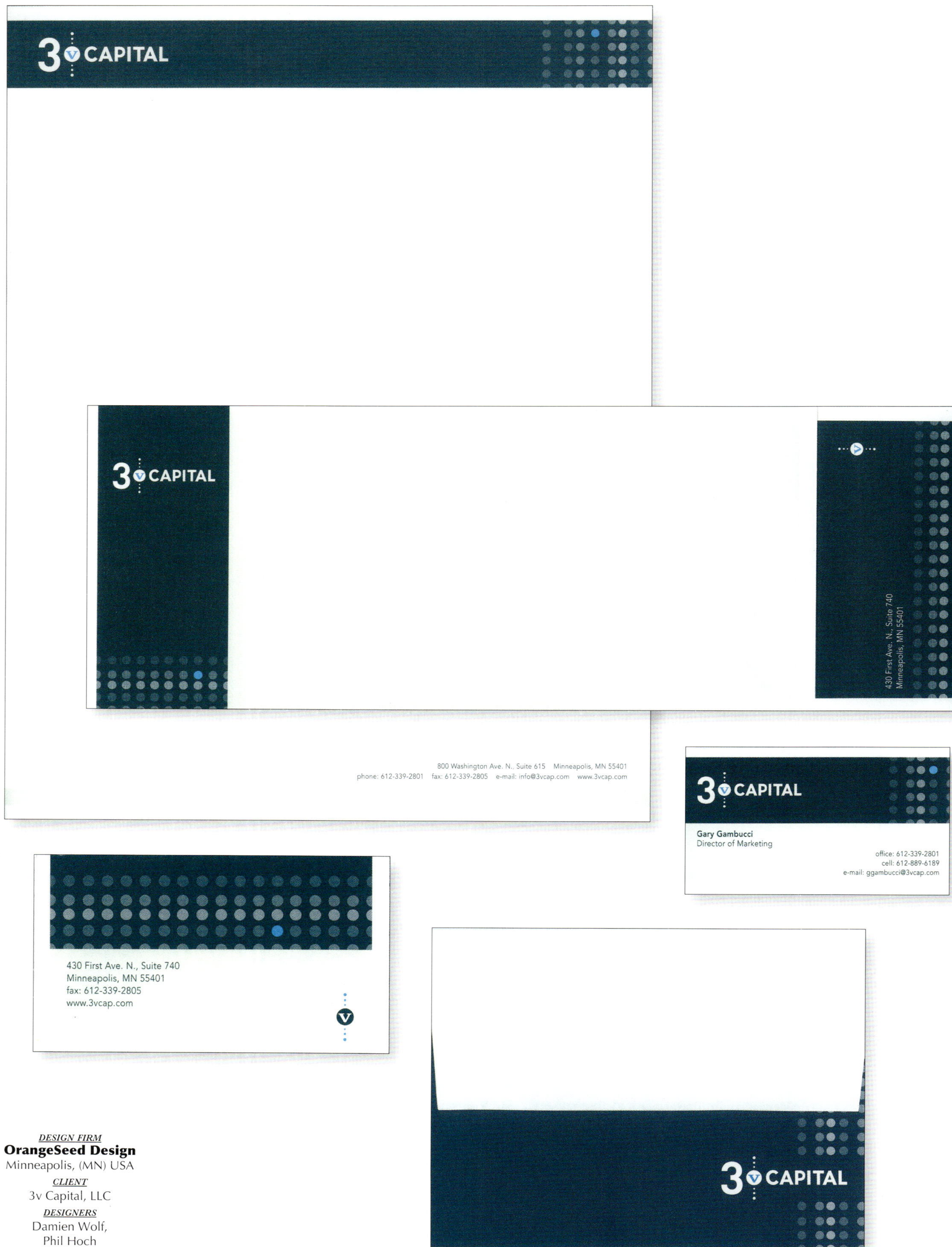

DESIGN FIRM
OrangeSeed Design
Minneapolis, (MN) USA

CLIENT
3v Capital, LLC

DESIGNERS
Damien Wolf,
Phil Hoch

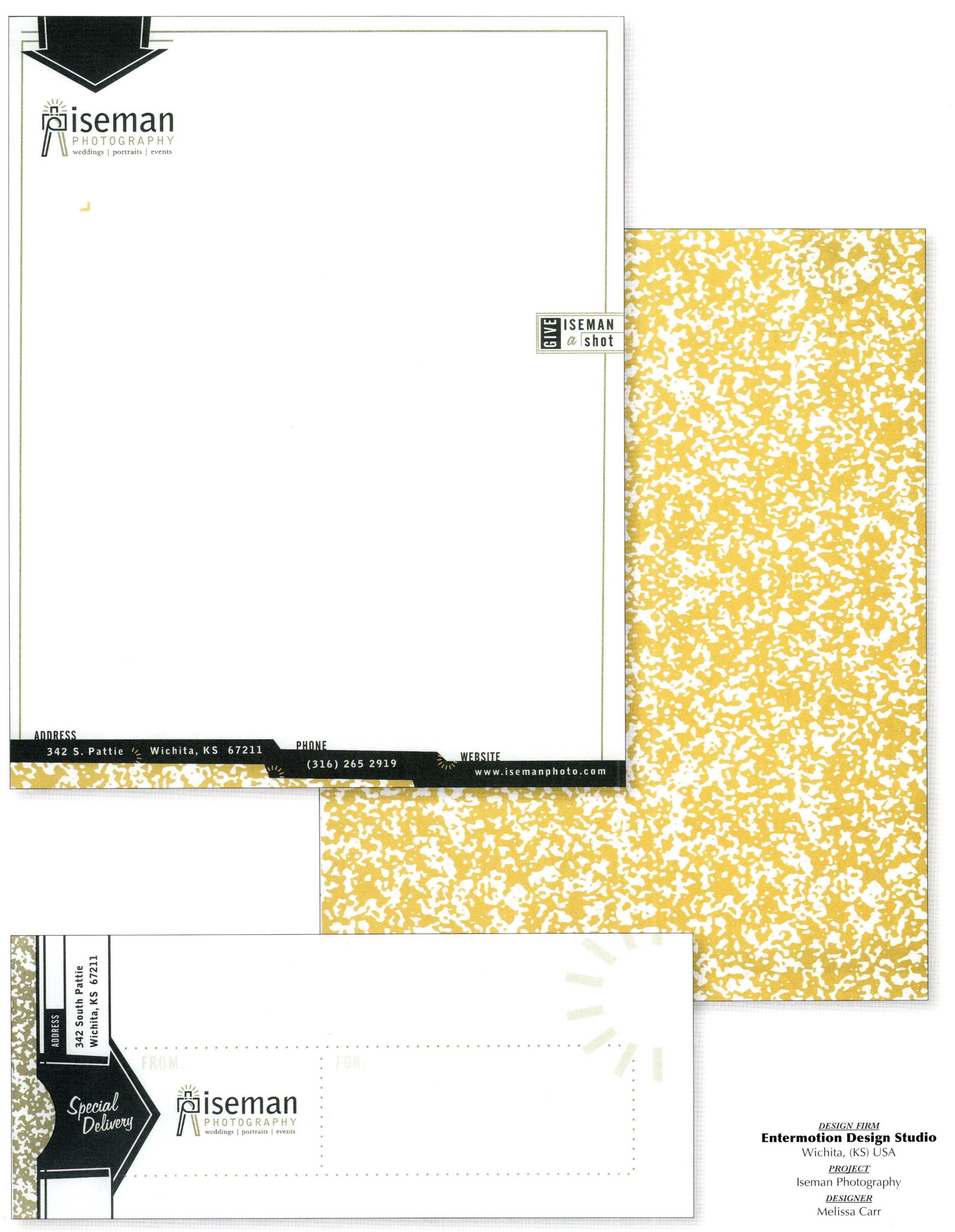

DESIGN FIRM
Entermotion Design Studio
Wichita, (KS) USA

PROJECT
Iseman Photography

DESIGNER
Melissa Carr

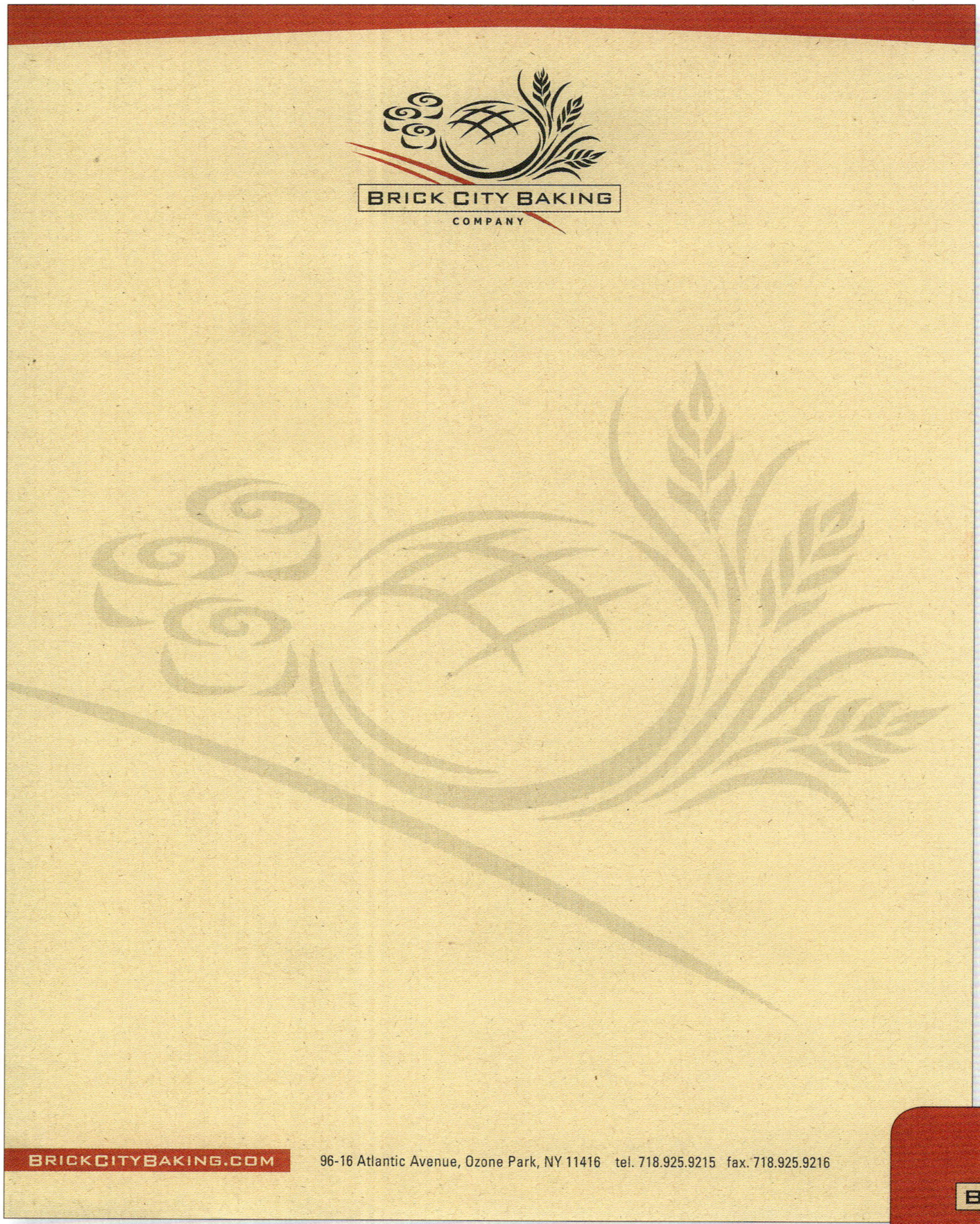

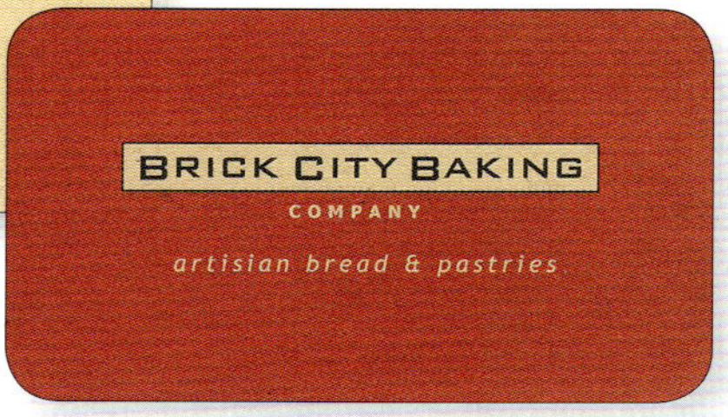

BRICK CITY BAKING
COMPANY

BRICKCITYBAKING.COM 96-16 Atlantic Avenue, Ozone Park, NY 11416 tel. 718.925.9215 fax. 718.925.9216

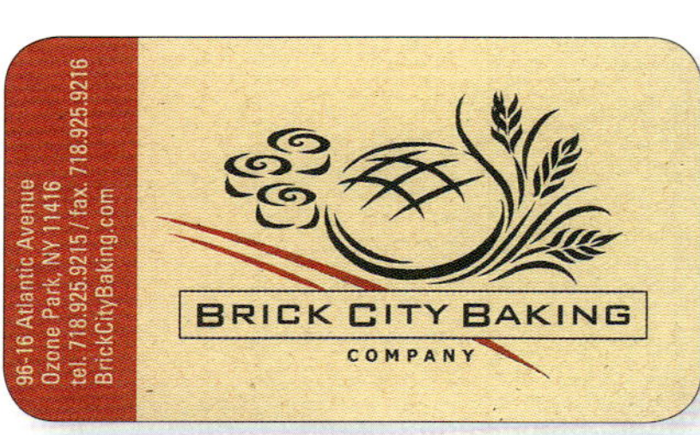

BRICK CITY BAKING
COMPANY
artisian bread & pastries

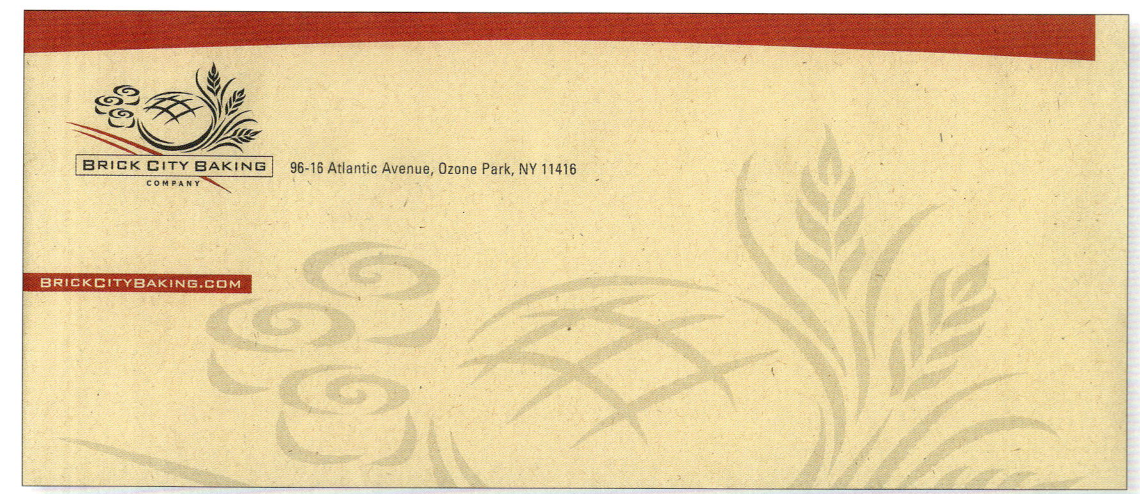

DESIGN FIRM
PM Design
Berkeley Heights, (NJ) USA
PROJECT
Brick City Baking
DESIGNER
Philip Marzo
ILLUSTRATOR
Sandy Haight

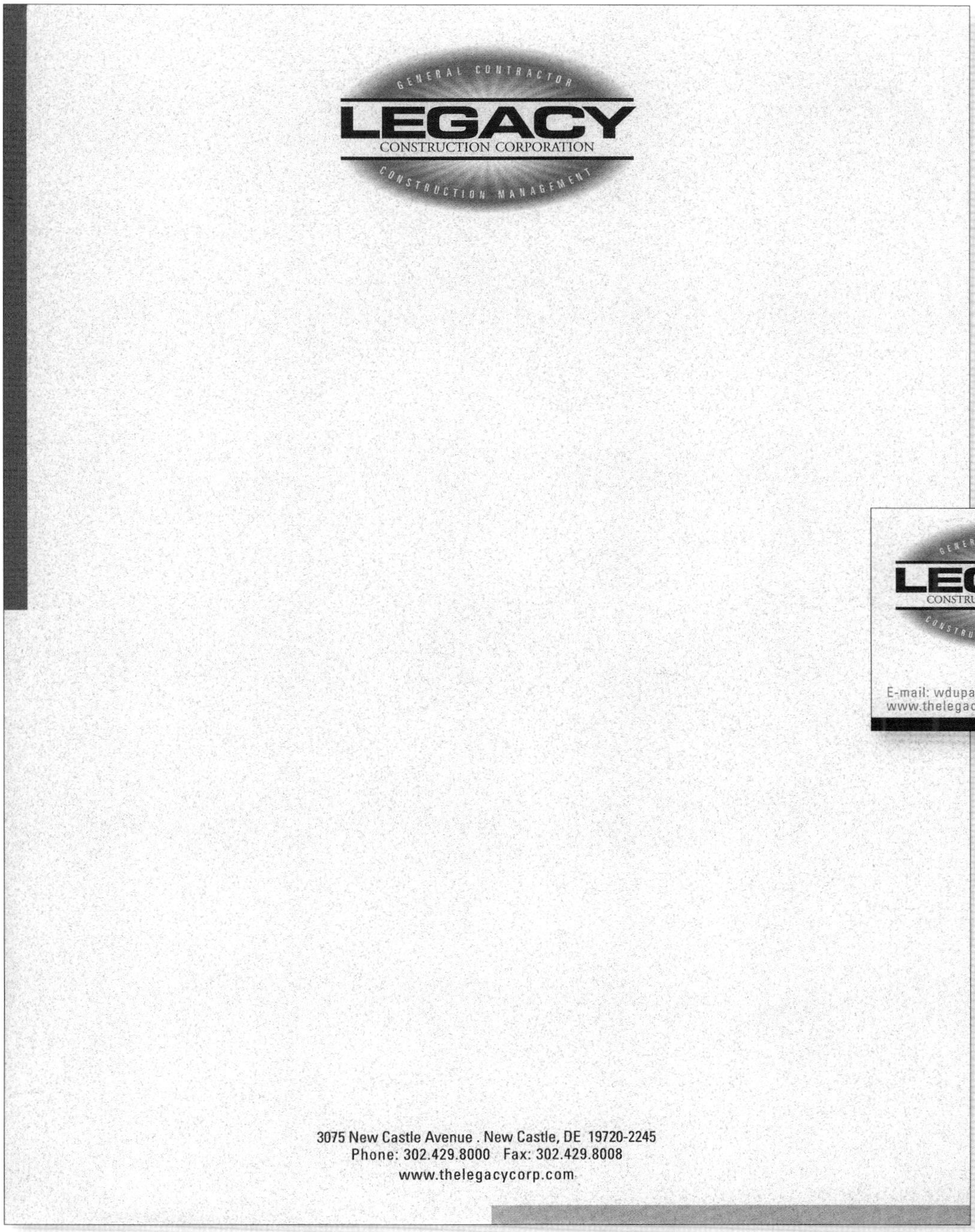

GENERAL CONTRACTOR
LEGACY
CONSTRUCTION CORPORATION
CONSTRUCTION MANAGEMENT

3075 New Castle Avenue . New Castle, DE 19720-2245
Phone: 302.429.8000 Fax: 302.429.8008
www.thelegacycorp.com

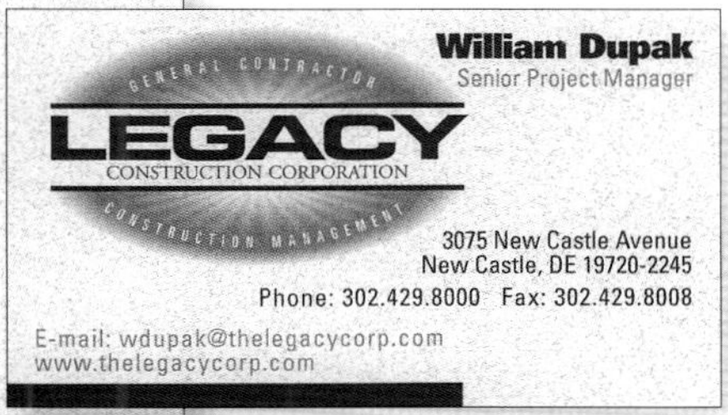

William Dupak
Senior Project Manager

GENERAL CONTRACTOR
LEGACY
CONSTRUCTION CORPORATION
CONSTRUCTION MANAGEMENT

3075 New Castle Avenue
New Castle, DE 19720-2245
Phone: 302.429.8000 Fax: 302.429.8008

E-mail: wdupak@thelegacycorp.com
www.thelegacycorp.com

DESIGN FIRM
McElveney & Palozzi Design
Rochester, (NY) USA
PROJECT
Legacy Construction Corporation
CREATIVE DIRECTOR
Steve Palozzi
ART DIRECTOR
Jon Westfall
DESIGNER
Matt Dundon

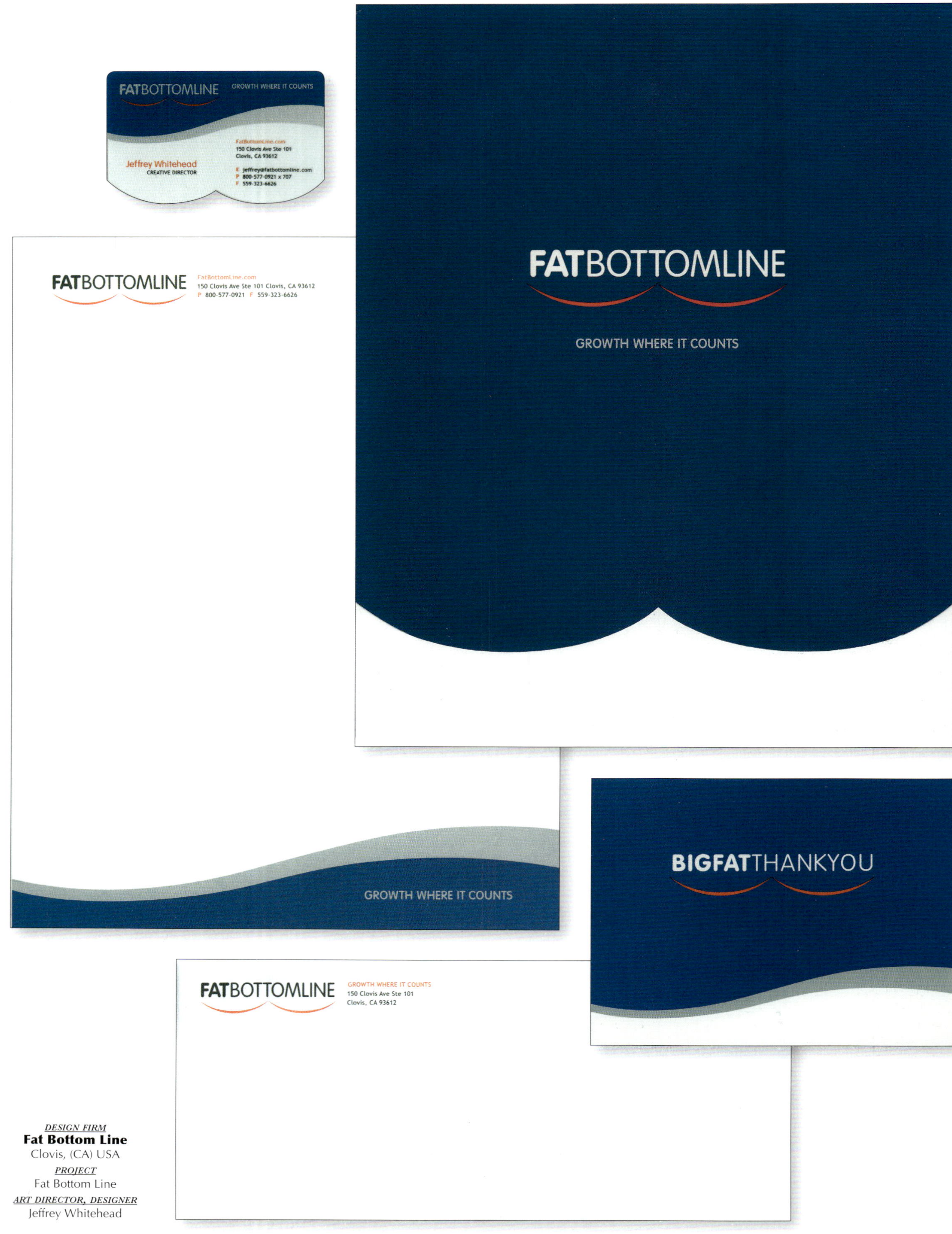

DESIGN FIRM
Fat Bottom Line
Clovis, (CA) USA
PROJECT
Fat Bottom Line
ART DIRECTOR, DESIGNER
Jeffrey Whitehead

INDEX

Design Firms

Clients/Projects